WHOLESALING

THEODORE N. BECKMAN
PROFESSOR OF BUSINESS ORGANIZATION
THE OHIO STATE UNIVERSITY

NATHANAEL H. ENGLE
PROFESSOR OF MARKETING
UNIVERSITY OF WASHINGTON

ROBERT D. BUZZELL
ASSISTANT PROFESSOR OF BUSINESS ORGANIZATION
THE OHIO STATE UNIVERSITY

Third Edition

THE RONALD PRESS COMPANY · NEW YORK

4

Library of Congress Catalog Card Number: 59–10138

PREFACE

In the ten years since publication of the preceding edition of this book, the field of wholesaling has been characterized by a steady flow of dynamic changes and a general quickening in tempo. Not only have many important developments taken place in the technology of wholesaling, but there has been among wholesale concerns a growing awareness of the need for professional and scientific management. Evidence of the latter is found in the multiplication of "management development" programs for wholesalers, in trade association educational activities, and generally in a greater emphasis on managerial techniques in the trade periodical literature. These developments have necessitated a complete and thorough revision of the book in order to reflect the changing patterns of wholesaling and the effects of technological and managerial improvements. At the same time an effort has been made to preserve the best features of the previous editions and to emphasize fundamentals in the form of principles and sound theory.

This book deals with wholesaling as it exists in the United States. While designed primarily as a textbook for college and university courses in the subject, it is intended also to serve as a guide and reference for those engaged in managing wholesale enterprises. The needs of both students and practitioners have thus been kept in mind throughout the process of revision. Briefly stated, the objectives of the book may be summarized as follows:

First, to provide a sound conceptual basis for the study and practice of wholesaling. Every effort has been made to introduce and explain in concise fashion the major concepts and basic terminology requisite to meaningful analysis.

Second, to analyze the historical development and modern status of the wholesaling system and its component parts. An understanding of this system is essential both to an intelligent appraisal of the role of a particular type of institution and to an analysis of the competitive forces at work in marketing at the wholesale level.

Third, to depict the environment—economic, social, and legal—within which wholesaling operates. Like other economic and social institutions, wholesale concerns must function within their environment; they are indeed influenced by, and in turn exert an influence on, this environment.

Fourth, to analyze the tasks of management in a wholesale enterprise. Since the book is intended to cover the entire field, emphasis is placed both on the development of principles having broad application and on subject matter that helps to cultivate sound and logical approaches to management problems in wholesaling. Because principles flow from an analysis of sound practice and experience and are illustrated with specific applications from a number of industries and trades, no distinction should be made between sound theory and good practice.

Fifth, to evaluate managerial and technological advancements in the field and their impact on traditional methods of doing business in a wholesale manner. As in the previous editions, newer methods, techniques, and institutions are placed in their proper perspective.

Several major changes have been made in the present revision. Most important, much greater emphasis has been placed on the managerial viewpoint. This is reflected in the increased number of chapters devoted to managerial aspects of wholesaling, as well as in the approach used in analyzing the conceptual framework, institutional structure, and the environment within which the individual firm must operate.

Some entirely new chapters have been added in providing a comprehensive treatment of wholesaling management. These are Productivity and Efficiency in Wholesaling, Establishing a Wholesale Enterprise, Financing a Wholesale Enterprise, Stock Turnover and Merchandise Planning, and Performance Measures and Standards. Obviously, part of the subject matter contained in these new chapters has been treated in the previous editions; nevertheless, they indicate the nature and extent of the shift in emphasis. In addition, all other chapters have been reorganized and substantially revised, with emphasis on the analytical and use of the descriptive only to the extent that it is essential to a correct understanding of the subject matter under discussion.

Special attention has been devoted in this volume to significant new concepts in wholesaling, including the notions of value added, productivity, and the use of performance measures in managerial control, all of them to an extent previously unknown or unutilized. Likewise, all important developments in technology affecting wholesaling are discussed, including those that pertain to materials handling, cost accounting, and electronic data processing.

All quantitative data have been revised and updated. Results of the 1954 Census of Business have been incorporated; in addition, many more recent figures have been used; and certain phases of the subject have been given quantitative expression for the first time.

To facilitate the use of the book in teaching and in management training programs, specially prepared case problems have been included in an Appendix. These are correlated with the contents of appropriate text chapters and are designed to focus attention in an illustrative manner on some major problems confronting the management of a wholesale enterprise.

The authors are indebted to the many persons who contributed ideas and information to past and present editions, including their colleagues in the teaching profession, executives of wholesale firms, and government and trade association officials. Wherever possible, these contributions have been acknowledged at appropriate points in the text. Special thanks are due to Professors William R. Davidson and James H. Davis of The Ohio State University, to Professor Henry D. Ostberg of New York University, and to Professors Charles J. Miller and Guy G. Gordon of the University of Washington, who have given the authors the benefits of their experiences in teaching and consulting.

THEODORE N. BECKMAN
NATHANAEL H. ENGLE
ROBERT D. BUZZELL

May, 1959

CONTENTS

PART I

Wholesaling in the American Economy

PART II

Scientific Management of a Wholesale Enterprise

FIGURES

xi

TABLES

I

Wholesaling in the
American Economy

1

GENERAL NATURE
OF WHOLESALING

The subject of this book is the complex of marketing activities and institutions known as *wholesaling*. All goods, both finished consumer products and those destined for industrial or commercial uses, pass through the wholesaling system. For this reason, its effective functioning contributes directly to our high and rising standard of living. For the same reason, a study of wholesaling is worthwhile to many persons other than those directly engaged in the field. Everyone, in fact, has a stake in wholesaling.

What Is Wholesaling? Wholesaling embraces all business activities connected with the marketing of goods at the wholesale level or in a wholesale manner. Contrary to popular belief, it is not confined to the operations of *wholesalers,* although they are of course an important segment of the system. Neither is wholesaling restricted to specialized wholesale institutions, which include establishments owned by manufacturers, retailers, and functional middlemen, as well as by wholesalers proper.

The true conception of wholesaling embraces all activities related to *wholesale transactions,* in which goods are *bought for business or institutional purposes* as distinguished from personal or ultimate consumption. Thus all of the marketing activities of manufacturers and other producers of physical goods should, strictly speaking, be regarded as parts of wholesaling whether or not conducted in separate and specialized establishments. In fact, if the true concept were strictly applied, all of the marketing system other than retailing could be treated as wholesaling. For practical purposes, however, this concept of wholesaling is too broad. In the first place, an adequate quantitative measurement of wholesaling in its true sense has never yet been accomplished. We are therefore restricted to a somewhat narrower definition for purposes of any statistical analysis of the past and present structure of the field. In the second place, many areas of wholesaling are in themselves sufficiently broad and complex to merit treatment as separate fields of study. Agricultural marketing, for example, is the subject of an extensive literature of its own. The same is true of foreign trade and freight transportation, both of which are parts of the wholesaling system. While some attention is given to these subjects herein, no attempt has been made to cover them in comprehensive fashion.

For purposes of organized study in a limited time period, then, the true concept of wholesaling is probably too broad and includes too many highly specialized subjects for treatment as an integrated whole. As a consequence, this book is devoted largely to the operations of *specialized wholesaling institutions engaged in domestic marketing*. Attention is also given to some of the wholesaling activities of manufacturers and other form-utility producers, which are not basically different from those of separate wholesale establishments owned by them or by wholesale middlemen.

THE PLACE OF WHOLESALING IN THE ECONOMY

In any economy which has progressed beyond the most primitive stages, wholesaling activities comprise a necessary part of the production process. The importance of wholesaling increases, moreover, in direct proportion to the long-run development of the economy as a whole. In present-day United States and in other advanced industrial nations, wholesaling affects millions of persons more or less directly and the performance of wholesaling tasks requires a large and specialized institutional structure. Attention may now be turned to the role of wholesaling in our economy and the reasons for its present importance.

Groups Affected by Wholesaling. Most directly affected by wholesaling are the many persons employed in the field. In early 1958 about 3.2 million persons were employed in wholesale trade. This total includes only employees of specialized establishments, and makes no allowance for the additional hundreds of thousands employed in wholesaling jobs by manufacturers, other physical goods producers, and by other marketing agencies. No reliable data are available to measure, with careful study and analysis, the magnitude of wholesaling employment in the broad and more proper sense of the term. In any case, wholesaling provides employment for a large army of workers. All of them, and especially those in managerial or sales capacities, must necessarily be concerned with the study and improvement of wholesaling performance.

Almost as directly concerned with wholesaling as those working in the field itself are the millions of persons employed in business activities closely related to it. This includes, in the first place, almost all *manufacturing firms*. It is true that some larger concerns, especially in the industrial goods field, utilize wholesaling institutions only to a small extent. It is rare, however, to find a manufacturer who is completely self-reliant in this area. Thus, to most manufacturers, the wholesaling system, even in the relatively restricted sense used herein, represents the primary market for the goods produced. Moreover, this system provides a constant flow of information about demand which should enable the manufacturer to coordinate the quantity and quality of production as needed.

Also affected by the wholesaling system and its performance are the many *retailers* who rely on it for their supplies of goods. Without a specialized wholesaling structure, most of these retail merchants would be unable to procure goods for sale except perhaps from local sources of supply. In a like manner, *industrial, commercial,* and *institutional* users of goods buy from wholesale establishments. Without a reliable source, especially for raw materials, parts, and operating supplies, industry would be subject to numerous costly interruptions.

Other segments of the economy engaged in or directly affected by wholesaling include *transportation agencies,* such as railroads and trucking companies, which handle goods in the course of their physical distribution; *storage companies,* such as public warehouses; and *financial institutions,* especially commercial banks, which facilitate the flow of products through the wholesale channels of distribution.

Finally, and most important of all, the *consuming public* is affected by the wholesaling system, although obviously not as directly as the business groups just mentioned. Although most consumers are not familiar with wholesale institutions or their activities, the effectiveness with which these tasks are carried on contributes ultimately to their high and rising standard of living.

The Essential Nature of Wholesaling. In its broadest and truest sense wholesaling includes all marketing transactions at the wholesale level, i.e., all purchases and sales other than those made to ultimate consumers. Under this concept the only goods not sold at wholesale are those distributed by manufacturers, farmers, and fishermen direct to consumers—an insignificant fraction of total output. Wholesaling is thus seen to be a necessary and integral part of marketing, one which pervades all lines of commerce and geographic regions.

Evidence of the essential character of wholesaling may be found in a study of economic history. As shown in some detail in Chapter 5, wholesaling activities and institutions have existed from the earliest times, references being made to them in the surviving writings of ancient Egypt, Babylon, and Sumeria. By the time of the Roman Empire, large-scale specialized wholesale enterprises were well established. Only in primitive societies, in which production is limited to the barest of necessities and is accomplished on a very small scale, is wholesaling absent.

A striking proof of the importance of a smooth-functioning wholesaling system is afforded by the experience of Communist Russia in the 1920's and early 1930's. During these years the marketing system that had grown up prior to the revolution was practically eliminated, but no adequate substitute was devised for it. Under the Tsarist rule the wholesaling business of Russia was largely free from governmental regulation and was organized on the independent proprietorship, the corporate, or joint stock company basis, and into consumers' cooperatives typical of other parts of Europe and of the United States. During the short-lived Lvoff and Kerensky regimes which followed the overthrow of the older form of government in March, 1917, the Provisional Government found it necessary to regulate the marketing system. Foods, especially, were brought under state control, and the private monopolies in grain and flour were confiscated. Following the October, 1917, Revolution, internal as well as foreign trade became a part of the state's economic activities. This status continued until the establishment of the New Economic Policy (the N. E. P.), early in 1921. At that time the Russian authorities deemed it wise to stop and appraise their progress. The tremendous task they had set for themselves needed to be reorganized on a sounder basis, and economic planning was injected into the picture. Some temporary relaxation of complete socialism gave private trading establishments, both wholesale and retail, a renewed opportunity. Such trade, however, was supplemental to the consumers' cooperatives and the state-owned trading establishments and was, moreover, subject to strict regulation.

In 1928 the temporary freedom of trade was greatly restricted under the first "Five-Year Plan," developed in that year. While this plan provided for most segments of the economy, there appears to have been no definite thought given to the requirements of an adequate system of wholesale and retail distribution, but rather a blind effort to weed out private traders and replace them with state and cooperative substitutes.

What actually took place in Russia during the first Five-Year Plan which extended from 1928 to 1933 is best summarized by one who was living there throughout that period in the capacity of an observer. W. H. Chamberlin, journalist and historian, points out:

The limited concessions which were made to private business enterprise under the New Economic Policy have been swept away, and no one in the Soviet Union today may own or operate the smallest kind of store, workshop, or restaurant, while private farming is also well on the way to elimination.[1]

This widespread planless elimination of private trading had many dire consequences, as might be expected. It had particularly unfortunate effects

[1] W. H. Chamberlin, *Russia's Iron Age* (Boston: Little, Brown & Co., 1934), p. 268.

upon Russia's available food supply. Discussing this particular phase, Chamberlin describes the changes which took place between 1921 and 1928 and what happened during the first Five-Year Plan in the following words:

The greatest change in the daily life of the Soviet citizen during recent years has been in the matter of food supply. From 1921, when the New Economic Policy came into effect, until 1928, there was no trace of rationing in the Soviet system. Foodstuffs were bought, without limitations as to quantity, in stores, just as in other countries, the only difference being that under the Soviet system there were fewer private shops and more state and cooperative stores.

The first pinch of food shortage was felt in 1928, and by the end of 1929 a widespread rationing system was in operation. At the same time a merciless drive of expropriation and confiscation was launched against the private traders. At the present time there is not a private business enterprise of any size and consequence throughout the length and breadth of the Soviet Union. The only private "traders" who remain are old ladies of the former régime who maintain a miserable existence by disposing of brooches, bits of lace, and other finery; individual peasants who bring a few carrots or a pat of butter to the market; and street hawkers of such commodities as worm-eaten apples and children's toy balloons.[2]

Another result of the neglect of wholesaling under the first Five-Year Plan was a lack of coordination in the wholesaling task of physical distribution. Whereas in the United States it is found to be more efficient and economic to ship most commodities in carload lots from the producer to the wholesale markets, and there to redistribute them by rail or truck to the retail stores, in Russia there has been inadequate transportation to distribute the products of Russian industry to the great consuming centers. It is interesting to note that G. Zberzhkhovski, a Russian writer, attributes some of the transportation problems to a "widespread underestimation on the part of some trading organizations in 1930 and 1931 of the importance of developing wholesale trade," which led to an excessive volume of small orders "direct from the factories to shops."[3] This disregard of the wholesale buying function "led in 1930 and 1931 to an increase in the number of underloaded goods wagons (freight cars) on the railways, retardation of traffic, and increased cost of transport, and what was most serious of all, an increase in the number of unassorted consignments to retail shops." Continuing, he adds:

All this prevented the distribution of goods from being properly regulated with a view to satisfying the specific requirements of consumers in different parts of the Union. Goods were sent to retail shops either in excessively large consignments which made it difficult for trading organizations to pay for them,

[2] *Ibid.*, p. 209.

[3] Leonard E. Hubbard, *Soviet Trade and Distribution* (London: Macmillan & Co., Ltd., 1938), p. 24.

or in excessively small consignments in which case it was impossible for retail shops to make the necessary assortments required to cater for the everyday needs of consumers.[4]

Direct distribution thus failed to meet the needs of the Union of Soviet Socialist Republics' system of distribution at two major points. It proved to be wasteful of transportation resources since it attempted to eliminate the valuable function of assembling merchandise in carlots at strategic points from which they could be redistributed in small quantities to the retailing outlets. It also failed to provide the retail units with adequate assortments of goods. The retail stores were allotted either too large quantities, with resultant overstocking and deterioration, or too small quantities, with frequent delays in delivery, leaving them short of needed stocks. The importance of wholesaling and the functions which a wholesaling system can perform for an integrated, socialized structure of production, distribution, and consumption are thus laid bare. Steps have since been taken to improve the transportation facilities of Russia, which will in turn help to put distribution on a more scientific basis. The experience of the 1920's and 1930's reveals the basic nature of wholesaling functions, which are fundamentally identical whether found in the Union of Soviet Socialist Republics or in the United States of America.

Functions of Wholesaling. The lessons of history and comparative economics prove the necessity for an organized wholesaling system. To find the reasons for this, however, it is necessary to go further and to examine the functions performed by wholesaling institutions. Analysis of these functions comprises a large part of this book. At this point they can only be summarized in the briefest fashion.

Buying and Selling. A basic function of wholesaling is the exchange of commodities between physical goods producers and retail outlets and between successive stages in the manufacturing process. While it may be argued that exchange functions can be partly eliminated through vertical integration, or even wholly eliminated through public ownership and control of business, it is noteworthy that even in these cases some *substitute* for exchange must be found. In socialist and communist countries, for example, governmental agencies must serve the same ends by systems of quotas and allocations. Likewise, in integrated companies it is often found more efficient to buy and sell goods between divisions in open competition with outsiders. Thus, in a free enterprise system, as long as the market mechanism is relied upon to direct the use of resources, buying and selling at the wholesale level will remain vital phases of the wholesaling task.

Transportation. As previously noted, much of the transportation system is part of the wholesaling structure in the broad sense of the term. The

[4] *Ibid.,* pp. 24–25.

necessity of moving goods from producing areas into consumer and intermediate markets is so obvious that it requires no explanation.

Storage. The most conspicuous and characteristic function of the wholesaling system is that of storage. To the layman this is probably the first thing that comes to mind when the words "wholesaling" and "wholesaler" are used. This is due, of course, to the presence in every city and town of warehouses operated by wholesalers and by others. In these facilities and in others less familiar, such as the great terminal grain elevators, goods are stored until needed for consumption or for use in business activity. Closely allied to this static *holding* of goods is the dynamic process of *assembly* in which goods from many manufacturers in all parts of the nation are sorted and distributed to the even greater number of customers served by wholesaling.

Risk-bearing. As goods pass through the channels of trade, risks attach to them constantly. There are *market* risks arising from changes in the price level and from other factors that cause losses in value. In addition, *physical* risks must be borne on account of contingencies, such as fire, theft, and weather. Bearing many of these risks is a basic contribution of the wholesaling system.

Financing. Like risk-bearing, financing is an inherent function in the marketing of all products. At each stage in the distributive channel and between these stages, someone must provide the capital needed to support inventories of goods and receivables created by their sale. The wholesaling system provides this capital down to the retail level, and often including the retail level through the extension of credit to the majority of retailers.

Marketing Information. The efficiency of any economy in satisfying the needs and wants of its consumers depends, in part, on the skill with which these needs and wants are determined and interpreted. In a complex industrial economy the collection and analysis of such information becomes a difficult and specialized job, which is accomplished partly by the business institutions in the wholesaling system.

Standardization and Grading. Another important phase of satisfying consumers' wants is the development of standards of product quality as well as standards of measurement and the application of these standards in production. Here again the wholesaling system is of major importance, especially in the formulation of standards for packaging and labeling, and of performing some of these tasks in their own places of business.

Other Functions. The foregoing comprise the basic marketing functions accomplished by the wholesaling system. In addition to these, certain other tasks are generally associated with wholesale distribution. For one thing, wholesaling institutions provide *marketing management services* to manufacturers and to retail and industrial customers, and especially to smaller retail stores. These include many different forms of assistance, ranging from accounting techniques to "store engineering" and advice on major policy problems. Another function not specifically covered by the list is that of *incidental manufacturing and processing* operations, such as assembling goods shipped "knocked down," and grinding and roasting of foods. These activities, while not properly included in wholesaling in a definitional sense, nevertheless have become customary parts of the operations of wholesale enterprises. Likewise, various kinds of *product service,* such as installation and repair, are commonly offered by certain kinds of wholesale enterprises.

All of these functions, taken together, comprise the task of wholesaling. The necessity for wholesaling, in turn, depends on the need for each of its functions. These may be and are performed in part by manufacturers, farmers, and other physical goods producers; in part by retailers; and by others. In advanced economies, however, the benefits of specialization dictate that a separate wholesaling system be developed. The existence of this system can be seen, then, as a natural outgrowth of economic development in the performance of the essential functions just described.

Value Added by Wholesaling.[5] It is common to separate marketing (including wholesaling) from "production," the latter term usually connoting physical changes in the products themselves. This dichotomy is misleading to the extent that it implies that marketing is not part of the production process and therefore is unproductive.

Actually, in the true economic sense, production consists in the creation of utilities, which, in turn, may be defined as want-satisfying power. Production, therefore, becomes the means for satisfying human wants. Wholesale marketing activities contribute to production through the creation of certain economic values or utilities, although such utilities are distinct from the change of form which is usually considered by the layman as *production.* Utilities created by wholesaling are those of time, place, and ownership. Time utility results from the greater capacity to satisfy human wants which a given commodity or service possesses at one point in time as compared with another. Thus the utility of a bushel of wheat which has been stored in a wholesale grain elevator from the time of harvest until the following spring is much greater normally in the spring than it was at the time of harvest. Similarly, place utility is the greater capacity to satisfy wants which a commodity possesses at a point of scarcity than at a point of plenty. Finally, ownership utility issues from the enhanced power of want satisfaction which a commodity usually has in the hands of a consumer over that which it enjoys when in the possession of a manufacturer or middleman.

Since wholesaling creates time, place, and possession utilities, it is properly regarded as a *type of production,* one which necessarily follows the

[5] See Chapter 14 for a more detailed consideration of the subject.

extraction of raw materials and their conversion into products. *Production* in this sense includes *all* business activities that create economic values in the form of utilities, from the extractive industries, through manufacturing, down to and including wholesaling and retailing. As a product passes through this process, a certain amount of value is added at each stage.

The values contributed by wholesaling through the creation of *time* and *place* utilities are generally recognized and understood though often not fully appreciated. It is more difficult, however, to understand that *possession* utility also constitutes a true addition to value. To explain this, it is helpful to refer to the concept of *marginal utility* as originally developed by Carl Menger and other Austrian and German economists in the nineteenth century. Utility refers to the usefulness, ability, or capacity of a good or service to satisfy human wants; and marginal utility is the utility of the *last* or marginal unit in a series of identical units of, say, a commodity in possession of an individual consumer. While the repercussions are to be felt throughout the channels of trade and in all the processes by which raw materials are transformed into finished goods, this can best be explained in terms of the ultimate consumer.

It has been established by observation, and one can verify it in his own experience, that marginal utility varies inversely with the quantity possessed for most products for most people. Thus, a man with no automobile would normally attach a high rate of utility to such a product. Already possessing one car, he would rate the utility of a second car exactly like it somewhat less; and for a third unit of the same product the utility would probably be very low or even nonexistent as he may have little or no use for it. This means that as the number of units of a given product increases in the hands of an ultimate consumer, the marginal utility diminishes. A corollary of this law of decreasing marginal utility is that *total* utility is equal to the total number of identical units of a commodity multiplied by the measure of the utility of the marginal unit. This law (of marginal utility and its corollary) lies at the nub of value creation by marketing and deserves more thorough familiarity by marketing students than it has had. A concrete illustration of this concept by means of a marginal utility schedule follows:

Number of Units	Commodity		
	A	B	C
1	10	15	7
2	9	14	6
3	8	13	5
4	7	12	4
5	6	11	3

Let us assume three commodities A, B, and C with marginal utility schedules as indicated in the above example. One unit only of Commodity

A would have a marginal utility measured by the number 10. With two units of Commodity A the marginal utility would fall to 9, and so on for the varying number of units and for the other commodities. Let us now assume that one man has four units of Commodity A and another has three units of Commodity B. The first man would thus have a marginal utility measured by 7 and a total utility measured by 28. The second man would have a marginal utility of 13 and a total utility of 39. The combined total utility of the two would then be 67.

Next, let us inject an exchange transaction in this situation, and for the sake of simplicity let it be in the nature of a barter. The first man wants a unit of Commodity B and offers the second man two units of Commodity A in exchange, and the offer is accepted. What effect has this simple exchange transaction had on the utility or value pattern? The first man now has two units of Commodity A and one unit of Commodity B, so that his total utility has increased from 28 to 33. The second man now has two units of each of the two commodities and his total utility has risen from 39 to 46. The combined total utility of the two men has thus increased from 67 to 79, a net gain of 12 created by the exchange opportunities (buying and selling) afforded by the marketing process.

THE STUDY OF WHOLESALING

Although wholesaling has existed since the beginnings of civilization, little attention has been given to it until fairly recently. There are several reasons for this, not the least of which is the continuing prevalence of certain basic misconceptions about the subject. There is evidence of a growing interest in wholesaling, however, and much progress has been made in a relatively short time toward the development of scientific wholesale distribution.

Neglect of Wholesaling in the Past. The idea that wholesaling is worthy of serious and scientific investigation is rather new. Prior to World War I, economists for the most part neglected marketing, including wholesaling. Even after the emergence of marketing as a separate field of study in the 1920's, wholesaling was usually regarded as a necessary evil rather than an integral part of marketing. Indeed, the attacks on "middlemen" and attempts to eliminate them, which can be traced back to ancient times, increased rather than diminished during this period. Predictions of the imminent disappearance of wholesalers appeared frequently in the trade and popular press. Thus wholesaling did not share in the intensified efforts of economists and businessmen to understand marketing which occurred in such comparable fields as, for example, retailing.

Several factors account for the general neglect of wholesaling up until the late 1920's. Probably the most important of these is the *complexity of the subject.* As shown in Chapters 2–4, it is difficult even to arrive at a satisfactory definition of wholesaling, much less to analyze its structure and functioning. The great diversity of conditions in various industries and areas, the tremendous variety of products passing through the system, the impact of legislation, are but a few of the many influences which make the principles of wholesaling so elusive.

A second reason for neglect, both by the general public and by economists, is the persistence of certain *misconceptions about wholesaling*. Among the more important of these are:

1. The belief that wholesaling is confined to the operations of *wholesalers*
2. The belief that the wholesaler is an anachronism
3. The belief that wholesaling differs in no important way from retailing insofar as internal management and operation are concerned

These ideas are obviously related. If the first two are accepted, then there would be no point in studying a vanishing phenomenon. If the third is believed, then nothing is to be gained by duplicating the existing knowledge of retailing. All of these are, however, mistaken notions, as will be evident from the contents of succeeding chapters.

A third factor contributing to neglect of wholesaling lies in the fact that the operations of wholesale establishments, unlike those of retail stores, are not open to public observation. Some wholesale organizations have unfortunately compounded this problem by maintaining an atmosphere of secrecy and even hostility toward attempts to study their activities. This attitude is gradually disappearing as progressive wholesaling executives have come to appreciate the mutual benefits of exchanging their experience and problems with others.

The Renaissance of Wholesaling. Since about 1925 there has been a real rebirth of interest in the field of wholesaling. Since that time the importance of the subject has been gaining wider recognition, and considerable research has been undertaken which throws much light on this little-known segment of our national economic life. For the first time in its history, the American Economic Association provided in its 1927 convention program for a discussion of wholesale trade. Other developments tending to bring the subject to the forefront occurred at about the same time.

The First National Distribution Conference, called by the Chamber of Commerce of the United States, met in January, 1925, to study various marketing problems, including wholesaling. Early in 1928 the same organization called a National Conference of about 300 wholesale executives to discuss problems in the wholesaling field. This was the first nationwide conference devoted to wholesaling. For some time there had been a widespread feeling that in many lines of trade wholesalers had been confronted with new and trying conditions which had not always been met successfully and that there existed a state of flux which did not augur a stable future in the industry. It was therefore deemed desirable for wholesalers to convene for a free and frank discussion of the common problems facing them.

A second conference with similar objectives met in the spring of 1929, at which time reports were submitted by committees which had been assigned at the 1928 meeting. These reports constitute some of the earliest efforts to analyze the operations of wholesale enterprises on a systematic basis.

Soon after the National Wholesale Conferences, the Bureau of the Census conducted the first census of business, covering operations for the year 1929. This census covered wholesale, retail, and service establishments, and has since provided the main source of quantitative information about wholesale trade. Subsequent censuses were taken for the years 1933, 1935, 1939, 1948, and 1954; others are scheduled for 1958 and every five years thereafter.

Developments since World War II have further intensified interest in the study of wholesaling. During the war, the armed services made great improvements in existing techniques for handling and storing goods. The urgency of improving these methods, and the availability of virtually unlimited funds for studying the subject, compressed many years of ordinary technological progress into three or four years. After the war, many of these ideas were adopted by private business. Indeed, even ten years later, the backlog of new techniques was still to be exhausted by most wholesale enterprises. During the same period there were strong incentives to raise the level of productivity in wholesaling, due to the loss of experienced personnel, the emergence of strong labor unions, and the rapid increases in wage rates that took place. As a result wholesaling became much more dynamic in the 1950's than at any time previously.

Not only has the U. S. Department of Commerce, as well as the various wholesaling trade associations, recognized the economic significance of wholesaling, but numerous other governmental agencies, notably the Departments of Agriculture and Labor, the Federal Trade Commission, and the Internal Revenue Service of the Treasury Department, have given the matter similar recognition. Attention to this subject has also been given by the Board of Governors of the Federal Reserve System and by many other public and private agencies. Bureaus of Business Research and Schools of Business or Colleges of Commerce in the leading universities have contributed substantially to our knowledge of wholesaling. Research foundations, such as the Brookings Institution, The National Bureau of Economic Research, and The Twentieth Century Fund, have published studies which contribute directly or indirectly to the growing literature on wholesaling. In short, as revealed in detail in the following pages, wholesaling has definitely and most assuredly come of age.

2

WHOLESALING
IN TERMS OF
TRANSACTIONS

Basic to any scientific treatment of the subject matter covered in this book is a full understanding of the true meaning of wholesaling conceptually. As in all science, including the social sciences of which wholesaling is a part, scholars in the field of wholesaling are in constant search for the truth regardless of where it may lead or of its possible adverse effects upon anyone. Much of this search has been directed toward a discovery and clarification of the fundamental nature of wholesaling and to what extent this true concept may properly be modified for specific practical applications without doing violence to its sound theoretical mooring.

In this effort the scholars have been handicapped by the widespread misapprehension and confusion in business and economic thinking concerning the nature of wholesaling. In this confusion legislative bodies and governmental administrative agencies have shared fully and sometimes contributed to it. Selfish business interests have added their part and in this have at times been abetted by conforming governmental organizations with an eye on appropriation sources and assistance. All of this has given rise to certain misconceptions that have stood in the way of objective study and research and an earlier clarification of this most important subject. To be sure, as will be pointed out later in this chapter, other reasons have been responsible for both the rise of some of the misconceptions and the tenacity with which they have held sway in certain quarters.

In the first edition of this book an attempt was made to clear some of the underbrush and to explore the basic nature of wholesaling in a preliminary way. Since then much work has been done in the field, important laws have been enacted that bear on the subject, considerable light has been shed in certain decisions handed down by both state and federal courts, and much experience was gained by the authors through both study and consulting work in that special area. It is hoped that the more comprehensive discussion presented in this chapter and the two immediately following will contribute to a better understanding of the concept of wholesaling and lead to generally sounder thinking on the subject.

Common Misconceptions. As an approach to a clarification of the basic concept of wholesaling it seems appropriate to examine a few of the more persistent errors currently found in discussions of wholesaling. There is, in the first place, no little confusion as to the fundamental distinction between *wholesaling* and *retailing*. A considerable part of this chapter will deal with this problem.

A second major difficulty is the failure to distinguish clearly between *wholesaling* (*wholesale trade*) and *wholesalers*. Much of the erroneous thinking and unwarranted interchangeable use of these terms can be traced to a failure to define the terms carefully before using them. Since *wholesalers* are engaged in *wholesaling* activities, it is very easy to fall into the error of identifying all *wholesaling* as the activities of *wholesalers*.

The fallacy of such an assumption becomes evident once the nature of a wholesaling transaction, discussed later in this chapter, is understood. Just as there is a difference between *retail sales* (which may be made by farmers and manufacturers as well as by retailers) and *sales of retailers,* so there is of necessity a distinction between *wholesale transactions* (which may be effected by various wholesaling institutions, including wholesalers, as well as by farmers, manufacturers, and retailers) and *transactions made by wholesalers*. As revealed in the discussion of the wholesaling structure in Chapter 6, *wholesalers* constitute but one segment of the field and account for about 40 per cent of the wholesale trade according to the *census concept* and a still smaller proportion of such trade in the broader view. Just as not all retail business is done by retailers, so it is true that not all wholesale business is done by wholesalers.

A third misconception that is closely allied to the one just discussed is the one in which the term *wholesaling* or *wholesaler* is treated as synonymous with that of *wholesale establishment*. As will be shown in the detailed discussion of Chapter 3, a wholesale establishment may be operated by a wholesaler or by someone else. The latter may be a functional middleman, a retailer, a manufacturer, or a group of farmers or other producers of raw materials. Thus the term *wholesale establishment* comprehends more than the activities of *wholesalers,* but less than the activities embraced in the term *wholesaling* when broadly conceived. The total business of all wholesale establishments is synonymous, however, with the total wholesale trade according to the Census viewpoint discussed in Chapter 3.

A fourth misconception of wholesaling, and a very common one, is that which identifies wholesaling with the activities of *wholesalers* only to the extent of their *sale* of goods *to retailers*. This fallacy of identifying the part with the whole grows out of the prevalence of the better known types of wholesalers in such trades as groceries who do sell largely to retailers. Even here, however, substantial amounts are sold by such wholesalers to restaurants, hotels, and institutions that are in the nature of commercial users of foods rather than retailers of such products. In other lines of trade, even regular wholesalers sell substantially to manufacturers, other industrial users, and to commercial concerns for business purposes rather than for resale. Furthermore, it excludes altogether the operations of all wholesale functionaries other than wholesalers. Consequently, the viewpoint conveyed by this misconception of wholesaling is as narrow as it is both impractical and theoretically fallacious.

A fifth and equally narrow use of the term "wholesaling" limits it to the operations of those wholesale middlemen who take title to the goods in which they deal. This of necessity excludes many legitimate and bona fide wholesaling groups and their functions from the field of wholesaling. Among others, it excludes the operations of all agents and brokers who do not normally take title to the goods in which they deal, nor does it include the activities of manufacturers' sales branches and other vertically integrated wholesale establishments. Such a concept is as capricious as it is arbitrary.

A sixth and final important misconception is one in which the term "wholesaling" is confined to wholesalers who handle the goods and otherwise perform all functions of the so-called regular, service, or full-function wholesaler. This is one of the narrowest concepts, as it does not even embrace all wholesalers, i.e., all wholesale middlemen who take title to the goods in which they deal, and excludes from its compass such wholesalers as drop shippers or desk jobbers, cash-and-carry wholesalers, and other limited-function wholesalers.

MAJOR CAUSES OF MISCONCEPTIONS ABOUT THE NATURE OF WHOLESALING

There are a number of factors accounting for the confusion and the misconceptions with regard to the true nature of wholesaling. In this discussion only the major causes are being considered.

Lack of Knowledge. The dearth of thoroughgoing research in the field of wholesaling until the 1930's and the consequent scarcity of literature on the subject contributed in no small measure to the confusion and misunderstanding current in many quarters about the true nature of wholesaling and its place in the economy of this nation and the world. As research in this area continues, the vast body of comparatively new and raw data on the subject becomes better assimilated, and the real nature of wholesaling finds expression in legislative acts and in court decisions, a correction of the false impressions and fallacious notions briefly discussed above will necessarily evolve. Traditional inertia and the usual time lag between correct interpretations by students of the subject and wide acceptance by the business community, let alone the public at large, militate against a rapid dissipation of views long grounded in ignorance or a disappearance of mistaken conceptions.

Varying Definitions for Purposes of Different Laws. While lack of knowledge may be the most common cause, there are other reasons for the confusion and misconceptions about the nature of wholesaling. One of them is to be found in the varying definitions and interpretations of the terms "wholesaling," "wholesale transaction," "wholesaler," or "wholesale establishment" in connection with different laws. For example, for purposes of the Robinson-Patman Act the Federal Trade Commission may define a wholesale transaction *narrowly* in order to confine the functional discounts or other benefits offered by suppliers on such transactions to a smaller volume of purchases and thereby prevent possibly unjustified price discrimination. For similar reasons it has refused to consider as a wholesale establishment any place of business that also engages in retail business, even when the preponderant part of the business is in the form of wholesale transactions. A similarly narrow interpretation is usually given to a wholesale transaction or a wholesale establishment by a State Tax Commission in its enforcement of a *retail* sales tax law.

On the other hand, for purposes of the Fair Labor Standards Act, which specifically exempts from its minimum wage and maximum hour provisions retail and service establishments (unless over one-half of their business is in interstate commerce), wholesaling is likely to be interpreted *broadly,* in order to limit the exemption from the law as much as possible. All of this is in line with the legal dictum that for purposes of coverage under a given statute the interpretation should be broad, while for purposes of exemption it should be narrowly construed.

For trade practice conference rules promulgated for an industry by the Federal Trade Commission, wholesaling may be defined broadly or narrowly, more or less in line with customary practice of the industry and depending upon how much industry viewpoints can prevail, although the effect upon competition is being constantly kept in mind by the Commission. A correct interpretation of wholesaling is illustrated by the definition of the Wholesale Plumbing and Heating Industry, which covers all those "engaged in the wholesale distribution and sale of industry products to dealers and distributors for resale and to other purchasers, such as, but not limited to, plumbing, heating, sheet-metal, and piping contractors, commercial and industrial users, governmental bodies, and institutions purchasing for business uses."[1] A similarly correct definition is to be found in the rules promulgated for the Fine and Wrapping Paper Distributing Industry, May 16, 1950. By way of contrast is the narrow definition of the business of the Wholesale Confectionery Industry of the Philadelphia Trade Area as consisting "primarily in purchasing these products from manufacturers and reselling and distributing the same to retailers."[2]

Varying Definitions for Statistical Purposes. Despite the fairly accurate definition of wholesale trade in terms of establishments by the U. S. Bureau of the Census, which will be discussed and utilized at various points throughout this volume, the Bureau of Labor Statistics, U. S. Department of Labor, defines wholesale trade in a completely different fashion. Here it is defined in the unusually and unrealistically restrictive sense as "selling merchandise to retailers."[3] Presumably, most of such trade is transacted by wholesalers; yet in its Index of Wholesale Prices no prices charged by wholesalers are included by the same governmental agency. Again, in the Wholesale Trade Series used by the Office of Business Economics of the U. S. Department of Commerce there is considerable adherence to the basic definitions and classifications used by the Bureau of the Census, but even here there are significant deviations as explained in its biennial supplements to the monthly *Survey of Current Business.*

It is perhaps not too difficult to understand differences in definition or concept of wholesaling on the part of businessmen, as individuals or collectively through the expressions of trade associations. In part they may be explained by lack of technical knowledge and more often by selfish motives. When, however, different parts of the federal government disagree substantially in this respect, the explanation may not be easy to find.

To be sure, the persons making the original decisions, while perhaps expert in statistical techniques and other aspects of government service, may have lacked basic knowledge of our business system as a whole and of wholesaling in particular. This was no doubt true of those who worked originally on the classifications of businesses based on income tax returns. They singled out commission merchants as one classification and "all other

[1] The "industry products" include plumbing and heating equipment and supplies and such air-conditioning equipment and supplies as are marketed for permanent installation. Trade Practice Rules Promulgated by the Federal Trade Commission, April 14, 1955.

[2] The products referred to include packaged candy, candy bars, chewing gum, and related confectionery items, as well as certain allied lines of merchandise. Trade Practice Rules Promulgated by the Federal Trade Commission, July 30, 1946.

[3] "Employment and Earnings," Annual Supplement Issue, Vol. 2, No. 12, June, 1956, p. 8–E.

wholesale trade" was lumped together into one other classification, despite
the fact that commission merchants account for only about 3.5 per cent of
all wholesale trade. Even in the days when the income tax was born, they
did not represent a major part of wholesale trade. It is quite probable that
the person playing a leading role in that decision may have had some
familiarity with and hence an exaggerated sense of the importance of the
commission method of operation on the wholesale level. Yet this ridiculous
classification has persisted through the years and is so presented to date in
Volume II of the annual corporation income tax returns by the Internal
Revenue Service. Such is often the price that is paid for sheer laziness or
for the dubious advantages of continuity and comparability. Whatever the
reason, it perpetuates errors and ignorance and thereby makes the existing
confusion worse confounded.

Obviously, differences in objectives will account for variations in the
scope of wholesale trade to be considered. If employment is the basic
consideration of the statistical collecting agency, the information may be
limited to those parts of wholesale trade in which large numbers of persons
are normally employed. Similarly, for certain purposes it may be felt that
only that part of brokers' business should be included that is represented by
the fees they collected rather than by the volume of business transacted.
Nevertheless, even though such deviations from a correct concept should
be justified, which may be highly questionable, the results should be designated by different terms rather than using the term "wholesale trade" with
entirely different sets of data.

Another possible explanation may lie in the extent to which different
agencies succumb to pressures, and their philosophy about it. It has become fashionable to resort to the services of advisory committees from the
various areas interested in statistics collected by governmental bodies. Depending upon the membership of such committees, especially of other than
professional and scientific societies, pressures may be exerted not so much
in the interest of truth as for the private benefit of some group. There are,
unfortunately, some statistical agencies of the government that either believe that such committees know best what the business facts are, or feel
that it is their duty to give those who contribute or use the information
what they want rather than what is true in the light of basic knowledge
and authoritatively recognized principles of business and economics. It
may take courage and involve loss of support for necessary appropriations
to resist such pressures, but fortunately in most instances the agencies hew
to the line established by intellectual integrity and high-purpose concomitant with a continuous search for the truth wherever it may lead.

Protective Motive. A desire to protect a certain group of wholesale
organizations in the way of trade discounts from suppliers or ineligibility
for membership in a given trade association may be the cause for differ-

ences in definition and interpretation of such terms as wholesaling, wholesaler, or wholesale establishment. For such restrictive purposes, which may
from a given point of view be justified, the concept may exclude concerns
selling primarily to commercial and industrial users rather than to retailers
for resale. Some authorities are inclined to consider such transactions as
in a so-called twilight zone between retail and wholesale, or as a third
basic category of marketing.

This point is illustrated by the historical case of the *Federal Trade Commission v. The Wholesale Dry Goods Institute, Inc.* For some years the
Institute published a list of wholesalers of dry goods and kindred lines, the
list including general and specialty dry goods wholesalers serving principally the retail trade. It did not cover ready-to-wear wholesalers, nor
wholesalers selling predominantly to manufacturers as would be true of
some piece goods wholesalers selling mainly to the cutter-up trade. Even
for dry goods proper, for purposes of listing, the Institute adopted a definition of a *wholesaler* as consisting of a

person, firm or corporation—
  (1) That is organized primarily to sell goods to and render service to re-
       tailers generally, and is not primarily interested in securing for a single
       retailer, or a limited group of retailers, price advantages which are not
       to be made available to other retailers;
  (2) That transacts business in sufficient volume to handle goods in whole-
       sale quantities and sells through salesmen, advertising and/or sales
       promotion devices;
  (3) That carries at all times at its principal place of business a representa-
       tive stock of the goods it sells, and from which it can fill the orders of its
       customers;
  (4) That extends credit to its customers and carries its own accounts.

The Commission claimed that this definition was too narrow, as it excluded "(a) buying offices or syndicates representing retailers; (b) their
stock carrying affiliates; (c) chain store central offices or warehouses; (d)
drop shippers; (e) brokers; (f) commission merchants; (g) selling agents;
(h) job lot dealers; (i) second hand dealers." It further contended that
"In numerous other instances concerns which are listed as wholesalers by
commercial agencies such as Dun & Bradstreet have been refused membership in the Institute or listing in its directory of wholesalers on the ground
that their operations did not conform to the Institute's definition of a
wholesaler."

While it may be argued that the Institute's definition was perhaps too
restrictive, it may be equally well argued that the Commission's concept
of a wholesaler was entirely too broad and in many respects out of line
with custom and the state of knowledge about wholesaling. Nevertheless,
the Commission enjoined the Institute from "preparing, maintaining, and

circulating any list of buyers considered or recognized by respondents as 'wholesalers,' or any similar list of preferred buyers."[4] This decision was upheld by the Circuit Court of Appeals;[5] the U. S. Supreme Court in 1944[6] denied certiorari proceedings, and thus the case ended.

Variations in Trade Custom and Tradition. Largely because of failure to distinguish clearly between the two types of consumption—personal or ultimate on the one hand and industrial, commercial, or business use on the other[7]—significant differences are to be found among the various lines of trade about what is regarded as a wholesale transaction. For example, in most lines of trade, including hardware, electrical, and plumbing, sales to contractors are properly regarded as wholesale transactions. In other lines of trade, as in the distribution of many building materials, such sales are considered to be retail in character. All of this gives rise to such conundrums as what is "ethical distribution," a "legitimate" distributor or wholesaler, or a "regular" dealer. These are more than differences of opinion. Each side is girt for battle, partly, as already indicated, because of a belief in the rightness of its position, and partly in order to protect its status and method of doing business deemed to be the most profitable. To confound the issue still more, for purposes of the 1954 Census of Business, sales to contractors were considered to be retail and establishments primarily engaged in making such sales were classified for the first time in Retail Trade.

Institutional v. Functional Approach to the Concept. A fifth cause for confusion and misconception of what is to be embraced by the terms wholesaling, wholesale, or wholesaler is to be found in differences in methods of approach and in viewpoints. There is, for example, an essential conflict between the institutional and functional approaches to the subject. This may be best illustrated from experience in the wholesale optical industry. In that line of trade wholesalers normally sell to oculists and ophthalmologists (both groups consisting of doctors of medicine specializing in eye treatment and surgery), optometrists, and dispensing opticians, the ophthalmic goods being sold on a stock or prescription ($\mathbb{R}$) basis.

That such transactions are wholesale is readily conceded by everyone. The disagreement arises, however, when such a wholesaler also engages in what is known in the trade as "wholesale dispensing," i.e., selling ophthalmic goods to a patient of an oculist or ophthalmologist (sometimes also to the patient of an optometrist) on the latter's prescription. If this type of transaction is viewed *institutionally* (i.e., from the legal arrange-

---

[4] Docket No. 3751, Findings and Order to Cease and Desist as of November 24, 1941.

[5] 139 F.2d 230 (CCA–2, 1943).

[6] 321 U. S. 770, 64 S. Ct. 258.

[7] Further developed later in this chapter.

ment viewpoint), it may be regarded as a wholesale transaction in so far as the wholesaler is concerned; for in such a case he merely acts as agent for the physician (often on the basis of a contractual arrangement to that effect) and retains for himself only the wholesale price of the goods plus a small charge as a fitting fee for the extra service rendered. On the other hand, it may be properly contended that the so-called "wholesale dispensing" is *functionally* retail in character, as the wholesaler deals directly with the consumer, sets the price for the goods, makes and fits the glasses, and collects the money from the ultimate consumer of the product.

After considerable litigation of this entire matter a Consent Decree was entered into by the defendants with the U. S. Department of Justice. It perpetually enjoined any doctor or other refractionist from accepting from any dispenser any payment arising out of or connected with dispensing to any of his patients. It makes no difference whether the dispenser acts or purports to act as an agent of the doctor or other refractionist. Nor does it make any difference whether the payment is in the form of a rebate, credit, credit balance, gift, dividend, participation in or share in profits, or anything else. It enjoined similarly all wholesalers and manufacturers from making such payments to a doctor or other refractionist.[8] Thus, the functional approach to this problem finally prevailed. This does not mean, however, that under other circumstances a different approach may not be equally justified both theoretically and legally.

DEFINITION OF WHOLESALING IN TERMS OF TRANSACTIONS

The Wholesale Transaction as a Basis for Defining Wholesaling. To understand the true nature of *wholesaling,* it is essential to comprehend the essence of a *wholesale transaction;* for it is the composite of such transactions that gives character to the business in which a person, firm, or corporation is engaged and that makes up the total of wholesaling or wholesale trade. It thus becomes necessary, first, to define a wholesale transaction and, second, to differentiate it from a retail transaction.

Prior to the first Census of Distribution taken for the year 1929, whatever definitions of such terms were used were clothed in vague and more or less general phraseology. To be sure, the veil which shrouded these definitions is to be explained in part by the fact that no clear-cut distinction between wholesale and retail trade was practicable until ample facts became available, and partly by the pioneering nature of studies in wholesale marketing which necessitated blazing a trail into hitherto unexplored areas of economic thought.

---

[8] *United States v. American Optical Company et al.* In the U. S. District Court for the Northern District of Illinois, Eastern Division, Civil Action No. 46 C 1333 (1951).

In preparation for the field canvass of the first census of wholesaling it became necessary to provide accurate answers to the many practical questions raised by enumerators and supervisors. In doing so, the senior authors, then in charge of the wholesale census, were compelled to draw a sharp and practical distinction, first between wholesaling and retailing, and later in more refined fashion between various parts of wholesaling itself. These definitions were further refined and elaborated for publication in the first edition of this book, and in the latter form served a useful purpose as a partial guide to certain decisions by the U. S. Supreme Court[9] and for some of the work of several governmental agencies. Since then the authors have continued their studies in this area and on the basis of the cumulated knowledge and added experience it is believed that correct and fully developed concepts are formulated and presented herein.

Definition of a Wholesale Transaction by Exclusion or Indirection. An easy way to define a wholesale transaction is by first defining a retail transaction and then considering all nonretail transactions, i.e., all other than retail sales, as wholesale. For example, a *retail sale* is typically defined as a sale (of goods or services) made to an ultimate consumer rather than to a dealer or merchant for resale. Since an ultimate consumer is an individual who buys the goods or services for his own use or for the consumption by his family, transactions involving any other type of consumer (commercial, industrial, institutional, governmental), with certain exceptions noted below, are nonretail or wholesale. Following this approach, a wholesale transaction is one that is nonretail. By exclusion, therefore, all transactions are wholesale that are not retail; by indirection, all nonretail transactions are wholesale.

To this kind of definition of a wholesale transaction there are two objections. One is based on the assumption that there may be more than two general types of transactions. Some students of marketing contend that there may be three classes of *marketing* categories: retail, wholesale, and a third involving transactions in industrial goods when goods are purchased not for resale but for commercial or industrial consumption. There is little justification for this position either in theory or in practice. An examination of the activities of middlemen in the industrial market reveals the fact that no separate classification is necessary for them. Most businessmen engaged in that field think of themselves as wholesale distributors, and a close scrutiny of their business methods indicates that they are right.

A dichotomous classification of marketing transactions into wholesale and retail (nonwholesale) or into retail and wholesale (nonretail) affords a natural and adequate basis for the scientific analysis of marketing phe-

[9] *A. H. Phillips, Inc. v. L. Metcalfe Walling,* 65 S. Ct. 807 (March 26, 1945); *Roland Electrical Company v. L. Metcalfe Walling,* 66 S. Ct. 413 (January 28, 1946).

nomena. This position is further strengthened by the fact that many business concerns cannot possibly be classified on the basis of whether they deal in the industrial market or in the ultimate consumer market. There are, for example, few wholesalers of electrical products or hardware who do not sell large quantities of their goods to industrial users, even though their major business may consist in the handling of merchandise intended for household or ultimate consumers.

More basic is the objection that in defining a wholesale transaction by exclusion or indirection nothing is learned of the essential character of such a transaction. Such a definition lacks positive identification and is devoid of essential characteristics. Above all, it fails to shed light on the real nature of wholesaling.

Questionable Criteria for Defining a Wholesale Transaction. In approaching the matter in more positive fashion, it has been suggested that wholesaling be defined by the *nature of the goods,* on the basis of whether they are industrial or consumer, and treating all transactions in industrial goods and those in consumer goods for resale as wholesale. This assumes, however, that industrial goods can always be identified and separated from consumer goods. To be sure, some commodities (like iron ore, steel, or crude oil) are seldom purchased by other than industrial users and can be readily labeled industrial goods. For most products, however, such a distinction is impossible. Products like coal, fuel oil, automobile tires, and so on ad infinitum are used by industrial and household consumers alike. This criterion is thus unrealistic.

The matter of price is sometimes injected; if not as a determining factor, at least as a test in distinguishing between a wholesale and a retail transaction, especially when coupled with the quantity concept. It is thus asserted that there are reasonably definite limits as to the quantities in which ultimate consumers buy certain goods and that on such quantities there are more or less normal retail prices, though not uniform or fixed and perhaps varying even in the same community. It is therefore assumed that sale of a given commodity at a lower than the so-called normal retail price is probably in the nature of a wholesale transaction.

While it is generally true that retail prices are by and large higher than wholesale prices, the assumption that retail prices are of necessity higher than wholesale prices because the retailer must add his margin (consisting of his cost of doing business and a reasonable net profit) to the net invoiced cost is entirely unwarranted. If that were so, there would be no need for the Fair Trade Laws and the Unfair Trade Practices Acts, both of which are essentially intended to prevent retailers from cutting the price below cost plus a relatively small margin.

Moreover, there is no such a thing as *a* retail price or *a* wholesale price. There are retail prices, a whole range of them for the same article, and the same is true of wholesale prices. In retailing much depends upon what type of store is patronized. If a consumer chooses to buy from a chain store or from a self-serve store operated by an independent, a lower price will be paid than that asked for the same goods by a service store. A supermarket—chain or independent—may undersell by still more. Again, it depends upon the method of buying. If an ultimate consumer wishes to buy a plumbing fixture from one of the nationally operating mail order houses by ordering it from the catalog, the price paid for it is that listed in the catalog plus freight charges in certain instances; if, however, the same fixture is to be purchased from one of the stores operated by the same mail order house, the price will in all probability be higher than that listed in the catalog by some 15 or 20 per cent. In addition, numerous special sales make the same goods available at substantially lower prices.

BASIC CRITERIA IN DEFINING A WHOLESALE TRANSACTION

In formulating a scientifically correct or theoretically sound definition of a wholesale transaction, consideration must be given to three basic factors or criteria, including:

1. Status or motive of the purchaser, i.e., the position of the customer and his purpose in making the purchase
2. The quantity of goods involved in the transaction
3. Method of operation of the concern

Status or Motive of the Purchaser. The single soundest basis for defining a wholesale transaction, especially for the purpose of differentiating it from a retail transaction, is afforded by the status or motive of the purchaser, i.e., the position of the purchaser or customer and his purpose in making the purchase. *On this basis a wholesale transaction is one in which the purchaser does not buy for his own private or personal use or that of his family and friends but is actuated by a profit or business motive in making the purchase.*

Approached from the vendor's viewpoint, the questions are in any one case: To whom was the sale made? What was the purpose of the customer in making the purchase? Obviously, all sales made to individual or ultimate consumers who buy the goods for their own use (including use by the family and other home consumption) are retail sales. It is equally clear that all sales, regardless of quantity involved, made to customers *for resale* by them to others are wholesale in nature. Thus, when a druggist orders from his wholesale supplier two-twelfths of a dozen of a certain item to be resold to consumers or when a gasoline filling station owner buys a single tire from the wholesaler to fill an order from a customer, the transaction is conducted in a wholesale manner and is beyond question wholesale.

A problem arises, however, in the treatment of sales of goods not for resale by the purchaser but for the use or consumption (commercial, industrial, or institutional) in his business, which may be operated for profit or as a nonprofit enterprise. This confusion can no doubt be traced to the failure to distinguish, as all marketing authorities have done, two types or classes of consumers, commonly designated as ultimate and industrial.

In the first class of consumers are included all people who consume or use up goods or services in the process of living. In this sense every person is an ultimate consumer. Goods bought for such consumption are known as consumer goods, and the final buyers of such goods are designated as individual, household, home, or ultimate consumers. Likewise, sales of goods to such consumers are universally regarded as retail sales, regardless of whether they are made by retail stores, directly by manufacturers or farmers, or occasionally by wholesalers.

Industrial consumers, on the other hand, are those consumers who use up the products they buy in the conduct of their business, whether the business be manufacturing, mining, road-building, residential construction, oil well drilling, farming, fishing, or lumbering. It also includes the consumption of goods in the operation of a wholesale house, a retail store, an office, a hotel, a restaurant, or an institution like a penitentiary or a hospital. Industrial consumers are, therefore, often divided into: industrial (in a narrower sense but including contractors), commercial, institutional, and governmental. The goods purchased for such consumption include raw materials and semimanufactures used for further processing before resale; parts used in connection with other goods when reselling; and machinery, equipment, and supplies used in the operation of the business.

If the *status* of the purchaser or the *purpose* in making the purchase is the only criterion in the definition of a wholesale transaction, all of the following types of transactions fall within the province of wholesaling:

1. Sales by manufacturers, directly from their factories or through their sales branches, to wholesalers and to other types and classes of wholesale middlemen
2. Sales to retailers of all types and classes
3. Sales to restaurants, hotels, and institutions (educational, fraternal, eleemosynary, social, or penal)
4. Sales to manufacturers, mining concerns, oil well companies, fisheries, railroads, public utilities, and government departments including the armed forces
5. Sales to farmers for use in operating the farm as a business enterprise, as distinguished from purchases by farmers for personal consumption. It is unfortunate that in the 1954 Census all sales to farmers were included with sales to household consumers.

6. Sales to barbers in the form of supplies and equipment. In this category are included all sales of equipment and supplies by so-called supply houses, so long as such equipment and supplies are not purchased from the supply house by ultimate consumers for their own use.
7. Sales of laboratory or office equipment and supplies to professional men, such as doctors, dentists, attorneys, optometrists, and accountants
8. Sales of building materials to construction contractors, except perhaps when they act as agents for and in behalf of the home owners
9. All activities and operations of middlemen who in some way aid in the transfer of title to goods to others than ultimate consumers. In this group fall the operations, involving purchases or sales, as the case may be, of brokers, resident buyers, purchasing agents in business for themselves, selling agents, manufacturers' agents, commission merchants, auction companies, and certain others
10. All purchases of farm products for resale to others than ultimate consumers, irrespective of whether such purchases are made directly from the farmers or from middlemen
11. All sales or purchases of raw materials, from whatever source, for resale on a wholesale basis

Quantity Involved in the Transaction. The very term "wholesale" or sale in *whole,* rather than in small quantities, etymologically suggests a definition based upon the quantity of goods involved in the transaction.[10] A wholesaler is thus commonly thought of as one who buys and sells in large quantities, whereas a retail store, in contrast, is characterized by numerous small sales. It is in line with this concept that in a number of important court decisions handed down over the years the test of the amount or size of the sale was applied, as illustrated by the following statement:

To retail means, generally, to sell by small quantities in broken parts, in small lots or parcels, not in bulk.[11]

It is this kind of thinking which accounts also for such statements as the following:

The quantity test [for distinguishing between retail and wholesale business] is a well-recognized business concept. . . . Quantities which are materially in excess of such a standard [referring to the quantity of a commodity which the general consuming public regularly purchases at any given time at retail] are generally regarded as wholesale and not retail quantities.[12]

[10] "Grosshandel" in the German language is the analogous word used for wholesale trade in contrast with "Einzelhandel" for retail trade. Similar connotations are conveyed by the French words *"en gros"* for wholesale and *"en détail"* for retail.
[11] *State v. Hawkins,* 91 N.C. 626.
[12] Interpretative Bulletin, Part 779, Retail and Service Establishment and Related Exemptions, Wage and Hour and Public Contracts Division, U. S. Department of Labor, April, 1954, p. 15.

Despite this and contrary to the layman's conception actual practice during this century has vitiated quantity as a basis for characterizing a transaction as wholesale or retail. While this basis for distinction may have been justified generically, it does not generally apply, as many wholesalers and other wholesale middlemen and establishments frequently buy and sell in very small quantities. It is the general practice for grocery and drug wholesalers, for example, to sell many items in dozen, half-dozen, or even single-unit lots. Retailers, on the other hand, sometimes sell in substantial quantities. The appearance of hand-to-mouth buying has caused wholesalers as well as retailers to buy in small quantities. It would thus appear that, while the quantity of goods involved in a transaction may be used as a rough gauge or as an *aid* in differentiating between wholesale and retail business, *it is by no means an ultimate consideration.*

Indeed, certain federal court decisions have specifically pointed out that the quantity factor cannot be taken as a sole determinant of the wholesaling character of a business. As early as November 10, 1915, the U. S. Circuit Court of Appeals, Second Circuit, ruled in the case of *The Great Atlantic and Pacific Tea Company v. The Cream of Wheat Company* that, while a wholesaler usually buys in comparatively large quantities, it is "the character, not of his buying, but of his selling," that "marks him as a wholesaler."[13] The same court stated again on March 13, 1923, in the case of *The Mennen Company v. The Federal Trade Commission,* that: "Whether a buyer is a wholesaler or not does not depend upon the quantity he buys. It is not the character of his buying but the character of his selling which marks him as a wholesaler."[14] Unfortunately, in neither case does the decision present any further enlightenment as to what really constitutes wholesaling or just how the "character of his selling" is determinative.

That the decisions in the above cases were amply justified on practical grounds, however, is apparent from the fact that many retailers make quantity appeals; i.e., they emphasize low prices based on quantity sales to ultimate consumers. Yet no one would regard such retailers as being engaged in the wholesale business. Among retailers of this type may be mentioned so-called consumers' wholesale supply houses and supermarkets. On the other hand, sales to retailers by manufacturers or by bona fide wholesale firms, when made in small quantities, cannot be regarded as retail transactions in the ordinary sense of the term.

[13] 227 Fed. 46 (CCA–2, 1915).
[14] 288 Fed. 774 (CCA–2, 1923); certiorari denied (U. S. Sup. Ct., 1923). While neither of these two cases specified the "character of selling" that would justify classifying a purchaser as a wholesaler, subsequent decisions rectified the omission pretty much in line with the conclusion reached in this discussion (see, for example, the cases involving the sale of nitrogen and other agricultural inoculators, all in 1938: 26 F.T.C. 320; 26 F.T.C. 303; and 26 F.T.C. 296).

The quantity concept is of definite value, nevertheless, in two respects. First, when viewed in the light of normal experience and practice in a given line of trade, it tends to indicate, though not to determine, the general nature of the transaction—whether wholesale or retail. Second, it is especially helpful in resolving a difficulty of practical application in connection with sales to commercial, industrial, governmental, or institutional buyers. Technically, on the basis of the status of the purchaser, such a transaction is to be regarded as wholesale. In many instances, however, such sales are made by what are normally regarded as retail establishments, and it may be most difficult if not impossible to distinguish between an ultimate consumer and an industrial or commercial user. In such cases the quantity in the transaction throws light on the question: if the purchase is not materially larger than the quantity which might reasonably be purchased by a private or ultimate consumer, it may well be regarded from a practical standpoint as retail; similarly, if the quantity involved in a particular transaction is materially in excess of that which might reasonably be purchased by an ultimate consumer for his own use, the transaction is wholesale in character. In neither of the two sets of instances, however, is quantity per se decisive.

Method of Operation of Seller. From the vendor's method of doing business much can be learned of the wholesale or retail character of the enterprise. Normally, a retail establishment is characterized by the following: (1) it is open to the general consuming public; (2) sales are made over the counter; (3) usually in small quantities; (4) in large numbers; (5) to ultimate consumers who buy for direct consumption; (6) at so-called retail prices that are not subject to various types of discounts. Even to these general attributes there are exceptions. The warehouse of the mail order retailer is not normally open to the public and sales by such a concern are not made over the counter, nor are sales technically made over the counter in a supermarket.

Just as there are attributes characterizing a retail establishment, so there are certain principal attributes of a wholesale establishment. (1) A wholesale establishment is not open to the general consuming public. (2) It does not normally make sales over the counter to any substantial degree. (3) It may specialize only in buying. (4) If engaged in selling, it usually employs outside salesmen. (5) The prices quoted are generally subject to discounts —trade, quantity, and special. (6) Its terms of sale are peculiar, usually involving cash discounts and free credit periods, as are its credit operations from the standpoint of both procedure and services used for securing information. (7) Its affiliations with and memberships in trade associations and credit groups are different from those with which retail stores generally affiliate or in which they hold memberships. Even the business terminology used in dealing with customers is distinctive.

This concept is helpful in supplying prima facie evidence of the whole-sale or retail character of a given transaction. However, not all sales even of bona fide wholesalers are made at wholesale, for to some extent they may and do sell at retail. Similarly, not all sales by retailers are made at retail. Practically every large department store, for example, operates a so-called contract department which handles sales made to institutions and offices in a wholesale manner, not for the ultimate consumption by the buyer but for business use by the institution or office. In some department stores such sales are not segregated. It would, therefore, seem most prac-tical, in the absence of knowledge to the contrary about purpose or quan-tity, to treat a transaction as wholesale if it is made by a wholesale estab-lishment and as retail if it is made by a retail establishment. *In no event can this criterion be considered final and determinative.*

Formulating a Definition of Wholesaling. From the foregoing discussion it appears that the *motive of the purchaser* is by far the most basic criterion in defining a wholesale transaction and in distinguishing it from a retail sale and, consequently, in differentiating between wholesaling and retailing and between wholesale and retail trade. *In fact, it is the determining factor.* The factors of quantity and method of operation cannot be overlooked, however, under certain conditions, but even then they are merely pre-sumptive. While not determinative or decisive in themselves, they must be used in conjunction with the purpose for which the goods are bought in reaching a decision as to the nature of the transaction when the facts are otherwise not sufficiently clear. The distinction between wholesaling and retailing, in the basically conceptual sense, may therefore be drawn in the following terms:

Wholesaling includes all marketing transactions in which the purchaser is actuated solely by a profit or business motive in making the purchase and, if the goods are bought from a concern operating substantially as a retail establishment and such goods are not intended for resale, the quan-tity is materially in excess of that which might reasonably be purchased by an ultimate consumer.

Retailing includes all marketing transactions in which the purchaser is actuated solely by a desire to satisfy his own personal wants or those of his family or friends through the personal use of the commodity or service purchased; it also includes transactions involving the purchase of goods for industrial consumption, from a concern operating substantially as a retail establishment, in quantity not materially larger than that which might reasonably be purchased by an ultimate consumer.

The definition of a wholesale transaction, in line with the above state-ments, is therefore based solely on the motive of the purchaser and is one involving a purchase for resale or for use in business. When, however, a purchase is made in a retail store, it is assumed that the transaction is of a retail nature unless (1) the goods are bought for resale or (2) are bought in a quantity substantially in excess of what is normally bought in such goods by an ultimate consumer. In any event, price is irrelevant in determining whether a given transaction is wholesale or retail.

Conclusion. As may be gleaned from some of the discussion in the two chapters that follow, the definition of wholesaling herein formulated, in terms of the totality of wholesale transactions, is directly in line with the thinking of the Federal Trade Commission, the Wage and Hour and Public Contracts Division of the U. S. Department of Labor, and the federal courts including the U. S. Supreme Court. It is also substantially in line with the thinking as expressed by some of our state legislatures in their more recent enactments of unfair sales, sales below cost, or unfair trade practices acts. A wholesale sale, under these laws, is thus commonly deemed to be a transfer of goods to the purchaser "for purposes of resale or further processing or manufacturing."[15] This, it is evident, gives no consideration whatever to the matter of quantity nor does it spell out the fact that a wholesale sale may be made for purposes other than resale or further processing or manufacturing. That the latter is probably contemplated, even though not clearly stated, is evident from a more recent definition of a wholesaler in such a state law which includes any organization selling or supplying "any commodity, article, goods, wares, or merchandise to retailers, industrial buyers, restaurants, institutions, or the selling on the part of one wholesaler to another wholesaler."[16]

[15] Arizona Revised Statutes, 1955, Volume 5, Title 44, Chapter 10, Article 4, Section 44–1461(7); also Massachusetts General Laws, 1932, Chapter 93, Section 14E(e), as amended by Chapter 494, 1941.

[16] Minnesota Statutes of 1953, Chapter 325, Section 325.01, Subdivision 3, as amended in 1957.

3

WHOLESALING IN TERMS OF ESTABLISHMENTS

It is not sufficient to define wholesaling in terms of transactions. For many important practical purposes the wholesale "establishment" concept is of greatest value or concern. This is obviously true in the choice of wholesale outlets for the distribution of goods and in the claim to such choice where that is relevant. Again, in taking a census of wholesale trade, as in all other censuses, the enumeration must be made by some physical unit in order that (1) such unit may be readily discerned and canvassed and (2) the results may be presented by geographic areas, i.e., by regions, states, counties, and cities. Similarly, for purposes of the Fair Labor Standards Act it would be most difficult to enforce some of its provisions on any basis other than the establishment. Most important, since practically all of the statistical facts pertaining to wholesaling are in terms or on the basis of establishments, it is best to treat the subject largely in such terms. To do so, however, it is essential first to define a wholesale transaction, as the sum of such transactions volume-wise determines, for example, whether the establishment is wholesale or retail in its operations. Thus the material presented in the preceding chapter is prerequisite to an understanding of the subject matter discussed in this chapter.

What Is an Establishment?

One of the questions in this area of thought on which there has been considerable controversy relates to the nature or concept of an establishment. On the one hand it is contended that an establishment is a company, an enterprise, a business, or an organization. Opponents to this view, on the other hand, contend that the term must be restricted to a single place of business. Even then it is not clear as to what is a place of business, whether it must be physically or organizationally separate and distinct from other places or just what physical segregation connotes. The implications of a correct definition of the term, as revealed in the following discussion, are important and far-reaching.

Correct Meaning of the Term "Establishment." When not used loosely or in nontechnical parlance, the term "establishment" refers to a single physical place of business. It does not refer to a company, a business, an organization, or an enterprise unless such company, business, organization, or enterprise is coextensive with the single physical place of business. The physical place of business need not, however, be an entire building, a floor of a building, or even an entire room. It may consist of but part of an office, store, or warehouse, or even of part of a home from which the business is transacted, so long as it is physically segregated and identifiable as a physical unit.

This view is in line with the concept adopted by the Bureau of the Census, which is in conformity with the requirements of the *Standard Industrial Classification Manual,* Volume II, Nonmanufacturing Industries, 1949 edition, issued by the Bureau of the Budget, Executive Office of the President. In the census publications it is spelled out in the following manner:

Wholesale trade as defined in the *Standard Industrial Classification Manual,* and as covered in the 1954 Census, includes establishments or places of business primarily engaged in selling merchandise directly to retailers; to industrial, commercial, institutional or professional users; or to other wholesalers; or acting as agents in buying merchandise for, or selling merchandise to, such persons or companies.

The concept of the term "establishment" as used in the census of Retail Trade is of the same essence. The same is true of the censuses of Manufactures and of Services.

Similar treatment is to be found in the administrative interpretations used under the Fair Labor Standards Act. On this score, the Office of the Administrator of the Wage and Hour and Public Contracts Division of the U. S. Department of Labor is quite explicit when it states that:

The term "establishment" . . . means a distinct physical place of business. The term is not synonymous with the words "business" or "enterprise" as applied to multi-unit companies. . . . Each physically separate place of business must be considered as a separate establishment.[1]

Just what constitutes a physically separated place of business must be construed in the light of a given situation. For example, in the lumber

[1] Interpretative Bulletin, Part 779, April, 1954, p. 3.

business an establishment comprises the yard with its offices, stock room, lumber sheds, grounds, and appurtenant structures. Similarly, a bulk tank station as *an* establishment includes many physically separated bulk tanks, together with the offices, and other structures at a given location; such an establishment may cover a considerable area and comprise many physically separated places in the literal sense, but they are all operated and managed as a single establishment. Again, a large department store with many segregated and departmentized lines of merchandise and numerous nonselling departments, if there is unity in ownership of all the departments and they are all operated as a single store, is a single establishment; leased departments in such a store, because of differences in ownership, are, however, separate establishments.

On the other hand, if part of the business is operated *functionally* on a different basis, even though it is under the same ownership and is physically connected with another part of the business, it is regarded as a separate establishment. Pertinent to this viewpoint is the decision by the U. S. Circuit Court of Appeals, Seventh Circuit, on November 29, 1945, in the case of *Walling v. Goldblatt Bros., Inc.,*[2] operators of a chain of department stores. These stores were being served by six warehouses, all located in Chicago. One of these warehouses "is just back of and across the alley from defendant's retail store on State Street, the warehouse and store being connected by three passage-ways, two of which are overhead and one underground. The warehouse is connected with no other building. This store and warehouse are heated by a single heating plant which is located in the State Street store."

Despite that close physical connection the warehouse was considered a separate establishment, although its employees were not brought under the Wage and Hour Law, simply because they serviced only the needs of the State Street store and hence were not deemed to be engaged in interstate commerce. At the same time, a drapery workshop maintained in this warehouse (which, among others, serviced the defendant's stores at Hammond and Gary, Indiana, and was therefore deemed to be engaged in interstate commerce) was ruled to be a separate establishment, and its employees became subject to the provisions of the Wage and Hour Law. By the same token the central office was ruled to constitute a separate establishment even though it was housed in part of the State Street store building; its employees were deemed to engage in wholesaling functions "which are neither retail nor local" and were therefore not exempt from the minimum wage and maximum hour provisions of the law.

Judicial Interpretations. One of the earliest cases in which the matter of what constitutes an establishment was faced squarely is that of *Fleming v.*

[2] 152 F.2d 475 (CCA–7, 1945); certiorari denied (U. S. Sup. Ct., May 27, 1946).

American Stores, Inc., decided by the District Court on December 30, 1941.[3] At that time the company operated 2,300 retail stores and food markets in several states, 11 warehouses, a main office, and a number of manufacturing and processing plants. Of the 14,000 persons employed by the concern, some 400 were employed in the central or main office and about 2,800 workers were used in its other offices, warehouses, manufacturing and processing plants, bakeries, transportation facilities, repair and machine shops, printing and multigraphing plant, and other nonretail selling units. The company contended that all of its employees were exempt from the wage and hour provisions of the Fair Labor Standards Act, because they were all employed in a "retail establishment." In its brief it took the position that "The retail establishment of the business of the defendant is the entire business of the defendant . . ." and that it takes all of the offices, warehouses, etc., as well as the retail units of the system "to make the retail establishment known as the American Stores Company."

In rendering its decision, the court put the question thus:

Specifically, is a $33,000,000 chain store organization, employing more than 14,000 workers, with gross annual sales of $115,000,000 which directly and through wholly-owned subsidiaries operates 2300 retail grocery stores and eleven warehouses in seven states and the District of Columbia, along with food-processing and manufacturing plants, etc., a "retail establishment"?

"That," the court said, "is the paramount issue in this action." It then proceeded to state its view in the negative in the following relatively strong terms:

I cannot subscribe to the defendant's view. To do so would be to do indescribable violence to the word "establishment" in section 13(a)(2). It does not follow that because a unit of an enterprise is a component or necessary part of that enterprise, that it is to be so regarded as part and parcel of the whole enterprise as to lose its individual and separate identity as an establishment.

In its decision on February 11, 1943, the U. S. Circuit Court of Appeals, Third Circuit,[4] affirmed the lower court's decision with some minor modifications that had no bearing on the definition of an establishment.

Another early case in which a similar decision was rendered by the U. S. Supreme Court is that of *A. H. Phillips, Inc. v. Walling.*[5] The company operated a chain of 49 retail grocery stores in Massachusetts and Connecticut and maintained a separate warehouse and office building in Springfield, Massachusetts, for the servicing of the stores. It claimed that its retail

---

[3] 133 F.2d 840.
[4] *Walling v. American Stores, Inc.* (CCA–3, 1943).
[5] 65 S. Ct. 807 (1945).

stores, warehouse, and central office together constituted a "retail establishment." To this the Supreme Court replied: "The lack of merit in this
claim is obvious." It continued with the following statement:

Even if, as petitioner urges, the word "establishment" referred to an entire
business or enterprise, the combined retail-wholesale nature of petitioner's interstate business would prevent it from properly being classified as a local "retail
establishment." But if, as we believe, Congress used the word "establishment"
as it is normally used in business and in government—as meaning a distinct
physical place of business—petitioner's enterprise is composed of 49 retail
establishments and a single wholesale establishment.

In a much later decision by the U. S. Supreme Court[6] the conclusion was
so clear and decisive that any controversy as to the nature of an establishment should have been laid to rest. In this case the company contended
that its five physically separated warehouses located in downtown Los
Angeles and used in its business of moving and storage of household and
commercial goods had been operated for years as a single unit under
central office management and with an interchange of employees and should
therefore be considered a single establishment. With this point of view
the trial court (U. S. District Court) agreed on the basis of the employer's
historical unit of operation and control, and the Circuit Judges affirmed it.
The Supreme Court, however, reversed the decisions of the lower courts
on the same grounds and with the same reasoning that it used in the
Phillips case quoted above and to which specific reference was made by
it. Accordingly, it was ruled that while all five warehouses were engaged
in what may be properly considered "retail" business and were therefore
exempt from the wage and hour provisions of the law, one of those warehouses (considered as an establishment) lost the exemption because more
than 50 per cent of its business in dollar volume was interstate.

OWNERSHIP OF WHOLESALE ESTABLISHMENT IRRELEVANT

From time to time the question is raised as to whether ownership of
the place of business is determinant in establishing its wholesale character.
Such a question is usually connected with the treatment of chain store
warehouses and the warehouses maintained and operated by department
stores.

Economic Basis. It is sometimes contended that a warehouse maintained
and operated by a department store for the servicing of the retail store
with merchandise is not a wholesale establishment but an integral part

---

[6] *James P. Mitchell v. Bekins Van and Storage Company,* Docket No. 122, March
11, 1957; 231 F.2d 25 (CCA–9, No. 14, 618, March 1, 1956).

of the retail business. This point of view seems to be so prevalent that no attempt has been made to date to include such establishments in the census of Wholesale Trade. It is similarly contended that warehouses operated by chain store systems for the supplying of merchandise to the retail units of the system and otherwise servicing such stores with records and supervision are but part of the retail business of the enterprise and are not engaged in wholesale operations, except to the extent that they may sell to retail stores not belonging to the chain or to other wholesale establishments not part of the system. Even the Bureau of the Census has succumbed to this untenable position in its treatment of chain store warehouses. In its first two censuses of business taken for the years 1929 and 1933 chain store warehouses were treated, as they properly should be, as wholesale establishments and data for them were included in the census of Wholesale Trade. For some reason they were dropped from the Wholesale Trade censuses taken for the years 1935, 1939, 1948, and 1954, despite protestations from authorities and recommendations of a committee representing a scientific group.

The entire matter hinges upon whether the character of a business establishment is to be determined by ownership or by functioning, whether the important thing is: *who owns it or what it does.* If the ownership basis is to be pursued, in line with the contentions for not including chain store warehouses or department store warehouses in the wholesale category because they are part and parcel of a retailing organization or system, the same treatment for the sake of consistency must be accorded to wholesale branches maintained and operated by manufacturers, since these are used primarily or entirely for the disposal of the manufacturer's output and hence they should be considered part of the manufacturing business. For similar reasons marketing cooperatives owned by farmers must not be considered as wholesale establishments but an integral part of farming, the products of which they are designed to market.

The very statement of these points reveals the fallacy of such a position. A manufacturing plant is a manufacturing plant no matter who owns it, and it should be covered by the Census of Manufactures. By the same token a wholesale establishment is a wholesale establishment whether it is owned and operated by a wholesaler, a commission merchant, a manufacturer, a retailer, a group of farmers, or anyone else, and it should be included in the Wholesale Census. Whether a given place of business is a wholesale establishment is purely a matter of what it does, how it functions, and whether it operates basically in a wholesale manner. In the words of the census authorities it is *generally* true that "Selling on a wholesale basis is selling primarily to retailers, dealers or distributors who buy the goods for resale, or selling to institutional and industrial users who purchase for business use rather than for the purpose of reselling the goods in the same form." The word "selling" is and has been used by the Census in a broad way to include transfers of goods from a manufacturer, for example, to his own wholesale branches or to his own retail stores.

Judicial Views. It is interesting to note that in all important decisions by the courts of the land in which this question was involved the functional basis was used in ascertaining the character of the establishment. Thus, in the District Court's decision of *Fleming v. American Stores, Inc.,* referred to above, the following significant statements appear:

The defendant's warehouses perform essentially the same functions as those performed by independent wholesale grocers, and their mode of operation is substantially the same. . . .

It is patent that the cost of operation of these seven warehouses [servicing stores in other states] is reflected in the cost of operation of the retail stores which they serve, since each retail store is debited by the defendant with the overall charges of the servicing warehouse. The prices charged by the defendant's retail stores for the commodities which they sell are affected by the operating cost of the stores which, in turn, reflect the operating cost of their servicing warehouse. . . .

Since wholesalers who sell in interstate commerce to non-chain store grocery stores and meat shops, which are engaged in competition with the stores operated by the defendant, are compelled to comply with the Act, an exemption of similarly operated warehouses would result in a burdensome differential to the complying warehouses and their customer retail stores.

Not only was it ruled that the chain store warehouses were not retail establishments, but the Circuit Court of Appeals went one step further and ruled that "The maintenance of the warehouse . . ." is not to break the continuity of the movement of the goods until they reach the defendant's retail stores, "but to make it even, economical and uninterrupted." Because of that (i.e., since the goods bought by and delivered to the warehouse from out of the state did not come to rest at the warehouse but continued in the flow of commerce), it was concluded that all of the company's warehouse employees were engaged in interstate commerce even though a given warehouse serviced only stores within the same state in which it was located.[7]

Much more pointed is the Supreme Court decision in the case of *A. H. Phillips, Inc. v. Walling* briefly discussed above, as shown by the following excerpts from the decision:

We hold . . . that the warehouse and central office of petitioner's chain store system cannot properly be considered a retail establishment. . . .

[7] *Walling v. American Stores, Inc.* (CCA–3, 1943).

A warehouse and a central office such as petitioner maintains are vital factors in this integration of the retail and wholesale functions. They are necessary instruments for the successful performance of the wholesale aspects of a multi-function business of this type. . . .

The disappearance of the independent middleman, together with his separate operations and charges, does not mean, however, that this essential intermediary or wholesale function of moving goods from producer to retailer has been abolished. In this instance it has only been taken over by the retailer, acting through its own distinct wholesale units. . . .

These duties [referring to the duties of the warehouse and central office employees], rather, are economically, functionally and physically like those of the independent wholesaler's employees. . . . We fail to perceive [any intent on the part of Congress or the law] to discriminate against chain store employees engaged in wholesale activities or to give to chain store warehouses a competitive advantage in labor costs over independent wholesalers.

Similar reasoning was followed by the U. S. Circuit Court of Appeals, Seventh Circuit, in the case of *Walling v. Goldblatt Bros., Inc.,* referred to previously in this chapter. This case dealt with warehouses maintained by a chain of department stores, but in the light of the decision of *Walling v. American Stores, Inc.* by the U. S. Circuit Court of Appeals, Third Circuit, if such decision should prevail, it would seem that this reasoning would apply even to a warehouse servicing a single department store located within the same state as the warehouse. In overruling the judgment of the District Court in the *Goldblatt* case, the Circuit Court concluded that:

Under this decision we feel impelled to hold that a majority of the defendant's employees working in its central office, located in the State Street store, in the bakery, in the drapery shop, located in the State Street warehouse, and in the five warehouses, not including the State Street warehouse, are engaged in wholesaling and manufacturing functions which are neither retail nor local. . . .

There is not the slightest doubt but that, in states where a chain store tax is imposed upon retail units only, a wholesale establishment would be exempt regardless of whether it is owned by a retail chain, by a wholesaler, or by a manufacturer and that such exemption would be determined solely by the method of operation or "character of the selling" by the establishment and not by its ownership. Again, in any consideration of local price-cutting practices and other possible injuries to competition that might be prohibited under state or federal law, especially when levels of competition are involved, the functioning of the specific establishment in question—whether on the manufacturing, wholesale, or retail level—is of significance and relevant rather than its ownership.

Proportion of Wholesale Business Required for a Wholesale Establishment

For the vast majority of wholesale establishments there is no problem in deciding how much of its business must be wholesale in order to qualify it as a wholesale establishment. This problem arises only when an establishment is engaged in more than one type of operation or more than one level of distribution, the usual combination of the latter being that of retail and wholesale.

Varying Viewpoints. For purposes of membership in a given trade association the requirement may be that practically all of the business be conducted on a wholesale basis. It may well be against the rules, explicitly or by implication, for any member to sell at retail, presumably in the interest of fair treatment of retailers and others operating at that level who are the normal customers of the wholesale establishment. Quite often the percentage of wholesale business is fixed at a minimum of 75 per cent or 80 per cent.

For census purposes, the requirement for such classification is a majority or over 50 per cent of the business, in dollar volume, at wholesale. This can be seen from the following statement in the census reports on Wholesale Trade:

Many business concerns do not fall clearly in either the retail or the wholesale division. Since it is impracticable, as a rule, to classify any single business establishment in more than one phase of the census, the *major-portion-of-business* or the *50-per cent* rule is followed for the most part. Establishments are placed in one classification or another according to their major activity.

That similar treatment is accorded to such establishments by the Census of Retail Trade can be gleaned from the following statement appearing in its publications:

Wholesalers-retailers are included in their entirety in whichever of the two censuses the *major* portion of their business applies.

For purposes of the wage and hour provisions of the Fair Labor Standards Act the Administrator at first adopted the "greater part" rule, which was expressed in G–37 on May 21, 1940, and in other releases of rulings in the following language:

For purposes of enforcement it is our position that any establishment which is engaged exclusively in the distribution of merchandise may be considered a retail establishment if 50 per cent or more of the dollar value of its total sales are retail sales.

In connection with these statements a warning was sounded, however, that the courts might not approve of such an arbitrary division but place emphasis instead on whether it also does a *substantial* wholesale business[8] and that in determining what is substantial dollar volume may be insufficient. When Interpretative Bulletin No. 6, issued December, 1938, was completely revised in June, 1941, the latter included the statement that:

> . . the Administrator will ordinarily consider the nonretail selling of an establishment to be substantial if the gross receipts from such selling constitute more than one-quarter (25 per cent) of the total gross receipts of the establishment.

The reason for the change from "the greater part" concept to the "substantial" concept as expressed in terms of over one quarter of gross receipts or sales was the feeling, first, that the concept of what is a retail sale has been broadened in the revision and, second, that exemption from the law should be construed narrowly. Thus the adoption of the 25 per cent rule was partly an expedient and a compromise but was no doubt motivated largely by a desire to widen the coverage of the law. On this basis it means that an establishment which in the ordinary course of business engages both in wholesale and retail selling is considered to be a wholesale establishment if more than one-fourth of its business (gross receipts) is done at wholesale or is nonretail.

The waters were muddied still more in a later revision which defined a retail or service establishment as:

> . . . an establishment 75 per centum of whose annual dollar volume of sales of goods or services (or of both) is not for resale and is recognized as retail sales or services in the particular industry;[9]

Instead of clarifying the matter, this revision raises many questions, some of which it attempts rather unsuccessfully to answer in succeeding pages. For example, what is meant by the words "for resale"? How about purchases of goods for business use, as in the purchases of equipment and supplies, that are not resold directly or indirectly? Does it mean that the same type of transaction might be considered retail in one line of trade and nonretail in another simply because the businessmen in those trades treat it that way? If that is so, there would be no such thing as a retail sale per se; and, hence, such sales can never be measured and compared.

Finally, in its work the Federal Trade Commission has generally refrained from classifying an establishment as wholesale or retail, but has insisted instead on treating each type of transaction on its own merits. This is illustrated by its decision in the *L. & C. Mayers Co., Inc. v. Federal Trade Commission* case discussed in the next chapter, in which the company was prohibited from representing itself as a wholesaler when selling to consumers, involving three specified types of transactions, but was free

[8] *Wood v. Central Sand and Gravel Company,* 33 F. Supp. 40.
[9] Interpretative Bulletin, Part 779, April, 1954, p. 2.

so to represent itself for the other types of bona fide wholesale transactions. This decision, which was approved by the U. S. Circuit Court of Appeals, Second Circuit, on June 6, 1938, although reached in a case brought under authority of Section 5 of the Federal Trade Commission Act, would appear to be applicable to the provisions also of the Robinson-Patman Act, discussed in the next chapter to some extent, and of other pertinent acts under the jurisdiction of the Commission.

The "Greater Part" of Business as Determinant. There are many arguments in favor of using the majority or more than 50 per cent of the business of an establishment in characterizing its wholesale or retail nature. That principle has been followed by the U. S. Bureau of the Census from the very first censuses of wholesale and retail trade and has been found highly workable. It follows the traditional classification of marketing organizations and avoids the necessity for the creation of nondescript, hybrid groups of marketing agencies not susceptible of classification and for multiplying the number of classes or groups of such agencies. Besides, the majority rule is ingrained in democratic tradition and usage; it is a truly democratic rule. It is used not only for electing representatives for government service, including the President of the United States, but also for U. S. Supreme Court decisions, the enactment of legislation, and for most other purposes in which the democratic process finds expression. In all matters pertaining to bankruptcy proceedings a majority of the creditors, in number and in amount of claims, usually governs. In fact, application of the majority rule is the standard in business usage and in practically all matters pertaining thereto; it is deeply rooted in democratic thinking and is taken for granted, except where a specific limitation is imposed establishing a different standard for a special purpose. Finally, any substitute is arbitrary and may be unreasonable. Once a departure is made from the "greater part" principle, arguments can be advanced with as much (or as little) reason for one percentage as for another as a basis for differentiating a wholesale from a retail establishment.

Four possible objections may be raised against the use of the majority principle under all circumstances. One is the fact that a majority of dollar sales does not necessarily reflect a majority of the business in physical units. Assume, for example, that the establishment does $100,000 of business a year and that 45 per cent of it is at wholesale and 55 per cent at retail. Such an establishment under the majority principle would be classified as a retail establishment. Suppose, however, that the margin or markup in terms of selling prices is 20 per cent on the wholesale part of the business and 40 per cent on the retail phase. The actual sales made at wholesale on a *cost* of goods basis is thus $36,000 against only $33,000 at retail, making the sales in terms of physical volume larger at wholesale than at retail.

Second, a smaller percentage than 50 of the total business done at retail, because of the higher retailing costs in contrast with the cost of selling at wholesale, may be sufficient to endow the establishment with the principal characteristics of a retail establishment. It may therefore be advisable to consider not only the proportion of business but such factors as annual sales per establishment, sales per employee, payroll as a per cent of net sales, and total operating expenses as a per cent of net sales. If the amount of retail business is such that it causes the establishment to resemble a regular retail place of business in that line of trade, then from the standpoint of these factors it might well be regarded as a retail establishment. If, however, in terms of these factors the establishment resembles a wholesale place of business in that line of trade and the volume of wholesale trade is substantial though not over 50 per cent, it may well be regarded as a wholesale establishment. This is so partly because the effects of a certain portion of retail and wholesale business will vary considerably with the size and volume of the total business of the establishment.

Third, for regulatory ends it may be advisable to interpret certain provisions of a law broadly for purposes of coverage and narrowly for the sake of exemption. This policy may justify a departure from the majority rule, but radical departure is likely to produce inequities and may result in arbitrary and unreasonable procedures. Whether or not economists fully agree on this, such has been the dictum of the courts and hence actual practice.

Fourth, and most important, is the conviction of enforcing agencies, and especially the Federal Trade Commission, that treatment of an establishment (or firm) as wholesale when some substantial part of its business is done at retail would inevitably lead to price and other discriminations that might prove injurious to competition and would certainly injure a competitor—a matter that is presumed to be prohibited, with specified exceptions, under the Robinson-Patman Act. Further discussion of this position is reserved for the next chapter.

Failure To Treat a Wholesale Establishment as a Unit. Regardless of what percentage or proportion is used in characterizing an establishment as wholesale, grave difficulty arises from failure to treat the establishment as a unit. If it is assumed, for example, that functional discounts to a wholesaler are to be allowed, under a certain construction of the Robinson-Patman Act, only on that part of the business which he transacts with his customers at wholesale, what happens to a wholesaler who sells 85 per cent of the merchandise that he buys from his sources of supply at wholesale and 15 per cent at retail? Would such a wholesaler be entitled to a functional discount on only 85 per cent of his purchases? Suppose, again, that on a given item *all* of his business is at wholesale, would he be entitled on purchases of that item to a functional discount on *all* his purchases? But suppose that a given highly standardized item, on which the wholesale business amounts to 79 per cent, is obtained from eight different sources of supply, the merchandise from which source was sold at wholesale and from which at retail? Obviously, unless a separate stock is kept, by each of the thousands of items and by the sources of supply for each item, it would be utterly impossible to know just what was sold at wholesale and what at retail. The only possible solutions to such a problem are: (1) to establish a separate organization and maintain a physically segregated stock of goods for the retail division of the business and, if that is impractical, (2) to eliminate the *retail* part of the business altogether. For purposes of the Fair Labor Standards Act, on the other hand, if such a construction were placed, it would be necessary either to segregate the two kinds of business or to discard the *wholesale* phase of it in order to secure exemption from the law for the "retail establishment."

Thus, failure to treat the wholesale establishment as a unit, while perhaps legally justified under the strictest construction, from the standpoint of practical and logical application it is as impossible as it is undesirable. It would force business into a strait jacket, to all intents and purposes prohibiting it from engaging in more than one level of distribution through a single establishment or doing so either at considerable risk of running afoul of the law or at substantial additional expense in record-keeping, stock segregation, and other physical and accounting divorcement of each class of transaction.

Basic Classifications or Groupings of Wholesale Establishments

A full understanding of the nature of wholesaling necessitates not only a sound conception of wholesaling in general and of wholesaling establishments but also a thorough grasp on the component parts of the wholesaling structure. It is difficult to comprehend the field of wholesaling because of its intricate character and structure. Wholesaling pervades all lines of trade and in any given trade there are a great many varieties of wholesaling methods and functionaries to be found at the same time. It is therefore necessary to understand, first, how wholesaling may be subdivided to bring out distinctive trade or commodity differences, and second, how such establishments may be classified to reveal significant functional and other bases for specialization within a trade or commodity group. Since the pioneer effort to disentangle these ambiguities was made by the first Census of Distribution and followed since then, the basis for census classification will be utilized in the following discussion. This method will serve the secondary purpose of affording guidance in the correct use of the basic census data in the field of business research.

Wholesale Establishments by Trade or Commodity Groups. One of the first classifications necessary to an understanding of wholesale trade is that by commodity groups, lines of trade, or, as the Census calls it, kinds of business. Three significant bases may be utilized in setting up such classifications:

1. Channel of distribution
2. Source of supply of raw material
3. Utilization of the commodity

One or more of these bases may be used in arriving at a final decision on the proper classification of a particular wholesale business. For example, a dealer in laundry soap is classified in the grocery trade since the great bulk of this kind of soap is normally handled through grocery *distribution channels*. Again, a wholesaler of needles, a product made of steel, is included in the dry goods trade because needles are generally sold by dry goods concerns as part of their notions department. Other dealers may be classified on the second basis, the *source of supply* of raw material for the commodity or commodities under consideration. A business house dealing in hides and skins or in raw cotton should be classified in the farm products group on this basis. The same would be true of establishments selling, at wholesale, fresh fruits and vegetables. Again, saddlery and harness wholesalers come under the leather trade classification for the same reason. Finally there is the *utilization of the commodity* by ultimate purchasers. On this basis, dealers in fish, meats, and the like are classified in the food products trade, dealers in stoves, in the heating trade classification, and dealers in shoes, even though shoes are made of leather, are placed in the clothing and apparel trade classification. It is often necessary to consider all three of the bases in determining the proper classification of an enterprise by kinds of business. Radio and television dealers, for example, may be classified in the electrical trade if based on the source of supply; in the amusement trade classification if based on the main use of the product; or if classified on the basis of channels through which radios are distributed, they may be placed in the furniture field, automotive equipment field, hardware trade, electrical trade, and in several others, since the channels for distribution of such a product are not as clearly defined as are those of many other commodities.

Classification by Wholesaling Institutions. Classification of wholesaling businesses into trade or commodity groups is only the beginning of the problem. A second step, essential to a full understanding of the wholesaling structure, is the further classification of different types or varieties of wholesaling establishments within each of the important trade groups. It is this classification by *types* which brings into relief the fact that *wholesalers,* for example, are but one of several types of wholesaling institutions, thereby dispelling one of the illusions mentioned at the beginning of the preceding chapter. In a broad sense some of the functions of wholesaling are performed by all who sell goods in a wholesale manner. In this are included farmers and manufacturers who sell at wholesale, as well as all places of business engaged principally in wholesale trade. They are also performed by agencies and institutions that specialize in *buying* or as aids in the buying of goods for wholesaling purposes.

In order to arrive at a sound and practical classification of the various *types* of wholesale establishments, it is necessary to follow a similar procedure to that used in classifying by trade groups. For all practical purposes one or more of the following bases may be used in developing such a classification:

1. Functions performed
2. Ownership
3. Agency status

It is possible theoretically to classify wholesale establishments on the basis of the variety of wholesale *marketing functions* which they perform. On this basis, however, wholesale businesses would be dispersed in a continuous, as contrasted with a discrete, series since functions performed vary by almost imperceptible gradations from a single activity, such as buying or selling for certain wholesaling agencies to the full gamut of wholesaling functions which are normally performed by the wholesaler of popular conception. This fact would make classification on this basis alone very difficult, if not impossible. In actual practice it is therefore necessary to distinguish between different types of wholesaling establishments on other than the functional basis, although functions are not entirely excluded from consideration and are actually helpful in establishing certain categories. The *ownership basis* is helpful in classifying such establishments as the wholesale warehouses operated by retailing chain systems. Here the integrated nature of the entire business structure makes the ownership basis of classification essential. For the same reason manufacturers' wholesale branch houses must be classified on the basis of ownership.

The third basis for classification, namely, the *agency status* of the wholesale place of business, is often helpful in arriving at a practical segregation of such wholesale establishments as agents and brokers who do not normally take actual title to the merchandise which they handle or in which they deal but rather operate on a commission basis. Such types are in sharp contrast with wholesaling establishments which purchase outright all of the goods in which they trade.

Functional differentiation is apparent in such categories as wholesale merchants, cash-and-carry wholesalers, and wagon distributors. The ownership basis appears in the separate classifications of chain store warehouses and manufacturers' sales branches. Examples of the third basis of classification appear in such types as manufacturers' agents, selling agents, brokers, export agents, and import agents.

Conclusion. From the very nature of *wholesaling,* as discussed in this and the preceding chapters, it is apparent that *wholesalers* are not the only type of institution engaged in wholesaling. Brokers, commission merchants, and other nontitle-taking middlemen engage in wholesaling, perform wholesaling functions, as truly as does the regular service wholesaler. Similarly, business establishments (such as mill supply houses, steel warehouses, hotel supply houses, and dental supply firms that distribute goods to industrial, commercial, and institutional enterprises) are a part of our wholesaling structure. The same reasoning applies to the activities of manufacturers who sell through branch houses or otherwise, either to wholesalers or to retailers and industrial concerns. Furthermore, the wholesaling picture would be incomplete if confined only to domestic trade. A substantial volume of foreign trade is carried on with other nations. For that reason one must include many of the organizations engaged in exporting and importing, directly or indirectly. Finally, there are a number of wholesale establishments operated by retail institutions, such as chain store warehouses and supply depots, which also constitute a part of the wholesaling mechanism. In this category should no doubt be included the warehouses servicing department stores and supermarkets even when a single store or supermarket is thus provided with goods from the wholesale place of business.

4

PRACTICAL IMPORTANCE OF WHOLESALING CONCEPT

From the contents of the two preceding chapters it should be crystal clear that the basis for any concept of wholesaling is the *wholesale transaction*. To reiterate, it is the composite of all such transactions that spells total wholesale trade. Similarly, it is the volume of all such transactions by a given place of business that normally determines whether it is a wholesale establishment for most purposes.

Parenthetically, it should be stated that, from the standpoint of the institution or establishment whose business volume is being considered, a wholesale transaction may be a purchase or a sale, depending upon whether its business is that of selling (which is true of most of them) or one of buying as with resident buyers, buying brokers, or purchasing-agent middlemen. This is unlike a retail transaction, which is always in the nature of a sale. Consequently, it is quite erroneous to treat wholesale trade as consisting only of *sales* on the wholesale level or in a wholesale manner.

THE TWO MAIN CONCEPTS OF WHOLESALING

It is equally clear from the discussion in the two preceding chapters that wholesaling or wholesale trade may be conceived of in one of two ways: (1) in terms of the totality of wholesale transactions no matter by whom made or where they are performed and (2) in terms of establishments primarily engaged in such business. The first is by far the broader view of wholesaling, but the second view is the more practical for the collection and dissemination of data about the subject and for a study of structural composition, and hence it is more useful in application.

Erroneous Concepts Frequently Held About Wholesaling. The above statement concerning the two main ways of viewing wholesaling does not disregard the fact that in many quarters, usually as a result of true misconceptions and misunderstanding or for business motives, the matter is looked at otherwise. The variety of ways in which wholesaling is conceived may be gleaned from an examination of qualifications for membership in certain trade associations and from the many speeches on the subject at the numerous conventions.

In its most narrow aspect to which, unfortunately, many business interests subscribe and which is quite acceptable to the layman *wholesaling* is confined to the operations of *wholesalers* who sell exclusively to retailers. This, unfortunately, is the view most widely held by laymen and by many businessmen who have not given much thought to the problem or who are interested only in the types of wholesale operations their businesses represent. This narrow view even restricts the definition of *wholesalers* to those wholesale middlemen who take title to the goods they buy, and who sell them subsequently to bona fide retailers for resale to ultimate consumers. Sometimes, only *service* or *full-function* wholesalers are embraced in the definition; and newer types of wholesalers, even though they take title to the goods they buy, and sell them to retail merchants, are excluded on the theory that they are not "legitimate." This concept invariably excludes the business of functional middlemen as well as the activities of chain store warehouses, manufacturers' sales branches, and certain other types of wholesaling establishments.

To show that this narrow concept (although held by many practical businessmen) is highly abstract and unrealistic, it is but necessary to call attention to the fact that few indeed are the wholesalers who sell exclusively to retailers. Practically every so-called regular wholesaler of any consequence in certain trades sells quantities of goods to industrial users and to institutional buyers. This situation obtains, in varying degrees, in practically all lines of business. On the other hand, many of the functional middlemen and others excluded under this narrow conception sell substantial amounts of merchandise to retailers.

Wholesaling Broadly and Properly Conceived. In the truest and most comprehensive interpretation wholesaling represents the totality of all wholesale transactions and affords the most complete picture of the field. It includes all activities relating to the purchase or sale of goods at wholesale in the light of the criteria discussed in Chapter 2. This view recognizes no fundamental distinction between the sale of goods by prime producers, by manufacturers or other processors, by wholesalers, or by any of the functional or nontitle-taking middlemen engaged in wholesale trade; nor does it differentiate, save within the field of wholesaling, between sales of goods to retailers, to industrial consumers, or to wholesale organizations so long as the purpose of the customer in buying such goods is not for personal gratification and the quantity, if bought from a concern operating substantially as a retail establishment and not for resale, is materially in excess of that which might reasonably be purchased by an ultimate consumer.

Establishment Basis for Wholesaling Concept. Because of the difficulties in securing data for wholesaling on the broad base, wholesaling or wholesale trade is determined on the basis of the business done by wholesale establishments. This conception of wholesaling has been substantially adopted by the Bureau of the Census for its censuses of business. In general, this view includes the activities of all *places of business* operating in a wholesale manner and was a compromise position dictated by technical statistical considerations of both enumeration and presentation of results by geographic areas. It does not include wholesale sales made by manufacturers, except through branches specially maintained for that purpose; nor does the term include wholesale sales made by farmers or by operators of mines, quarries, or oil wells.

It is generally impossible for the Bureau of the Census to make the term all-inclusive, that is, to use it in the *broadest aspect,* since the censuses are taken on an establishment basis and are therefore restricted to specialized wholesaling establishments. Were the scope of the wholesale census broadened to include such sales, it would be necessary to secure a separate distribution report from every goods producing establishment in addition to the report which it submits on production activities to the Census of Manufactures, the Census of Mines and Quarries, or the Census of Agriculture. This is a desirable objective which may be achieved ultimately. To date, sporadic attempts have been made to secure a part of such data from manufacturers and to a limited extent from farmers.

On the other hand, it would have been equally impracticable for the census to confine the term to service wholesalers or to any other single type of wholesaler, inasmuch as a clear-cut functional division between different types of wholesale organizations does not exist. Much of the wholesale business, even in the sense in which *service* wholesalers operate, is being done by bulk tank stations, by manufacturers' sales branches, and by other types of wholesale establishments. Moreover, the Bureau of the Census would have had a very inadequate census of distribution had it not included all of the places of business engaged in distribution which it could discover.

The student of wholesaling must always bear in mind that this main viewpoint of wholesaling that is based on Census data for the most part is at best but a compromise conception, dictated by practical limitations upon the scope of operations of a particular research agency and not by scientific analysis of the field of wholesaling. It deserves attention primarily because it is the basis upon which the largest body of data on wholesaling now available is collected. Because of this limited concept, a very large part of the field of wholesaling has not yet been adequately covered by extensive research methods. One must not therefore make the mistake of identifying the area covered by the various censuses of wholesaling with *all* wholesaling.

Practical Aspects of Wholesaling Concept

In the interest of scientific truth alone there is ample justification for earnest efforts to probe into the real nature of wholesaling. There are, however, important practical implications in the concept of wholesaling and especially in a proper and adequate differentiation of it from retailing. Some of them have to do with a scientific study of the subject and the effective quantitative measurement of wholesaling and its component parts. Some arise out of various types of taxation. Others issue from the regulations to which competitive marketing enterprises are subjected. Finally, there are the implications coming from attempts to prevent unfairness in competition and thus making the competitive system more effective.

Scientific Study and Quantitative Measurement. Science is essentially a body of classified and systematized knowledge. Before items of knowledge can be classified, they must first be defined in order that all those possessing the same basic characteristics may be grouped together for study and analysis. This applies to the nature of the transaction as well as to the character of the establishment. Thus the essence of wholesaling and the manifold problems that are peculiar to it can be understood best when the term is properly defined and comprehended.

Without a correct definition, the field of wholesaling cannot be delineated and delimited for quantitative measurement or any other statistical treatment. Indeed, no census enumeration is possible nor can changes or trends in wholesaling or parts thereof be properly gauged except on a sample basis that would deal with but an unknown segment of the field. Finally, no analytical study of quantitative data is possible without knowledge of what exactly is encompassed by the data, both in terms of transactions and establishments.

Tax Implications. Many states impose a tax on retail sales. In some of the statutes the term "retail sale" is specially defined for the peculiar purposes of the law, but in most of them the determination of the nature of the sale and what sales or purchases are subject to the tax is within certain broad limits left to the interpretation of the appropriate enforcing agency. Under such circumstances it is natural for the enforcing agency to define a retail sale broadly and to subject to the tax many transactions that are truly wholesale in the light of the criteria discussed in Chapter 2. Especially is this true of sales made to institutions and to others for commercial and industrial consumption, even though the quantity involved may be substantial and materially in excess of any quantity of such product that might reasonably be purchased by an ultimate consumer. For such purposes a correct concept of the transaction—whether wholesale or retail—is of prime importance.

A number of states impose a chain store tax that usually applies only to retail *establishments*. To be exempt from such a tax it behooves a concern to prove that its business is nonretail. Such an exemption was obtained, for example, in one of the states for a chain of several feed stores when it was demonstrated that the sales made by such stores were to dairy farmers and others who used it for the production of milk for sale. The purchasers of the feed were therefore buying it for business purposes, in substantial quantities, and the transactions were considered wholesale. In all such instances the character of the *establishment* is a primary consideration.

Again, practically all states have laws imposing taxes on inventories of merchandise, but the tax rate on retail inventories is considerably higher than that levied on wholesale inventories. Finally, in some states there is a gross receipts tax law, according to which the tax rate is much smaller on wholesale transactions than on retail. Under all such circumstances it is extremely important to make the distinction, mainly in terms of transactions, first, for the purpose of complying with the provisions of the law and, second, to take advantage of the preferential treatment allowed by the law.

Regulatory Implications. For purposes of complying with certain laws or in securing exemption from them, it may be necessary to distinguish clearly between wholesale and retail transactions or establishments. Illustrative are the several relevant types of laws, state and federal, briefly discussed below.

Sales Below Cost Laws. In 26 states including Hawaii there are sales below cost laws of general application in effect. Except as specified in the law, a vendor is prohibited from selling his merchandise below cost, plus, in most cases, a specified markup percentage. In 15 of these states the law does not apply to manufacturers; in 18 states service trades are not subject to it at all, while in 2 others they are subject to it only in part. Furthermore, for wholesalers either no markup is specified or the markup is a much lower percentage than that specified for retailers. What all of this means is that for purposes of this type of law it is essential to know exactly what kind of business is involved, both in terms of transactions and total character of the establishment.

For Compliance with the Robinson-Patman Act. For purposes of complying with the explicit provisions or with the general spirit of the Robinson-Patman Act, it may be necessary for a vendor to classify customers into wholesale and retail or even into subgroups in each of these two main categories. It may also be necessary to distinguish between wholesale and retail transactions of customers.

From time immemorial vendors have been classifying their customers into certain groups for specific purposes. The motives for such classifications have been many and varied and may have issued from a desire to eliminate from the list certain groups deemed undesirable, to graduate price differentials usually in the form of trade discounts, or to differentiate in services to be rendered. The widespread use of customer classification for pricing purposes is a matter of common knowledge, has been sanctioned by the courts, and may even be regarded as traditional.

Prior to the enactment of the Robinson-Patman amendment to the Clayton Act it was held lawful, for example, for a manufacturer to sell to wholesalers at one price and to retailers at another price, even though purchases in both cases involved the same quantity. This principle was well established in the case of *The Mennen Co. v. Federal Trade Commission,* where the court declared that:

> The company is engaged in an entirely private business and it has a right freely to exercise its own independent discretion as to whether it will sell "wholesalers" only or whether it will sell to both "wholesalers" and "retailers," and if it decides to sell to both it has a right to determine whether or not it will sell to the "retailers" on the same terms it sells to the "wholesalers."[1]

A Senate amendment to the Robinson-Patman Act was designed to protect this common practice of classifying customers according to *function,* such as wholesalers or retailers, and of granting a different trade discount to each such class of customers. This amendment was eliminated in conference, as it was no doubt considered superfluous and may have made the practice mandatory. Inasmuch as customer classification was held lawful prior thereto, it would seem to remain lawful, since there is nothing in the Robinson-Patman Act to prohibit it, so long as it does not result in unlawful price discrimination.[2] For this purpose is would seem necessary that:

1. The division of customers into classes shall be reasonable and bona fide, not arbitrary;

[1] 288 Fed. 774 (CCA–2, 1923), certiorari denied, 262 U. S. 759.
[2] *Standard Oil Co. v. Federal Trade Commission* (CCA–7, March 11, 1949).

2. Discount *classes* must not be unduly large and too few in number. In other words, the boundaries between classes must be reasonably placed, usually at points where the costs of doing business change most conspicuously.

3. The discounts must be available to all who qualify for placement in a given class, and no one may be kept out because of a capricious and arbitrary definition of the class of customers in question. Thus if a discount is offered to those who render a specified service, it must be made available to any purchaser who is willing and able to render such service.

That functional discounts, which will be discussed in some detail in Chapter 15, are obviously permissible under the Robinson-Patman Act is generally recognized. Judging by the Federal Trade Commission's "closed files," a wholesaler can be given a discount as a wholesaler if the supplier so desires. The law neither requires nor prohibits such differentials or so-called "functional" discounts. But when a seller chooses to grant wholesalers a functional discount, he must know exactly who is entitled to such a discount; and for that purpose the term "wholesaler" must be carefully defined, in line with the basic criteria previously discussed, to make sure, on the one hand, that such discount is not granted to those who are not in that customer classification and, on the other, that those who do qualify for such a classification are not excluded. The same reasoning applies to functional discounts and other price differentials allowed to classes of customers on other levels of distribution; when that is done, it is essential that the same treatment be accorded to all customers in a given class, subject only to the specific exceptions provided by the law. All of this requires comprehensive knowledge of the nature of (1) a wholesale transaction, (2) a wholesale establishment, and (3) the various types and levels of wholesaling in the American economy.

For Application of Wage and Hour Regulations. Another federal law that is extremely pertinent to this discussion is the Fair Labor Standards Act, commonly known as the Wage and Hour Law. Section 13(a)(2) of this Act grants an exemption from the minimum wage and maximum hour provisions with respect to "any employee engaged in any retail or service establishment the greater part of whose selling or servicing is in intrastate commerce." In making this exemption, it was apparently the intent of Congress, judging from the legislative history and the declared purpose of the Act, first, to provide exemption to local retail and service establishments which are situated near state lines, and which might otherwise come within the scope of the Act because they make retail sales across state lines; second, to provide exemption to establishments of a retail character which might come within the purview of the Act merely because they purchase goods outside the state; third, to apply the exemption only to such retail or service establishments as are comparable to the local merchant, grocery store, filling station operator, and similar places of business that sell to or serve ultimate consumers for their personal use.

It is but natural that the Administrator of the law should attempt to define the terms "retail" and "service" narrowly, in order to bring under the provisions of the law as many employees as possible and to restrict the exemptions therefrom to a minimum. This is in line with pronouncements by the courts that for purposes of coverage the provisions of the law shall be interpreted broadly and that exemptions from it shall be construed narrowly.[3] It is equally natural that objections to such interpretations should be raised by various concerns. These contests, when finally decided by the courts, are helpful in clearing up misunderstandings and misinterpretations and facilitate operation under the law.

One of the important cases bearing on this point that was decided by the Supreme Court of the United States on January 28, 1946, is that of *Roland Electrical Company v. L. Metcalfe Walling.*[4] At the time of the controversy the company was engaged in "commercial and industrial wiring, electrical contracting, and dealing in electrical motors and generators, for private, commercial, and industrial uses." It served approximately 1,000 active accounts, 99 per cent of which consisted of commercial and industrial concerns. The company claimed exemption from the law, principally because it was a "service establishment." The court ruled, however, that the words "retail" and "service" are used "so closely together in the statute as to require them to be interpreted similarly. This makes it appropriate to restrict the broader meaning of service to a meaning comparable to that given in the narrower term retail. The words are put on a like level by their use in the alternative with the single word establishment." The court proceeded to say that "The word retail because of its ready contrast with wholesale is generally more restrictive than the word service" and that retail refers to the sale of goods to ultimate consumers for personal or household purposes. Since the company dealt almost altogether with industrial customers, it did not qualify for the exemption. "These," the court ruled, "are not retail customers in the same sense as is the customer of the local merchant, local grocer or filling station operator who buys for his own personal consumption." It was therefore immaterial that the customers did not buy the goods for resale or redistribution in any form after processing but were consumed instead in the hands of such customers. Thus the distinction between the two general classes of consumers—ultimate and industrial—is clearly drawn.

At first blush it would appear that, insofar as criteria in distinguishing between a retail and wholesale transaction is concerned, the decision in

[3] *Fleming v. Hawkeye Pearl Button Co.*, 113 F.2d 52 (CCA–8); *Bowie v. Gonzales*, 117 F.2d 11 (CCA–1); *Wood v. Central Sand and Gravel Co.*, 33 F. Supp. 40.
[4] 66 S. Ct. 413 (1946).

this case was based solely upon the status of the customer and the purpose for which such goods and services were purchased by the customer. To be sure, that was, as it should be in the light of sound theory, the principal consideration. Attention was also given, however, to the matter of quantity, as is evident from the statement that "In the suggested use of the word retail as opposed to the word wholesale, a distinction appears not merely between the size and volume of the sales but between types of purchasers."

For Trade Practice Conference Rules. As will be discussed in Chapter 15, one of the functions of the Federal Trade Commission is to encourage members of industries and trades to work with it in the development of trade practice conference rules applicable to a given industry or trade. When approved by the Commission, the rules are promulgated and they become binding upon all members covered. The principal purposes of this activity of the Commission are to eliminate or prevent unfair methods of competition, to foster and promote fair competitive conditions, and to promote standards of ethical business conduct in harmony with public policy. One of the rules in some of these sets for certain industries or trades declares it illegal under certain circumstances for a member of the particular industry to fail to differentiate between wholesale and retail transactions. The following wording is illustrative:

When an industry member sells industry products at both wholesale and at retail in the same establishment, it is an unfair trade practice for such industry member to sell any such products under circumstances having the capacity or effect of causing purchasers to believe that they are buying at wholesale when such is not the case.[5]

Competitive Implications. An illustration of how the definition of a wholesale transaction, as distinguished from a retail sale, may be used to prevent alleged unfair competitive practices and to that extent protect the interests of bona fide wholesalers and retailers from such competition is afforded by the case of *L. & C. Mayers Co., Inc. v. Federal Trade Commission.*[6] This case, prosecuted under authority of Section 5 of the Federal Trade Commission Act, also illustrates the use by the Federal Trade Commission of the three basic criteria, in defining a wholesale transaction, discussed in the preceding section of this chapter.

The principal question in this case was whether the respondent, L. & C.

[5] Wholesale Plumbing and Heating Industry, Effective May 14, 1955, Rule 3. Substantially similar wording is to be found in a number of other sets of rules. See, for example, Bedding Manufacturing and Wholesale Distributing Industry, as Amended, September 15, 1955, Rule 8; and Wholesale Optical Industry, Effective July 30, 1950, Rule 7.

[6] F.T.C. Docket No. 2038 (Order to Cease and Desist, issued October 30, 1935), 97 F.2d 365 (CCA–2, 1938).

Mayers Co., Inc., was selling jewelry at wholesale as claimed by the company or at retail as charged in the complaint. In the decision, handed down on October 30, 1935, the Commission concluded that "the acts and practices of respondent . . . are to the prejudice of the public and respondent's competitors and constitute unfair methods of competition." The Commission, therefore, issued an order to the company to "cease and desist from representing itself . . . to be a wholesale jeweler or wholesaler" in so far as certain kinds of sales are concerned.

It is interesting to note in the light of the preceding discussion of criteria for defining wholesaling transactions that the Federal Trade Commission used the following definition:

A wholesaler of jewelry is one who sells to the trade for resale and seldom, if ever, to the purchasing public, with the exception that sales to industrial concerns, public utilities, banks and other similar organizations, which purchase in quantity lots, i.e., simultaneous sales of more than one of a given item, not for resale, but for use of such organizations, are considered as wholesale transactions. It is the character of sales to the trade that makes and distinguishes a wholesaler.

The Commission added that "It is the character of sales to the trade that makes and distinguishes a wholesaler." This important decision included an analysis of a number of the criteria developed in the foregoing pages. The *quantity* factor was recognized but not stressed. The *method of operation* was developed in the elaboration of the term "character of sales," when the Commission pointed out that the use of catalogs, discounts, and "list prices" are wholesaling devices and are so recognized by the purchasing public. The *nature of the goods* was implied in the recognition of industrial sales as wholesale business. The *use of the product* criterion was recognized in the distinction which the Commission made in sales "not for resale" and in differentiating "industrial concerns, cooperative buying bureaus, state governments, municipal governments and purchasing clubs" from the usual consuming public. The main emphasis of this decision, however, was placed upon the *motive of the purchaser* as the basic criterion for defining wholesale business as opposed to retail trade.

The Commission's decision was appealed and on June 6, 1938, the U. S. Circuit Court of Appeals, Second Circuit, handed down its decision, affirming the Federal Trade Commission's order to cease and desist, and granting the order of enforcement. In restating the case, the Circuit Court gave the gist of it as follows:

The theory of the Commission's complaint is that the company sells to ultimate consumers; that in aid of such sales it uses catalogues designating itself as a wholesaler and that the purchasing public regards it as such—one selling to retailers at a price lower than the price at which the retailer sells; that consumers infer from this representation that they are buying at the prices at which retailers purchase, thereby saving an amount equal to the retailer's profit, and that the prices as fixed in the catalogues are wholesale prices; but such is not the fact and the consumer purchaser is thereby deceived.

The court misinterpreted, however, some of the facts in the case, when it stated:

The groups to whom the petitioner is directed not to sell representing itself as a "wholesaler" are consumers. . . . Since the jewelry was sold to customers "not for resale" they are the ultimate purchasers. The evidence of experts as well as of other manufacturers and jewelers justifies the conclusion of the respondent that the petitioner was not a wholesaler.

The court was no doubt correct in its general interpretation of the essential facts in the case and certainly in its conclusion that "It is in the interest of the public to prevent the sale of commodities by the use of false and misleading statements and representations." It showed some confusion, however, as to what was really alleged by the Commission and failed to distinguish between the two general classes of consumers (ultimate and industrial) as the Commission did. The complaint by the Commission was not against the company's parading as a wholesaler with respect to *all* of its sales but only with regard to those sales that were in the nature of retail transactions. Furthermore, in what were deemed retail sales were not included *all* sales to customers "not for resale" but only those sales made to customers "not for resale" that were not in quantity lots, i.e., sales that were in quantities normally purchased by an ultimate consumer for personal use. Finally, it failed to distinguish ultimate *purchasers* from ultimate *consumers*.

In a number of other cases the Federal Trade Commission ordered the offending business concern, called the respondent, to stop certain practices similar to those covered in the case just discussed. One of them was to cease representing himself as a "wholesaler" when he was not a wholesaler. Another was to cease using the terms "list prices" and "discount" usually associated with wholesaling operations; in effect, it ordered the respondent to cease representing that the prices at which the goods were offered for sale were wholesale prices or at a discount from his normal prices.[7] More recent action of this type was taken by the Commission against sellers of home freezers who claimed that their respective plans or wholesale buying schemes would allow purchasers of freezers to buy food from a wholesaler at wholesale prices.[8] Occasionally the respondents con-

[7] For example, such orders to cease and desist were issued, among others, in the following cases: Adding machines, Docket No. 3110 (1937); Clothing, Docket No. 3747 (1943), affirmed in *Progress Tailoring Co. v. Federal Trade Commission* (CCA–7, 1946); Fur garments, Docket No. 5870 (1951); Jewelry, Docket No. 4087 (1941), affirmed in *Macher et al. v. Federal Trade Commission* (CCA–2, 1942).

[8] F.T.C. Docket Nos. 6131 and 6140 (1953).

sented to the cease and desist orders; more often settlement was made by stipulation whereby the respondents agreed to cease and desist from making the misrepresentation of which they were accused and signed agreements accordingly.[9]

All of the foregoing analysis indicates beyond any shadow of a doubt the importance of knowing the real nature of a wholesale transaction and of a wholesaling institution, as distinguished from a retail transaction or retailing institution. One must also bear in mind that the applications referred to above are but illustrative and by no means indicate the widespread use of such knowledge, even for purposes of determining only unfair methods of competition or unfair and deceptive acts or practices.

[9] See, for example, stipulations 3609 (luggage), 3651 (automobile tires), 7840 (athletic equipment), 7985 (watches), 8112 (textile goods).

5

HISTORICAL BACKGROUND OF MODERN WHOLESALING

"Past is Prelude." So reads an inscription chiseled in a lintel of the nation's Archives Building in Washington, D. C. Actually, it is much more than an introduction to the present, for a knowledge of the past is essential to a thorough understanding of modern wholesaling, just as a study of history is essential to an understanding of a people or any phase of human experience.

Apart from the pleasure to be derived from such human interest stories as those of Sinbad, a noted merchant of Arabian Nights fame, the history of wholesaling may serve utilitarian ends and certainly provides the background for an understanding of the system as it now exists. Much truth inheres in the adage, *there is nothing new under the sun*. A searching study of the history of wholesaling may well reward the searcher with valuable ideas.[1]

Modern research in marketing looks more and more toward interdisciplinary analysis, especially in the field of social science. In this context history has much to contribute to a fuller comprehension of wholesaling.

[1] A study of the history of the plumbing industry by the senior author was used in litigation. The defendants were acquitted in an antitrust action. *The United States of America v. The Central Supply Association et al.,* No. 16750–Criminal. In U. S. District Court for the Northern District of Ohio, Eastern Division, April, 1947. The study revealed the evolution of each step in the marketing channels of the plumbing supplies industry and contrasted it with developments in other hard goods lines. From the historical evidence it was clear that economic conditions rather than arbitrary or artificial restrictions had determined the pattern of marketing channels in the plumbing supplies business.

Moreover, awareness of the long tradition back of wholesaling provides a warm feeling of kinship with evolving humanity and pride in one's profession. But history needs no apology. It is quite able to stand on its own achievements.

WHOLESALING IN ANCIENT TIMES

Early wholesaling appears to have been largely interregional and international. It was the natural extension of commerce as primitive societies became more economically sophisticated. From self-sufficiency in the provision of goods and services for individuals and families with little or no exchange, specialization gradually evolved. With the growth of specialized physical goods production, markets emerged to facilitate the fuller satisfaction of needs and wants. At first these markets were local and rudimentary in scope and function, perhaps no more than open spaces set aside for convenience in trade on a barter basis.

Evidence of the existence of interregional trade, possibly only incidental to warfare, has been found in various parts of the world. For example, one of the authors has in his possession an obsidian tool used for the shaping of stone knives from softer materials. This tool was discovered in a cave on the seacoast of Sicily. No obsidian occurs naturally in this area but is plentiful in an adjacent island. The Sicilian cave-dwellers had discovered an overseas source of a needed raw material. How they got it, whether by trade, raiding, or mere exploration and exploitation, may never be known. Similarly, research by archaeologists and anthropologists has uncovered evidence of prehistoric trade between areas as distant as upper Egypt and India.

Biblical Reference. Much of the wholesale trade during biblical times was carried on over caravan routes which were characterized by poor roads, deserts, and rugged mountain passes. Beasts of burden or human portage afforded the usual means of transportation; hence trading was confined to articles of small bulk and relatively high value, such as precious stones, gold, silver, copper, tin, amber, spices, gums, incense, fine fabrics, dyes, wool, silk, skins, and furs; or to certain necessities of life, such as salt; or to other goods which were unequally distributed among the different lands, such as honey, and woods of cedar, fir, and ebony.

Wholesale traffic in human beings (slavery) made up altogether too large a share of early commerce. One of the early references to such traffic may be found in the Bible in Genesis which recounts the sale of Joseph: "and they (Joseph's brothers) lifted up their eyes and looked, and, behold, a caravan of Ishmaelites came from Gilead, with their camels bearing spicery and balm and ladanum, going to carry it down to Egypt. . . . And there passed by Midianites, merchantmen; and they drew and lifted up Joseph out of the pit, and sold Joseph to the Ishmaelites for twenty pieces of silver."[2] The sale was apparently made by others before Joseph's brothers had an opportunity to pull him out of the pit in order to sell him themselves, indicating rather extensive travel of merchants via that caravan route.

The Far East. One of the earliest records of organized markets imputes to Shen Nung, a Chinese emperor, who ruled some 5,000 years ago, credit for establishing "the practice of holding markets for the exchange of commodities."[3]

Highly developed markets and both overland caravan trade and waterborne commerce in and out of China were reported by Marco Polo in his classic "Travels." While he wrote about A.D. 1295, the marketing institutions he described had been long established by that date. Archaeological research in the lower Mesopotamian lands substantiates the existence of well-established commerce with the Far East as early as 4,000 years ago.

Sumeria. Historical research suggests that "Sumerian outlanders moved into the delta of the Euphrates and Tigris, bringing with them a mature culture, a system of writing, and a corpus of law,"[4] perhaps more than 6,000 years ago. Excavations in the late 1920's by the British archaeologist, Leonard Woolley, at the site of ancient Ur led to a much fuller knowledge of the Sumerians than was possible before. He has been able to compile a chronology which dates the First Dynasty of Ur at 3100–2930 B.C.[5] Less accurate records trace much earlier beginnings, back to antediluvian times.

By 2000 B.C. a thriving trade existed between the cities at the head of the Persian Gulf, overseas points, and communities to the north. Woolley tells of a "bill of lading of a ship commissioned by the temple of Nin-Gal at Ur for the Gulf trade." After an absence of two years at Dilman it unloaded at Ur about 2048 B.C. The cargo included gold, copper ore, ivory, precious woods, and fine stone for statues and vases. "The merchants of the south had their agencies or branch houses in distant towns with whom they kept up a correspondence and did business by letters of credit, or they entrusted their goods to independent commercial travellers who sold to the best advantage and had to render account on their return, receiving a share of the profits; the law dealt harshly with such as failed to

[2] Genesis 37:25, 28. Translation according to the Masoretic text, The Jewish Publication Society, Philadelphia, 1944.

[3] H. H. Gowen, *An Outline History of China* (Boston: Sherman, French & Co., 1917), p. 26.

[4] C. W. Ceram, *Gods, Graves, and Scholars* (New York: Alfred A. Knopf, Inc., 1951), p. 303.

[5] C. Leonard Woolley, *The Sumerians* (2d impression, May, 1929; Oxford: Clarendon Press, 1928), pp. 29 ff.

keep accounts or otherwise cheated their employers, but allowance was made for loss by robbery on the road."[6]

The trade routes, apart from the sea lanes, which were early developed in the Far East, linked the cities at the mouths of the Tigris-Euphrates with upstream market centers, such as Carchemish. Wooden boats were loaded with silver and copper ore, cedar from Lebanon, walnut wood, lye, and cystas-gum and floated down the river where the cargoes were unloaded and the boats broken up and the timber sold.[7] Gold and silver were used to facilitate distant trade but always had to be verified as to quality. Barley was the standard of value in local trading. Credit also played an important role in ancient Sumer. Legal interest rates ran as high as $33\frac{1}{3}$ per cent per annum on grain and to 20–25 on silver.[8]

Egypt, Babylon, Phoenicia. As the delta of the rivers became silted and as rival civilizations from the north gained strength, centers of commerce and culture moved upstream. Thus, Babylon became a great wholesaling center in Mesopotamia. A somewhat parallel development had been evolving further to the west in Africa. The Egyptian civilization centered largely on the Nile Valley had grown apace. It was but natural that interregional trade should have developed between these great cultures.

The "Cappadocian Tablets," business archives of a colony of merchants, and other records discovered through archaeological research in the Near East and in Egypt, give evidence of considerable wholesale trading activity in all leading countries of the ancient world, particularly in Egypt, Babylonia, and Phoenicia. Because of her strategic location, Babylon occupied a prominent position in the commerce of the times. Trade was fairly well developed and even specialized. A different term was used for wholesaler from that used for retailer; the former referred to the exporter and importer who sold to the retailer.[9]

Even greater development in wholesaling occurred in Phoenicia, which enjoyed trading advantages arising from its strategic location between the great empires along the Nile and the Tigris-Euphrates river valleys. In its day the city of Tyre was the commercial mart of the world, and merchant princes constituted the aristocracy of the kingdom.

Wholesaling in Greece. The era of Greek supremacy saw an even greater development of wholesaling. The Greeks indeed recognized wholesaling

---

6 *Ibid.,* p. 116.

7 A variation on this pattern is described by Herodotus (Book I, Ch. 194) who reported that boats were made of willow wood covered with skins. Loaded with merchandise in Armenia, they were floated down the Tigris and Euphrates with the current. On reaching Babylon, the boats were taken apart after unloading; the wood was sold, but the skins were returned via caravans to be reused.

8 Woolley, *op. cit.,* p. 118.

9 C. A. Herrick, *History of Commerce and Industry* (New York: The Macmillan Co., 1917), pp. 31–32.

and wholesalers as a distinct branch of commerce. Despite the prominence of wholesaling in the Far East, Sumeria, Egypt, Babylon, and Phoenicia, there is little or no evidence of its recognition as a separate business institution in the thinking and language of the people before the time of the Greeks. While much of the earlier wholesaling had been largely exporting and importing, wholesaling in Greece included a substantial volume of internal trade resulting from the differentiation of production in the various parts of the country. Moreover, wholesaling was sharply differentiated from retailing, although to a considerable extent the two were combined in actual business. The term "emporia" was used to designate wholesalers while retailers were known as "kápeloi."[10] The *émporos* was the merchant who imported foreign goods and sold them "by wholesale." He also owned ships as a rule and sold his wares either to other wholesalers, to smaller traders, or to broker-like agents. The term *kápelos,* on the other hand, normally referred to the retail dealer, the translation of the term being "a retail dealer, petty tradesman, huckster, a tavern keeper, a cheat, rogue, knave," which indicates the lack of esteem for the retail trade in ancient Greece.[11]

Further evidence of specialized wholesaling activities may be gleaned from the following quotation from Becker: "The sale of goods was variously effected. The wholesale dealer, émporos, seems usually to have sold by sample." These samples were either displayed at special market places, not unlike our modern exchanges, or were carried about from place to place.[12]

Rome. Roman history reveals that the successors to Greek world power were in general adverse to trade. Roman civilization was essentially agrarian rather than commercial. However, large dealings, i.e., on a wholesale basis, advanced in public esteem as the higher classes became more dependent upon them and even participated in them.[13] Trade was largely in imports of food supplies from the provinces and colonies. The nearest approach to the present-day wholesaler in the days of Roman domination was the *"negateatore"* who was a middleman dealing both in merchandise and money. He was usually an independent Greek shipowner who tramped from port to port, buying and selling whatever cargo promised the greatest

[10] For a distinction between the two terms, see: *The Works of Plato—A New and Literal Version,* Vol. I, trans. by H. Cary and others (London: Bell & Daldy, 1861–1872); for a literary translation of these passages, see Plato's *Protagoras,* trans. by James A. Towle (Boston: Ginn & Co., 1889). In such literary translations the term *"émporos"* is usually translated as wholesaler.

[11] Plato's *Protagoras,* p. 242.

[12] Becker's *Charicles: or Illustrations of the Private Life of the Ancient Greeks,* trans. by the Rev. F. Metcalfe (5th ed.; London: Longmans, Green & Co., Ltd., 1880), pp. 277–92.

[13] Tenney Frank, *An Economic History of Rome* (2d ed.; Baltimore: Johns Hopkins Press, 1927), pp. 321–22.

profit. Some wholesale warehouses (*horrea*) were located at strategic points for the receipt of goods from foreign lands and for distribution to the retail dealers at home. According to a description left by Benjamin de Tudela, a Spanish rabbi, some of these *horrea* were immense structures. He relates that one of them had 360 windows and a circumference of three miles, making it more than twice the size of the Grand Central station in New York.[14] While some of these large warehouses were owned by the government and leased to importers and wholesale dealers, others were erected by rich knights and senators.

Practically every harbor had a wholesale market where "the incoming merchant unloaded whatever wares he thought he might sell, and displayed them in the market while his ship stood at anchor. . . . To the same market, came, of course, the small shop keepers of the town to buy for their retail trade."[15] Traces may be found, also, of functional middlemen of the broker or agent type, who were stationed in Rome as representatives of exporters in eastern cities. To these agents goods were frequently consigned, much as to present-day commission merchants.

The Middle Ages (a.d. 500–1500)

With the decline of Rome the wholesaler seems to have suffered an eclipse for some centuries, mainly through integration with retailing. The Middle Ages, which according to historians began roughly with the Fall of the Roman Empire in A.D. 476 and ended about A.D. 1500, was characterized by a system of social organization known as feudalism with the economic and political life centered about the lord of a manor; by a philosophy of scholasticism; and during the last two centuries of the period by an economic system of guilds. Almost to the thirteenth century a very simple independent domestic economy existed in Europe. Agriculture was held in high esteem, manufacture of the handicraft type was tolerated, but trade was looked upon with disfavor except in a few of the Mediterranean cities.

Trade Routes. During the early Middle Ages wholesale trade was confined largely to commerce with the East where traffic in spices and luxury goods predominated. The ancient trade routes continued to be followed from the Far East to the Near East whence some trade found its way into Europe.

During this era the Italian cities of Genoa, Pisa, and Venice waxed rich and powerful on a foundation of foreign commerce. Shakespeare's play, *The Merchant of Venice,* reveals the importance of the merchant in the social and economic life of the times. Venice was one of the earliest

14 C. G. Herbermann, *Business Life in Ancient Rome* (New York: Harper & Bros., 1880), pp. 33–34.
15 Frank, *op. cit.,* p. 312.

of the European cities to build up a great trade with the East. Genoa and Pisa also developed into great trading centers. The traders from these cities collected the products of Europe, such as furs, lumber, and fish, which came down the rivers and through the passes from the north and carried them to the trading ports of Asia Minor and Africa. Here they picked up the rich cargoes of luxury goods and spices which were in great demand in Europe. During the crusading period an added impetus was given to trade by the requirements of crusaders for transportation to the Holy Land. Merchants constructed larger ships to accommodate them and consequently brought back increasingly larger cargoes. Often they made direct arrangements with caravan traders and picked up their freight at agreed points outside the regular trading cities.[16]

During the fourteenth century trade and commerce flourished throughout Europe with thriving centers in London, Paris, Bruges, Avignon, Nice, Arles, Perpignan, Aiguesmortes, Lisbon, Barcelona, Catalonia, as well as the Italian cities. Despite the very rough times fraught with wars, plagues, robbers, and bad roads, merchants carried on their business. This era is clearly set forth in a recent study of the very comprehensive letters and archives of an Italian merchant of those days, Francesco Di Marco Datini. This man, born in Prato near Florence about 1335, set out as a poor boy of fifteen for Avignon to seek his fortune. After a brief apprenticeship with Tuscan merchants he very early tried his own wings. He became very successful, establishing branches in Genoa, Pisa, Majorca, Barcelona, Valencia, Florence, and Prato. His records show that he traded in armor and weapons, cloth, wool, veils, metals and hides, spices, pictures, and jewels. He combined the roles of wholesaler, retailer, exporter, importer, and banker. His archives reveal letters in Latin, French, Italian, English, Flemish, Catalonian, Provençal, Greek, and even some in Arabic and Hebrew. Despite his very extensive and successful dealings, Datini was but one of a large company of small- or middle-sized merchants, a *grande mercante* (big or international merchant) to be sure in contrast with the *piccolo mercante* (little merchant), but not one of the great companies, such as the *Alberti*.[17]

As the period of the Middle Ages drew to a close, a new interest in geography and navigation began to make itself felt. The Portuguese under the stimulus of Henry the Navigator had been venturing farther and farther from their own shores until they had finally reached the Cape of Good Hope. Following this discovery an expedition with the main purpose of locating the Spice Islands was fitted out under the leadership of Vasco da

[16] James Harvey Robinson, *History of Western Europe* (Boston: Ginn & Co., Inc., 1925), p. 243.

[17] Iris Origo, *The Merchant of Prato* (New York: Alfred A. Knopf, 1957); for the distinction between the big (international) merchant and the little merchant (both of which traded at wholesale as well as at retail), see p. 78.

Gama. Included in the cargoes was a small amount of each sort of spice to be shown as a sample of what they sought. After various interesting and exciting episodes, Vasco da Gama arrived in 1497 at Calicut, the center of the spice district in India.[18] The Mohammedan spice merchants were suspicious of the Portuguese but were powerless to interfere with their trade which grew and prospered. By 1515 Portugal was the greatest maritime power in the world, the Portuguese became keen traders, and Lisbon became a great trading center where cargoes of spice arrived regularly.[19] The Portuguese control continued for nearly a century before they were supplanted by the Dutch.

Oriental Trade. The exact status of wholesale trade in the Orient during the medieval era is even less well known than that of the West. There is evidence, however, in the accounts of travelers like Marco Polo that commerce was highly developed. There is record of a high development of commerce in India during the sixteenth century:

Kanishka, the Indo-Scythian ruler of India, took such a great personal interest in the trade between China and the West that he was known as "the illustrious middleman."[20]

Markets and Fairs in Europe. In Europe no distinction is to be found between wholesale and retail trade until late in the Middle Ages, although merchant trading was undoubtedly very largely wholesale in character. Most dealers sold both *"en gros"* (at wholesale) and *"en detail"* (at retail), as the opportunity presented itself.[21] When the distinction was finally made, it first applied to sellers of foodstuffs, the term "grocer" applying to a dealer who sold pepper and spices *en gros* and that of "spicer" referring to the retail dealer in such commodities. The wholesaler was finally recognized as a separate institution in a decree issued by England early in the fourteenth century, sometimes called the Magna Charta of Commerce:

The merchants of Germany, France, Spain . . . and all other foreign parts, who shall come to traffic in England, shall and may safely come with their merchandise into all cities, towns, and ports, and *sell the same by wholesale only,* as well to natives as to foreigners, except for groceries and haberdasheries which could also be sold by retail.[22]

[18] W. S. Lindsay, *History of Merchant Shipping and Ancient Commerce* (London: S. Low, Marston, Low & Searle, 1874–1876), Vol. II, pp. 4–13.

[19] W. H. Coates, *The Old "Country Trade" of the East Indies* (London: Imray, Laurie, Norie & Wilson, Ltd., 1911), pp. 14–17.

[20] Herbert H. Gowen, *Asia, a Short History* (Boston: Little, Brown & Co., 1936), p. 43.

[21] J. W. Thompson, *Economic and Social History of Europe in the Later Middle Ages* (1300–1530) (New York: The Century Co., 1931), pp. 451–52.

[22] H. G. Selfridge, *The Romance of Commerce* (London: John Lane Co., 1918), p. 176. (Italics by the authors.)

Internal trade at wholesale was relatively small in volume during the Middle Ages and more or less insignificant. Wholesaling was mostly international in character; consequently wholesaling was largely synonymous with importing and exporting. Much of the trade, both wholesale and retail, was transacted at fairs. To these points gravitated large numbers of merchants, manufacturers, and artisans from foreign lands and from distant communities for the purpose of buying and selling goods of various descriptions, as well as for amusement. Fairs, such as those of Nizhni Novgorod and Kiev (Russia), Champagne and Lyons (France), Sinigaglia (Italy), Kiachta (Mongolia), and Kanbalu (China)[23] became established institutions and were known to traders everywhere. It was in the thirteenth and fourteenth centuries that the European fairs had their greatest period. A considerable amount of business was transacted at these fairs, which were held at intervals of from 3 to 12 months, many of them lasting a month. Because of lack of communication facilities, they afforded the only practical way of bringing together a large number of traders. Located at inland points for the most part, they supplemented the seaports as communication centers in addition to performing their primary function of merchandise distribution.[24]

At these fairs the merchant was permitted to sell both at retail and at wholesale, depending somewhat on the nature of the product. The wholesaler was a large-scale assembler who sold his goods for further processing to retailers, and sometimes also directly to consumers. During the Middle Ages and through the handicraft stage of economic development, agricultural production was limited, manufacturing was highly localized and on a small scale, and retailing was confined to markets held on certain days, in addition to the fairs. The various so-called fairs of today are really *expositions* and serve entirely different purposes.

The Guilds. It was about this time that the guild system became all-powerful. Whether one could engage only in wholesale trade, sell also at retail, or trade at all with foreigners in foreign markets depended upon the trade superstructure of the guild. Most famous among these superstructures was the Hanseatic League; it supervised the activities of German merchants who operated as international wholesalers, selling at wholesale and sometimes also at retail at the various fairs and in other markets. The trade of the Baltic and North seas, and of northern and central Europe

[23] *The Travels of Marco Polo* (Garden City, N.Y.: Doubleday Publishing Co., Inc., 1930), chap. xxii. "To this city everything that is most rare and valuable in all parts of the world finds its way." Both foreign and domestic commerce are included. "No fewer than a thousand carriages and pack-horses loaded with raw silk, make their entry daily."

[24] For a good description of fairs, see S. Colwell, *The Ways and Means of Payment* (Philadelphia: J. B. Lippincott & Co., Inc., 1859), chaps. vii, viii, and xii; and C. Walford, *Fairs, Past and Present* (London: Elliott Stock, 1833).

generally, was thus largely in the control of the Hanseatic League during this era. The League was made up of a group of Free Cities which banded together to protect trade from the many difficulties of the period. It maintained great warehouses for the concentration and storage of the products of their respective districts pending redistribution by way of the Rhine or Danube, through the Alpine passes and down the Rhone or Po to the cities of the south.[25]

Exchanges. The supremacy of the guild system in the Middle Ages saw the development of extensive trading facilities, which were, however, frequently designed as a means for the collection of taxes and fees and for the supervision of transactions. For example, when a German merchant reached Venice, he was immediately taken to a special hotel provided for traders. Here his wares were invoiced for taxation purposes, and an inspector was appointed to accompany him. The inspector acted as interpreter and broker, in addition to seeing that none of the Venetian trading regulations were broken.

The hotel served both as office and warehouse, where much of the trade was transacted. Fairs, as already indicated, had early developed as places for trading, while the guild halls or trading posts maintained by the various guilds constituted still a third place. The trading posts of the Hanseatic League, known as factories, were among the most famous of these latter, including the widely known "Steelyard" with its branches in England. In Bruges, the Hanseatic "factory" housed over three hundred traders, serving as offices and warehouses. A fourth facility maintained for trading was the central exchange. In Bruges it was called the "Bourse," after a rich burgher who lived adjacent to it.[26]

The merchant, i.e., the wholesaler, performed practically all the marketing functions. In addition, another wholesale middleman of the broker type flourished. A commentator points out that "The merchants of Bruges, in a word, were nothing but intermediaries between the merchants of the various nations of Europe. They were the brokers who, in Bruges, played the important social and economic role elsewhere played by mere ship-

---

[25] Clive Day, *A History of Commerce* (New York: Longmans, Green & Co., Inc., 1907), pp. 38, 79–83.

[26] For interesting accounts as to the type of commerce prevailing during the Middle Ages, the fortunes amassed by such great merchant families as the Medicis and the Fuggers, and for other items of pertinent information concerning the wholesale business conducted during this time, see: Selfridge, *op. cit.*, chaps. iii–xvii; H. Pirrenne, *Medieval Cities,* trans. from the French by F. D. Halsey (Princeton: Princeton University Press, 1925), chaps. iii–viii; H. Zimmern, *The Hansa Towns* (New York: G. P. Putnam's Sons, Inc., 1893); W. J. Ashley, "The Beginnings of Town Life in the Middle Ages," *Quarterly Journal of Economics,* X (1896); G. B. Adams, *Civilization During the Middle Ages* (New York: Charles Scribner's Sons, 1894); and A. Schulte, *Geschichte des Mittelalterlichen Handels und Verkehrs Zwischen Westdeutschland und Italien* (Leipzig: Dunker & Humboldt, 1900).

owners. The Brugeois were the great middlemen of Europe."[27] The experience of Bruges, incidentally, illustrates the limitations of *arbitrary* restrictions in attempting to force upon the business world and the public uneconomic trading channels. While for a long time Bruges was a meeting place for merchants from all over the world, its trade dwindled when its rich and autocratic burghers passed a rule that all exchange between foreign merchants had to be made through local brokers. This lesson from history should be heeded by modern legislators who seek arbitrarily to interfere with distribution systems which have been generated by economic forces.

THE COMMERCIAL ERA (1500–1800)

Mercantilism was essentially the economic counterpart of the political philosophy of nationalism which had its inception during the period following the Middle Ages. Based upon an excessive emphasis upon the complete identity of money and wealth, it encouraged the importation of gold and silver through restrictive legislation. There was a sound political reason for this attitude in the necessity for war chests to defend the newly formed nations. Economically, however, mercantilistic legislation proved to be suicidal to national progress and practically impossible to enforce by ordinary methods. Even more shortsighted than the monetary and foreign trade policies were the restrictive measures imposed upon all trade and industry. The French government went so far as to specify in minutest detail the conduct of business and ruthlessly enforced the laws to the letter. In England the system purported to protect and encourage home industries, to accumulate and retain large stocks of money, to encourage shipping as a basis for an efficient navy, to increase revenue, and to protect native grain growers in order to make the country self-sufficient.

Trade could not be restrained, however, even by the strait jacket of mercantilism. Abundant evidence of extensive wholesale trade is to be found in the writings of Adam Smith. The importance of the wholesale middleman is further indicated by the prevailing system of production; the "putting out" system, in which capitalist middlemen in the textile industry, for example, provided the raw materials and paid the master weavers for processing them in their own households. The wholesaler organized production and assumed control of the selling function, and his importance grew apace with the expansion of demand for industrial products.

Wholesaling Institutions. Exchanges, one of the earlier types of wholesale institutions, were developed further during the mercantilistic era. The first exchange was established in Antwerp in the sixteenth century. Here men gathered daily for the exchange of goods, without the actual display of commodities; spices, pepper particularly, being among the principal

[27] Thompson, *op. cit.,* p. 333.

commodities traded in at the time. On the Royal Exchange of London goods were offered for sale by the method of candle auction, an arrangement whereby a parcel of goods was sold to the highest bidder before an inch of candle burned away. Sales of single parcels of silk, indigo, or spice sometimes amounted to a half-million dollars in value. A further insight into the importance and functioning of the exchanges may be had from some of the provisions of the law passed by Parliament in 1697 for the regulation of brokers dealing on the exchange. The law permitted brokers to operate in London "for the making of bargains between merchants and traders for merchandise and bills of exchange." Since, however, some of the brokers indulged in unfair practices, the law required that brokers obtain a license from the lord mayor and aldermen. Furthermore, the number of brokers operating on the exchange was limited to 100, their names being written on the Royal Exchange, and a penalty of £200 being imposed upon a broker who "dealt for himself," i.e., bought on his own account any merchandise, stocks, or other items.[28]

Another interesting glimpse into the trading of the day may be obtained from the description of dealings in corn by Daniel Defoe, author of Robinson Crusoe. The system he describes is one of buying and selling corn by sample only, and appears to be the prototype of the regular corn exchange later developed. A sample was brought by the farmer to the market town where he stood at a place "where such business was done." The corn factors, mealmen, bakers, and millers came along, looked at the sample, asked the price, bid, and then one of them bought the entire amount. The two parties then went to a nearby inn and adjusted the bargain, as to manner of delivery, time, and method of payment. The corn was then hauled into the nearest town where it was put on boats and sent to London. In commenting on this type of trading, Defoe says:

Now although this is openly done, nor do I see it can be practicable to prevent it, yet it must be acknowledged that it is really a clandestine trade, utterly unlawful, and may sometimes be very inconvenient; as it opens a door to the fatal and forbidden trade of ingrossing, regrating, forestalling the markets, and the like.[29]

A second wholesale institution of the mercantilistic era was the auction, a general method of wholesale trading on exchanges and in other whole-

[28] A. Anderson, *An Historical and Chronological Deduction of the Origin of Commerce from the Earliest Accounts* (London: printed at the Logographic Press, 1787), Vol. II, p. 630.

[29] Daniel Defoe, *The Complete English Tradesman* (London: 1727), Vol. II, p. 182. During the eighteenth century it was customary for merchants (wholesalers) to meet their customers at the well-known city inns or taverns of London on days specified by their "trade cards" and, on the basis of samples displayed by them, transact business. Defoe apparently looked upon sale by sample as new in his day whereas we have seen that the Greeks used the device centuries earlier.

sale markets, though at times separate establishments were maintained. Sales were made by auction on the Antwerp Exchange, on the Royal Exchange in London, and by the East India Tea Company for the disposal of imported goods.

A third and very important institution, which was used for both wholesale and retail trading, consisted in markets and market halls. These markets were held at frequent intervals, many of them weekly. They generally specialized in the handling of products of local manufacture or production, so that certain towns became famous for specific products, like Norwich for fine crepes and Devon for dyeing and finishing serges. At these markets the small-scale artisans would gather with their merchandise which would be disposed of to factors, merchants, and other buyers within an hour after the opening bell struck and the market began.[30]

While fairs continued to be an important marketing institution throughout the major part of the mercantilistic era, during the eighteenth century their importance declined rapidly, principally because of the development of the postal system, canals, and better roads. Fairs generally attracted the most important wholesale merchants from distant communities and foreign lands.

Wholesale Middlemen. During the mercantilistic era trading interests began to displace rapidly the old feudal aristocracy. This period gave rise to the "merchant princes," and wholesale middlemen multiplied in number and variety. Partnerships and associations of merchants had developed during the Middle Ages, but the great trading companies which were the predecessors of the modern corporation did not make much progress until mercantilism was substituted for the manorial system. Examples of these large trading companies were the East India Company, founded in 1601; the Dutch West India Company, founded in 1621; The Hudson's Bay Company, chartered in 1670; and the Royal African Company. The companies were either regulated or joint stock.

Another type of wholesale middleman common to the times was the traveling merchant, who visited small shopkeepers with a stock of goods carried through the country by pack-horse trains. Such merchants were often called "Manchester Men," "Chapmen," and, when they dealt in farm and dairy produce, "Badgers." Often they were the link between the fairs and the industrial centers, buying at fairs or markets in one district and selling in another. Their itinerary and means of travel were sometimes carefully defined in the license granted them by the local authorities.[31] Much of the cloth in England was sold in this fashion to the retail trade.

[30] For a good description of such a market, see L. W. Moffit, *England on the Eve of the Industrial Revolution* (London: P. S. King & Son, 1925), pp. 216–18.
[31] J. Parkes, *Travel in England in the Seventeenth Century* (London: Oxford University Press, 1925), p. 271.

As the roads improved, still another variation appeared in the form of traveling merchants who began to cover their territory on horseback, carrying with them only samples of the merchandise. Orders were taken and later delivered by wagon. This new method of soliciting business by a "rider out" became very popular and made big inroads on the business of the established London wholesalers who had been accustomed to having the country draper come into the city to buy his cloth. Thus, the London wholesalers were forced to send riders (probable prototype of the modern traveling salesman) at great expense to promote their business in the country.

Despite the traveling merchant, however, wholesale merchants with established places of business occupied an important position in the large market centers. Writing in 1727, Daniel Defoe frequently mentioned London wholesalers. Apparently wholesalers were regarded primarily as warehousekeepers, although they performed certain other essential functions. The function of the regular wholesaler in the cloth trade is indicated by the following quotation:

Nor do the shopkeepers go or send to all the several countries where those goods are made; that is to say, to this part for the cloth, or to that for the lining; to another for the buttons, and to another for the thread; but they again correspond with the wholesale dealers in London, where there are particular shops and warehouses for all these; and they not only furnish the country shopkeepers, but give them large credit, and sell them great quantities of goods, by which they again are enabled to trust the tailors, who make the clothes, or even their neighbors who wear them.[32]

Adam Smith, as indicated previously, also makes frequent mention of wholesalers.

From the foregoing analysis it appears that the operations of wholesalers prior to the nineteenth century were not different essentially from those of the modern wholesaler. They stored stocks of merchandise, arranged for transportation, engaged "riders out" to solicit business, and bought from various sources either directly or through factors and brokers.

Factors constituted another type of wholesale middleman of this era. The factors of old were much like the brokers of today, their function being to buy and sell goods for others on a commission basis, although some of the factors resembled more the commission merchant of modern times. The literature of the period gives us some idea of the degree of specialization in types of wholesale middlemen. Clive Day, for example, refers to a writer of the seventeenth century who distinguished between five classes of factors: those who bought goods for others, those who sold for others, those who made collections for principals (for bankers or businessmen), forwarders who received and forwarded merchandise which

[32] Defoe, *op. cit.*, Vol. I, p. 267.

had to be transshipped, and those who acted as agents for carriers.[33] The factor became increasingly important toward the end of the mercantilistic period. In the textile industry, for illustration, the factors of London became the outstanding agency for mercantile capital. They exercised extensive control over a large part of the cloth trade, so much so that in 1739 it was complained that the factor who started as a servant of the cloth maker became his master.[34]

Colonial America. Wholesale trade in the United States began with grants by European monarchs of the sixteenth and seventeenth centuries to merchant companies for the purpose of colonizing the New World. The mercantilistic doctrines of that era dictated the colonial policy of the European powers. Trade was foremost among the motives which underlay the early efforts at empire-building. Colonies were sought for two major purposes: (1) as sources of raw materials for domestic industry in the parent country and (2) as markets for the products of the same industry.

One need but recall the colonial history of the United States to be impressed with the early importance of trade: the lumber, fish, and shipping industries of New England; the fur trade of the north and west; the tobacco culture of Virginia and the South. This traffic was largely water borne and consisted of coastwise trade and of exporting to and importing from Europe, both of which are primarily wholesale trading activities.[35] It required many years of intensive effort to develop the vast hinterland of the Atlantic coastal colonies. Transportation was a limiting factor, and was confined largely to rivers and Indian trails until such time as roads could be carved through the wilderness. With the growth of population the pioneers gradually sifted westward, first along natural routes but later over highways of their own devising. Towns sprang up at the intersections of water and land routes, and trade grew with the towns. Records of the times indicate that much of the trade at interior points was essentially wholesaling.[36]

The political transition from colonial to independent national status in 1776 was less significant to the evolution of wholesaling than were the *economic* changes of the late eighteenth and early nineteenth centuries. Economic forces, indeed, are held by modern historians to have been the fundamental causes of the political controversy which culminated in the birth of a new nation. The interruption of commerce occasioned by the Revolution and by postwar political readjustments was but a minor ob-

---

[33] Day, *op. cit.,* p. 142.

[34] L. B. Numier, "A Mid-eighteenth Century Merchant," *English Historical Review* (October, 1927), 517.

[35] E. R. Johnson, T. W. VanMetre, G. G. Huebner, and D. S. Hanchett, *History of Domestic and Foreign Commerce of the United States* (Washington: Carnegie Institute of Washington, 1915; Reprint, 1922), Pt. II, p. 193.

[36] *Ibid.,* pp. 202, 204.

stacle to the continuous expansion of the same flow of commerce which has been traced through the colonial period.

THE EMERGENCE OF MODERN WHOLESALING

The Industrial Revolution. The broad foundations of modern wholesaling were fairly well laid by the close of the eighteenth century. The structure remained to be erected. A chief architect in this building was the industrial revolution. The closing decades of the eighteenth century and the early years of the nineteenth witnessed the great inventions in textiles manufacture which launched a new economic era. Hargreaves patented his spinning jenny in 1770, a year after Arkwright invented the water frame. Crompton followed with his *mule* in 1779, later made self-acting by Kelly in 1792 and improved by Roberts in 1825. Cartwright's power loom, patented in 1785, completed these basic innovations. These mechanical improvements, following closely on Watt's steam engine, set the stage for rapid growth in the textile industry and the appearance of the *factory system,* which soon displaced the earlier *domestic system.*[37]

It is debatable whether the industrial revolution had a greater impact on wholesaling than wholesaling had on the industrial revolution. Certain it is that wholesale merchants were not slow to reap the benefits of the new application of power to machinery. It must be recalled that wholesalers were among the more opulent of the population and in a better position than many others to raise the necessary capital to embark on production. Toynbee points out that "to secure a sufficient supply of goods it became the interest of merchants to collect weavers around them in great numbers, to get looms together in a workshop, and to give out the warp themselves to the work people."[38] Thus, the wholesalers of that day may be said to have anticipated vertical integration by combining the manufacturing with the wholesaling functions.

Other Changes Affecting Wholesaling. Among the most important developments affecting wholesale trade favorably may be mentioned the changing modes of transportation, improvements in communication, development of organized banking, and the changing attitude of governments.

During the latter half of the eighteenth and the early years of the nineteenth centuries, European countries launched upon an era of canal-building and the making of roads. Canal boats on the one hand and the "Fly-Waggon"[39] on the other displaced the pack horse and accelerated the decline of fairs as marketing institutions. Railroads, which came later, facilitated wholesale trade even more. Steamships were another factor in

---

[37] Arnold Toynbee, *The Industrial Revolution* (London: Longmans, Green & Co., Ltd., 1925), pp. 70–71.

[38] *Ibid.*

[39] Great lumbering wagon drawn by half-a-dozen horses.

the progress of transportation, followed by widespread improvements in highways, under the leadership of two Scottish engineers, Thomas Telford and John Macadam.[40]

The movement toward larger scale production and growth in urban population was given considerable impetus by the discovery of the Bessemer steel process in 1855 and the open hearth process in 1870. When the telegraph was invented in 1840, followed by the invention of the telephone and the establishment of cheaper postal service, rapid strides were made in the field of communication, so essential to the best use of exchanges and the establishment of world prices. Regular banking organizations were founded during the century in the most important countries of Europe, replacing in large part the private bankers or joint stock companies of merchants.

Above all, wholesaling benefited by a change in the attitude of the governments toward trade, particularly toward the large trading companies which operated as monopolies. Individuals grew restive under the system of mercantilism and the severe restrictions placed upon business by government; hence the development of a demand for a laissez faire policy. The factory system of production gave a marked impetus to this individualistic philosophy. Many restrictions upon trade were removed and some of the powers formerly given exclusively to trading companies were considerably modified. Wholesale trade was further aided by the codification of the commercial laws of various countries, inaugurated by France in 1807 and followed by Belgium, Italy, Spain, and several other European nations. Germany established a general code of commerce in 1861, which was followed by Austria, Hungary, Switzerland, and other countries.[41]

RISE OF TRADING CENTERS

Europe. During the nineteenth century much shifting was in evidence among various wholesale marketing institutions in Europe. Fairs were gradually supplanted by more permanent markets, although a few continue to this day. Important developments also stimulated the growth of exchanges and auctions. In London alone there were established during this period a wool exchange, a wool auction, a corn (grain) exchange, a metal exchange, a coal exchange, a shipping exchange, and one exchange—the Baltic—where dealings took place in all commodities. About 1820, during the severe depression then existing, cooperatives for the marketing of flour were started at Rochdale and Leeds, England.

[40] F. A. Ogg and W. R. Sharp, *Economic Development of Modern Europe* (New York: The Macmillan Co., 1926), pp. 229, 233, 237–41.
[41] *Encyclopaedia of the Social Sciences*, Vol. IV, p. 17.

Much the same types of middlemen operated during the nineteenth as in the preceding century. In the grain markets of England during the nineteenth century, the *corn merchant* and the *corn jobber* occupied prominent positions. The operations of these two middlemen overlapped, both engaging in speculation, although the jobber speculated more in time relations, while the merchant speculated in place relations. The former bought and sold according to his estimates of the future prices in a particular market, while the latter bought and sold in many markets, domestic and foreign, according to the prices prevailing or likely to prevail in each of these markets. Consequently, the corn merchant was primarily an exporter and importer, while the corn jobber was the wholesaler operating in the domestic markets. *Factors,* who bought corn by sample, as already described, were another type of wholesale middleman in the grain trade as was also the *badger* who engaged factors to go to the markets and large estates to buy up grain and care for its shipment to their principal. Corn *chandlers* sold primarily at retail, although they sometimes bought on commission for stable keepers.

In the textile industry the *draper* or wholesale merchant employed *bagmen* who went from town to town with samples of merchandise, soliciting orders which were later delivered. Factors operated in the cloth markets, buying and selling to drapers, merchants, and manufacturers. *Linen merchants* dealt in imports and exports of cloth.

In the meat industry there were *graziers* who bought cattle for fattening, *carcass butchers* who were the wholesale butchers and meat dealers, and *meat jobbers.* In the coal industry there were the *coal factors* who operated more like present-day selling agents in the same industry, and *coal undertakers* whose main function was to take charge of loading and unloading operations.[42]

Wholesaling in England had definitely come into its own. With the decline of trading companies and fairs as marketing institutions, there came a tremendous growth of established markets and wholesale firms using the "Warehouse System," of export and import houses specializing in wholesaling, of exchanges and organized auctions, followed by a multiplication in the number of middlemen and a higher degree of specialization on the part of such middlemen by commodities and by functions. Establishment of a permanent place of business in the form of a warehouse caused the wholesaler to adopt different methods of selling. First an attempt was made to bring the customer to the warehouse, through the employment of "hookers-in" and "canvassing clerks" who haunted the coaching houses and inns for new arrivals who might be prospective customers; "riders-out"

---

[42] For a good description of the middlemen in England, see R. B. Westerfield, "Middlemen in English Business," in *Transactions of the Connecticut Academy of Arts and Sciences,* Vol. XIX (New Haven: Yale University Press, 1915).

who would go out part of the way to meet such prospects; and other such devices. Later travelers were sent out with samples to call upon customers.

Similar developments took place in time on the European continent. In France the fairs declined in importance, and established markets like the Halles Centrales[43] of Paris came into prominence and an increase in the number of specialized wholesale middlemen took place. Being largely agrarian, France led all other countries in the development of produce markets.

In Germany fairs held an important place in the wholesaling structure until about the middle of the century. Even as late as 1841 the business transacted at the fair of Leipzig amounted to £4,905,000, exclusive of the large volume of business done through a clearing house or cancellation system known as sales in the books, for which the Leipzig fair was famous.[44] By 1850, however, fairs showed a tendency to decline, and traveling or itinerary merchants made their appearance. With the decline of the Hansa towns German trade fell off very rapidly, so that by 1860 relatively little wholesale trade was carried on in Germany. But with the coming of the canals, railroads, improved surface roads, political unity, the Industrial Revolution, and the opening of colonies of other nations to foreign trade, German wholesale trade advanced rapidly. In 1886 Berlin organized its food markets and created a central hall for wholesale dealings.[45]

In Russia, as in a number of the European countries in the same stage of commercial development, the commerce of the nineteenth century was much like that which prevailed in France and in England during the latter part of the Middle Ages. Largely agrarian, fairs still constituted the principal means for the exchange of goods on a wholesale basis in these backward nations. The Fair of Nizhni Novgorod in Russia, for example, was important throughout the century for the sale of iron, corn, furs, salt, tea, fish, wine, pottery, and certain manufactures. Merchants from Russia, from Iran (Persia), and from Armenia were the chief traders at these fairs. On the frontiers of China, Russian trade was transacted principally through the Fair at Kiachta, Mongolia. A small amount of trade was also carried on by traveling wholesale merchants whose main dealings were in the grains shipped by river to Odessa for export, or by way of German seaports.[46]

[43] The Halles Centrales is a large produce market, in which goods are sold both at wholesale and at retail, although wholesale operations predominate.

[44] Stephen Colwell, *The Ways and Means of Payment* (Philadelphia: J. B. Lippincott & Co., 1859), p. 285.

[45] J. H. Clapham, *The Economic Development of France and Germany, 1815–1914* (London: Cambridge University Press, 1928), p. 369.

[46] For a description of "The Great Fairs and Markets of Europe," see article by R. H. Horne, *Harper's Magazine*, XLVI (1873), 376–85.

The United States. Up to the nineteenth century the internal trade of the
the United States had undergone very little change from colonial days.
The country was still a frontier community with two-thirds of its population on the Atlantic seaboard. Even as late as 1802, according to a
description by the French traveler Michaux, goods (consisting largely of
firearms, small metal articles, dry goods, and other valuable commodities)
were transported from Philadelphia to Pittsburgh in large covered wagons,
drawn by four horses, two abreast.[47] There appears to have been relatively
little competition in internal wholesale trade, possibly because none of the
powerful wholesaling concerns which were to make their appearance later
had yet been established.

Most of the wholesaling of the period was divided between the frontier
trading posts and the country general stores on the one hand, which continued as in colonial days to assemble the raw produce of the land, and, on
the other hand, importers who also dealt in the more profitable goods of
domestic manufacture. Items in the latter category, however, amounted to
but a few million dollars per annum in value. They included textile products, pig and bar iron, lumber, carpentry, wheelwrighting, furniture,
wagons, harness, hats, shoes, and meat products. As domestic manufacture
increased, a number of specialized middlemen sprang up to market them.
About 1808 the first wholesale house to be entirely divorced from importing was established in the United States at Eaton, Ohio, by Cornelius
Vanausdal, who in 1828 opened a similar place of business in Cincinnati,
Ohio. Both houses presumably dealt in dry goods.[48] ·

In 1809 John Jacob Astor, the German fur merchant, who was said to
be the only millionaire in this country at the turn of the nineteenth century,
founded the American Fur Company, followed by the Pacific Fur Company in 1810, and the South-West Company in 1811, thus becoming the
leading wholesaler of his day.[49] Astor, in common with other East India
merchant princes of that time, also engaged in importing spices, tea, sugar,
coffee, fruits, wines, and liquors. Thus the wholesale grocery trade during
the early part of the century was definitely associated with general importing, although it was beginning to show signs of a distinctive existence.

The War of 1812 stimulated the development of American manufactures,
which in turn gave impetus to the wholesale business of the country. The
first rolling mill was opened in Pittsburgh in 1812.[50] The period of 1815–
1818 marked the beginning of quantity canning in tin in the United States,
following the introduction of the secret of hermetically sealing food in tin

[47] E. L. Bogart, *Economic History of the American People* (New York: Longmans,
Green & Co., Inc., 1930), p. 350.

[48] *Directory of Preble County, Ohio, for 1875* (Eaton, Ohio: B. F. Morgan, pub-
lisher and compiler, 1875), pp. 73, 75.

[49] Selfridge, *op. cit.*, pp. 331–32.

[50] M. Keir, *The Epic of Industry* (New Haven: Yale University Press, 1926), p. 30.

cans by Ezra Daggett,[51] and in 1818 the meat packing industry started in Cincinnati.[52] This increase in industry called for greater marketing facilities. By the end of the first quarter of the nineteenth century enough wholesale houses were established in different parts of the country to provide American manufacturers with ample channels for the distribution of their goods. In 1828 Boston and New York jobbing houses were selling over a million and a half dollars' worth of shoes annually. After 1830 similar houses handling boots and shoes, as well as hats and caps, were in existence in all the larger cities of the South and West.[53] Wholesalers apparently made an effort to serve retailers by sending out traveling salesmen to the trade.[54]

Evidently it took some time for these wholesale establishments to break entirely away from retailing as a side line. The transition was as gradual as the separation of wholesaling and importing which has been mentioned above. Probably the first establishment in the United States to divorce wholesaling from retail trade was the wholesale dry goods house established at the close of the War of 1812 by Elisha Riggs, a draper, in Georgetown, Maryland, now a part of the District of Columbia.[55] Later, in 1834, a census taken in Detroit by A. E. Hathon of all wholesale and retail businesses of that city, revealed the fact that of the 64 stores and warehouses recorded, only 2 establishments were listed as strictly wholesale.[56]

Wholesaling developed at different times in the various lines of trade, depending, no doubt, on the economic conditions affecting a given line of goods. In the boot and shoe trade the wholesaler dates back to about 1810, wholesale dealers of New England selling boots and shoes to "grocers, dry goods, and hardware dealers throughout the country as well as to shoe dealers proper."

In the drug business the development also came early. In fact, one firm, Schieffelin & Company of New York, is reported to have been established in 1794; another, the firm of Powers & Weightman of Philadelphia, was organized in 1818 as Farr & Kunzi; and McKesson & Robbins was founded in 1833 under the name of Olcott & McKesson. The last-mentioned concern was the first wholesale drug house to operate a separate laboratory on a large scale for the purpose of manufacturing a general line of pharmaceuticals. The formation of the Western Wholesale Druggists' Association in 1876 was hailed as an epochal event of the century

[51] C. M. Depew (ed.), *1795–1895, One Hundred Years of American Commerce* (New York: D. O. Haynes & Co., 1895), p. 396.

[52] E. C. Semple, *American History and its Geographic Conditions* (Boston: Houghton Mifflin Co., 1903), p. 358.

[53] Depew (ed.), *op. cit.*, p. 571.

[54] M. Welker, *Farm Life in Central Ohio Sixty Years Ago* (Wooster, Ohio, 1892), pp. 67–68.

[55] Elbert Hubbard, *Little Journeys to the Homes of Great Business Men* (New York and Chicago: Wm. H. Wise & Co., 1916), Vol. XI, p. 316.

[56] Friend Palmer, *Early Days in Detroit* (Detroit: Hunt and June Pub., 1906).

for the drug trade. In 1882, when many Eastern wholesale druggists joined with those of the West, the National Wholesale Druggists' Association was formed, numbering toward the end of the century 258 active and 153 associate members.

In the wholesale stationery business records show that jobbing came a little later. In 1837 an exclusive wholesale stationery house selling not only to retailers but also to jobbers was operated by L. I. Cohen, an importing stationer of prominence. In 1845 Richard Bainbridge came to New York and introduced to this stationery concern the English and Continental method of traveling with samples, which proved very successful.[57]

Additional evidence of the early establishment of wholesale trading in the United States may be found in the special studies growing out of the first Census of Distribution.[58] With the expansion of wholesale trade and the differentiation by lines of merchandise came also the development of wholesaling centers. Detroit was one of the earliest to appear in this role in the West. By 1840 St. Louis took its place as the "great emporium" of commercial activity of the upper Mississippi Valley, rivaling such other centers as Pittsburgh, Cincinnati, and Louisville. The Merchants' Exchange was opened in Cincinnati in 1846, and its jobbing and wholesale houses supplied country merchants with a complete line of dry goods, hardware, groceries, and drugs. In the South, according to the best statistics available, Savannah, Georgia, in 1848, had 263 merchants, factors, and wholesale dealers, and 136 shopkeepers and retail grocers. By 1850 New York City had a total of 740 importers operating in 18 different lines of trade, dry goods importers leading with 139, followed by 108 importers of wines and liquors, and 107 importers of hardware.[59] Internal trade was growing rapidly, so that the trade of a single New York market in 1850 exceeded the total foreign trade of the United States of a century earlier.

Specialization in goods began to develop during the second quarter of the century, but "it was about the year 1850 that the custom of making a specialty of a certain kind of merchandise became general."[60] Goods were offered for sale in much greater detail as to items stocked, and both retailers and wholesalers carried the matter of specialization in a single type of merchandise to a fine point. Thus, in the dry goods trade alone, different importers and wholesalers specialized in such lines of goods as

[57] Depew (ed.), *op. cit.,* pp. 571, 612, 617–18, 643–44.

[58] T. N. Beckman, *The Wholesale Hardware Trade,* Fifteenth Census of the United States, Census of Distribution, Distribution No. W–203 (Washington, D. C.: Government Printing Office, 1933), pp. 24–25; also N. H. Engle, No. W–205, same series.

[59] R. S. Fisher, *Statistical Gazetteer of the United States of America* (New York: J. H. Colton, 1858), pp. 579, 773.

[60] G. D. Hunt, *History of Salem and the Immediate Vicinity* (Salem, Ohio: 1898), p. 135.

notions and small wares; white goods and linens; silks and dress goods; hats and caps; and hosiery, underwear, and gloves.[61]

The further development of wholesale centers is apparent during this period. By 1850 Chicago was a prominent wholesale center. Cooley, Wadsworth and Company, a firm which engaged largely in the wholesale business, was the most notable in the city and was the forerunner of the present Marshall Field and Company.[62] The large development of the wholesale hardware business of St. Louis dates back to the establishment of the Simmons Hardware Company in 1855. Edward C. Simmons, who started the enterprise, introduced traveling salesmen into the hardware field. When finally incorporated in 1874, this concern is said to have been the first mercantile firm to incorporate in the United States.[63] By 1856 there were some 200 wholesale and jobbing houses in Boston alone, selling shoes, while New York boasted of 56 such business houses.[64]

Wholesaling After the War Between the States. The total volume of wholesale trading done in the United States internally prior to 1860 is not known. That it was quite extensive just before the War between the States, however, can perhaps be gauged from an estimate that in 1860 New England sent to the South some $60 million worth of merchandise, comprising cotton and woolen manufactures, fish, molasses, and shoes, while the South in turn sold to New England naval stores, cotton, hemp, flour, and animal products to the extent of $55 million.[65] At this time the organization of commerce appears to have been fairly complex. Merchandise apparently passed through a number of hands before reaching the consumer.

Industry was growing apace, and there must have been corresponding activity in the field of distribution. Cotton mills, boot and shoe factories, plants producing hardware, rubber goods, and machinery turned out a rising tide of commodities, all of which had to be marketed. The war further stimulated domestic manufacture because of the loss of ships and interference with foreign trade. Railroads were built on a large scale, replacing canal transportation. By 1890 the value of manufactures produced in the United States amounted to over $4 billion, and the production of mineral and metal products exceeded $0.5 billion in value. This is in contrast to an annual domestic production of but a few million dollars' worth

[61] Depew (ed.), *op. cit.,* p. 556.

[62] S. H. Ditchett, "Marshall Field and Company—The Life Story of a Great Concern," *The Dry Goods Economist* (1922), 15.

[63] B. C. Forbes, *Men Who Are Making America* (New York: B. C. Forbes Publishing Co., 1917), p. 352.

[64] Depew (ed.), *op. cit.,* p. 572.

[65] "The South in the Building of the Nation" (Southern Historical Publication Society, 1909), Vol. V, p. 408.

of manufactured goods produced at the beginning of the century.[66] From 1850 to 1900 the increase in the value of manufactured goods amounted to 1,100 per cent. Likewise, the value of agricultural products increased tremendously, being tripled during the same period.[67]

The marketing structure of the United States appears to have been patterned on that evolved in Europe. Most classes of domestic manufactures were handled through middlemen, such as brokers, jobbers, or commission houses, who in turn distributed the goods to wholesalers. In some lines of merchandise the manufacturer dealt directly with the wholesalers, but since many of the plants were small and widely scattered, the broker carved for himself a definite groove in the marketing structure of the latter half of the nineteenth century.

Wholesalers, as well as wholesaling, played an important role in the economic development of the nation. Wholesalers themselves were held in great esteem. Writers of this period have referred to the keenness of the mercantile mind, the integrity and skill of the great merchants, and the knowledge required for trading with all parts of the globe.[68] Through their stimulation of trade throughout the extent of the country, the wholesalers contributed to the development of steam transportation, and also provided a significant factor in reviving trade after the war and after the depression of 1873. The early Marshall Field organization, for example, operating at the time as Field, Leiter and Company, acted as its own banker after 1865, rendering financial assistance to the merchants in the small country towns in the vicinity of Chicago.[69]

In the foregoing pages a number of distinct trends in wholesaling worthy of reiteration have been mentioned. One of the first was the separation of wholesaling from importing. A second trend was the separation of wholesaling from retailing. A third was a growing specialization in certain types of merchandise. A fourth trend lay in the introduction of a number of middlemen of different types and in the growth in the number of wholesale middlemen of each type. Brokers and commission houses became important. Even wholesalers who took title to the goods were of several varieties. In addition to the regular type of wholesaler, and the jobber, was the wholesale peddler (a wagon peddler or perambulating wholesaler); the canal or river-boat wholesaler; and the coastwise boat wholesaler. Branch-house wholesaling was practiced as early as the mid-century. There was also the integration of wholesaling with manufacturing.

[66] Depew (ed.), *op. cit.,* p. 42.

[67] H. U. Faulkner, *Economic History of the United States* (New York: The Macmillan Co., 1928), p. 162.

[68] James Hall, *The West; Its Commerce and Navigation* (Cincinnati: H. W. Derby & Co., 1848), pp. 12, 21; and F. Hunt, *Lives of American Merchants* (New York: Derby & Jackson, 1858), Vol. II, p. 245.

[69] Ditchett, *op. cit.,* pp. 29–30.

Growth of Wholesaling in the Twentieth Century. The dawn of a new century saw no revolutionary transition in wholesaling. Rather, a continuation of the evolutionary processes we have been following characterized the early years of the century. Changes which have taken place have been primarily quantitative rather than qualitative.

Moreover, great progress has been registered in statistical data on wholesaling which permits a more accurate appraisal and evaluation of the field. For example, wholesale trade was made a part of the first census of distribution (for 1929) and has continued to be covered in subsequent censuses of business. These censuses cover the number of wholesale establishments by type of operation and line of merchandise, and provide data on sales, employment, payrolls, operating expenses, etc. The Bureau of Labor Statistics publishes data on wholesale prices, employment, hours of labor, wage rates, and related information. The Treasury Department publishes data on sales, profits, taxes, advertising expenditures, and other facts on wholesale corporations. The contribution of wholesale trade to the national income is compiled and published by the Office of Business Economics of the U. S. Department of Commerce. The U. S. Department of Agriculture conducts much research on wholesale trade in farm products. Trade and financial groups collect and publish data on wholesaling. In short, businessmen and students interested in wholesaling now have a wealth of invaluable data of immense practical value to a knowledge and understanding of wholesaling.

During the first half of the twentieth century, and with every prospect of continuing, wholesaling has shown a steady growth. The wholesaler of tradition, however, has faced a rising tide of competition. While many have stemmed the tide, casualties have been heavy. The struggle has been to discover new ways of performing the tasks of wholesaling. Manufacturers have greatly expanded their own wholesaling activities, making use of sales branches or offices, and thereby channeling their output largely around the wholesaler. At the same time large-scale retailers—department stores, mail order houses, chain stores, and supermarkets—have tended to purchase directly from manufacturers and other primary or secondary producers and to perform their own wholesaling, chiefly by use of wholesale warehouses. Despite these changes, which are examined more fully elsewhere in this book, the wholesaler continues to be the dominant type of wholesale institution in the American wholesaling structure.[70]

General Conclusions

From this brief and highly condensed review of the history of wholesaling a few significant generalizations may be drawn.

[70] See N. H. Engle in Richard M. Clewett (ed.), *Marketing Channels* (Homewood, Ill.: Richard D. Irwin, Inc., 1953), chap. iii.

1. *Wholesaling is of ancient lineage, deeply rooted in the past.* It has been present to some degree wherever commerce existed among civilized men. This seems to warrant the conclusion that wholesaling is a fundamental function of every economic order beyond the primitive.

2. *Wholesaling is dynamic, constantly changing in response to evolution in economic and political conditions.*

3. *The development of wholesaling institutions, middlemen, and methods of operation has, on the whole, been evolutionary and orderly.* This is to be noted in the emergence of certain wholesaling institutions at about the same stage of economic and political maturity in different countries. It is observed also in the timely appearance of a given type of wholesale middleman in the distribution of the different lines of merchandise.

4. *Large-scale wholesaling, differentiated in form both by type of wholesale organization and by degree of specialization in merchandise and functions, is usually attained at an advanced stage of a country's industrial and commercial development.* In a sense, therefore, wholesaling may be regarded as a concomitant of civilization. It flourished in Sumeria, Babylonia, Phoenicia, Egypt, Persia, China, India, Greece, Rome, Venice, and Genoa when these countries and cities were at their height in the arts, philosophy, religion, political rule, or social conduct for the times. However, its greatest development did not take place until after the Industrial Revolution.

5. *The basic pattern of the modern wholesaling system was laid for the most part during the nineteenth century and was established in its major essentials by the end of that period.* Since then, changes which have taken place have been mainly in internal organization, method of operation, and in relationships of wholesale institutions with suppliers on the one hand and with customers on the other, rather than in basic form.

6

THE WHOLESALING
STRUCTURE IN THE
UNITED STATES

To accomplish the great task of distributing at wholesale the vast output of our economy, a highly complex institutional system has evolved. From the contents of the preceding chapter it is evident that the modern wholesaling system is largely an outgrowth of past institutions as they have been modified and adapted in response to an ever changing economic and social environment. An understanding of the present-day structure and the competitive forces at work within it is obviously of basic importance to the student of the field. It is also important to the wholesaling executive, since his enterprise must function within this system and compete not only with concerns similarly operating but with other types and classes of wholesaling institutions as well.

In this chapter the modern wholesaling structure in the United States and its component parts are described, analyzed, and critically evaluated. In subsequent chapters each of the major types or classes of institutions is examined separately. First, however, it is necessary to obtain a broad view of the structure as a whole.

The Wholesaling Structure Defined. In the commonly accepted sense, as covered by census data, the wholesaling structure or system may be defined as that complex of business *establishments*, which, like the cilia in certain parts of the human organism, are constantly functioning to move the products of industry through the channels of trade from primary and other producers to retail outlets or to industrial consumers. It includes all public and private agencies (except the specialized service agencies noted below) which contribute, as their major activity, to the physical flow of merchandise or to change in ownership up to the point where the goods reach the hands of retailers or industrial users.

From the broadest viewpoint the *wholesaling system* of the United States is synonymous with *wholesaling* and embraces all *marketing* activities of farmers, mine operators, lumbering concerns, fisheries, oil producers, and manufacturers, except the relatively small volume of sales which these physical-goods or form-utility producers make directly to household consumers. It includes *all* activities of the multitude of agents, brokers, assemblers, and other types of wholesale middlemen who function *between* such producers and the better known types of wholesale distributors and merchants. It includes, of course, *all* operations of the so-called *regular* wholesalers, who take title to the goods in which they deal, and also the work of industrial distributors, exporters, and importers, as well as the activities of such wholesale dealers as cash-and-carry wholesalers and wagon distributors who specialize in the performance of selected functions.

To the above activities must be added the work of the specialized *wholesaling* divisions, departments, or warehouses which are *integral parts* of manufacturing, refining, and retailing firms. Among these types of wholesaling establishments, which must not be confused with the nonspecialized wholesaling activities above mentioned, are the wholesale branch houses of manufacturers, the bulk tank stations of petroleum refiners, and the warehouses maintained by retail chain systems, department stores, and mail order houses.

The cooperative movement also contributes to the scope of the wholesaling structure in the United States. For example, the wholesale units of consumers' cooperative organizations, the wholesale divisions of cooperative groups of retailers, and the wholesaling activities of agricultural cooperatives, all are a part of our great wholesale marketing system.

The discussion of the wholesaling system as herein contemplated generally covers the activities of wholesale establishments only and excludes the specialized service agencies which *facilitate* the wholesale marketing process. The transportation system—including rail, water, truck, pipe line, and air transport—while performing wholesale distribution functions, and for that reason theoretically part of the wholesaling *process,* is excluded from a consideration as part of the wholesaling *structure* or system proper, partly because it does not confine itself exclusively to wholesaling functions, but primarily because it is sufficiently differentiated from other economic activities to justify separate treatment. The communications system—including mail, express, telephone, telegraph, cable, and the radio—is similarly excluded, as are the highly specialized financial institutions such as the commercial banks, savings banks, investment houses, and insurance companies. The student of wholesaling should not ignore any of these institutions, however, because some of them perform essential wholesale marketing functions and a full understanding of the subject must embrace them all.

THE TASK OF THE WHOLESALING SYSTEM

The institutions which make up the wholesaling structure exist in the long run only because they perform essential economic functions. In a narrow sense their task may be conceived of as the marketing on the wholesale level of the physical output of factories, mines, farms, and other goods-producing organizations. In a truer sense wholesaling serves also to coordinate the supply of goods with demand and to provide useful services to both suppliers and customers. As the American economy has expanded, the magnitude of this task has grown. The nature of this growth and the reasons for it are analyzed briefly in this section.

Value of Goods Marketed at Wholesale. The magnitude of the wholesaling task may be measured in part by the quantity of physical output marketed at wholesale. This is practically synonymous with the total quantity of goods produced in a given period, since only a small fraction of total output is not initially marketed at the wholesale level. The only exception to this is the relatively small volume of merchandise sold by manufacturers and farmers directly to ultimate consumers, i.e., for personal use, which amounts to only about 2 per cent of total output under normal conditions.

The goods marketed include a great many different kinds of products, which can be combined for measurement purposes only in terms of a monetary common denominator. Hence total output is designated as the *value of goods marketed at wholesale,* with each product counted once at its value f.o.b. point of physical production or importation. These goods come from many sources—including manufacturers, mines and quarries, oil wells, farms, forests, fisheries, and hunters and trappers in the domestic economy, as well as from similar sources in other lands whose goods are imported into this country. These goods must be distributed to an even greater number of ultimate consumers (via retail outlets) and to industrial users, commercial users, and institutional buyers.

While virtually all goods are marketed *at wholesale,* by no means all of them pass through the *wholesaling structure* as herein defined. Probably about 60 per cent of total output is handled by wholesale establishments, and less than 30 per cent is handled by wholesalers. Wholesale channels of distribution for different commodities vary greatly, of course. For consumer goods, as much as 75 per cent passes through wholesale establishments and almost 50 per cent is sold by wholesalers; while for industrial goods, only about 40 per cent of total output goes through wholesale establishments, and less than 15 per cent through wholesalers. Furthermore, within the two broad categories of consumer and industrial goods, equally great variations in marketing channels exist.

Unfortunately, it is not possible to measure the relative importance of different wholesale channels of distribution or to show the flow of various commodities through these channels. To do this it would be necessary to know the distribution of sales by manufacturers and other form-utility producers to different classes of customers, such as sales to industrial users, to wholesalers, to retailers, for export, and so forth. This type of information was last collected on a broad basis for 402 of the 446 industries through the "Distribution of Manufacturers' Sales" inquiry in the 1939 Census of Manufactures.

For the 1954 Census of Manufactures an inquiry similar in scope was planned, but for various reasons, some of doubtful validity, such data were collected only for 28 industries or commodity groups.[1] A principal reason for this limitation was that industries covered were the only ones which typically maintain records of shipments by class of customer. Furthermore, the inquiry was adapted to the customer channels thought to be used by the particular industry, which makes comparison of one industry with another extremely difficult. Despite these shortcomings it should be possible for the limited number of industries or commodity groups to ascertain the proportion that is in the form of interplant transfers and the percentages of shipments to retailers, wholesalers, government, and for export. Such information is extremely useful, not only to students of marketing for purposes of analysis, but also to marketing executives in selecting and evaluating channels of distribution and in marketing management generally. It is hoped that in future censuses of manufactures such information will be properly collected and on a much broader scope.

Volume of Wholesale Trade. The *value of goods marketed at wholesale* is not to be confused with the *volume of wholesale trade*. The latter concept is a measure of wholesale *transactions* rather than of commodities per se. Thus, in comparing the value of goods marketed with the volume of wholesale trade, several factors would account for the much larger figure for the latter:

1. In measuring the *value of goods* marketed at wholesale, the goods are counted but once and are taken at f.o.b. prices or values at point of physical production or importation. In measuring the *volume of wholesale trade,* however, the volume or value of all *transactions* in such goods

---

[1] Confectionery; soft drinks; hosiery; carpets and rugs; linoleum; printing and publishing; drugs and medicines; paints and paint products; essential oils, perfumes and cosmetics; petroleum products; shoes and slippers, other than rubber; heating and cooking apparatus (including electric); service-industry and household machines; refrigeration and air-conditioning equipment; storage batteries; sporting and athletic goods.

on the wholesale level is used. In this are included, for one thing, all *duplicate* transactions as, for example, when the goods are marketed by a manufacturer, through a broker, to a wholesaler, and by the latter to a retailer or to an industrial consumer; in such a case the same goods are reported in the sales of the manufacturer, in the business volume of the broker, and in the volume of trade of the wholesaler.

2. In the volume of wholesale trade are included the *transportation* costs incurred in moving the goods through all the wholesale channels of trade, starting with their origin at point of physical production or importation.

3. In the volume of wholesale trade are included the *margins* added to the cost of the goods to cover the distribution expenses and net profits of all those engaged in the wholesale marketing of the goods after they leave the point of production or importation.

From this it may be correctly surmised that the volume of wholesale trade, if it could be measured in its true sense, would greatly exceed the value of goods marketed at wholesale. Estimates for recent years indicate that, in fact, the volume of wholesale trade is about twice as great in amount as the value of goods distributed. Accurate data for wholesale trade volume in this sense are not, however, available. Census data measure, instead, the volume of trade conducted by *wholesale establishments*. In this latter sense wholesale trade volume is actually somewhat smaller in amount than the value of goods marketed, because of the substantial share of such goods not passing through the specialized wholesaling structure.

The volume of wholesale trade is a more useful measure of the magnitude of the wholesaling task than is the value of goods marketed at wholesale, because it reflects all transactions made on the wholesale level. Even though some of these are "duplicate" transactions they are properly considered part of the task of the wholesaling system and require the performance of wholesaling functions. Changes in the wholesaling task can best be evaluated, therefore, by examining changes in the volume of wholesale trade.

Trends in Wholesale Trade Volume. Data for the volume of wholesale trade in each of four Census of Business years since 1929 are presented in Table 1. Since these are census data, they reflect only the sales of wholesale *establishments,* and do not measure total wholesaling activity. The significance of this limitation is indicated by the fact that wholesale sales in the broad or true sense (counting *all* wholesale *transactions*) are usually more than two times as great as the sales of wholesale establishments as measured by the Bureau of the Census. Since the analysis of the wholesaling structure must be confined to the census concept, however, and comparisons can probably be made on that basis just as well, total sales of establishments must necessarily be accepted as the measure of whole-sale volume for purposes of analysis.

As shown in Table 1, the volume of wholesale trade has increased from slightly less than $69 billion in 1929 to over $247 billion in 1954, or by more than three and a half times. Much of this increase, obviously, re-sulted from the approximate doubling of wholesale commodity prices which took place during the period. Adjustment must therefore be made for this factor in appraising the growth in wholesale trade. This is done by converting the volume of wholesale trade *at current prices* in each year to its equivalent at constant (1954) prices, or what is popularly called "physical volume." For this purpose, adjustments have been made on the basis of the Index of Wholesale Prices compiled and published by the U. S. Bureau of Labor Statistics, which reflects changes in the prices of some 2,000 commodities (900 prior to 1947) at the wholesale level as reported by manufacturers and as obtained for agricultural products in the primary markets.[2] The various commodities in the index are weighted for the most part according to their relative importance in terms of value added. Thus the index, insofar as commodity coverage is concerned, corresponds reasonably well to the "mix" of products sold by wholesale establishments and is, therefore, the most appropriate available index for the purpose.

After adjustment for price changes, the volume of wholesale trade in 1954 was slightly more than double that of 1929. Its growth was not, of course, regular or consistent throughout the period. In 1939 wholesale trade volume was only slightly higher than ten years previously, having recovered from the decline which took place in the early 1930's. By 1948 volume stood 57 per cent higher than in 1939, reflecting the impact of World War II and the prosperous postwar years. This rate of growth continued unabated up to 1954, when wholesale trade was almost 24 per cent higher than its 1948 level.

These data serve to show, in quantitative fashion, the magnitude of the wholesaling task and of the changes that have taken place in the recent past. It is not enough, however, to measure this task in absolute terms alone. Some change would naturally be expected in consequence of the over-all growth of the American economy. Has wholesaling kept pace with this over-all growth, fallen behind it, or exceeded it? The answer to this question lies in a comparison of the trends revealed in Table 2 with certain measures of over-all economic growth.

Trends in Commodity Output. One basic measure of the growth of the economy since 1929 is the quantity of physical goods produced. Since a substantial proportion of these goods is handled by establishments in

[2] For a full understanding of the index of wholesale prices, see "A Description of the Revised Wholesale Price Index," *Monthly Labor Review* (February, 1952), 180–87.

TABLE 1

VOLUME OF WHOLESALE TRADE AT CURRENT PRICES AND AT 1954 PRICES,
UNITED STATES, SELECTED CENSUS OF BUSINESS YEARS, 1929–1954

(Amounts in Thousands of Dollars)

Amount or Index	1929	1939	1948	1954
Volume at Current Prices[a]	$ 68,950,108	$ 57,797,363	$189,657,630	$247,474,422
Index of Wholesale Prices[b] (1954 = 100)	56.1	45.3	94.7	100.0
Volume at 1954 Prices[c]	$122,905,718	$127,587,998	$200,271,942	$247,474,422
Index of Volume at 1954 Prices (1954 = 100)	49.7	51.6	80.9	100.0
Per Cent Change in Physical Volume from Previous Census Year	—	+3.8%	+57.0%	+23.6%

[a] Include sales of chain store warehouses. Data for 1948 were retabulated on a basis comparable with 1954 when establishments without paid employees and milk-bottling plants were excluded. Such establishments are included, however, in the data for 1929 and 1939.

[b] Index of Wholesale Prices for All Commodities, U. S. Bureau of Labor Statistics. Base shifted by the authors from 1947–49 = 100 to 1954 = 100.

[c] Actual volume at current prices, divided by the index of wholesale prices and multiplied by 100.

Source: Compiled and computed from data published by the U. S. Bureau of the Census at current values.

the wholesaling structure, it is pertinent to compare the growth of whole-sale volume with trends in commodity output. A measure of this output is presented in Table 2, based on indexes of goods produced in the manu-facturing, mining, and agriculture sectors of the economy.

TABLE 2

Indexes of the Value of Goods Produced and Marketed, at Constant Prices, by Major Economic Sectors, United States, Selected Census of Business Years, 1929–1954

(Index Numbers, 1954 = 100)

Economic Sector	1929	1939	1948	1954
Manufacturing[a]	45.7	44.9	81.1	100.0
Mining[a]	61.3	61.3	95.5	100.0
Agriculture[b]	68.5	74.1	96.3	100.0
Total Commodity Output[c]	50.2	50.3	84.4	100.0
Per Cent Change from Previous Census Year	–	+0.4%	+67.7%	+18.5%

[a] Federal Reserve Board indexes of production (1947–49 = 100) as published in the *Federal Reserve Bulletin,* with base shifted by the authors to 1954 = 100.

[b] U. S. Department of Agriculture index (1947–49 = 100) as published in *Agricultural Statistics,* with base shifted by the authors to 1954 = 100.

[c] Average of output indexes for the economic sectors, weighted in accordance with their value added (net output) in 1954. The total value added for each sector and the corresponding percentage weights were as follows: manufacturing, $116,915,000,-000, 78.06 per cent; mining, $11,415,000,000, 7.65 per cent; agriculture, $21,400,-000,000, 14.29 per cent. Data for manufacturing from 1954 *Census of Manufactures;* for mining from 1954 *Census of Mineral Industries;* for agriculture from *Survey of Current Business* (February, 1956), 27.

Sources: Compiled and computed from data published by the U. S. Bureau of the Census, Board of Governors of the Federal Reserve System, and the U. S. Department of Agriculture.

This index may be used to adjust the volume of wholesale trade *at con-stant prices* shown in Table 2, as follows:

Year	Volume of Wholesale Trade at 1954 Prices	Index of Commodity Output (1954 = 100)	Volume of Wholesale Trade at 1954 Prices Discounted for Changes in Commodity Output
1929	$122,905,718,000	50.2	$244,832,107,000
1939	127,587,998,000	50.3	253,654,071,000
1948	200,271,942,000	84.4	237,289,030,000
1954	247,474,422,000	100.0	247,474,422,000

When this kind of adjustment is made, it appears that practically no change in the volume of wholesale trade has taken place *relative to* the physical quantity of goods created by our economy. This is simply another way of saying that wholesale trade, after discounting the effects of changes in prices, has maintained its relative position in the economy because it has grown right with it from 1929 through 1954.

This may be regarded as a mark of great stability in wholesale trade, and it may be concluded that the share of total output of physical goods passing through the wholesaling structure has remained about the same during the 26 years beginning with 1929 and ending with 1954. As a matter of fact, it may also be concluded that the share of total commodity output expected to go through wholesale establishments that did go through them has actually increased in view of the fact that, compared with 1929, a larger and larger proportion of gross national product consisted of physical goods and transactions that normally do not go through the wholesaling structure at all or to a much lesser degree than is true of the remainder of the physical goods output. To illustrate, in 1929 new construction, producers' durable goods, government purchases, and gross government product made up only 30.3 per cent of gross national product. In 1939 these items constituted 32.4 per cent of gross national product, but in 1948 they amounted to 35.0 per cent, and in 1954 they reached 41.2 per cent.

Wholesaling Compared with Retailing. Another approach to evaluating changes in wholesale trade is afforded by a comparison with corresponding trends in the sales of retail establishments. As shown in Table 3, retail sales include all sales of retail stores, mail order houses, door-to-door selling organizations operating out of specialized establishments, and vending machine organizations. Retail sales in current dollars increased from about $48 billion in 1929 to almost $170 billion in 1954, or by about three and a half times. As with wholesale trade, however, much of this gain can be attributed to rising retail prices during the period in question. It is necessary, therefore, to adjust the reported figures for retail sales by an appropriate price index. Here, the proper price index to employ is the Index of Retail Prices compiled by the U. S. Department of Commerce. This index is not to be confused with the Consumer Price Index ("Cost of Living Index") published by the Bureau of Labor Statistics. While the Index of Retail Prices is based on *commodities sold in retail stores only,* the Consumer Price Index also includes such *services* as rent, utilities, and medical care.[3]

After allowance for price changes, the volume of retail sales increased by 106 per cent between 1929 and 1954. This closely parallels the increases in both wholesale trade and commodity output, which were 101.4

[3] The significance of this distinction may be illustrated by comparing recent trends in the two price indexes. Between 1929 and 1954, the Index of Retail Prices increased by 72.5 per cent, while the Consumer Price Index went up by 56.6 per cent. From 1948 to 1954, however, the Consumer Price Index outgained the Index of Retail Prices, 11.7 per cent to 8.2 per cent. This indicates that, in the post-World War II period, the prices of services purchased by consumers, such as those mentioned in the text discussion, have gone up more rapidly than those of physical goods.

TABLE 3

SALES OF RETAIL ESTABLISHMENTS AT CURRENT PRICES AND AT 1954 PRICES, UNITED STATES, SELECTED CENSUS OF BUSINESS YEARS, 1929–1954

(Amounts in Thousands of Dollars)

Amount or Index	1929	1939	1948	1954
Sales at Current Prices[a]	$47,768,656	$41,444,507	$128,849,252	$169,967,748
Index of Retail Prices[b] (1954 = 100) ...	58.0	47.5	92.4	100.0
Sales at 1954 Prices[c]	$82,359,752	$87,251,594	$139,447,242	$169,967,748
Index of Sales at 1954 Prices (1954 = 100) ...	48.5	51.3	82.0	100.0
Per Cent Change in Physical Volume from Previous Census Year	—	+5.9%	+59.8%	+21.9%

[a] Data for 1929 were revised to exclude automotive service establishments, and data for 1929, 1939, and 1948 were revised to exclude retail milk dealers, both of which have been reclassified outside of retail trade for census enumeration purposes. Data for 1948 were also revised on a basis comparable with 1954 census coverage, but this was not possible for 1929 and 1939. The differences involved represent only a small fraction of retail establishments and an even smaller fraction of sales, however, and do not have any appreciable effect on the comparisons made herein.

[b] Index of Retail Prices (1947–49 = 100), U. S. Department of Commerce, as published in the *Survey of Current Business*, with base shifted by the authors to 1954 = 100.

[c] Sales at current prices divided by Index of Retail Prices, times 100.

Source: Compiled and computed from data published by the U. S. Bureau of the Census at current values.

per cent and 99.2 per cent, respectively. Moreover, the changes from one Census of Business year to the next within the period are almost identical to the corresponding changes in wholesale trade volume. Thus, there appears to be a very stable relationship between the wholesaling structure and the retailing system which is its largest single market.

It may be noted from the data in Tables 1 and 3 that the volume of wholesale trade in each of the years covered is considerably greater than the volume of retail trade for the same year, whether the figures are compared in current dollars or in dollars of constant value. This is still a source of surprise to many, and calls for further explanation. The relationship between wholesale and retail trade volume, each in constant dollars, for the four Census of Business years in question is as follows:

Year	Volume of Wholesale Trade at 1954 Prices	Volume of Retail Trade at 1954 Prices	Ratio of Wholesale Trade to Retail Trade
1929	$122,905,718,000	$ 82,359,752,000	149.2%
1939	127,587,998,000	87,251,594,000	146.2
1948	200,271,942,000	139,447,242,000	143.6
1954	247,474,422,000	169,967,748,000	145.6

It may be seen from these data that wholesale trade volume as measured by the Census normally exceeds retail trade volume by about 45 per cent to 50 per cent and has done so consistently since 1929.

When census data for wholesale and retail trade were first collected, many businessmen and economists expressed amazement that wholesale sales should be as great as retail sales, much less about 45 per cent larger. Indeed, there are at least two seemingly good reasons why retail sales should exceed wholesale volume, rather than the reverse:

1. Not all goods sold by retail establishments are obtained from wholesale establishments. This can be seen from the fact that approximately 20 per cent of all manufacturers' sales is made directly from the factories to retailers and another 3 per cent is sold from the factories to the manufacturers' own retail branches. Similarly, some of the farm products sold by retail stores are obtained directly from farmers, without the intervention of any wholesale establishment. Thus, in the retail trade volume are included many goods which have not passed through wholesale establishments and are not, therefore, included in the wholesale trade data.

2. The prices charged at retail must generally be higher than those charged at wholesale, since the former must include transportation costs incurred in moving the goods from sources of supply to the retail stores and the retailer's gross margin, including net profits and operating expenses.

While these factors would seem to support the view that retail sales must exceed wholesale trade volume, there are good and sufficient reasons for the facts as indicated in census statistics. For one thing, wholesale trade volume includes *sales by wholesale establishments to industrial and commercial users*. These goods do not pass through retail stores, since they are not sold to ultimate consumers until they have been further processed, if at all, as in the case of machinery, equipment, and supplies used in the operation of the business or other enterprise. Such sales represent about 35 per cent of all sales of wholesale establishments.[4]

Second, wholesale sales include a considerable amount of *duplicate counting* growing out of sales by one wholesale establishment to another. As the sales of both such establishments are included in the wholesale trade totals, the merchandise involved is counted twice. This form of duplication accounts for about 22 per cent of wholesale trade. There is very little similar duplication in the volume of retail trade, the only exception being used car trade-ins and the limited amount of other secondhand merchandise which returns to the channels of trade.

A third factor explaining the larger volume of wholesale trade is the fact that it includes a certain amount of *export business* which, obviously, does not go through retail stores in this country and is not, therefore, counted in their sales. Export business represents about 4 per cent of total sales by wholesale establishments.

Fourth, wholesale trade volume includes some *sales by wholesale establishments to ultimate consumers,* amounting to about 1.5 per cent to 2 per cent of the total. This is offset, however, by an approximately equal amount of wholesale sales made by retail establishments and included in their volume of business.

Finally, in wholesale trade volume are included certain *purchases* made by functional middlemen for others and reported as "sales." In this category are the transactions negotiated by buying brokers, resident buying offices, purchasing agent middlemen, and commission buyers of farm products. In 1948 the volume of transactions reported to the Census of Business by these buying agents and brokers represented about 2.5 per cent of total wholesale trade. There is no comparable type of transaction in the volume of retail trade, since retail establishments do not act as buying functional middlemen.

When all of these factors are taken into account, sales to retailers are seen to comprise only between 35 per cent and 40 per cent of the total trade of wholesale establishments. Nevertheless, retailers are the most important single class of customer of wholesale establishments as a whole, so that the comparisons between wholesale and retail trade made on

---

[4] The data for wholesale sales by class of customer cited in this discussion are estimates based on 1948 figures and on partial results of the 1954 Census of Business. It was not possible to compute an over-all distribution of sales by customer class for 1954, because petroleum bulk stations and certain important classes of manufacturers' sales branches were unfortunately not required to report such information.

preceding pages do serve to show changes in the status of wholesaling relative to its potential market.

Conclusion on the Status of the Wholesaling Structure. In spite of periodic swings in the attitudes of economists and business journalists toward wholesaling, the relative status of the wholesaling structure as herein defined has displayed a remarkable stability throughout the 26 years from 1929 through 1954. As the volume of output has grown, so has the wholesaling structure grown to accommodate it. The close relationship between these, through a major depression, a World War, and a period of unprecedented prosperity suggests that the future growth of the wholesaling structure will be in direct proportion to the long-run expansion of output in the economy.

CLASSES AND TYPES OF WHOLESALE ESTABLISHMENTS

Within the wholesaling structure are more than 250,000 establishments, encompassing a wide variety of different kinds of business enterprises. At one extreme are one-man organizations handling a few items and serving a limited number of customers in a single metropolitan area; at the other are full-line houses employing one hundred or more persons and serving customers many miles distant from the establishments. The diversity of the wholesaling structure gives rise to the need for *classification* of the establishments so as to permit scientific analysis of their sales and operations. This need is clearly recognized by the Bureau of the Census and is also reflected in the distinctions commonly made by wholesale trade associations in gathering and publishing various statistics.

Possible Bases of Classification. Wholesale establishments can be classified in many different ways, depending on the purpose for which the classification is intended. Some of the more important bases of classification include:

1. Ownership
2. Method of operation
3. Kind of business
4. Size
5. Location
6. Extent of trading area served
7. Extent of merchandise line handled
8. Functions performed
9. Legal form of organization

At appropriate points in this and subsequent chapters, attention is given to all of these bases.

Major Segments of the Wholesaling Structure. A fundamental division of the wholesaling structure is made in terms of six major types of establishments. Actually, this division represents a hybrid classification of wholesale establishments, based on ownership, method of operation, and certain other factors. The six major segments are:

1. *Wholesalers,* also called "distributors," "jobbers," or "wholesale merchants." These include establishments primarily engaged in buying, taking title to, and, where customary, physically storing and handling goods, and selling them at wholesale to retailers or to commercial and industrial users. Wholesalers generally handle goods made by others, but often perform certain processing or assembling functions incidental to marketing, such as installing machines and roasting coffee.

2. *Manufacturers' sales branches, sales offices,* which are owned and operated by manufacturers or mining companies separate from their physical-production establishments. Sales *branches* are distinguished from sales *offices* in that the former maintain warehousing facilities for goods handled, while the latter act solely as selling organizations.

3. *Agents and brokers* are primarily engaged in selling *or* buying merchandise on behalf of others. They are usually compensated in the form of fees or commissions on their sales or purchases. Agents and brokers dealing in real estate, securities, financial transactions, and the like are not included in the wholesaling structure, which is confined to the marketing of tangible goods.

4. *Chain store warehouses* are operated by retail multi-unit organizations for the purchasing, assembly, and distribution of goods for their retail stores. These establishments are unrealistically not classified as wholesale by the Bureau of the Census.

5. *Petroleum bulk plants, terminals,* are distinguished from other types of wholesale establishments by the peculiar character of the physical facilities used in the storage and handling of gasoline and other bulk petroleum products. Bulk plants may be operated by wholesalers ("independents"), as manufacturers' sales branches ("refinery stations"), or as chain store warehouses by retail chains of service stations. Bulk plants are not to be confused with wholesalers of packaged petroleum products, which are classified as such.

6. *Assemblers* are comprised of establishments primarily engaged in buying and assembling farm products and shipping them to terminal markets. In 1948 and prior censuses this classification also included a few assemblers of fish and seafood, but in 1954 these were classified as wholesalers. Assemblers' establishments may be independently owned or may be operated by food canners or packers, by retail chain organizations, or by farmers' cooperative marketing organizations. In any event they are distinguished from other types of wholesale establishments in that the usual relationships of buying and selling are reversed. In most wholesale establishments goods are bought in large quantities and sold in relatively small lots; assemblers, on the other hand, typically buy in relatively small quantities and sell in large ones.

TABLE 4

NUMBER AND SALES VOLUME IMPORTANCE OF TYPES OF ESTABLISHMENTS
WITHIN THE WHOLESALING STRUCTURE, UNITED STATES, SELECTED CENSUS OF
BUSINESS YEARS, 1929–1954

Institutional Segments of the Wholesaling Structure	Number of Establishments		Net Sales Per Cent of Total			
	1929	1954	1929	1939	1948	1954
TOTAL[a]	169,654	255,232	100.0	100.0	100.0	100.0
I. Wholesalers	79,784	165,153	42.5	40.9	40.4	41.0
Regular or service wholesalers (domestic market)[b]	74,476	151,328	36.8	35.6	35.1	35.7
Export merchants	754	2,361	2.2	1.4	1.8	1.8
Import merchants	2,262	2,571	2.6	2.4	1.5	1.7
Limited-function wholesalers[c]	2,292	8,893	0.9	1.5	2.0	1.8
II. Manufacturers' sales branches	17,086	22,590	23.7	23.4	26.8	28.2
With stocks (warehouse facilities)	n.a.	14,759	n.a.	15.3	15.1	14.9
Without stocks (sales offices)	n.a.	7,831	n.a.	8.1	11.7	13.2
III. Merchandise agents, brokers (functional middlemen)	18,388	22,131	20.7	19.4	17.3	15.9
Selling agents	3,260	2,336	3.8	3.0	3.2	2.5
Manufacturers' agents	6,987	8,720	2.6	2.4	1.9	2.9
Brokers	3,689	4,359	5.8	5.9	4.9	4.4
Commission merchants	3,018	3,586	6.3	4.7	3.8	3.5
Other types of agents, agencies[d]	1,434	3,130	2.2	3.4	3.5	2.6
IV. Petroleum bulk plants, terminals	19,611	29,189	3.4	6.6	5.5	6.5
Refiner-marketer plants, terminals	n.a.	17,837	n.a.	n.a.	n.a.	4.4
Other petroleum bulk plants[e]	n.a.	10,482	n.a.	n.a.	n.a.	2.0
Wholesale L. P. gas facilities	n.a.	870	n.a.	n.a.	n.a.	0.1
V. Chain store warehouses[f]	559	2,914	2.8	4.4	4.8	4.7
VI. Assemblers of farm products[g]	34,226	13,255	6.9	5.3	5.2	3.7

n.a. = not available.

[a] Totals for sales volume are as follows: 1929, $68,950,108,000; 1939, $57,797,363,000; 1948, $189,657,530,000; 1954, $246,116,531,000. The *Census of Business—Wholesale Trade, 1954* differs in several respects from earlier Censuses. In 1954 establishments without paid employees and milk-bottling plants were excluded, although covered previously. Data in this table for 1948 have been retabulated by the U. S. Bureau of the Census on a basis comparable with 1954 procedures, but this has not been possible for 1929 and 1939. Differences in Census procedures may account for some differences shown for various years, especially for limited-function wholesalers and some specific classes of agents and brokers, but do not have a significant effect upon major trends revealed for the major segments.

[b] Includes all regular wholesalers of consumer goods, industrial distributors, converters, and terminal market wholesalers of agricultural raw materials.

[c] Includes cash-and-carry wholesalers, drop shippers, wagon distributors, and retailer cooperative warehouses.

[d] Includes auction companies, export agents, import agents, purchasing agents and resident buying offices operated on an agent basis.

[e] Includes plants operated by wholesalers or jobbers, retail chains of gasoline service stations, and cooperative marketing organizations.

[f] Chain store warehouses were included in the Census of Distribution for Wholesale Trade in 1929, but in the Census of Business for Retail Trade in 1939 and 1948, although tabulated separately from retail establishment data. Because such establishments operate in a wholesale manner, they are included in this and all other tabulations of total wholesale trade data in this text, except as otherwise indicated. For 1954 the data cover central administrative offices and warehouses (both of which are really chain store warehouses), with sales to others and billings to own stores of $11,142,109,000.

[g] Data for assemblers in 1948 and prior censuses include some establishments handling fish and seafood. In 1954 these establishments were classified as "Fish and seafood wholesalers."

Sources: Compiled and computed from data published in Census of Business publications for the years indicated.

Data for these six major segments are presented in Table 4, as well as for certain subdivisions of some of the segments. These data show, for selected Census of Business years beginning with 1929, the number of establishments in each class and the share of total wholesale trade accounted for by it. For the six major segments, trends in relative importance are also shown in Figure 1.

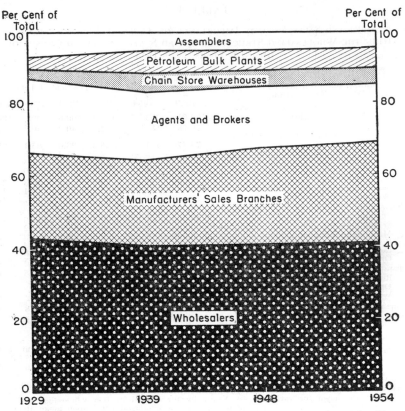

FIGURE 1. Distribution of Sales of Wholesale Establishments, by Major Type, United States, Selected Census of Business Years, 1929–1954

Source: Table 4.

Analysis of the data in Table 4 and Figure 1 supports certain conclusions about the six major segments of the wholesaling structure. For the sake of brevity, these may be summarized as follows:

1. There has been a consistent tendency for the total number of wholesale establishments to increase since 1929. In 1954 the number of establishments (253,618) was 49.5 per cent higher than in 1929 (169,564). Moreover, the number increased from each Census of Business year to the next throughout the 26-year period. The increase was not, however, as great as the approximate 100 per cent increase in sales volume at constant prices.

2. *Wholesalers* are the most numerous type of establishment as well as the most important in terms of volume, as they have been throughout the period. In 1954 the number of establishments operated by wholesalers was more than twice as great as in 1929; in fact, the net increase

in the number of wholesalers' establishments was greater than the net increase in all wholesale establishments combined. This apparent contradiction is explained by the partially offsetting decline in the number of assemblers' establishments.

3. Despite the belief of many that the wholesaler is diminishing in importance, the share of total wholesale trade accounted for by this segment remained quite stable during the 26-year period. Moreover, since the total volume of wholesale trade doubled during this period, the total volume handled by wholesalers (after allowance for price changes) almost doubled also.

4. The largest gain in relative sales volume importance was made by manufacturers' sales branches, although both chain store warehouses and petroleum bulk plants improved their status more *relative to* their respective positions in 1929. Losses in relative sales importance were suffered by agents and brokers and by assemblers, the latter losing almost one-half (46 per cent) of their share of the total business. Both of these classes actually *gained,* however, in terms of absolute sales volume. This is true even after allowance for price changes; assemblers, for example, had sales of $9,050,816,000 in 1954 compared with $7,262,804,000 in 1929 *in 1954 dollars.*

5. The largest relative gain in number of establishments was achieved by chain store warehouses, which numbered about 1,300 in 1954 as compared with only 559 in 1929.

6. In general the major segments of the wholesaling structure have displayed considerable stability in their relative positions, when considered in light of the great changes in the American economy which transpired during the period.

Certain reservations should be kept in mind when interpreting the data shown in Table 4. These arise primarily from changes in census coverage during the period in question, which might account in part for some of the changes indicated. In 1954 establishments without paid employees were excluded from the Census of Business for the first time. Data from the 1948 Census were retabulated so as to exclude these places of business, but no such retabulations could be made for earlier years. Another change in coverage resulted in the exclusion from the 1954 Census of certain manufacturers' sales branches, on account of their being included with reports to the Census of Manufactures instead. It is estimated that between 5 and 10 per cent of sales branches with stocks, and an even larger percentage of those without stocks, were so treated.[5] There were other minor differences from one Census of Business to the next, largely because of continuing confusion as to the treatment of integrated establishments and wholesale establishments owned by manufacturers or retailers. While

[5] 1954 *Census of Business, Wholesale Trade, Sales by Class of Customer,* Bulletin W–2–4 (Washington, D. C.: Government Printing Office, 1957), pp. iii–iv.

every effort has been made to adjust reported figures to compensate for
these factors, it has not always been possible to do so. For chain store warehouses, for example, the figures shown in Table 4 and Figure 1 are only
approximations resulting from the way the data are published by the Bureau
of the Census.[6]

Wholesaling by Merchandise Lines. The foregoing analysis of the
various types of wholesale establishments, while helpful to an understanding of the wholesaling structure, leaves out of consideration for
the most part the important factor of merchandise specialization. Not
only may wholesaling establishments be distinguished by the various types
discussed above—each of which is, in many ways, quite closely akin to
others of its type regardless of the line of merchandise handled—but they
may also be distinguished primarily by the kind of merchandise handled.
On this latter basis there are food wholesalers, hardware wholesalers, and
wholesale establishments which handle electrical goods, farm products, and
a great variety of other commodities.

There are many thousands of different kinds of merchandise flowing
through the wholesaling system of the United States. These commodities,
however, may be grouped together into related classes, which are quite
realistic if in their formulation the trade practices of wholesaling establishments are closely followed. The two senior authors distinguished 343
of these detailed commodity groupings for purposes of classifying wholesale establishments by kind of business in the first census of wholesale
distribution.[7] For statistical purposes these detailed classifications were
summarized into 88 major classifications which were in turn condensed
for some purposes into 24 trade groupings. A similar method was followed
in later censuses. In 1954 wholesalers were classified into 160 kinds of
business, 56 trade classifications, and 17 major groups. A somewhat different procedure was followed for manufacturers' sales branches, which
were classified according to 67 industry groupings, depending on the
manufacturing industries served by them.

The classification of businesses by the type of merchandise (by commodities and classes of commodities) used by the Census for statistical

[6] In 1929 and in 1933, chain store warehouses were included in the Census of
Wholesale Trade and classed as one of the major segments of the wholesaling
structure. In later censuses, however, such establishments were classified in the retail part of the census as a result of requests to this effect by certain retail chain
executives. In the opinion of the authors this change is in violation of sound statistical practice as well as contrary to any logical concept of a wholesale establishment. Chain store warehouses are physically and functionally wholesale in character,
and there is no more reason for classifying them as retail than there is for classifying
a manufacturer's wholesale sales branch as a "factory" or for classifying as a retail
establishment a manufacturing plant merely because it is owned by a retailer.

[7] See Classification by Kind of Business, Fifteenth Census of the United States,
1930, *Distribution*, Vol. II, *Wholesale Distribution*, pp. 36–41.

TABLE 5

ESTABLISHMENTS AND SALES OF WHOLESALERS BY SELECTED KINDS OF BUSINESS, 1954, AND PER CENT CHANGES 1929–1954 AND 1948–1954, UNITED STATES

(Ranked in Order of Magnitude of Per Cent Change in Sales Between 1929 and 1954)

Kind of Business	Number of Establishments			Net Sales		
		Per Cent Change			Per Cent Change	
	1954	1929–1954	1948–1954e	1954 (000)	1929–1954	1948–1954e
TOTAL^a	165,153	+108.6%	+27.9%	$101,100,941	+246.2%	+32.1%
Above-Average Increases:						
Amusement, Sporting Goods	2,514	+332.7	+32.9	952,711	+955.8	+75.3
Machinery, Equipment, Supplies	27,150	+288.5	+38.7	10,039,852	+691.3	+49.3
Electrical, Electronic Appliances	7,123	+226.4	+41.3	6,337,718	+648.5	+47.1
Lumber, Construction Materials^b	10,314	+173.3	+85.0	6,586,207	+413.0	+69.3
Scrap, Waste Material	8,189	+109.0	+27.2	2,405,590	+407.0	+ 9.7
Metals, Metalwork	3,235	+277.9	+89.6	3,362,585	+400.0	+72.3
Paper, Allied Products	5,057	+120.2	+39.3	2,961,049	+320.4	+57.5
Tobacco and Products	2,858	+ 66.1	+ 5.8	3,208,929	+273.9	+29.0
Approximately Average Increases:						
Hardware, Plumbing, and Heating	6,183	+109.4	+19.2	4,397,711	+262.6	+19.5
Drugs, Chemicals, Allied Products	5,837	+145.7	+41.5	3,369,865	+255.5	+50.2
Beer, Wine, Distilled Spirits	7,309	—f	+ 9.1	5,686,934	—f	+40.4
Below-Average Increases:						
Automotive	15,540	+350.3	+14.6	3,977,513	+187.6	+ 1.5
Grocery, Confectionery, Meat }^c	29,795	+ 23.1	+11.7	22,057,824	+161.1	+29.2
Farm Products (Edible)						
Dry Goods, Apparel }^d	14,713	+ 61.1	+15.0	7,964,269	+140.4	+17.5
Furniture, Home Furnishings						
Coal	700	- 15.0	-26.0	794,189	+ 16.9	-60.3

a Kind-of-business groups shown do not add to total because some groups have been omitted.

b 1954 data are not comparable with those for previous years. In 1954 some establishments formerly classified as lumber and construction materials wholesalers were classified as retail establishments instead. Also, better coverage of "nonrecognizable" establishments was obtained in the 1954 Census, which was taken by mail. The latter fact probably more than offset the reclassification of some establishments as retail outlets.

c Data for these groups were not reported separately in 1954.

d Not reported separately in 1954, due to the reclassification of certain kinds of wholesalers between the two groups.

e Comparisons with 1948 data as retabulated for comparability with 1954 coverage. This could not be done, however, for 1929 data.

f Not sold in significant quantities in 1929 due to "prohibition."

Source: Compiled and computed from publications of the U. S. Bureau of the Census for the years indicated.

purposes has its limitations, chief of which is the danger of confusing the sales of a particular *kind of business* with the sales of *commodities* of the same or related names. Thus it is quite easy to assume that the sales of drug wholesalers are synonymous with the sales of drug products at wholesale. In the first place, drug products are dealt in at wholesale by others than wholesalers, as a considerable volume goes through agents and brokers and manufacturers' sales branches. Second, the designation "drug wholesaler" really means a wholesaler who specializes in drugs *and related items,* so that not all of his sales are in drugs. Third, drug products are also sold by wholesalers in the grocery trade and in other kinds of business.

A summary of establishments and sales of wholesalers in selected kinds of business in 1954 is shown in Table 5. Also shown are changes in the number of establishments and in sales volume from 1929 to 1954 and from 1948 to 1954. For all lines of business the number of establishments in 1954 was 108.6 per cent higher than in 1929, while sales were 246.2 per cent higher. Similarly, there were 27.9 per cent more establishments in 1954 than in 1948, with sales volume 32.1 per cent in excess of the 1948 level. These over-all changes can be used to evaluate relative changes in the importance of different kind-of-business groups. None of the figures in Table 5 are corrected for price changes, and this must be borne in mind in the interpretation of some of the changes that took place.

The greatest increases in both sales and number of establishments were achieved by groups handling relatively new products or products affected by major changes in consumer spending patterns and by those handling goods affected by industrial expansion or construction activity. New products probably account for a major proportion of the sales of electrical and electronic appliance distributors, for example. In fact, one of the kinds of business within this group (electronics parts and equipment distributors) was an entirely new classification in the 1954 Census. The impact of shifts in consumer spending is illustrated by the amusement and sporting goods group, which experienced nearly a tenfold sales expansion from 1929 to 1954, and a 75.3 per cent gain even from 1948 to 1954. This, of course, reflects the higher income levels and increased leisure time for sports activities.

At the other extreme from the "growth industries" noted above are a few kinds of business experiencing sales increases well below the average, or even declines. Coal wholesalers' sales were 16.9 per cent greater in 1954 than in 1929; but if the data were adjusted to discount the effect of price changes, it is certain that a decline actually took place. Even in the six years between 1948 and 1954, sales of coal wholesalers fell by over 60 per cent, while the number of establishments declined by 26 per cent. This reflects the general decline of the coal industry, in which output decreased substantially after 1929—by an average of almost 2 per cent annually for bituminous coal and between 3 and 5 per cent for anthracite.[8]

In between these two extremes wholesalers in most lines of trade showed increases in sales and establishments closer to the over-all average. For two of the traditional "jobbing lines" (hardware and drugs) 1954 sales exceeded 1929 levels by almost exactly the average for all kinds of business. The other "jobbing lines" (groceries and dry goods) achieved gains somewhat lower than the average.

Wholesale Trade by City Size. Much can be learned from an analysis of wholesale trade by location of the establishments engaged in it. It is possible to use several different methods of classifying locations, including states, metropolitan areas, and counties. One of the most revealing, however, is a classification of establishments and sales by size of city.

TABLE 6

PER CENT DISTRIBUTION OF ESTABLISHMENTS AND SALES BY CITY SIZE,
WHOLESALE TRADE BY TYPE OF ESTABLISHMENT, UNITED STATES, 1954

Type of Establishment	Cities of 500,000 or More	Cities of 100,000– 499,999	Cities of 25,000– 99,999	Cities of 5,000– 24,999	Remainder of U. S.	Total
	Per Cent of Establishments					
Wholesalers	34.8%	20.5%	15.7%	14.0%	15.0%	100.0%
Manufacturers' Sales Branches	39.7	32.4	16.0	7.0	4.9	100.0
Petroleum Bulk Plants	1.6	3.7	8.3	23.6	62.3	100.0
Agents and Brokers	48.6	21.2	8.5	7.7	14.0	100.0
Assemblers	2.4	3.0	4.1	12.9	77.6	100.0
TOTAL	30.9%	18.7%	13.6%	13.9%	22.9%	100.0%
	Per Cent of Sales					
Wholesalers	44.3%	23.9%	13.6%	8.9%	9.4%	100.0%
Manufacturers' Sales Branches	62.4	24.8	6.4	3.1	3.3	100.0
Petroleum Bulk Plants	12.4	15.1	16.1	18.8	37.5	100.0
Agents and Brokers	55.2	19.3	8.2	6.7	10.6	100.0
Assemblers	7.9	9.2	8.9	16.1	57.9	100.0
TOTAL	47.9%	22.3%	10.5%	7.7%	11.6%	100.0%

Source: Computed from data in 1954 *Census of Business, Wholesale Trade, Size of Establishment or Firm,* Bulletin W–2–2 (Washington, D. C.: Government Printing Office, 1957), pp. 2–95.

Data in Table 6 show the concentration of wholesale establishments and sales in different sizes of cities, further classified by type of operation. As might be expected, wholesale trade is shown to be highly concentrated in large cities, with 30.9 per cent of all wholesale establishments and 47.9 per cent of total sales located in cities of 500,000 or more population. The relatively greater concentration of sales compared to establishments further reveals the fact that the bigger establishments tend to be located in the larger cities.

[8] Cf. "A New Look at Production Growth Rates," *Survey of Current Business* (April, 1957), 5–12.

Considerable variation exists in the degrees of concentration for different types of wholesale establishments. The three major types which deal primarily in manufactured goods (wholesalers, manufacturers' sales branches, and agents and brokers) all exhibit high degrees of urban concentration. In contrast, petroleum bulk stations and assemblers are more widely dispersed both in terms of establishments and in terms of sales. The explanation of this fact for assemblers is readily apparent; these middlemen are engaged in buying unprocessed farm products in local producers' markets. Such markets are not generally found in large cities. For petroleum bulk stations the explanation is to be found primarily in the dispersion of their customers (mainly gasoline service stations), in the prohibitive costs of urban land for such large physical establishments, and in the high cost of transportation to the retail establishments of bulky commodities (gasoline and oils) by expensive equipment (tank trucks).

While wholesale trade is still quite centralized relative to population or to retail trade, there has been a definite tendency toward decentralization since 1948. This is evidenced by the fact that wholesalers located in cities over 500,000 did 49.5 per cent of total wholesalers' sales in 1948, compared with 44.3 per cent in 1954.[9] The proportion of sales made by wholesalers located in cities of 100,000 to 499,999 also declined slightly, from 24.1 per cent to 23.9 per cent. All of the smaller city-size classes enjoyed gains, however, with the largest increase coming in the "remainder of the United States" (cities under 5,000 and rural places). The latter geographic division's share of the total grew from 5.8 per cent in 1948 to 9.4 per cent in 1954.

The decentralization of wholesale trade, while still relatively small, is nevertheless significant. In part, it is associated with the shift to suburban locations and the development of one-story warehouses which has taken place in some trades, as discussed further in Chapter 23. To some extent, however, the decentralization results from shifts of population and retail stores away from larger cities and from the economic advantages of local wholesale operations. Since both of these factors are still operative, further dispersion of wholesale trade may be expected in the future, although it will no doubt be gradual in character.

[9] 1954 *Census of Business, Wholesale Trade, Size of Establishment or Firm*, Bulletin W–2–2 (Washington: Government Printing Office, 1957), p. vii.

7

THE REGULAR
WHOLESALER

The most important single type of *wholesaling* institution in the marketing structure of the United States is the *wholesale merchant* who is oftentimes known as the *regular* wholesaler, *service* wholesaler, *full-function* wholesaler, or merely *the wholesaler*. It is this type of organization which is commonly but erroneously thought as comprising the entire field of wholesaling by those who adopt the very narrow view of the term as discussed briefly in the early part of Chapter 4.

The approximate nature of the regular wholesaler is indicated by the definition used by the U. S. Bureau of the Census in its 1954 Census of Business for what it terms "Wholesale Merchants, Distributors," which is as follows:

Merchant wholesale establishments primarily engaged in buying and selling in the domestic market who perform most of the principal wholesaling functions. They buy and sell merchandise on their own account; sell principally to retailers or to industrial, commercial, or professional users; usually carry stocks; assemble in large lots and generally redistribute in smaller quantities, usually through salesmen; extend credit to customers; make deliveries; service merchandise sold; and render advice to the trade.

This type of wholesaler is distinguished by the Census from other types of what it classifies as "Merchant Wholesalers,"[1] a designation which

[1] It would seem that the term "merchant wholesaler" is somewhat redundant, since every wholesaler is a merchant in the sense that he takes title to the goods in which he deals. That being the case, it would be more accurate merely to use the term "wholesaler" for the broader designation intended for the term "merchant wholesaler."

embraces, in addition, foreign trade wholesale merchants commonly known as exporters and importers, and limited-function wholesalers of the cash-and-carry, drop-shipper, and wagon (truck)-distributor types. It is also more or less in line with the less clearly differentiated statements contained in the *Standard Industrial Classification Manual,* Volume II, Non-manufacturing Industries, 1949 edition, issued by the Bureau of the Budget, Executive Office of the President.

STATUS OF THE REGULAR WHOLESALER

As pointed out in a preceding chapter dealing with the history of wholesaling, the wholesale merchant in one form or another has been a part of our distributive organization from the earliest Colonial days. At first he operated mainly as an importer, later he combined wholesaling with retailing, and finally he emerged as a specialized middleman occupying a position between producers of form utility on the one hand and retailers and other business customers on the other. In Colonial times domestic production was limited and on a small scale; consequently there was little need for wholesalers. With the advent of factory production and specialized retailing, wholesaling became more prominent in the marketing of domestic products as well as foreign goods, until, during the nineteenth century, the wholesaler in the United States reached full stature. By the 1870's regular wholesalers were operating in almost all consumer goods trades and in some of them handled virtually all of the goods produced except those marketed by manufacturers in local markets. Even at this time, however, there was a generally unfriendly attitude toward wholesalers, and certain forces were in operation which eventually would have serious consequences for them.

Antagonism Toward Wholesalers. Despite his long history and service, much criticism has been leveled against the wholesaler and many attempts have been made to eliminate him from the marketing structure. He has been accused of performing unnecessary functions, of failure to render essential services in a reasonably efficient manner, and of gross neglect in a number of other frequently unspecified ways. In general it may be said that the wholesaler has been on trial before a prejudiced and unsophisticated jury which, through ignorance of or blindness to his true place in our economic order, has looked upon him with suspicion and has been ready to condemn him a priori. The wholesaler's existence has, consequently, been deemed precarious and his complete disappearance has been freely predicted by self-appointed prophets and others unfamiliar with the facts.

Criticism of wholesalers is not a new phenomenon. Economists generally have taken their cue from John Stuart Mill, whose writings served as textbooks for many generations. Mill's attitude is reflected in his statement that:

. . the class of mere distributors, who are not producers but auxiliaries of production, and whose inordinate numbers, far more than the gains of capitalists, are the cause why so great a portion of the wealth produced does not reach the producers . . .[2]

Evidence of the existence of the same attitude toward the close of the last century in the mind of the layman is found in a letter written in 1897 to a young man who had been recently employed by a wholesale hardware firm. The letter expressed the following convictions:

It is very unwise of you to start your business life in the wholesale jobbing trade, because any time you spend upon it will be wasted. The wholesale merchant has no place in these progressive times. You may take my word for it that within ten years there will be no more wholesale establishments in the United States.[3]

Moreover, ever since marketing efficiency has become a subject of general interest, the wholesale merchant has been widely condemned as a clog to progress. It has been urged that a shortening of the chain of middlemen between primary producer and ultimate consumer would inevitably eliminate much of the waste and inefficiency of marketing and hence reduce marketing costs.

So widespread did these attitudes become, and so firm was the conviction that wholesalers in fact *were* disappearing, that some observers expressed great surprise in the persistence of such institutions after World War II. When Census data showed that wholesalers were not only maintaining but improving their status, it was hailed as a "comeback" for wholesalers.[4] Actually, the use of such a term is grossly misleading, since it implies a return from an oblivion to which wholesalers never, in fact, were consigned. The so-called "comeback" might perhaps better be termed a "rediscovery" except, perhaps, when the comparison is made with some period prior to 1920.

There are several reasons for the generally unfriendly attitude toward wholesalers. In part, this attitude is merely part of a broader antagonism toward marketing in general, which in turn may be traced to the popular idea that distribution does not create any economic values. A second reason lies in the fact that wholesalers are *middlemen,* and as such may be

[2] J. S. Mill, *Principles of Political Economy,* Ashley Edition (London: Longmans, Green & Co., Ltd., 1923), p. 789.

[3] J. R. Sprague, *The Middleman* (New York: William Morrow & Co., Inc., 1929), p. 2.

[4] Edwin H. Lewis, "The Comeback of the Wholesaler," *Harvard Business Review,* XXXIII (November–December, 1955), 115–25. See also "Comeback for Wholesalers," *Business Week* (May 26, 1956), 45.

regarded as parasitic.[5] This point of view is reinforced by the unfamiliarity of the general public with this institution. While the retailer is also a middleman, his contributions are apparent to all who buy goods in stores and hence receive much less criticism. A final reason for the unpopularity of the wholesaler, and most unfortunate of all, lies in the lack of appreciation, among wholesalers themselves, of their true role. Too often their thinking has been restricted by a narrow viewpoint, with consequent failure to develop and maintain good public relations.

Competitive Position of Regular Wholesalers. Notwithstanding the attacks made on regular wholesalers and the predictions of their impending disappearance, their share of total wholesale trade has remained approximately stable since 1929, and in actual current dollars their volume of business more than trebled. The status of regular wholesalers may be judged from these Census statistics:

| | | | Per Cent of Total | |
Year	Number of Establishments	Net Sales (Add 000)	Wholesale Establishments	Wholesale Trade Volume
1929	77,492*	$28,687,143*	45.7%	41.6%
1939	96,872	22,754,876	48.0	39.4
1948	125,199†	72,759,935†	57.6	38.4
1954	156,260	96,560,196	61.2	39.2

* Revised data for 1929 from *Sixteenth Census of the United States: 1940, Census of Business,* Vol. II, *Wholesale Trade, 1939* (Washington, D. C.: Government Printing Office, 1942), p. 1045.

† Retabulated on a basis comparable with 1954, when establishments without paid employees were excluded.

These data belie the assertions made by various persons that wholesalers are declining in number and importance. The number of establishments operated by regular wholesalers has, in fact, increased much more rapidly than the total number of wholesale establishments. In 1954 the number of regular wholesaler establishments was slightly more than double (201.6 per cent) that of 1929, while all wholesale establishments combined increased by only 50.4 per cent during the same period.[6] Moreover, the increase in establishments of regular wholesalers was also substantially greater than the 16.9 per cent gain registered by retail establishments during the period.[7]

More important than changes in the number of establishments are changes in the share of total wholesale trade accounted for by regular wholesalers. This share remained almost constant over the entire 26-year

[5] A survey of consumer attitudes toward marketing revealed that "misunderstandings and confused thinking" characterize beliefs and opinions on middlemen and their functions. See *Consumer Attitudes Toward Distribution,* Committee on Consumer Relations in Advertising, Inc. (New York, 1947).

[6] See Chapter 6.

[7] The number of retail establishments in 1929 was 1,472,377; in 1954, 1,721,650.

period covered by the Census data. This should not, however, be interpreted as merely a maintenance of status quo. Some decline in regular wholesalers' share of total wholesale trade would be expected, for two reasons:

1. Products not ordinarily handled by wholesalers increased in importance during this period. In this category are such lines as automobiles, which were primarily sold direct to retail dealers by manufacturers throughout the period.
2. Regular wholesalers were confronted with new types of competition during the period, both from so-called "limited-function" wholesalers and from various forms of integrated wholesaling.

The fact that regular wholesalers have been able to meet these problems and still maintain their share of the market is good evidence of their continuing vitality. The reasons for this vitality may be found, first, in the competitive environment in which regular wholesalers operate, which is the subject of the remainder of this chapter; and, second, in the essential character of the functions performed by them, which are examined in the next chapter.

COMPETITION AND SPECIALIZATION AMONG REGULAR WHOLESALERS

Regular or service wholesalers compete with direct selling manufacturers on the one hand and with direct buying chains, department stores, mail order houses, and other retail groups on the other. They also compete for business with wholesalers whose services are limited, abbreviated, or modified. But, above all, regular wholesalers compete among themselves. There are several aspects of this latter kind of competition, including that from:

1. Other wholesalers in the same trade who carry similar merchandise lines
2. Wholesalers in separate but related trades or kind-of-business groups
3. Wholesalers in the same trade but carrying different kinds of merchandise lines
4. Wholesalers who operate on a sectional or national scale
5. Establishments in multi-unit wholesale enterprises.

A given wholesaler may face any or all of these kinds of competitors. The nature and significance of this keen rivalry for business may best be appreciated by examining the various elements involved in this competitive struggle.

Classification by Kind of Business. A basic division of regular wholesalers may be made according to the trade or kind of business in which they operate. This is the commonest grouping used in business directories and by trade associations. An analysis of sales trends for wholesalers in various kind-of-business groups has already been presented in the preceding chapter. At this point it should be added that the lines of division between the trade groups are seldom sharply defined. Wholesalers in one trade frequently face direct competition from those in other trades. Hardware products, for example, are handled by wholesalers in some 24 different kinds of business—including such diverse trades as groceries, electrical, lumber and millwork, and petroleum, as well as hardware wholesalers proper. Similarly, drugs and drug sundries are sold by more than a dozen different kinds of wholesalers, and auto parts and accessories by about 15.[8] In most cases, of course, products in one line of merchandise are handled only incidentally by wholesalers in another line. Nevertheless, the overlapping of lines represents a source of real competition in most trades. This overlapping has been greatly encouraged by the "scrambling" of lines that has taken place at the retail level since about 1950. Diversification by supermarkets, for example, makes handling of drugs, housewares, and hardware a necessity to some grocery wholesalers. Similar developments have taken place in the retail drug, hardware, variety, and other trades.

CLASSIFICATION BY EXTENT OF MERCHANDISE LINE

In addition to the classification of regular wholesalers by *kinds* of merchandise, a division may also be made on the basis of the *extent of the line handled* within a given trade. On this basis regular wholesalers of consumer goods may be identified as *general merchandise wholesalers, general line wholesalers,* and *specialty wholesalers.* A similar classification is used among industrial distributors, as explained in Chapter 9.

General Merchandise Wholesalers. Such wholesalers carry a general assortment of goods in several distinct and unrelated lines of merchandise. They operate in the Middle West, the West, and to a considerable extent in the South, as well as in certain sections of the East, where the country general store still holds sway in rural communities. In 1929 there were 246 general merchandise wholesalers in this country with a total volume of sales for the year of $453 millions, or 1.5 per cent of the total sales of all wholesalers. By 1954, however, although the number of general merchandise wholesalers had increased to 594 and their sales to $814 millions, their relative importance had declined to less than 1 per cent of total sales of all wholesalers.

General merchandise wholesalers usually carry goods which are nonperishable and easily portable over relatively long distances and to

---

[8] Based on reported analyses of sales by commodity lines for wholesalers in the various trade groups as revealed in the Census of Business publications.

out-of-the-way communities, such as dry goods, hardware, electrical supplies, sporting goods, furniture, plumbing and heating equipment and supplies, and farm implements. Occasionally some general merchandise houses may also carry limited assortments of groceries. While a wholesaler is classified in this category only when he sells substantial proportions in each of several distinct lines of goods, frequently one line such as hardware or dry goods dominates the business. In many general merchandise houses these two lines together represent the bulk of the business. This wide variety of merchandise enables such establishments to meet competition from more specialized concerns, particularly in selling to country general stores or to stores located in small communities. In their turn these stores can concentrate their purchases, thereby making it economical for the wholesaler to cultivate such trade. As long as there are many small stores handling a wide variety and assortment of merchandise—and there are still nearly 18,000 independent general stores with food and probably some 10,000 to 20,000 other independent stores in the general merchandise group exclusive of department stores—it will be feasible for this type of wholesaler to render a useful service. The trend among these wholesalers, however, has been away from handling general merchandise in several unrelated lines and toward a general line of goods in one trade. In other words, general merchandise wholesalers are becoming general line whole-salers and are thereby increasing the competition among the latter type of service wholesaler.

General Line Wholesalers. In this group are included the large number of service wholesalers who carry complete stocks in their respective fields. For example, the general line wholesale grocer carries a complete stock of canned fruits and vegetables, canned sea foods, cereals, coffee and tea, extracts and spices; in addition, he handles flour, sugar, cheese, smoked meats, soaps and soap powders, and numerous other items closely related to the food or grocery business.

Similarly, the general line hardware wholesaler carries stocks consisting of hardware proper, including builders' hardware, shelf or light hardware, tools and cutlery, heavy hardware, and the like. He also carries goods that are closely allied to hardware, some of which may even be regarded as a part of the hardware line of goods. In this latter group are included such goods as electrical appliances and supplies, china and glassware, sporting goods, paints and varnishes, plumbing supplies and equipment, industrial chemicals, mill supplies, radios and refrigerators, house furnishings, and toys and games. The items in this group, however, seldom represent over a third of the entire business volume of a general line hardware wholesaler.

Again, a general line electrical wholesaler counts in his stock of goods electric household appliances; motors, generators, and control apparatus; interior electric construction materials, including fixtures; storage batteries;

radio sets, parts, and accessories; electric refrigerators; and electrical supplies.

The general line dry goods wholesaler handles merchandise ranging from ready-to-wear clothing to window shades. Although in its strictest sense the term "dry goods" is confined to piece goods, ready-to-wear clothing, knit goods, and notions, the average stock of the general line dry goods wholesaler contains also furnishings, floor coverings, luggage, millinery, and many other items.

The above are merely illustrative for, in individual cases, classes of merchandise are constantly added to or dropped from a line to keep pace with changing demand and opportunities. The distinction between these general line wholesalers and the general merchandise wholesalers discussed above is that the latter may handle several distinct and unrelated lines, such as hardware, electrical goods, dry goods, and groceries, each in substantial proportion.

The assortment of merchandise stocked by a general line wholesaler corresponds roughly to that of a single-line store at the retail level, although the wholesaler handles a much greater number of items than any one retail store. Since most retail stores are of the single-line type, at least in convenience goods fields, they find the general line wholesaler an invaluable source of supply. A drugstore, for example, can obtain almost all of its requirements from a general line wholesale druggist, which facilitates concentration of purchases by the retailer and greatly simplifies his buying problems. The same is true in the other traditional "jobbing lines" of dry goods, groceries, and hardware. A comparison of general line wholesalers with specialty wholesalers in each of these four lines of trade is shown in Table 7. These data indicate the important position occupied by general line wholesalers, despite the fact that they have lost

TABLE 7

GENERAL LINE AND SPECIALTY WHOLESALERS IN FOUR KINDS OF BUSINESS, UNITED STATES, SPECIFIED CENSUS OF BUSINESS YEARS, 1929–1954

Kind of Business	Number of Establishments				Per Cent of Total Sales			
	1929	1939	1948	1954	1929	1939	1948	1954
Drugs:								
General Line	494	297	303	392	80.7%	69.8%	61.9%	58.6%
Specialty Lines	514	1,321	1,902	2,409	19.3	30.2	38.1	41.4
Dry Goods:								
General Line	867	222	182	132	33.2	17.4	11.0	10.2
Specialty Lines°	2,939	3,875	6,418	5,005	66.8	82.6	89.0	89.8
Groceries:								
General Line	5,748	3,424	3,649	3,127	69.9	51.0	47.7	37.8
Specialty Lines	3,337	12,045	13,080	17,295	30.1	49.0	52.3	62.2
Hardware:								
General Line	953	772	673	606	93.7	91.1	84.5	78.5
Specialty Lines	296	571	1,480	1,531	6.3	8.9	15.5	21.5

° Includes piece-goods converters.

Source: Compiled and computed from data published in the Censuses of Business for the various years.

some ground to their narrow-line competitors. In both drugs and hardware general line wholesalers still account for a majority of the total business, while in groceries their share amounts to almost 40 per cent. The figures also suggest the larger scale on which general line wholesalers operate. In drugs, for example, general line wholesalers represented only 14 per cent of all establishments in 1954, but handled almost 60 per cent of total sales. In actual dollar amount the 392 general line establishments had sales of almost $1.3 billion, while the 2,409 specialty establishments did only about $900 million.

Specialty Wholesalers. Just as the *general line* wholesaler is more specialized than the *general merchandise* wholesaler, so the *specialty* wholesaler is another link in the chain of increasing specialization among service wholesalers. Specialty wholesalers, often referred to as short-line distributors, confine their activities to a narrow range of products in a single line of merchandise. In the grocery business such wholesalers may handle canned goods exclusively, or coffee, flour, sugar, or some other single class of merchandise. Some of them may not even handle a *general* line of canned goods but confine their effort to canned fruits, vegetables, or seafoods. The degree of specialization in merchandise varies considerably even with specialty concerns. While some of them handle coffee exclusively, other coffee houses may add teas and spices to their line. In hardware, specialty houses may deal exclusively in cutlery, in heavy hardware, in builders' hardware, or in some other limited group of commodities. Specialty wholesalers in drugs may limit their stock to pharmaceuticals, to patent medicines, or may specialize in some of the toilet articles or preparations. In dry goods, the specialty wholesaler may handle only knit goods, notions, or piece goods. Specialization in this latter line of business is carried to such lengths that some wholesalers confine their entire activity to dealings in silks and velvets, others to woolens and worsteds, and still others to cotton goods.

Development of Specialty Wholesaling. Specialty wholesalers came into being with the development and territorial expansion of trade. As pointed out in Chapter 5, specialization in merchandise began shortly after the Civil War because of certain inherent advantages. In some trades, such as dry goods, many of the successful specialty wholesalers started as offshoots from general line dry goods jobbing houses from which one line after another had been split away until the remaining lines were so reduced in number that the business assumed the characteristics of a specialty house. Occasionally the failure of a general merchandise or general line jobbing firm or the voluntary withdrawal of such a firm from business has resulted in the establishment of specialty houses by former employees, who sought to capitalize their skill in buying and selling limited classes of merchandise in a given line and their general knowledge of the trade. A good example was the withdrawal of Marshall Field & Company of Chicago from its jobbing business. The company, 70 per cent of whose wholesale business consisted of goods manufactured in its own plants prior to the change, decided to concentrate all its activities on its own merchandise instead of serving to any extent as a wholesale outlet for the goods of other manufacturers. As soon as this decision was reached, no less than six new specialty houses in the dry goods trade were incorporated by some of the former employees of the company. Another reason for the formation of specialty wholesale houses lies in the limited financial resources of the organizers. Many firms start with a limited capital. Hence they face two alternatives: one, the operation of a general line house with inadequate stocks; the other, the establishment of a business stocked only with a short line. A further reason for organizing specialty houses to handle new lines is that the old general line wholesalers are at times too slow to recognize and appreciate opportunities in new fields.

Status of Specialty Wholesaling. Table 7 shows the extent to which specialty wholesaling has invaded certain lines of wholesale trade and thus throws light upon the growth of competition among service wholesalers. In all four lines of business for which data are shown specialty wholesalers operate in larger numbers than general line wholesalers, but only in dry goods do they obtain a correspondingly dominant share of total sales.

The statistics in Table 7 suggest that specialty houses generally operate on a small scale. For instance, specialty drug wholesalers represent 86 per cent of the number of establishments, but account for only 40 per cent of the total business. In groceries, specialty concerns constitute 85 per cent of the number of houses, but absorb less than two-thirds of the business. The situation is most accentuated in the hardware trade, where about 70 per cent of the establishments are operated by specialty wholesalers, but general line wholesalers do about 80 per cent of the business. In some lines of trade (such as industrial chemicals, metals, paper, petroleum products, or tobacco products) specialty wholesalers do practically all the business. There is, however, in each field a further degree of specialization. Not only is there *intertrade* specialization as *between* lines of goods, but there is the additional division of activities as *within* a line of goods which may be called *intratrade* specialization. Thus, while some wholesalers handle a general line of tobacco and its products, others limit their stock only to cigars, and still others sell only cigars and cigarettes but do not handle snuff, packaged tobacco, or smokers' supplies. Again, in the automotive wholesaling business the handling of replacement parts or of ignition apparatus has tended to be separated from automobile supplies and accessories. Specialization has also taken place in the jewelry trade, where some wholesalers carry only clocks and watches, others specialize in precious stones, still others in flat silverware or in jewelry specialties.

Advantages of Specialty Wholesaling. In addition to being the only practical alternative for founders with small capital and limited knowledge and skill, specialty wholesaling is in many ways well suited to meet the demands of the competitive market. In the first place, buyers are attracted to such houses because of a complete assortment of goods carried in a given line. This appeals particularly to specialty stores and to the larger retail institutions where buying is more specialized than in stores dealing in a general assortment of goods in a particular line. Furthermore, salesmen become more expert in the handling of a restricted number of items, and are able accurately to determine the customer's needs, and to give intelligent and satisfactory service. Such skill depends in a measure, of course, upon the degree of restriction in the line of goods stocked. Prompt service is another advantage generally accruing to the trade of a specialty jobber. Finally, from the standpoint of the owners themselves, the specialty wholesaling organization is advantageous since it permits a simplified control of stock and thereby prevents the accumulation of unsalable goods. Simplification of business practices may permeate the accounting department, the shipping department, and every other part of the business with resulting economies in operation.

Disadvantages. Specialty houses, however, when compared with their major competitors—the general line wholesalers—are handicapped in that their entire overhead expense must be borne by relatively few items. This accounts in part for the higher operating expenses which are normally incurred by such firms. The extent of the disparity in operating expenses between general line and specialty wholesalers is shown in the following comparison for 1954:[9]

Kind of Business	Operating Expenses, Per Cent of Net Sales, 1954		Ratio of Specialty Wholesalers' Expenses to General Line Wholesalers' Expenses
	General Line Wholesalers	Specialty Wholesalers	
Drugs	13.6%	16.9%	1.24
Dry Goods	14.4	12.1	0.84
Groceries	7.8	10.4	1.33
Hardware	17.6	20.8	1.18

In three of the four trades, specialty wholesalers had operating expenses 20 per cent to 30 per cent higher than their general line competitors. The exception is again the dry goods trade, where specialty wholesalers enjoyed a substantial advantage. This is to be explained by the relatively large-scale operation of specialty dry goods wholesalers dealing in piece

[9] Computed from published figures reported in the 1954 Census of Business.

goods that are sold in substantial quantities to cutters-up (manufacturers of clothing), to large retailers, and to general line wholesalers—a situation peculiar to this type of operation.

A second disadvantage of specialty wholesaling lies in the difficulty of adequate market coverage. Having relatively few items to sell, the specialty wholesaler cannot afford to cultivate the smaller customers, since their orders would be unprofitable to him. Consequently, he may confine his efforts to "skimming the cream" by selling only to large buyers in large cities; or he may cultivate intensively a small area. He cannot, by the same token, provide intensive coverage of a large area as a general line wholesaler can.

From the point of view of the typical retailer, another disadvantage of dealing with specialty wholesalers is the effect on buying problems. If he deals with specialty wholesalers, the retailer is prevented from concentrating his purchases, which may result in his spending excessive time and expense in negotiating with salesmen, handling invoices, and in related activities.

A fourth limitation to the activities and growth of specialty wholesalers is to be found in the awakening of the general line wholesaler to the idea that he, too, can specialize by establishing separate departments for certain lines on which he wishes to concentrate his effort. Some general line wholesalers select what may be termed "blue-ribbon-lines" for special sales effort, the choice being determined by the profit margins, sales possibilities, and by the manufacturers' distribution policies. Other wholesalers employ specialty salesmen for certain items in their line, providing the same sales expertness that characterizes specialty concerns. Still other general line wholesalers devote a certain amount of time, possibly two weeks each year, to a selected line of goods for special sales campaigns, rotating their intensive sales effort from one class of merchandise to another. It would, therefore, appear that the general line wholesaler could meet the specialty wholesaler's competition successfully if he would take advantage of his opportunities.

CLASSIFICATION BY RADIUS OF OPERATION

Regardless of the kind of merchandise carried or the extent of the line stocked, regular wholesalers differ markedly in the extent of the trading areas served by them. On this basis three classes may be distinguished: *local wholesalers, sectional* or *regional wholesalers,* and *national wholesalers.* The kind of area served by a wholesaler depends in part on the nature of his market, but often it is largely a matter of policy adopted after consideration of alternatives.

Local Wholesalers. The term "local wholesaler" applies to a service wholesaler who operates within a single city, covering all or part of it, or within a radius of 75 to 150 miles outside the community in which the house is located. Not only is his market area small but his volume of business seldom exceeds several million dollars a year, although in the aggregate the volume of business done by this class of wholesalers is very large. The local wholesaler predominates in the distribution of foodstuffs and is particularly strong in the wholesaling of nationally advertised products as well as unbranded staples and private brands of his own.

Numerically, as well as in total volume of business, local wholesalers predominate greatly over sectional and national wholesalers. Moreover, the tendency seems to be toward increased relative importance of local wholesalers both in number and in the aggregate volume of sales. The economic basis for this trend seems to lie in the fact that local wholesalers operate on a lower cost margin than do wholesalers covering large territories. In particular, the expenses of salesmen tend to be lower since there is not much travel out of the adjacent urban district, inasmuch as the city trade for local wholesalers frequently amounts to half or more of their total business. Even the traveling salesmen incur less expense for hotel accommodations and other "on the road" living, as they return to their homes for week ends and holidays. Furthermore, local wholesalers do not incur as much advertising expense for the promotion of private brands as do sectional or national concerns. Costs may also be lower, at least in part, as the result of the type of business organization. Most of these organizations are single proprietorships, partnerships, or close corporations, which allow for immediate supervision of the business by the owners themselves. This reduces many administrative expenses and removes the necessity for high-salaried hired executives. Since only a small territory is covered, the manager-owner can keep in close touch with the credit aspects of his business, thereby reducing bad debt losses to a minimum. Inventory control is also a simpler and less expensive operation for the local firm because, as a general rule, it does not have to stock as many items as the large concern which is attempting to draw business from a wide area.

In addition to the advantages incident to low costs of doing business, the local distributor has an important advantage in lower transportation costs. The transportation costs on incoming goods may be as high for him as for other types of wholesalers since he must stock his warehouse from sources far and near; but on outgoing orders he has the benefit of a close proximity to his customers. Thus, while it may be difficult for a *national* wholesaler to ship into a given territory because he has to contend with high cost l.c.l. shipments over long distances, a *local* wholesaler has only a short haul. Moreover, the local dealer has the advantage of being able to give prompt service to his trade through the use of trucks, either his own or public motor truck carrier service. In many lines of trade, orders from customers usually call for rush shipment. For example, when a printer requires a certain kind of fine paper stock for a given job, he places the order with his local paper wholesaler or converter, expecting to get immediate delivery; and it behooves the vendor to maintain adequate stock and to render prompt delivery service if he is to justify his existence. The same is true of mill supply houses when orders are received from local industrial consumers. The local wholesale house has a decided advantage over competitive wholesalers in fulfilling these exacting requirements. A final advantage accruing to the local wholesaler is that his close contact with his trade enables him to build up institutional prestige and good will among his customers, making it easier to effect repeat business.

Sectional Wholesalers. The district, regional, or sectional wholesaler covers a territory of two or more states, but does not operate nationally. He is usually located in one of the larger cities which dominates the area that lies tributary to it. The volume of business of such firms usually is in excess of several million dollars per annum. Sectional wholesalers are of greater relative importance in lines of business where the number of retail outlets is not large. For example, in the hardware trade sectional wholesale organizations are more significant than in the grocery trade, because hardware wholesalers naturally tend to extend their radius of operation in order to reach a number of outlets which will be large enough to support a profitable volume of sales on the numerous slow-selling items which must be carried in stock.

When a sectional wholesaler goes beyond the local trading area of his community, competition from local jobbers in adjacent communities increases, higher transportation costs are incurred, deliveries on customers' orders are delayed, sales expenses in traveling to far points rise, and sales of certain lines may be limited, since not all items warehoused can be shipped economically to distant markets; such items as heavy and bulky goods require too high transportation costs. To meet the competition from local wholesalers, the sectional wholesale house has resorted to private branding, which in turn frequently leads to manufacturing. It is largely this group of wholesalers that is responsible for the rise in the private brand problem, which has exerted a profound influence on the methods of distribution used by a number of manufacturers. Branding has been used primarily as a means of avoiding direct price competition, since it is difficult if not impossible to make direct price comparisons on items bearing different labels. This tendency is in itself evidence that local wholesalers have a competitive advantage in most if not all lines carried and particularly in nationally advertised goods and staple merchandise.

National Wholesalers. National wholesalers, i.e., wholesalers who sell in several sections or over the entire United States, are few in number but account for a substantial volume of business. Most of them are very large concerns either handling a general line of goods or distributing a narrow line of specialties, with the emphasis shifting toward the latter type of business.

Not many general line national wholesalers have developed in the grocery trade because of problems arising from the expense of shipping goods over a long distance and selling them in competition with local or sectional wholesalers who bring identical or similar merchandise into an area in carload lots. Chicago has led in importance as a center for this limited number of national wholesale grocers, followed by New York and St. Louis. Some of the more prominent concerns in this field are Francis H. Leggett & Company; Reid, Murdock, and Company; and R. C. Williams & Company.

In the hardware business national wholesale houses occupy a more prominent position. The Belknap Hardware Company of Louisville, Kentucky; Hibbard, Spencer, Bartlett & Company of Chicago; the Winchester, Simmons Company of St. Louis; and the Shapleigh Hardware Company of St. Louis are all well-known national hardware houses.

A few outstanding national wholesalers in the dry goods trade are Butler Brothers, Carson-Pirie-Scott and Company, and Wilson Brothers.

Among the general line service wholesalers in the electrical trade there are three national concerns operating numerous branches and doing a very substantial proportion of all the business of general line wholesalers of electrical merchandise. These three companies are: The Graybar Electric Company, The General Electric Supply Corporation, and the Westinghouse Electric Supply Corporation.

For the hardware business, New York, Chicago, and Louisville seem to be the leading centers for national distributors; and for dry goods, New York, Chicago, and St. Louis are the principal centers. The McKesson & Robbins Company chain of wholesale druggists is a leading example of national distributors in the drug trade.

Most of the firms mentioned above operate on a *multi-unit* basis, that is, through separate houses located in a number of different cities. Only a small area is served from each establishment, and the so-called national wholesalers operate in fact as an aggregate of *local* wholesalers. Salesmen function out of a given house, goods are shipped to it in carloads, and deliveries are made out of it. The cases in which a wholesaler covers the entire nation or even a substantial part of it from a single *establishment* are rare indeed, the most important of which are the first two mentioned above for the hardware trade.

Multi-Unit Wholesalers

When two or more establishments are owned and operated by a single wholesaler, the business is designated as a *multi-unit* enterprise. Multi-unit wholesalers account for only about 15 per cent of all establishments and less than 30 per cent of total sales by wholesalers. Even most of the multi-unit firms are relatively small, firms of 25 or more establishments being exceptional.

Census data for multi-unit wholesalers should, for purposes of analysis, be further divided into two distinct types of multi-units: *chain wholesalers* and *branch-house wholesalers*.

Chain Wholesalers. The chain method of operation, as it is popularly conceived, is by no means confined to retailing, as many important wholesale organizations also operate on the multiple-unit principle. Some of these were mentioned in the discussion of national wholesalers, such as the Graybar Electric Company, McKesson & Robbins, Inc. in the drug trade, and Francis H. Leggett & Co. in groceries. Some regional wholesalers also function as chains. For some of these organizations the growth has been from within, while for others the multiplication of wholesale units resulted from the acquisition of existing wholesale houses. A few chain wholesalers have been established as such from the very beginning.

The gigantic buying power represented by a chain of several wholesale houses may be greater than the buying power of most retail chains. Such an organization can buy the entire output of certain plants and thus secure substantial price concessions. It can maintain an elaborate buying organization in all the important markets at home and abroad. Goods can be imported without the use of intermediate agencies. Economies may also be effected in administration and in selling. A uniform accounting system may be perfected and installed in all the establishments. The rivalry between the different houses in the chain may help to maintain low operating expenses and promote sales. Private brands may be introduced simultaneously over a wide territory, and extensive advertising campaigns become feasible. Chain wholesaling also usually leads to control of manufacturing, which may in consequence tend to modify the nature of the wholesale business of the organization.

Despite these advantages chains have never attained the status in wholesaling that they have in retailing. In 1954 there were only 1,314 establishments in chains of 100 or more, meaning that there were at most 13 such firms. These firms had sales of about $4 billion, or 4 per cent of the total for wholesale merchants. In contrast, chains of 101 or more retail stores owned 44,241 places of business in 1954 and accounted for total sales of $21.4 billion, or 12 per cent of all retail sales.[10]

The reasons for the lesser importance of chains in wholesaling than in retailing seem to lie in the smaller relative advantage which chain

[10] Based on data contained in the *1954 Census of Business, Retail Trade, Single Units* and *Multi-units,* Bulletin R–2–4 (Washington, D. C.: Government Printing Office, 1956), Table 4A.

wholesalers have over independents. Within a given line of business there is no clear-cut tendency for operating expenses to decline with the number of establishments operated by a firm. For example, single-unit general line drug wholesalers had expenses of 13.1 per cent of sales in 1954 compared with 13.9 per cent for firms with 10 or more establishments. Similarly, independent general line grocery wholesalers had a cost advantage over those with 25 or more houses, 8.3 per cent as against 10.9 per cent. It may well be that a single-establishment wholesaler is able to attain a sufficient size to take advantage of most of the economies of scale, so that little additional savings are realized through integrated operation of several places of business.

Branch-House Wholesalers. Technically there is a distinction between branch-house wholesaling and chain wholesaling, although for census or survey purposes it is almost impossible to discern it. In the first place, chains of wholesale houses are usually formed from without, through consolidation, while branch houses develop from within as a means of growth and expansion. Again, all units of a wholesale chain generally operate in similar fashion, while branches may vary not only in size but also in their method of operation. For instance, some branches of a given wholesaler may render all services characteristic of a regular service wholesaler, others may operate on a cash-and-carry basis, depending upon the nature of the customers served. The various units of a chain are also as a rule larger than ordinary branches of a parent institution, and retain a high degree of autonomy with regard to internal management and operation, being responsible to headquarters only for the major policies and methods and for final results. The parent organization of a chain is frequently a holding company or a large manufacturing organization. On the other hand, branch houses are usually supervised closely by the parent organization, which was in existence before the branches were established, and which is engaged primarily in the distribution of goods at wholesale. The branches are seldom distinct organizations but rather represent physical extensions of the main establishment.

In actual practice, however, it is very difficult to distinguish between these two types. In fact, the structure may be so complicated as to overlap, and even to involve branches of branches. An example is the Midland Wholesale Grocery Company operating in central Ohio. The company owns several so-called branches, one of them known as the Monypenny-Hammond Company, which is of the regular type, located in Columbus, Ohio, and which in turn has several cash-and-carry branches.

Several advantages are claimed for branch-house wholesaling. It affords a practical means for expansion, combining ability to render quick service with the advantages of large-scale buying and operation. A company thus operating can cater to the varying needs of its customers by similarly varying the degree of service. Thus, some of the branches sell for cash only and make no deliveries, others operated by the same parent institution may render full service. Inasmuch as the branches are controlled from the main house, little administrative expense is incurred and a simplified accounting system is maintained at each branch, although probably the best branch systems are those which give the manager a considerable amount of autonomy. When the latter practice is pursued, the branch manager works on a certain budget, keeps his own books and records, does some of his own buying, grants credit without reference to the home office, supervises the collection of accounts, and is in other ways directly responsible for the operations of his branch. The branch under such circumstances is also recognized as a home institution in the community in which it is located, thereby strengthening relations with customers. This is particularly true of main branches but not so much of the smaller or subbranches which are found in growing numbers.

8

FUNCTIONS OF THE REGULAR WHOLESALER

Despite generally unfriendly attitudes and in the face of increasing competition, regular wholesalers have maintained their competitive position in the wholesaling structure. Throughout the period since 1929 for which Census data are available, regular wholesalers have handled about 39 per cent of total wholesale trade, and in actual volume reckoned in current dollars their sales have more than trebled. In part, this is explained by certain adaptations made by wholesalers, some of which were discussed in the preceding chapter. A more basic explanation lies in the functions that the regular wholesaler performs.

Some critics assert or imply that the wholesaler performs *no* useful functions. This, of course, reflects an ignorance of the facts. Regular wholesalers perform certain essential marketing functions, which must be performed regardless of the channel of distribution used for a product. Moreover, wholesalers generally function more efficiently and effectively than could their customers and suppliers. This is due to the fact that wholesalers serve many customers and suppliers, respectively, and are able to operate on a *large scale,* with a considerable degree of *specialization* in their tasks. As a result regular wholesalers add values to goods at a lower total cost than could be done without them. There are, of course, exceptions to this statement that obtain under certain conditions and which will be pointed out at appropriate points in this and later chapters.

GROUPS AFFECTED BY THE FUNCTIONS OF THE REGULAR WHOLESALER

Inasmuch as the regular wholesaler operates *principally* between the manufacturer and the retailer, it is convenient to analyze his functions from the viewpoint of each of these parties. The values added by regular wholesalers also benefit the consuming public. The functions of the regular wholesaler and their importance to each of these three interest groups, discussed in some detail in this chapter, may be summarized briefly as follows:

1. What the regular wholesaler does for his customers:
   a) Anticipates their requirements
   b) Assembles goods for them from many sources of supply
   c) Buys for them in economical quantities
   d) Maintains a reservoir of goods from which they can draw on short notice
   e) Makes prompt deliveries
   f) Makes possible a faster inventory turnover
   g) Extends credit
   h) Guarantees goods and adjusts complaints
   i) Renders advice and assistance of various kinds
2. What the regular wholesaler does for his suppliers:
   a) Plans distribution in his territory
   b) Establishes and maintains connections with customers to whom he sells their goods
   c) Cultivates his territory intensively
   d) Aids in stabilizing production
   e) Provides storage facilities and ready stocks near points of demand
   f) Simplifies their accounting and credit problems
3. What the regular wholesaler does to benefit the consuming public:
   a) Adds value to the goods he handles
   b) Reduces total marketing cost
   c) Coordinates supply and demand

Assumed Framework for Analysis. Several assumptions must be kept in mind as these functions are discussed:

First, for the *retailer,* it is assumed that most retailers operate on a *small scale;* that most stores must handle an *assortment of merchandise from many manufacturers;* and that most retailers have *limited financial resources at their disposal.* That these assumptions are substantially true in most lines of trade may be easily verified.

Second, for the *manufacturer,* it is assumed that most plants operate on a *small scale;* that in most cases only a *narrow line of products* is manufactured; that *financial resources must be devoted primarily to manufacturing;* and that the products must be *widely distributed through many retail outlets.* Again, it may readily be shown that these assumptions correspond to the facts in most industries. While the popular notion of a manufacturer may be that of a large, diversified, integrated, and financially strong company, this is still true only of a relatively small proportion of our manufacturing enterprises.

Finally, it must be assumed that the *wholesaler operates with a reasonable degree of efficiency*. The validity of this assumption rests on the active competition of wholesalers with other channels of distribution and among themselves, as described in the preceding chapter.

This should not be taken to mean that regular wholesalers are used *only* when these assumptions are warranted. There are, indeed, many circumstances to which none of the assumptions apply, but in which the products are nevertheless marketed through wholesalers. An example is the distribution of electrical appliances by full-line manufacturers to franchised outlets.

How the Regular Wholesaler Serves His Customers

Planning for Customers. One of the first functions of the wholesaler is to anticipate his customers' requirements and to be ready at all times to fill their needs. To perform this function, it becomes necessary for the wholesaler to have the right merchandise, at the right time, at the right price, and in the right amounts. Outside of a limited number of staple products, the demand for goods usually varies with the different communities in the wholesaler's territory. Among the factors affecting such demand may be mentioned race, nationality, religion, income, wealth of the population and its distribution, education, and custom. A formal analysis of consumer demand is sometimes necessary before decisions can be made by the wholesaler as to what kinds of goods to buy, but generally such information is collected by his salesmen continuously on an informal basis. Not only is the problem one of the determination of *what* to buy, but it involves also a determination of quantities to be bought at any given time, and the sources from which to make such purchases.

The task of planning for customers is not a one-time proposition, but is rather a continuous process. Figuratively speaking, the wholesaler constantly sweeps his territory with his eye and studies its needs. As soon as changes in demand are ascertained, he proceeds to look for the merchandise that will satisfy the new needs. That is why he can often tell the retailer of a demand that will be felt in his territory next spring or fall, long before the retailer becomes aware of it himself. The progressive wholesaler must look ahead, and anticipate the needs of consumers, and hence of retailers, in his territory. This forward look stands him in good stead not only in searching out new sources of supply for items that will be wanted by the trade months hence, but also in foreseeing the coming doom of certain items which should be quickly disposed of before they become "frozen" stock on the shelves of retailers or in his own warehouse.

In a well-managed wholesale house, merchandise planning takes the form of a systematic *merchandise budget* which is drawn up periodically.[1] Such budgets specify the amount of goods to be bought, usually on a monthly basis, for a period of six months to a year ahead. They also serve to focus the thinking of buyers on changes in the kinds of goods to be bought. Few retailers are in a position to formulate systematic plans of this kind. It is interesting to note, however, that large-scale retail organizations such as department stores, mail order houses, and chains utilize budgets of the same type for their buying.

The Wholesaler as an Assembler. The planning functions of the wholesaler are not recognized as such by the average retailer. The retail dealer is more apt to think of the wholesaler as a source of supply for the goods he sells, which emphasizes the *assembling* function of the wholesaler, who must assemble his stock from hundreds if not thousands of different sources. This function requires the maintenance of a competent staff of buyers who must be on the alert for new sources of supply; price changes; natural factors, such as storms, earthquakes, or drought, which may affect the supply; for artificial factors, such as legislation; and for many other influences upon the supply of a great variety of merchandise.

There are in the United States alone about 42,000 plants manufacturing food and kindred products; nearly 40,000 plants engaged in the production of textiles and their products; over 11,000 manufacturing plants producing chemicals, drugs, and druggists' sundries; and approximately 20,000 plants producing items that are normally handled by hardware stores. In the absence of the wholesaler who carefully selects from this large number of plants those producing the items in which he deals, retailers of groceries, dry goods, drugs, and hardware would be faced with the necessity of buying directly from thousands of manufacturers. It is true that a single manufacturer may own a number of plants, and hence there would not be as many manufacturers in all the trades indicated as there are manufacturing plants or units. It is also true that no retailer handles the goods manufactured in all the plants making the type of merchandise in which he deals. Nevertheless, direct buying would necessitate the establishment of direct contact with thousands of manufacturers in order to select several hundred of them as regular sources of supply. Such contact would have to be established and maintained by the manufacturer through his salesmen and his catalogs, or by the retailer calling upon the producer at his place of business.

The manner in which the wholesaler simplifies the problem of assembly for his retail customers is indicated in Figure 2. To receive the hordes of salesmen from hundreds or thousands of manufacturers, were a retailer attempting to buy directly from them, would require the entire time of

[1] For a discussion of the process of merchandise planning, see Chapter 20.

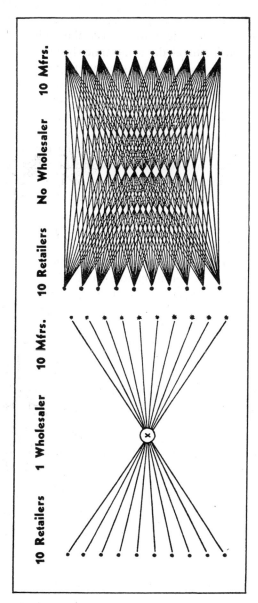

FIGURE 2. How the Wholesaler Simplifies the Task of Supplying Retailers

Reproduced with permission, through the courtesy of the National Association of Tobacco Distributors, New York, N. Y.

This chart graphically demonstrates: (1) How the operation of supplying multiple retail outlets with the products of multiple manufacturers is simplified by the facilities of the wholesaler; (2) the complications resulting from the absence of a wholesaler when retailers find it necessary to obtain shipments direct from manufacturers.

In this chart we have used the simple example of only 10 retailers and 10 manufacturers, with one distributor as the middleman. Actually, a single distributor serves many hundreds of retail outlets and warehouses the products of scores of manufacturers. A chart showing 1,000 retailers and 100 manufacturers, with one distributor as the middleman, would need only 1,100 lines, but a chart de noting the direct transactions between 1,000 retailers and 100 manufacturers (with no wholesaler) would be unimaginably complicated with 100,000 lines.

one or more individuals in the retailer's place of business. Similarly, to place orders by mail would necessitate the handling and filing of a truckload of manufacturers' catalogs, kept up to date with the latest price sheets, and constant searching for the items wanted by consumers. This, too, would require an amount of work sufficient to occupy the full time of more than one person and would incur, at the same time, heavy expenses for the retailer. To buy goods from manufacturers by visiting the market is even more out of the question for most lines of merchandise. There are a few exceptions to this rule, as in such lines as women's ready-to-wear apparel and furniture, where retailers visit organized central markets. Such exceptions are few, however, and it would, therefore, be most unwise for retailers in most lines of trade to attempt to do their buying direct. The geographic diffusion of such sources as food canneries and factories making hardware or drug items throughout a country as large as the United States would clearly render impractical, if not impossible, the direct purchasing by retailers of most varieties of merchandise.

Some idea of the task of assembly which the wholesaler performs for the retail outlets can be gained from some of the mathematics of wholesaling, by noting, for example, the number of items carried by the various stores. The small retail grocer, for example, is said to handle from 1,200 to 3,000 items and the average supermarket handles about 5,000 items in the grocery departments alone; the average hardware dealer stocks from 3,000 to 8,000 separate items, while for the independent retail druggist the number of articles averages about 6,000. Thus any attempt to assemble his own stock in trade would prove rather costly for the retail merchant. The procedure must be shortened by use of the wholesale system. A single letter, a telephone call, a visit to the nearby wholesaler, or a call from the wholesaler's salesman puts the retailer in touch with virtually hundreds of manufacturers and other sources of supply.

The wholesaler's stock often represents thousands of items. For example, a typical electrical goods wholesaler may carry in stock about 4,500 separate items which have been assembled from 140 different manufacturers for the benefit of his 800 or so customers. Larger firms in this line of business may carry as many as 30,000 items assembled from more numerous sources. It is not exceptional to find wholesale tobacconists who stock in excess of 3,000 items. Some grocery wholesalers who have attempted to streamline operations by eliminating all slow-moving and duplicated items have found that they still have about 3,000 items in stock, whereas some of the large firms in this field may carry between 10,000 and 20,000 items. The retail druggist has at his command the wholesaler's inventory of around 20,000 to as high as 60,000 items. The hardware dealer can choose from a selection of from 20,000 to 60,000 items in the jobber's stock, and the dry goods wholesaler's stock may run into 250,000 individual items.

Even in lines of trade where the number of items is deemed to be limited, the assembly function of the wholesaler is a matter of great import. To illustrate, in the paper trade, depending upon whether the wholesaler handles only fine paper, only wrapping paper, or operates what is known in the trade as a "dual house," the goods are assembled from around 100 up to 500 manufacturers and converters. Thus it is a great convenience, if not an absolute necessity, for the retailer to have the burden of assembling fall on the wholesaler. If the wholesaler were not here today, he would have to be invented, if for no other reason than for the performance of this function alone.

Large-Scale Purchasing. A function of the wholesaler closely related to assembling is that of *large-scale* buying. Long before the chain store systems brought the advantages of large-scale buying into public notice the wholesaler had practiced this business method to the general advantage of his retailer clients and the consuming public, as well as for his own profit.

While the quantity bought or sold is not an essential characteristic of wholesaling, the wholesaler generally buys in large quantities which he then breaks down into amounts that suit the retailer's convenience. He usually buys by the car or gross and sells by the case or dozen, although he often sells also by the single package. This large-scale buying is particularly true of grocery, drug, and hardware wholesalers, who buy many of their goods in full carloads or in truckloads.

Large-scale buying enables the wholesaler to effect economies which the forces of competition compel him to pass on to the retailer or other customers in the form of reasonable prices, considering the services rendered. These economies are twofold in character. In the first place, judicious large-quantity buying enables the wholesaler to secure the goods at lower prices. The price concessions may take the form of quantity discounts, "free deals," superior credit terms, or merely lower price quotations. In the second place, the wholesaler effects economies in transportation. By buying in carlots he lowers the cost of transportation, since on many items freight rates on shipments in carlots are one-half to less than one-third the charges made for less-than-carlot (l.c.l.) shipments. In this wise, the wholesaler brings the goods close to his customers at freight rates much lower than such customers could receive on orders placed with manufacturers. Only a short haul is then required at the higher local rate. Furthermore, in shipping goods in l.c.l. amounts payment must be made for a certain minimum weight even though the shipment is less than the minimum. In ordering from a wholesaler, where a wide selection of goods is afforded, the retailer can always make the minimum weight by consolidating many items on one order, thereby reducing the cost of transportation still further.

An example of the freight economies achieved by wholesalers on certain types of goods is afforded by a comparison of transportation costs on the items listed in a single invoice of a grocery wholesaler in Cincinnati, Ohio.[2] This invoice included 22 different items from as many different manufacturers. Total freight costs on these items, when bought in the quantities typical of wholesalers, amounted to $5.17. To this must be added the cost of truck delivery to retailers of $1.02, for a total cost of $6.19, or about 6 per cent of the amount of the invoice. This may be compared with a total transportation cost of $23.88, or almost 24 per cent of the total value of the goods, if bought by retailers direct from manufacturers in the quantities typical of retailers' purchases. This difference in freight cost *in itself,* in the actual example cited, is greater than the total gross margin of a general line grocery wholesaler, which is in the neighborhood of 9 per cent or 10 per cent of sales. Thus the wholesaler, by buying in large quantities, effects substantial savings which may offset or at least partially offset his costs of doing business.

Finally, since the wholesaler buys in large amounts, he is often the logical medium for grading and sorting commodities according to size, quality, type of package, and the like, in conformity with local demand. By virtue of the large scale of his operations and his superior knowledge, the wholesaler can perform this function to better advantage than can the retailer.

Maintains a Reservoir of Goods for His Customers. Not only does the wholesaler assemble a large assortment of merchandise which he buys in large quantities at any given time, but it is his duty to maintain both the complete assortment and the volume of both regular and emergency goods in a reservoir that can be tapped by any of his customers on short notice. He must carry the reserve stock for his territory which enables his customers to keep their merchandise investment down to a minimum and to avoid the risk of loss due to deterioration or price declines. Were the wholesaler abolished, the retailer would be forced to buy in large amounts in order to prevent "outs," or else adopt an elaborate system of stock control and perpetual inventories. The latter is impractical and too expensive for the average store dealing in a large variety of merchandise, and the former practice would result in sluggish movements of goods, few stock-turns, and much obsolete merchandise.

Because of the scale of his operations, the wholesaler can operate economically a warehouse which is flexible, not only from the standpoint of changing seasonal requirements, but also with regard to the special requirements involved in the storage of certain kinds of goods. The seasonal nature of the production of many goods, particularly raw materials, complicates the storage problem. Some goods are obtainable only at certain

[2] Milan R. Karas, *The Contributions Made by Wholesalers to the Economy of Hamilton County, Ohio* (unpublished doctoral dissertation, The Ohio State University, 1951), p. 125.

seasons, although the demand for such items may be continuous, as is true of certain fancy grocery products. Such goods must therefore be bought in large enough quantities to last until the following season. Other goods, though they can be purchased at any time, may have but a short selling season; hence large purchases must be made in advance, and different merchandise is chosen to take their place afterward.

Technical problems of storage or warehousing add to the difficulties. Some products are heavy, some are light and bulky, some deteriorate more rapidly than others, some are odoriferous, and still others absorb moisture. Special treatment is needed for many types of merchandise normally carried in the wholesaler's warehouse, all of which is part of the function of maintaining large reserves of stocks for customers. In addition to the limitations mentioned in the preceding paragraph, retailers would find that the assumption of the wholesaler's storage function would involve the substitution of numerous small and inflexible storage areas for the wholesaler's warehouse. Not only would this be grossly uneconomical from the standpoint of operation, but it would also be clearly beyond the financial capacity of most of our retail store owners.

Delivers Goods Promptly. A retailer can get his orders filled by most wholesalers on the same day that they are received and have the goods delivered to the store in a short time. This is made possible, first, by the fact that the wholesaler ordinarily carries adequate merchandise stocks in anticipation of requirements; second, by the convenient location of the wholesaler's warehouse close to his trade; and third, by the choice of transportation facilities for delivery purposes. In ordering directly from the factory, it is frequently necessary to wait until the goods are produced, particularly during peaks of seasonal activity. Besides, the factories are usually at a considerable distance from the retailer. Finally, distant shipments can often be made only by railroad or water transportation, whereas the wholesaler can utilize trucks as additional means of transportation. Local wholesalers often deliver the goods on the same day that they are ordered, at least to customers located in the same city or in the area directly tributary to it and within truck delivery radius. Rapid truck delivery may be further supplemented by the maintenance of a sales counter or display room in the wholesale house for the convenience of customers who prefer to pick up goods themselves. In this manner a retailer can obtain merchandise almost immediately if desired.

Prompt delivery service rendered by wholesalers is responsible to no small degree for their success in a number of lines of trade. The adoption on the part of retail merchants of the policy commonly known as "hand-to-mouth" buying has helped considerably in bringing the wholesaler's service to the forefront. Such a policy, obviously, cannot be adhered to unless prompt delivery of orders is assured. When quick delivery service is available, there is no longer any need for "starving" the stock in some lines and overstocking on others, nor is there any valid reason for being "out" on some items for any length of time. Prompt delivery service also enables the retailer to keep his stocks fresh and clean since he can quickly replenish items currently demanded and make the necessary seasonal adjustments with little waste of time and effort. All this helps to maintain a good will that is essential to the wholesaler's success as well as that of the retailer.

Makes Possible a Faster Retail Stock Turnover. The speedy delivery of a large assortment of carefully selected and reasonably priced merchandise by the wholesaler makes possible a more rapid rate of stock turnover for the retailer. This is a great advantage to the retailer since it permits him to operate with a smaller capital and at the same time provides him with an adequate stock of fresh merchandise. Contrast this with pre-Civil War days when sources of supply were so remote and transportation facilities so inadequate that the retailer had to maintain as much as a six months' supply of many items. Not only does the modern method improve the retailer's profit opportunities but it provides the ultimate consumer with much fresher merchandise.

It is almost axiomatic that successful business is predicated in large part on a reasonably rapid stock turnover. Speeding up turnover, through purchases from the wholesaler, generally results in the reduction of the retailer's operating expenses, involving less interest on the investment in stock, less insurance cost on merchandise, smaller store space for a given volume of business, and less heat and light expense. It eliminates the investment of working capital in sluggishly moving goods and substitutes for it an active investment in fresh, salable merchandise.

The faster turnover achieved by retailers on goods bought from wholesalers is often more than enough to offset any price advantage obtained through direct buying, even without taking other factors into account. In the drug trade, for example, a test showed that on proprietary items, a higher margin was secured by buying direct (39.5 per cent vs. 33.4 per cent), but that the annual rate of turnover on items purchased direct was much lower (2.19 times) than on similar goods bought from wholesalers (4.81 times).[3] The effect of these differences may be illustrated by comparing the investments in inventory needed to support a given volume of sales, as follows:

Source of Supply	Sales	Sales at Cost*	Turnover Rate	Inventory Investment
Manufacturers—Direct	$10,000	$6,050	2.19	$2,760
Wholesalers	10,000	6,660	4.81	1,380

* Based on assumed gross margins cited in text paragraph above—39.5 per cent on goods direct from manufacturers and 33.4 per cent on goods bought from wholesalers.

[3] *The Case of Clyde Earnest,* National Wholesale Druggists' Association (New York, not dated).

While the cost of goods sold in this illustration was higher by $610, the investment in inventory required to support the same sales volume was lower by one-half, or by $1,380, when the goods were bought from wholesalers. This means that not only was less capital required for inventory purposes, but that the total savings resulting therefrom substantially offset the differences in the gross margins. Though the specific figures used here are hypothetical, they are believed to reflect actual conditions reasonably well.

Extends Credit. Through the extension of credit to his customers the wholesaler furnishes a much needed financial assistance. Many small retailers are ineligible for a line of credit from banks.[4] They rely solely or largely on the wholesale house for financial help. Without this aid many retailers would be forced out of business and others would be prevented from entering business regardless of ability and merit. In some lines of wholesaling as much or more money is tied up in the wholesaler's financing of receivables as in merchandise inventories. It is quite possible that the wholesaler has gone too far in this direction and inadvertently assumed the role of banker, but it is indicative of the vital necessity of this service to retailers.

The importance of the wholesaler's financing function is evidenced by the fact that over 80 per cent of all sales by wholesalers is made on a credit basis, and that almost 90 per cent of all wholesalers make at least part of their sales on credit. The relative importance of credit sales varies by line of business, ranging from about a third of the total for beer and ale distributors to around 98 per cent for general line dry goods wholesalers. At least some credit sales are made in every line of trade; even cash-and-carry food wholesalers reported a small share of their business on credit.[5]

In the absence of the wholesaler there is no doubt that some credit would be extended to retailers by the manufacturer. That is certainly true of manufacturers who operate sales branches with stocks, over 90 per cent of which do a credit business with 80 to 85 per cent of their business being on credit. However, a much larger number of retailers would be refused

[4] It is of course possible for commercial banks to extend credit to retailers, but the fact remains that they do not cover the retail field apart from the larger-scale stores, especially for the financing of inventories. Many of the small retailers cannot qualify as credit risks for bank loans, and those who do qualify are limited in the amounts they can borrow. It may be argued that the wholesalers should turn this function over to the banks; but until the banks broaden their policy or change their essential nature and function, namely, that of financing receivables and seasonal peaks in inventories, this would prevent many retailers from receiving needed credit services.

[5] Statistics cited in this paragraph are based on data reported to the Bureau of the Census and contained in the *1954 Census of Business, Wholesale Trade, Credit, Receivables, Bad-Debt Losses—Merchant Wholesalers,* Bulletin W–2–3 (Washington, D. C.: Government Printing Office, 1957). The national figure for beer and ale wholesalers is artificially low because of legal restrictions on the extension of credit for such goods in many states.

such accommodations, partly because the amount of business, when buying in small quantities from a manufacturer, would be too small to justify a credit investigation and the opening of an account, and partly because of the distance separating buyer and seller. The latter would even handicap retailers who are in good financial circumstances. From the standpoint of the manufacturer the loss of an order from a retailer because of refusal to sell to him on credit, would mean very little, as compared to the relative difficulty and costliness of securing necessary credit information, keeping in touch with local situations, and in collecting overdue accounts at a distance. On the other hand, the wholesaler who sells a large number of items finds an important outlet even in the smallest retailer. Consequently, each retailer is treated with deference and special consideration. Furthermore, the wholesaler's proximity to the trade and his constant personal contact, usually through his salesmen, make it possible for him to collect accounts with a minimum of expense and effort.

The credit arrangement is also advantageous to the retailer from still another viewpoint. Instead of arranging his credit with several hundred manufacturers, the retail merchant establishes his credit with a limited number of wholesalers in his territory. The annoyances involved in establishing credit, which usually makes necessary the furnishing of references, a financial statement, and other details, aside from the delay incident to a credit investigation, are well known.[6] It is also much easier and simpler for the retailer to keep his credit in line and in sound condition, and to take cash discounts, when dealing with fewer sources of supply. Thus, the wholesaler facilitates the establishment of credit relations and, because of the retailer's concentration of purchases and the wholesaler's continuity of selling contact, more credit is extended to the retailer than would have been made available to him by manufacturers.

Guarantees the Goods and Adjusts Complaints. Even though the goods sold by the wholesaler do not bear his own label, he usually guarantees the quality of the merchandise. Instead of investigating the merits of each item, the retailer relies upon the wholesaler to give him sound information because he knows that the wholesaler, through his trained buyers, is in a better position to study the merits of the goods and to investigate the guarantees made by the manufacturers. The retailer depends upon the wholesaler's ability to measure the quality of the goods and the reliability of their makers, and to stand between the retailer and manufacturer with the assurance that all factory claims and guarantees are enforced. The wholesaler thus provides the retailer in effect with a double guarantee.

This service is of particular moment in lines of merchandise that are of a technical or mechanical nature, such as automotive equipment, certain

6 See T. N. Beckman and R. Bartels, *Credits and Collections in Theory and Practice* (6th ed.; New York: McGraw-Hill Book Co., Inc., 1956).

types of hardware, and electrical goods. Complaints are at best annoying both to the complainant and to the vendor. If such complaints had to be made by the retailer to scores or hundreds of factories, the annoyance might become unbearable, let alone the expense involved in correspondence. The wholesaler serves as the clearinghouse for all complaints and adjustments, which are handled by the same personnel in a single office. He becomes quite familiar with the problems of the retailer and the best way of handling them, usually to the satisfaction of all concerned.

Advice and Assistance to Customers. Since the wholesaler's welfare—in fact, his very existence—depends in the last analysis upon the success of his customers, it behooves him to render to the retailer whatever assistance he can in the solution of his merchandising and store management problems. The wholesaler must devote a great deal of time and intelligence to the upbuilding of this retailer on whom he so definitely depends. It is, of course, the wholesaler's first duty to supply the retailer with a well-rounded stock of good merchandise, but with this his task is but partially accomplished; it is not complete until he has provided the retailer with a merchandising service which enables him to maintain a satisfactory sales volume at a reasonable rate of profit.

A comprehensive list of services provided by various kinds of wholesalers to their customers is beyond the scope of this discussion. For present purposes it will suffice simply to mention some of the more important areas in which merchandising and general management assistance are given:[7]

1. *New Product Information.* The wholesaler's salesmen supply the retailer with a steady stream of information about new products, which manufacturers often introduce through wholesalers so as to get national distribution in a short time. From the wholesaler the retailer also secures advice on the suitability of new items for his particular clientele, which the wholesaler is well suited to evaluate. At times new product information goes beyond the day-to-day contacts of salesmen and is expanded into a formal advisory service.

2. *Inventory Control.* Wholesalers' salesmen often act in the capacity of "stock clerks" for retailers, especially in small stores which lack formal inventory control systems. The salesman checks shelf stocks, points out items that are running low or are slow-moving, and recommends appropriate action to keep stock fresh and in balance. Sometimes this service is systematized through the provision to retailers of stock control forms, model-stock plans, and other materials.

3. *Sales Planning.* Modern wholesalers often render a more or less complete merchandise planning service to their customers, including as-

---

[7] Customer services are discussed from a managerial point of view in Chapter 26.

sistance in planning and executing special promotions, provision of "specials" to be featured in advertising and displays, and more or less permanent "leaders" handled on narrow margins and used for price appeal purposes. In addition, some wholesalers sponsor cooperative advertising programs among their customers.

4. *Pricing.* In some lines of trade it is customary for wholesalers to supply retailers with lists of suggested resale prices for their goods, often based on a comparison shopping service provided by the wholesaler. This service is important to smaller stores in groceries and drugs, in which many items are stocked and active price competition from chains must be met.

5. *Store Engineering.* The advent of self-service and self-selection at the retail level has brought the importance of proper store layout, fixturing, and decoration to the forefront. Many wholesalers have rendered a valuable service to their customers by helping them to remodel existing structures or to design new ones.

6. *Other Services.* The foregoing are merely illustrative of the wide range of services made available by regular wholesalers. Others include training of retail store personnel, provision of showrooms to display complete lines, and even operation of model stores where improved methods may be developed and demonstrated. It is probably a fair statement that every conceivable form of managerial assistance has been given by at least one wholesaler at some time to one or more of his customers. In all of this the regular wholesaler is guided by the basic principle that whatever helps his customers, helps his own business in the long run.

It may be said that such advice and assistance would, no doubt, be given by the manufacturer and his salesmen, were the wholesaler nonexistent. This is, however, a matter of conjecture; certainly the advice would not be likely to be as unbiased and impartial. Each manufacturer's salesman would, in all probability, attempt to push his own line of merchandise at the expense of competing goods, even though such procedure might prove detrimental to the retailer on whom he would call at relatively infrequent intervals. Because of the pressure brought to bear by a horde of manufacturers' salesmen, the average independent retailer would be loaded up with excessive inventories, resulting in less frequent purchases, slower stock-turnover, poorer merchandising, and consequent higher prices to consumers.

As a rule, high-powered salesmanship and constructive dealer aid do not go together. The average wholesaler has learned that such a policy is not sound. His salesman, very often carefully trained, usually calls upon a given retailer year after year. He knows that it is not to his advantage to discriminate between the goods of different manufacturers. He will normally recommend goods which he knows can be sold best in his territory.

He may, however, be partial to goods which bear the wholesaler's private label; but he realizes that his success is bound up with that of his customers, and he will not ordinarily attempt to oversell or consciously misdirect their purchases.

Helps Customers in Time of Stress. It is a well-known fact among credit managers that, in the handling of any adjustment of an embarrassed debtor, the small creditors are the most troublesome. They invariably insist upon full payment or upon the liquidation of the account probably because they have so little at stake, and they know that their vociferousness and stubborn attitude will result in full payment, even though it be at the expense of the large creditors. Thus should a retailer buy directly from hundreds of manufacturers, the amount owing each of them would be so small that in time of stress he would be pressed for payment of many small amounts coming due simultaneously, which might jeopardize his entire business. On the other hand, when a retailer purchases his goods from wholesalers, he generally concentrates his buying and confines his patronage to a few well-selected houses. In times of financial embarrassment the wholesalers, having much at stake in the account and anxious for continued patronage of the retailers, are likely to treat the account with great care. They frequently make every effort to preserve the business and give the retailer another chance so long as he is honest and has an opportunity to extricate himself from his financial difficulties, even though it necessitates an extension of time or a composition settlement.

The value of this aid afforded by the wholesaler was dramatically demonstrated during the several years of severe depression beginning with 1929. During this time many retailers would have been forced to close their doors had it not been for the special consideration shown them by the wholesaler. A study of the commercial history of the United States reveals the fact that such was also the practice of wholesalers immediately following the Civil War, in the years of depression beginning with 1873, and again during the depressed period commencing with 1893. It is a service and an extra protection which mean a great deal to every thoughtful and farsighted merchant in this country.

How the Regular Wholesaler Serves His Suppliers

Contrary to the proverbial admonition, the regular wholesaler can and does serve two masters; and when his business is efficiently operated, the benefits inure to all parties concerned, including the consuming public. In the preceding section the wholesaler's service to the *retailer* and to other types of customers who buy from him was discussed. Attention may now be turned to the wholesaler's work as a distributor of the output of the *manufacturer of consumer goods.*

Plans Distribution for the Manufacturer. Because of his peculiar and strategic position in the marketing process, the wholesaler is thought to be in the most favorable position to interpret and evaluate the facts bearing on consumer demand. This is an important function, since it is the basis for all manufacturing, wholesaling, and retailing activities. Neither the average manufacturer nor the average retailer has thus far qualified for the position. It has already been pointed out that the typical manufacturing establishment is a small business unit. The manufacturer is generally preoccupied with factory problems since the successful production of even a single article is an accomplishment that usually calls for the continued application of all his ingenuity. Most of them are too far removed from the ultimate consumers to make a comprehensive quantitative and qualitative market analysis easily. Furthermore, the cost of a well-rounded consumer research program similar to those which are carried on economically by the very large manufacturers would be too much of a financial burden, if not an utter impossibility. The retailer, on the other hand, is too close to the consumers and is overly influenced by unimportant local movements and conditions. Frequently, he "cannot see the woods for the trees." The perspective of both the average retailer and the average manufacturer is comparatively narrow and too limited to gauge accurately consumer wants and attitudes.

The wholesaler, however, is well qualified to take over this work for the manufacturer. He specializes in selected lines of merchandise and in dealing with certain types of customers in a given territory. He knows, or is in a position to discover, the existing and potential demand of his trade and that of ultimate consumers. Thus he is in a strategic position to solve with skill such problems as the determination of the nature of the goods that can be sold in his territory; how much of these goods can be profitably sold; the type of package that will be most suitable; the size of the unit that will make the greatest appeal to the trade; and many other pertinent points which can be adequately appraised only by a specialist in distribution. Unfortunately, the typical wholesaler, although in a position to appraise the market scientifically and accurately, has not taken full advantage of his opportunities. His neglect of modern techniques of marketing research has been one of the contributing causes of his unpopularity with manufacturers. However, as will be shown in a later part of this book, there is ample evidence that many progressive wholesalers are awakening to their responsibility and are adopting a more scientific attitude toward marketing management.

Establishes and Maintains Connections with Customers and Sells to Them. The wholesaler, once he becomes well established in his area, provides the manufacturer with a definite clientele of relatively permanent customers. The personal acquaintances which his salesmen develop with buyers through frequent contacts with the trade (in many lines of business as often as twice a week) enable them to break down unfounded sales resistance and insure more favorable consideration of their sales arguments when presenting new lines of merchandise. In connection with Figure 2 it was pointed out that the retailer would find it practically impossible to contact the thousands of manufacturers to procure his supply of goods. The manufacturer is faced with the same problems, for he in turn would find it costly and unsatisfactory to attempt to reach the retailers, who are legion. There are in the United States about 1,720,000 retail outlets alone, about 90 per cent of which are independently owned, and which would require separate contacts. In the grocery business alone there are about 280,000 retail stores. To these must be added about 170,000 eating places; about 20,000 candy, confectionery, and dairy stores; and probably another hundred thousand stores handling food items, including country general stores, some large superdrugstores, certain department stores and what the Census terms "all other food stores." Thus, there must be between 500,000 and 700,000 retail outlets for food products. For any manufacturer of a grocery article or of a small line of groceries to attempt to establish and maintain contacts with even a small fraction of these outlets would be most difficult and costly if not impossible.

It may be objected that the foregoing example is misleading because it deals with food products, which are among the most widely distributed of all goods. While the problem may not be quite as great in other lines, it is nevertheless beyond the capabilities of most manufacturers. For dry goods there are about 150,000 retail outlets; for drugs, about 56,000 drugstores in addition to a substantial number of food and other stores handling drugs; in hardware, about 50,000 outlets. With relatively few exceptions, therefore, manufacturers cannot attempt to reach their retail outlets directly because of their great number and geographic dispersion.

It should not be inferred from the foregoing that selling through wholesalers eliminates the need for a manufacturer's sales force. When the factory is small, it may be that a single wholesaler or very few such concerns will absorb the entire output. Under such circumstances all the manufacturer's selling can be done by one of the executives and a sales force may be unnecessary. However, when the plant is large and the output is greater than the amount which a few wholesale houses can handle, or when the manufacturer is unwilling to concentrate his selling lest his position become precarious in the future, a sales force must be maintained by the manufacturer in order to call upon wholesalers and other customers.

The sales force, however, need not be very large. Instead of cultivating perhaps 100,000 to 250,000 retail outlets for food products, the manufacturer of a food product need but call upon a substantial representation of some 3,320 wholesale grocers handling a general line of groceries, and if specialty concerns are to be used as well, upon part of another 10,000 to 12,000 such establishments. In the dry goods trade most of the retail stores can be reached through some of the 132 general line dry goods wholesalers. Certainly it can be excellently cultivated through a selected number of the 4,600 or more wholesale establishments dealing in all kinds of dry goods, including wholesalers who specialize in piece goods, in knit goods, and related lines. Likewise, instead of the drug manufacturer having a possible clientele of 56,000 retail drugstores to canvass, he can confine his activities to a portion of the 392 general line wholesale drug houses and some of the 2,409 specialty concerns in that field. Again, in place of calling upon some 35,000 hardware stores, such stores can be reached through a number of the 2,137 general line and specialty hardware wholesalers. If the manufacturer desires to be more aggressive in the promotion of sales, he may enlarge his sales force to include missionary salesmen in order to cultivate the retail trade directly.

Cultivates the Field Intensively. Through the activities of wholesalers goods are distributed to more retailers and sales calls are made with greater frequency than could possibly be done by the manufacturers themselves. This is due to the great geographic dispersion of retail outlets throughout the United States. While there has been some tendency for retail establishments to become more concentrated in urban areas, widespread distribution still characterizes most lines of merchandise. Nearly one-half of all retail outlets (44.5 per cent), accounting for over 35 per cent of all retail store sales, are located outside of the 172 metropolitan areas. Especially for convenience goods lines, such as groceries, drugs, and hardware, coverage of outlets in smaller towns and rural areas is essential. Manufacturers would find it uneconomical to cultivate these outlets, however, because of the small quantity of goods that could be sold on a call.

From the foregoing facts it would appear that with few exceptions no manufacturer dealing in consumer goods can afford to cover his territory very intensively with his own sales staff. The expense involved would definitely prohibit him from calling upon retailers located in small towns and in rural areas. The wholesaler, on the other hand, because of the large variety of merchandise which he has to offer to his customers and the many manufacturers represented, usually can afford to cover his market very thoroughly by penetrating to retailers in every city, town, village, and hamlet. Because of the great number of items carried, the average order from even a small retailer may be expected to return a gross profit sufficient to cover necessary traveling and other expenses incident to securing the order. Without this service, a large number of merchants and consumers located in small towns and in other rural areas would be seriously handicapped and inconvenienced. Many very small-scale retailers would no doubt be forced out of business altogether. It should be noted here that many wholesalers have gone too far in attempting to service uneconomic retail outlets of this type. While this may prove to be a service to the manufacturer in disposing of his wares, it results in an undue burden and frequent loss to the wholesaler. The latter would be much better advised to restrict his sales to profitable accounts through a more scientific use of selective selling.

Except for those retail establishments that specialize in a limited line of goods, such as gasoline and oil, men's shoes, or millinery, most stores operate on such a small scale that their individual orders on any item or group of items cannot be large enough to justify direct contact between manufacturer and retailer. A comprehensive study,[8] involving an analysis of a number of typical wholesalers' invoices for the year 1950 in five lines of trade (dry goods, drugs, groceries, hardware, and tobacco), revealed the fact that the average invoice for all these lines taken together totaled $107.14, involved over 24 items ($4.42 per item), and called for merchandise from about 17 manufacturers ($6.52 per manufacturer). For groceries the average order was $177, with 40 items and 26 manufacturing sources; for drugs it was $88, with 30 items and 20 manufacturing sources; for dry goods it was $117, with 20 items and 13 manufacturing sources; for hardware it was $94, with 18 items and 13 manufacturing sources; and for tobacco it was $59, with 14 items and 11 manufacturing sources. It would be economic folly, therefore, for any manufacturer of a single product or of a limited line of merchandise to cultivate such trade; but, for reasons pointed out above, the wholesaler may be in a position to render economical service to many of these small retailers in the larger cities as well as to those in the rural sections and less populated territories.

As long as great distances separate manufacturers and retailers, as long as many manufacturers are relatively small-scale operators and produce a limited line of merchandise, as long as many retailers are located in small communities and in otherwise inaccessible places, and as long as large numbers of retailers operate on a small scale and buy in very small quantities, so long will wholesalers be an indispensable medium for translating concentrated production into widely diffused retail distribution.

Aids in Stabilizing Production. The wholesaler usually orders his goods from the manufacturer considerably in advance of the needs of retailers and consumers, which enables the manufacturer to take fuller advantage of a planned production schedule. For example, canneries of food products sometimes regulate the quantities they produce almost entirely by the volume of advance orders placed by wholesalers. Many dry goods factories book future orders from wholesalers for large quantities of merchandise. Similarly, manufacturers of seasonal hardware items, such as wire screens,

8 Milan R. Karas, *op. cit.*

lawn mowers, sleds, ice skates, stoves, and numerous other products of like nature, depend upon the wholesaler to place his orders in advance, and to carry seasonal stocks of such merchandise in his own warehouses. This relieves the manufacturer of the risk involved were he to produce for stock. In this wise the manufacturer can better gauge his markets with more intelligent control of raw material purchases and production schedules. A more uniform utilization of plant and equipment resulting from a somewhat stabilized demand tends toward increased efficiency in production, which in turn should enable the manufacturer to charge the wholesaler lower prices.

The wholesaler's activities, which bring about advance ordering from sources of supply as just noted, exert a stabilizing influence in another way. In critical times the manufacturer who sells through wholesalers does not feel the curtailment as sharply as if he sold directly to retailers. In other words, the wholesaler acts as a shock absorber, and the producer has additional time to make adjustments.

Provides Storage for the Manufacturer. As has been pointed out previously, one of the most important functions of the wholesaler is to maintain a complete and adequate stock of goods for the convenience of retailers. In carrying out this function, the wholesaler also renders a valuable service to the manufacturer. It was noted in the preceding section that the wholesaler places his orders considerably in advance of demand by retailers and consumers. This enables the manufacturer to ship his goods as fast as they are produced, thus transferring the storage function to the wholesaler.

It is generally recognized that the wholesaler can probably store goods with greater economy than either the manufacturer or retailer. Given a certain amount of storage space, labor, and equipment, the wholesaler can utilize them to greater advantage by virtue of the comparative evenness with which goods flow in and out the year round and the quantity of merchandise that is being stored regularly. Unlike the manufacturer the wholesaler obtains his goods from various sources, serving as a reservoir into which the products of many producers constantly flow, so that the facilities may be utilized to capacity. Furthermore, a given space may be assigned to several types of merchandise if the demand for such goods is of a seasonal nature and the seasons dovetail. Thus, it is not uncommon for a hardware wholesaler to store in a given space such items as sleds and, as soon as the season changes and most of the sleds are sold, to devote the same space to wire screening and the like.

It is no doubt true that the full-line manufacturers, or those operating on a large scale and supported by ample financial means, may provide their own warehouses at certain distributing centers; but the smaller or short-line producers usually find it to their advantage to pass the bulk of this function on to the wholesaler. This leaves the manufacturer free to devote his time and energy to production. He need not provide facilities for the storage of large quantities of goods, or worry concerning methods of financing these inventories, or assume the hazards resulting from deterioration, theft, destruction by fire, or unfavorable price fluctuations. Any attempt by wholesalers to shift the responsibility of performing these functions tends to jeopardize their usefulness if not their very existence. When the wholesaler strives to speed the flow of goods through his warehouses beyond certain limits, he fails to discharge one of his most important functions. In fact, in view of the retailer's desire to buy frequently and in small amounts, the assumption of the storage function by the wholesaler takes on greater significance. He should not, therefore, try to shift this function back to the manufacturer, unless he wants to subject himself to just criticism and endanger his position. Once a manufacturer provides the necessary storage facilities at points of demand, he may next be led to undertake direct selling to the retailer, a procedure which may be quite uneconomic for all concerned.

Additional Functions. The wholesaler performs other important services for the manufacturer. For one thing, he effects savings in transportation charges for the manufacturer as well as for the retailer. In selling to wholesalers, the manufacturer makes a few large shipments instead of the many small ones which would be necessary when selling directly to retailers. The consequent reduction in the number of orders and shipments results in substantial economies in packing and shipping.

The wholesaler also gives valuable assistance to some manufacturers by supplying them with financial support. Sales of goods through the wholesaler enable the small- and medium-sized manufacturer to operate on limited capital. Since the wholesaler provides for the warehousing or storage of the manufacturer's output, it is on his shoulders that the cost of carrying adequate inventories devolves. Because of his stronger credit position the wholesaler normally pays for merchandise immediately upon delivery, discounting his bills when presented for payment, or very shortly thereafter. In some lines, as in the fruit and vegetable canning industry, where the entire output of a plant may be purchased by a wholesaler on contract for future delivery, financial assistance is rendered by the wholesaler at the beginning of the production season in the form of a direct loan, or by indorsing the canner's promissory notes which can then be discounted at the bank. Furthermore, as was pointed out previously, the wholesaler carries the accounts of retail dealers which, in his absence, would have to be carried and financed to some extent by the manufacturer.

The wholesaler also aids the manufacturer by simplifying the latter's accounting procedure. Relatively few accounts are carried on the manufacturer's books, and overhead is reduced through the employment of a smaller clerical force for the bookkeeping department. Orders from whole-salers are larger than those which retailers normally place, and fewer in number. These factors result in a considerable reduction in sales record-ing, invoicing, billing, and in other office expenses.

Finally, the wholesaler reduces the manufacturer's cost of credit granting. When a manufacturer uses the wholesaler channel of distribution, he sells his goods to concerns which, for the most part, enjoy a high credit rating, are well financed, and whose chances of failure are much reduced. Not so in the case of sales to retailers: most retailers are poorly financed, have a low credit rating in the mercantile agency books, and present hazardous credit risks in other than the prosperous years when nearly every business-man is successful. In the absence of the wholesaler the manufacturer would naturally be forced to assume some of these risks which the wholesaler, partly because of his proximity to the trade, is better able to assume.

How the Regular Wholesaler Benefits the Consumer

In preceding paragraphs the regular wholesaler's services to his customers and suppliers have been analyzed. Important as these are, they do not provide a complete explanation of the status of the wholesaler in the economy. In the long run this depends on the benefits derived by the con-suming public from the functions performed by the wholesaler. These benefits have been implied, in part, by the discussion of how the wholesaler serves customers and suppliers. Now they may be summarized briefly with an explicit consumer point of view.

Adds Value to Goods. The basic contribution of the wholesaler is that he *adds value* to the goods he handles. This is done by the creation of time, place, and possession utilities. *Time utility* results from the storage of goods in the interval between their manufacture and the time of pur-chase by retailers. This is one of the regular wholesaler's most conspicu-ous functions, and he bears most of the burden of maintaining adequate local stocks.

Place utility is created by bringing goods closer to the point of con-sumption, where they have greater value than at points of manufacture. Regular wholesalers contribute to this type of utility through their opera-tion of delivery equipment as well as by their part in arranging for shipments to more distant customers via common carriers.

The wholesaler helps to create *possession utility* in several ways. His buying and selling activities, of course, contribute directly to this end. As goods are transferred in ownership from manufacturers to retailers and eventually to ultimate consumers, they become progressively more valu-able. Wholesalers play a major role in this process of title transfer. In addition to buying and selling as such, several of the wholesaler's functions facilitate the movement of title, including the activities of planning, financing, guaranteeing, and the furnishing of various forms of managerial assistance.

Reduces Marketing Cost. The fact that the wholesaler adds value to goods explains his role in the production process, but does not explain his successful competition with other marketing channels. Time, place, and possession utilities could be created by others; but the wholesaler has a basic advantage which enables him to accomplish his task at a lower cost to the consumer. The sources of this economy are twofold: *simplification* of the marketing task and *greater productivity* through large scale and specialization.

Assuming that the products of many small manufacturers must be distributed to numerous small retailers, fewer transactions are needed when wholesalers are used. This means that the wholesaler simplifies the ex· change process, which can be accomplished by a smaller number of sales· men and buyers with a consequent reduction in its total cost. Similarly, the wholesaler substitutes a single, flexible storage area for many small and inflexible ones, reducing the total quantity of goods that must be stored to support a given level of consumption. The same reasoning can be applied to the other functions, and in each case it can be shown that the over-all marketing process is simplified and its cost reduced to the consumer, who must ultimately pay for it.

Because the wholesaler operates on a large scale, he can generally perform his functions *more productively* than retailers or manufacturers, that is, with a lower total expenditure of labor and capital resources. In storage, for example, the wholesaler employs modern materials-handling equipment which can be used only if a large volume of goods is handled. In transportation, the largest semitrailers can be used for store deliveries, which would not be possible if it were not for the larger orders obtained by wholesalers from each customer. In brief, the wholesaler does for all of his customers and suppliers what each would have to do individually in his absence. It is not surprising, therefore, that he can attain a degree of specialization in personnel and equipment not usually possible under direct marketing.

Coordinates Supply and Demand. Coordination of supply and demand is a basic task of marketing institutions in a free economy. For reasons already given, the wholesaler is generally in the most advantageous position to collect, interpret, and transmit the information necessary for this purpose. As a result of this coordinating function, the kinds of goods manufactured are better attuned to the needs and desires of consumers. Not only are the broad preferences of the nation as a whole made known, but the special and unique demands of each area are reflected back to manufacturers through the intimate knowledge of the wholesaler in his trading area.

Coordination of supply with demand also implies a better adjustment of the quantities turned out and the timing of their manufacture. Finally, it includes the continuity of supply of which consumers are assured because of the storage of adequate stocks in wholesalers' warehouses.

SUMMARY

The effects of the regular wholesaler's functions on his customers, his suppliers, and the consuming public have been shown in preceding pages. By way of summary, the performance of the wholesaler can be viewed as consisting of several well-defined marketing functions:

1. *Buying* in economical quantities from a number of suppliers, based on estimates of the requirements of customers
2. *Selling* through an established and trained sales force and by mail and telephone, reaching all or most potential customers in a trading area, and assisting in the coordination of advertising and promotional programs
3. *Transportation* of goods to customers, making possible prompt local deliveries, and reducing transportation costs between manufacturer and points of demand by buying in economical shipping quantities
4. *Storage* of a reservoir of goods near the point of demand, utilizing efficient methods and equipment through large-scale operation
5. *Financing* of inventories and customers' purchases
6. *Risk-bearing* through the purchase of goods in advance of customers' needs, carrying of stocks, and the guarantee of merchandise sold
7. *Standardization and grading,* especially as these functions apply to packaging and packing. Wholesalers also work closely with suppliers and customers in developing mutually acceptable product standards.
8. Collection and dissemination of *marketing information* through continuous and systematic study of the market, and assistance to customers and suppliers in utilizing such information

In addition to these basic marketing functions, many regular wholesalers also render *technical product services,* including installation and repairs.

As long as these functions are performed with reasonable efficiency, and so long as the assumptions stated at the outset of the chapter remain substantially true, it is safe to predict that the regular wholesaler will maintain his traditional role in the marketing of goods.

9

THE INDUSTRIAL
DISTRIBUTOR

It is often assumed that what are commonly known as regular whole-salers are important only in the marketing of goods destined for resale in the same form to ultimate consumers, usually through retail stores. Actu-ally, wholesalers also sell substantial quantities of goods to business users. There is hardly a wholesale grocer who does not sell to hotels, restaurants, and various kinds of public or private institutions. Similarly, few hardware wholesalers do not sell substantial amounts to manufacturers and other industrial users. Again, virtually all drug wholesalers have as regular ac-counts hospitals, clinics, and physicians buying for institutional use or for dispensing to patients.

In addition to these industrial sales by wholesalers of consumer goods, there are many wholesalers who *specialize* in cultivating the industrial market, i.e., who sell principally or entirely goods which do not reach ultimate consumers in the same form. The term "industrial distributor" is used to designate this type of wholesaler.

Industrial distributors are quite similar to wholesalers of consumer goods, but there are also some distinctive features which serve to differenti-ate them from other wholesalers. The main distinctions, by definition, are in the nature of the market served, which is comprised of industrial and other business users rather than of retail outlets, and often in the type of merchandise handled. Another difference lies in the greater competition with direct marketing channels which industrial distributors generally face. Finally, there are differences in the kinds of functions performed and their relative importance.

151

The Industrial Market

Despite a substantial body of literature on the subject, there is much confusion about the meaning of the terms "industrial market," "industrial marketing," and "industrial distributor." Some definitions center around the *nature of the goods* handled, while others focus attention on the *type of purchaser*. Whichever alternative is followed, there are still differences of opinion as to the *scope* of the industrial market and industrial marketing institutions.

Industrial vs. Consumer Goods. From the standpoint of the nature of the goods, several conceptions of the industrial market are current among businessmen and economists. A narrow and unrealistic view restricts the field to machinery, equipment, and supplies used in the manufacturing and processing of finished goods. This conception leaves in doubt the status of semimanufactured goods and parts bought by industry, as well as all goods purchased by wholesalers, retailers, institutions, and others for use in the conduct of the respective business enterprises but not for resale. If these are included, the industrial market may be broadened to include all *manufactured* goods not intended for ultimate consumers. A much broader concept, however, and one on which most marketing authorities agree, also includes all *raw materials* that come from the farms, mines and quarries, forests, oil wells, or as a result of fishing, hunting, and trapping.

Industrial Users. When viewed from the standpoint of the purchaser of the goods, the term "industrial marketing" is again subject to several diverse interpretations. In the narrowest sense it is said to apply to goods bought or used by industry, the term "industry" applying only to manufacturing concerns. While many businessmen still hold to this narrow view, ordinarily the term "industry" is used to include all industries in which extensive mechanical installations are used, i.e., manufacturing, mining and quarrying, construction, lumbering, and even public utilities and transportation. A third and somewhat broader concept of industrial marketing from the point of view of purchasers includes service industries, such as hotels, restaurants, theaters, and barber shops; institutions, whether privately owned or governmentally operated, such as schools, hospitals, churches, and clubs; and local, county, state, and federal governmental bodies.

A fourth view, much broader than those just stated, also includes purchases of goods by commercial organizations such as retailers and wholesalers, financial institutions, office buildings, and the like, when such goods are not bought for resale. However, none of the aforementioned concepts embraces the purchases by farmers when such goods are bought for business purposes, namely, agricultural production. Even the broadest definitions now generally in use omit the latter from their scope.

It is the authors' considered judgment that the terms "industrial marketing" and "industrial market" should be used in a very broad and true sense to include all goods (whether in the form of raw materials, semi-manufactures which must be converted into more finished products, machinery, equipment, supplies, parts which are embodied without change in the finished product, containers and packaging materials, or other materials such as chemicals and wood pulp) that are bought for further processing, or that are consumed or used for business purposes, regardless of whether they are bought by farmers, manufacturers, construction contractors, commercial organizations, the service industries, governmental bodies, or others engaged in business pursuits, *so long as such goods are not bought for personal consumption or for resale in the same form*. Any other definition of industrial marketing appears to be arbitrary and in violation of both sound logic and recognized marketing principles.

Importance of the Industrial Market. Industrial goods comprise almost one-half of the total value of manufactured goods produced, when the goods are valued at f.o.b. prices at point of manufacture or import. If the goods are valued instead at *final selling prices* to ultimate and industrial consumers, respectively, consumer goods are much more important because of the wider total marketing margins (including transportation) normally incurred in their distribution. Finally, when reckoned in terms of sales volume, the consumer goods market looms even much larger, generally amounting to about three times the size of the industrial market. This is to be accounted for by the wider marketing margins on consumer goods already mentioned; by the longer channels for their distribution and the resulting duplication in counting the volume of business transacted; and by the fact that there are many duplicate transactions on the same goods even within a given level of distribution.

The relative importance of industrial and consumer goods varies from year to year according to the stage of the business cycle. This is due to the fact that one significant category of industrial goods, composed of major *installations,* such as diesel engines, turbines, and the like, is extremely sensitive to fluctuations in general business activity, as is the construction of additional plant capacity. Primarily because of the sensitivity of these capital goods, the industrial market tends to decline and expand more than proportionally with material fluctuations in business. Thus, in a depression or even a mild recession, industrial goods fall off to much less than one-half of total output, while in peak years of prosperity they may represent substantially more than the normal share.

Channels of Distribution for Industrial Goods.[1] Industrial goods issuing from the factories are generally distributed through four principal channels:

1. Direct from factory to user
2. Through the manufacturer's own sales branches to user
3. Through agents or brokers
4. Through industrial distributors or through ordinary wholesalers who also deal in industrial goods although their principal business is in consumer goods

Complete data showing the relative importance of the several channels through which industrial goods move from point of production or import to destination are not readily available, nor can such computations from existing data be easily made. From all the facts studied by the authors, however, there is no question as to the relative ranking of these channels. Direct selling from the factory to user is by far the most important channel, followed by wholesalers and industrial distributors, manufacturers' own sales branches, and finally by agents and brokers, in the order listed.

For purposes of this chapter it is best to divide industrial goods (other than semimanufactures) into two broad categories. In the first are such industrial goods as machinery and factory installations. These items have a rather high unit value and therefore require a relatively heavy investment on the part of the purchaser. In addition, they are complicated and thus necessitate high-grade technical engineering service from the seller for the benefit of the buyer.

The second category of manufactured industrial goods consists of the great variety of parts, equipment, and supplies, and includes small machines, mechanical devices, and tools. This group of commodities does not require a major investment; neither is the necessity for engineering salesmanship a major factor in their marketing. The great preponderance of direct selling of industrial goods by manufacturers either from the factory or through their own wholesale outlets is undoubtedly in the first of these categories of industrial merchandise. This is a field which lies outside the scope of the average industrial distributor except in the far West, and it is therefore unlikely that a very large expansion of business by such distributors may be anticipated in the sale of this type of goods. The unit cost of the separate items sold is usually great enough to justify the expensive selling techniques of direct marketing, and the complicated nature of most

---

[1] As noted in Chapter 1, the analysis in this book is restricted to the wholesaling of *manufactured* goods. Thus, even though most agricultural products are properly classed as industrial goods and their marketing as part of industrial marketing, no attention is given to such products herein.

products in this group requires the combined efforts of engineering and selling which only the manufacturer can adequately provide.

The sphere of the industrial distributor therefore lies in the second category of industrial goods, which lend themselves to the specialized selling technique of such wholesalers. As might be expected, the available data indicate that a much larger proportion of such industrial goods is sold through wholesalers and industrial distributors than is true of industrial manufactured goods as a whole. In fact, the industrial distributor and other wholesalers are apparently the most important sales channels for this type of merchandise.

The Distributor and His Position

Just as the terms "industrial market" and "industrial marketing" may be interpreted in more than one way, so the term "industrial distributor" has varying definitions. Even when a narrow interpretation is placed on the term, there is some controversy over the kinds of firms to be included. A basic distinction may be made between the broad, theoretically correct concept of "industrial distributor" and the narrower but still somewhat ambiguous popular usage of the term.

TABLE 8

WHOLESALERS OF MANUFACTURED INDUSTRIAL GOODS, UNITED STATES, 1954
(Amounts in Thousands of Dollars)

Kind of Business	Number of Establishments	Sales
TOTAL, MANUFACTURED INDUSTRIAL GOODS	62,569	$30,804,809
Air Conditioning, Commercial Refrigeration	1,860	484,070
Commercial Machines, Equipment	3,219	660,125
Construction Machinery, Equipment	1,640	1,401,359
Farm, Dairy Machinery, Equipment	1,112	534,379
Industrial Machinery, Equipment	5,746	2,618,986
Industrial Materials, Supplies	4,393	2,009,740
Professional Equipment, Supplies	2,912	853,153
Service Establishment Supply	5,264	1,101,992
Transportation Equipment	1,004	376,048
Industrial Chemicals, Explosives	1,878	923,242
Office Furniture	918	234,195
Trucks and Tractors	666	265,603
Garage Equipment, Tools	207	55,731
Electrical Apparatus, Supplies	3,159	2,910,458
Wiring Supplies	1,989	1,105,922
Paper, Allied Products (Except Wallpaper)	4,864	2,915,424
Lumber, Millwork	4,304	3,805,942
Construction Materials	6,010	2,780,265
Metals, Metalwork	3,235	3,362,585
Scrap, Waste Materials	8,189	2,405,590

Source: 1954 Census of Business, Vol. IV, *Wholesale Trade—Area Statistics,* (Washington, D. C.: Government Printing Office, 1956), Table 1–A, p. 1–6.

Broad Concept. All wholesalers who deal primarily in industrial goods may be regarded as industrial distributors in the broad sense of the term. This includes many different kinds of business. The principal ones are listed in Table 8, which also shows the number of establishments and sales volume of each kind for the year 1954. Altogether, there were 62,569 establishments operated by wholesalers who specialized in manufactured industrial goods. These represented almost 40 per cent of the total number of establishments operated by wholesalers (165,153) and their sales of just under $31 billion amounted to over 30 per cent of all sales by wholesalers.

Popular Concept. Strictly speaking, the broad meaning of "industrial distributor" as illustrated by Table 8 is the only correct one with reference to manufactured goods. This is not the meaning, however, that is usually attached to the term in business parlance. As used by trade associations and in periodicals in the field, an industrial distributor is one who handles supplies, equipment, machinery, and parts for manufacturing establishments, mines, oil wells, public utilities, railroads, and similar types of customers.

While this concept is much narrower than that employed in the preceding section, it is still subject to differences in interpretation. Despite continuing efforts to arrive at a satisfactory and specific definition since the late 1920's and especially since the formulation of the NRA codes in the early 1930's, there is still much controversy on the subject.[2] This can be traced to several causes. First, industrial supplies, equipment, and parts are often sold in combination with other lines of goods. Many of the supply houses grew out of retail and wholesale hardware firms, and while most of them have long since been divorced from retail store operations, they often maintain their wholesale hardware businesses. This presents no problem so long as one line is clearly subordinated to the other; but when substantial amounts are sold both to industrial users and to retail hardware dealers, it is difficult to assign a satisfactory status to the enterprise. In similar fashion industrial supplies are frequently sold in conjunction with electrical goods, plumbing and heating, and other predominantly consumer goods lines.

A second source of confusion has to do with the distinction between an industrial distributor and various types of *machinery* wholesalers. Industrial distributors do not ordinarily handle machinery lines except as an adjunct to supplies and equipment, for reasons discussed previously. There is no clear-cut line, however, between "equipment" and "machinery." Quite often an industrial supply house will sell materials-handling equipment or machine tools, some of which are mechanically complex and high in price.

---

[2] For statements of varying viewpoints from members of the trade and from authorities in business and economics, see George L. Bottari, "What's Your Definition of an Industrial Distributor?" *Industrial Distribution* (October, 1957; November, 1957), 82–84; 82–87.

The distinction between supply and machinery distributing is still a valid one, however, as evidenced by the common practice of setting up a separate department or division for machine tools even when it is owned by a supply house.

A third problem is that the customer groups served by various "supply houses" overlap considerably. Traditionally, distributors devote most of their efforts to serving a particular type of customer. In the northeast, where metalworking industries are concentrated, the distributors were and are called "mill supply houses." In coal mining regions similar distributors are "mine supply houses," while in the southwest they might be "oil well supply houses." While these terms have some descriptive value, it is rare for distributors to sell *only* to one type of customer. Their products are also used in the operation of service establishments, such as garages and gasoline service stations; by transportation agencies; and by contractors in various types of construction activity. Thus the markets served by the industrial distributor overlap to some extent those served by other specialized wholesalers, such as railroad equipment and supply houses, ship chandlers, construction materials wholesalers, and so on. In an attempt to bring in all of the wholesale distributors who compete substantially with one another in supplying business users, it is virtually impossible to stop short of the list used in Table 8. Even this more or less comprehensive list is confined to wholesalers *specializing* in the marketing of industrial goods or in goods sold to business and institutional users.

A final factor entering into the controversy over definition lies in the desire of established distributors to exclude smaller, newer, or unconventional operators as "unorthodox" or "illegitimate" links in channels of distribution. Thus, various definitions advanced by the large, general line distributors exclude specialty line distributors and drop shippers. In similar fashion, some definitions have attempted to set up minimum criteria of the number of lines handled, value of inventory carried, number of salesmen traveled, and the like. As in many other industries these attempts to restrict distribution to a particular *type* of wholesaler are ultimately doomed to failure since any quantitative criteria established are bound to be arbitrary and possibly illegal, except possibly for purposes of membership in an association, and since no such definition can stand in the way of dynamic changes in the makeup of the wholesaling structure.

Because most of the available data deal with the *industrial distributor* in the narrow sense of the term, it is primarily in this sense that the term is used in the remainder of the chapter. But it should be kept in mind that the analysis of the distributor's status and functions is, for the most part, also applicable to other wholesalers of manufactured industrial goods.

Competitive Position of the Industrial Distributor. Because there is no Census classification exactly corresponding to the meaning of the industrial distributor given above, it is not possible to evaluate the status of such distributors with any certainty. The importance (as measured by 1954 Census data) of the kinds of wholesalers most nearly corresponding to the popular concept may be judged from these data:

Kind of Business	Number of Establishments	Sales (Thousands)
Abrasives, Abrasive Materials	141	$ 77,400
Mechanical Power Transmission Equipment	335	113,349
Mechanical Rubber Goods	280	100,031
Rope, Cordage	117	94,120
Valves, Fittings	214	139,320
Other Industrial Materials, Supplies	2,934	1,420,160
Oil Well Supply	1,208	914,479

All of the distributors listed above with the exception of oil well supply houses are classed by the Bureau of the Census in the broad group of "Industrial Materials, Supplies Distributors." The above figures doubtless include many wholesalers not properly regarded as industrial distributors. It is impossible, however, to separate these from the kinds of business listed. The difficulty in defining and classifying these distributors is evident, in fact, from the large number of them designated by the Census simply as *"Other* Industrial Materials and Supplies Distributors."

For many products the industrial distributor is the most important channel of distribution. Surveys of industrial buying practices made by the magazine *Industrial Distribution* reveal that from 75 per cent to 90 per cent of manufacturers' requirements of such products as files, hack saws, machine and socket screws, bearings, mechanics' hand tools, drills and reamers, and V-belts are bought from distributors. In addition, distributors are the dominant outlet for many kinds of mechanical equipment, including small motors, portable electric tools, and light machine tools.

Variations in Product Lines and Territories. Like consumer goods wholesalers, industrial distributors differ among themselves as to the extent of the merchandise line carried. The traditional industrial supply house stocks a *general line* of goods. From 1935 to 1948 the Census Bureau defined "industrial distributors" as ". . . establishments dealing in a fairly *complete line* of materials, equipment, and supplies for mines, factories, oil wells, public utilities, and similar industries, and selling primarily to industrial users."[3] In the 1954 Census of Business this classification was no longer employed, presumably due to the impracticality of applying any such vague concept in practice.

[3] Census of Business, 1948, Vol. IV, *Wholesale Trade—General Statistics and Commodity Line Sales Statistics* (Washington, D. C.: Government Printing Office, 1952), p. 15.03. Emphasis supplied.

Besides the general line industrial distributors, there are many *specialty houses* that concentrate on one product line or on a few related product lines. Some of these houses handle nothing but bearings; others limit their efforts to power transmission equipment; while still others sell only abrasives or rubber goods such as V-belts. Such specialty distributors compete directly with the so-called "department stores of industry," and therefore must be classified as industrial distributors even in the narrow sense of the term.

A third type of industrial distributor is sometimes distinguished, namely, the "selected lines" house.[4] This type of wholesaler concentrates on a relatively small number of lines, but does not specialize in *related* lines. As an example of this type of distributor, one concern in 1958 handled 29 manufacturers' lines in four broad categories: cutting tools, abrasives, bearings, and machine parts. Adoption of this compromise course between traditional methods of general line and specialty operation is based on a simple criterion of handling only profitable lines on which full cooperation can be secured from the manufacturers.[5] This is not a practical alternative for most distributors, because their customers depend on them to meet their requirements even for unprofitable, slow-moving lines. The policy has been successful, therefore, only in major industrial centers where users can readily patronize two or more distributors, so that one of them can "skim the cream" by offering superior service on selected lines.

The advantages and disadvantages of general line and specialty houses in the industrial field are similar to those in consumer goods wholesaling, as outlined in Chapter 7. Specialization in merchandise is perhaps even more advantageous, due to the greater importance of technical proficiency in designing, installing, and servicing industrial products. For this and other reasons there appears to be some tendency for specialty houses to increase in relative importance. General line distributors are still dominant, however, in most markets.

SERVICES TO INDUSTRIAL USERS

Although the *functions* of the industrial distributor differ but little from those rendered by the service wholesaler in the distribution of consumer goods, the differences being largely in application rather than in kind, the subject of industrial marketing is so important from the standpoint of volume of business and specialized interest in the subject that it is deemed advisable to discuss briefly at least some of the functions of the industrial distributor despite some duplication in concepts.

[4] For a comparison of the general line, specialty, and selected lines distributors, see "Organizing for More Sales," *Industrial Distribution* (September, 1953), 90–120.

[5] Based on an interview between one of the authors and the general manager of the firm in question.

The Industrial Distributor Acts as a Purchasing Agent for His Customers. One of the principal functions of the industrial distributor is to act as a purchasing agent for his customers—the industrial users or consumers. In doing this it behooves the distributor to gather under one roof thousands of products from manufacturers located in every part of the United States and even abroad. A typical mill supply house is said to handle a representative stock of 5,000 to 6,000 different items when it specializes in certain lines of supplies; distributors handling a more general line of supplies carry from 20,000 to 30,000 items each, and in a number of instances the inventory runs as high as 65,000 items. The great diversity of distributors' inventories can be gleaned even from a partial enumeration of the merchandise classifications normally carried, which include supplies, pipe, fittings, valves of all types, tools, files, saws, chain hoists, power-transmission equipment, nails, spikes, bolts, belting, grinding wheels, packing and shipping materials, wire and Manila rope, gauges, machine tools accessories, wire wheel and other brushes, drills, reamers, car movers, ladders, factory trucks, wheelbarrows, hacksaw blades, metal plates and bars, mechanical rubber goods, chemicals, paints, and numerous other types of merchandise.

The distributor's buyers, like those of regular wholesalers, are constantly on the alert to select items from the numerous offerings of manufacturers, and to determine the adaptability of new products to the trade. In the absence of the distributor the industrial user would have to select from the thousands of manufacturers producing industrial supplies and equipment the relatively small number who could supply him in the most efficient manner with the goods desired. That this task is impractical for most industrial users unless operations are on a very large scale and other conditions are propitious is evident from the fact that there are almost 1,000 manufacturers of screw machine products, 99 manufacturers of handsaws, about 1,000 manufacturers of metalworking machinery attachments, 136 manufacturers of insulated wire and cable, and over 500 manufacturers of valves and fittings. Under the distributor system the user can reach most of the manufacturers producing machinery, equipment, or supplies through the mail, the telephone, or through a single interview with the distributor's salesman. In addition, the distributor's catalog facilitates the work of the purchasing agent, doing away with the large number of manufacturers' catalogs.

Furthermore, buying from an industrial distributor minimizes the bookkeeping and other purchasing details of the user. Only one account is maintained, instead of many, representing hundreds of manufacturers. Instead of ordering 20 or 30 items on one order, in direct buying the purchasing agent would frequently have to write 20 or 30 separate orders and pay as many separate bills. All of this would multiply purchasing detail and expense out of proportion to whatever savings might be effected by direct buying.

Makes Deliveries Promptly. Closely tied up with the maintenance of complete and diversified stocks for the benefit of customers, is the advantage arising out of the distributor's ability to make deliveries quickly. Orders are normally filled within 24 hours which might take a week or so to get direct from the factory. Prompt delivery is facilitated, first, by the distributor's close proximity to his customers, and second, by the variety in methods of transportation used. The average distributor has about five inside telephone order expediters and uses three or four trucks to make deliveries to city customers once or twice daily. When a customer needs something immediately, a salesman is not above putting it in his car and driving right over with the article. In addition, almost all industrial distributors have extensive showrooms and counter sales departments, which accommodate pickups on rush orders. In many cases these counters have a steady stream of traffic almost all day, which may require the full-time attention of several countermen.

The advantages to the consumer issuing from the fact that distributors deliver goods promptly are several. In the first place, it helps the customers to operate with less capital by carrying minimum inventories. More important, prompt delivery helps to minimize delays in production and factory shutdowns. An analysis of the orders received over a period of time by an industrial distributor in the Middle West showed that over 70 per cent of all the orders received required rush shipments and were of an emergency or semiemergency nature.

Maintains Service Department. Engineering or technical service to industrial consumers usually takes one of two forms. It may be given in anticipation of a sale of some large installation, or it may take the form of servicing existing installations and equipment in order to keep the plant running. Although many industrial users provide their own servicing, it is true that the industrial distributor's activities along this line are also most useful, especially to small-scale users. He often provides complete machinery overhauling facilities and employs expert mechanics to serve the trade. Machine shop facilities are frequently offered where special lengths of staple products can be cut to meet the requirements of customers, and pipe-threading machines can handle pipe of different sizes; other types of service are rendered involving periodic inspection to insure satisfactory operation of equipment previously installed. This function, however, for heavy machinery and more expensive installations, generally can be performed better by the manufacturers of the equipment who sell direct.

Information and Advice to Customers. The distributor's salesman calls more frequently upon a given industrial user than a sales representative from a direct selling manufacturer. He thus learns at first hand of the customer's maintenance needs. He arouses the interest of foremen in new ideas; supplies some technical information on the use of certain items under consideration; gives immediate price information without having to refer the matter to a distant home office; suggests new applications for products; and informs the consumer of the newest improved machinery and equipment. Users are usually anxious for information on uses of certain products, typical installations, working data, cost data, new mechanical features, service applications, how the products are made, and market conditions. The distributor generally knows the markets and the territory in which he operates, and is able to aid the customer in anticipating changes in prices or new product requirements.

SERVICES TO MANUFACTURERS

In the discussion immediately preceding, some services of the industrial distributor have been examined from the standpoint of the user to whom he sells. The distributor also serves the manufacturer whose goods he buys, stores, and resells to the trade. In order to view him in his full stature, therefore, it is essential that the distributor's economic position in relation to the manufacturer be briefly appraised in terms of certain of his functions for the supplier.

Provides a Competent Sales Force. The industrial distributor furnishes the manufacturer a definite clientele of permanent and presumably pleased customers. Connections have already been established with hundreds or thousands of consumers who are called upon by the distributor's salesmen at frequent intervals. The manufacturer is thus relieved of the task of hiring, training, and supervising an adequate sales force, a task with proportions determined by the size and type of business involved and the extent of coverage sought.

The importance of this service to the manufacturer should not be underestimated. It is true, of course, that the industrial market is more concentrated than that for consumer goods, in the sense that it contains a smaller total number of customers and that they may be located primarily in a few industrial centers. For any one manufacturer, however, the market is still rather large and diffuse for direct contacts. This is especially true for smaller manufacturers, and even for large ones direct marketing is difficult. The reasons for this are apparent from a brief examination of the number of potential customers for industrial products.

An extreme case is afforded by the market for certain standardized items, such as files or cutting tools (taps, dies, etc.). These products are used in practically all of the 287,000 manufacturing establishments in the United States; in many of the 275,000 establishments engaged in automotive services and repair; in a substantial proportion of the 180,000 transportation, communication, and public utility enterprises; in most of the 39,000 places of business in the mineral industries; and in some of the 480,000 contract construction firms. Thus, altogether, there may be as many as 1,260,000 potential customers for some industrial goods.[6] To call on all these customers or on any substantial proportion thereof direct, even infrequently, would require a field sales force of hundreds of men. In contrast, most of these potential customers can be reached more effectively and more often through perhaps 1,000 or at most 2,000 wholesale distributors.

Even where the market is more specialized than that just described, the distributor serves to simplify a manufacturer's distribution problems greatly. Each distributor services several hundred customers, which reduces selling costs by spreading them over the dozens, hundreds, or thousands of items carried.

Stores Goods for the Manufacturer. Storing of finished products is indispensable to continuous and regular production. The manufacturer of industrial goods may choose to store the finished goods in his own warehouses until demanded by consumers or he may allow the distributor to perform this function. Both from the manufacturer's and the social points of view, the latter method is generally by far the more economical. The distributor's warehouse, like that of any wholesaler, may be likened to a reservoir into which products from hundreds of manufacturers are constantly flowing and from which they in turn flow out to the trade. Unless the manufacturer resorts to the use of public storage facilities for warehousing stocks in consumer centers, which may be practical for relatively few of them, he cannot escape the inefficiencies in production arising out of seasonal fluctuations in demand.

The industrial distributor also aids the manufacturer in various other ways. For instance, by his customary ordering of goods far in advance of actual need by his trade, the distributor gives the manufacturer the opportunity to operate according to schedule and to produce to order instead of for stock. He also is able to extend financial assistance to many manufacturers of industrial products who operate on a relatively small scale, and frequently require aid which, because of their size, they cannot secure from commercial banks or from other financial institutions.

Other Services. The distributor also serves the manufacturer by simplifying his accounting problems. When a manufacturer sells through distributors rather than direct to users, he need but carry a relatively small number of accounts on his books. Moreover, since distributors place large

[6] Figures on number of businesses in various groups from *Statistical Abstract of the United States, 1957* (Washington, D. C.: Government Printing Office, 1957).

orders, a few substantial shipments are made in the place of numerous small ones to consumers, which effect savings in packing, shipping, billing, and record-keeping. In addition, the distributor also reduces risk to the producer by placing orders in advance, and by carrying large inventories; he thereby assumes risks incident to unfavorable price fluctuations and deterioration or obsolescence of goods. Another advantage to be gained from the use of the distributor method of marketing is that it tends to minimize costs of servicing products. The ability of the distributor to provide local service and repairs may make it possible to perform this function more economically than could the distant producer. This type of service, moreover, reduces the number of orders from users for special or non-standard commodities. Many other kinds of expense, such as those arising out of adjustments, are also reduced to a minimum by the distributor's close contact with the market.

Conclusion. The term "industrial marketing," while used in many different ways, seems best defined when used in the broadest possible sense to include all goods which require further processing or which are consumed in the process of production, trading, and in the performance of various services. In this sense the industrial market, measured either in terms of physical output or dollar volume, is truly a significant segment of the entire wholesale market. In the marketing of industrial goods which come from the factory, direct contact with consumers, either by selling directly from the factory or through wholesale branches maintained by the producer, constitutes the principal channel of distribution, followed by the manufacturer-distributor-consumer channel and the manufacturer-broker or agent-consumer channel.

The choice in distribution channels naturally depends on many factors, such as the number of potential industrial users, average unit of sale, geographic distribution of consumers, credit standing of users, regularity of demand, amount of technical sales service required, servicing and repairs after the product has been installed, degree of promptness in delivery required, opportunities for economy in shipping in carlot quantities, amount of sales promotional work demanded by the manufacturer, and the size of the manufacturing organization and its financial strength. When the number of potential users of a given product is large, the market scattered, the unit of sale low, the credit standing of users limited, demand irregular, prompt delivery of major importance, economies in shipment possible, little or no technical sales service required, repair service essential, the manufacturer operates on a small scale or needs financial assistance, and relatively little sales promotional effort produces satisfactory results; then the distributor channel is the most economical means, provided, of course, that the distributor operates with a reasonable degree of efficiency.

10

LIMITED-FUNCTION
WHOLESALERS

In the chapters immediately preceding, attention has been given to the operations of the service or regular wholesaler, who acts as a purchasing agent for retailers and industrial consumers and as a distributor for manufacturers' products; who carries stocks adequate to meet the requirements of his trade; and who performs the whole range of wholesaling functions as discussed in Chapter 8. This and the following three chapters are devoted to a discussion of various developments within the field of wholesaling which have had the effect of providing increased direct or indirect competition for the regular wholesalers as a class.

Some Factors Affecting Wholesaling. Since the 1920's many social and economic changes have taken place which have tended to affect the regular wholesaler adversely and certain other segments of the wholesaling structure favorably. Detailed consideration of these developments is given at various places throughout this book. At this point suffice it merely to enumerate a few of the more important of the developments which have caused the regular wholesaler serious concern:

1. A quickening in the style tempo, accompanied by a growing interest of consumers in fashion, which reacts upon the retailing and wholesaling structure as well as upon the maker of the goods
2. A growing tendency for consumers to shop for many goods in reasonably large trading communities or their satellite shopping centers, thereby reducing the relative importance of the small store which the wholesaler generally serves
3. The growth of chain systems and the multiplication of chain store units. Such retail systems generally buy their goods directly from manufacturers in quantities which equal and frequently exceed those bought by

wholesalers and at prices that are often more advantageous than those which the regular wholesaler can obtain from his sources of supply.

4. Development of large department stores and mail order houses which buy most of their requirements directly from manufacturers

5. The growth of supermarkets, particularly for the distribution of food products, drugs, and certain other nonfood merchandise

6. Group buying by independent retail outlets, through resident buying offices or through cooperative buying associations, thereby going around the regular wholesale distributor

7. Manufacturers' attempts to sell directly to retailers and industrial users, in hopes of reducing expenses or of increasing or maintaining their volume of business

8. Use by manufacturers of facilitating agencies like warehouses for the maintenance of inventories from which to fill orders from retailers that are solicited directly by manufacturers' salesmen

Changing Pattern of Wholesaling. The wholesaler has been vigorously crowded as a result of these changes, which, in combination with the years of constant criticism by businessmen, economists, legislators, and the public at large, have made his position precarious. Partly yielding to the pressure from without and partly on his own initiative, therefore, the wholesaler of the old school has been obliged to find new methods. Some of these changes have been of an internal nature, such as a reduction in the number of parallel lines of merchandise carried, a constant alertness to technological developments that would enhance efficiency, the relinquishment of one or more of the usual wholesaling functions as a means of reducing operating expenses, or the development of private brands. Other changes have involved different external relationships with manufacturers on the one hand and with retailers on the other.

Some of the important changes within the field of wholesaling which have come about as the result of the changing economic conditions that were listed above might be summarized as follows: (1) the development of wholesalers who do not perform all the regular wholesaling functions; (2) widespread efforts of retailers and manufacturers to establish more direct methods of distribution by circumventing the wholesaler; (3) the integration of wholesaling with retailing and manufacturing operations, coupled with the horizontal expansion of wholesaling establishments under a single ownership and management; and, (4) the growth of retailer-cooperative and wholesaler-sponsored voluntary chain organizations.

Many of the wholesalers referred to in (1) above owe their existence to a modification or curtailment in wholesaling functions and services, and for that reason they have been called "limited-function" wholesalers. In that group belong the "drop-shippers" who do not take physical possession of the goods in which they deal, the "cash-and-carry" wholesalers who have largely eliminated credit and delivery services from their operations, and the "wagon distributors" who sell and deliver simultaneously from a truck which serves as warehouse and delivery vehicle combined.

Another development has been an increase in the number of manufacturers who as a result of special circumstances, dissatisfaction, misconceptions, or lack of knowledge have attempted to shorten channels of distribution for their products by going around the wholesaler and selling direct to the retailer or industrial user. This tendency has been accentuated by the practices of numerous large-scale retailers who have taken the initiative in attempts to go around the regular wholesale merchant by purchasing directly from manufacturers.

A third development, sometimes directed toward circumvention of the wholesaler and sometimes opposed to this end, has been integrated wholesaling: that is, the practice of combining wholesaling functions with other levels of business operation. Some manufacturers, in attempting to sell direct, have set up regular wholesale branches with stock and, not infrequently, have undertaken the wholesaling of noncompeting products of other manufacturers in order to utilize their facilities more fully. Large-scale retailers, such as department stores and chain stores, have integrated wholesaling with retailing activities by establishing their own wholesale warehouses and, in some cases or in some degree, by selling to other retailers as "semijobbers."

Integrated wholesaling has also come about as the result of actions of regular wholesalers who, being adversely affected by the direct distribution policies of certain manufacturers, have reached out and secured control of their sources of supply, manufacturing goods for distribution under their own private brands. To a more limited extent other wholesalers have gone in the opposite direction and have integrated their operations by the acquisition or direct establishment of retail outlets. Very often, successful attempts at vertical integration, as just noted, have led to a horizontal expansion of activities on the wholesale level of operation, giving rise to multi-unit concerns such as chain and branch house wholesalers. An additional development, somewhat related to each of the above, has been the rise of voluntary chain systems. One form of the voluntary chain has been developed by retailers who, by taking the initiative in meeting chain store competition, have attempted to cut costs by setting up their own cooperative wholesale establishments.

The second and more successful type of voluntary arrangement was brought into being by regular wholesalers who organized groups of independent retailers into a system functioning much like a corporate chain organization with the wholesaler furnishing advertising, sales promotion, store layout, accounting, and other types of assistance.

It should be emphasized that all these developments are very closely related, and that it is often difficult to draw sharp lines of distinction between them. For example, a retailer-cooperative voluntary organization may operate a limited-function wholesale establishment of the cash-and-carry type. Such an organization no doubt came into being as the result of a desire on the part of the retailer members to circumvent the wholesaler. Furthermore, it will have integrated wholesaling with retailing functions and, if operations are on a large scale, may also have entered into some manufacturing activity.

In the pages that follow, the important special types of limited-function wholesalers are given detailed consideration, while circumventing the wholesaler, integrated-wholesaling, and cooperative wholesale distribution form the subject matter of the next three chapters.

Not all wholesalers perform all of the recognized functions of the *regular* wholesaler discussed in the preceding two chapters. Some, indeed, have deliberately *limited* their performance of certain functions, either by modifying them or by shifting them backward to manufacturers and other suppliers or forward to retailers and other customers. Such wholesalers are designated, consequently, as *limited-function wholesalers*. It is important to keep in mind that a shifting of any essential wholesaling activity does not eliminate it and may result in less efficiency and higher *total* cost.

Importance of Limited-Function Wholesalers. Among the types of establishments classified by the U. S. Bureau of the Census as limited-function wholesalers are *drop shippers, wagon* or *truck distributors,* and *cash-and-carry wholesalers.*[1] The relative importance of these wholesale organizations has often been exaggerated because of their early rapid and dramatic growth. Their activities have attracted a great deal of attention because, in part, their development paralleled that of large-scale retail organizations, particularly corporate chains. The limited-function wholesalers came into prominence at a time when there was considerable dissatisfaction with traditional methods of distribution, and played their part in the far-reaching competitive adjustments which took place in many lines of trade. Another factor accounting for the disproportionate attention to limited-function wholesalers is found in their unusual and unorthodox methods of operation, which distinguish them from regular or service wholesalers.

After a period of rapid growth limited-function wholesalers have accounted for a stable or only slightly increasing share of total wholesale

[1] Data published by the U. S. Bureau of the Census also include retailer-cooperative warehouses as a type of limited-function wholesaler. These warehouses are not operated by independent wholesale merchants, however, and are not properly regarded as wholesalers. Hence, they are not treated in this chapter; and, wherever possible, adjustments have been made in Census data to eliminate them from data for wholesalers, although such treatment may be questioned when operated as corporate entities.

trade since the late 1930's. Trends in the number of establishments operated by such wholesalers and their volume of business can be ascertained from appropriate Census data:[2]

Year	Number of Establishments Operated by Limited-Function Wholesalers*	Sales of Limited-Function Wholesalers		
		Amount (000 omitted)	Per Cent of Total Wholesale Trade	Per Cent of All Wholesalers
1929	2,292	$ 601,077	0.9%	2.0%
1939	4,533	664,052	1.2	2.8
1948†	3,658	3,105,829	1.6	4.1
1954	8,633	3,871,693	1.6	3.8

* Include wagon or truck distributors, drop or direct-mill shippers, cash-and-carry wholesalers, and miscellaneous types such as mail order wholesalers. Original Census figures were retabulated to exclude retailer-cooperative warehouses; this adjustment for 1954 is based in part on estimates by the authors.

† Data for 1948 were retabulated on a basis comparable with the 1954 Census of Business, which excluded establishments without paid employees. This was not possible, however, for 1929 and 1939 data.

These figures indicate that while the number of establishments operated by limited-function wholesalers and their total sales volume have increased substantially, their *relative* volume of business status has increased only slightly since 1939 in relation to total wholesale trade and even declined somewhat between 1948 and 1954 in relation to sales of all wholesalers. This conclusion must be qualified, at least in part, because of changes in Census coverage. Thus, for example, the large increase in the number of limited-function wholesalers' establishments between 1948 and 1954 is probably more apparent than real, since the 1954 Census (taken by mail) covered many "nonrecognizable" places of business, not enumerated in 1948, which were listed in Old Age and Survivors' Insurance records as employers.

Despite this and other qualifications, the general conclusion to be drawn seems clear. Limited-function wholesalers as a class account for but a small part of the establishments and sales of wholesalers and of total wholesale trade, and have not changed significantly in relative importance in the post-World War II period. The reasons for this are best explained by examining each of the major types of limited-function wholesalers, since they differ fully as much from one another as they do from regular wholesalers.

Drop Shippers. The most important type of limited-function wholesaler in terms of sales volume is the drop shipper or "desk jobber." In 1954 there were about 2,600 establishments operated by drop shippers, with

[2] Statistics in this tabulation and other data employed in this chapter are based on information published in the Censuses of Business for the various years, unless otherwise noted.

total sales of approximately S2.2 billion. When a shipment of goods is made directly from the factory to a retailer or to an industrial user on an order secured by a wholesaler and transmitted to the factory, it is generally known in the trade as a *drop shipment*. Practically every wholesaler on occasion resorts to this practice; but when a wholesaler does the bulk of his business in that manner or fully specializes in such operations, he is designated as a *drop shipper, desk jobber, parlor wholesaler,* or *direct-mill shipper*. The drop shipper usually operates from an office, maintains no warehouses since he does not actually handle the goods, and, apart from the selling function, renders very little service to the manufacturer whose goods he distributes. He is a type of wholesaler, however, for he takes title to the goods which he orders from producers, assumes all risks incident to the ownership of such goods, extends credit to his customers on his own responsibility, and collects from his accounts. He operates most successfully in those lines of trade where the goods are economically bulky, and where the retailers or business users can buy in carload lots or in original packages, i.e., in units in which the manufacturer normally packs or ships his product.

Because of the limited number of functions performed, the costs of operation of a drop shipper are considerably below those of service wholesalers in the same lines of business. He passes back to the manufacturer the cost of maintaining warehouse inventories, and many other expenses incident to drayage, cartage, and the performance of administrative functions. The differences in operating expenses between drop shippers and regular wholesalers are particularly notable in bulky types of merchandise, such as lumber and building materials. In that line of trade, drop shippers in 1954 had a cost of doing business of 6.7 per cent of net sales, while regular wholesalers of lumber and building materials with yards operated at a cost of 12.5 per cent.

Despite the economies effected by eliminating physical handling and storage of the goods, drop shippers are confined to only a few lines of trade. This is because of the requirement that customers buy in substantial quantities, usually carload lots, to make direct shipment from mills or factories economical. Two lines of business, lumber and millwork and coal and coke, account for about 80 per cent of all drop shippers' establishments and an even higher proportion of their total sales. In coal the number of establishments and sales of drop shippers have decreased substantially, but this was due to an industry-wide decline rather than to any shift from drop shippers to regular wholesalers. Other bulky products in which drop shippers are of some importance include metals and metal work (mostly iron and steel scrap), petroleum and products, machinery and equipment, hardware, plumbing and heating, and furniture. A few also operate in the dry goods trade, where they solicit orders from a list of well-rated retailers at prices substantially below those charged by regular wholesalers.

It is claimed that drop shippers came into being largely because regular wholesalers failed to supply large-scale dealers with merchandise at reduced prices by this method. It is relatively easy to enter the drop shipment business, particularly in such lines as dry goods. A wholesaler's salesman who has been discharged or who has voluntarily severed connections with his house can secure sample cards from certain mills and solicit business, first from his old customers and later from others. To meet competition from drop shippers, regular wholesalers sometimes choose to cultivate their own drop shipment business since they can thereby reduce operating expenses and at the same time secure trade which might otherwise go directly to manufacturers. This method may also be used in the handling of "outs" and fill-in orders.

Drop shipment business, however, is not without disadvantages. Most retailers cannot buy in large enough quantities to justify such shipments unless it be on initial or preseason orders. Drop shipments are usually handled by regular wholesalers at lower prices than orders which are filled from warehoused stocks. In many cases the price reductions made on drop shipments exceed the cost savings involved, and such orders may actually result in net losses after proper allocation of all costs. Moreover, once price concessions are given to a customer on drop shipments, they may be expected on ordinary purchases. Such precedents may prove troublesome in later dealings. Finally, many manufacturers resent the general practice of drop shipment, for it requires the assumption on their part of additional functions. They prefer to sell to wholesalers in large quantities in anticipation of demand from retailers, and to transfer certain functions to the wholesaler who generally can perform them more economically and thereby reduce the manufacturer's own costs of storage, risk, packing, billing, and accounting.

In some lines of trade, as in plumbing, heating, building materials, or paper, drop shipments by regular wholesalers even in carload lots have proved troublesome. Anxious for volume and increased business, a wholesaler may sell a carload of merchandise to a contractor or dealer as a drop shipment on a 5 per cent margin when his margin on warehoused merchandise may be around 20 per cent. He justifies this action by assuming, first, that such sales represent "plus" business which he would not otherwise secure and, second, that the 5 per cent charge is adequate to cover costs and even yield a net profit. That neither of these assumptions is fully warranted is reflected in a provision in some of the Trade Practice Rules promulgated by the Federal Trade Commission that the differential of, say, between the 5 per cent and 20 per cent referred to above may result in a prohibited discrimination in violation of law.

Wagon Distributors. One of the types of wholesalers that has come into prominence in recent years, especially in the food trades, is the wagon distributor. This middleman, who at one time was regarded somewhat condescendingly as a wholesale peddler, is now generally designated as the *wagon jobber, truck wholesaler,* or *truck service distributor,* the newer appellations usually connoting his utilization of modern vehicles. Not unlike the ordinary service wholesaler, the wagon distributor performs the functions of buying (usually direct from manufacturers), of selling to retailers and institutions, of warehousing, and delivery. Occasionally, he extends credit to his customers, takes orders over the telephone, and renders other recognized wholesaling services. He differs from the regular service wholesaler principally in that he combines the functions of selling and delivery. Instead of first soliciting orders from the retailer and subsequently delivering the goods ordered, the wagon distributor sells and delivers simultaneously. Consequently, he maintains no separate sales force, the dual functions of selling and delivery being performed by salesmen-drivers. A second point of distinction is in the amount of business done on credit. Normally the wagon distributor sells for cash, collecting for the goods at time of sale. Another important difference lies in the variety of goods handled, the wagon distributor being confined to narrow specialty lines which require special promotion or handling.

Development and Present Status. Periodical literature has generally treated the wagon distributor as a development of the late 1920's. Others attribute the origin of the idea to Charles Fleischmann who, in the early 1870's, discarded the basket which was used for carrying orders of fresh yeast and substituted for it a horse and wagon driven by a uniformed salesman. As indicated in Chapter 5, however, wagon distributors, known at the time as wholesale peddlers or perambulating wholesalers, carrying a general assortment of articles, were prominent factors in the distribution of goods in New England in the early part of the nineteenth century, with some traces extending back even to Colonial days. Later, certain products came to be sold direct to retailers from wagons but the extensive development of this type of wholesale merchandising occurred after 1927.

Among limited-function wholesalers, wagon distributors are now second in importance in terms of sales volume and are the most numerous in terms of establishments. In 1954 there were 5,071 establishments with total sales of $1.4 billion. This compared with only 1,065 establishments (excluding those with no paid employees) in 1948 with sales of $147 million. The apparent increase in wagon distributors between 1948 and 1954 is quite misleading, however, on account of the previously mentioned change in the method of conducting the census.

Even with the better coverage obtained in the 1954 Census, the total number of wagon distributors is far less than estimates made by those in the trade. Various writers have estimated that there were as many as 10,000 wagon jobbers as early as 1930.[3] Apart from the fact that wagon distributors without separate places of business were not counted prior to 1954, several factors may explain the discrepancy between official figures and private estimates. One of these arises from the definition of wagon distributor which is employed. Private estimates no doubt include as wagon distributors *manufacturers* who sell to retailers by the wagon distribution method. Such companies as Standard Brands, Inc., Best Foods Corporation, and General Foods use trucks in marketing their products to the trade. In fact, the economies of distributing a fairly wide line of products simultaneously from a single fleet of trucks may have played a part in the mergers which created these companies.[4] Such manufacturers cannot be regarded, however, as *wagon distributors,* for they are not wholesalers, but are merely engaged in the distribution of their own products. The term "wagon distributor" applies properly only to *wholesalers* who buy goods from one or more manufacturers and resell them to their customers.

A second factor which may account for the disparity in the figures is the inclusion of *regular wholesalers* who distribute some of their products by methods resembling those of wagon distributors. These wholesalers should not be regarded as wagon distributors, however, since they do not specialize in such methods but employ them only incidentally.

Finally, some private estimates of the number of wagon distributors may be exaggerated as a result of confusion between the number of *distributors* and the number of *trucks* which they operate. While there are many distributors who have but a single vehicle, most of them have two or more and some organizations operate fleets of 75 or more trucks.

Products Handled and Methods of Operation. Wagon distributors operate principally in the food trade, over three-fourths of their establishments and sales being in this field. By its very nature wagon distribution is suited primarily to perishable or semiperishable products, such as frozen foods, dairy products, potato chips, specialty processed meats, and the like. Some wagon distributors also operate in the petroleum business, in automotive lines, and in the books, periodicals, and newspaper trade. A later development in the field is the *rack jobber,* a type of wagon distributor who handles nonfood lines sold mainly in food stores of the supermarket type, including housewares, paper products, health and beauty aids, apparel, toys, and hardware. There were about 800 to 1,000 rack jobbers handling

[3] H. A. Haring, "What the Wagon Jobber Can/Can Not Do for the Manufacturer," *Advertising and Selling* (May 14, 1930), 20.
[4] Frank M. Bass, "Wagon Jobbing in Modern Distribution," *Current Economic Comment,* Bureau of Economic and Business Research, University of Illinois, XV, No. 3 (August, 1953), 36–43.

these lines in the late 1950's, almost all of them concerns established after World War II.[5]

The common characteristics of products handled by wagon distributors include a need for frequent distribution, specialty selling, and regular servicing of displays; high margins; and (in the case of the rack jobber) unfamiliarity of the retailers with the products and their trade channels. Most wagon distributors handle very narrow lines of merchandise and can presumably give them special attention, which regular wholesalers cannot do because of the large number of items which they typically carry.

Wagon distributors purchase goods from manufacturers and call on their customers at regular intervals, each truck making 35 to 50 calls a day. In some cases large territories are covered, the drivers returning to headquarters only on week ends. At each store visited, the driver inspects the displays of his goods, refills them from the stock in his truck, sets up point-of-purchase promotional materials, and discusses new items with the customer. Sales are usually made for cash, but some kinds of wagon distributors sell on what amounts to a consignment basis, collecting on each visit only for goods sold since the previous trip. In either case the distributors commonly assume all merchandising risks, since they take back unsold merchandise. Rack jobbers "rotate" merchandise among their customers, attempting to sell items in one store that fail in another.

Advantages. One of the big advantages claimed for this method of wholesaling is the ability to apply specialty selling to the products carried. This involves calling the retailer's attention to each of the products handled by the salesman-driver; a determination of the quantities of each product the retailer should carry in his store; proper adjustment of intervals between calls to the needs of each retailer, and special care to see that only fresh and salable goods are kept in the retailer's stock, and that such goods are properly displayed.

Another advantage of the wagon distribution method of wholesaling is that it enables the retailer to buy in small quantities, thus keeping down his overhead; increasing his stock turnover by, placing it on a weekly basis on the items sold; and offering the consumer fresher merchandise. Since the wagon distributor calls on his customers at frequent intervals, at least once a week, there is no need to overstock. It is to the interest of the driver-salesman not to overload the dealer.

Wagon distributors may also provide certain services to customers which they would otherwise be required to perform themselves. Rack jobbers, for example, usually price-mark their goods before putting them into the stores. The drivers actually put the goods on the shelves, which is normally done by stock boys or by the proprietor in a smaller store. In

[5] *National Directory of Rack Jobbers* (2d ed.; Detroit: Gale Research Co., 1957), contains 840 listings, a few of which are branch establishments.

some cases the distributor provides the display itself, although it is now more common for stores to maintain uniform fixturing of their own rather than use the jobber's "rack." It is also claimed that the rotation of goods among stores makes possible the offering of a much greater number of items in limited floor space, which is especially important in the case of nonfood lines handled by supermarkets, many of which are of an impulse character.

Costs and Other Disadvantages. It is frequently claimed that the wagon distributor, through his combination of selling and delivery, affords an economical method of wholesaling. Logic is drawn on to show why certain economies are effected through this type of wholesale distribution. Among the reasons given are that one man is used for both selling and delivery; that one motor vehicle is used for both purposes; that only one trip is required for the performance of the two functions; that orders are subject to but a single handling; that cash sales are facilitated, and hence fewer administrative expenses are incurred as a result of credit and collection activities; that deterioration of samples is somewhat less than that of ordinary salesmen; and that record-keeping and accounting procedure are simplified. It is also pointed out that wagon distribution involves practically no rent charges and storage costs, since the place of business may consist only of a garage for the housing of the trucks, together with a little surplus merchandise. When the goods are of a perishable nature, they may be stored in a public cold-storage warehouse. From these many advantages claimed for the wagon distributor it might be expected that his costs would be considerably lower than those incurred by other types of wholesalers. This is not true, however. The data available from the Census of Business indicate that wagon distributors experience operating expenses above those incurred by general line wholesalers who provide the full range of regular wholesaling services.

It has already been pointed out that the majority of wagon distributors operate in the grocery trade. In this field the operating costs of regular general line wholesalers are about 8.2 per cent of sales, whereas the expenses of wagon distributors, as a class, are over 14 per cent of sales. Data from the first Census of Business, which provided a breakdown of operating expenses of wagon distributors by line of business, showed that such distributors had considerably higher operating expenses in both the dairy products field and in the petroleum trade than did regular full-service wholesalers. An outstanding exception to this generalization was in the tobacco products business where regular wholesalers incurred operating expenses well above those of wagon distributors.

Some explanation for the relatively high operating expenses of wagon distributors may be found in the very combination of functions which are alleged to make for economy. In the first place the driver-salesman is often a poor businessman, having had very inadequate training. Many of them were originally drivers of delivery trucks for wholesalers or manufacturers who, when their savings permitted, bought trucks and went into business for themselves, capitalizing upon their knowledge of the trade. Incidentally, it might be mentioned that this, no doubt, accounts for the fact that a driver is usually required to sign an agreement not to enter business in his territory for a certain period of time after he severs connections with his employer. An additional element of increased cost grows out of the fact that the wagon distributor is forced to let his expensive vehicle stand idle much of the time while he makes sales and arranges the stock in the stores.

The relatively high operating expense of wagon distributors should not, of course, be interpreted as an indicator of inefficiency. Higher costs are to be expected in view of the special services given by these distributors, who probably resent their classification as "limited-function" wholesalers. Rack jobbers, in fact, designate themselves as *service distributors.*

From the manufacturer's point of view, there are also several advantages and limitations to the use of wagon distributors as their wholesale outlets, except as supplements to the usual type of wholesaler. In the first place it is frequently difficult to establish connections with these distributors, particularly the small ones, since many of them are not listed or classified anywhere, usually possess no office, and are constantly out on the route. Most trucks are loaded and on the way by 7:00 A.M., returning to the warehouse or garage between 6:00 and 7:00 P.M., making it hard for a manufacturer's salesman to contact them. Furthermore, since many of the wagon distributors operate on a small scale and are not usually well established, the manufacturer assumes considerable risk in extending credit on goods sold. Again, the ability of driver-salesmen to do specialty selling for the manufacturer has been considerably overrated. The long hours that are required of driver-salesmen in order to make from 35 to 50 calls per day, the heavy physical labor, the need to make minor repairs on the vehicle, and the requirement to wear a uniform are some of the drawbacks that militate against the employment of good salesmen by wagon distributors. Most of these handicaps hold true even for the independent operator who owns and operates his own wagon or truck. It is for this reason that manufacturers who have adopted this method of distribution do not rely on it altogether to open new accounts or to introduce new products, but employ true specialty salesmen for the purpose.

Cash-and-Carry Wholesalers. As the term implies, cash-and-carry wholesalers sell for cash only (do not extend credit) and do not deliver the goods to their customers. This type of wholesaler grew out of the turbulent competitive conditions of the late 1920's, in which independent retailers were feeling the first real impact of the chains. Despite an impressive beginning, cash-and-carry wholesalers have never succeeded in obtaining a very large share of total wholesale trade. In 1954 there were only 922 cash-and-carry establishments, with total sales of less than $300 million. This reflects a substantial relative decline from 1948, when 978 establishments made total sales of over $350 million.

While some cash-and-carry establishments operate independently, most of them are units of multi-unit firms. In the grocery trade, for example, out of a total of 291 cash-and-carry depots, 170 (58 per cent) were in multi-unit firms of 25 or more establishments.

The typical cash-and-carry establishment has few employees (average about 3 per establishment) and renders a minimum of services to its customers. Merchandise lines are restricted to fast-moving staples. Outside salesmen are usually not employed and little is spent for advertising, price circulars being the usual medium. Thus several important functions are curtailed in addition to those of credit and delivery.

Because of these limited services such houses have lower operating costs than those incurred by full-function wholesalers. Inasmuch as the chief appeal of cash-and-carry wholesale houses is that of price at the expense of service, their patronage comes largely from the smaller retailers who are facing unusually keen competition from chain stores, and whose time is not fully occupied by the selling end of their business. That is probably why the grocery and food trades account for about 30 per cent of the cash-and-carry establishments and about 50 per cent of the cash-and-carry business of the country. Many of the remaining houses are in the tobacco trade.

In the grocery field, cash-and-carry wholesalers had a cost of doing business in 1954 of 4.2 per cent as compared to an average cost of 8.2 per cent for service wholesale grocers. In the handling of tobacco and its products, the operating expenses of cash-and-carry houses have been correspondingly lower than those of regular tobacco wholesalers. Thus, through the curtailment in stock assortment, the elimination of salesmen, and credit and delivery service, and through the reduction in general administrative expenses which such restricted service entails, cash-and-carry wholesalers are able to reduce their expenses by a third or one-half of those incurred by regular wholesalers. Consequently, the prices of many staple commodities charged by such houses vie successfully with those charged by retailer-owned cooperatives, and in some instances are considerably lower. Limited inventories confined to staple merchandise are advantageous in that they tend to minimize any possibility of stock accumulations and obviate the necessity for any elaborate system of stock control.

Against the somewhat lower prices of the cash-and-carry wholesaler must be set up certain disadvantages, such as the cost to the retailer of driving his own motor vehicle to the wholesale branch, of paying cash, and of consuming time which may be utilized to better advantage in the management of the store. The service necessarily lacks appeal for the retail merchant who desires credit accommodations, convenience of buying under one roof small quantities of many types of merchandise, advisory service from salesmen, delivery service, or the advantages accruing from a concentration of purchases. These are some of the definite limitations to the further development of this type of wholesaling and may have been responsible for its slow growth to date. From a general economic point of view one must also keep in mind the fact that the cash-and-carry method of wholesaling does not result in an absolute decrease or in the elimination of function; it merely transfers some of the wholesaling functions to the retail merchant whose cost of performing them may be considerably higher. Moreover, if such method of wholesaling should expand, it would tend to increase the service wholesaler's cost of doing business, inasmuch as it would reduce his volume in the staple, fast-moving items. Thus it is conceivable that whatever the retailer would save in patronizing the cash-and-carry wholesaler in the purchase of staples may be consumed in the higher prices charged for nonstaple merchandise obtainable from regular wholesalers.

In summary, it might be pointed out that probably the greatest good which has come from this method of merchandising has been the awakening of the service wholesaler to the realization that expenses must be reduced in order that goods may be sold to retailers at lower prices. Looking at the problem objectively, there seems to be no reason why a well-conducted service wholesale house cannot, in an orderly manner, fill 500 orders, for example, and deliver them to as many different merchants more cheaply than the 500 merchants can secure the goods themselves by coming to the cash-and-carry branch in an unsystematic and hurried fashion.

Mail Order Wholesalers. Mail order wholesaling, which eliminates the personal salesman, is a type of limited-function wholesaling that has been steadily declining in importance in the United States for some time. By 1930 there were but 41 mail order or catalog wholesalers who sold all or the bulk of their goods by mail, by methods similar to those used by mail order houses in the retail field. By 1940 the Census of Business no longer provided a separate classification for such establishments. Some concerns, however, still operate successfully on a mail order basis. One Milwaukee house, for example, is said to have sold $33 million worth of goods in 1956, and issues an annual catalog listing some 18,000 items. Such mail order houses sell primarily to small-town retailers, including general stores, which cannot stock adequate assortments in all lines and utilize the wholesaler's catalog to make sales that would otherwise be lost. Frequently, the retailer acts only as a "catalog order office" on these transactions, and the wholesale catalog may be used to create an atmosphere of discount selling on such items as small electric appliances.

Mail order wholesaling is of little importance today because of changes in the conditions that made it originally feasible. Improvements in transportation had a dual effect on mail order operations. First, customers were lured away from the rural general stores which were always the most important market for mail order wholesalers. Second, salesmen of regular wholesalers were enabled to extend their sphere of operations and reach many retailers in smaller towns and rural areas. The development of chain stores and voluntary chains further accentuated the difficulties of mail order wholesaling. Consequently, many mail order firms began sending out representatives, first as "good will men" and later as full-fledged salesmen. Some of these concerns became quite successful as regular wholesalers, notably the Butler Brothers house which sponsors the Ben Franklin voluntary chain of variety stores.

Mail order wholesalers generally have higher expenses than regular wholesalers, despite their elimination of field salesmen. Moreover, little service is obtained by retailers from mail order companies. The retailer must make out his own order, is unable to examine samples of the goods before buying, and then must wait for the goods to be shipped. As a result, mail order selling in the wholesale field is now largely confined to "fill-in" orders which must be placed by the retailer between the regular calls of the wholesaler's salesman. This method of selling is also used to some extent by regular wholesalers who wish to provide service to small retailers whose purchases are not large enough to warrant the expense of a salesman's call. This may be an economical method of serving such customers, if catalogs do not have to be revised too frequently.

11

INTEGRATED
WHOLESALING

In preceding chapters the various types of wholesalers operating in the present-day economy have been analyzed and evaluated. Attention may now be turned to the specie of *integrated* wholesaling in which the independent middleman is circumvented, and his functions are assumed by others.

While it is common to think of the wholesaler as occupying a place in the "regular" or "usual" channel of distribution, such a middleman is by no means always used. Indeed, less than one-half (about 45 per cent) of all manufactured consumer goods and about 20 per cent of industrial goods are sold through wholesalers. This means that, overall, in any one year wholesalers handle between 30 and 35 per cent of all manufacturing output, since consumer and industrial goods are normally of about equal volume importance at f.o.b. factory prices. The remainder, comprising about two-thirds of all output, does not require the performance of wholesalers' functions or is marketed through one or more of the channels designated herein as integrated forms of wholesaling. By "integrated" it is meant that the task of wholesaling is combined in ownership (and often in physical facilities as well) with manufacturing, retailing, or both. It involves the incorporation within a single business organization functions that are normally performed by separate and distinct business entities. Strictly speaking, this should be termed *vertical* integration, as distinguished from the *horizontal* integration of units on the same level of distribution, such as multi-unit wholesalers of the chain or branch types.

Forms of Integrated Wholesaling. Several distinct methods are used in circumventing the wholesaler. At one extreme, integration may serve to eliminate both wholesalers *and* retailers, as when a manufacturer sets up his own retail stores or sells by mail or through house-to-house canvassers to ultimate consumers. This form of integration is relatively uncommon, accounting for only about 4 per cent of all manufactured *consumer* goods. It is of considerable importance in certain lines, however, including men's suits, shoes, and tires.[1]

A more common form of integrated wholesaling occurs when a manufacturer sells directly from the factory to retailers or business users. Sales may be made by mail or by salesmen who travel out of a central sales office. Sometimes, customers visit the factory to make purchases, as in the ready-to-wear apparel trade where buyers come to a central market. In any event, some provision must be made for wholesaling the goods at the factory, including storage, order assembly, performance of necessary services to customers, granting of credit if needed, and so on. About a third of all consumer goods and more than two-thirds of all industrial goods are marketed at the wholesale level in this manner.

A third form of integrated wholesaling involves the operation of separate *wholesale establishments* under the ownership of the manufacturer. As shown in Table 4 in Chapter 6, there were 22,590 manufacturers' sales branches in 1954, accounting for over 28 per cent of total wholesale trade as encompassed by the Census concept. Sales branches handled about 10 per cent of all consumer goods and 12 per cent of all industrial goods. These data in reality understate the importance of manufacturers' sales branches, since they do not cover the oil refining industries. Wholesale establishments owned by refining companies are shown in the table as "Petroleum bulk plants, terminals" rather than as manufacturers' sales branches. Of the total of 29,189 bulk plants, 17,837 (or 61 per cent) were owned by refiners, accounting for 68 per cent of all bulk plant sales. If these are added to the manufacturers' sales branches in other industries, this form of integrated wholesaling represents about a third of total wholesale trade.

A final type of integrated wholesaling is found in the operation of *wholesale establishments* by retail organizations. Sales by manufacturers to these establishments are included in the figures previously given for sales by manufacturers to retailers, so that the importance of this channel cannot be measured separately. Some idea of its quantitative status may be gotten, however, from the data in Table 4 for chain store warehouses. These establishments handled 4.7 per cent of the total wholesale trade in 1954. Not included in this figure are department store or mail order

[1] For further discussion of direct-to-consumer marketing, see T. N. Beckman, H. H. Maynard, and W. R. Davidson, *Principles of Marketing* (6th ed.; New York: The Ronald Press Co., 1957), pp. 136–37, 247–52.

house warehouses, both of which are essentially similar to the facilities operated by chains.

As may be apparent from the foregoing brief descriptions, the various forms of integrated wholesaling differ from one another *functionally* fully as much as they differ from independent wholesalers, and in some cases much more. The circumstances in which these methods are used are also quite different, as will be shown in the following analyses of reasons for circumventing wholesalers and conditions favoring direct relationships.

REASONS FOR CIRCUMVENTING THE WHOLESALER

Direct contact between retailers or industrial users on the one hand and manufacturers on the other may be initiated by either the buyer or the seller for a variety of reasons. In general, five principal motives account for direct manufacturer-retailer or manufacturer-industrial consumer relationships. They are (1) the nature of the goods, (2) desire for economy, (3) competition, (4) dissatisfaction with the wholesaler's method of distribution, and (5) pressure from retailers and industrial users.

Nature of the Goods. Direct distribution may arise, for example, from the perishability of goods. As perishable commodities should be sold in the shortest possible time, the reduction in the number of handlings is often attempted. Perishability may be due to progressive physical deterioration of the goods. Thus, in the distribution of such goods the wholesaler occupies an inferior position, as the manufacturer seeks to sell the goods directly to retailers or even to ultimate consumers, or he may operate his own wholesale branches. Such distribution practices are designed to speed the movement of the product. Furthermore, they are desirable because they enable the manufacturer to safeguard the good will of the consuming public by preventing the sale of stale and unsuitable merchandise.

Perishability may also lie in the depreciation in the value of goods because of changes in style. Millinery and women's ready-to-wear, in general, decline in value within a short time because of frequent changes in style. Here, too, time is the very essence of profitable distribution; consequently, direct channels of distribution flourish. In ready-to-wear, because of the extreme style risks, only small quantities are produced in advance of a season. Samples are shown to retail store buyers, and if enough orders are secured, a cutting is made. Even after the beginning of a season, retailers order only in small lots for experimental purposes, then later reorder the styles that are accepted by consumers. It is almost inconceivable that this process of trial orders and reorders, with the need for speed in filling them, could be handled through the medium of a wholesaler. Hence wholesalers, unless they also engage substantially in manufacturing, are important only in the marketing of the more staple kinds of ready-to-wear, such as house dresses.[2]

A similar situation exists in the marketing of shoes. It is estimated that only about 15 per cent of the total output of shoes passes through wholesalers.[3] While some of the remainder is warehoused by manufacturers and by retail chains, the bulk of it is shipped directly from factories to stores in order to capitalize on rapid changes in styles.

Another aspect of the product which may lead to the circumvention of wholesalers is the need for technical services. This is especially true in the industrial field, where major capital installations require highly trained factory representatives for sales and installation. Often such goods are built to order or practically so, and direct contact is absolutely essential. They may also require repair and maintenance services which can best be supplied by the manufacturer.

Service requirements may also be important in consumer goods. In the tire industry manufacturers' sales branches were established at the outset partly because there were few competent servicemen available.[4] Similar considerations arise in the marketing of automobiles, electrical appliances, and many other products.

Desire for Economy. A manufacturer may be prompted to go around the wholesaler in the hope of reducing his costs and thereby increasing his own net profit. To do this, he strives for greater volume than he feels he can secure from the wholesaler, who may not push the sale of the former's goods. In his desire to reduce the costs of marketing, the producer errs when he assumes that going around the wholesaler automatically results in the elimination of the wholesaler's functions. The fact of the matter is that when a manufacturer sells directly to retailers he assumes the wholesaler's functions himself, thus actually entering the wholesaling business; or else he transfers them to the shoulders of the retailer. Whether the manufacturer or the retailer will assume the services formerly rendered by the eliminated middleman depends largely upon their relative strength and position. Because of their adequate financial resources and warehousing facilities, large-scale retailers (such as chain stores, department stores, and mail order houses) may assume at least some of the wholesaler's functions, particularly those of warehousing, assembling, and credit, provided they can secure the goods at prices low enough to justify the performance of these functions. If the manufacturer sells to small retailers, he must ordinarily assume the wholesaling functions himself.

---

[2] John W. Wingate and Raymond B. Voorhees, in Richard M. Clewett (ed.), *Marketing Channels for Manufactured Products* (Homewood, Ill.: Richard D. Irwin, Inc., 1954), pp. 346–50.

[3] William Girdner, in Richard M. Clewett (ed.), *op. cit.*, p. 296.

[4] Warren W. Leigh, in Richard M. Clewett (ed.), *op. cit.*, pp. 124–25.

Regardless of who assumes the wholesaler's functions under a more direct method of distribution, costs incident to their performance must be incurred. The question, then, is whether they will be higher or lower, i.e., one of relative efficiency in the performance of the task. Ordinarily, it is assumed that direct sale invariably spells lower costs and hence lower prices to customers. Whether this is true or not depends upon a great many factors, some of which are analyzed and evaluated in this chapter. At this point suffice it to state that the wholesaler *usually* has an economic advantage which results in direct marketing actually costing *more* rather than less. The reasons for this have been explained in earlier chapters. Basically, they revolve around the fact that the wholesaler performs essential functions on behalf of his suppliers and customers, which in his absence they must perform for themselves. Because he performs these functions for many manufacturers and customers simultaneously, the wholesaler is able to simplify the task of distribution, i.e., reduce the total amount of work to be done. Moreover, because he operates on a large scale, the wholesaler is able to specialize and thus to perform his functions with maximum productivity and greater efficiency.

Despite the logic of the foregoing analysis, many manufacturers, retailers, and industrial users believe that direct marketing is *inherently* more economical than distribution through wholesalers. Thus one paper manufacturer, advertising a new policy of direct sale and delivery, claimed that "Double freight, double warehousing, and double sales expenses are eliminated." A careful examination of the discussion in Chapter 8 will show the fallacy of this appeal. There is, in fact, every reason to believe that freight, warehousing, and selling costs will be *greater* under direct selling. Nevertheless, the superficial "common sense" of the thesis that eliminating the middleman eliminates his costs still has its effect.

It is not meant to imply that wholesalers *always* have an advantage over others who seek to assume their functions. In subsequent pages many contrary examples will be cited. Moreover, the fact that two-thirds of all manufactured goods are distributed without wholesalers belies any assertion that wholesalers are inevitable. Still, in the absence of compelling evidence to the contrary, it must be assumed, especially in the area of consumer goods, that wholesalers can do the job of marketing at the wholesale level more efficiently and economically than alternative channels.

In many cases it may be questioned whether the expressed desire for economy is the true motive for going around the wholesaler. Usually there are other reasons for making the change, such as the impact of competition, and the plea of seeking greater economy is used to rationalize the action taken.

Competition. In recent years the steady growth of large-scale manufacturing has made the competitive struggle increasingly severe. While most manufacturers operate on a small scale, a substantial amount of our fabricated products comes from relatively few factories controlled by still fewer companies. Such large-scale production demands wide markets, and the resulting competition for business becomes keener and keener. Not only does a large-scale producer compete with small-scale producers, but he must also compete with other giant enterprises in the same line of business, and in other industries, all of which are striving to secure a portion of the consumer's dollar. To attain success in this competitive struggle, some manufacturers believe it necessary to secure more direct control over the distribution of their goods. Some have gone so far as to sell directly to consumers and thereby retain control over all marketing activities while others have been satisfied to reduce the number of links in the chain of distribution and to sell to retailers.

The desire for control over marketing at the wholesale and retail levels is generally associated with the development of heavily advertised brand names. In industries dominated by a few large manufacturers, each promoting a branded and differentiated product, the need for coordinated advertising programs and intensive sales promotion activities leads to dissatisfaction with wholesalers and sometimes to their elimination. A good example is afforded by the household washing machine industry in the 1920's. In 1921 an estimated 60 per cent of output was sold through wholesalers and only about 40 per cent went direct to dealers. Most manufacturers at this time were small and their brand names had little acceptance. During the ensuing years, "as distribution widened so that markets for various brands overlapped, competition between manufacturers became inevitable . . . manufacturers had to replace wholesalers by extending the scope of their direct-to-dealer operations."[5] As a result, by 1928 only 15 per cent of output went through wholesalers, the remainder being sold direct to dealers and to ultimate consumers.

This process tends to become a vicious circle. A manufacturer first feels that he must control the market in order to dispose of the large quantities which he wants to produce. He needs the larger demand to enable him to reduce his costs and his prices. As soon as a substantial demand has been created, he is fired with ambition to expand his operations still further in hopes of again reducing the per-unit cost of production, increasing his profits, and becoming a leader in his industry. The effect is cumulative, and success at one stage gives rise to the necessity for additional demand and still greater control of the market. The process may indeed continue until it falls of its own weight, since there is a limit in the competitive struggle beyond which it is unsafe to proceed. After a certain point is reached, costs no longer decrease, and increased demand means reduced profits.

[5] Anthony E. Cascino, in Richard M. Clewett (ed.), *op. cit.,* pp. 183–84.

Dissatisfaction with the Wholesaler's Method of Distribution. Quite frequently a manufacturer decides to go around the wholesaler because he is dissatisfied with the latter's services and general attitude toward his goods and policies. Several charges have been laid at the door of the wholesaler on this score, such as (1) lack of aggressive selling, (2) general apathy toward the manufacturer's advertising and sales promotional program, and (3) pushing his private brands at the expense of the manufacturer's competing brands.

Lack of Aggressive Selling. The manufacturer who is unsympathetic toward the wholesaler channel of distribution often claims that his products are not cultivated intensively, that his product is not aggressively represented, that insufficient time is devoted to the sale of his goods, that the wholesaler's salesmen are mere order-takers and sell what the trade demands without attempting to direct or influence such demand in favor of the manufacturer's products.

Insofar as these allegations are directed to the general line wholesaler, their general validity must be recognized. Such a wholesaler carries a wide assortment of merchandise consisting of thousands of items coming from hundreds of factories. Since it is the wholesaler's function to supply any commodity for which there is a demand, he is forced to handle many competing or parallel lines of merchandise. This militates against the possibility of applying specialty selling technique to any one item. It is a physical impossibility for his salesmen to devote any considerable amount of time to each item on every call upon a customer or prospect. Few, if any, salesmen could be expected to know the merits of all products in a general line wholesale establishment, so as to present an adequate number of talking points concerning each item. Constant and ceaseless effort is required to keep the salesmen acquainted with some of the merits of a few selected lines of merchandise handled by such a wholesaler.

There are, however, conditions under which it is legitimate for the wholesaler to cultivate the field intensively for a particular product line. It would be unfair and discriminatory to push the goods of one manufacturer at the expense of those of another, unless some particular inducement is offered as compensation. A wider margin of profit may be offered the wholesaler by the manufacturer; the product may enjoy a better reputation and hence sell more readily; or it may be handled by the wholesaler on an exclusive agency basis in his territory. Under these conditions the wholesaler may be justified in concentrating his efforts on the sale of a given product because vendors of competing goods have the prerogative of utilizing similar methods.

A manufacturer can also take other steps to secure and retain the cooperation of wholesalers in his promotional programs. Specialty salesmen may be sent out from the factory to work with the distributors' salesmen, or "missionary" men may be sent to retailers, sending any orders obtained back through the wholesaler. Another frequently used measure is to establish and publicize a policy of selling only through wholesalers.

Apathy to Manufacturer's Promotional Activities. The wholesaler has also been accused of indifference to the manufacturer's advertising and sales promotional work, sometimes bordering on hostility and antagonism. He is particularly charged with failure to cooperate in the distribution of dealer-helps to the trade and with neglect to synchronize his sales effort with that of the manufacturer. Such an attitude on the part of the wholesaler may be explained by his desire for self-preservation. If the manufacturer's advertising and other sales promotional activities result in an increased demand for his products, he may insist that his goods be handled on a smaller margin or else he may go around the wholesaler. Enough such instances can be cited in justification of this fear. Had it not been for the successful demand creation for its products it is quite unlikely that the Procter & Gamble Company would have attempted in the early 1920's to sell directly to retailers, a policy which was pursued for several years but subsequently modified because of its failure to solve the distribution problem. The action of the Winchester-Simmons Company at about the same time, equally unsuccessful, is another example. While in both instances the companies returned largely to the wholesaler method of distribution, there were attendant losses for the wholesaler as well as for the manufacturer.

The basic explanation of the friction between manufacturers and wholesalers regarding promotional activities lies in the very nature of the wholesaler's operation. It is virtually impossible to give what most manufacturers regard as "adequate cooperation" to each and every one of the numerous suppliers served, especially in convenience goods fields. Consequently, while wholesalers may favor aggressive promotion because of its effect on stock turnover and sales volume, they are seldom able to participate in it as fully as manufacturers would like.

Competition from Private Brands. Many wholesalers carry some goods under their own labels. Naturally, such merchandise is pushed by the sales force in preference to articles bearing manufacturers' labels, particularly since private brands are generally used on the most profitable kinds of merchandise. Manufacturers resent and oppose this practice, feeling that it is direct competition, since a wholesaler who emphasizes his own brands ceases to that extent to serve as a distributor for manufacturers' brands. While this method estranges the manufacturer, the wholesaler is reluctant to abandon his private branding policy, and the problem continues as a great source of annoyance.

Desire of Retailers and Industrial Users To Buy Direct. Quite frequently the manufacturer is forced to sell direct instead of through wholesalers because of the pressure brought to bear upon him by retailers and by larger industrial consumers. In the hope of securing the goods at lower prices, department stores, mail order houses, and chain stores attempt to purchase directly from producers. Even the small retailers often combine into cooperatives for the same purpose. Similarly, contractors buy appliances for new homes directly from manufacturers. These demands may be so insistent that manufacturers are forced to circumvent their regular channels against their wishes, or large-scale direct purchases may be regarded as "plus business" which would not be obtained otherwise and handled on a very narrow gross margin.

Large-scale retailers who buy direct usually assume the wholesaler's functions themselves and set up integrated wholesale divisions. This form of integration is examined in more detail at a later point in this chapter.

Conditions Favoring Direct Manufacturer-Retailer Contacts

Motivated by the factors described above, many manufacturers have undertaken to go around the wholesaler, but with varying degrees of success. Unless conditions of manufacturing and customer-buying definitely favor direct contact, circumvention of the wholesaler is neither feasible nor economical. The conditions which favor direct contact may conveniently be summarized in five categories: (1) the nature of the product, (2) the circumstances of the manufacturer, (3) the character of the retailer or business user market, (4) availability and competence of wholesalers, and (5) availability of partial substitutes for the wholesaler.

Nature of the Product. As indicated in the preceding section, the nature of the product is one of the reasons for attempting to short circuit the wholesaler. Sometimes the nature of the product makes it *necessary* to sell direct, as in the case of made-to-order items, perishable goods, and high-style merchandise. In other cases product characteristics make it feasible, but not necessary, to go around the wholesaler. One such characteristic is *high unit value.* Generally speaking, the higher the unit value, the more practical it becomes to sell direct to retailers or industrial users, because orders for even small quantities of such goods represent sizable dollar amounts and hence may justify the costs of direct contact.

It should be noted in this connection that the higher unit value of such products as automobiles, appliances, or furniture, merely diminishes the wholesaler's *relative* advantage, but does not eliminate it altogether. This may be illustrated as follows: suppose the cost of calling on retailers is $5 per salesman's visit. Obviously such a high cost would prohibit direct selling by a manufacturer of a tobacco item who might obtain orders for only about $10 per call, while the tobacco wholesaler can secure an order for a number of items amounting to, say, $100. On the other hand, the producer of an item worth $100 may be able to get a much larger average order from retailers—say, $200—which brings the percentage of selling cost down within reason. Nevertheless, the wholesaler may still have some advantage. He might obtain an average order of $500 from the same retailers, which would make his selling cost still substantially lower than that of the direct-selling manufacturer. The *relative* advantage is less, however, which may be enough to encourage direct marketing, especially in the presence of other motivating forces.

For many mechanical products of high unit value, installation and repair services must be made available and supplies of replacement parts maintained at convenient points. For these reasons, it is argued, it is best for a manufacturer to establish and maintain direct connections with retailers. Not only that, but such relations should be as close as possible, frequently attained through exclusive agency agreements. An example of this belief is to be found in the practices of furniture manufacturers who sell about two-thirds of the output direct to retailers.

Many manufacturers of commodities of high unit value continue to utilize wholesalers despite these alleged reasons for direct selling. In the electrical appliance field, for example, there has been a trend toward increased use of distributors since the end of World War II. In this and certain other trades the wholesaler typically handles a manufacturer's line on an exclusive agency basis in a territory which is cultivated intensively. The explanation given for selling high unit value commodities through wholesale distributors is fourfold. First, the wholesaler obligates himself in advance to dispose of a certain quota of the product, which leaves the manufacturer free to plan his production according to a definite schedule. Second, the wholesaler provides financial assistance, either directly through loans and advances or indirectly through purchases on short terms followed by prompt payment. The wholesale distributor is also in a better position to maintain satisfactory repair service in his territory than are the retailers. Finally, manufacturers have found that distances from retailers make it extremely difficult to select proper and adequate representation, and to supervise their work. If the wholesaler is relied upon, these matters can be delegated to him, since he is in close contact with the trade.

Circumstances of the Manufacturer. The position of the manufacturer has a direct bearing on the feasibility of going around the wholesaler. Among the factors conducive to direct selling are large-scale production, routinized production, manufacture of a long line, and capable management.

Large-Scale Production. No small manufacturer can afford to market his goods directly to the retail trade unless his market is confined to his immediate locality. The size of his plant and his limited output do not permit him to organize and maintain a sales force of sufficient size to cover the trade adequately. The expense of direct distribution would prove prohibitive and handicap the producer competitively. Even when the manufacturer operates on a fairly large scale and wishes to experiment with direct methods of marketing, he may be precluded from carrying out his wishes by lack of financial resources. It requires considerable capital to maintain an adequate sales force to call upon retailers and to finance the latter's purchases on the usual credit terms. The manufacturer's financial weakness often makes it imperative that he rely on the wholesaler's assistance, and when this is coupled with small-size operation the wholesaler becomes practically indispensable.

Routinized Plant Operation. The condition of a manufacturer's plant organization may be a determining factor in choosing channels of distribution for his products. If the organization is in its early stage of development, preoccupied with manufacturing problems, it behooves him to leave the marketing task to the wholesaler. If, however, the work of the plant has become fairly routinized, authority for its supervision may be delegated to a responsible factory manager, which leaves the general management ample time to delve into possibilities of modifying and altering the existing method of distribution. The feeling may be strong that, inasmuch as the manufacturing problems have been solved satisfactorily, there is no reason why the marketing problems cannot be solved equally well. The fact is often overlooked that the techniques of marketing and manufacturing are quite different.

Manufacture of Long Line of Merchandise. Most manufacturers are highly specialized, short-line producers, making a single item or a very limited number of items. Under these conditions, other things being equal, direct distribution is not feasible except at rather high cost. It should be avoided unless very unsatisfactory selling conditions make improved distribution at almost any cost essential to the success of the business. This explains the use of wholesalers in the fur trade, for instance, despite the importance of the fashion element.[6]

If, on the other hand, a long line of products is sold by one manufacturer, large orders can be obtained from retailers or industrial users. This may justify the costs of direct contact in the same way that high unit value does. In some companies this consideration is of sufficient importance to encourage the filling out of a line via mergers or diversification from within. A wave of mergers in the electrical appliance industry in the 1940's and 1950's was attributed in part to the marketing advantages derived from full-line manufacturing. Similarly, the acquisition of a line of

[6] John M. Wingate and Raymond B. Voorhees, in Richard M. Clewett (ed.), *op. cit.,* p. 356.

cake mixes and a line of paper products by the Procter & Gamble Company facilitated direct contact by it with retailers.

The number of manufacturers that produce complete lines, or families of related products, which are capable of supporting the cost of direct cultivation of retail trade is small indeed. Examples are furnished by producing organizations which have resulted from mergers, such as the Standard Brands Company and the General Foods Company, or by such large corporations as the General Electric Company and the Westinghouse Electric Corporation. It is interesting to note, however, that while the completeness of the lines produced by such organizations makes direct contact with retailers possible and economical, they have apparently found that indirect distribution for many of their items is even more economical, as witnessed by the fact that large quantities of their goods flow through wholesalers' warehouses.

Capabilities of Management. A practical consideration that must be taken into account when decisions are made regarding the use or nonuse of wholesalers is the kind of management personnel available to a manufacturer. Even when other considerations seem favorable to the operation of an integrated wholesaling system, if executives are strictly factory-oriented and lack marketing "know how," it may be best to sell to wholesalers and let them assume the task of marketing management. Conversely, if capable executives with experience and aptitudes in the field of marketing are available, a company may undertake its own wholesaling activities despite some unfavorable circumstances. This, however, should never be the *major* consideration in arriving at such a decision.

Character of the Market. For most manufacturers it is impractical to sell direct because of the dispersion of the market and the small quantities in which retailers and industrial users normally purchase. For others, the nature of the market is such that these problems do not arise. This may result from sale to large-scale retailers or users, quantity purchases by small retailers, sale to a small number of customers, or geographic density of the market.

Large-Scale Buyers. Chain stores, department stores, mail order houses, and certain stores handling shopping and specialty goods, ordinarily buy a share of their merchandise directly from manufacturers at wholesaler prices, or through representatives, such as resident buyers, agents, and brokers. In the grocery trade, for example, some manufacturers classify as "direct accounts" any group of five or more stores with a warehouse. The exact dividing line is often difficult to determine, but size is usually the governing factor.

Large-scale retailers buy in large quantities, secure quantity and other discounts, obtain economies in transportation, may be able to store the goods as efficiently as a wholesaler, and retain for themselves the whole-saler's net profit. In fact, their savings may be even more substantial, because they need not employ wholesale salesmen or create outlets for the goods they buy, and are often able to secure special allowances for advertising purposes. Moreover, they obtain favorable credit terms including large cash discounts, and succeed in passing on to the manufacturer some of the wholesaling functions while retaining the wholesaler price advantage. Whether a manufacturer is justified in giving such preferential treatment to some of the large-scale retailers is a much disputed question that is discussed elsewhere in this book.

Large-scale buying is even more common among industrial users. Many of the manufacturing concerns, railroads, mining companies, public utilities, and other customers in the industrial market operate on a very large scale and buy in correspondingly large quantities. The situation is further accentuated by the common practice of buying many raw materials and supplies on a forward basis, i.e., on contracts covering up to a year's requirements in advance. Purchasing agents for industrial users often insist on dealing direct on large purchases, even when these are out of the ordinary run of business. Needless to say, the loss of business on occasional large transactions is damaging and irksome to wholesalers, who are frequently left to handle the "cats and dogs" parts of the business. In general, it appears to be an unwise policy for a manufacturer to deal direct with industrial users on *occasional* large purchases because of the resulting ill will with distributors. On the other hand, if a buyer regularly purchases in substantial quantities, direct contact may well be desirable.

Quantity Purchases by Small Stores. Large retail organizations are not the only ones to buy in substantial quantities. Many small retailers buy cooperatively in groups or through a resident buyer, and obtain the advantages incident to large-scale buying. Others purchase in large quantities individually and independently because of the nature of the merchandise in which they specialize. Men's clothing stores are an illustration. Even the relatively small store in that line of business can buy in large enough amounts to warrant direct contact with the manufacturer.

In the first place, such a store generally confines its stock of merchandise to the product of a single manufacturer, often on an exclusive agency basis. Occasionally, two or more nationally known brands are combined, but seldom is it necessary for men's clothing stores to buy from a large number of manufacturers.

In the second place, the goods are seasonal in character. This means that a substantial proportion of the merchant's requirements for the entire season is bought at one time, generally when the manufacturer's representative makes his visit. "Fill-in" orders for the remainder are placed almost automatically by mail as the exigencies of the season's business demand. Furthermore, producers of such goods as men's clothing generally manufacture a complete assortment of sizes, styles, and colors, so that the consumer's needs may be satisfied by the retailers with the products from a single source of supply.

What has been said about stores specializing in men's clothing also applies to stores handling shoes, furniture, typewriters, automobiles, electrical appliances, and musical instruments. Only the less expensive varieties of these goods are usually sold through the wholesaler, except when they are intended for the small country store, when other factors militate against direct-to-retailer selling, or when the wholesaler is used as a supplementary channel.

Small Number of Customers. Direct selling may be feasible when only a small number of customers is to be served. In the consumer goods field this is often true when a manufacturer distributes on a highly selective basis, i.e., to a single store or a few selected stores in a given community. One manufacturer of costume jewelry, for instance, covers the entire United States with only three salesmen. No calls at all are made in cities of less than 100,000 population, and in larger cities only a few stores are chosen. In effect, the manufacturer is "skimming the cream" from his particular market. Similar policies are often adopted by producers of specialty goods such as musical instruments, but for a different reason. For these commodities the total number of potential retail outlets is small and close cooperation is needed with retailers for effective servicing and promotion.

Direct marketing to a limited number of customers shows up even more clearly in the industrial field. If a manufacturer produces an item used only in a particular industry, which itself is highly concentrated in a few plants, wholesalers are superfluous. Thus, suppliers of parts and semi-manufactured goods to the automobile industry almost always deal directly with the few customers for their goods.

Geographic Density of the Market. Other things being equal, it is more feasible to go around the wholesaler when the manufacturer sells in a densely populated area than in a market where population is sparse and retailers are widely scattered. Even small retailers dealing in convenience goods might be cultivated with reasonable economy in populous communities. Goods can be shipped in carload lots to such a market, from which they are distributed to the stores by truck with stops at short intervals. Under such conditions the maintenance of local warehouses may be warranted as well as the employment of salesmen to solicit the business. Thus, direct selling in the New England, New York City, and Chicago markets may be practical, while an attempt to follow a similar policy in other parts of the country might prove burdensome and expensive.

Geographic density, like large-scale buying and small number of customers, is more characteristic of the market for industrial goods than for consumer goods. An over-all measure of this concentration is the fact that almost two thirds (64.83 per cent) of the total value added by manufacture in 1954 originated in 64 major metropolitan areas in the United States.[7] In individual industries, markets may be even more confined. Textile mills are concentrated in New England and a small section of the South; automobile manufacturers are highly concentrated in the Detroit area. Furthermore, Census data do not fully reflect the geographic density of some industrial markets. In many industries most of the corporate headquarters, where actual purchase decisions are made, are located in a single city.

Availability and Competence of Wholesalers. Some manufacturers have established branch wholesaling systems largely because they were unable to find enough interested and competent wholesalers to handle their products. The shift to direct selling of washing machines in the 1920's, for example, was attributed in part to the "apathetic, disinterested approach of the wholesaler."[8] This is no doubt explained by the fact that washers were a side line at that time, being handled by hardware, farm implement, and other types of wholesalers not primarily concerned with or dependent on the new item. Similar reasons have been given for the establishment, during the same period, of a system of branch warehouses by one of the largest manufacturers of electrical apparatus and supplies.

In a broader sense any wholesaler faces the possibility of elimination from the channel of distribution if he does not perform his functions with reasonable efficiency. While critics of the wholesaler have exaggerated the problem, many wholesalers have been and are guilty of failure to change traditional methods quickly enough. This was no doubt a contributing factor in the rapid growth of the chains with their integrated warehousing systems in the grocery field.

Availability of Partial Substitutes for the Wholesaler. Apart from the possibilities of taking over the wholesaler's functions or shifting them to customers, some manufacturers have been able to utilize the services of organizations which take on part of the task. Physical distribution activities may be provided by a *public merchandise warehouse,* while selling may be done by a *functional middleman.*

Public Merchandise Warehouses. A public merchandise warehouse, as the name implies, offers storage space and associated services on a fee basis. In 1954 there were 1,197 warehouses primarily engaged in storing general merchandise (as distinguished from household goods, farm prod-

---

[7] Based on a special computation by the authors from basic data contained in the *1954 Census of Manufactures.*

[8] Anthony E. Cascino, in Richard M. Clewett (ed.), *op. cit.,* p. 183.

ucts, and the like) with total occupiable floor space of over 108 million square feet.[9] Such warehouses are found in every large city and in many medium-sized communities. They provide the manufacturer with a flexible substitute for his own branch warehousing system and a number of additional services as well.

The basic services of the public merchandise warehouse are storage, order filling, and delivery. The manufacturer can rent space for the maintenance of local or "spot" stocks at as many distribution points as he desires without making any capital outlay or committing himself to a lease. The amount of space used can be contracted or expanded as conditions warrant; it is thus more flexible than space provided in owned or leased warehouses. Under the public warehouse system it is just about as economical for the manufacturer to maintain 100 small stocks of goods close to his customers as 10 large stocks farther removed from them. This circumstance makes it possible for the manufacturer to ship goods as far as possible in carload lots, effecting important savings in transportation charges. As warehouses are located along railroad sidings or docks, intermediate transportation and handling charges are usually eliminated. Merchandise which has already been sold by the manufacturer may be shipped to the warehouse as a "pool" car, i.e., a car containing merchandise for several customers. Such a car is broken by the warehouseman and delivered or reshipped immediately to customers. In the more usual case the manufacturer ships merchandise to the warehouse, where it is stored until sold by the manufacturer's salesmen or until it is ordered from the warehouse by customers. The use of an "accredited list" of customers makes it possible for the warehouse to provide immediate delivery service upon receipt of a customer's order, without awaiting instructions from the home or branch office.

Since many warehouses are in a position to guarantee overnight delivery service within a radius of 400 to 500 miles, it is usually much easier and more economical for a manufacturer to make his goods conveniently available to customers by using public warehouse services than by establishing a number of his own branch houses. Furthermore, in the public warehouse the cost of storage and handling is on a unit basis. Thus a large part of the distribution expense is exactly known in advance, because such costs are a fixed amount per unit of product instead of varying with the volume of business as is true when the manufacturer provides his own facilities.

The use of public warehouses instead of branch houses solves many administrative problems for the manufacturer who sells direct. He is provided with the services of trained personnel experienced in the handling,

[9] *1954 Census of Business,* Vol. III, *Wholesale Trade—Summary Statistics* (Washington, D. C.: Government Printing Office, 1957), p. 11–21.

storage, and delivery of goods, but without the worry of added personnel problems. Risks of physical deterioration may be reduced through the specialized facilities of the warehouse. Since most warehouses are of modern construction and are provided with sprinkler systems and watchmen, insurance rates are frequently lower than for a company-operated branch. The manufacturer's financial problems may be simplified by the use of the warehouse receipt. This instrument has full negotiability and has become recognized as a valid security acceptable to all banks. Warehouse receipts issued on stored goods which are not required for immediate sale may thus serve as the basis for easily obtained working capital loans.

In acting in a "branch house capacity" for manufacturers, public merchandise warehouses have developed a wide range of special services. Many of them have office space for rent. The use of this space permits the client's sales force to keep a close watch over the stock of goods, making sure that such stocks do not get too low nor out of line with sales possibilities. Some warehouses also have display rooms where customers may be shown goods which cannot be carried about by salesmen. Breaking of packages and the storing of technical repair parts in open bins are commonly rendered services. In addition, most merchandise warehouses will repackage, weigh, and stencil merchandise. Furthermore, they make C.O.D. collections, render accounting service, make rough sales or market analyses, provide traffic information, supply jobbing or dealer lists, and develop other types of services and facilities according to the needs of their manufacturer clients.

The distribution service which is rendered by warehouses has had the effect of increasing the territory of operation of many manufacturers and has increased the amount of direct selling by permitting manufacturers to substitute the warehouseman for the wholesaler without establishing branch houses. It may also have the effect of reducing the number of manufacturers' branches with stock for the simple reason that the warehousemen, operating on a large scale in all strategic distribution centers, can provide more rapid service in a more economical manner than can the great majority of manufacturers.

The factor limiting this type of distribution is that other conditions already enumerated must be present in order that it may be economically feasible or possible for the manufacturer to set up his own selling organization. The warehouseman offers no substitute for the performance of the buying, selling, credit-granting, and risk-bearing functions of the regular wholesaler. Thus he cannot be expected to supplant the wholesale merchant in the distribution of the great bulk of the convenience and shopping goods flowing from typical manufacturing enterprises. In fact, the public merchandise warehouse is not always used to circumvent the wholesaler. Some manufacturers, whose typical sales to jobbers are too small to justify carlot shipments, utilize warehouses to *facilitate* rather than supplant a program of nationwide distribution through regular wholesalers.

Functional Middlemen. Whereas the public warehouse is a substitute for the wholesaler's *physical* distribution functions, functional middlemen may be used as substitutes for his *selling* function. The various types of agents and brokers and the circumstances governing their use are discussed in Chapter 13. At this point it should be emphasized that even when *both* public warehouses and functional middlemen are used in selling direct to retailers or industrial users, some of the wholesaler's functions still remain to be assumed by the manufacturer himself. Neither the warehouseman nor the agent is ordinarily equipped to handle problems of product service or credit extension. Moreover, their services are sometimes open to the same objection as the wholesaler's, namely, lack of cooperation and limited interest in the manufacturer's promotional programs.

OPERATION OF WHOLESALE ESTABLISHMENTS BY MANUFACTURERS AND RETAILERS

Conclusive proof of the essential character of wholesaling functions is found in the experiences of manufacturers and retailers who have, for one reason or another, eliminated wholesalers. Often these direct-selling manufacturers and direct-buying retailers find it necessary to set up wholesale establishments separate from their main places of business and under separate management. As indicated in Chapter 6, these establishments are properly regarded as part of the wholesaling structure and have been treated as such in this book.

Manufacturers' Sales Branches. Among the larger manufacturers who have adopted policies of direct selling, the use of branch warehouses or sales offices has developed largely as a substitute for the wholesaler. Sales branches have increased substantially in number and in both absolute and relative sales importance since 1929. By 1954 this segment of the wholesaling structure accounted for over 28 per cent of the total business of all wholesale establishments.

Types of Branch Systems. Three distinct types of manufacturers' branch wholesaling systems may be distinguished: (1) the branch-sales-office system that carries no stocks but ships directly from one or more factories; (2) the completely decentralized branch-house-sales system with sales staffs, warehouses, and full-function wholesaling services; and (3) the branch-sales-office system that carries limited stocks, usually in a public merchandise warehouse.

Under the first system the manufacturer divides his market, which may be regional, national, or world-wide, into districts. In each district a sales office is established in the leading wholesaling city with a district sales manager in charge and a staff of salesmen under him. The degree of autonomy extended to the district sales manager varies. Usually the district manager is responsible to the general sales manager of the company for results in his territory.

In general, these offices specialize in the selling function, although frequently they are expected to service the accounts, especially where the product is complicated. The normal procedure for such sales offices is to secure orders that are filled at the factory and shipped directly to the customer. The branch-sales-office system does not, as a rule, entirely displace the wholesaler. Often the wholesaler is supplemented by the sales office system. Occasionally orders are taken that are routed to the nearest wholesaler for filling. More frequently the sales offices are restricted to a few large-volume wholesaling centers, wholesalers being used in other parts of the country where large volume is harder to secure.

The second type, the completely decentralized branch-house-sales system, may divide the market into regional, district, and even local wholesale territories. In each wholesaling center a warehouse and sales office are maintained, the size depending upon the requirements of the market. Usually the physical plant is undistinguishable from that of a large, progressive, independent wholesaler in the same line of business. The location is in the wholesaling district of the city adjacent to rail, water, or truck transportation facilities. The warehouse is designed to maintain adequate stocks of the company's products and oftentimes related noncompetitive items obtained from other manufacturing sources. To this extent manufacturers' sales branches act in the capacity of regular wholesalers. The predominance of one company's products is indeed the chief differentiation from the regular wholesaler. Trucks and delivery systems, the sales department, the credit and collections department, the accounting office—all are typical of the more modern of the regular wholesale houses.

Where such branch-house systems are used, normal practice is to allow the regular wholesalers to list the products of the manufacturer but not to stock them in any large quantities. Rather does the wholesaler rely upon the stocks locally carried by the branch house, "picking up" such quantities as he needs to fill orders. The wholesaler is allowed a special discount on such purchases. As a rule, however, he makes little effort to sell the product, limiting his activities to filling orders that customers prefer to give to him rather than to the manufacturer's branch house.

The third type of manufacturer's branch wholesaling system, that of sales offices with limited supplies of stocks, is a compromise between the first and second methods of achieving integrated distribution. Less expensive than the complete all-function branch system, it adds to the more limited functions of the branch office system a local source of supply of the company's products. Arrangements with public warehouses are flexible enough to permit the manufacturer to supplement his field sales offices with as much storage, warehousing, and delivery service as the territory warrants. Of the three systems, the last seems to offer the greatest economy coupled with adequate service for all but the very largest manufacturers who feel the urge more fully to integrate wholesaling activities with those of manufacturing.

The relative importance of these three types of branch systems cannot be measured exactly from Census data. The Bureau of the Census distinguishes only between sales *branches,* which maintain facilities for the storage and handling of goods, and sales *offices,* which do not. Included in the latter category, presumably, are offices which sell goods stored in local public warehouses as well as those shipped from the factory or its own warehouses. In 1954, 14,759 or 65.3 per cent of the 22,590 manufacturers' branches had stocks, and these accounted for 52.9 per cent of the total sales volume of the two types combined.

Operating Expenses of Sales Branches. One of the principal reasons for attempting to go around wholesalers is the belief that this will result in lower marketing costs. The validity of this assumption may be tested in part by a comparison of costs under alternative channels, i.e., the wholesaler vs. the sales branch.

Direct comparisons of wholesalers with manufacturers' sales branches in terms of operating expenses are difficult to make. For all kinds of business combined, regular wholesalers had total operating costs in 1954 of 14.2 per cent of sales, as against 10.5 per cent for sales branches with stocks. These figures are in no sense comparable, however, largely because of the great difference in products represented. Sales branches are known to handle a much greater proportion of industrial goods, for example, which are of higher unit value and are bought in larger quantities, which would result in lower percentage costs. For this and other reasons valid comparisons can be made only for establishments handling similar product lines and operating under similar conditions with reference to types of customers served and the like. This kind of comparison is frustrated for the most part by the Census Bureau's use of different kind-of-business classifications for the two classes of establishments.

A rough comparison can be made between regular wholesalers and manufacturers' sales branches in only two lines of trade. Branches with stocks operated by manufacturers of food and kindred products had total costs of 10.3 per cent in 1954, compared with 7.5 per cent for general line grocery wholesalers and 9.6 per cent for specialty line grocery wholesalers. The lower expenses of wholesalers, especially those handling a general line, clearly reflect the economies of spreading such expenses as selling and administration over many different items, which few manufacturers are in a position to do. In the general purpose industrial machinery field, on the other hand, sales branches with stocks incurred expenses of 18.0 per cent of sales, somewhat lower than the 20.8 per cent for wholesalers in the same field.

If appropriate data were available, it is probable that most manufacturers' sales branches would generally be found to incur somewhat lower costs than those of wholesalers in the same lines. An analysis of 30 lines of trade in 1948 showed that in 19 this was so. There are several reasons for this. For one thing, manufacturers' sales branches do not perform the wholesaler's buying function, inasmuch as all or most of their goods are furnished by the parent company. Credit may be centralized at headquarters, and its cost not allocated to the branches. Another factor leading to lower costs is that a substantial proportion of their business is with other wholesale organizations and industrial consumers who buy in large quantities. Furthermore, some manufacturers have set up branches to "skim the cream" by selling direct to the large retailers and to the stores or industrial users located in concentrated markets while leaving the wholesaler to do the more expensive job of cultivating smaller and more scattered customers.

Retailers' Warehouses. Large-scale retailers may physically assume wholesalers' functions by a process of backward vertical integration, in which they establish warehouses with facilities for buying, storage, and delivery to stores. This is common practice among chain organizations, department stores, and mail order concerns. Smaller retailers achieve somewhat the same end by participating in retailer-owned cooperatives, which are discussed in the next chapter.

Chain Store Warehouses. Physically the typical chain store warehouse has the appearance of a wholesaler's warehouse or a manufacturer's branch warehouse handling the same kind of merchandise. The chief difference is that the accounting department is larger, since the accounting records for all of the retail units of the chain in the territory covered by the warehouse are handled in the warehouse, which also houses the general headquarters staff of the chain or district. The location is in the wholesaling section of the market center, adjacent to transportation facilities. Incoming merchandise is unloaded from cars or trucks and stowed in the appropriate department, ready for order filling. Because of its later development, the typical chain store warehouse is more modern than the typical wholesaler's place of business, making use of the latest developments in labor-saving equipment such as conveyor systems, lift trucks, pallets, and accounting devices.

Chain store warehouses are also similar to independent wholesalers in their functions. They do some central buying, maintain stocks, break bulk, deliver and bill the merchandise to the retail outlets, operate an accounting department to keep records of purchases and deliveries, and employ a supervisory force of store inspectors which works in much the same manner as the sales force of the typical wholesaler. These supervisors do not normally make sales or take orders, but they do perform the important function of liaison officers and keep the warehouse headquarters informed as to the actual marketing conditions and new developments in the field.

There are several important differences between chain store warehouses and regular wholesalers. For one thing, for more than 80 per cent of the goods handled by the chain store warehouse there is no selling problem, for the goods are delivered to the retail units of the same company. For the same reason, there is no problem of making credit investigations or of bad debt losses. Again, a considerable proportion of the goods handled by the retail stores of a chain does not pass through the warehouse but is drop-shipped by manufacturers and other suppliers directly to the stores. This practice minimizes the amount of handling, storage, and breaking of bulk in the warehouse, since these functions are shifted back to the suppliers. Another difference arising from the integration of wholesaling with retailing is the better coordination which can be achieved between the two, especially on ordering procedure and delivery schedules and routes. The economies of this coordination are so important that many wholesalers have emulated them in their sponsorship of voluntary chains discussed in the next chapter.

On account of these differences chain store warehouses typically have lower operating expenses than do regular wholesalers. In the general line grocery business, for example, chain store warehouses operate on expenses of 4 per cent or even less of their sales and billings. Since only about 80 per cent of "sales and billings" actually passes through the warehouse, this is really equivalent to about 5 per cent of sales. Regular wholesalers in the same trade have total expenses of about 8.2 per cent of sales. On the other hand, progressive wholesalers sponsoring voluntary chains appear to function with fully as much productivity as the best of corporate chains. All of this suggests that there is no *inherent* economic advantage for chain store warehouses in terms of operating efficiency.

Department Store Warehouses. Unlike the chains, which have one warehouse to service many retail outlets, the department store may have two or more warehouses to service the one large retail store. Thus it is common for the larger department stores to have separate furniture warehouses, service warehouses, and one or more storage houses for other merchandise. Department stores handle such a wide range of merchandise and such a large volume that separate warehouses are necessary to permit large scale purchasing. Moreover, the seasonal character of many lines necessitates purchasing large quantities in advance and storing them against the time the season opens.

Physically the department store warehouses are similar to wholesalers' warehouses and to chain store warehouses in both appearance and layout. Differences lie mainly on the shipping side of the operation. The department store warehouse not only supplies the various departments in the main store with shelf stock and such reserves as may be required close at hand but also has the problem of delivery to the ultimate consumers. Especially is it customary for department stores to make deliveries of furniture and other bulky merchandise from the warehouse, using the floor exhibits only as sales aids. Unlike the chain system, the accounting departments and credit and collection offices on the retail level are usually found in the department store proper rather than in the warehouse; only a minimum of stock records, receiving records, etc., is maintained at the department store warehouse.

Mail Order Warehouses. Perhaps nowhere in the marketing system has the wholesaling function been more effectively integrated into other activities than in the mail order houses. The larger of such concerns have developed the conveyor belt system to a high degree of perfection. From the handling of incoming letters to the shipping of the filled orders, an efficient, smoothly functioning system of mass distribution of a widely diversified line of merchandise has been achieved. Merchandise arrives in carlots at the warehouse, which is located in the wholesaling center close to rail or other means of transportation. Goods are routed to designated areas in the building where they are stored in such a way as to permit easy access to them in filling orders. A high rate of turnover on most items insures a steady flow into and out of the warehouse. Standardization and simplification of all operations from order-handling to final shipment characterize the work of the larger and more successful mail order operators.

INTEGRATION BY WHOLESALERS

Manufacturers' sales branches and retailers' warehouses illustrate vertical integration *into* wholesaling by others. In some lines of business it is also common for wholesalers themselves to engage in vertical integration either forward into retailing or backward into manufacturing.

Integration into Retailing. Some wholesalers actually operate retail stores, either as outlets for their merchandise or as "model" stores in which merchandising methods may be tried out. Much more common is the wholesaler who makes a portion of his sales to ultimate consumers out of his wholesale establishment. Such a wholesaler is designated as a "semijobber."

The term "semijobber" is also used in another sense, to apply to a retailer who engages to a limited extent in the wholesale business. In various Census of Business years, almost 2 per cent of all the business reported by retail stores has consisted of sales to other retailers, or strictly wholesale business. The automotive trade has occupied a prominent position in this type of business, followed by stores in the food classification. The retailer has assumed the wholesaler's functions in certain lines of trade in order to augment his volume of sales and to secure jobber prices from manufacturers. Retail sales frequently being limited, the enterprising retailer may endeavor to dispose of his surplus purchases to smaller merchants in his community. When such an experiment has proved successful, his jobbing ambitions sometimes lead him to issue a modest catalog, and perhaps also to employ a traveling salesman to sell to smaller merchants in neighboring towns. He thus becomes known as a wholesaler and is placed by manufacturers on the jobbers' list, which entitles him to certain discounts. These lower prices, however, are not apt to be justified by the quantity he buys or by the amount of actual wholesaling he does, since most of his goods are still sold at retail through his retailing establishment. Furthermore, under the Robinson-Patman Act, he is entitled to the functional discount only on the merchandise he resells at wholesale. Frequently, small stores are responsible for the development of wholesaling by larger establishments. It may begin by the small merchants calling for pickups from the larger stores, which in the end develops into the habit of buying small quantities from such sources regularly.

In some lines of trade, the integration of retailing and wholesaling has caused considerable difficulty and strained trade relations. Jewelry wholesalers often take advantage of their central location in the community and sell substantial quantities of goods at retail though they do not ostensibly operate retail stores. Naturally, retail jewelers resent this practice and have, at their various conventions, seriously considered steps to curb the practice. Wholesale jewelers feel the same way about retailers in that business who sell to other stores. Manufacturers, on the other hand, are called upon to sell to retailers at "jobber" prices, receiving little practical service for their concessions.

Unless the wholesaler maintains separate establishments for his retail business, his semijobbing practice may result in the loss of trade from retailers who resent such competition. For this reason a wholesaler may operate retail stores in one territory and sell at wholesale elsewhere, thus avoiding direct competition with his retailer customers.

At best the entire practice of semijobbing, especially when the two functions are combined in the same establishment, may be seriously questioned on historical and economic grounds. It will be recalled that in the early days of the evolution of the wholesaler these two functions were generally combined, but since the middle of the last century a complete segregation of functions was found profitable and economical. Semijobbing may, therefore, be regarded as a backward step which is justified only under special circumstances.

Integration into Manufacturing. For some years there has been a growing tendency for wholesalers to do a certain amount of manufacturing in their wholesaling establishments, in separate plants of their own, or have it done by other producers under the wholesaler's label. Many wholesale grocers roast their own coffee, grind spices, package preserves, and engage in light manufacturing generally. Other wholesalers who produce some of their own goods are the confectionery wholesalers, a number of jewelry wholesalers, and most drug wholesalers. This is particularly true of the larger concerns located in the major distributing centers.

In the wholesale grocery trade, manufacturing activities are encountered more frequently and amount to a larger proportion of total sales among specialty wholesalers than among those handling a general line of groceries. In the paint and varnish business the number of manufacturing wholesalers is small, but some of those who do manufacture have a considerable sales volume on their own products. Manufacturing by wholesalers in such lines as hardware is rarely encountered, probably because few items of this type can be produced without the benefit of expensive machinery and substantial plant equipment. Again, as in the grocery trade, the practice is more common among specialty concerns than among general line houses. In conclusion, it may be said that manufacturing by wholesalers is not general, but is confined to certain lines of trade. Furthermore, it is largely restricted to operations which can be carried on economically on a small scale without the aid of expensive installations.

12

COOPERATIVE
WHOLESALE
DISTRIBUTION

One of the most important developments in the field of marketing since 1900 has been the continued growth of various types of large-scale retailers. Commencing with department stores in the 1860's and their rapid growth during the first decade of this century, a series of waves has spread over the retail merchandising system, including the mail order houses in the early 1900's and their rapid growth following World War I, the tremendous expansion of chains in the 1920's, the advent of supermarkets in the 1930's, and the development of discount houses in the late 1940's and in the 1950's. Each of these has had its impact on wholesaling. As indicated in the preceding chapter, the increasing importance of large-scale retailing not only injures the small retailer but also adversely affects his chief supplier, the regular independent wholesaler. Large-scale retailers often buy direct from manufacturers, may organize their own wholesale establishments, and invite the growth of manufacturers' branch wholesaling systems.

The response of independent retailers and wholesalers to these competitive developments has taken several forms. Some have attempted to take refuge in sponsoring restrictive legislation, such as chain store taxes and resale price maintenance laws. The lessons of history show, however, that this is a poor defense and at best but temporary economic crutches, though invariably the first reaction to unusual competitive developments. Legal restrictions are in themselves or in the long run seldom effective in the face of changes in basic economic conditions, and such has proved to be true in twentieth century America just as in other times and places.

Fortunately, not all independent retailers and wholesalers placed their reliance on propaganda and legislation. Many of them early recognized that mass distribution had innate advantages and was becoming firmly entrenched in our economy. Large numbers of them turned to methods of self-help, with the idea that the answer to their problems was not in eliminating the advantages of the distribution giants, but in obtaining for themselves through a massing of strength, quantity discounts, advertising allowances, access to important advertising media, modernized store operations, the assistance of specialists, and the like. Thus it was that cooperation on the wholesale level of distribution came about; it is one type of defensive or response mechanism of the independent wholesaler or retailer in his struggle for self-preservation against new forms of competitive strength, particularly the corporate chains.

Degrees and Types of Cooperation. Cooperative organizations on the wholesale level are of two types, the classification depending upon who organized and continues to control the organization. The first type consists of retailers who take the initiative and act cooperatively by themselves in obtaining advantages in buying, advertising, or in the performance of other merchandising activities. The degree of cooperation within these associations may range from a loose relationship among a group of merchants who combine their efforts to form a *buying pool,* to a highly complex organization which performs all the marketing functions itself. In the grocery, drug, and hardware trades, informal buying pools have failed in so far as meeting chain store competition in general is concerned, and therefore they have not become of quantitative significance. In the dry goods, clothing, and furniture trades, cooperative buying has been more important. The term "buying group" is in common use in these lines of business.

The *most complex* form of retailer cooperation, as found particularly in the grocery trade, involves the ownership and operation of a wholesale warehouse on a cooperative basis. Such an organization is called a *retailer-owned cooperative.* The individual members contribute capital, elect a board of directors to manage the wholesale establishment and to coordinate activities, and share whatever profits there may be, on a patronage basis. Generally, retailer-owned cooperative warehouses operate on a limited-service basis, similar to the cash-and-carry wholesaler. In the drug business, the term "mutual" is somewhat erroneously applied to such organizations. It arises from its use in the title of the Mutual Drug Company of Cleveland and other cities. Such companies, while having many cooperative features, are not strictly cooperatively owned enterprises. Retailer-owned cooperatives are also often erroneously designated as "retailer-owned wholesalers," both in the trade and by the Bureau of the Census. This terminology is misleading; a *wholesaler* is an independent middleman, which retailer-owned cooperatives may not be so considered.

When a wholesaler takes the initiative and induces a number of retailers to affiliate with him contractually for purposes of cooperative action in buying, advertising, or other merchandising activities, the resulting organization is known as a *wholesaler-sponsored voluntary chain*. In these associations the wholesale house remains under private ownership. Usually, the sponsoring wholesaler and the independent retailers enter into a formal written agreement. Retailers may obligate themselves to do such things as to promote the sale of private brands furnished by the wholesaler, concentrate a substantial proportion of their total purchases with the sponsor, use standardized accounting systems, and to cooperate in the sale of advertised merchandise at the stipulated prices for the period covered by the advertising. For their part, wholesalers, in addition to providing all the regular wholesaling services, may agree to provide merchandising advice, assist in store modernization, furnish merchandise that may be used as sales leaders, prepare advertising and sales promotion campaigns, and provide uniform accounting systems for the members. Thus sponsoring wholesalers usually provide even a greater variety of services than the regular wholesalers. The retail members of organizations of this kind maintain stores which are more uniform in appearance, and their operations usually resemble more closely the operations of a corporate chain system than is true of retailer-owned cooperatives.

Similar to the wholesaler-sponsored voluntary in many respects is the *corporate chain with voluntary affiliates*. The difference lies in the fact that instead of a wholesaler sponsoring the retail outlets, a chain organization franchises them as supplements to its own outlets. An example is the Western Auto Supply Company, which owns some 365 stores but has 3,600 "associate stores" or independent franchised stores in 47 states and the District of Columbia as of early 1957. The services provided by the chain organization are similar to those furnished by the wholesaler in a regular voluntary group.

Both retailer-owned cooperatives and wholesalers sponsoring voluntary chains engage in a further degree of cooperation through their participation in *federations* or *alliances* of such organizations. These central agencies make a further pooling of buying power possible, especially for merchandise sold under a common private brand. In addition, the federations are active in promoting and advertising the private brands of the group and in obtaining advertising allowances from manufacturers. Another service involves the carrying on of research activities and the employment of merchandising experts for the benefit of the entire group. Furthermore, most of them publish a weekly or monthly house organ, and sponsor periodic conventions or meetings for their affiliated members.

The most notable examples of federations are the Independent Grocers' Alliance, which includes about 50 wholesalers and 6,000 retail stores and the National Retailer Owned Grocers' Association, with a reported 25,000 member stores.

Development and Present Status of Cooperative Wholesaling. From the outset, cooperative wholesaling has been associated primarily with the grocery trade, because of the intense competition that has existed between independents and chains in this line of business. The development of retailer-owned cooperatives preceded that of the wholesaler-sponsored chains. The oldest existing retailer-cooperative in the grocery trade is the Baltimore Wholesale Grocery, which was organized in 1887. It was followed closely by the Frankford Wholesale Grocery Company, organized in Philadelphia in 1888. At almost exactly the same time similar organizations were beginning to appear in the drug trade.

The first wholesaler-sponsored voluntary chain was the General Purchasing and Distributing Company which was organized in San Francisco in 1916. However, the Red and White Corporation, organized by the S. M. Flickinger Co. of Buffalo about 1920, was the first such firm to appear that has continued to be a prominent organization until the present time. During the decade of the 1920's there was a rapid growth of wholesaler-sponsored voluntaries, paralleling the expansion in the chain store field. The Independent Grocers Alliance of America (I.G.A.) was organized in 1926 in Chicago. Other well-known groups having their inception during the same period are the Clover Farm Stores, Nation-Wide Stores, and the Quality Stores Group. A few alliances were organized which were little more than "racketeer" groups. These had for their purpose only the collection of advertising allowances for groups of stores or wholesalers that claimed to be affiliated according to voluntary principles. Most of them have ceased to exist. All these developments revived interest in the retailer-owned type also, but during that decade the increase in membership was not as great as it was for the wholesaler-sponsored type.

The status of cooperative wholesaling in the grocery trade since 1929 can be judged from the data in Table 9. Comparable figures are not available for other lines of business because such organizations have never attained a sufficient degree of importance to justify separate treatment in the presentation of statistical data.

In 1929 there were 306 voluntary group wholesalers, whose sales of about $355 million represented 8.4 per cent of the total for all grocery wholesalers. Retailer-owned cooperatives were not reported separately in 1929, presumably because they were of little importance in terms of sales volume. The greatest impetus to both types of cooperative wholesaling

TABLE 9

NUMBER OF ESTABLISHMENTS AND RELATIVE SALES IMPORTANCE
OF RETAILER-OWNED COOPERATIVES AND VOLUNTARY GROUP
WHOLESALERS, GROCERY TRADE, UNITED STATES, 1929–1954

Type of Enterprise	1929	1939	1948	1954
Retailer-Owned Cooperatives:				
Number of Establishments .... n.a.		136	211	193
Sales as a Per Cent of Total for				
All Grocery Wholesalers* ...... n.a.		3.8%	5.2%	7.5%
Voluntary Group Wholesalers:				
Number of Establishments 306		638	634	574
Sales as a Per Cent of Total for				
All Grocery Wholesalers* 8.4%		16.1%	14.5%	14.2%

* Including unaffiliated general line wholesalers and wholesalers of confectionery, fish and seafoods, meat, and other specialty food lines.

Source: U. S. Census of Business publications for the various years.

came in the depression of the 1930's, when chain store competition became even more intense and was compounded by the advent of supermarkets. By 1939 the two types combined accounted for about a fifth (19.9 per cent) of all grocery wholesalers' sales.

The growth of cooperative grocery wholesaling since 1939 has been more gradual than it was during the 1930's. Overall, the share of total sales of grocery wholesalers made by retailer-owned cooperatives and voluntary group wholesalers has increased slightly to 21.7 per cent. Wholesalers sponsoring voluntary chains have actually declined in number and relative sales importance. Retailer-owned houses have gained substantially, however, almost doubling their share of total sales from 3.8 per cent to 7.5 per cent.

Retailer-owned cooperatives and voluntary chain wholesalers together reached a point, in the 1950's, of equal competitive standing with the corporate chains. Estimates of the division of *retail* food sales among stores in these three groups show the growth of cooperatives and voluntaries in the post-World War II period:[1]

	Per Cent of Total Retail Food Sales Made by		
Year	*Stores Belonging to Cooperative or Voluntary Chains*	*Corporate Chains*	*Unaffiliated Independents*
1947	29%	37%	34%
1956	44	37	19

[1] Estimates made by the staff of *Progressive Grocer* and published in "Mass Marketing Through Wholesalers—The Food Industry's Newest Success Story," address by Robert W. Mueller at the annual convention of the National-American Wholesale Grocers Association, Chicago, March 18, 1957.

These figures indicate that the competitive position of the chains has been approximately stable during the postwar period, but that voluntaries and cooperatives have increased their "share of the market" by about 50 per cent, while unaffiliated independents have suffered corresponding losses in relative status mostly, no doubt, through joining voluntaries.

Very little information is available concerning the development or current importance of voluntaries in fields other than groceries. This is no doubt due to their limited growth in other areas, but there is some indication that cooperative distribution activities in other areas are on the increase. An outstanding example is the Butler Brothers Company of Chicago and St. Louis, which sponsors the Ben Franklin variety stores; the Homecrest stores in floor covering; and the Federal stores in wearing apparel. Chain organizations and mail order houses have even turned to the voluntary as a means of reaching communities that cannot support regular retail units and to make more efficient use of their central office and wholesaling facilities. In the drug field the Walgreen Company has organized a number of retailers on a voluntary basis. The Western Auto Supply Company of Missouri and the Gamble-Skogmo Co. of Minneapolis, both of which operate their own units in large communities, have greatly expanded their operations by taking in associate dealers in the smaller communities.

FUNCTIONS OF COOPERATIVE CHAINS

Large-Scale Buying. Retailer-owned cooperatives in the grocery and drug trades, and buying groups in the several shopping goods trades, are essentially *buying* organizations. Being organized and controlled by retailers, their main desire continues to be that of eliminating the wholesaler, his net profits, and as much of his costs as possible. The retailer-owned cooperative warehouse can buy at lower prices direct from manufacturers than the individual members can buy from the local service wholesaler. Thus, the warehouse obtains the discounts and allowances which regularly accrue to the wholesaler. To the degree that wholesaling costs can be cut, merchandise is received in the retail units at lower prices than would be possible in purchasing from a service wholesaler. Since this is accomplished by the assumption of wholesaling functions on the part of the retailers, the *true costs* are usually not appreciated. The advantages resulting from centralizing purchases through an owned warehouse are probably exaggerated, because *true* savings imply a more efficient operation than can be provided by the regular wholesaler. Savings through centralized wholesale buying have not appeared so significant to the members of wholesaler-sponsored groups, since the regular wholesaler is already established and buys at the usual "jobber-list" prices.

However, purchasing at prices which are customarily granted to regular wholesalers was not the sole goal of the voluntary chains, because corporate chains and other mass distributors have habitually enjoyed substantial price concessions which were not available even to regular wholesalers. In order to obtain these additional savings in prices, the federations or alliances of voluntaries were formed. Thus such firms as the National Retailer Owned Grocers Association, with its some 100 wholesale establishments and 25,000 retail units, and the Independent Grocers Alliance, with its 50 or so wholesalers and some 6,000 fairly large retail units, amass a centralized buying power roughly equivalent to that of the Great Atlantic & Pacific Tea Company or of some of the other large corporate chains. Even outside of the federations, some cooperatives and voluntaries are large enough in themselves to permit volume buying. Butler Brothers with its more than 2,000 Ben Franklin variety stores and Certified Grocers of Los Angeles, serving an estimated 1,400 retail outlets, illustrate this point.

Through the late 1920's and the 1930's, these and other associations imitated the practices of the corporate chains by inducing manufacturers to pay brokerage fees and grant advertising allowances in addition to substantial quantity discounts. After the passage of the Robinson-Patman Act, some of the voluntary groups set up subsidiary corporations, ostensibly independent of the parent organization, for the purpose of collecting brokerage fees from sellers and passing on such fees to the voluntary organization in an indirect manner in the form of periodic advertising allowances. In a case which concerned the Red and White stores the Federal Trade Commission was upheld by the courts in its order which called for the cessation of such practices.[2] A similar complaint against the Clover Farm group was dismissed when the company dissolved the subsidiary which had been receiving prohibited brokerage.[3]

A more recent case of the same character involved one of the largest wholesaler-sponsored voluntaries. Here the Federal Trade Commission found that the grocers alliance acted for and on behalf of its affiliated wholesalers in purchasing transactions and not for and on behalf of sellers from which the brokerage was received. Such findings were based upon: (1) franchise agreements between the so-called brokerage concern (grocers alliance) and its wholesalers; (2) license agreements of the "broker" with sellers authorizing the latter to use brands, labels, and trade marks belonging to it; (3) the ownership and management of the alliance; and (4) disbursements made by the so-called broker of the fee it received on the buying transactions. Accordingly, the Commission pro-

[2] *Modern Marketing Service, Inc. et al. v. Federal Trade Commission,* 109 F.2d 970 (CCA–7, 1945).
[3] *Clover Farm Stores Co. et al. v. Federal Trade Commission,* Docket No. 4334.

hibited acceptance of brokerage fees from sellers of grocery products and related commodities and this order was affirmed by the courts.[4]

In an analogous manner the Robinson-Patman Act has operated to reduce the importance of advertising allowances and quantity discounts. Particularly in the purchasing of nationally advertised merchandise, the advantages of voluntaries, like those of the corporate chains, have been lessened substantially. Under conditions where competitive purchasers are involved, the cooperative chains can now receive *legally* only such advertising allowances as are available on proportionally equal terms to all purchasers. Furthermore, only such discounts or price concessions may be obtained as can be justified by the seller's savings (actually effected by virtue of differences in method of sale, method of delivery, quantity, or cost of manufacture) or as are necessary to meet in good faith the lower price of a competitor.

Considerable savings can still be effected through centralized buying, however, especially in connection with merchandise which is to be packed under the group's private label. Frequently such merchandise is obtained from fairly small manufacturers or processors who do not have their own brand of merchandise or at least do not have widely known brands. In such cases the voluntary organization may be able to negotiate for the entire output of the plant or at least the entire output of a specified grade or quality, with the result that the question of price discrimination does not arise. When this can be accomplished, very favorable price quotations are usually obtained, especially when a buyer's market prevails. Another important advantage of large-scale buying is that the central organization can keep in much closer touch with markets and sources of supply over the entire country and thus is in a much more favorable position to take advantage of any bargain or distress offerings than is an individual wholesale establishment.

Cooperative Advertising. Cooperative advertising is of two types: horizontal and vertical. Horizontal cooperative advertising implies a coalition of distributors on the same level of marketing, who join efforts toward the accomplishment of a common objective. Vertical cooperative advertising comes about when a manufacturer or processor induces retailers or other dealers to participate in his advertising programs by granting allowances to compensate them for featuring the manufacturer's or processor's products in local or point-of-sale advertising. For voluntary chains, the practicing of horizontal cooperative advertising has been greatly facilitated by the willingness of manufacturers to engage in policies of vertical cooperative advertising.

[4] *Independent Grocers Alliance Distributing Co. v. Federal Trade Commission,* 203 F.2d 941 (CCA–7, 1953).

Until the arrival of the wholesaler-sponsored groups, retailer-owned cooperatives did little joint advertising. Emphasis in these latter groups centered upon buying, not selling. Occasionally a small group of stores would indulge in some community-wide advertising or announce a city-wide sale. The individuality of the cooperating store, however, remained unchanged in most instances.

One of the first to organize an association within an association was the Frankford Grocery Company with its Unity Stores. Members of this smaller group displayed a common sign and paid for an advertising and merchandising service. This type of work developed rapidly with the growth of the wholesaler-sponsored groups, in which advertising was given special attention, and cooperative advertising of all kinds, very similar to that of the corporate chains, was utilized. The sponsoring wholesaler has been in a position to see the benefits accruing from mass selling by retailers and so is willing to offer weekly specials and to help plan advertising. Members of the group, or committees of them, meet regularly with the wholesaler and agree in advance upon weekly specials which are to be featured. The wholesaler, through his advertising or sales promotion manager, prepares and places the advertising, utilizing suggestions and technical aids provided by the headquarters organization.

The cost of the advertising is borne in part by nominal fees paid by the retailers, but to a larger extent by the manufacturers, who, acting on their own initiative or succumbing to the pressure exerted by the central wholesaling agency, grant advertising allowances to the organization. Even though the amount of these allowances has been limited by the Robinson-Patman Act, many manufacturers continue to grant allowances on a percentage of purchases basis to all customers. Through horizontal cooperative advertising, the voluntary chain is admirably situated to take advantage of the greater part of these grants. By pooling efforts, it is in a position to make use of full-page expensive newspaper space and local radio or television time. All these media are usually inaccessible to the unaffiliated independent retailer, because of the small scale of his operations. It is common today to find both types of voluntaries advertising regularly on a scale comparable to that of the large corporate chains.

Promotion of Private Brands. Both types of cooperative chains have been favorable to private brands, as a merchandising device which places the independent retailer above or beyond his competition. This method, used more commonly by the service wholesalers in the grocery trade than elsewhere, became a basic part of most wholesaler-sponsored groups from the outset and has been copied in varying degrees by the retailer-owned cooperatives. A number of reasons involving competitive strategy account for the aggressive promotion of private brands by voluntary groups.

In the first place, it strengthens the retailers' hold upon their trade once a reputation has been established for the brand. Insofar as customers are induced to make repeat purchases, the advantages of the advertising are retained by the merchants rather than accruing to the manufacturer of the goods.

Second, private brands usually provide a larger gross margin and afford a means of avoiding direct price competition. Well-known brands of manufacturers are frequently used as "price leaders" by large distributors and therefore carry low margins. The voluntaries can advertise these national brands at competitive prices in order to combat the impression that chains sell for less, and recoup their margins by applying sales pressure to private brands of merchandise—a practice which has also been followed by many of the corporate chains.

An additional reason is that private branding gives the voluntaries greater freedom in selecting sources of supply. Merchandise is purchased strictly on a basis of quality specification rather than brand reputation, and can often be obtained at lower prices than branded goods which have been aggressively advertised by the manufacturer. This is especially true where the headquarters organization can contract for the entire output of certain producers who thus have little or no selling expense. Of course, the voluntary groups then have to assume the burden of demand creation which involves considerable expense, so it does not follow necessarily that any *net* savings are enjoyed by ultimate consumers purchasing private brands.

It is for reasons such as the above that national groups like I.G.A., Red and White, Clover Farm, and the National Retailer Owned Grocers have developed their own brands as the central feature of their organization, providing a common rallying point for their retailer members. These private brands, which can be advertised nationally by the central organization and locally by cooperative advertising, can become just as strongly entrenched in the minds of consumers as many of the manufacturers' brands.

There seem to be two important developments which may tend to restrict the further progress of private brands on the part of voluntaries. One of these concerns the possible savings to be effected in the purchase of merchandise packed under the private label. There have been cases where the Federal Trade Commission has held that the practice of selling special or private brands to large distributors at lower prices than those at which other brands of like size, grade, and quality were sold to independent dealers constitutes illegal price discrimination. This interpretation largely nullifies the price advantages to be obtained in cases where producers are selling to competing purchasers, and it may have the effect of concentrating more and more private brand purchases with smaller producers whose entire output may be so obtained.

A second development is the continued trend toward self-service operation among retail food stores. In the past private brands could be promoted in part by the personal salesmanship of store clerks. In supermarkets, however, this factor is largely or entirely absent. Most stores belonging to cooperative and voluntary groups are now of the supermarket type.[5] In such stores brand selections are made primarily on the basis of impulse, with advertising and display assuming a more prominent role. Other things being equal, the consumer is more likely to choose a heavily advertised manufacturer's brand than a private brand. This means that voluntary and cooperative groups, to succeed in the promotion of private brands, must employ the same techniques. In spite of both these adverse developments, however, private brands continue to be an integral part of voluntary chain operations, particularly because they tie good will to the distributor rather than to the manufacturer.

Warehousing. Practically every retailer-owned cooperative chain started with the distribution of incoming purchases directly from the railroad car or from the back room of one of the larger members. In order to secure wholesale prices and discounts, it became advisable for each group to hire a manager and open a warehouse, as soon as possible, in which were usually carried a limited line of merchandise and a relatively small stock. For many years most of the retailer cooperatives limited their inventories to fast-moving staples, operating in much the same fashion as cash-and-carry wholesale houses. This proved to be a false kind of economy, however, since members were forced to buy many of their requirements elsewhere. Most cooperatives, like those sponsored by wholesalers, now carry full lines of groceries as well as some of the nonfoods commonly handled by supermarkets. In fact, trade surveys indicate that both types of cooperative wholesale establishments carry a larger number of items, on the average, than do unaffiliated wholesalers. The practice of selecting items to be carried by means of a committee probably does help to reduce inventory carrying costs, however, since a stricter attitude can be taken on the handling of "accommodation goods" which are unprofitable to the group as a whole.

Delivery. In the 1920's and 1930's, most retailer-owned cooperatives sold goods on a cash-and-carry basis, with retailers picking up their merchandise from the warehouse. This particular limitation in service did

[5] The term "supermarket" is used here to designate a large retail food store emphasizing self-service and open display. According to estimates by *Progressive Grocer,* in which supermarkets are defined as stores with annual sales of $375,000 or more, over half of the sales of both voluntary and cooperative groups are made by such stores. ("Mass Marketing Through Wholesalers," *op. cit.,* p. 19.)

not provide any true economies, however, except where idle retail personnel and equipment could be used. As more and more of the stores shifted to supermarket operations, and as sales volume increased during World War II and the postwar years, fewer retailers had such idle personnel or trucks. It became more economical to schedule deliveries by regular trucks out of the warehouse, just as the voluntary group and regular wholesalers had always done.

Delivery affords, nevertheless, a good illustration of how the quasi-integration of cooperative wholesaling results in important operating economies. In an independent wholesale house deliveries must often be made to suit the whims of small customers, and the number of "emergency" orders may be substantial. These problems do not arise in a corporate chain, because store managers are subject to the control of division executives at the warehouse and must adhere to predetermined schedules. While voluntary groups do not have the same degree of central control, they can and do reduce delivery costs by minimizing the number of orders handled outside of regular routings. In addition, much time can be saved by the retailer helping to unload the truck and by eliminating the waiting time of the driver while the retailer checks his order.[6]

Merchandise Planning and Other Services. The early retailer-owned cooperatives offered few services to their members. Sales were made on a cash-and-carry basis, no salesmen called on the stores, and little or no help was given members on their advertising or store operations. The explanation for this policy lay in the fact that the retailers who formed cooperatives were interested only in reducing merchandise costs and saw little need for rendering services to themselves.

The wholesaler-sponsored group started at the other end of the service scale. Most of them were service wholesalers in the grocery, drug, and hardware trades, accustomed to carrying large stocks of merchandise, extending credit liberally, making almost instant deliveries, and not averse at times to giving some advice as to how the retailer could improve his operations.

To some extent these differences still prevail, but in most cases the two types of cooperative wholesale groups have tended to converge in most respects. Many voluntary wholesalers ceased to extend credit, for example, while the cooperatives started to make deliveries, engage in cooperative advertising, and perform various merchandising services.

There are few or no salesmen in either voluntary or cooperative groups. Since the retailers have agreed in advance to concentrate their purchases

[6] See *Methods of Handling and Delivering Orders Used by Some Leading Wholesale Grocers,* Marketing Research Report No. 13, U. S. Department of Agriculture, Production and Marketing Administration (Washington, D. C.: Government Printing Office, 1952), p. 33.

with the wholesale establishment, there is little need for selling in the usual sense. Instead, *supervisors* call on member stores to communicate information and give advice to store managers on merchandise, display, advertising, personnel problems, and general management. In addition, a *sales planning* service is provided through headquarters in which items are selected for special promotional emphasis and plans are made for coordinated advertising and displays.

Both voluntaries and cooperatives help their members in *store planning and engineering.* Prospective new members may be aided in selecting a store site and in securing long-term credit accommodations for constructing a store. Members are also assisted in remodeling their store, including design of the layout, selection of fixtures, and financing. One Midwestern wholesaler sponsoring about 600 stores reported helping in 31 new store constructions, 79 remodelings, and 24 enlargements of stores within a single year.[7]

In addition to the aids indicated above, many voluntaries and coopera-tives provide *uniform accounting systems* for members, sponsor *trading stamp or other premium plans,* and render a wide variety of miscellaneous services.

Operating Expenses of Voluntaries and Cooperatives. In view of the fact that voluntary group wholesalers usually provide more services than retailer cooperatives, it is to be expected that their operating expenses should be higher. The disparity between the two has, however, steadily narrowed, as shown by the following Census data:

	Operating Expenses, Per Cent of Sales			
Type of Operation	*1929*	*1939*	*1948*	*1954*
Retailer-Owned Cooperatives	n.a.	5.2%	4.6%	4.4%
Voluntary Group Wholesalers	9.9%	10.6	8.3	7.4

The expense ratio for retailer cooperatives is quite similar to that of cash-and-carry wholesalers (4.2 per cent). Voluntary group wholesalers, on the other hand, have expenses of 1.5 points below those of unaffiliated general line service wholesalers in the same trade (8.9 per cent). Since wholesalers sponsoring voluntaries give *more* service than unaffiliated houses, their lower expenses presumably reflect true economies of coordi-nation between wholesaling and retailing and larger scale of operation.

All the foregoing data are *averages,* and as such they conceal sig-nificant variations in operating expense levels. Thus, some retailer-owned cooperatives have higher costs than some voluntary group wholesalers, depending on individual differences in services given, wage rates paid, and

[7] Rudolph L. Treuenfels, "New Conceptions of the Wholesale Trade," Third Inter-national Congress on Food Distribution (Rome, 1956), p. 14.

the general efficiency of management. Conversely, some voluntary group wholesalers are known to have operating expenses of 4 per cent.

Conclusion. Despite the weaknesses and limitations pointed out in this discussion, there can be little question that cooperative wholesaling has been eminently successful, at least in the grocery trade. Census data reflect a rapid growth up to 1939 and relative stability since that time. All this has been attained, furthermore, in the face of severe competition from the chains. When all things are taken into account, voluntaries and retailer cooperatives seem to be every bit as efficient as chain store warehouses.

An indirect effect of the development of cooperative wholesaling has been to stimulate improvements in the operating methods of unaffiliated wholesalers. Total operating expenses of general line grocery wholesalers *not sponsoring voluntary groups* amounted to 9.6 per cent in 1939, but declined to 8.9 per cent in 1954. Since it is likely that *more* services were given by such wholesalers in 1954 than formerly, this indicates a true gain in productivity, in which the competition of cooperative organizations undoubtedly played no small part.

It must be recognized that cooperative wholesale organizations are not a panacea for the competitive problems of independent retailers. The failure of such groups to develop in lines other than groceries suggests, for one thing, that this method is not readily applicable except where purchases can be concentrated almost altogether with a single wholesale source of supply. Even in lines where this is feasible, cooperatives are not a substitute for sound business judgment and experience. Within these limits, cooperative wholesaling is both economically sound and socially desirable.

13

MERCHANDISE AGENTS AND BROKERS

An integral and vital part of the wholesaling structure of the United States is represented by the large number of trading organizations which *do not acquire title* to the goods in which they deal. The institutions falling in this classification are commonly designated as functional middlemen, since they seldom, if ever, perform all the wholesaling functions but specialize instead in a limited number of such activities. At times they confine their operations to a single wholesaling function or to a part thereof. Ordinarily, they do not buy or sell outright but merely act as agents for others for whom they make purchases or sales. They operate as independent enterprises, taking the place of the client's buying or selling department, and deal principally in negotiatory functions, but not in the risks and duties which inhere in the ownership of goods. The two principal subdivisions of functional middlemen are agents and brokers, respectively, the distinction being based primarily upon the continuity of representation of the principal rather than on legalistic grounds or trade usage.

The discussion in this chapter is confined to those agents and brokers who deal in *merchandise,* as distinguished from the same types of middlemen in the fields of real estate, insurance, and securities. The latter types are beyond the province of this book.

Importance of Functional Middlemen. The relative importance of agents and brokers as a major segment of the wholesaling structure is indicated by the data in the tabulation which follows.[1]

[1] For breakdown by detailed types of agents and brokers, see Table 4 in Chapter 6.

Year	Number of Establishments	Volume of Transactions	
		Amount (add 000)	Per Cent of Total Wholesale Trade
1929	18,388	$14,256,695	20.7%
1939	20,903	11,201,035	19.4
1948*	18,138	32,839,667	17.3
1954	22,131	39,250,509	15.9

* Retabulated on a basis comparable with the 1954 Census of Business, when establishments without paid employees were excluded.

These figures must be interpreted with care because of certain changes in the coverage by the Census of Business, particularly the exclusion from the 1954 data of establishments without paid employees. The importance of this change is suggested by the fact that there were 6,239 establishments operated by functional middlemen without paid employees in 1948, representing over 25 per cent of the total. If the same proportions existed in 1954, there were probably 30,000 establishments in this segment of the wholesaling structure.

In the above tabulation strict comparability obtains only between 1929 and 1939 and between 1948 and 1954. Even when all differences are taken into account, it can be concluded that there has been a tendency for the number of establishments operated by agents and brokers to increase, while their share of total wholesale trade has declined steadily. These conclusions do not, however, apply equally to all classes of agents and brokers, as will be seen in the subsequent discussion of the major individual types.

Common Characteristics of Agents and Brokers. The major types of functional middlemen are *brokers, commission merchants, manufacturers' agents,* and *selling agents,* listed in order of sales importance. Others included in the general category are *auction companies, export and import agents, purchasing agents,* and *resident buyers.* While there are many differences among these types, they share certain common features which may be examined before turning attention to points of distinction.[2]

In the first place, and by definition, agents and brokers *specialize in the performance of a limited range of marketing functions.* Most of them confine their operations primarily to the exchange functions, more often to selling than to buying. Some types, such as purchasing agents and resident buyers, obviously specialize in buying; but most functional middlemen represent sellers in negotiating with industrial and commercial users or with merchant middlemen on the wholesale and retail levels. Occasionally

[2] There are additionally some functional middlemen operating on the wholesale level of marketing that are not as yet included in the wholesale trade part of the Census of Business. This is true, for example, of freight forwarders who facilitate the performance of the transportation function, and of factors in the field of financing inventories and receivables thereby facilitating the marketing process.

functional middlemen also do business on their own accounts, but this is the exception and to that extent they are wholesalers. In 1948 less than 20 per cent of agents and brokers reported such transactions to the Census. This practice is confined largely to certain trades such as fresh produce, where commission merchants often act as merchants in fact as well as in name.

Second, most agents and brokers are *small business enterprises* in terms of employees and facilities. Over three-fourths are unincorporated and the average number of paid employees is small, ranging in 1954 from about 3 for manufacturers' agents to 17 for auction companies. These figures do not tell the entire story, because an agent with only a few salesmen can handle a substantial volume of business ranging up to and over a million dollars. Nevertheless, most functional middlemen are clearly small concerns by any standards.

Third, agents and brokers are *found in all lines of trade,* although their relative importance varies greatly from industry to industry. The ubiquity of functional middlemen suggests that their usefulness depends primarily on factors other than the type of product alone.

Fourth, agents and brokers are *compensated by commissions or fees, usually on a percentage basis.* As a result their compensation varies directly and proportionally with the volume of transactions handled. This factor is a major inducement to manufacturers who wish to avoid the risks incident to establishing their own sales forces. The use of functional middlemen in effect shifts these risks to them, since there is seldom (if ever) any minimum payment guaranteed. This is especially attractive to manufacturers of industrial goods, for which demand is often quite unstable.

Finally, it should be pointed out that agents and brokers are *not substitutes for wholesalers.* They seldom provide storage space or local delivery service, rarely finance their customers, and in general do not afford the same breadth and depth of services as regular or even as most limited-function wholesalers. Partly as a result of these differences in functions performed, agents and brokers do not in most cases sell to the same customer groups served by wholesale merchants. While almost one-half of the sales of wholesalers are made to retailers, this customer class accounts for only about one-sixth of sales made by agents and brokers. Conversely, a much larger proportion of agent and broker business (about 35 per cent) is represented by sales to other wholesale establishments than is true for wholesalers (less than 15 per cent). An even larger segment of their business is done with industrial and commercial users, amounting to over 40 per cent of the total. These data show that agents and brokers are used by sellers in several different ways, of which distribution to retailers is one of the least important.

BROKERS

From the standpoint of sales volume the most important class of functional middlemen consists of *brokers*. They negotiate transactions between buyers and sellers without having physical possession of the goods, operate with very limited authority as to prices and terms of sale, and usually do not maintain continuous relationships with any one set of principals. It is this last feature, the absence of continuous relationships, that distinguishes brokers from agents. For the broker every transaction stands alone, although the same broker may, if his services prove satisfactory, be called upon by a given client to represent him in a series of transactions.

Importance of Brokers. Brokers operated 4,359 establishments in 1954, with total business volume of $10.8 billion. This represented more than one-fourth (27.5 per cent) of the total business of all kinds of agents and brokers. Of this total almost 90 per cent ($9.4 billion) was handled by brokers representing sellers rather than buyers. Some brokers, of course, represent either sellers *or* buyers, depending on circumstances, but most of them devote the bulk of their efforts to negotiations on behalf of sellers.

Lines of Trade. Although brokers operate in practically every line of merchandise, they are highly concentrated in a few. Of all brokers representing sellers, over half are in the grocery trade, although many of these so-called "food brokers" probably should be classed as manufacturers' agents instead (see below). Brokers are also important in both the purchase and sale of agricultural raw materials, such as cotton, grain, hides, livestock, tobacco, and wool. Lines of lesser significance include dry goods, drugs, furniture, automotive products, lumber and construction materials, and machinery and equipment.

Methods of Operation. Services of the broker to his principals are confined almost entirely to those of negotiation. As noted previously, the broker does not have a continuous contractual relationship with his clients. Instead, a manufacturer may call on a broker to dispose of a specific lot of goods. The broker's stock in trade is his expert knowledge of markets and prices, and he is in a better position than the seller to determine where, and to whom, the sale should be made at any given time. The broker proceeds to find a buyer or, in some cases, to obtain bids on the goods. He then secures confirmation from the seller and advises him where to ship the merchandise. Normally brokers do not assume physical possession of the goods they sell; in 1954 brokers reported inventories of only $16 million, which is an insignificant amount relative to a business volume of $10.8 billion. They do not usually handle invoices, these being sent directly from the principal to the customer.

Because of the limited services rendered, brokerage rates are typically quite low relative to the commissions of other types of functional middlemen. On the average, brokerage fees represent about 2 per cent of the value of sales or purchases. There are, of course, variations from one line of trade to another, from one part of the country to another, and according to the scale of operation. In such lines as automotive equipment, construction materials, or plumbing and heating equipment, brokerage fees run as high as 6 per cent or 7 per cent. At the other extreme, fees on cotton, grain, and livestock are between 0.5 per cent and 1.0 per cent. Frequently fees are quoted as dollar-and-cent amounts per unit of commodity (bale, barrel, box, etc.) rather than as percentages of dollar value.

Like other types of functional middlemen, brokers are used by manufacturers who are too small to maintain their own sales force or who wish to sell in distant or scattered markets which cannot be reached as economically in any other way. In addition, as the broker's distinctive feature is his noncontinuous representation, he is an ideal representative for producers of seasonal goods or for others who do not need the day-to-day representation afforded by agents. When production is seasonal, it is usually not feasible for a manufacturer to establish a sales force, since the cost of compensating salesmen for an entire year would be prohibitive; at the same time, salesmen cannot satisfactorily be hired to work only during a short season. This situation prevails in many food-processing industries and, accordingly, brokers are of considerable importance in handling such goods. The broker must attempt to offset the seasonal fluctuations of his lines by obtaining complementary lines (i.e., lines with opposite seasonal patterns), or else he would suffer from many of the same drawbacks which prevent the manufacturer from performing the selling task himself.

Another factor which may affect the use of brokers is the anonymity which a buyer or seller can achieve through their use. The broker does not reveal the name of his principal until a transaction is completed. Moreover, because his relationships are noncontinuous, the broker is not associated with any one principal or set of principals by the trade. This enables buyers or sellers to shield their identity in transactions negotiated by brokers, which is important, for example, in the gray cotton cloth field, where large industrial users often prefer not to be known by the mills during the negotiation process.

Brokers are best suited to selling standardized goods, because the main factor affecting negotiations on such goods is price. When other factors such as terms of sale or reputation of seller become important, it is necessary either for manufacturers to contact customers directly or to employ one of the agents who render more complete services than the broker.

"Food Brokers." In the grocery trade the term "broker" is commonly applied to a class of middlemen who, by the nature of their operations, are more properly classified as manufacturers' agents. Many of these food brokers belong to the National Food Brokers Association, in which they subscribe to a common code of ethics and operating methods. Even a cursory examination of these typical operating methods reveals that most so-called food brokers are not brokers in the true sense of the term.

Food brokers represent manufacturers of canned, processed, frozen, or dried foods, sugar and flour, and (more recently) nonfood products of the kinds handled by retail food stores. The representation provided by the food broker is continuous, usually contractual, and often on an exclusive agency basis in a given territory. Since the theoretically and historically distinguishing feature of the *broker* is lack of continuity in his relationships, most food brokers should no doubt be regarded as manufacturers' agents instead. Nevertheless, most of them are reported in Census data as brokers. In 1948 the Census showed 2,590 brokers representing sellers of groceries, confectionery, and meat, but only 158 manufacturers' agents in the same lines. Since there are about 1,800 food brokers listed in the directory of the National Food Brokers Association, most of them obviously reported to the Census Bureau as brokers.[3]

In addition to negotiating sales, food brokers offer a relatively wide range of services to their principals. Like wagon distributors, they set up displays, develop related-item promotions, and perform other merchandising services at the local level. Unlike wagon distributors, however, they do not stock or deliver goods except in unusual circumstances. In most respects the operations of food brokers are like those of other manufacturers' agents, described in a later part of this chapter.

COMMISSION MERCHANTS

Commission merchants resemble brokers in that they do not ordinarily maintain continuous relationships with any fixed group of principals. They differ from brokers and agents except auction companies in their performance of physical handling functions not usually associated with functional middlemen.

Importance. At one time commission merchants constituted the most important group of functional middlemen. In 1929 they accounted for over 6 per cent of all wholesale trade; since that time, however, their relative status has declined steadily. By 1954 commission merchant sales represented only 3.5 per cent of total wholesale trade volume. Actually, commission merchants did not suffer an *absolute* decline during this period, but instead stood still while most other kinds of wholesale establishments made substantial gains.

[3] This is to be expected in view of the Census policy of assigning establishments to the various classifications on the basis of "self-designation," i.e., traditional or otherwise devised trade terminology modified by the interpretation of Census definitions made by the person reporting.

Lines of Trade. Commission merchants are highly concentrated in a few lines of trade. About two-thirds of their establishments and almost 90 per cent of their sales are in farm products. The most important single line is livestock, followed by fresh fruits and vegetables, grain, cotton, dairy, and poultry products. As previously indicated, agricultural marketing is for the most part beyond the scope of this book. Consequently, no attention is given to the operations of commission merchants in such lines.

In the marketing of manufactured goods, commission merchants are of less significance. It is estimated that about 1,000 establishments with total sales of about $1 billion operate in manufactured lines, chiefly in piece goods, lumber and millwork, and industrial supplies. The reasons for their limited use in the distribution of manufactured goods should be apparent from the following description of their methods of operation.

Methods of Operation. Commission merchants transact business in their own names, take possession of the consigned merchandise, usually store it in their places of business, condition the goods, and otherwise prepare them for the market, sell them at the most advantageous prices, make deliveries to purchasers, extend credit at their own risk, deduct the commissions and other charges, and remit the remainder of the proceeds to their principals. Although they have direct physical control over the goods which they handle on a consignment basis, commission merchants do not take title to the goods they sell for clients. This does not mean that commission merchants do not occasionally buy goods outright and operate as merchants rather than agents. In certain lines of trade it is quite common for commission merchants or commission houses, as they are frequently called, to combine some merchant business with that of commission dealing. In fact, some commission firms, particularly among those dealing in consumer farm products, have gradually increased the proportion of merchandise bought and sold on their own account until they have become regular wholesale merchants.

When commission merchants act in the capacity of brokers, they always represent sellers who may be producers, or shippers located in local growers' markets and in secondary market centers. Shippers often consign goods to commission merchants without advance notice, but the relationship between such a broker and his clients is not continuous in a contractual way as is true of manufacturers' or selling agents. In the raw cotton trade commission merchants are usually designated by the term "factor," which must not be confused with the factor operating in the textile trade. Factors in the raw cotton trade actually engage in the distribution of the commodity. They usually advance funds to growers or country buyers of cotton; warehouse the product when it is delivered to them; grade it; sell it; and remit the proceeds after deducting commissions, interest on the money advanced, the amount of the loan, and other charges. In addition, commission merchants supply shippers with market information and, in the grain trade, may also help their clients in procuring freight cars, and look after the inspection, weighing, and grading of the goods.

In brief, a commission merchant is a broker to whom goods are consigned, located in an organized central market, who is given considerable freedom in negotiating prices by the sellers whom he represents. This type of operation practically requires the existence of a terminal market through which goods must pass, since otherwise sellers would have little incentive to entrust their goods to a distant middleman. Indeed, even in agricultural products the commission method of dealing is declining in importance because of the growing tendency to bypass terminal markets.[4] In most lines of manufactured goods such terminal markets never existed in the first place. Hence commission houses are not, and never have been, of major importance.

MANUFACTURERS' AGENTS

Third in importance among functional middlemen as measured by sales volume, and most numerous of all the types, are manufacturers' agents, sometimes referred to as manufacturers' representatives. In many respects their operations are similar to those of brokers on the one hand and selling agents on the other, but there are distinguishing features. Quite commonly, the manufacturers' agent represents two or more manufacturers in a limited geographic territory. Like the selling agent, he maintains continuous contractual relationships with his principals, but does not handle their entire output as does the selling agent. Like the broker, the manufacturers' agent has little authority over prices and terms of sale, but continuity of representation distinguishes him.

Importance. Manufacturers' agents operated 8,720 establishments in 1954, accounting for total sales of over $7 billion, or about 2.9 per cent of wholesale trade. Census data indicate wide swings in the relative importance of this type of functional middleman. In 1929 they accounted for 2.6 per cent of total wholesale trade volume, but this declined to 2.4 per cent in 1939 and only 1.9 per cent in 1948. These figures must be interpreted, however, in light of the change in Census coverage in 1954 which resulted in the inclusion, for the first time, of many functional middlemen who operate out of "nonrecognizable places of business," such as private residences.

A distinction is made between manufacturers' agents *with stocks* and

---

[4] For an analysis of changes in agricultural marketing patterns as they affect the commission merchant, see T. N. Beckman, H. H. Maynard, and W. R. Davidson, *Principles of Marketing* (6th ed.; New York: The Ronald Press Co., 1957), pp. 364–67.

those *without stocks*. The latter type is much more numerous, including 6,238 establishments or 71.5 per cent of the total number.

Lines of Trade. At least a few manufacturers' agents are to be found in virtually every line of manufactured goods, with emphasis on industrial goods, such as machinery, equipment, and supplies. Other important lines include electrical apparatus and wiring supplies; automotive equipment, tires, and tubes; clothing, furnishings, and footwear; iron and steel products; and hosiery, underwear, and piece goods. As previously indicated, manufacturers' agents are also important in the marketing of processed food products although their sales are reported under the category of "food brokers."

Methods of Operation. The "typical" manufacturers' agent is an independent proprietor or member of a partnership, with perhaps 2 or 3 paid employees. He represents several manufacturers, the maximum being about 25.[5] A given agent usually represents manufacturers of related but noncompetitive lines. Thus, for example, an agent in the electrical goods trade might sell one line of fittings and switches, another line of clamps, still another of heaters and fans, and so on, comprising in the aggregate a reasonably full line of apparatus and wiring supplies.

The principal service of the manufacturers' agent is that of negotiating sales. This is done at prices and terms specified by the manufacturers, but the agent is sometimes given authority to bargain or to modify terms. Because of his continuous representation of a group of manufacturers, the agent is likely to provide a better kind of selling than brokers, who handle each transaction more or less separately. Consequently, "selling" as practiced by manufacturers' agents tends to include more sales development and planning activities in addition to negotiating per se.

Relationships between the agent and the manufacturers represented are almost always provided for in a written contract, which is automatically renewed on a year-to-year basis unless terminated by one of the parties for cause. Common provisions of such contracts include: the territory to be covered; the exclusive rights of the agent; the class of purchasers to be solicited; frequency of calls; description of the line, prices, and terms of sale; terms for returns and allowances; authority of the agent (if any) to change prices, discounts, or terms of sale; a minimum sales quota (if any) which must be attained by the agent; the rate of commission and amount of fees for special services (if any) and the manner of their payment; and a termination clause, usually stipulating thirty days' notice of such intent by either party. Other details concerning special services, additional sales promotional work, and shipping specifications may be included.

[5] Thomas A. Staudt, *The Manufacturers' Agent as a Marketing Institution* (Washington, D. C.: Government Printing Office, 1952), p. 127.

Territories covered by manufacturers' agents vary considerably according to the type of product, density of the market, amount of service given by the agent, degree of competition, stage of sales development of the product, and other factors.[6] Agents designated as "food brokers" may cover only a single metropolitan area with its numerous retail food stores and institutional buyers. Industrial machinery agents, on the other hand, may cover an entire state or an even greater area, since the market is thinner and customer purchases are more infrequent.

In addition to selling, manufacturers' agents often provide other services to their suppliers and customers. Agents who service retail outlets for consumer goods manufacturers may coordinate dealer promotion programs, arrange for cooperative advertising, and take care of trade shows and exhibits. All manufacturers' agents furnish marketing information to their principals, usually on an informal basis but sometimes as a result of systematic marketing research. This information gives clients a localized picture of outlets, competition, and other demand factors not otherwise obtainable.

About a fourth of manufacturers' agents provide warehousing facilities and make deliveries of goods. Agents with stocks are dominant in certain lines, such as farm and dairy machinery, industrial chemicals, and paints and varnishes. This service is essential in lines where continued availability of supply is necessary to insure operation of a customer's plant. In consumer goods lines stocks are carried only for display purposes, as in the case of sporting goods. Even when the agent does not actually carry stocks, he may arrange for public warehouse space, help to make up pooled cars, and authorize their distribution by the warehouseman after receipt.

Circumstances Favoring the Use of Manufacturers' Agents. It appears that the services of manufacturers' agents are best utilized when:

1. A manufacturer has ample financial strength for production purposes; hence does not require the assistance of a selling agent, but lacks additional pecuniary strength to organize and maintain his own sales force.
2. A manufacturer produces a single product or a narrow line of goods of low unit value. Under these conditions it may be too expensive to maintain a separate sales force.
3. A manufacturer is subject, by the nature of his product, to wide cyclical fluctuations in demand.
4. The market is at a distance, making sales cultivation from the home office too expensive.
5. The market is sparsely populated and customers and prospects are located at a distance from each other. The cost incurred in traveling long distances between calls and the time consumed in such travel make it

[6] Staudt, *op. cit.*, pp. 75–78.

impractical and uneconomical for the producer to sell through his own organization.

6. A new product is being introduced by a new manufacturer or by an established manufacturer entering a new field. In these cases the manufacturers' agent who is usually well known in his territory lends his prestige to the unknown product. After the market has been established the producer may undertake to sell his goods through a controlled sales force of his own, without incurring any undue risks.

7. A manufacturer has his own sales force which is operating satisfactorily in a limited territory, but wishes to expand operations to other areas where the expected sales volume does not justify an expansion of his own sales force.

8. Salesmen with considerable technical knowledge are needed, but are not available as employees.

9. A manufacturer wishes to secure entrance to a certain group of prospective customers, particularly railroads and large industrial users, whose purchasing agents are more or less inaccessible.

10. Continuous representation in the market is necessary and brokers cannot be used to advantage.

Commission Rates. The rate of commission charged by manufacturers' agents varies considerably with the nature and unit value of the product, degree of competition, extent of sales effort required, fertility of the trade territory to be covered, class of customers to be cultivated, amount of repeat business to be expected, and similar considerations. The number of functions performed for the client in addition to selling, such as warehousing, credit, and repair service, is another factor. Rates may vary from as low as 2.5 per cent, on a line where average sales run into four-digit amounts and are readily made, to more than 25 per cent of sales on lines where sales are in small quantities and surrounded by difficulties. The average commission rate for all manufacturers' agents with stocks in 1954 was 6.9 per cent, while those without stocks averaged 5.3 per cent.

SELLING AGENTS

Of all the types of functional middlemen, the selling agent performs the widest range of marketing functions. Selling agents handle the entire output of their principals, operate without territorial limitations, and are given considerable authority to determine prices, terms of sale, customers to be solicited, and other policy matters. In effect, the selling agent serves his principals as a complete "marketing department." Relationships are continuous and contractual, and, generally, a selling agent represents the same group of mills or factories for a considerable period of time.

Importance. A total of 2,336 establishments were operated by selling agents in 1954, with sales of $6.2 billion. Thus selling agents accounted for 2.5 per cent of total wholesale trade, which is somewhat less than their share in former years. In 1929, for example, selling agents secured 3.8 per cent of total wholesale volume.

Lines of Trade. Selling agents are traditionally associated with the textile trades. About 30 per cent of them are in dry goods and apparel, accounting for over half of all sales made by such middlemen. A later development has been in coal, where a substantial number now operate. Other important lines are industrial machinery, equipment, and supplies; electrical goods; hardware, plumbing, and heating; and iron and steel products.

Methods of Operation. Selling agents, also known in some trades as "commission houses," "commission agents," or "selling houses," are independent business enterprises operating on a commission basis, whose distinctive feature is that they normally handle the entire output of their clients, with whom they maintain continuous contractual relationships. They are authorized to sell everywhere and have no restrictions on their power over prices, terms, and other conditions of sale. In addition to performing the selling function, they furnish market and style information to the mills they represent and, frequently, also extend financial assistance. The latter function may take one of several forms, such as a direct advance against the client's warehoused goods on which a lien is obtained as security, endorsing the client's promissory notes so that they may be more readily acceptable at the commercial banks for discounting purposes, or cashing sales in advance and guaranteeing the mill's accounts. When financial assistance takes this last-mentioned form, selling agents also perform for their clients the credit and collection function.

The number of selling agents engaging in a multiple type of operation is small. A few of them, particularly among the larger firms, do a small amount of brokerage business, and a limited number also sell a small amount of goods on their own account as merchant wholesalers.

In the textile trades and in the canning industries selling agents have persisted for many years, largely because of their early entrenchment and the relatively small size of the mills in these fields of manufacturing. It is economical for the sales force of a single selling organization to handle the goods of 20 to 30 plants and mills rather than for each manufacturer to maintain his own sales force. The same reasoning applies to the maintenance of a trained staff to gather style and market information. Moreover, many of the mills are financially weak, unable to wait until the expiration of the normal credit period for payment from customers. Such firms need some financial assistance so that they may continue with their production program before the selling season is opened. Again, close personal relationships frequently exist between selling agents and their clients. Very often there are interlocking directorates, or the treasurer of a mill may be a direct representative of the selling agent who, in turn, may be financially interested in the manufacturing organization. Under such conditions it becomes embarrassing and even impossible for a manufacturer to sever his relations with the selling agent even at the expiration of the annual agreement.

The selling agent form of marketing seems to be best when the manufacturer operates on a small scale, needs financial assistance, produces a limited variety of merchandise which requires fairly wide distribution, and when he needs continuous representation in the markets. Because of the lines of merchandise in which they deal, selling agents are important in various segments of the industrial market. Approximately half of their sales have been made to industrial users, the remainder being divided between wholesalers and large retailers.

The average commission rate for all selling agents in 1954 was 3.6 per cents of sales. Commission rates vary, naturally, with the kind of merchandise and with the degree of service that is rendered a given client. On staple goods in the textile trade it may be about 2 to 3 per cent if the accounts are not guaranteed, and for style goods with their attendant risks the commission may be as high as 5 per cent, while on novelty goods it may run to 10 per cent. Even in a single trade the commission may vary with the type of merchandise. Thus, on silks the amount charged when no credit service is involved is around 3.5 per cent. When loans are made to a client a separate commission is charged and still another fee when accounts receivable are guaranteed.

OTHER TYPES OF AGENTS AND BROKERS

Brokers, commission merchants, manufacturers' agents, and selling agents are the principal types of functional middlemen in the marketing of manufactured goods. In addition to these, there are several other kinds of agents and brokers of lesser significance.

Auction Companies. In the marketing of certain kinds of agricultural products, wholesale auction companies are of great importance. Such concerns do not take title to the goods, but handle them for clients on a commission or fee basis. They provide a place for the public inspection and sale of merchandise that has been consigned either directly to them or to auction receivers. On their own responsibility auction companies may extend credit to purchasers, but after the sale has been consummated the company must remit the proceeds, less the commission and other charges, to their clients. In many respects auction companies operate like commission merchants, the principal distinguishing characteristics being that with the auction companies the sales are public rather than private and are usually made to the highest bidder.

The largest number of auction companies operate in the leaf tobacco and livestock trades. Fruits and vegetables, floor coverings, furs and skins, jewelry, and furniture are the other fields in which auction companies operate to some extent, their relative importance being more or less in the order listed.

The charges made by auction companies for their services vary with the different lines of merchandise and the different sections of the country even when the same goods are involved. For fresh fruits and vegetables the commission ranges from 1.5 to 3 per cent, the customary charge being around 2 per cent. In addition, there is a charge to the seller for unloading the car and assorting the shipment, and the buyer may be required to pay a certain amount per package for handling the goods for him and making delivery. Auctions operating in the leaf tobacco market usually charge about 3 per cent, with a minimum charge applying to all shipments handled. This fee includes the selling service, warehousing, handling, and insurance on the consignments.

Auction companies, like commission merchants, always represent sellers or shippers. Their employment is best adapted to goods that are highly standardized and graded, and of which there is an ample supply from day to day and from year to year in order continuously to attract large numbers of buyers. They are also to be recommended when quick disposal of goods is desired and there is little or no confidence in the commission method of dealing through private negotiations. The auction method is at times an economical means of marketing, presumed to allow free play of supply and demand. The publicity attending auctions tends to assure fair treatment of vendors, and is useful in establishing prices which are used as a guide in private dealings.

On the other hand, drawbacks are that the buyers attending auctions have little opportunity to shop around; sellers must take the price offered or withdraw the goods; bidding is sometimes sluggish, with resultant low prices to shippers; malpractices, such as collusion of buyers (especially when the number of buyers patronizing the auction is small), and puffing on the part of sellers have developed, so that expected economies have not always been realized. While the commission charges of auction companies are low, there are other marketing costs incident to the auction method. To the commission fee of the auction company must be added the commission charged by *auction receivers,* to whom the bulk of the goods handled by the auction method in the fruit and vegetable business is consigned; also the commission charged by buying brokers when retailers and jobbers seek to have such representation at the auctions. When all of these charges are considered, auctions are probably fully as expensive as commission merchants in the same lines of business.

Purchasing Agents and Resident Buyers. The purchasing agent is an independent functional middleman who specializes in rendering a market information and purchasing service to a group of clients who must assemble goods from very numerous and widely scattered sources. The most important of these clients are wholesalers of groceries, hardware, electrical products, automotive products, and mill supplies. This type of agent may be distinguished from a buying broker in that his relationship with his clients is a continuous one. Furthermore, he is generally compensated by a fixed fee rather than by a commission on the goods which he purchases. The purchasing agent who is a functional middleman must also be distinguished from the purchasing agent who is not in business for himself but is merely an employee in a manufacturing or other business.

Among well-known organizations of this type are the Biddle Purchasing Company and Oliver Bros., Inc., both of New York. These firms, and others in the field, contact thousands of small manufacturers, examine and test their wares, and obtain from them prices and descriptions of goods which are sent out to clients for insertion in loose-leaf books and card-index files. These are kept up to date by information supplied by manufacturers and by the continuing contacts of the agent. The subscribers to this market information service, numbering in the hundreds or thousands, pay the purchasing agent a fixed amount per month, which in the aggregate constitutes the income of the purchasing agent.

In addition to this market information, the purchasing agents also provide a purchasing service. Prior to certain proceedings under the Robinson-Patman Act, subscribers often placed orders for merchandise through such an agent, who combined separate orders and transmitted them to suppliers. Because of the large volume of operations, it was possible for the agent to collect a brokerage fee from the seller in nearly all cases. These commissions were generally passed on to the purchasing agent's clients through separate credit memoranda, and thus constituted a price advantage which was not available to other purchasers buying direct from the manufacturer or through a bona fide broker who retained for himself his legitimate fee. Inasmuch as the purchasing agent was a representative of the buyers, the courts upheld the Federal Trade Commission in ruling that the receipt of brokerage fees from sellers, under such circumstances, constituted a violation of Section 2(c) of the Robinson-Patman Act.[7] It was generally felt at the time that such a ruling would greatly diminish the importance of purchasing agents. It is true that any such firms that owed their existence primarily to their ability to secure from sellers special discounts in the way of brokerage fees have little basis for existence today.

[7] *Oliver Bros. Inc. et al. v. Federal Trade Commission*, 102 F.2d 763–71 (CCA–4, 1939); and *Biddle Purchasing Co. et al. v. Federal Trade Commission*, 96 F.2d 687–93 (CCA–2, 1938).

However, it was reported in one case that the brokerage fee "rebates" received by 86 per cent of the purchasing agents' clients were less than the amount paid by them for the market information service.[8] This would indicate that the market information service was of greater importance to the customers than was the price advantage obtained.

There are still some advantages to be derived from placing orders through a purchasing agent, but these are important only in a limited number of cases, with the result that only a small proportion of the wholesaler's orders is now so placed. Among advantages that might be mentioned are faster delivery, ease of establishing credit, and ability to purchase less than the manufacturer's minimum order quantities. Some manufacturers are willing to make these concessions because it is of benefit to them to have their products publicized by the purchasing agent, who often provides their most important contact with the trade.

The importance of purchasing agents should be judged not so much by the volume of wholesale trade transacted by them as by the nature of the market information which they provide. This service has probably become more important because of the large number of very small manufacturing firms which came into being during World War II. Many of these were formerly subcontractors for larger firms engaged in the production of war materials and have continued to manufacture one or a few products of limited demand. Such firms frequently have no sales force and are often unable to do any advertising. Furthermore, the size of their average shipment, particularly in some hardware and mill supply items, may be so small that manufacturers' agents or other middlemen are not interested in handling their business. About the only way a wholesaler can find out about the products of many such firms is to have available the information service of the purchasing agent which furnishes the latest specifications, prices, terms of sale, and other required information.

Organizations similar to purchasing companies, functioning in the dry goods and women's apparel trade, are known as *resident buyers*. Normally they represent buyers in the retail trade and, unlike the purchasing agent in the wholesale trade, they confine their contacts with manufacturers to a single central style market. The service of a single purchasing agent may suffice for a hardware wholesaler, whereas it may be necessary or advisable for a department store to utilize the services of a number of resident buyers located in New York, Chicago, Los Angeles, Dallas, St. Louis, and other manufacturing centers. Resident buyers keep their clients informed regarding prices, style movements, and sources of supply. Their purchasing activities consist of buying goods for which large combined orders can be placed, making fill-in purchases as required by each client, and serving as guides for store buyers visiting the market.

[8] *Oliver Bros. Inc. et al. v. Federal Trade Commission,* supra.

Brokers and Agents in Foreign Trade. Finally, there are numbers of agents and brokers who facilitate the handling of our foreign commerce through their negotiatory functions. Some of them specialize in exports and are known as export brokers, export commission houses, export manufacturers' agents, and export selling agents. To these might be added customs brokers who are expert in all matters pertaining to imports and exports, such as duties, consular fees, necessary legal documents, invoices, the tariff laws, and in the proper packaging and routing of shipments. Such brokers are commonly found in or near our importing and exporting centers.

Export commission houses generally represent foreign clients in the purchase of American products. They may furnish their clients with market information and perform incidental functions connected with the technique of shipping. They may also sell for American firms goods consigned to them, such sales being made to buyers located in the countries in which they sell. These houses more often specialize in markets rather than in commodities, as is also true of other export agents.

Despite the variety of export agency types, their importance is but slight, accounting for about 0.5 per cent of the business reported by all wholesale organizations in various Census of Business years. The business of import agents is even less, varying from 0.1 per cent to about 0.6 per cent of the business of all wholesale institutions. Among these import agents are to be found import commission merchants, manufacturers' agents, and selling agents who represent foreign sellers in the American market. Normally, a single agent represents a number of clients whose imports are too small to justify setting up their own importing staffs. The agents also attend to customs formalities and receive their compensation in the form of commissions.

14

PRODUCTIVITY AND EFFICIENCY IN WHOLESALING

In the preceding eight chapters the institutional structure of modern American wholesaling has been discussed and its functioning analyzed. Attention has been given to the nature of the various types of wholesale establishments, the functions and services performed by them, and their role in the wholesale distribution of goods. A full understanding of the wholesaling system requires, however, more than this. In addition, a question must be raised regarding *how well* the system and its component parts accomplish their tasks. To make such an evaluation, concepts and measures of productivity and efficiency in wholesaling are introduced in this chapter.[1]

NATURE AND SIGNIFICANCE OF PRODUCTIVITY AND EFFICIENCY

The related concepts of productivity and efficiency are among the most important in the fields of economics and business management. Leaders of industry, labor, and government all recognize this and make frequent

---

[1] This chapter is based largely on studies of productivity and efficiency conducted by the authors. Basic concepts of productivity and statistical measures applying to wholesale trade are drawn from Robert D. Buzzell, "Productivity in Marketing with Special Reference to Drug and Hardware Wholesalers," unpublished Ph.D. dissertation on deposit in the library of The Ohio State University and carried out under the supervision of Theodore N. Beckman (1957). See also Theodore N. Beckman and Robert D. Buzzell, "Productivity—Facts and Fiction," *Business Horizons,* Bureau of Business Research, Indiana University, Vol. I, No. 1 (Winter, 1958), pp. 24–38.

reference to these concepts in wage bargaining, in public speeches, and in legislative hearings. A clear understanding of productivity and efficiency and of their relationships to the general standard of living, to wages, to prices, and to profits, is, therefore, essential.

Productivity and Efficiency Defined. The terms "productivity" and "efficiency" are often confused or even used interchangeably. While the two are closely related, there is an important difference between them which should be apparent from an examination of the discussion that follows.

Productivity is a ratio of output to the corresponding input of economic resources in a business institution or process, both during a given period of time. "Output" consists of the results of some productive activity, in the form of physical goods and/or services, so long as it has some market value. "Input," on the other hand, denotes the factors of production used in obtaining a given output, including labor, capital, land, and other resources. As applied to wholesaling, productivity is a ratio of the output of wholesaling functions and services to the input of resources. This ratio may be computed for an establishment, a firm, a trade group, or for the system as a whole.

The *efficiency* of a process or institution is its productivity as compared with an optimum or ideal level possible under given conditions. Efficiency measures are frequently used in engineering and the physical sciences to appraise the performance of a process or of a type of equipment. To illustrate, a gallon of gasoline has a definite maximum number of energy units in terms of Btu's (British thermal units). If an internal combustion engine could be developed capable of using the total energy content of its fuel, the engine might be designated as "100 per cent efficient." Because it is impossible, or at least prohibitively expensive, to build such an engine, actual efficiency is considerably less, perhaps 70 per cent or 80 per cent of the maximum. Similar measures are sometimes applied to the operations of factory workers where output can be reckoned in physical terms.

As applied to economic activities including wholesaling, the concept of efficiency is more complex and subject to varying interpretations. In the first place, what is efficient from one standpoint may be inefficient from another. Thus, for example, a business yielding high profits but paying low wages is efficient from the owners' point of view but inefficient from that of the employees, and vice versa. Moreover, what is efficient in the short run from any viewpoint may be inefficient in the long run. The early practices in cutting timber and drilling for oil produced high immediate returns but were wasteful of resources in the long run; recognition of this fact led to reforms in such practices.

Still another difficulty in applying the "physical" efficiency concept to wholesaling is that of measurement, which presupposes an adequate method of measuring productivity, and further, of determining the maximum level possible under given circumstances. For reasons explained in subsequent parts of this chapter, this is not yet possible. The level of wholesaling efficiency can, therefore, only be roughly estimated.

Productivity and Living Standards. In the long run, consumers' living standards depend primarily on the productivity of the economic system, including the wholesaling segment of it, and the degree of efficiency achieved in actual operation. In oversimplified fashion the relationship between living standards and productivity may be stated as follows:

1. Living standards depend on the volume of output (goods and services) relative to population.
2. The volume of output depends on the proportion of the population working, their hours of work, the amount and quality of capital and natural resources employed in production, and the efficiency with which these labor, capital, and other resources are used.
3. Of the basic factors affecting output, several are relatively stable except over long periods of time. In this class are the proportion of the population working, hours of work, and the natural resources (land, minerals, and the like) available.
4. Therefore, the two factors with the most direct effects on living standards are the *productivity* of labor, capital and other resources, and the rate of capital accumulation.

Since wholesaling is an integral part of any advanced economy, its productivity has an important effect on consumption levels. Because many economists believe productivity in marketing (including wholesaling) to be static or even declining, criticisms have been made of the marketing system as a deterrent to economic progress. The validity of these criticisms is examined in a subsequent section of this chapter.

Productivity, Wages, and Prices. Much of the interest in productivity in recent years has centered around its role in determining wages and prices. The true nature of this role has all too often been obscured by the claims and counterclaims of groups with essentially conflicting motives, such as organized labor on the one hand and the executives of large corporations on the other. Without entering into the merits or fallacies of the statements made by the contending parties, a brief explanation of how productivity affects wages and prices may be given.

As previously indicated, productivity is a ratio of output to the input of an economic resource or of all resources combined. Since the payments made to the factors of production must come from the sale of output, the rate of output relative to factor input is naturally a basic determinant of wages as well as of the other distributive shares: profit, interest, and rent. Thus it is just as valid to speak of the role of productivity in determining interest rates, rents, or profits as it is to discuss productivity-wage relationships. Primary attention has usually been given to wages, however, for several reasons. First, labor is the largest single type of input, accounting for between 60 and 70 per cent of national income. Second, and probably more important from a practical standpoint, much of the demand for productivity information has come from industry and organized labor in connection with wage disputes. Naturally, labor input is of principal interest in this context. Third, and partly as a result of the second factor, the most important source of productivity measures is the Bureau of Labor Statistics of the U. S. Department of Labor. Here, again, it is natural that emphasis would be placed on labor input.

While there are valid reasons for focusing attention on *labor* productivity, there is a danger of confusing it with *total* factor productivity. The inference can be drawn (purposely or mistakenly) that labor is *responsible* for increased productivity and entitled to all of its benefits. This, of course, is fallacious. In fact, the principal cause of the long-run upward trend in output per man-hour lies in improved management, resulting in the substitution of more and better capital equipment for labor. This is not to say that *none* of the results of enhanced productivity should accrue to labor; the truth lies somewhere between this and the other extreme. It would be highly desirable to develop methods of allocating productivity gains (or declines) among the various factors of production responsible for them. Unfortunately, no objective techniques for this purpose have yet been fully developed.

The relationship between productivity and prices is closely connected to that with wages. Productivity gains might, instead of being distributed in the form of higher wages, be passed on to customers in the form of lower prices; or a given increase might be used *partly* to raise wages and the shares of other factors of production and *partly* to decrease prices. What has happened more often in the post-World War II period is that wage increases have exceeded productivity gains, resulting in *higher* prices. Some economists conclude from this that organized labor is responsible for "creeping inflation," while others argue that price increases tend to *precede* wage improvements, so that labor is simply trying to keep abreast of a rising cost of living. Whatever the truth of the matter, it is well recognized that productivity trends have a joint effect on wages and prices.

Productivity and Profits. Of even more direct interest to wholesaling executives is the effect of productivity changes on net profits. In this connection it is necessary to speak of *capital* and entrepreneurial *management* productivity rather than labor productivity, since net profits are primarily a compensation for the use of capital and owner-management risks in an enterprise. Furthermore, the effects of productivity on net profits are more difficult to isolate than are those on wages, because profits are treated by accountants as a *residual* after all costs. Hence net profits are affected by many factors, especially by general business conditions. Nevertheless, it is safe to say that, *other things being equal,* net profits tend to vary directly with the level of productivity achieved. As a result, it behooves management to devote some attention to changes in productivity and to the factors underlying them. For this purpose, it is desirable to establish *internal* measures of productivity for the various segments of a business. This type of productivity measurement is treated in Chapter 30.

MEASUREMENT OF PRODUCTIVITY IN WHOLESALING

While productivity and efficiency concepts in themselves provide a valuable guide to managerial thinking, their principal significance is in the *quantitative* analysis of business results to which they are applied. Accordingly, both economists and business executives have devoted considerable effort to measurement techniques. The authors know of one large manufacturing concern, for example, which assigned several highly trained persons for a period of several years to a project involving productivity measurement. In the field of wholesaling and marketing generally, however, little has been done along this line. There is no valid reason why such measures cannot be developed and profitably used in the management of wholesale enterprises and in the analysis of the wholesaling system. The conceptual foundations for such an application, together with illustrative statistical measures, are discussed in this section.

Nature of the Measurement Problem. Productivity measurement is a difficult task at best. Basically, it requires the development of stable and meaningful *units* of measurement for the two terms of the ratio, namely, output and input. In manufacturing, mining, and agriculture it is customary to measure output in *physical* units such as tons of steel or bushels of wheat. Such measures have the merit of simplicity, but suffer from several limitations. First, different physical measures cannot be combined—apples cannot be added to oranges. For the same reason, physical output measures cannot be compared directly between industries. Third, physical units do not allow for changes in *quality*—a 1959 automobile of a given make is treated as equivalent to the corresponding 1928 model. Even if it were not for these limitations, physical measures would have little application in wholesaling, since there is usually no "physical product" in a wholesale establishment in the same sense as in the output of a farm or a factory. As a result the traditional output measures cannot be used in analyzing the productivity of the wholesaling system.

Input is equally difficult to measure. As previously indicated, it is customary to relate output to *labor* input only, measured in man-hours. Much of the information published by the Bureau of Labor Statistics is based, in fact, on just one *type* of labor—so-called "production workers." These include direct factory workers and others "immediately associated with production operations."[2] Productivity measures related only to "production" workers are misleading, since the proportion of "nonproduction" employees engaged in supervision and certainly in such activities as sales, advertising, product service, and personnel management has been steadily increasing over the years. Furthermore, as the basis of classifying workers is their participation in *physical* production, no such distinction can meaningfully be made in the field of wholesaling. In any event, inasmuch as all workers make some contribution to a firm's output, *all* should be included in measures of labor input. The distinction, it must be further noted, is based on an archaic and even originally false conception of the nature of production.

Apart from labor, other types of input should also be related to output, including at least capital and land. Because these inputs are measured in different units, they cannot be combined with labor into any single measure of "total input." The result is that a *series* of productivity measures should be used, relating output to each major class of resources used and perhaps to subdivisions of each class.

Measurement of Wholesaling Productivity. In measuring the productivity of a wholesale enterprise, trade group, or the system as a whole, certain special problems are encountered in addition to those already mentioned. The most important of these is the *intangible* nature of the "product," which prevents the use of physical measures such as those used to quantify factory output. Actually, since wholesaling involves dealing in and handling of physical goods, physical measures do have some significance and have been used. For example, in the grocery trade, a common measure of output is *tons* of product handled, and productivity is expressed in *tons per man-hour*. Such a measure is not valid, however, as an expression of *total* output in a food wholesaling business. It merely measures *warehousing* output and has little significance for such other functions as buying, selling, or general management. This is not to say that tonnage measures are of no value. In fact, analysis and control of over-all productivity is best achieved by developing a series of specific internal measures for the various functions of a business.[3] These measures should not be confused, however, with the *total* output or productivity of a business, which includes *all* of its functions.

Another special problem of measuring productivity in wholesaling lies in the traditional emphasis on *cost reduction* in marketing generally. This, in turn, is based on the doctrine that marketing is altogether unproductive. This belief is an outmoded concept derived from the ideas of the Physio-

[2] For a fuller statement of the distinction between "production" and "nonproduction" workers, see "Nonproduction Workers in Factories, 1919–56," *Monthly Labor Review*, LXXX (April, 1957), 435.

[3] See Chapter 30.

crats and other economists of the eighteenth and nineteenth centuries. If it is accepted, then naturally costs should be minimized, since nothing is received for them. Modern economic theory recognizes, however, that marketing activities including wholesaling *are* productive despite the fact that they do not generally alter the physical form of products. The "output" of wholesaling consists of the *value added by it* to products as they pass through the system. The nature of this value added is examined next.

Value Added by Wholesaling. The output of a wholesale enterprise or of the wholesaling system is best measured by the value added to products as a result of the performance of wholesaling functions. From the brief explanation of the marginal utility concept and other related subject matter discussed in Chapter 1, it should be obvious that wholesaling does add such value. A refrigerator, for example, may be sold by its manufacturer for $200. The distributor, in turn, resells it to a retailer, say, for $240. Unless the distribution of the product is arbitrarily restricted, it is *worth* $40 more in the second transaction than in the first. This $40 addition to value represents, of course, the distributor's gross margin. Most of it (but not all) is *value added* by the wholesaler. Some part of it, say $4 or $5, comprises the value of goods or services bought by the wholesaler from others, such as packaging materials, supplies, or professional services. But most of it is value added by the wholesaler himself in the performance of his functions, including warehousing, selling, extension of credit, product service, and so on.

In the 1950's, considerable interest has developed in the measurement of value added by wholesaling and other segments of marketing.[4] Measures of value added by marketing would be useful for a number of reasons apart from their use in the measurement of productivity, for they would:

1. Provide the best available *absolute measure* of the economic contributions made by wholesaling and other marketing activities.
2. Permit *comparisons* between different types of wholesale institutions, between wholesaling and other parts of marketing, and between marketing and other major segments of the economy.

[4] The authors have, with others, participated in the development of the value added concept and measures based on it. The term was first applied to marketing in the first edition of this book in 1937. See especially Theodore N. Beckman, "The Value Added Concept as Applied to Marketing and Its Implications," *Frontiers in Marketing Thought* (Bloomington, Indiana: Bureau of Business Research, Indiana University, 1955), pp. 83–99; *Value Added by Distribution* prepared under the supervision of Theodore N. Beckman by Robert D. Buzzell and David D. Monieson (Washington, D. C.: Domestic Distribution Committee and Business Statistics Committee, Chamber of Commerce of the United States, 1956); Theodore N. Beckman, "Value Added by Distribution," in the proceedings of the *Twenty-Eighth Boston Conference on Distribution* (Boston: Retail Trade Board of the Boston Chamber of Commerce, 1956), pp. 43–47; and "Value Added as a Measurement of Output," *Advanced Management* (April, 1957).

3. Place marketing costs, including those of wholesaling, in their proper perspective, rather than overemphasize cost reduction as has traditionally been done.
4. Provide a sound foundation for a more positive approach to the management of wholesale and other marketing enterprises.
5. Emphasize the productive character of wholesaling and other marketing institutions.
6. Improve the accuracy of national income accounting, especially the measurement of gross national product which must now be estimated in large part in so far as marketing is concerned.
7. Help in the evaluation of different forms of taxation and facilitate the development of more equitable tax burdens.

For these reasons many leading authorities in the field of marketing have encouraged the collection and publication of value added data by the Bureau of the Census.

In the computation of productivity, value added serves as the *numerator* or output measure of the ratio. The advantages of this measure over other possible measures are several. First, since value added is expressed in monetary units, it permits the measurement of output for different kinds of wholesale enterprises on a comparable basis. The output of a hardware wholesaler can be compared with that of a grocery wholesaler, for example, even though the physical products handled by the two are quite dissimilar. Second, value added is an *over-all* output measure reflecting the contributions of all functions in a business, including buying, selling, warehousing, credit extension, delivery, and so forth. Third, value added measures reflect changes in the quantity and quality of services performed between firms or over a period of time. For example, if a wholesaler added a store engineering service for his customers, it would result in a higher value added figure, whereas no account would be taken of such a change in any physical measure. Finally, by the use of an appropriate price index, value added data can be adjusted to eliminate the influences of inflation or deflation in the value of money.

Illustrative Measures of Productivity. Application of productivity concepts to marketing is a relatively new idea, and very little research has been done in the field. This is evidenced by the fact that a very comprehensive bibliography of some 900 books, articles, and reports dealing with productivity contained fewer than two dozen references specifically oriented to marketing.[5] Consequently, it is not possible to present statistical data reflecting changes in wholesaling productivity except on a very limited scale. Productivity measures for wholesalers in two trade groups are analyzed in the following paragraphs mainly as illustrative of the kinds of

[5] *Productivity: A Bibliography*, Bulletin No. 1226, Bureau of Labor Statistics, U. S. Department of Labor (Washington, D. C.: Government Printing Office, 1957).

TABLE 10

VALUE ADDED AT 1954 PRICES, MAN-HOURS WORKED, AND VALUE ADDED
PER MAN-HOUR, GENERAL LINE DRUG AND HARDWARE WHOLESALERS,
CENSUS OF BUSINESS YEARS, 1929–1954

	Drug Wholesalers			Hardware Wholesalers		
Year	Value Added (000)	Man-Hours (000)	Value Added per Man-Hour	Value Added (000)	Man-Hours (000)	Value Added per Man-Hour
1929	$132,838	43,479	$3.06	$262,323	88,367	$2.97
1935	88,941	30,109	2.95	129,675	42,258	3.07
1939	110,804	36,319	3.05	253,629	77,893	3.26
1948	124,368	46,216	2.69	370,670	101,815	3.64
1954	203,571	54,226	3.75	314,241	87,492	3.59

Source: Robert D. Buzzell, "Productivity in Marketing with Special Reference to Drug and Hardware Wholesalers," unpublished Ph.D. dissertation on deposit in the library of The Ohio State University, 1957, Tables 5, 7, and 10.

studies that can be made when the necessary information is collected and tabulated.

Measures of value added, man-hours of labor, and output per man-hour for general line drug and hardware wholesalers are presented in Table 10.[6] The technique employed in developing these measures may be summarized briefly:

1. Net sales for the two groups were obtained from the appropriate Census of Business publications.
2. Typical ratios of value added to net sales were computed on the basis of expense and margin figures reported by the National Wholesale Druggists' Association and the National Wholesale Hardware Association, respectively. These ratios were developed by deducting from average gross margin percentages those expense categories that represent payments to other firms for goods and services used in operation, such as telephone and telegraph, office supplies, tabulating equipment costs, legal and collection expenses.
3. Measures of value added in dollars were computed by applying the ratios described in (2) above to net sales.
4. Value added measures were adjusted to eliminate the effects of price changes, using price indexes developed especially for that purpose.
5. The total number of persons employed in each trade group was determined from the Census of Business for each of the years in question.
6. Average hours worked per week were estimated from average figures for "all wholesale trade" as reported by the Bureau of Labor Statistics.
7. Total man-hours worked during each year were computed on the basis of the estimates described in (6) and (7) above.

[6] Buzzell, "Productivity in Marketing with Special Reference to Drug and Hardware Wholesalers," op. cit.

As shown in Table 10, there has been a substantial increase in output per man-hour for both drug and hardware wholesalers since 1929. The over-all improvement averaged about 0.8 per cent per annum in each group, belying the idea that wholesalers' productivity is static or declining. Increases in productivity were not regular from year to year, however, with declines actually being registered during some parts of the 26-year period. Drug wholesalers exhibited an especially high rate of growth between 1948 and 1954, averaging almost 6 per cent (5.8 per cent) per year.

Productivity measures for the aforementioned groups of wholesalers will inevitably be compared with trends in output per man-hour in manufacturing and in the economy as a whole. While the data are not exactly comparable, the average annual increases for the same period were:

> For the economy as a whole .... 2.4 per cent per year
> For all manufacturing .... 2.0 per cent per year[7]

It should not be concluded from these figures that drug and hardware wholesalers lagged far behind other segments of the economy. The main problem in comparisons of this kind is that the broad averages shown above reflect many *shifts* in output and employment among the industries making up the averages. It is possible, in fact, for the average productivity of the economy as a whole or of all manufacturing industry to increase despite *decreases* in all or most individual industries. This could happen as a result of shifts from an industry with low productivity to one with high productivity.

Even if this factor could be taken into account, there is no question that output per man-hour *has* grown more rapidly in manufacturing and probably also in mining and agriculture, than in the field of wholesaling. The primary reason for this is the much greater degree of mechanization in these other segments of the economy than has been possible among wholesale enterprises. Also, it is likely that the managements of many wholesale firms have adopted conservative attitudes toward innovation, thus delaying improvements in productivity. The rapid gains made by drug wholesalers in the post-World War II period, however, show that there is no inherent reason for the slower growth of wholesaling productivity. These gains have no doubt been matched or exceeded by wholesalers, chain store warehouses, and manufacturers' sales branches in the food and certain other trades not represented in Table 10.

Capital Productivity Trends. In Table 11 are presented measures of output per dollar of assets employed by general line drug and hardware wholesalers, comparable with the labor productivity measures shown in

---

[7] Beckman and Buzzell, "Productivity—Facts and Fiction," *op. cit.,* based on data in Tables 1 and 2.

TABLE 11

VALUE ADDED, VALUE OF ASSETS EMPLOYED, AND VALUE ADDED PER
DOLLAR OF ASSETS, GENERAL LINE DRUG AND HARDWARE WHOLE-
SALERS, CENSUS OF BUSINESS YEARS, 1929–1954

	Drug Wholesalers			Hardware Wholesalers		
Year	Value Added (000)	Assets Employed (000)	Value Added per Dollar of Assets	Value Added (000)	Assets Employed (000)	Value Added per Dollar of Assets
1929	$ 63,563	$188,367	$0.34	$119,383	$424,129	$0.28
1935	41,660	122,238	0.34	51,455	154,665	0.33
1939	53,542	129,375	0.41	109,796	246,242	0.45
1948	128,858	241,163	0.53	348,282	627,789	0.56
1954	203,571	411,851	0.49	314,241	609,650	0.52

Source: Robert D. Buzzell, "Productivity in Marketing with Special Reference to
Drug and Hardware Wholesalers," unpublished Ph.D. dissertation on deposit in the
library of The Ohio State University, 1957, Tables 3, 8, and 12.

Table 10. In this case, however, no adjustment was made for price
changes, on the theory that such changes would affect value added and
asset values about equally. Somewhat surprisingly, the figures reveal a
more rapid gain in capital productivity than in output per man-hour. This
is in contrast to most manufacturing industries, in which the substitution
of capital for labor has prevented any rapid increase in output relative to
investment during the period of rapid capital expansion. After World War
II, however, a change in this pattern has become apparent. During this
period many wholesalers constructed one-story warehouses, installed mechanical tabulating systems, and otherwise mechanized their operations.[8]
As a result, output per dollar of investment actually fell slightly between
1948 and 1954 but would be expected to rise once the effects of the capital expansion begin to be felt in substantial measure.

Significance of Productivity Trends. Measures of labor and capital productivity in and of themselves reveal little of interest or value to business
executives and economists. The usefulness of such data lies in the relationship to the various *causes and effects* of productivity changes. Again as an
illustration of productivity analysis, these factors may now be examined
briefly.

Because productivity as herein discussed is a measure of over-all performance in a business, it is affected by virtually all of the forces bearing
on the business. These include *external factors,* such as government taxation policies and price regulation; general economic forces, such as population trends, and consumer income and tastes; and natural factors, such as

[8] See Chapters 23, 24, and 25 for further discussion of these developments.

the discovery of new resources. Even more important are *internal factors* —technology, the quality of management, and the skills and efforts of workers.

During the period in question a number of these factors operated to encourage an increasing level of labor and capital productivity. Higher rates of taxation, a rapidly increasing wage scale, and the dislocations caused by the depression of the 1930's and by World War II, all disrupted the traditional patterns of wholesaling and forced managements to seek new and better ways of accomplishing their tasks. Within wholesale enterprises technology of materials handling and warehousing improved tremendously during the period and especially after World War II, during which great strides were made by the armed services in their warehousing and handling of war materials. Management methods also improved particularly in the areas of sales, planning, and control of operations. It is also apparent that the quality of the typical wholesaling worker has been raised, especially among sales and merchandising personnel. Many jobs formerly regarded as suitable for persons with little formal education are now filled by highly trained specialists, and this trend has been accelerated in the 1950's.

The *effects* of changes in labor and capital productivity are more difficult to isolate. For wages and prices, available information suggests that money wages increased much more rapidly than did output per man-hour, which is consistent with the approximate doubling in prices during the period. This is quite similar to the over-all pattern of wage and price increases in the total economy, and indicates that wholesaling has probably been affected by the same basic economic trends. Profits, on the other hand, seem to have increased but little relative to assets employed, if consideration is given to the much higher level of taxation prevailing in 1954 than in earlier years. The dual impact of higher wages and higher taxes, together with continuing pressures by manufacturers and retailers on gross margins, seem to have prevented any improvement in relative profits.

Measures of Efficiency. In addition to measures of productivity such as those just discussed, various measures of efficiency are useful in appraising the performance of a wholesaling enterprise. Since the definition of efficiency adopted depends on one's viewpoint, several kinds of measures are possible. From the viewpoint of workers, *wage rates per hour* provide a convenient measure of efficiency, but must be modified in the light of working conditions, "fringe" benefits, and other factors. *Profit on invested capital* is a commonly used measure of financial efficiency as conceived by the proprietors or stockholders of a business. Owners of land can compare alternative uses in terms of *rental rates per square foot* or *per acre*. Finally, from a broader social viewpoint, any over-all measure of efficiency must take into account the total benefits and costs to society associated with an activity, including such factors as effects on national security, depletion of resources, and injuries to workers.[9]

CRITERIA OF PRODUCTIVITY AND EFFICIENCY

The statistical measures of productivity discussed in the preceding section are merely *examples* of quantitative productivity analysis. At the present time it is not possible to extend this analysis to cover wholesale trade systematically. In the absence of such measures qualitative judgments must be made of the level of productivity and efficiency and of changes therein. This can best be done by applying certain *criteria* of productivity and efficiency, the presence and extent of which determine or condition effective performance. Of these factors, the following are believed to be the most important:

1. Specialization in functions and in goods, and the degree of division of labor
2. Standardization in functions performed and in goods marketed
3. The use of labor-saving devices
4. Organization for the coordination of effort
5. Provision of incentives for employees
6. The dynamic nature of the wholesaling system
7. The degree and nature of competition
8. The kind and amount of research
9. The amount and quality of organized education and training for work in the field[10]

Specialization in Wholesaling. It is generally conceded that specialization is the very cornerstone of efficiency. In the field of manufacturing, the benefits of specialization, and the division of labor which is a corollary of specialization, are widely recognized and taken for granted. Manufacturing, however, has no monopoly on specialization. Wholesaling in a broad sense is in itself a field of specialized activity involving all necessary intermediate steps, exclusive of manufacturing and processing operations, in the movement of goods from manufacturers, agricultural producers, or extractive industries to the point at which consumer goods, or the services flowing from industrial goods, are to be distributed for personal or household consumption.

---

[9] For an interesting analysis of the various factors to be considered, see "Underlying Objectives of Marketing Efficiency Programs," in *Marketing Efficiency in a Changing Economy,* Report of the National Workshop on Agricultural Marketing, U. S. Department of Agriculture (Washington, D. C.: Government Printing Office, 1955), pp. 179–92. See also "Marketing Efficiency," by N. H. Engle, in *Journal of Marketing* (April, 1941).

[10] Theodore N. Beckman, "Criteria of Marketing Efficiency," *Annals of the American Academy of Political and Social Science,* Vol. 209 (May, 1940).

Within this specialized field of economic activity, there is a division and subdivision of the various distributive tasks in order that the process may be carried on more economically. Witness, for example, the large number of varied types of middlemen who bear little or no market risk but specialize in the performance of a limited number of marketing functions. Among those who might be mentioned are brokers, commission merchants, selling agents, manufacturers' agents, factors, purchasing agents, resident buyers, auction companies, export and import agents. Then there are the numerous types of wholesale merchants, including regular wholesalers, voluntary group wholesalers, industrial distributors, and those who have limited their service to some degree such as cash-and-carry wholesalers, retailer-owned cooperatives, drop shippers, and wagon distributors. The very presence of such a variety of institutions in a highly competitive segment of the economy is prima facie evidence that each of these specialized types of middlemen performs a service more efficiently under given conditions and circumstances than other types.

Specialization in wholesaling exists by lines or kinds of merchandise as well as by types of services rendered or methods of operation. Thus some brokers specialize in manufactured food products, others in consumer farm products, still others in grain, and so on. Similarly, manufacturers' agents usually specialize in restricted lines of merchandise such as automotive accessories, industrial equipment, construction materials, or grocery specialties. As only one of the many examples that may be drawn from the field of wholesale merchants is the distributor of industrial goods: some carry a rather full line of smaller items of factory equipment and all kinds of mill supplies, others handle specific types of merchandise such as nonferrous metals or industrial chemicals, and still others specialize in serving specific types of purchasers such as dental supply houses and barber and beauty supply houses.

Then there is the division of labor within individual business organizations. In a typical wholesale house, for example, there are executives such as the general manager, merchandise manager, warehouse superintendent, sales manager, treasurer, and credit manager, as well as all sorts of specialized employees at various operating and staff levels.

It is believed that the benefits resulting from specialization in the field of wholesaling are on a level comparable with those in the field of manufacturing and that, *within* the field of wholesaling, a degree of specialization and division of labor in individual organizations that is encountered only in the larger and most highly integrated retailing organizations has become rather commonplace. Retailing is less specialized than manufacturing or wholesaling, because of the preponderance of institutions which, because of size or location factors, or because of consumer shopping habits, must necessarily be substantially nonspecialized.

Standardization. Closely allied to specialization as a factor in efficiency is the degree of standardization in goods marketed and functions performed. Standardization in goods marketed results from the practice of producing goods to conform to predetermined specifications or, in the case of agricultural commodities or products from the extractive industries, the grading or classification of goods according to standards previously set up and generally recognized.

Standardization in goods marketed contributes to productivity and efficiency in wholesaling in many ways. It makes possible economical and speedy exchanges by *description* in contrast to the costly and more cumbersome methods of sale or purchase by *inspection* or *sample* that are necessary in the absence of standardization. Standardized or graded commodities may be mixed or pooled in storage or in transit, packed in uniform shipping containers, and in many cases formed into unit loads, thus effecting substantial economies in storage and transportation. Risk is reduced and business carried on with greater confidence in certain lines because of the practice of hedging futures contracts in highly standardized storable commodities subject to a large volume of trading. The financing of wholesaling activities is facilitated through the ability to obtain larger loans on a given amount of collateral when the collateral represents standardized rather than nonstandardized commodities. This is true because the prices of standardized goods fluctuate less violently than those of nonstandardized goods, what those prices are at any given time is readily ascertainable and, since there is a ready market for most standardized goods, the collateral can be quickly disposed of should the need arise. Standardization in goods marketed also contributes to efficiency in wholesaling through the greater quantity of market information available and the intelligence with which this information can be interpreted. The foregoing is necessarily an incomplete listing of advantages flowing from standardization and can be interpreted only as illustrative of the many advantages derived from dealing in such goods.

Standardization in goods marketed has also contributed to progress in standardizing some of the marketing functions. As more efficient methods are developed, they are imitated by other concerns. Certainly many of the procedures in buying, receiving, warehousing, stock control, selling, order-handling, credit-granting, delivery, and the handling of expenses and records, while necessarily varying somewhat from establishment to establishment, have been the subject of standardization throughout the field of wholesaling. Within specific lines of trade where wholesalers are bound together in progressive trade associations and within individual organizations, standardization in functions has been facilitated by time-and-duty studies and other standard measures of performance which are used to raise the level of efficiency of employees.

Although additional economies in distribution can undoubtedly be effected through further progress in standardization, the benefits already derived are substantial. It is equally important to recognize that, in a competitive capitalistic economy, there are definite limits beyond which standardization cannot be carried without unduly restricting the buyer's freedom to pick and choose from a variety of offerings of goods and services.

Use of Labor-Saving Devices. The important role played by labor-saving devices in the more efficient manufacturing of goods in our economy is a matter of common knowledge. Not so commonly recognized by the layman is the degree to which such devices are used in marketing. For the *internal* movement of merchandise in wholesale houses, witness the use of skids and pallets handled by hand jacks and electric lift or fork trucks, spiral and straight-ramp chutes, portable gravity conveyors, power-driven roller and monorail conveyors, "dumb-waiters," and elevators. Then, for accounting and statistical purposes and other office activities, there are typewriters, addressographs, duplicators, mechanical dictating equipment, and various billing, bookkeeping, computing, and tabulating machines; also witness the use of such internal communication devices as telephones, pneumatic tube systems, and the telautograph.

Labor-saving devices are not restricted to items of machinery and equipment. Also involved is the proper design of the physical plant, including the correct use of light and color to facilitate the economical performance of necessary tasks, a factor concerning which much progress has been made in wholesale distribution. Noteworthy are various types of merchandise layouts in an assembly line manner designed to be used in connection with preprinted order forms. Also important is the use of the newer systems of stock control which, with the aid of special tabulating and computing equipment, make possible order transcription, physical inventory control, inventory control in terms of value, sales analysis, invoice writing, and other operations. The proper design of forms to facilitate subsequent operations in the office or warehouse is another area in which many wholesaling firms have made notable progress.

Organization. Another important factor in efficiency is the organization that is necessary to coordinate the effort of many specialized employees. In a majority of wholesale houses of medium or large size, a logical allocation of specific duties on a *functional division* basis has been adopted; thus there are generally *merchandise, operating, sales,* and *finance and accounting* divisions, each in charge of a specialized executive.

Another aspect of organization is the departmentization of merchandise stocks in accordance with the nature of the goods handled, volume of sales, profitableness of items, experience of the personnel, storage and handling facilities available, and amount of sales effort required.

By segregating the various divisions of the enterprise according to the type of work and line of merchandise, tending toward decentralization, there are formed largely self-governing units, subject only to the general supervision of the management. In this way effective control of merchandise inventories, purchases, and sales is secured; responsibility for various activities is clearly defined and coordinated; and a sound basis for planning is provided.

Incentives. The provision of opportunity to employees in the form of incentives encourages productivity in the performance of assigned tasks. Although this is an area in which much progress can still be made in all segments of our economy, certainly wholesaling stands in a favorable position relative to other segments. Practically all selling work in wholesaling, whether broadly or narrowly conceived, is on an incentive basis with compensation varying according to accomplishment. Various forms of compensation plans involving commissions, bonuses, and profit-sharing devices, are common in wholesaling. With regard to all employees in medium- and large-sized wholesaling firms, lines of promotion are usually fairly well defined in a functional system of organization. Since wholesaling establishments operate without the great masses of routine employees characteristic of large manufacturing industries, promotion comes easier to those able to demonstrate their efficiency. Furthermore, because the size of the average wholesale establishment is large enough to provide a variety of opportunities, it appears that incentives in the nature of promotion possibilities are greater than in retailing, when the latter field of activity is viewed as a whole. Finally, there is the higher level of average wage rates available in the field of wholesaling, which is in itself an incentive.

Dynamic Nature of the Business. The ever changing character of our marketing system and its institutions prevents stagnation and encourages progress and efficiency. That wholesaling has been highly dynamic, almost in a state of flux, will be readily conceded when attention is called to the gradual supersedence of the wholesaling activities of the early trading posts and general stores by strictly wholesale establishments, largely of a general merchandise type. Then developed the custom of specializing in certain kinds of goods as a larger assortment of merchandise became available from a firmly established factory system. This evolutionary process continued through the nineteenth and twentieth centuries witnessing, as the need arose, the emergence of a large number of specialized types of wholesaling middlemen, most of whom have already been mentioned in connection with the preceding discussion of specialization in wholesaling. The wholesaling system has been equally dynamic in the matter of policies, methods, and the manner of performing specific functions— present-day practices being those which have evolved through a competitive struggle that has tended to eliminate or minimize the importance of the less efficient.

Competition. Competition is a factor in efficiency, for under a competitive system only the more efficient tend to survive in the long run. Unlike the manufacturer who is usually on his own level of operation the exclusive seller of a product differentiated to some degree, the wholesaler is generally in direct competition in his own market with other wholesalers selling, for the most part, identical goods. Not having as one of his functions the creation of demand for a differentiated product, the wholesaler must compete more aggressively on the basis of prices offered or services rendered.

Not only must a wholesaler meet the competition from other wholesalers of the same type located in his own city and in surrounding market centers, but he must also compete with different types of wholesale organizations as a class that are similarly located. Thus the regular wholesale grocer, as one example, must compete not only with other wholesale grocers in his territory, but also with specialty and limited-function wholesalers in the grocery trade, with wholesale grocers who have a voluntary tie-up with retailers, with retailer-owned cooperative warehouses, with manufacturers' sales branches, with chain store warehouses, and to some degree with functional middlemen who sell to the larger retail grocers. As a result of this kind of competition there is no question that all those engaged in most lines of wholesale trade have become vastly more efficient than their predecessors.

Research. One of the most potent corrective forces in business today is to be found in research. Although much more in this field remains to be accomplished, the great expansion in the application of marketing research techniques in the years immediately prior to and following World War II has certainly contributed to the more effective and economical cultivation of markets. By constantly adding to the body of organized knowledge concerning sound business policy and practice, research provides for sound decisions based on pertinent and properly interpreted facts.

Within wholesaling organizations, this is accomplished by location studies, continuing and occasional sales analyses of various types, cost analyses, and time-and-duty studies of salesmen's and inside employees' activities. Trade associations in various lines of wholesale business have been very active in research work of various types. Some of these carry on or sponsor cost and operating studies that provide great benefit to their memberships. Particularly noteworthy are the operating cost studies, published annually by a number of such associations, providing detailed functional cost data for firms classified according to size and geographic location. Also of great importance is the research work carried on in the field of wholesaling by various Bureaus of Business Research, such as those at The Ohio State University, Harvard, and the University of Washington, and the numerous master's theses and doctoral dissertations written and in progress at leading colleges of commerce. In addition, there is the vast amount of research undertaken by government agencies, particularly the U. S. Department of Commerce, which results in the many important operating studies of the types frequently referred to throughout this book.

Education and Training. A final factor in productivity efficiency is the amount and quality of organized education and training for work in any given field of activity. There are now many schools of commerce on the collegiate level and courses in wholesaling are offered in many of the leading schools. In addition, many of the functional courses in marketing such as sales management, credits and collections, distribution cost accounting, and marketing research deal largely with wholesaling activities. There are also other business courses in accounting, business organization and management, business correspondence, office management, advertising, personnel administration, and transportation which are applicable to wholesaling and provide a foundation for work in the field. Furthermore, in almost all colleges that have any kind of a curriculum in business administration, a course is provided in general marketing dealing to a considerable extent with wholesaling activities and institutions.

Many business organizations provide sales and other types of training for their employees. Thousands of men and women actively engaged in marketing attend evening classes for the purpose of acquiring more education in their chosen fields of work. Such classes are provided in colleges and universities, in adult education programs, and under other auspices. While this education and training movement is belated, the rapid progress being made should certainly contribute to enhanced efficiency.

15

GOVERNMENTAL
IMPACT UPON
WHOLESALING

Wholesaling, as all of marketing, is an integral part of economics. Like our economic system as a whole, exclusive of what are known as the regulated industries, such as railroads and public utilities, it is necessarily governed by the same basic philosophy that underlies the relationship of government and *all* private competitive business enterprise. That philosophy, in short, has as its primary objectives the maintenance and promotion of competition on the one hand and the prevention or removal of unfairness in competition on the other.

By the same token all those engaged in wholesaling must operate within the same legal context or environment that affects or surrounds all private competitive economic activity. This context consists for the most part of what is commonly referred to as antitrust legislation and its enforcement, which is aimed largely at the regulation or control of business activity in the market place and on the wholesale level. Illustrative are all matters touching agreements or conspiracies in restraint of *trade,* unfair methods of competition, price discrimination, selection and classification of customers, exclusive dealings, tying sales contracts, and the regulation of industry *trade* practices.

Finally, wholesaling, like all economic activity, is subject to certain general public policies, which may be in line with the basic philosophy and its legal implementation referred to above or may, for varying durations, seriously deviate from them. For example, since the 1930's it has been public policy to *support the prices* of certain agricultural products at specified levels determined from time to time by legislation and gov-

255

ernmental administrative decision, instead of allowing the prices to fluctuate in obedience to the forces of supply and demand at work in a competitive market. Again, it has been the declared public policy to *maintain full employment,* even at the expense of competitive determination of certain costs, prices, and profits. Closely allied to this is the public policy that calls for *economic stability,* with emphasis on anti-inflationary effort, even though some of it may threaten to run athwart our basic desire for competition and its implementation through antitrust policy.

Obviously, those operating on the wholesale level must know *how* to do business within the appropriate legal framework and in line with declared public policies that may be pertinent. More than that, they must know *why* they should so operate; that comes only from a proper understanding and appreciation of the reasons and bases for the laws and public policies in question and the method of their enforcement. Even that may not be enough, for it is far better to conduct a business on the highest level of morality even beyond any legal or public policy requirements. Verily, a man's goodness cannot be fully trusted if it rests solely on his fear of arrest or social opprobrium. It is intended that the contents of this chapter, though limited in scope, should provide some of the fundamentals for appropriate as well as successful wholesaling.

Essence of Basic Philosophy. As already indicated, a principal objective in the relationship of government and private competitive business enterprise is the maintenance of competition and possibly its further promotion. It is believed in this country that the greatest economic good for all of society can thus be best achieved, for it is the self-interested and independent rivalry of private competitors that tends, in the long run, to guide the flow of economic resources toward the most productive uses, that provides incentives through improved technology and management for innovation and cost reduction, and that makes for an equitable distribution of proceeds from economic effort among the factors of production. More specifically, maintenance and promotion of competition spells competitive opportunity for both buyers and sellers, commercial freedom including entry into and exit from business, as well as public benefits. This is summed up in Section 2(a) of the Small Business Act of 1958,[1] which made the Small Business Administration a permanent and independent federal agency, as follows:

The essence of the American economic system of private enterprise is free competition. Only through full and free competition can free markets, free entry into business, and opportunities for the expression and growth of personal initiative and individual judgment be assured. The preservation and expansion of such competition is basic not only to the economic well-being but to the security of this Nation. . . .

[1] Public Law 85–536, signed by the President in August, 1958.

A second principal objective is the prevention or removal of unfairness in competition, including the prevention of public injury that might result from certain competitive practices. This, in a sense, puts bounds to, and places a bridle upon, competition. In general, then, it may be said that it is the composite of these two objectives that forms our antitrust policy.

Concept of Competition. Competition is conceived variously as pure, perfect, monopolistic, oligopolistic, imperfect, workable, effective, or normal, depending upon (1) the model used by the economist for theoretical analysis and (2) the degree of reality it is desired to depict. Obviously, the concepts of pure and perfect competition are merely tools of theoretical analysis; the very listing of the prerequisites for such competition as well as the literal meaning of those terms are convincing proof of their abstract character. The concept contemplated for this discussion is that of workable, sometimes referred to as effective or normal, competition. Some of the factors bearing on the identification of the existence and extent of such competition are:

1. The number of effective competitors—buyers or sellers—and their relative size
2. Freedom of opportunity for entry of new rivals and withdrawal of old ones
3. Genuine independence of business rivals, each pursuing its own individual advantage
4. Absence of predatory preclusive practices, which are usually symptomatic of monopoly or intent to monopolize
5. Rate of growth of the industry or market as an indirect indicator of the state of competition
6. Nature and extent of market incentives to competitive devices, as measured perhaps by the response of customers and prospects to a competitor's move
7. Product differentiation or homogeneity, price competition usually being more active the more homogeneous the products of rival sellers are
8. Degree to which prices and other competitive devices are met or matched by competitors
9. Certain types of price discrimination
10. Existence of unused or excess capacity under normal conditions, which would presumably stimulate competition in order to make use of it[2]

Implementation of Basic Philosophy. While consideration in this chapter is confined to the various laws that constitute the framework of our antitrust policy, businessmen operating on the wholesale level are also concerned with other laws which have no direct bearing on competition.

[2] For a summarized discussion of these factors, see *Report of the Attorney General's National Committee To Study the Antitrust Laws* (Washington, D. C.: Government Printing Office, 1955), pp. 324–36.

Among these are the Fair Labor Standards Act designed to protect the worker by placing a floor on wage rates and a ceiling on hours worked per week at the minimum or other agreed wage rate; the Food, Drug, and Cosmetic Act aimed to protect the health and welfare of the public; and the many promotive measures enacted for the benefit of business like those having to do with weights and measures.

Not all the laws bearing on competition exert a similar influence on it. To be sure, theoretically and in the long run, all of them are presumed to cause us to maintain or promote competition in one way or another. Some of them, however, have the effect of *preserving* competition by maintaining a status quo. Others tend to *promote* competition by making it more vigorous or more workable. Still others tend to *restrict* competition by inhibiting the freedom of competitors, especially in pricing. Usually, when a law does not help to maintain or promote competition, it may have been enacted pursuant to a declared public policy which, to that extent, supersedes and deviates from the basic philosophy.

On the federal level the core of our antitrust policy consists of three statutes and amendments thereto. They are: the Sherman Antitrust Act (1890), as amended by the Miller-Tydings Act (1937); the Clayton Antitrust Act (1914), as amended by the Robinson-Patman Act (1936) and the Antimerger Act (1950); and the Federal Trade Commission Act (1914), as amended by the Wheeler-Lea Act (1938) and the McGuire Fair Trade Act (1952). These, together with the Wool Products Labeling Act of 1939, the Fur Products Labeling Act (1951), the Flammable Fabrics Act (1953), and the Textile Fiber Products Identification Act (1958, effective March 3, 1960), are often regarded as the basic laws dealing with trade regulation. In addition, there are many federal laws of varying impact upon private business. Some of them, like the Pure Food and Drug Act (1906), as amended in 1938, and the Small Business Act of 1958, are of widespread application. Others, like the Automobile Franchise Act (1956) and the Commodity Exchange Act (1922), are aimed at specific situations or commodities.

On the state level there are "Little Sherman Antitrust Acts," Fair Trade Acts, Sales Below Cost Laws, Price Discrimination Acts, Chain Store Tax Laws, Sales or Gross Receipts Tax Laws, and others that may affect wholesaling. Even at the local level there are laws affecting the taxes paid by wholesale organizations, requiring licenses of one kind or another, and the like.

It must be remembered that the legal context in which a wholesale business must function consists of more than legislation. Laws must be administered and for that purpose they have to be interpreted and applied to specific situations. The regulations and interpretations prepared by the administering agency to that end at times go beyond the intent of the legislators or, if unsympathetic, may so restrict the application as to nullify the original intent of the law. Moreover, some of the agencies are more competent and perhaps more objective than others. One must therefore become familiar with the machinery for enforcement, especially the U. S. Department of Justice and the court system under its jurisdiction, the Federal Trade Commission, the U. S. Department of Agriculture, and other federal government agencies that may be charged with the administration of specific laws that are applicable. Finally, the legal context includes the vast number of decisions by the various state and federal courts, the Federal Trade Commission, and other pertinent administrative and semijudicial agencies, including stipulations and consent orders and decrees.

RESTRAINT OF TRADE AND MONOPOLY

That part of our national policy that has to do with the maintenance of competition and the prevention of monopoly is presumed to be attained through the statutory prohibitions of restraints of trade, monopolizations, and mergers. On the federal level the most pertinent of these prohibitions are contained in the two basic laws discussed below.

Background. Throughout the greater part of the nineteenth century, rugged individualism and free-for-all competition characterized the business structure of the United States. Little demand for government regulation of commerce was evident during the great era of the conquest of the West. Business, expanding steadily under the impetus of the Industrial Revolution, was ever alert for new devices and mechanisms of progress. Energetic and aggressive leaders of industry found in the corporate form of organization the means for accumulating the great blocks of capital required to untilize to the full the advantages of large-scale operations. Combinations, pools, and trusts were developed to concentrate control in the hands of relatively few capable, but often ruthless, captains of industry. The small, independent operator became more and more disturbed as these giant enterprises waged unequal warfare against him.[3]

[3] This development is well summarized in the following statement:
"Efforts to obtain monopolistic control of the market have existed to a greater or less extent in almost all periods of civilization. . . . The recent development of large combinations and monopolies in the United States, as well as in various foreign countries, has been especially striking, because it followed an era in which competition had been strongly developed. This pronounced competitive era was apparently the result of several historical circumstances, among which may be mentioned the development of the factory system of production, the improvement of means of transportation and communication, the development of more liberal laws of commercial intercourse between nations, and the influence of the economic doctrine of free trade and free industry."
Report of the Commissioner of Corporations on "Trust Laws and Unfair Competition," Department of Commerce, Bureau of Corporations (Washington, D. C.: Government Printing Office, 1916), p. 1.

Following the pattern of Great Britain, the *common law* of the United States traditionally favored competition and opposed monopoly. Various court decisions under the common law indicated the intent of the courts to prevent the development of trusts, holding companies, price-fixing agreements, and other devices which were held to be in restraint of trade or unfairly competitive. But the common law and the court decisions under it were clearly inadequate to preserve competition. Action could be taken only upon the complaint of an injured competitor and in his behalf. All that the courts were able to do in the majority of cases was to declare contracts unenforceable. Thus there was no way in which the interests of the *public* could be safeguarded.

During the latter part of the 1880's the public became fearful of the increasing trend toward bigness in industry, feeling that this trend was contrary to the American tradition of rugged individualism. The clamor for legislation to control the industrial giants resulted in the passage of a number of state "antitrust" laws before the first federal enactment, the Sherman Antitrust Act, which became effective on July 2, 1890.[4]

The Sherman Antitrust Act. This act was intended to remedy the defects of the common law under which the enforcement of competition in interstate commerce was practically impossible. The two major provisions of the act, which represent the central core of antitrust concepts, were directed against restraints of trade and monopoly. They are as follows:

SEC. 1. Every contract, combination in the form of a trust or otherwise, or conspiracy, in restraint of commerce among the several states, or with foreign nations, is hereby declared to be illegal . . .

SEC. 2. Every person who shall monopolize, or attempt to monopolize, or combine or conspire with any other person or persons, to monopolize any part of the trade or commerce among the several states, shall be deemed guilty of a misdemeanor. . . .

Early decisions under the Sherman Antitrust Act cast some doubts upon the value of the act. In the *Knight* case, for example, an attempt was made to break up the rather complete domination of the sugar industry by the "sugar trust." In this case the court ruled that manufacturing (which was monopolistically controlled by the trust) was not *commerce* and was not therefore subject to the provisions of the federal law. Other decisions, notably the Trans-Missouri Freight Association, the Joint Traffic Association, and the Addyston Pipe & Steel Company cases, were more

4 Among the states that enacted legislation prohibiting trusts and other combinations in restraint of trade or tending to monopoly, before the passage of the Sherman Act, were the following: Maine, 1889; Michigan, 1889; Texas, 1889; Iowa, May 6, 1890; Kentucky, May 20, 1890. Several states also had constitutional provisions declaring monopolies or combinations in restraint of trade unlawful. Among these states are Arkansas, Georgia, Kentucky. Tennessee. and Texas.

encouraging to the control of monopoly. Later victories by the government against the oil and tobacco trusts strengthened the belief that monopolies might be prevented in the United States. It was in 1911, in *The Standard Oil Company* case, that the Supreme Court practically amended the Sherman Act by declaring that only when contracts and combinations restrain trade *unreasonably* are they to be regarded in violation of the law.[5] While this interpretation provided the basis for the breaking up of rather complete monopolies, it created much confusion regarding the legality of integrations and loosely knit agreements that were trade-restraining to a less marked degree.

Since the early cases referred to above, numerous actions have been taken under each of the two sections of the Sherman Act. One case worth noting because it probably serves as a landmark in some respects is that of *United States v. Trenton Potteries Co.*[6] For one thing it established the doctrine that the *unreasonableness* previously enunciated by the Supreme Court with reference to restraint of trade may be "conclusively presumed," so that some restraints may be unreasonable per se as in the *Trenton Potteries* case. Second, reasonableness does not depend upon the *effect* of the agreement, as revealed by the following quotation from the decision:

The aim and result of every price-fixing agreement, if effective, is the elimination of one form of competition. The power to fix prices, whether reasonably exercised or not, involves power to control the market and to fix arbitrary and unreasonable prices. . . .

The Sherman Act is enforced by the Department of Justice through suits for injunctive relief or for criminal penalties, or both, at the discretion of the court. Until the 1955 amendment[7] violation of the law was a misdemeanor punishable by a fine not exceeding five thousand dollars, or by imprisonment not exceeding one year, or both. At that time the fine was raised to an amount not exceeding fifty thousand dollars. Nor is it possible, since 1956,[8] for private parties to sue for treble damages under this law; instead, any such action must now be taken under Section 4 of the Clayton Act discussed below.

The Clayton Antitrust Act. The inadequacies of the Sherman Act and the confusion resulting from the early Supreme Court decisions culminating in its "Rule of Reason" pronouncement in 1911 led to a demand for ad-

---

[5] See *United States v. Trans-Missouri Freight Association,* 166 U.S. 290; *Addyston Pipe & Steel Company v. United States,* 175 U.S. 211; *United States v. E. C. Knight,* 156 U.S. 1; *United States v. Joint-Traffic Association et al.,* 171 U.S. 505; *United States v. American Tobacco Co.,* 221 U.S. 106; *Standard Oil Company of New Jersey et al. v. United States,* 221 U.S. 1.

[6] 273 U.S. 392, 47 S. Ct. 377 (1927).

[7] Public Law 135; 15 U.S. Code, Secs. 1, 2, and 3.

[8] Public Law 137, Sec. 7.

ditional legislation to curb big business and prevent unfair and monopolistic practices. This agitation led, among other things, to the passage of the Clayton Antitrust Act in 1914. This law supplemented the Sherman Act by defining and prohibiting the following practices "where the effect will be substantially to lessen competition or tend to create a monopoly":

1. Discrimination in price between purchasers of a like grade, quality, or quantity of the commodity sold
2. "Tying contracts" which obligate the buyer of a commodity to purchase supplementary and perhaps undesirable lines of merchandise in order to secure the desired items handled by the seller
3. Interlocking directorates in directly competing corporations (except banks and common carriers) of more than $1,000,000 capital, surplus, and undivided profits
4. The acquisition by a corporation of more than a limited amount of stock in a competing corporation

Coming largely under this law are also some of the restrictive features that are sometimes connected with exclusive dealings under franchise or other arrangements.[9] Prominent among them are those that require or have the effect of full line forcing, the exclusion of competing products, limitations of dealers' or distributors' sales territories, and price restrictions other than those allowed under Fair Trade laws.

In 1936 this law was amended by passage of the Robinson-Patman Act to be discussed later in this chapter, mainly in order to elaborate and put teeth into old Section 2 which prohibits price discrimination. Another significant amendment was adopted in 1950 in the form of the Antimerger Act, in order to cover mergers consummated by other than stock acquisition and to overcome rather narrow court interpretations of old Section 7. The new law is intended to cope with tendencies toward monopoly or a substantial lessening of competition *in their incipiency,* thus making it sufficient to establish a *reasonable probability* of such tendencies resulting from a merger.[10]

UNFAIRNESS IN COMPETITION

It is not sufficient to have effective competition at any given time. There must be assurance that there is no unfairness in it if effective competition

[9] For a comprehensive discussion of this subject, see "Exclusive Distributorships and Dealerships," by Robert Edward Dillon, an unpublished doctoral dissertation supervised by the senior author and on deposit in the library of The Ohio State University (1958).

[10] For further light on this, see the Initial Order to Cease and Desist issued by the Federal Trade Commission Examiner in the *Matter of Pillsbury Mills, Inc.* on March 11, 1959. The Commission charged Pillsbury with unlawful acquisition of the assets of Ballard and Ballard Company and Duff's Baking Mix Division of American Home Products Corporation, resulting in monopolistic tendencies in the flour industry (F.T.C. Docket No. 6000).

is to endure. To provide for this the Federal Trade Commission Act was passed in 1914, almost simultaneously with the Clayton Antitrust Act just discussed. This organic law established the Federal Trade Commission (1) as an expert administrative agency for antitrust law enforcement and (2) as an authority to define, determine, and prevent unfair methods of competition and unfair or deceptive acts or practices under authority of Section 5 of the law.

The Federal Trade Commission. Under the jurisdiction of the Federal Trade Commission comes the enforcement of the Federal Trade Commission Act (1914) as amended by the Wheeler-Lea Act (1938) and the Oleomargarine Act (1950); the Clayton Act (1914) as amended by the Robinson-Patman Act (1936) and the Antimerger Act (1950); the Webb-Pomerene Export Trade Act (1918); the Wool Products Labeling Act (1939); Public Law 15 relating to the regulation of the business of Insurance (1945); the Lanham Trade Mark Act (1946); the Fur Products Labeling Act (1951); the Flammable Fabrics Act (1953); and the Textile Fiber Products Identification Act (1958).

This does not mean that the Commission has sole and exclusive jurisdiction over each of these laws. For example, the Clayton Act makes the U. S. Department of Justice and the Federal Trade Commission each responsible for enforcement of Sections 2, 3, 7, and 8. Again, though the Sherman Act specifies enforcement responsibility only to the Department of Justice (Attorney General), the Supreme Court has held that the Commission may declare conduct prohibited by the Sherman Act as "an unfair method of competition" under Section 5 of the Federal Trade Commission Act and that there is no reason why the enforcement of that law by the Department of Justice cannot be supplemented through the administrative process of the Commission.[11]

Whenever such dual enforcement is specified in the law or is otherwise deemed desirable, there is need for effective cooperation. Thus each agency notifies the other before initiating any action in a case in order to avoid unnecessary overlapping (in the matter of investigation, for example) or possible conflict. Furthermore, there is an understanding as to which agency would usually bring action under a given section of a law with dual enforcement. Finally, it may be a matter as to which agency is best fitted to do a given job. Thus the Department of Justice is no doubt better able to handle evidence involving criminal prosecution, while the Commission is better fitted to utilize the *administrative* process in the handling of a case. There may be other considerations, such as prior proceedings in a given case or industry, but at no time must the two agencies proceed in the same matter.

[11] *Federal Trade Commission v. Cement Institute,* 333 U.S. 683, 693 (1948).

There are also laws under the jurisdiction of the Commission in which other agencies have even more important functions. For example, while the Commission has responsibility for matters involving false advertisements of food, drugs, cosmetics, and devices, in all such cases it must take account of the labeling requirements of the Food and Drug Administration before any corrective action is applied to the advertising. Under such circumstances close cooperation between the agencies concerned is essential.

Principal Functions of the Federal Trade Commission. Obviously, the over-all function of the Commission is to enforce the laws for which it must or can assume responsibility as indicated in the preceding paragraphs. A major responsibility with which it is charged under the organic law is the determination and outlawing of *unfair* competition. To do this, the Commission in a given instance undertakes an investigation upon its own motion or upon written application of an interested party. If warranted, following a preliminary investigation, a complaint is issued, hearings are held before an examiner, and if found to be in violation of law, a cease and desist order may be issued by the Commission.

Illustrative of such action, later appealed to and finally adjudicated by the courts, are two cases involving the nature of wholesale as distinguished from retail transactions and the definition of a wholesaler as formulated and used for certain restrictive purposes by a trade association, respectively.[12] Another typical cease and desist order was that issued to a national association of wholesalers, 22 regional trade associations, and nearly 100 paper distributors requiring them to stop combining or conspiring to fix the prices of fine and wrapping paper. Among other things, they were forbidden to establish and maintain markups or percentages of markups in arriving at selling prices; to establish or maintain differentials for different quantities, color, cutting, trimming, packaging, or delivery; disseminate to each other price lists or terms or conditions of sale; publish or distribute any publication of national average percentage markups, and so forth; or hold or participate in any meeting or exchange of information for the purpose or with the effect of devising or establishing any method of fixing prices for fine or wrapping paper.[13] While the prohibitions contained in this order are far-reaching in scope, it must be remembered that they do not prohibit any one wholesaler from entering into agreements with any of his suppliers or customers to buy or sell at any price or on any terms or conditions independently determined in any bona fide transaction when such an agreement is not for the purpose or

[12] *L. & C. Mayers Co., Inc. v. Federal Trade Commission,* 97 F.2d 365 (CCA–2, 1938); and *Wholesale Dry Goods Institute, Inc. et al. v. Federal Trade Commission,* 139 F.2d 230 (CCA–2, 1943), certiorari denied (U.S. Sup. Ct., 1944).

[13] *National Paper Trade Association of the United States, Inc., et al.* Order to Cease and Desist, F.T.C. Docket No. 5592 (1954).

with the effect of restraining trade or competition. Nor does the order bar any wholesaler from quoting prices, terms, or conditions, for the purpose of effecting bona fide transactions.

Instead of formal legal proceedings, the Commission has developed over the years two types of informal settlement procedures which save time and expense and which under certain conditions may be equally useful as an enforcement device. One of them is settlement by *stipulation* to cease and desist. This process is usually limited to cases of unfair methods of competition or deceptive practices or acts where it is felt that the law was violated unintentionally through misunderstanding or carelessness. It is never used for certain types of cases like those involving acts inherently dangerous or injurious to health or restraints of competition through conspiracy, discrimination, or monopolistic practice. The stipulation is in the nature of an agreement, usually by the lawyers of the contending parties, as to facts and jurisdiction and to cease and desist from the acts or practices deemed in violation of law. While it does not constitute an admission of guilt, the stipulation is admissible as evidence in later proceedings that may be instituted if relevant to the issues. Sometimes a settlement by stipulation may be reached after an order to cease and desist has been issued, as was the case in which a petition for review of such an order, made by an association of electrical wholesalers charged with a combination to fix prices in the sale of rigid steel conduit, was withdrawn in consequence of a stipulation.[14]

A second type of informal settlement procedure is the *consent order* to cease and desist, which permits the disposition of a case as a whole or as to some of the issues by consent at any stage of the proceeding. A consent order has the same effect as a regular order by the Commission, but in the former the respondent must waive any right to appeal to a court for the purpose of testing the order's validity.

Another function of the Commission is to promulgate trade practice rules for industries as discussed in some detail later in this chapter. The Commission is also charged with the task of making investigations of business practices, undertaken on its own initiative or at the request of Congress or the President. These investigations serve three important purposes: (1) they supply background information for proposed congressional action; (2) they provide businessmen with information which is valuable in planning their own activities; and (3) they provide information as a background for its cease and desist orders. Finally, the Commission advises the President and the Congress with reference to changes in existing law, new laws, or other matters of public interest which are its concern.

[14] *National Electrical Wholesalers Ass'n. et al. v. Federal Trade Commission* (CCA–7, 1945).

The Wheeler-Lea Act. Since the enactment of the legislation of 1914, the activities of the Federal Trade Commission have expanded both as a result of a more liberal interpretation of the original legislation and by the passage of new legislation. The Commission has been charged with the enforcement of the Clayton Act and the Robinson-Patman Act. In addition, in a number of cases the Supreme Court has ruled that violations of the Sherman Act may be interpreted as "unfair methods of competition" subject to the control of the Commission.[15] Control of unfair methods of competition by the Commission was made much more comprehensive by the passage of the Wheeler-Lea Act in 1938.

This law, which was an amendment to the Federal Trade Commission Act, effected three important changes. First, it broadened the Commission's jurisdiction, to include practices that injure the public but which may or may not injure a competitor. A defect of the original act was that action could be taken only when a competitor was presumably injured by an unfair practice. Because of this defect, the Commission was overruled by the courts in such cases as one involving a manufacturer who used harmful and even fatal drugs in the preparation of an obesity cure. Because other manufacturers of similar products also used the same drugs, no injury to competition could be established, and the manufacturer was not stopped from continuing the practice. Under the present law, the Commission may take action of its own accord at any time that *public* injury can be shown.

A second change shortens the process of enforcement of the Commission's cease and desist orders. Unless appealed to the Federal District Courts, orders to cease and desist now become effective after 60 days. The enforcement process is also strengthened by the provision for violation suits in the District Courts where substantial penalties may be inflicted. A $5,000 civil penalty is provided for each violation of a cease and desist order after it becomes final.

The third and most important of the principal changes made by the Wheeler-Lea Act pertains to advertising. This provision definitely prohibits false advertising of food, drugs, cosmetics, and therapeutic devices. Certain infractions of these items are rendered criminal when injurious to health or when involving intent to deceive or defraud, and are punishable by fine and imprisonment. Temporary injunctions are provided to stop these practices pending issuance of a complaint and determination of the charges.

Control of Unfair Trade Practices. As a result of the more liberal interpretation of the original Federal Trade Commission Act and the enact-

---

[15] *Federal Trade Commission v. Pacific States Paper Trade Association*, 273 U.S. 52; *Fashion Originators' Guild v. Federal Trade Commission*, 312 U.S. 457. See also fn. 11.

ment of new legislation, the Commission now has very broad control over unfair methods of competition. The unfair methods and unfair or deceptive acts and practices condemned by the Commission from time to time in cease and desist orders may be classified into three major groups.

First, the Commission has jurisdiction over all methods that are *unfair as against good morals,* if used in interstate commerce and if the action is in the public interest. These are characterized by fraud and deception and must result in injury to competitors or the public. Misrepresentation of one's own goods as to origin, quantity, quality, price, and so on, or misrepresentation of one's business as to identity, character, and status are cases in point. Commercial bribery, deceptive selling schemes, disparagement of a competitor's goods, lottery, style piracy, and other immoral methods are illustrative of other unfair practices falling in this category.

The second class of unfair methods controlled by the Commission includes those that are *trade restraining or of a monopolistic nature.* Among these may be listed cooperation and combination through contracts and conspiracies in restraint of trade, illegal agreements and codes, trust agreements, holding companies, illegal mergers, and interlocking directorates. Similarly treated are coercion and restraint through tying contracts, full-line forcing, exclusive dealing, price discrimination, resale price maintenance (except as permitted by the Miller-Tydings Act and the McGuire Act), and imposition of arbitrary terms, conditions, and rates.

Finally, the Commission exercises power over *destructive competitive practices.* Included in this group are selling below cost, boycotts, harassing devices like interference with a competitor's supply of goods, or other economically unjustified hindrances to his sales and operations.

Trade Practice Conference Rules. In order to assist an industry in voluntary compliance with trade law and the prevention or removal of unfairness in competition, machinery has been set up by the Federal Trade Commission for the promulgation of trade practice rules for an industry desiring them. To date, such rules have been promulgated for some 300 manufacturing, wholesale, retail, and service trade or industry groups. Among the more recent in the wholesale field are one for the Wholesale Optical Industry (1950) and one for the Wholesale Plumbing and Heating Industry (1955).

Proceedings for establishing trade practice rules are instituted upon application made by members of an industry. Upon receipt of such an application the Commission arranges a trade practice conference at which suggested rules are considered and adopted by the industry, subject to the approval of the Commission. A draft of the proposed rules is then published for the information of interested parties and public notice is given concerning an additional hearing at which all interested or affected persons or organizations may present objections or suggestions for amendments. After full consideration of the matter, final action is taken by the Commission whereby it approves and promulgates the rules, which generally become operative within 30 days.

The trade practice rules are divided into two groups. In the first group are listed the rules which are considered to be unfair methods of competition, unfair or deceptive acts or practices, or other illegal practices prohibited under laws administered by the Commission. This group includes all the three types of unfair practices discussed in the preceding section. Appropriate action will be taken by the Commission to prevent the use of such unlawful practices in commerce by any firm that is a member of the industry for which the rules have been promulgated.

Violations of the rules listed in the second group do not in themselves constitute violations of law. In this group are included rules concerning actions which are considered by the industry to be unethical, uneconomic, or otherwise objectionable; or, when in the nature of positive pronouncements are considered to be conducive to sound business methods which the industry desires to encourage and promote. The observance of these rules is accomplished through the cooperation of the members of the industry concerned. Whenever such practices are used in a manner that they become unfair methods of competition in commerce or a violation of any law over which the Commission has jurisdiction, appropriate proceedings are instituted by the Commission as in the case of violations of rules in the first group.

Following the promulgation of the rules, a *trade practice committee* is usually established by the industry to work with the Commission in securing compliance with such rules. It is the function of the Industry Committee, formed by the industry at its option, to assist in keeping the rules active by periodically bringing them to the attention of the members; to disseminate among all members of the industry any Commission action relating to practices covered by the rules; and to meet periodically with Commission personnel for the purpose of discussing the rules, their administration, and possible revision.

It is important to bear in mind that trade practice rules do not make new law. Their function and effect is to:

1. Interpret the important provisions of existing laws applying to an industry.
2. Codify for the industry the existing laws that are applicable.
3. Clarify the laws by giving them concreteness and meaning through appropriate examples rooted in industry practice.
4. Evolve rules that are in consonance with the law and at the same time practical and workable.

5. Provide industry members with guidance by which they may judge the lawfulness of their activities.
6. Render, through the procedure, an educational service in eliminating or preventing unethical as well as illegal practices and acts, thus raising the moral level of industry conduct.
7. Provide an opportunity for an industry to clean house and for moral self-discipline.
8. Remove the pressure to engage in questionable practices to meet equally questionable practices of competitors.

PRICE DISCRIMINATION IN ITS SEVERAL FORMS

As previously indicated, the Clayton Antitrust Act prohibited certain discriminations in price to purchasers of the same goods under like conditions, but this provision of the law was ambiguous, narrowly interpreted, and seldom enforced. At the same time the need for such a prohibition stemmed from a different source and became urgent in the 1920's with the tremendous growth in chain stores and other mass distributors which allegedly received economically unjustified price and other concessions from suppliers. All of this was at the expense of the smaller competitors—retailers and wholesalers—and much to their detriment as well as in restraint of trade and tending toward monopoly.

In pursuance of Senate Resolution 224 adopted in 1928, the Federal Trade Commission conducted a "Chain Store Inquiry," as a result of which it has submitted as Senate documents over a period of several years 33 factual reports on various phases of the chain store industry. In its final report, transmitted in December of 1934, it recommended legislation which finally resulted in the passage in 1936 of the Robinson-Patman Act, sometimes referred to as the "Equal Opportunity Act," the "Anti-Price-Discrimination Act," or the "Anti-Chain Act," depending upon one's feelings and viewpoint.

The Robinson-Patman Act. Section 1 of this law is an amendment of Section 2 of the Clayton Antitrust Act, but to all intents and purposes is new law on matters of price and other forms of prohibited discrimination and is to be referred to as Section 2. Also important is Section 3, which prohibits *participation* (agreement with competitors) in discrimination between competing purchasers, or between purchasers in different areas, or charging unreasonably low prices, for the purpose of destroying competition or eliminating a competitor. Violation of this section carries with it a fine of not more than $5,000 or imprisonment for not more than one year, or both, and is the only part of this Act on which criminal action can be taken. The principal provisions of amended Section 2 are discussed in the pages that follow.

In addition to being enforced by the appropriate governmental agencies, the "antitrust laws" (involving principally the Sherman Act and the Clayton Act) can also be enforced through private suits for injunctive relief or for treble damages. Since Section 1 of the Robinson-Patman Act is an amendment of Section 2 of the Clayton Act, suit by private parties for treble damages are in order for any violation of that section of the law. The same cannot be said for violations coming under Section 3 of the Robinson-Patman Act. There is no express statutory authority for private treble damage actions or any other private action for price discrimination under this section of the law, and there is no express statutory statement that the Robinson-Patman Act is an "antitrust" act. As a matter of fact, such were the two rulings handed down in 5–4 decisions[16] by the U. S. Supreme Court on January 20, 1958. This means that price discriminations which violate Section 3 do not give rise to private actions for treble damages.

Provision Prohibiting Price Discriminations. No doubt the most important provision of the Robinson-Patman Act is that embodied in Section 2(a). It makes it *unlawful for sellers to discriminate in price between different buyers of goods of like grade and quality where the effect of such discrimination may be substantially to lessen competition or to tend to create a monopoly, or to injure, destroy, or prevent competition with any person who grants or knowingly receives the benefit of such discrimination or with customers of either of them.*

This section sets up certain defenses under the law. Price differentials which make only due allowances for differences in cost, including cost of manufacture, sale, and delivery for varying quantities, are not affected. The defense under this "cost savings proviso" is most often utilized in appropriate cases. It was used successfully, for example, by Sylvania Electric Products, Inc., in justifying an average price differential in favor of Philco Corp. in the sale of radio tubes for replacement purposes.[17] There was no question that Sylvania sold the tubes at the lower price to Philco for resale to its distributors than it sold to its own distributors. The only points at issue were whether certain items of savings should be allowed in the computation, whether a weighted average difference in prices and cost savings was proper or whether the difference would have to be established for each of the 400 types of tubes involved, and whether the savings must equal or exceed the price differential or may only approximate it. All of these points were resolved on appeal to the Commission in favor of Sylvania.

16 *Nashville Milk Co. v. Carnation Company,* No. 67, October Term, 1957; and *Safeway Stores, Incorporated v. Harry V. Vance, Trustee in Bankruptcy for Frank Melvin Thompson, Bankrupt,* No. 69, October Term, 1957.

17 *Federal Trade Commission v. Sylvania Electric Products, Inc., and Philco Corp.,* F.T.C. Docket No. 5728 (complaint dismissed in 1954).

Under certain conditions the Federal Trade Commission, which is charged with the enforcement of this section of the law, may set maximum quantity limits. This is done where it finds that available large-scale purchasers are so few as to render quantity price differentials unjustly discriminatory or promotive of monopoly.

Probably one of the most important court cases involving quantity discounts was that of the Morton Salt Company. In this case the U. S. Supreme Court upheld the Federal Trade Commission's order to the company to cease and desist from continuing its wholesale discount plan which gave a substantial advantage to large purchasers. The company had quoted standard prices of $1.60 per case of salt in l.c.l. quantity purchases, $1.50 in c.l. quantity purchases, $1.40 in 5,000 case-lot purchases in any consecutive 12 months, and $1.35 in 50,000 case purchases in any consecutive 12 months. These standard discounts were *nominally* available to *all* purchasers on equal terms, but functionally and practically they were not, for the record showed that no single independent retailer and probably no single independent wholesaler ever purchased as much as 50,000 cases of salt in one year. The company was not able to show that the price differentials were justified by reason of differences in the cost of manufacture, sale, or delivery resulting from the differing methods or quantities in which its salt was sold or delivered. Nor could it prove that the special discounts granted were made in good faith to meet a competitor's equally low price. A significant ruling of the court in this case was that the Commission may bar discriminatory prices upon the *reasonable possibility* that different prices for like goods to competing purchasers may substantially lessen or destroy competition; *actual injury* to competition need not be established.[18]

Not so successful was the Commission with its Quantity-Limit Rule imposed upon 49 tire companies. In this instance it fixed the maximum quantity discount limit on sales of tires and tubes at 20,000 pounds (approximately a carload) ordered at one time for delivery at one time. After several years of controversy the rule was held invalid mainly because the findings were in terms of dollar values, alleging that there were relatively few available purchasers in annual dollar volumes greater than $600,000, while the limit was established in physical units. There was also a serious doubt as to what constitutes fewness.[19]

A number of cases, prosecuted as violations of the Clayton Act as amended by the Robinson-Patman Act, have cast serious doubt upon the legality of any basing point, zone-delivered, or postage stamp *pricing system*. Single basing point systems of pricing were practically outlawed by cases against manufacturers of corn derivatives. In a matter concerning

[18] *Federal Trade Commission v. Morton Salt Co.*, 334 U.S. 37, 68 S.Ct. 822 (1948).
[19] *B. F. Goodrich Co. v. Federal Trade Commission*, 242 F.2d 31 (CA–DC, 1957).

the Corn Products Refining Company, for example, it was shown that the company had two plants, one at Chicago, Illinois, and another at Kansas City, Missouri. All bulk sales of glucose (corn syrup) were made on a delivered price basis. The delivered price was computed by taking the Chicago price and adding freight from Chicago to the point of delivery, regardless of the actual origin of the shipment. In this way purchasers in all places other than Chicago paid a higher price than did Chicago purchasers; on shipments from the Kansas City plant to points that were nearer to Kansas City than to Chicago, the purchaser thus paid *phantom freight*, i.e., a freight cost that was not actually incurred. The Supreme Court upheld the Federal Trade Commission in its ruling that the pricing practice of the company resulted in price discrimination as prohibited by the Robinson-Patman Act, because customers who paid phantom freight could not compete effectively with those who bought at the lower prices.[20]

A multiple basing point system of pricing was also declared illegal in a case involving the Cement Institute and leading producers of cement. The Supreme Court upheld the Commission in its ruling that the employment of a pricing system which resulted in all producers quoting the same identical delivered price to any given destination constituted a discrimination in price between different purchasers. The discrimination arises because *varying mill net returns* are received by the producers on sales to customers in different localities. The Court did not allow the claim of the cement producers that the discriminations were justified because they were made "in good faith to meet an equally low price of a competitor." It ruled rather that this defense does not permit a seller to "use a sales system which constantly results in his getting more money for like goods from some customers than he does from others."[21] The Commission has instituted proceedings against numerous other producers using some form of a basing point, freight equalization, or zone-delivered pricing system, on the ground that *systematically* varying the realized mill net return constitutes price discrimination among customers within the meaning of the Robinson-Patman Act.

This amendment to the Clayton Act permits the selection of customers where done in good faith and when not in restraint of trade. It permits price changes under certain specified conditions to meet market fluctuations, to dispose of perishables, to avoid obsolescence of seasonal goods; it permits distress sales under court order, and bona fide closing-out sales.

Any person may enter a complaint against another of discrimination in price, services, or facilities furnished. If proof of such discrimination is

20 *Corn Products Refining Co. et al. v. Federal Trade Commission,* 144 F.2d 211 (CCA-7, 1944), 324 U.S. 726 (1945) and *Federal Trade Commission v. A. E. Staley Manufacturing Co.,* 144 F.2d 221 (CCA-7, 1944), 324 U.S. 746 (1945).
21 *Federal Trade Commission v. The Cement Institute et al.,* 157 F.2d 533 (CCA-7, 1946), 333 U.S. 683, 68 S.Ct. 793 (1948).

given at a hearing, the burden of justification is placed upon the accused, who must affirmatively refute the testimony against him or the Federal Trade Commission may order the discrimination terminated. The defendant may offer in rebuttal the fact that the alleged discrimination was made in good faith to meet competition.[22] Other bases for justification appear to be that the sale was of services rather than of goods; that the transaction was in intrastate commerce rather than interstate; that the goods were sold for bona fide export trade; and that there was no discrimination because of actual cost differences. An important effect of the law has been the rather rapid development of distribution cost analysis which is required in most cases for the justification of different prices charged to customers of the same general class or to customers in different classes.

Discrimination in Payments of Brokerage Fees. The Act endeavors to correct a practice which has been strongly opposed by brokers and other types of wholesale distributors, namely, the granting of brokerage commissions to large-scale buyers who purchase directly from manufacturers. The payment of a brokerage fee by a seller to a buyer when a genuine brokerage service is not rendered to the vendor is merely an additional discount from basic price quotations that results in price discrimination among different purchasers. The payment of brokerage fees, except for services actually rendered, is prohibited by the following provision (Section 2(c)):

That it shall be unlawful for any person engaged in commerce, to pay or grant, or to receive or accept, anything of value as a commission, brokerage, or other compensation, or any allowance or discount in lieu thereof, except for services rendered in connection with the sale or purchase of goods, wares or merchandise, either to the other party to the transaction or to an agent, representative, or other intermediary therein where such intermediary is acting in fact—or on behalf, or is subject to the direct or indirect control, of any party to such transaction other than the person by whom such compensation is so granted or paid.

Various large chain organizations have been affected by this provision. The Great Atlantic & Pacific Tea Co., for example, allegedly required its salaried buyers to collect brokerage fees from suppliers and to remit them

[22] This matter was finally resolved in a 17-year legal controversy (*Federal Trade Commission v. Standard Oil Co.,* U. S. Sup. Ct., October Term, 1957, No. 24, dated January 27, 1958, 233 F.2d 649 (CA-7)) as to what constitutes good faith and whether the lower price of a competitor must be a *lawful* price. The latter point was introduced for the first time when the case reached the Supreme Court in the first round, but in its final majority opinion there was no reference to it. Furthermore, in a previous decision (*Standard Oil Company v. Robert K. Brown, d.b.a. Bob Brown's Standard Service,* 238 F.2d 54 (CA-5, 1956)) the Circuit Court ruled that the use of the word lawful by the Supreme Court "was not to establish a standard that must be met; it was rather a description of the facts presented in that case."

1958).
[29] This reasoning must be modified in the light of a Circuit Court of Appeals decision in a case involving payments made by food products suppliers for advertisements in a retail chain's wholly owned magazine (*Woman's Day*) distributed only in its own retail chain stores. In this case the payments were ruled to be in violation of

it is to indicate that the buyer who so long
was the one who, knowing full well that there was little likelihood of a defense for the seller, nevertheless proceeded to exert pressure for lower prices. Enforcement of the provisions of Section 2(f) against such a buyer should not be difficult.[30a]

Effects of the Robinson-Patman Act. In general, this legislation has had the effect of making competition between large-scale distributors and smaller dealers more equitable. Many mass buyers had previously enjoyed advantages that could not be justified on economic grounds, merely because of the importance of the volume of their purchases and the strategic position occupied by such buyers with respect to a given seller. Many of these buyers have been deprived of advertising allowances, undeserved brokerage fees, and outright price concessions that formerly were one of their principal sources of income.

To the extent that large-scale retailers suffer under the operation of the law, independent retailers and the wholesalers serving them have gained. This benefit to the latter has come about in two ways. First, large distributors have been deprived of unjustified price discriminations and hence are unable to reduce prices to their customers as much as formerly for the purpose of attracting trade. Second, since manufacturers are forced to charge higher prices when selling to mass distributors, it has been possible for them to reduce prices formerly charged to their other customers, thus tending to equalize somewhat their prices to all customers. Voluntary chains, most of which are wholesaler-sponsored, have also been deprived of many of their buying advantages with the result that nonaffiliated wholesalers have benefited at the expense of this group to some extent.

An important by-product of the Act has been the development of a more adequate system of accounting for costs of distribution. At the time of enactment, few even of the large and important companies had "worked out and installed cost-accounting systems which, for purposes of defense under the Robinson-Patman Act, are sound and adequate in their conception and at the same time suitable and practicable for the everyday use of the individual business concern."[31] Confronted with the burden of proof once a prima facie case of price discrimination is instituted by the Federal Trade Commission, many manufacturers and distributors have

[30a] Such was the reasoning in F.T.C. Order to Cease and Desist issued against *Mid-South Distributors,* etc. (Docket Nos. 5766 and 5767), March 12, 1959.
[31] Annual Report of the Federal Trade Commission for the fiscal year ended June 30, 1938.

to headquarters.[23] When this practice was outlawed, it was claimed that the company instructed its buyers to have sellers deduct amounts equal to brokerage fees from the invoices submitted for payment. Such deductions were nothing but rebates or discounts that could not be justified by any

Under Section 2(e), that is closely allied to the provision in Section 2(d), it is *unlawful for a seller to furnish services and facilities to one purchaser that are not accorded to all purchasers on proportionally equal terms*. Both of these sections call for *equitable* treatment of all customers at the same time satisfying legitimate business needs of both seller and buyer. The latter section covers such matters as cooperative advertising arrangements, furnishing of "demonstrators" in stores, special promotional services, special packaging as in providing toilet articles in "junior" sizes for certain types of stores but refusing to supply them to the regular wholesale and retail drug trade, and any other favored treatment such as in the acceptance of returned goods from or omission of warehousing charges to some customers but not available to others on proportionally equal terms.

After the mid-1950's numerous complaints were issued by the Commission under these two sections. In a number of them chain stores of the supermarket type were affected, and the alleged discriminations varied all the way from offering "specials" for store openings to payments for radio and television advertising of specific events.

Knowingly Inducing or Receiving a Discrimination. Section 2(f) makes it unlawful for any purchaser knowingly to induce or receive a discrimination in price which is prohibited by this section of the law. The governing case here is without doubt that of the *Automatic Canteen Co. of America v. Federal Trade Commission*.[30] In this case the Commission presented evidence that the purchaser (Automatic Canteen Co.) received or solicited prices it knew were as much as 33 per cent lower than those quoted other purchasers and apparently took this to be a prohibited price discrimination which the buyer should not have received or solicited. The Supreme Court concluded that

. . . a buyer is not liable under Section 2(f) if the lower prices he induces are either within one of the seller's defenses such as the cost justification or not known by him not to be within one of those defenses.

The Court rejected the Commission's insistence that the buyer should prove cost savings to the seller enough to justify the discrimination received by him, for to do so would require data not in the buyer's hands. Furthermore,

it would almost inevitably require a degree of cooperation between buyer and seller, as against other buyers, that may offend other antitrust policies, and it

is interesting to note, however, that the decision on appeal emphasized the following:

As a private trader in interstate commerce, Ronson not only could select its own customers but also could refuse to sell its merchandise to anyone and by so doing would in no way violate the anti-trust laws. It is settled law that a seller may either refuse to negotiate or may cease doing business with a customer without running afoul of the Act. It is also clear, however, that if a seller chooses to negotiate and to sell goods of like grade and quality to competing customers, he cannot discriminate in price or services either to the advantage of one purchaser or to the disadvantage of another.

Classification of Customers. The matter of classifying customers according to *function* for purposes, among others, of establishing functional discounts is discussed in some detail in Chapter 4. Suffice it to state here that functional discounts, which are trade discounts dependent upon the distributional status or classification of the customer and usually confined to those customers operating on some wholesale level, are a traditional pricing technique by which sellers compensate for distributive functions. A wholesaler, for example, may receive a functional discount of, say, 20 per cent from a list price to compensate him for the many functions he performs in the sale of a manufacturer's products as discussed in Chapter 8. Failure on the part of the manufacturer to allow such a discount does not mean that the wholesaler will not be compensated; it only means that the needed 20 per cent will be arrived at in a different manner through the computation of a margin that will enable the wholesaler to handle such goods profitably in the long run. No matter how it is determined, the wholesaler will have to secure enough of a difference between what he pays for the goods and what he receives for them from his customers to cover his cost of doing business and leave him a reasonable net profit to enable him to continue such operations. Obviously, the amount of such margin or functional discount has in reality little or nothing to do with the manufacturer's estimates of the value of such functions to him unless he has the alternative of performing them himself which is not normally true. It is an amount that must be provided for the movement of goods through a given channel and is usually determined competitively by the alternative channels of distribution that may be available and the kinds of services required.

It is no accident, therefore, that neither the *specie* of such discount nor the *size* of it has ever been questioned in bona fide uses of functional discounts. Thus, for example, all complaints charging a number of respondent companies in the sale of tile with the allowance of discounts varying from 5 to 15 per cent to certain customers designated as "wholesalers" while denying them to other customers designated as "contractors" were dismissed by the Federal Trade Commission.[35] In one case it was ruled

[35] F.T.C. Docket Nos. 2951, 3546, 3548, 3549, 3550, 3551, and 3553.

that the offering of sugar to distributors at lower prices than to a manufacturer was not a prohibited discrimination, because "When two purchasers are in different levels of the distribution process, differences in price or sales terms offered them do not violate the law."[36] The reasoning for this is spelled out a bit by the following statements on some of the historical aspects of functional discounts:

The single function middleman presented no problem of classification, for he bought as well as sold in one distributive role, that is, strictly as a wholesaler or strictly as a retailer. A discount granted to such wholesalers did not injure retailers who received no equivalent price reduction, since they did not compete for the consumer's business. By virtue of the "injury" prerequisite in Section 2(a) of the act, therefore, functional discounts to single-function distributors were considered above legal reproach.[37]

The controversy arises in connection with the split-function wholesalers or with other middlemen and with integrated concerns like the chain stores.[38]

FAIR TRADE AND ITS SUBSTITUTES

The term "fair trade" almost invariably refers to vertical resale price maintenance. Under such a policy a manufacturer or other original owner of a branded product stipulates the price at which the product is to be resold or below which it cannot be resold.

Origin and Early Development of Fair Trade Legislation. According to decisions of courts and Federal Trade Commission, such a policy could not be enforced prior to the enactment of special so-called Fair Trade legislation. Any agreement to maintain resale prices was held to be a conspiracy in restraint of trade under Section 1 of the Sherman Act[39] and an unfair method of competition under Section 5 of the Federal Trade Commission Act. Merchants also enjoyed the common law right to dispose of their own property, including branded products purchased by them for resale, in any manner desired.

Price-cutting tactics have been resorted to by some merchants from time to time in order to drive competitors out of business or to attract customers to whom other goods could be sold at regular or even higher than competitive prices. Such tactics became widespread when adopted by

[36] *Chicago Sugar Co. v. American Sugar Refining Co.,* 176 F.2d 1 (CA–7, 1949); U.S. Sup. Ct., certiorari denied (1950).

[37] *Doubleday and Co., Inc., Federal Trade Commission Order to Cease and Desist,* F.T.C. Docket No. 5897 (1955).

[38] For detailed treatment of the entire subject, see "Functional Discounts: Their Economic and Legal Implications," by Henry Dean Ostberg, an unpublished doctoral dissertation supervised by the senior coauthor and deposited in the library of The Ohio State University (1957).

[39] *Dr. Miles Medical Co. v. John D. Park & Sons Co.,* 220 U.S. 373 (1911).

Antitrust Acts.

2. Instead of confining the language to minimum prices as in the Miller-Tydings Act, it also legalizes contracts or agreements prescribing stipulated (absolute) prices.

3. It removes all doubt as to whether a brand owner may, if allowed by state law, require a vendee to enter into such an agreement with his customers in order to make the established minimum or absolute resale price effective. While the Miller-Tydings Act was silent on this point, the new law specifically legalizes it.

4. It specifically legalizes the nonsigner clauses of the state acts by providing that a vertical price agreement is binding "whether the person . . . is or is not a party to such contract or agreement," thereby nullifying the effect of the Supreme Court ruling in the *Schwegmann* case.

5. It provides that neither the contracts or agreements in question nor any rightful action taken to enforce them "shall constitute an unlawful burden or restraint upon, or interference with, commerce." Since the word commerce in federal legislation refers to interstate commerce, this provision was no doubt designed to overcome the decision in *Sunbeam Corporation v. S. A. Wentling* respecting the burden on interstate commerce which tended to favor such concerns as mail order houses. In any event, it can no longer be ruled that an effect on interstate com-

[43] *Schwegmann Bros. v. Calvert Distillers Corp.,* 341 U.S. 384.

[44] *Seagram-Distillers Corp. v. Greene, Inc.,* (Fla. Sup. Ct., 1951), and *Calvert Distillers Corp. v. Sach's* (Minn. Sup. Ct., 1951).

chains and other large-scale retailing institutions, especially during a buyer's market such as prevailed in the early years of the Great Depression of the 1930's. Among the injured parties were independent retailers, wholesalers serving them, and manufacturers whose products were used as loss-leader bait. Attempts at remedial federal legislation failed at first, so a drive was made on state legislatures to provide the necessary help in the form of *Fair Trade Acts*.

California was a pioneer in this upsurge of state legislation by enacting the Fair Trade Law of 1931. When it was amended in 1933 to include the so-called nonsigners' provision, it gave impetus to the movement and a number of other states passed fair trade laws in 1935 and 1936. The U. S. Supreme Court declared the California and Illinois statutes constitutional on December 7, 1936, and thereby provided a further impetus to this type of legislation.[40] In 1937 Congress removed the final barrier by passing the Miller-Tydings Act which directly amended Section 1 of the Sherman Act and by reference also amended Section 5 of the Federal Trade Commission Act. This law legalized vertical price agreements in interstate commerce with respect to trade in states having fair trade laws if such agreements, according to a court decision, did not place an undue burden upon interstate commerce.[41] Following these developments, such laws multiplied until they had been adopted in 46 states including Hawaii.[42]

Major Provisions of the Fair Trade Laws. The principal provision of the

merce is a cause for declaring fair trade pricing inoperative even on intrastate sales.

Confused Status of Fair Trade Legislation and Enforcement. By the middle 1950's it had become fashionable to cut prices, as a result of the tremendous growth of discount houses, excessive inventories in the hands of manufacturers, excess productive capacity in certain lines, and other pressures to move goods in larger and larger quantities and counteract the steadily rising cost of living. As a result more and more of the Fair Trade laws were subjected to constitutionality tests insofar as the state constitutions are concerned.

By 1959 the constitutionality had been tested in all but 12 of the 46 states which had enacted Fair Trade laws. In two of the states the law was declared entirely unconstitutional, in 14 others it was declared unconstitutional as applied to nonsigners, and only in 18 of the 34 states tested (including Hawaii) and in Puerto Rico was it declared constitutional on all counts. Furthermore, the trend was in direction of outlawing the statutes.

Even more important was the difficulty of enforcing the laws, the courts requiring, for example, more and more proof of diligence in the enforcement tactics of the brand owner.[45] Additionally, special types of violations mushroomed, including "phony" close-out sales, package deals and premiums, trading stamps, and arbitrary or fictitious trade-in allowances. All of this has given rise to more widespread use of the "agency" plan of distribution, "suggested" resale prices, and a demand for federal legislation that would obviate the need for separate state laws.

Effects of the Fair Trade Laws. As a result of the fair trade laws cut-rate retailers, principally large and integrated organizations, have been deprived of an important competitive and frequently uneconomic weapon. By the same token independent retailers and the wholesalers who serve them have benefited; in a way, also, their gross margins are recognized by law. Manufacturers and other brand owners have benefited from the protection afforded to the good will they have created for their products through advertising and other sales promotion efforts. To the extent that these effects tend to preserve, and perhaps also to promote, competition, by insuring the existence of large numbers of small enterprises on the one hand and the curtailment of monopolistic practices by the price-cutters on the other, they may be socially desirable and beneficial. On the other hand, operation under the fair trade laws may in some instances have restricted price competition on branded merchandise, especially when absolute prices are prescribed and such prices apply to efficient and inefficient outlets alike without regard to their differences in costs of doing business.

[45] *General Electric Co. v. S. Klein on the Square, Inc.*, 129 N.Y.L.J. 583 (N. Y. Sup. Ct., 1953).

It is easy, however, to overemphasize the general or net effect of these laws. First, they apply only to trade-marked or branded goods. Second, they are permissive in nature, not mandatory. Even when a product possesses distinctive characteristics in the minds of consumers, its owner may be reluctant to maintain resale prices: (1) when competing manufacturers do not follow such a policy; (2) when the product yields too narrow a margin per unit to justify the expense of maintaining prices; (3) when the product is sold through widely different types of outlets from a cost of operation standpoint; (4) when the retail price of the commodity normally fluctuates with the price of the raw material; or (5) when part payment for the retail purchase is in the form of a trade-in which offers an alternative means of price competition. Third, there is no conclusive evidence as to the effect on prices paid by consumers. While established prices may be higher than those previously prevailing at certain price-cutting stores, they may be set lower than those previously prevailing in the service stores. The result may be a leveling of prices to the consuming public on "fair-traded" merchandise. There is no doubt, however, that the prices on such goods have tended to become relatively rigid, as changes cannot be made often without much additional expense and undue confusion. In a period of rising prices, however, this relative price rigidity becomes an anti-inflationary force.

SALES BELOW COST

The objective of this section of the chapter is to analyze the extent to which goods may be sold by those engaged in wholesaling below cost under federal law and regulation and under certain state laws specially enacted for the purpose. Attention is also called to the problems involved in the determination of cost for purposes of such laws and regulation, and the business and economic consequences.

Applicability of Federal Law and Regulation to Sales Below Cost. While it is possible that selling below cost may under certain conditions be declared an unfair method of competition under Section 5 of the Federal Trade Commission Act, there are relatively few Commission rulings directly on this point; practically all of them that have any bearing on this had to do with intent to drive out competitors or otherwise stifle competition. To be sure, it is possible to sell below cost when it becomes necessary to meet the lower price of a competitor in good faith as permitted under the Robinson-Patman Act. It may, however, be an unfair trade practice under an industry's Trade Practice Rules to sell below cost when it is done with the intent or effect "to substantially injure, suppress, or stifle competition or tend to create a monopoly."

Unfair Trade Laws. This type of state legislation strikes more directly at purely predatory price-cutting, but does not affect price-cutting made possible by efficient operation. Some 30 states have enacted such legislation, known as "Unfair Trade Practices Acts," "Unfair Sales Acts," and the like, all of which relate to wholesalers and are of general application.

While there is more variability among the provisions of these laws than among those of the state fair trade laws, in essence they all forbid sales below cost, which in some of the laws is presumed to be the invoice price of goods plus a fixed percentage and in other laws is supposed to include the invoice price of the goods and all costs of doing business of the vendor, the latter types of costs often being fully spelled out in the law.

It is against some of these arbitrary provisions that objections have been raised, as illustrated by the court decision which declared the Maryland Unfair Sales Act unconstitutional[46] mainly for two reasons: the provision that a fixed percentage be added to the net invoice price of the goods regardless of the vendor's actual costs of doing business and the prohibition of deductions of cash discounts earned in determining the net invoice price of the goods.

These laws have fared better in the courts than have the fair trade laws. Of the 19 tested, only 6 were declared partly or wholly unconstitutional. They have suffered, however, from the varying and conflicting interpretations by the respective state courts. For example, the Colorado Unfair Practices Act was declared unconstitutional because the section of the law which defines cost of doing business was deemed by the court to be "too vague, indefinite, and impossible to comply with."[47] This came largely, if not entirely, from the court's interpretation that the statute intended the cost to be determined for each item in question and not the over-all cost of doing business to be applied to individual items. Obviously, the accounting profession has not advanced enough to solve the problems raised in any attempt to determine in a retail store, or anywhere else for that matter, the cost of doing business for each item of merchandise handled for sale.

A more reasonable viewpoint on this matter was taken in a decision in the Supreme Judicial Court of Massachusetts.[48] Here the Court stated:

We do not agree that the prohibition relating to advertising to sell below cost is too vague to be enforced. Nor do we feel able to hold that the legislature has imposed unreasonable restrictions upon private business.

[46] *Isaac Cohen, individually and trading as Capital Wholesale Grocery Co. et al. v. Frey & Son. Inc. et al.* (Court of Appeals of Maryland, May 7, 1951).

[47] *Standard Store v. Safeway Stores, Incorporated, and King Soopers, Inc. et al.* (In the District Court in and for the City and County of Denver and State of Colorado. Civil Action No. B–2671, dated October 5, 1955.)

[48] *Louis Fournier v. John P. Troianello* (No. 5430, dated June 3, 1955).

In this instance it was not necessary to establish the cost of doing business for a specific item, but the statute itself was more realistic in its intent and in express language.

The unfair trade laws differ from the fair trade laws in several important respects. First, the laws are *mandatory* in character and are not merely permissive. Second, they apply to *all* goods, whether trade-marked or not, sold by wholesalers and retailers and in some cases by manufacturers. Third, these laws are somewhat more justifiable on economic grounds since they permit variations based on differing original merchandise costs and costs of doing business. No wholesaler or distributor is required to charge more than his actual merchandise cost plus the actual overhead cost of handling an item. Proponents of this legislation claim that it is intended to prevent the destruction of competition by eliminating the unfair practice of cutting the price on some items even below cost of purchase and making up for the losses thus incurred on other items.

While the unfair trade laws are primarily directed at predatory price-cutting, most of them contain other provisions. Among other common prohibitions are those relating to false and misleading advertising, secret rebates, and special services, which tend to destroy competition, injure competitors, or in other ways violate the spirit of the act. Exceptions to the price-cutting provision are provided in the cases of such sales as are made in good faith to meet competition, genuine clearance or liquidation sales, sales of perishable or seasonal goods, or sales to charitable organizations.

II

Scientific Management of a Wholesale Enterprise

16

ESTABLISHING A
WHOLESALE
ENTERPRISE

The preceding chapters have dealt with the nature of wholesaling and the evolution of the modern American wholesaling system, both of which are essential to an understanding of its *raison d'être*. Much space was devoted to a discussion and analysis of the present-day wholesaling structure or system and its functioning, as well as the competitive forces at work in molding it and effecting changes therein, for it is in such a business environment that a wholesale enterprise must operate. Not only that, but it must be fully cognizant of the legal context within which it must function. Some of the treatment, to be sure, has been primarily from a broad business, economic, and social viewpoint, but even that provides an invaluable background for the practicing executive of a wholesale business in giving him a proper perspective and in indicating the nature and extent of the contribution such a business makes to our economy.

Of much more direct concern to those engaged in wholesaling are the principles, practices, policies, and techniques of managing such an enterprise in a manner conducive to the fullest accomplishment of its major objectives in a profit-motivated competitive economy. In this part of the book, accordingly, attention is turned to the managerial aspects of wholesaling. Each of the major phases of wholesaling management is treated, roughly in the same sequence as these problems arise in the establishment of a new enterprise. Obviously the discussion is not limited to new concerns, but has equal application to any established business operating at the wholesale level, including wholesalers, operating (as distinguished from dead storage) warehouses owned by retail chains, manufacturers' sales branches, and functional middlemen. In this first chapter of Part II, a foundation is laid for the more detailed treatment by considering some of the basic decisions that must be made in founding a new enterprise, which give a business its distinctive character and which, taken together, largely determine its probable success or failure. It should be noted that the same types of decisions are faced when an established business is expanding or modifying its operation.

BASIC DECISIONS

The maxim that an organization is "the lengthened shadow of a man" might well be modified to read "an organization is the projection of an idea." Every new business enterprise, including those in the field of wholesaling, begins as an idea in someone's mind. A wholesaler's salesman may decide that his territory has sufficient sales potential to support a new, independent wholesale enterprise; or a retailer may achieve such success with a new product line that he thinks it can be sold to other retailers, and thus becomes a wholesaler. Whatever the particular circumstances, the spirit of enterprise is traditionally strong in the United States, and many new wholesale firms are founded each year.

At the outset, and before any substantial amounts of capital or time are invested in a business, it is essential that certain basic decisions be reached. Among the most important of these are:

1. The kind of business or line of trade in which the enterprise is to be engaged
2. The extent of the merchandise line to be handled
3. The extent of the territory to be covered, whether it shall be local, sectional, or national in scope
4. The location of the enterprise
5. The method of operation to be employed, in terms of functions and services to be performed and the manner of their performance
6. The legal form of organization
7. Relationships with suppliers and customers

Each of these basic decisions is discussed in succeeding paragraphs. It should be pointed out that these problems are not confined to *new* wholesaling concerns. All of them are subject to change in established businesses as well, since the conditions governing such decisions may and often do change.

An illustration of such change is afforded by the experience of Butler Brothers, which was originally founded as a dry goods wholesaler in 1877. For many years this firm sold a general line of dry goods on a national scale, primarily by mail. Changing economic conditions affected the company adversely, however, and after the mid-1920's a basic alteration in the character of the business began taking place. By the late 1950's Butler Brothers bore little resemblance to its past in terms of merchandise handled, method of operation, or relationships with customers. The company had been converted into a general merchandise wholesaler, sponsoring a voluntary chain of over 2,400 variety stores throughout the United States. While such a drastic change was not made overnight, it does illustrate the process of successful adaptation to changing times.

Importance of Proper Initial Decisions. The critical importance of making the right initial basic decisions can hardly be overstated. Each year over 20,000 new wholesale firms are established, about as many are discontinued, including outright failures, and about 11,000 change hands.[1] In view of the intense competition characteristic of most wholesale markets, it is perhaps inevitable that not all of these new concerns can succeed. Indeed, some of them fail completely. About 1,000 wholesale firms annually are recorded as *failures*, that is, are involved in court proceedings or in voluntary actions likely to result in losses to creditors.

These figures point up the great risks inherent in any new and untried business venture. In many cases, no doubt, the persons engaged in the new enterprise lack the basic abilities needed for success, and no amount of education, training, or assistance would supply such need. In other cases, though, the cause of failure can be found in *improper basic decisions* on market opportunities and competitive situations. Too often the newcomer merely copies the pattern of existing concerns, relying on his personality or perhaps on some new and untried product line to insure success. The fallacy of this approach should be apparent from the discussion that follows.

Initial Decisions and Business Policies. The basic decisions discussed in this chapter have an important bearing on the major business policies that are formulated by management for the guidance of day-to-day operations. In order to clarify the discussion, a clear conception of the nature and significance of policies should be kept in mind. By a *policy* is meant "a definite course of action predetermined for the purpose of securing uniformity of procedure so long as substantially similar conditions exist."[2] A policy is, then, a sort of generalized solution to a class or group of business problems which arise with some frequency in the course of operations.

A distinction should be made between *major* and *minor* business policies. Major policies are those of such importance to the business, and/or

[1] Based on typical figures in the 1950's as reported in the *Survey of Current Business,* U. S. Department of Commerce, July, 1957, p. 3. See also *Survey of Current Business,* January, 1958, p. 6.

[2] Theodore N. Beckman, Harold H. Maynard, and William R. Davidson, *Principles of Marketing* (6th ed.; New York: The Ronald Press Co., 1957), p. 597.

with such broad effects on all of its operations, that they are formulated by top management, i.e., the directors or owners of the firm. Within the broad lines set down by these major policies, there are many relatively *minor,* though not unimportant, policies which are established by departmental or supervisory managers.

Some of the basic decisions treated in this chapter are in themselves major business policies. For example, one such decision has to do with the extent of the merchandise line to be handled. Suppose it is decided to handle a specialty line of abrasives and cutting tools within the general line of industrial supplies. This decision, in itself, serves as a guide to subsequent buying activities. In all likelihood, if the enterprise is successful, would-be suppliers of other industrial supply products outside the specialty line will seek to have their lines handled. As long as the original policy is adhered to, such offers will be rejected. This does not mean, of course, that the initial policy decision is irrevocable; indeed, many specialty line wholesalers gradually expand their stocks and ultimately reach a general-line status. In similar fashion all business policies should be kept *flexible* and responsive to changing conditions. But within the framework of these conditions, it represents a predetermined course of action to be followed until deliberately and consciously revised.

Other initial decisions that are in the nature of major policies are the extent of the territory to be covered, the method of operation, and relationships with suppliers and customers. The remaining decisions—kind of business, location, and legal form of organization—are not policies because they do not apply to repetitive and continuing problems. Instead, they are "one-shot" decisions which do not recur unless major expansion or modification of the enterprise is contemplated.

Need for Planning and Research. Decisions such as those treated in this chapter are not simply "grabbed out of the air." They must serve as guides to the operation of the business under given economic conditions and hence should be based on an accurate appraisal of those conditions. A prospective wholesaler would not, for example, decide to locate in New York City without any consideration of the need for his enterprise in that area in terms of market potential and competition. Neither should the location be chosen on the basis of vague rumors, unsupported statements, or crude guesses about available business. Instead, as indicated at some length in Chapter 17, the location of a wholesale house should be selected only after an exhaustive analysis of various market factors such as population, income, freight rates, and competition. The same is true of the other basic decisions and policies. They should reflect the application of accepted marketing principles to the facts of a particular situation and the latter must be ascertained as thoroughly and as accurately as possible.

The foregoing points up the need for systematic *marketing research* in the formulation of major policies for wholesale enterprises. Space does not permit the description of research methods in detail herein, except for certain specified problems treated in subsequent chapters such as that on location. For a more complete discussion of research techniques, one should consult any of several standards texts in that field.[3]

Choosing a Line of Business. Perhaps the most fundamental of all initial decisions is that of selecting the line of business in which the enterprise is to be engaged. Often this decision is governed largely by the circumstances and background of the persons establishing the firm. Seldom, indeed, does a prospective businessman have an unrestricted choice in this matter. Usually he will have had some experience in one line or another, perhaps as salesman or buyer. Such experience is essential, in fact, if the business is to have any chance of survival; it is well known that lack of experience is one of the major causes of business failures. This does not mean, however, that the choice of a line of business is always predetermined or narrowly circumscribed. Experience in one line may provide a sufficient foundation for entering any of several related lines. A person with experience in a wholesale hardware house, for example, may venture into builders' supplies, tools, construction materials, housewares, appliances, toys, paints, or any of several other closely allied lines. With that in mind, it is wise for one starting in the wholesaling field to attempt to secure his experience in a trade that offers possibilities of setting up his own firm at some future time.

The choice of a line of business is critical because the relative opportunity for the profitable employment of capital and managerial ability differs considerably with each kind of business. Some lines of trade, as a class, are known to offer very little opportunity, since the industries producing such goods are definitely on the decline. Lack of opportunity for the wholesaler also prevails in such lines as women's wear where the practice has become one of direct buying by the large department and specialty stores. Again, certain lines of trade such as the food industries, including confectionery, and the tobacco business are more or less in a static condition. Insofar as consumption and production potentialities are relatively constant or vary only with changes in population and with cyclical fluctuations, the future of wholesaling is limited in those fields. Opportunities are largely confined to situations where a temporary scarcity of establishments may be discovered in a given community or area of the country, or where the

[3] See, for example, Lyndon O. Brown, *Marketing and Distribution Research* (3d ed.; New York: The Ronald Press Co., 1955); Harper Boyd and Ralph Westfall, *Marketing Research: Text and Cases* (Homewood, Ill.: Richard D. Irwin, 1956); Richard D. Crisp, *Marketing Research* (New York: McGraw-Hill Book Co., Inc., 1957); Donald M. Hobart, *Marketing Research Practice* (New York: The Ronald Press Co., 1950).

newcomer has the ability to operate more efficiently than the existing agencies, which may have failed to keep pace with the changing times. There are also industries that are overexpanded, as illustrated by beer, wine, and spiritous liquor, although in the early 1930's, before the saturation point had been reached following the repeal of "prohibition," these industries appeared to offer an exceedingly bright future. Other lines of trade may be temporarily in the doldrums, as was the production and distribution of radio sets from 1929 through 1934. On the other hand, there are always many kinds of business that offer a real future for the wholesaler who wishes to pioneer and cast his lot with a *coming* industry. These are exemplified by sporting goods, commercial refrigeration, air conditioning, electronics and television, certain chemical and plastics lines, and the frozen food industry.

Some insight into relative opportunities in different wholesaling fields may be obtained from an examination of Table 5 in Chapter 6, in which trends in sales volume of wholesalers by kind of business are compared. Further information along these lines may be secured by reference to the publications of the Bureau of the Census in the periodic *Censuses of Wholesale Trade* and monthly *Wholesale Trade Reports.* Trade periodicals and special studies of specific lines of business may also shed light on the question.[4]

On the basis of all available information from such sources, the newcomer must seek to choose a kind of business that offers a real opportunity because of the growing character of the industry, the scarcity of distributing concerns in it, or the complacency of existing firms in a given area or line of trade, and, on the other hand, to avoid enterprises which may be largely doomed to failure at the outset because of the declining character of an industry, significant changes in methods of distribution, or the presence in that field of too large a number of competing and relatively efficient firms.

Extent of the Line to Be Carried. Closely related to the choice of a line of business is the determination of the *extent* of the line. Within the paper trade, for instance, a wholesaler may handle a *general line* of products and operate as a "dual house" or a *specialty line* and operate as a fine paper merchant or as a wrapping paper wholesaler. The advantages and disadvantages of general line and specialty wholesaling and shifts among these

---

[4] See, for example, *A Study of Tobacco Wholesalers' Operations,* Industrial Series No. 62, Office of Domestic Commerce, U. S. Department of Commerce (Washington, D. C.: Government Printing Office, 1946); *Dry Goods Wholesalers' Operations,* Office of Domestic Commerce, U. S. Department of Commerce (Washington, D. C.: Government Printing Office, 1949); "Hardware Wholesaling—The Giant Nobody Knows," and "The New Look in Wholesaling," special reports by the staff of *Hardware Retailer,* issues of May, 1956, and May, 1958, respectively.

types were analyzed in Chapter 7. As shown in Table 7 in that chapter, there has been a pronounced trend in favor of specialty wholesaling in several important lines of trade. In part this is a natural concomitant of the growing variety of goods manufactured and as such it suggests a probable advantage in this method of operation for a new concern. There is another important reason to explain the fact that most new enterprises are of the specialty type. This is found in the *limited capital* and *limited experience* of most newcomers to wholesaling, both of which favor the establishment of a specialty operation. Once such a firm is well entrenched, it may be possible to expand the line little by little, ultimately reaching a general line status. This, in fact, is probably the path that has been followed by most existing general line houses, except for the oldest that may have started as general merchandise concerns.

The difficulties of establishing a general line firm are illustrated by the experiences of a former student of one of the authors. This individual started a full line electrical goods concern "from scratch." He soon found, however, that his available capital was spread too thin over the hundreds of lines required. More serious, his company had little or nothing to offer its customers in the way of any real advantages over existing competitors. As a result it was necessary to liquidate much of the inventory and convert to a specialty line on a franchise basis, which proved very successful.

Although the general trend has been to specialty wholesaling, this term should not be too narrowly construed. It is possible to handle a limited number of lines without specializing in any *one* line. The determination of the extent of line to carry should be made through a careful analysis of market potential and competition in *each* major category of goods within a line in a given geographic area.

Extent of Territory To Be Served. A third basic decision refers to the *extent of the market* area to be cultivated. This decision depends in part on the nature and extent of the merchandise line and may be made before or after the selection of a specific city in which to locate. Within the limitations imposed by these factors, management must decide whether to cultivate only the local trade in a metropolitan area, to reach out into the smaller surrounding communities, to cater to trade over a large region, or to extend the sales effort to all or a large part of the whole country.

If the new firm plans to carry a very complete assortment of a narrow line of specialties, it probably will have to extend its operations over a fairly large area in order to attract a sufficient volume of trade, unless, of course, it is located in a very thickly populated area where customers in large numbers are highly concentrated.

If a general line of merchandise limited mainly to manufacturers' brands is to be carried, the firm may be largely confined to local operations because of the difficulty involved in meeting competition from other wholesalers who are bringing such goods into outlying markets in carload lots. On the other hand, if the general line contains a large selection of private brand merchandise, a much wider market can be cultivated because of lack of direct price competition on the controlled brands.

The kind of business may also influence the extent of the market to be covered. For example, a grocery wholesaler may easily find enough customers in a medium-sized city that would be too small to support a hardware or drug wholesale house. Except in the larger cities of the country, these latter firms are forced to reach out into a trade territory of considerable size.

The decision to operate on a local, a sectional, or a national basis may assist in the selection of the community in which to locate the business. Some communities are better suited for one purpose than are others. Occasionally, the decision as to market area may be determined by the location that has already been selected, for precisely the same reason.

Location. A fourth important matter to be decided in starting a wholesale business is the selection of a suitable location. This is a problem of the utmost importance, both to the newcomer and to the established concern, for a good location may be the firm's best asset, whereas a poor one may sometimes lead to failure. In locating a wholesale house, especially when it is being newly established, three distinct problems need to be considered. The first relates to the choice of a community which, together with the territory that is geographically tributary to it and which it thus dominates, will offer superior advantages for the kind of business contemplated. The second problem is whether to locate in or near the wholesale district in the chosen community and the third deals with the selection of a specific site. Because so much depends upon obtaining the most suitable location, each of these problems is discussed in considerable detail in Chapter 17.

Method of Operation. Another basic decision relates to the *method of operation* of a proposed new concern. As pointed out in Chapter 7, a general distinction is made between regular or full-service establishments and those operating on a limited-function basis such as cash-and-carry wholesalers or drop shippers. The choice is not as simple as this, because infinite variations exist in the nature and extent of functions performed by various wholesale enterprises and the extent and manner of their performance. For the new firm it is often possible to secure an important competitive advantage by offering to customers a slightly different "package" of services than those rendered by existing competitors. This gives the newcomer a distinctive "personality" and furnishes customers a tangible reason for switching suppliers.

An example of variation in method of operation is the adoption of *cost-plus* pricing for certain large customers.[5] This policy, copied from

___
[5] See Chapter 22 for a discussion of cost-plus policies.

retailer-cooperatives and voluntaries in the grocery trade, has been used by regular and cash-and-carry wholesalers in several lines of business. One tobacco wholesaler, for instance, bills his larger customers at his own cost plus 2 per cent. The remainder of his customers are too small to qualify for the plan and are served on a conventional basis.[6] This method offers real economies to large-scale buyers and provides the wholesaler's salesmen with important talking points in soliciting new accounts. It also illustrates the idea that even in long-established companies, methods of operation should—indeed, must—be under constant review and subject to continuous modifications.

Legal Form of Organization. A wholesale enterprise can be set up as a *proprietorship,* a *partnership,* or a *corporation* in terms of its legal form of organization. The decision on this point depends on several factors, including the desirability of *limiting liability, amount of capital needed, managerial considerations,* and *tax advantages.* Often these factors are conflicting in the sense that the best form of organization from one standpoint may not be the best from another. In such cases careful analysis must be made of all pertinent advantages and disadvantages.

Limited Liability. The original and basic reason for the evolution of the corporate form of organization is the limited liability which it makes possible for the owners of a business. The importance of this factor is reflected in the term "Limited" which is still used, for example, to designate a corporation in England and Canada. In an unincorporated business the liability of the owners for business debts generally extends to all of their assets, personal and otherwise. If one person has an interest in several enterprises, the assets of each and all can be used to satisfy debts of any one of them. This kind of liability is normally avoided by incorporating, since the legal liability is limited to the worth of the owners' equity in the business itself.

Capital Requirements. Partly because of the limited liability feature, the corporate form of organization is especially suitable to enterprises requiring large amounts of capital. For a relatively small concern it is often possible to secure enough equity capital from the savings of one person or a few partners. Indeed, for the small wholesale enterprise it is often an advantage not to be incorporated. Banks and other lenders are more willing to supply short-term financing to unincorporated concerns, *all other things being equal,* because of the unlimited personal liability of the proprietor or partners. If the proprietor or partners have substantial personal assets, these serve in effect as additional security for business borrowings which would not exist under a corporate structure.

[6] Harry B. Patrey, in collaboration with Joseph Kolodny, *Successful Methods of Wholesale Tobacco Distribution* (New York: Foresight Publications, 1957), pp. 136–38.

The basic limitation of unincorporated forms of organization is that, beyond a certain point, it becomes impossible to raise sufficient equity funds. Investors not directly concerned in management are not, as a rule, willing to risk their personal assets by becoming partners in a business. Since at least a minimum ratio must be maintained between equity and debt, lenders will refuse to supply additional capital beyond this point. Under such conditions incorporation is almost mandatory if further growth is to be possible. Thus it is not surprising that almost all large wholesale concerns are corporations.

TABLE 12

NUMBER OF ESTABLISHMENTS AND PERCENTAGE DISTRIBUTION OF
TOTAL VOLUME OF BUSINESS BY LEGAL FORM OF ORGANIZATION,
WHOLESALERS, AND AGENTS AND BROKERS, UNITED STATES,
1954

Type of Operation and Legal Form	Establishments		Per Cent of Total Volume of Business
	Number	Per Cent	
Wholesalers	165,153	100.0%	100.0%
Proprietorships	53,370	32.3	10.7
Partnerships	30,291	18.3	13.8
Corporations	74,196	44.9	68.2
Cooperative Associations	988	0.6	2.5
Other Legal Forms[a]	6,308	3.9	4.8
Merchandise Agents and Brokers	22,131	100.0%	100.0%
Proprietorships	9,911	44.8	24.4
Partnerships	4,764	21.5	26.7
Corporations	6,565	29.7	41.3
Cooperative Associations	294	1.3	4.5
Other Legal Forms[a]	597	2.7	3.1

[a] Includes establishments not reporting legal form of organization.

Source: Census of Business, 1954, Vol. III, *Wholesale Trade—Summary Statistics* (Washington, D. C.: Government Printing Office, 1957), p. 24.

The relationship between size and legal form of organization is brought out clearly by the data in Table 12. These figures, based on the 1954 Census of Wholesale Trade, show the distribution of establishments and sales among the different forms of organization. In terms of numbers unincorporated firms are obviously predominant, representing over half of all establishments operated by wholesalers and around two-thirds of all agents and brokers. Corporations are much more significant, however, when viewed in terms of business volume. This means, of course, that establishments operated by corporations are much larger, on the average, than those operated by proprietors or partnerships. Furthermore, these data really understate the larger size of corporate enterprises, since they are based on establishments rather than firms.

Managerial Considerations. In a single proprietorship there is no problem of conflicts in management. The proprietor may do as he sees fit, except possibly for restrictions imposed by creditors. Conflicts are likely to arise when partners are brought into the firm. Even good personal friends may disagree over proper management of a business and, unless authority is clearly divided, these disagreements may seriously hamper the enterprise. For this reason it is essential that a *partnership agreement* be drawn up in writing at the outset. This agreement should specify the duties and responsibilities of each partner, method of dividing net profits, salaries of each partner, the period of time for which the partnership is to exist, and provisions for dissolving the partnership. These are the points on which controversy is likely to arise in the absence of a written statement.

Whatever the provisions of the partnership agreement, it must be borne in mind that it is an agreement among the partners themselves and does not extend to outside parties. Under the law the actions of any one partner are binding on all of them unless the outside party is known to be aware of some of the restrictions on such action. Thus, for example, although one partner is not supposed to buy goods for the business, a purchase agreement made by him can be enforced by the vendor. Likewise, a partner whose duties exclude selling can bind the firm to an unprofitable deal with a customer. These problems are purely academic so long as all partners act in good faith with one another and exercise sound business judgment. Conflicts have often occurred, however, as attested by the long record of legal proceedings arising out of disputes among partners. All this means, in short, that *an inherent disadvantage of the partnership is its diffusion of authority among two or more persons,* and that the greater the number of partners the more likely conflicts are to arise.

In a corporation the problem of disputes among owners is minimized. Authority is definitely assigned to the firm's officers under its charter and bylaws, and stockholders cannot act on behalf of the firm except through their election of directors. This does not mean that conflict is automatically eliminated. Indeed, bitter dissension may exist in a small closed corporation just as in a partnership. But, in contrast to the unincorporated form of organization, those who hold a controlling interest in the corporation can make their authority prevail.

Tax Considerations. In general, the corporation operates at a considerable disadvantage, compared with the single proprietorship and partnership forms of organization, insofar as relative tax burdens are concerned. This is due principally to the fact that its earnings are taxed twice, once as corporate income and again, to the extent of the amounts distributed to stockholders as dividends, as personal income to the recipients. This "double taxation" of corporate earnings is especially burdensome to the smaller enterprise, yet this form of organization has much to recommend it for reasons previously stated and for some of the fringe tax benefits available to corporate employees like deductible group insurance, tax-free reimbursement of medical expenses, or exempt sick pay.

In 1958, however, the Congress enacted changes in the tax laws which may overcome some of the double taxation difficulty for the small corporation. It is now possible for the first time for a small corporation not having more than ten individual stockholders and not more than one class of stock, if agreed to by all the stockholders, to elect not to be taxed as a corporation, even though it is a corporation and operates as such in all other respects. When that is done, the undistributed taxable income of an electing small business corporation must be included in the gross income of its shareholders. By the same token, a net operating corporate loss is allowed as a deduction from the gross income of the shareholders.[7]

Other Factors. Limitation of liability, capital needs, management, and tax liabilities are usually the controlling factors in determining the legal form of organization. In addition, consideration should be given to continuity, transferability of ownership, and legal restrictions. By *continuity* is meant the life of the enterprise. A corporation, because it is a separate legal entity, has a continuity of existence beyond that of its owners. This may be a very important consideration, since the death or withdrawal of a partner from an enterprise automatically dissolves it. If a partner dies and his heirs demand cash settlement, the remaining partners may be forced to liquidate the business. In a corporation this does not happen.

Transfers of ownership are difficult in unincorporated firms, as the person withdrawing must find a purchaser for his interest who is acceptable to the other partners. The cumbersome mechanics of such transfers make the partnership form almost inconceivable in very large wholesale concerns such as McKesson & Robbins, Inc., or Butler Brothers.

The corporation has certain disadvantages in terms of the greater *legal restrictions* imposed on it. It must function within the powers given or implied by its charter from the state of incorporation, and these are subject to judicial interpretation. Moreover, corporations must make various reports to state and federal authorities not required of proprietorships and partnerships, and fees must be paid for incorporation. These factors are insignificant in a firm of any considerable size, but may be important in small companies.

Relationships with Suppliers and Customers. The wholesaler, by definition, is a *middleman* standing between manufacturers and other physical goods producers on the one hand and retailers or industrial users on the

---

[7] For more detailed information concerning the application of the new law, see Technical Amendments Act of 1958, Public Law 85–840, 85th Cong., 2d Sess., 72 Stat. 1013. Also see the interpretations with reference thereto in the tax services of Prentice-Hall, Inc., and the Commerce Clearing House, Inc.

other hand. Since the wholesaler must render satisfactory services both to his suppliers and to his customers, the importance of proper relationships with them is at once apparent. It is not surprising, therefore, that various types of agreements and arrangements have been evolved among these three groups in different lines of trade. At the inception of a new whole-sale enterprise, some attention must be given to the possibilities of enter-ing into such working relationships. Sometimes these are formal and con-tractual in nature, as with *exclusive agency agreements* with suppliers or *voluntary chain sponsorships* with retailers. More often the relationships are less formal and consist of *committee arrangements, policy statements,* or other devices for communication, arbitration of disputes, and perform-ance of specified services.

Exclusive Agency Agreements. An exclusive agency or "franchise" agreement is a formal, continuing arrangement between a wholesaler and a supplier, usually in the form of a written contract. In it the manufacturer gives an exclusive territory to the wholesaler, that is, an area in which no competing wholesalers will be allowed to handle the line. The wholesaler, on his part, agrees to give full support to the line. Specific contract pro-visions vary, but some of the more common ones can be summarized as follows:

Manufacturer Agrees to	Wholesaler Agrees to
1. Give sales support, in the form of mis-sionary salesmen, advertising assist-ance	1. Participate in the manufacturer's pro-motional program, by distributing dealer aids, conducting special promo-tions
2. Guarantee wholesaler's stocks against losses	2. Meet sales quotas established by the manufacturer
	3. Carry specified minimum inventories of the line
	4. Service specified customers or a mini-mum number of customers in his area

Exclusive agency contracts are commonly made on an annual basis but can be terminated at will by either party. By their very nature such con-tracts require actual support and participation and could not very well be enforced in the absence of voluntary compliance. Some manufacturers, in fact, operate without any written contracts for this very reason.

The wholesaler's decision on exclusive agencies is often governed largely by circumstances. In some lines of trade such arrangements are practically unknown, while in others they are quite common. In general, the system is employed when large inventories must be carried by wholesalers, when a coordinated promotional program is desired, when technical services must be provided to customers, or when introducing a new product into a market. Among wholesalers, exclusive agencies are most common in the electrical, industrial equipment and supply, hardware, and dry goods trades. In the last mentioned kind of business, a survey disclosed that over half of the wholesalers covered had at least one exclusive line, and that a wholesaler typically handled 3 to 5 such lines.[8] In contrast, exclusive agencies are practically unknown in the grocery and drug trades.

It should not be inferred that exclusive agencies are found *only* when the stated conditions obtain. Sometimes they are employed largely or entirely because of custom and tradition. For example, most of the leading brands of cigars are marketed in this fashion, although this product meets few if any of the requirements usually associated with exclusive distribution. It is not surprising, therefore, that the system does not work at all perfectly in this industry. "Bootlegging" of cigars by franchised wholesalers to large retailers who act as "subjobbers" for small outlets is a chronic problem in the trade, and around three-fourths of the wholesalers carrying franchised lines are said to engage in the practice.[9]

When a wholesaler has some choice in the matter, the decision to seek or accept a franchise should be governed by a careful analysis of its advantages and disadvantages. The main advantage, of course, is the relative freedom from competition. Since no other wholesalers in a given area would handle the line, the franchised distributor can be assured that his sales effort will benefit himself and will not be shared with other sellers. Moreover, there can be no direct price competition on the exclusive brand. A further advantage is in the close cooperation between supplier and wholesaler, especially in promotional activities, which should lead to a higher volume of sales than could be achieved otherwise. Finally, an exclusive line may be regarded as a prestige factor.

The disadvantages of exclusive agencies center around possible actions by the supplier. Many manufacturers have used the device to establish their lines, only to withdraw the franchises and "throw the line open" once brand acceptance has been achieved. Short of this, there are many sources of friction between manufacturer and wholesaler under a franchise agreement. Some manufacturers exert constant pressure for more sales. Inventory requirements may be so high that other lines are neglected by the wholesaler. Furthermore, the supplier usually controls the price, terms of sale, and services given with the line, and to this extent the wholesaler surrenders some of his independence.

The relative weight of these advantages and disadvantages obviously varies with individual cases. So long as the line is of good quality, competitively priced, and the manufacturer acts in good faith, the franchise is a definite asset to the wholesaler. When these conditions do not exist, the "game is probably not worth the candle."

[8] *Dry Goods Wholesalers' Operations*, by John R. Bromell, U. S. Department of Commerce (Washington, D. C.: Government Printing Office, 1949), pp. 99–100.
[9] Harry B. Patrey, in collaboration with Kolodny, *op. cit.*, pp. 23–29.

Informal Arrangements with Suppliers. Short of exclusive agencies, there are many less formal arrangements between wholesalers and their suppliers. Some manufacturers, for example, sponsor *wholesalers' committees* among their distributors. These groups meet periodically, often at the time and place of trade association conventions, to consider problems of mutual interest and to suggest changes in marketing policies or methods to the supplier. Such committees are fairly common in the paper trade, among others.[10] Mechanics of operation differ with lines of business, for obvious reasons, but the basic purpose of committees, meetings, and similar manufacturer-wholesaler arrangements is to provide better coordination of effort and to avoid the disputes that only too often characterize such relationships.

Relationships with manufacturers pose a difficult problem for the newcomer. Often a new enterprise is regarded with hostility by existing wholesalers. Manufacturers of established merchandise lines are skeptical about most newly formed distributors and will probably withhold their products from them at first. This may result, in part, from pressure applied by established competitors. Opposition from this source is likely to be particularly strong if the newcomer chooses to operate in an unconventional manner. Only after a fairly substantial level of sales is attained and the new firm has proved itself can it expect to secure the better-known brands and the cooperation of their manufacturers. For these reasons it behooves the owners of a new enterprise to (1) avoid incurring the enmity of competitors, insofar as possible, and (2) concentrate on building up a clientele of loyal customers so as to become important from the viewpoint of potential sources of supply.

Voluntary Chain Sponsorship. The most formal type of relationship between a wholesaler and his customers is that existing in a voluntary chain of retailers under the sponsorship of a wholesaler. The history, growth, and present status of voluntaries were discussed in some detail in Chapter 12. The advantages of such a relationship to a wholesaler are manifold. Most important, it practically assures him of a continuing volume of business, including most or almost all of the purchases of the retailer members, without the necessity of spending much effort or money on selling. In addition, since retailers usually agree to certain limitations in such services as delivery and credit, operating expenses can often be reduced substantially. From the standpoint of a new enterprise these advantages can frequently be translated into a very effective "opening wedge" with which to secure a place in the channel of distribution. Many voluntaries have been started, in fact, on account of dissatisfaction among retailers

[10] See F. K. Doscher, "Our Wholesaler Consultation Committee Is Paying Off . . . Says Lily-Tulip," *American Paper Merchant* (May, 1958), 32–33.

with orthodox wholesalers, spurred on by the active price competition of chain store systems.

The main drawback of the voluntary chain is the difficulty of enlisting a sufficiently large group of retailers carrying similar merchandise lines within a territory of workable size. As noted in Chapter 12, such organizations are confined largely to the grocery trade for this reason. There are several very successful voluntaries in hardware, drugs, and variety lines, but from an over-all point of view they are not a significant factor. Nevertheless, the success of such voluntary food groups as Independent Grocers' Alliance and Red and White continues to stimulate attempts at emulation in other trades.

Other Types of Customer Relationships. As discussed in Chapter 8, modern wholesalers have maintained their competitive position by offering to customers an ever widening range of customer services. The use of such services as a selling aid is considered in more detail in Chapter 26. At this point, suffice it to say that the type of relationship that exists between a wholesaler and his customers, including the kinds of services rendered and the prices charged therefor, is a basic policy decision which contributes to the over-all complexion or "personality" of the business. Variations between individual firms are virtually infinite. Underlying all of these variations is a more fundamental alternative in the philosophy of the organization itself. A wholesale enterprise can adopt the viewpoint that its function is to sell the goods to retailers or industrial users and that its responsibility ends there; or it can seek to assist retailers in all ways to carry the marketing process on through to ultimate consumers. There is no question but that the general trend has been from the former concept to the latter, and that the greatest opportunities for establishing and developing new firms in the future lie in this direction.

17

LOCATING A WHOLESALE ESTABLISHMENT

One of the first problems that arises in the formation of a new wholesale enterprise is that of selecting a location. The proper location is of vital importance, for the wrong choice may spell failure of the business. As explained in the preceding chapter, location decisions must be made in conjunction with certain other basic considerations, including the line of goods to be sold, the extent of the merchandise line, and the method of operation. All of these are interrelated, and any analysis of location problems must be made with this fact in mind.

Decisions about location are not confined to *new* wholesale enterprises. In an established business constant attention must be given to shifts in market factors which may call for *re*location. Also, expansion may be accomplished through a setting up of new establishments of the chain or branch types. Thus, although location problems arise rather infrequently, management must be constantly alert to the possibilities.

A basic prerequisite to an analysis of location problems is an understanding of the geography of wholesale trading centers and of trading areas as they have developed in the United States. Within this framework actual choices are made by a systematic evaluation of pertinent factors affecting potential sales and costs, as explained in the concluding part of this chapter.

WHOLESALE TRADING CENTERS AND AREAS

For political administration the United States is divided into states, counties, municipalities, and other minor subdivisions. For statistical and other ends it is also divided into several regions. The boundaries between the political areas are of little significance, however, in the geography of wholesale trade. Trade flows freely across political lines in obedience to certain economic forces, on the basis of which it is possible to identify *trading centers* and *trading areas* for each major line of trade.

Trading Centers and Areas Defined. A trading center is a city or metropolitan area in which wholesale establishments are concentrated. As shown in Chapter 6, wholesale trade is much more centralized than either population or retail trade, but there has been a slight tendency in recent years toward some decentralization. While it is entirely possible, and sometimes advisable, to locate in some place other than a trading center, these centers do have basic economic advantages which account for their development.

For each trading center it is possible to measure a *trading area,* which is simply the territory served by wholesale establishments located in the trading center. The boundaries between adjacent wholesale trading areas cannot be drawn sharply, as there is considerable duplication and overlapping in the customers served by competing centers. Nevertheless, trading areas are almost completely self-contained. The criterion adopted in one study was that each trading area be at least 90 per cent self-contained; that is, that neither the outflow to, nor the inflow from, other trading areas be more than 10 per cent of the total.[1] The term "primary trading area" is sometimes used to designate the area from which the bulk of business (90 per cent or some other high arbitrary figure) is drawn. Parenthetically it should be stated that the Standard Metropolitan Area or even the city itself in which the establishment is located often accounts for the bulk of this volume. The more distant parts from which scattered trade is obtained are said to comprise the "secondary trading area."

Variations in Trading Areas. There is really no such thing as "the" trading area for a given trading center in the sense of rigid demarcations and for all lines of trade. A trading area must be conceived as a general geographic approximation. Each center has, therefore, in a sense, as many trading areas as it has wholesale establishments, although for any given line of trade they tend to converge and to approximate each other in size and shape. Variations in trading areas exist, first, and probably most significantly, between different lines of trade; second, between competing sellers in a given line of business; and third, but of least importance, over a period of years for an individual wholesale enterprise. In part these variations reflect true differences in underlying economic factors, but they

[1] *NWDA Drug Trade Market Data* (New York: The National Wholesale Druggists' Association, 1956).

also reflect differences in the interpretations of these factors by executives of wholesale firms and consequent application in the conduct of business.

Variations by Line of Trade. Of all the sources of variation in trading areas served by wholesale establishments, undoubtedly the most important is the line of trade. For some kinds of goods the typical trading area is quite small, perhaps only a few counties. In contrast, a few establishments located in such centers as New York, Chicago, or St. Louis cover virtually the entire nation. This practice is not common, however, outside of a few lines of trade.

The smallest trading areas are those served by wholesale establishments handling convenience goods, for which the retail and other outlets are many and often quite concentrated, transportation costs relatively high, and where there is need for frequent replenishment of stocks. Thus, for the wholesale grocery trade the U. S. Department of Commerce has divided the nation into no less than 184 trading areas. In contrast the same agency recognizes only 46 trading areas for wholesale dry goods.[2] Similarly, the National Wholesale Druggists' Association divides the country into only 37 "primary areas of wholesale influence."[3]

Several things enter into the variations in trading areas for different classes of commodities. These can best be understood by analyzing first the general factors that determine trading areas.

Theoretically, the trading area for a seller of any product is limited by differences in costs of selling to customers located at various points as between the seller and his competitors located elsewhere. Assuming that competitors have about the same merchandise outlays, variations in costs arise primarily from differences in transportation expenditures (including both inbound and outbound) and in sales costs, especially salesmen's traveling expenses. On this basis a given wholesale establishment would have a cost advantage over competitors located elsewhere up to a certain point in each direction; beyond this point it would be operating at a cost disadvantage.

By way of illustration, a schematic representation of a wholesale trading area is shown in Figure 3. A wholesaler located in City A would normally find it profitable to cultivate the territory bounded by Points P, Q, R, and S in each of the four directions, respectively. At each of these points he will encounter competition from wholesale establishments located in Cities B, C, D, and E on an equal-cost basis.

It will be noted that the trading area shown in Figure 3 is not symmetrical as might be expected. If cost differences consisted only of salesmen's

[2] Office of Domestic Commerce, *Atlas of Wholesale Grocery Trading Areas* (Washington, D. C.: Government Printing Office, 1938); *Atlas of Wholesale Dry Goods Trading Areas* (Washington, D. C.: Government Printing Office, 1941).

[3] *NWDA Drug Trade Market Data, op. cit.,* p. 72.

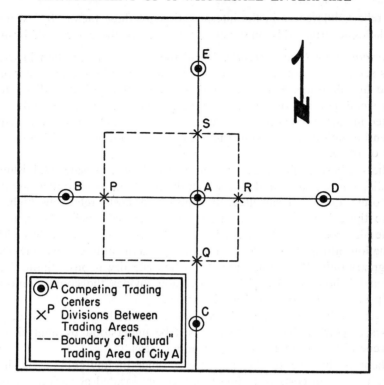

FIGURE 3. Schematic Representation of a Wholesale Trading Area

expenses and outbound transportation, the points dividing one trading area from another should be equidistant between competing trading centers. Point P might be expected (except for natural barriers such as mountains, rivers, etc.) to fall halfway between City A and City B. It does not do so, however, because consideration must also be given to differences in *inbound* transportation costs on goods shipped from suppliers to each competing wholesale establishment. In most lines of trade the flow of goods from manufacturing sources is primarily in one direction because of the concentration of manufacturing activity. For manufactured goods the traditional flow is from east to west and from north to south. In Figure 3, it is assumed that most goods are received by the competing establishments in cities A, B, C, D, and E from manufacturers to the east. If it can be further assumed that many incoming goods are received in railroad carlots while outgoing goods are shipped by truck or by lcl freight, then it is natural for the trading area of City A to extend farther west than to the east, since shipments back to the east represent "backhauling" and the point is soon reached (Point R) at which competitors to the east (City D) have a cost advantage. In general, for the reason just given as well as on account of the existing freight rate structure, a tendency may be noted for wholesale trading areas in the United States to extend farther to the west and south of their respective trading centers than to the north or east.

The foregoing analysis can be utilized to explain most of the variation in trading areas between lines of trade. For the different kinds of business trading areas vary because the goods are received from suppliers located in different places and because the goods differ greatly in bulk. The bulkier the goods, of course, the more important transportation costs become relative to total value; and, hence, the smaller the trading areas are likely to be because of the importance of shipping as far as possible in carload lots or other economic quantities. Also, the number and density of customers for different kinds of goods differ considerably, as previously mentioned. This is important because regardless of transportation costs a large enough area must be covered to support a wholesale establishment of some minimum economic size in each trade. The type of customer served is also important; a grocery wholesaler selling principally to small independent stores, or a tobacco wholesaler selling primarily to the same type of customer, cannot cover a large area because customers insist on buying frequently in very small amounts.

On account of these and other factors, there are substantial differences between the "normal" trading area of a grocery wholesaler or a chain store warehouse in the same trade and that of a wholesale establishment handling some other kind of goods. This still does not fully explain all actual differences among wholesale establishments, however, as will be seen from the discussion that follows.

Variations Within a Line of Business. Wholesale establishments in the same line of trade and located in the same trading center are frequently found to have quite different trading areas. In one study, for example, it was found that, although the "typical" trading area for a hardware wholesaler located in Minneapolis–St. Paul did not include any of Montana, 6 out of 27 wholesalers operating in the area did cover most of that state.[4] Other studies have disclosed similar variations in all lines of business and in many different trading centers.

Several reasons exist for variations in trading areas within a given line of trade. Among the most important may be mentioned size of establishment, extent of the merchandise line, policies on sales coverage, and knowledge of costs.

Obviously, there is a relationship between the size of an establishment and the size of its trading area. This relationship is not as clear cut and direct as might be expected, however. Although larger houses do tend to

---

[4] *Retail and Wholesale Trading Areas of Minneapolis and St. Paul* (Minneapolis: Chamber of Commerce, 1951), p. 9.

cover more extensive territories, other factors may be just as important or more important in trade area determination than size of the house per se.

The extent of the merchandise line carried affects the size and shape of the trading area in much the same way that the kind of goods itself does. Within a single line, such as hardware, are included many thousands of items coming from different manufacturing sources, sold to somewhat different customers, and varying in bulk, servicing requirements, and in other relevant respects. A general line wholesaler carries all or most of these items, and his trading area reflects a sort of "average" of the trading areas that might be covered for each item individually. If only part of the line is carried, however, a different kind of trading area may be in order. Thus, specialty wholesalers are usually found to cover territories that differ from those of their general line competitors. In general the trading area of a wholesale establishment carrying a specialty line is likely to be *larger* than that of a full-line establishment, because it is not profitable to cultivate all or most potential customers, and a wider area must be canvassed to yield a sufficient number of profitable accounts.

Finally, it is likely that the trading areas served by many wholesale establishments reflect a lack of accurate knowledge of selling and delivery costs. Measurement and allocation of these costs is a difficult task at best and may be virtually impossible with the accounting systems used in smaller firms. From studies made to date, there is no doubt that many customers are served at a loss and that a careful evaluation of the facts would lead to a realignment of territories.

SELECTION OF A COMMUNITY

In locating a wholesale house, especially when it is being newly established, three distinct problems need to be considered. The first relates to the choice of a community which, together with the trading area that is geographically tributary to it and which it thus dominates, will offer superior advantages for the kind of business contemplated. The second problem is whether to locate in or near the wholesale district in the chosen community or in some other type of district or area. The third deals with the selection of a specific site. Because so much depends upon obtaining the most suitable location, each of these problems is discussed in considerable detail in the following sections.

In selecting a community, it is first necessary to ascertain the trading area served by it for the kind of business in question. Then attention should be given to basic economic factors *for the trading area as a whole* which will affect the sales and profit opportunities available therein for that kind of business. Among the most important of these factors are population, consumer income, number and types of retail or industrial customers, competitive conditions, transportation facilities, labor conditions, the financial situation, tax burdens, and special inducements offered by the community.

Population. Wholesaling, a type of business activity operated on a fairly large scale and requiring the patronage of a large number of retail outlets or industrial users, is largely performed by urban institutions. Rather than being content with a superficial count of the number of retail outlets in his line of business, the new or prospective wholesaler must acquire a thorough understanding of the fundamental conditions in the market. A point of major importance is the population of the community and its wholesale trade area, because *size of the population* determines the number of potential ultimate consumers and provides a first indication of whether or not the area may be large enough to support the contemplated operation.

A knowledge of the size of the population, however, is not in itself sufficient; a question of at least equal importance is *the trend*. Some cities have been growing steadily and rapidly over a long period, some have barely kept pace with the general population increase, others have retained only about the same absolute number of inhabitants, and still others have declined in size. The advantages of locating in a growing community are obvious, but care should be taken to ascertain whether the growth is one that is firmly founded upon the natural development of the area, or whether it may be temporary because it has been occasioned by such a factor as the artificial stimulus of the government in connection with the development of defense industries. The fact that a city is more or less static as regards population size does not in itself mean that it is necessarily an undesirable location; but it does point up the need for a careful investigation of the reasons for absence of growth and a more careful weighing of other factors.

Still another question of great importance is the *composition* of the population. The number of people of various nationalities and races, the number professing membership in certain religious denominations, the number of homeowners and tenants, the number of persons of certain educational levels, and other similar questions are all matters that may be of major concern to a specific line of business. Finally, it is significant to know the *geographic distribution* of the population; how many are living on farms, in rural places, in cities, and in suburban areas.

The basic and most authoritative source of information on population size, trends, composition, and distribution is the decennial census taken by the Bureau of the Census of the U. S. Department of Commerce. At a given time Census figures, except for totals for the United States that are estimated for intercensal years, are unfortunately likely to be somewhat out of date. Current estimates for states, cities, and counties can be obtained from a number of sources. In most large cities Chambers of

Commerce or Planning Commissions may supply this kind of data. Data for all cities and counties are also summarized in convenient but estimate form in the annual "Survey of Buying Power" issue of *Sales Management* magazine, discussed in a subsequent section of this chapter.

Consumer Income. Even more important than population as a determinant of demand is the amount of *disposable income* available to consumers in the trading area. The pattern of income disposition among various goods and services may be estimated with reasonable accuracy, and from this the total amount of expenditures on a particular class of goods can be forecast.

As with population, it is not sufficient merely to know the total amount of consumer income; attention should also be given to the level of income *per household* or *per capita* and the *distribution* among various income groups. These factors may alter the spending pattern substantially.

Still another significant question has to do with the *sources* of incomes in an area, that is, the proportion of the total income that is derived from manufacturing industries, trade, agriculture, the professions, construction industries, and the government. Very important considerations are the diversification and stability of the industries of a community. Some cities (such as Gary, Indiana; Detroit, Michigan; and Akron, Ohio) are predominantly one-industry communities, whereas other cities are so well diversified industrially that an unfavorable condition, such as a strike or a depression in one of the more important industries, is not apt greatly to affect the total trade of the area. Some industries are on the decline, whereas others may be just developing with all the prospects of an extremely bright future. Seasonal variations may be of more importance in some communities because of the underlying character of the industries, while the influence of the business cycle may be of very serious consequence in others, particularly those that have a high concentration of manufacturers producing heavy industrial goods. Conditions such as these affect the earning power and consumption capacity of the population, which in turn supports or fails to support the wholesale business of the community.

Finally, attention must be given to the *trend* in disposable personal income in the trading area of a community. Because of changes in the industrial composition of employment in an area, changes in customs regarding multiple wage earners in families, and other social and economic factors, some areas have rising income levels while in others they are static or declining.

Reliable estimates of consumer income are published by the U. S. Department of Commerce in the *Survey of Current Business* and in biennial supplements to this periodical. These data are available for states but not for counties or smaller areas. Family income data for states, counties, and cities are available decennially from the U. S. Census of Population. Estimates for these smaller areas have been made in some states by Chambers of Commerce and university Bureaus of Business Research. Similar figures are prepared annually by *Sales Management* magazine in its "Survey of Buying Power," issued in May. For each county and city this survey contains estimates of population, disposable personal income, a distribution of households by income class, and retail sales by major kinds of business. Trade magazines in several important lines of business also publish periodic market guides with income and other data especially designed for use in evaluating potential markets for specific commodities.

In the absence of consumer income data, county data on payroll may serve as approximations. A further clue may be obtained from data on bank debits which are available on a county basis.

Number and Types of Potential Customers. The factors of population and consumer income affect potential wholesale sales only indirectly and even then only for consumer goods; that is, these factors determine *retail* sales, from which wholesale sales of consumer products must be derived. More direct measures of the potential market opportunity in a trading area are the number and types of retail outlets *and* business users in the area. This kind of information is also of vital importance in estimating the number of salesmen that will be needed to canvass the territory, which tends to vary primarily with the number of accounts to be serviced. The types of retailers or industrial users must also be determined, especially as to their size and ownership. Very small customers may not be regarded as worthwhile to be included in the estimates of potential sales. Conversely, very large retailers or industrial consumers may obtain most of their requirements in goods direct from manufacturers and afford little opportunity for sales by a wholesaler or a competing manufacturer's branch. Ownership of retail stores may be a critical factor; for example, chain units may not be prospective customers for a wholesaler. Finally, an attempt should be made to evaluate likely future trends in customer groups. For example, if the establishment under consideration is a chain warehouse, the company's plans for new retail outlets in the area should obviously be considered.

The authoritative sources of information on retail outlets and industrial establishments are the censuses of wholesale, retail, and service trades and for manufacturing, mining, and agriculture. These censuses are conducted periodically by the Bureau of the Census of the U. S. Department of Commerce. Supplementary sources include trade directories, city directories, and personal inspection of a community.

Competition. For all types of wholesale establishments except warehouses operated by retailers, competition constitutes a fourth factor to be surveyed before selecting a community in which to locate. The investigation must take into account the competition arising within the city under consideration and that emanating from other cities that compete for business within the wholesale trade area. This must go beyond a mere appraisal of the activities of other wholesale establishments of the same type. Rather, it must be extended to a careful study of all organizations handling the same types of merchandise on the wholesale level of distribution. For example, industrial distributors compete not only with each other but with hardware wholesalers who have industrial departments; grocery wholesalers compete with chain store warehouses; wholesale druggists compete to some extent with wholesale tobacconists; liquor wholesalers compete with wholesale druggists who operate liquor departments; general line dry goods wholesalers compete with the wide range of specialty concerns. Almost all types of wholesalers are in direct competition with manufacturers' agents and with manufacturers' sales branches that are located in the same market area. Therefore, a study of competitive conditions, if it is to provide a true picture of the actual situation, must encompass the total structure of wholesale distribution within the market area for the product class under consideration.

Some of the most important of these competitive conditions that must be taken into account are: the number and size of wholesale houses in the local community and in nearby cities; their policies on trade selection and market cultivation, whether intensive or extensive; the degree of specialization among establishments handling the line; the use of specialty salesmen and private brands; and the degree of style or uniqueness characterizing the merchandise handled. Considering only the first of these factors, for example, a general line hardware wholesaler locating in Columbus, Ohio, would soon run into competition to the north from similar firms in Cleveland, to the east from Pittsburgh, to the southwest from Cincinnati, to the west from Dayton and Indianapolis, and to the northwest from Toledo. Competition from the southwest and the northwest would be much more intense because of the presence in Louisville of the Belknap Hardware Company and in Chicago of the Hibbard, Spencer, Bartlett & Co., both of which are national concerns selling a very extensive line of merchandise over a large area. Thus, the new firm locating in Columbus would find that its market area would not extend very far from the city in any direction except possibly the southeast, whereas a decision to locate in some other city, such as Atlanta or Denver, would provide an altogether different set of circumstances.

Transportation Facilities. As explained in a preceding section of this chapter, transportation costs largely determine the "natural" trading area for a given community. For this reason careful analysis should be made of freight rate structures before choosing a city. It may be found that the trading area actually served by wholesale establishments in a given center bears little resemblance to that based on freight rates. One reason for this is that present trading areas are based in large part on trade practices and customs which grew up over a long period of time during which freight rate structures may have changed significantly.

Apart from the influence of transportation *costs* on the trading area itself, consideration must be given to the *adequacy* of transportation services from the standpoint of ability to handle the physical volume of shipments and the *variety* of available types of transportation and services. In connection with variety, railroads, motor carriers, water transportation, air service, freight forwarders, local cartage firms, and express and mail service, all are matters to be investigated. In addition, if the wholesaler plans to operate his own delivery service for outgoing shipments, a careful study of highway facilities and conditions must be made.

In most lines of business railroad freight is more important than the other services, at least for incoming shipments. A city that is situated on the main lines of several railroads obviously enjoys service superior to one serviced principally by branch lines. The *number* of railroads competing for freight business is in itself an important factor that usually affects the character and quality of service obtainable. Highway transportation has become increasingly important for both incoming and outgoing shipments, with the truckload often replacing the carload as an economical unit. In lines of business where that is the situation, there is a tendency toward a greater decentralization of wholesale business in order to place the "bulk-breaking point" as near as possible to the retail outlets. If the plan is to operate a business on a sectional or national basis, if the merchandise is not bulky, if the goods are highly perishable or are frequently ordered on a rush or emergency basis—under such conditions air freight facilities may be extremely important.

Obviously, the importance of the transportation factor varies greatly according to the line of merchandise handled, being determinative in lines like hardware or groceries and inconsequential in lines such as jewelry or optical goods. Even in a line of business like groceries, the fancier goods can be sold over a larger area than the more bulky items such as breakfast cereals and salt.

Labor Supply. A sixth important item to be considered in choosing a distributing center is the labor supply and the possibility of securing an adequate number of good salesmen. Adequacy of the supply of the various kinds of labor and of salesmen that will be needed should be carefully considered, particularly if the operation is to be of substantial size, or if it will require the employment of specialists, technicians, or other skilled labor as would be true in such lines as optical goods.

Wage and salary levels also vary considerably from one community to another for a given class of labor. These variations stem from several factors, including (1) differences in living costs, especially between large and small communities; (2) differences in the degree of unionization for warehousemen, truck drivers, and other workers; (3) variations in availability of labor; and (4) differences in competition for available workers.

Higher wage and salary levels in a community will, unless offset by correspondingly higher productivity (output per man-hour), cause higher labor costs. This is demonstrated by the data in Table 13, which reflect variations in the ratio of payroll expense to net sales for wholesalers in specified lines of trade. As shown there, differences in payroll cost are

TABLE 13

PAYROLL EXPENSE AS A PERCENTAGE OF NET SALES, WHOLESALERS IN
SPECIFIED LINES OF BUSINESS AND METROPOLITAN AREAS, 1954

	Payroll Expense, Per Cent of Net Sales				
Metropolitan Area	General Line Grocery	General Line Drug	Dry Goods, Apparel	Electrical, Electronic, Appliances	Hardware
Boston, Massachusetts	4.67%	8.89%	7.21%	8.46%	13.74%
Atlanta, Georgia	4.36	6.53	5.39	7.27	10.90
Indianapolis, Indiana	5.59	9.64	8.85	8.26	13.11
San Francisco—Oakland, California	4.73	9.16	9.37	8.81	9.09
St. Louis, Missouri	4.40	8.79	8.84	7.69	14.69

Source: Basic data from which computations were made, from *1954 Census of Business,* Vol. IV, *Wholesale Trade—Area Statistics* (Washington, D. C.: Government Printing Office, 1956), Table 103.

often as great or greater than the net profit margins in a given trade. Hardware wholesalers, for example, would, on the average, find payroll costs almost 50 per cent higher in Indianapolis than in San Francisco. Actually, this discrepancy in *average* labor costs may not apply in an individual case and a more detailed investigation is needed when market studies of potential community locations are made. Nevertheless, the figures in Table 13 are indicative of the magnitude of differentials that do exist.

Banking and Other Financial Facilities. A seventh consideration concerns the adequacy and variety of the financial services available in a community, together with the attitude of bankers toward supplying funds for business ventures. Most wholesale establishments require the use of outside sources for operating capital, some more or less regularly, and others largely in connection with seasonal or irregular needs. The banking institutions of different communities vary a great deal in their ability to provide needed funds and in their willingness to venture with a new enterprise. The investigation should determine whether control of the banking facilities is concentrated or diffused. In some cities all banks may be controlled by one family or by a very few cohesive families or groups with an ultraconservative attitude; hence the borrower is hindered by what amounts to a monopolistic condition in banking. In other communities there may be a high degree of effective competition in the money market as a result of the presence of a number of banks under varied ownership and with liberal attitudes toward new or expanding businesses.

For certain lines of business the existence of specialized financial institutions is significant. For wholesaling of consumer durable goods, such as electrical appliances, the presence of well-established, competitive sales finance companies, which finance dealer stocks as well as consumer purchases, is a favorable factor. In some lines of business the ability to take advantage of temporary low-price offerings on forward buying is enhanced by the presence of firms that render a field warehousing service. The use of the field warehouseman's receipt usually permits the wholesaler to secure a larger loan on a given amount of collateral stored in his own warehouse than would otherwise be possible.

Taxes. An eighth factor to be considered in selecting a community is the tax burden to be borne by the wholesale establishment. If the choice is to be made among cities located in different states, then state as well as local taxes must be investigated. Many states levy taxes of varying amounts on the income of proprietorships, partnerships, and corporations. Usually, this tax is paid on the net profit of the firm, but in some states it is levied on the gross income. Most states have some sort of business franchise or license fee for various lines of business. Some states also have taxes on real or personal property, which, although lower in amount than similar taxes assessed by cities or counties, are still items to be considered. In a few states the expanding multi-unit wholesaler will have to take into account the provisions of chain store tax laws that may apply to wholesale as well as retail units.

Local taxes, levied by cities, counties, school districts, and other governmental units with power to tax, consist largely of real property taxes to be paid if the physical facilities are owned, personal property taxes on inventories and other assets, and special license fees for particular kinds or lines of business or on specified merchandise items. In making a comparison of the tax situation in the various communities under consideration, three things are of primary concern: first, the kinds of taxes applicable to wholesaling; second, the tax rates that apply or the amount of fees that must be paid; and third, in the case of property taxes, the usual ratio of the *assessed* valuation to the *true* value of property. Information on the first two of these items may be obtained easily and accurately; the last one can only be estimated. However, since different communities may assess real or personal property at anywhere from 25 to 100 per cent of its actual value, some idea of this ratio must be obtained in order to make the tax information meaningful.[5]

Inducements. An additional matter to be considered consists of special offers or inducements sometimes made by municipalities or civic groups to attract new businesses to their community. The most common of these inducements are related to taxes and may include deferments, exemptions, special low rates, or promises of low assessment ratios. Other offers may be worked out by the local Chamber of Commerce or the city in connection with the consideration of a specific business or a specific location, such as free street pavement, construction of railroad sidings, very low electric power rates, or considerable amounts of publicity. Some communities have evolved elaborate programs of this character, whereas others have made no effort to attract new enterprises or, under the influence of certain selfish interests, have actually discouraged business growth from without. It would be dangerous for a new firm to place too much emphasis on this factor, for, in the absence of a binding contract, once the establishment is located some of the concessions may be withdrawn or neutralized by succeeding administrations holding different views. Special inducements are more or less artificial in nature, anyway, and should not rate the same importance as population, income, transportation, competition, and the other basic factors.

Information on special inducements available, as well as other data for a particular state, city, or county, can often be obtained from industrial development commissions especially established for purposes of attracting new businesses. According to *Industrial Development* magazine, there were as many as 6,700 such organizations operating on local, state, regional, and national levels as of late 1957.[6] Some of the information obtained from development commissions, like that secured from advertising media and Chambers of Commerce, should be interpreted cautiously. While the information they contain is almost always truthful and useful, it may fail to reveal *all* of the facts about an area including unfavorable or derogatory features.

Analysis of Potential Community Choices. Because community choice for the location of a wholesale establishment is of great importance, decisions about it are usually based on formal and comprehensive market analyses. In this process all of the factors briefly discussed above must be

---

[5] An outline of the various taxes imposed by different states can be obtained in the latest issue of *Tax Systems,* published by the Commerce Clearing House, Inc., New York. Estimates of the ratio of assessed valuation to actual values are contained in the report of the Citizens' Research Council of Michigan, "Tax Rates of U. S. Cities," *National Municipal Review* (January, 1955), 14–35. These ratios ranged from a low of 5 per cent in Greenville, S. C., to 90 per cent in Watertown, N. Y., and several other cities.

[6] "Site Selection Handbook Edition" of *Industrial Development* (October, 1957).

carefully considered, and on that basis estimates should be prepared of probable sales volume, operating expenses, and expected net profits.

Some specific sources of information for certain location factors have been indicated at proper places in the preceding discussion. It is appropriate, however, at this juncture to summarize this matter in a more or less general way even at the expense of some repetition. Furthermore, it should be emphasized that wherever possible two or more information sources should be used as checks against one another in order to minimize bias and inaccuracies.

As already indicated at a number of places, the federal government provides a wealth of quantitative information through its censuses of Manufactures, Population, Agriculture, and Business. Interim information on trends and shifts in business establishments, employment, and payrolls is available from the U. S. Department of Commerce reports compiled from records of the Old Age and Survivors Insurance Program. Special wholesale trading area studies for certain lines of business are available from the U. S. Department of Commerce. The Bureau of Labor Statistics supplies a vast amount of information on wage payments, wage rates, unionization, and similar matters.

State and local governments can provide the required information on taxes that apply to the business in question. Reports of the Interstate Commerce Commission and tariff schedules of transportation agencies provide the means for analyzing the transportation rate structure.

Various publications, such as general and trade magazines, have made important studies that are pertinent to location analysis. One notable example is the Survey of Buying Power issue of *Sales Management Magazine,* which provides annual estimates of retail sales, wholesale sales, effective buying income, and other data previously indicated for each county and city in the United States. In addition, numerous local media, such as newspapers and radio stations, have made detailed surveys of their own local markets that are usually available on request.

Some Chambers of Commerce, particularly in the larger cities, have market research staffs and can furnish a large amount of relevant data. Trade associations, banks, public utilities, and others interested in the development of an area may also be fruitful sources of information, including quantitative data.

In addition to the *quantitative* or statistical data that can be obtained from the above-mentioned and other sources, a great deal of information of a *qualitative* nature pertaining to such questions as the marketing policies of competitors and the attitude of bankers must be gathered. Frequently, this can be accomplished only by a personal investigation through interviews with informed persons within the various cities under consideration.

The collection, organization, and interpretation of all the quantitative and qualitative data required for a thorough market analysis is a rather substantial undertaking. An individual, not trained in proper research methods, would encounter grave difficulties in locating the right information and in bringing it together in usable form. In view of the presence throughout the country of many competent consultants and marketing research agencies, the best course of action is undoubtedly to engage the services of such a specialist. This procedure may prevent the management from becoming bogged down by the confusion of countless details and frees the executives to concentrate their attention on the important problem of weighing the alternatives after the facts have been gathered, analyzed, and properly presented.

SELECTION OF THE TYPE OF LOCATION WITHIN THE CITY

In every city of any considerable size there are two or more sections in which wholesale houses cluster together. In the smaller cities most of the concerns, except those dealing in produce, are located in a single wholesale district. In the larger cities there may be a principal wholesale district and a number of secondary clusters of wholesale establishments. These secondary clusters may consist of a variety of firms of different types operating in one line or in various lines of trade, or of a concentration of similar types of wholesale establishments within a given line of business. Thus there may be a wholesale produce area that includes brokers, commission merchants, and jobbers; a wholesale dry goods and wearing apparel center that includes wholesalers, selling agents, and manufacturers' branches dealing in general dry goods, specialty lines of dry goods proper, floor covering, millinery, dresses and coats, and similar items; a clustering of grocery or hardware establishments; or a concentration of wholesale jewelry firms. Each of these clusters may be more or less separated from the others.

In most cities the established wholesale districts are of long standing, and vacant land is seldom available within them. A suitable building may be vacant, however, in which case attention must be directed to the advantages and disadvantages of locating in such a district.

Factors Favoring Location in the Wholesale District. In some lines of business an important advantage of locating in the wholesale district is that it facilitates visits by customers to the wholesale house. The significance of this factor varies with the line of merchandise handled and with the method of operation of the wholesale concern. If the wholesaler deals in such lines as dry goods, clothing, millinery, or jewelry, it is highly important for him to be located in the principal wholesale district for his line of business. Such a location attracts trade from both city and out-of-town buyers who desire to visit several competing houses within a short period of time and compare the merchandise of each as to style, quality, price, and other factors. If the merchandise is highly perishable and subject to large variations in quality and price, as are fresh fruits and vegetables, the desire of retailers to visit the market and make purchases quickly makes a central location imperative. If the concern is to be operated on a limited-service basis, such as a cash-and-carry wholesale grocer, it must also be centrally located in order to be convenient to customers who assume the delivery function.

Another advantage of locating in close proximity to competing concerns is that it enables the wholesaler to pick up "shorts," that is, goods of which the seller is temporarily out and that are needed to fill an order. A central location is also convenient to traveling representatives of sources of supply. In a seller's market, as in periods of rising prices, wholesale houses that are not located along the beaten tracks of vendors' salesmen are more apt to be overlooked, particularly when such concerns operate on a small scale. Furthermore, a wider variety of transportation agencies and other facilitative services such as public storage, banks, and credit organizations are more immediately accessible from a wholesale district. A final consideration involves the type of building or amount of warehouse space to be occupied. If the concern can operate efficiently in a multistory warehouse, or if the amount of needed space is so small that it will require the leasing of only part of a building, then a location within the wholesale district will probably be desirable.

Factors Favoring a Location Outside of the Wholesale District. When the business is operated on a fairly large scale, the style element and quality variations are not of great importance, practically all sales are made by the salesmen of the house, and merchandise is delivered by the wholesaler to customers or to transportation agencies; then the advantages of locating in the wholesale district lose much of their weight. Under all or most of these conditions, a location in an outlying area that does not require proximity to competitors or allied firms may, in fact, be more desirable.

One of the most important advantages of such a location is relief from the increasing traffic congestion that characterizes almost all major cities. Such congestion greatly hinders trucking and delivery operations, delays of several hours not being too uncommon in "line-ups" at important transportation terminals. The congestion of a central district may also interfere with salesmen; for example, a major electrical supply company transferred most of its Los Angeles salesmen from the downtown office to suburban offices accessible to the freeways. As a result, it was estimated that each salesman could make an additional two calls per day.[7]

[7] "Aim Now Is Profit, Not Volume," *Business Week* (February 22, 1958), 114.

An outlying location is usually obtained at a much lower ground cost, so that ample parking facilities can be provided. Such a location may also afford an escape from the factory atmosphere of the wholesale district, which may involve smoke, noise, odors, lack of sunlight, and other disutilities. In addition, if the location is outside of an incorporated area or is in a suburban community, important tax savings may be realized.

As important as all these factors are, the main reason for the trend toward suburban wholesale locations is yet to be mentioned. This is the *type of warehouse building* to be used. Basically there are two types of warehouses in use in lines of business requiring a large amount of storage space. These consist of (1) the older multistory warehouses designed for vertical storage, and (2) the newer one-story buildings that provide horizontal storage of merchandise. As a result of the tendency to cluster wholesaling businesses in a concentrated area, the vertical warehouse has predominated in the regular jobbing lines. Since the middle 1930's, however, there has been a marked trend toward the single-story type, a trend that has been greatly accentuated by the experience of government warehousing operations during World War II when speed in the mass handling of equipment and supplies was a prime essential and when great experimental developments in horizontal handling methods by mechanical means could be undertaken without regard to cost. The advantages of horizontal handling of some types of products have thus become more apparent, with the result that most new buildings are being located in outlying areas where the ground cost permits the construction of a type of warehouse in which these advantageous features may be incorporated. Construction of such buildings in established wholesale districts is usually impossible, because sufficient land is not available and its cost would be prohibitive. A decision to construct a one-story warehouse is usually tantamount, therefore, to a selection of a suburban location.

The choice of the type of warehouse building is based primarily on the handling methods to be used rather than on location factors. For this reason, further discussion of the subject is postponed until Chapter 23.

SELECTION OF A SPECIFIC SITE

After a community has been selected and a decision has been reached as to the general area within the city or suburbs in which to locate the house, the problem of selecting a specific site still remains. The dynamic nature of a city's structure and the continual changes that take place within the field of marketing add to the difficulty of this choice. For a particular site to be considered a suitable location, special attention must be given to a number of factors. Among the more important are the rent-paying capacity of the business, availability of railway track service, proximity to freight terminals, accessibility to the trade, proximity to sources of supply, and opportunities for expansion.

Rent-Paying Capacity. Regardless of its suitability on other grounds, a site cannot be selected if its cost is beyond the "rent-paying capacity" of the business. Wholesale enterprises generally occupy a middle position between retailers and manufacturers. This explains why a wholesale house ordinarily cannot be located in a downtown district, where a retail business could afford to pay a much higher rent. On the other hand, wholesale establishments command better sites than those occupied by factories.

Even within wholesale trade there are considerable variations in rent-paying capacity of different lines of wholesale trade. Such differences arise in large part from the line of business, as shown in Table 14. The data in

TABLE 14

SALES PER SQUARE FOOT OF WAREHOUSE SPACE, WHOLESALERS IN SPECIFIED
KINDS OF BUSINESS, UNITED STATES, 1954
(Ranked in Order of Sales per Square Foot)

Kind of Business[a]	Sales per Square Foot[b]
ALL WHOLESALERS	$ 60.19
Wine, Distilled Spirits	171.28
Tobacco	164.08
Jewelry	100.21
General-line Grocery	89.56
General-line Drug	83.74
Specialty-line Grocery	68.89
Specialty-line Drug	67.54
Beer, Ale	66.15
Industrial Materials, Supplies	50.74
Plumbing, Heating	42.01
Paper and Allied Products	38.84
Automotive Equipment, Tire and Tube	35.62
Hardware	34.31
Paint, Varnish	31.09

[a] For each line of trade, the figures apply to those establishments which reported 500 or more square feet of warehouse space to the Bureau of the Census.

[b] The area figures represent "net warehouse floor space," exclusive of offices, receiving and shipping areas, and the like.

Source: Computed from data in the *1954 Census of Business, Wholesale Trade, Warehouse and Cold Storage Space*, Bulletin W–2–5 (Washington, D. C.: Government Printing Office, 1957), Table 5–A.

this table measure *sales per square foot of warehouse space* for specified kinds of business conducted by wholesalers. Lines of trade with high sales per square foot can, other things being equal, afford to pay more for a given site than those with low space sales productivity.

Sales per square foot as shown in Table 14 vary from a little over $30 in the paint and varnish kind of business to over $170 in wine and distilled spirits, the highest figure being almost six times as great as the lowest. This wide variation may be accounted for in part by differences in the value of the goods handled relative to their size. This is obviously a factor in the high ranking of wine and distilled spirits, tobacco, and jewelry, as opposed to automotive equipment, hardware, and paint and varnish. Another factor is the rate of stock turnover; for example, for general line wholesale druggists turnover averages around 5.5 times per year, as compared with about 3.5 for hardware wholesalers.[8] A third factor affecting sales per square foot is the use of *cubic* space, that is, the amount of goods stored in a given space area. In some lines such as groceries goods are stacked high through the use of pallets and mechanized handling equipment; in other lines, because of weight or other considerations, this is of little importance.

Availability of Railway Track Service. For the handling of groceries, hardware, drugs, electrical goods, and many other lines of trade, track service is essential to economical operation. Consequently, such firms locate their places of business, whenever possible, on sites that permit the construction of railroad spurs alongside or leading into the buildings from which cars may be loaded and unloaded with a minimum of labor, time, and expense. Some houses have sufficient space to accommodate five or more cars at a time, to be switched as desired. Goods may be unloaded directly from the car into trucks for local delivery instead of going through the warehouse. Track service also enables wholesalers more conveniently to combine purchases and thus "pool" cars to obtain lower freight rates.

Proximity to Freight Terminals. Whether or not railway track service is available, it is generally advisable to locate within a short distance of the freight depots. Such a location facilitates the handling of less-than-carlot shipments, both incoming and outgoing. A location near railroad terminal facilities prevents long-distance hauling to and from the cars; and since passenger stations are also nearby, buyers from out-of-town are attracted to the house. If the community is connected by water routes with important centers of supply, it may be advantageous to locate conveniently near the waterfront, particularly when the goods are bulky. The more general use of "store-door delivery" in connection with certain kinds of freight shipments and the increasing use of truck transportation have lessened the importance of both railway track service and proximity to freight terminals for wholesalers who operate on a fairly small scale in restricted market areas.

[8] Approximate figures based on averages reported by members of the National Wholesale Druggists' Association and the National Wholesale Hardware Association in recent years.

Accessibility to the Trade. Ease of reaching city trade with deliveries and of being reached by prospective buyers is desirable. In locating a new business or in relocating an established concern, it is desirable to spot all prospective or actual customers on a map in order to determine which of a number of alternatives will be most suitable in this respect. A location that is readily accessible to customers reduces delivery expense and serves to attract trade in lines where it is customary for buyers to visit the wholesale house frequently. With the growing use of motor vehicles for both freight and passenger transportation, accessibility to thoroughfares and parking facilities is sometimes the governing factor.

Proximity to Local Sources of Supply. If local sources of supply are significant, it may be advisable, other things being equal, to locate near them. This simplifies the assembly function, but may be offset by higher delivery costs to customers.

Expansion Possibilities. Since most business firms commence operations on a scale smaller than that which they hope to attain eventually, the possibility of expanding the physical facilities at a given location must be considered. This problem concerns the feasibility of adding one or more floors to a vertical warehouse, of acquiring sufficient ground space to expand a one-story warehouse, or the possibility of acquiring additional space in the same building in case only part of it is occupied at the beginning. If it is not possible to provide such safeguards, it is best to avoid any long-term commitments that would tie the firm to a location with definitely limited facilities.

18

FINANCING A
WHOLESALE
ENTERPRISE

Capital is a vital ingredient in any business enterprise. The tasks of planning capital needs, determining sources of funds, and controlling their use in the business comprise the major management function of *financing*. Problems of financing are especially acute in most new enterprises, and lack of capital has often proved to be the rock on which an otherwise well-conceived organization founders. In the established concern the problem is hardly less important; cash balances must be maintained to make payments when due, capital costs must be controlled, and provisions must be made for expansion when justified by market opportunities. The nature of the financing function and some general techniques for its performance are discussed in this chapter.

Objectives of Financial Management. Once the financial structure of the enterprise is soundly conceived and effectuated, organizational responsibility for financial management thereafter rests with a major specialized executive in large firms and with the owners or proprietors in smaller concerns. In carrying out this responsibility, several objectives must be kept in mind. First, capital needs must be *anticipated in advance* so that time will be available for careful planning and negotiating with potential sources. If this type of planning is not done, emergencies are likely to arise frequently, and the company's bargaining position will be weakened.

A second objective is to *minimize costs of acquiring capital*. In part this flows from proper planning. It also requires an intimate knowledge of financing methods and the costs of obtaining funds from available sources.

328

Third, financial management must seek to *maintain liquidity,* in order that bills may be paid when due and cash discounts taken on purchases, and yet *avoid the accumulation of idle cash* which is wasteful of capital resources and highly unprofitable.

Finally, a *sound financial condition* is a basic consideration in financing. This means that certain relationships must be maintained among the different types of assets, liabilities, and net worth. These will, of course, vary for different kinds of business. When such relationships are not observed, the firm may become vulnerable to changes in economic conditions and may be seriously damaged thereby.

DETERMINING CAPITAL NEEDS

The first step in financing a new enterprise is to determine the types and amounts of capital needed. A similar problem is faced by established concerns in providing for temporary or permanent expansions. In either case capital needs are determined on the basis of the various kinds of assets, current and fixed, that are required for carrying on operations. As a general approach, asset requirements can be estimated in terms of their relationships to anticipated sales volume in a given line of business, as is done in the discussion that follows.

Classes of Assets and Their Relative Importance. The conventional classification of assets, which is convenient for use in determining capital needs, makes for two basic groups: current and fixed. These are further subdivided as follows:

Current Assets:
Cash
Accounts and Notes Receivable
Merchandise Inventories
Other Current Assets

Fixed Assets:
Land and Buildings
Warehouse Equipment
Delivery Equipment
Other Fixed Assets

The financial structure of a business depends in large part on the relative importance of these asset requirements. Wholesaling is somewhat distinctive on this score, as may be seen from the figures in Table 15. These data show the distribution of assets among the major categories for selected kinds of wholesale business. Noteworthy is the similarity among the various trades represented in the table. There are some variations, to be sure, but for the most part wholesaling concerns have about the same distribution of total assets among the various categories.

TABLE 15

Typical Distribution of Assets by Major Categories, Selected Kinds of Wholesale Business, United States

Asset Class	Auto-motive Supply	Drugs	Dry Goods (General Line)	Electrical Appli-ances	Grocery (General Line)	Hardware	Industrial Supply	Lumber and Building Materials	Plumbing and Heating
Current Assets:									
Cash	6%	7%	7%	8%	8%	6%	6%	7%	6%
Receivables (Net)	26	35	30	35	21	26	36	35	30
Inventories	46	45	39	44	48	47	40	35	45
Other Current	2	0	2	1	1	3	3	2	1
Total, Current Assets	80%	87%	78%	88%	78%	82%	85%	79%	82%
Fixed Assets—Total	15	10	9	8	16	12	11	17	14
All Other[a]	5	3	13	4	6	6	4	4	4
Total	100%	100%	100%	100%	100%	100%	100%	100%	100%

[a] Includes prepaid expenses, such as insurance premiums; notes and accounts due from partners, officers, directors, stockholders, or others exclusive of customers; and all other assets.

Sources: Based on typical figures reported by members of trade associations and by firms analyzed by credit reporting and similar agencies, such as Dun & Bradstreet, Inc., and Robert Morris Associates.

The most important single class of assets in all kinds of wholesale business is *merchandise inventory,* representing from 35 per cent to 50 per cent of total capital needs. *Accounts and notes receivable* are second in importance, although in at least one trade group (lumber and building materials) this item is on a par with inventory. These two types of assets, together with cash and miscellaneous current assets (e.g., prepaid expenses) make up from 80 per cent to 90 per cent of all assets. Here an important difference between wholesaling and other forms of business activity such as manufacturing is revealed. Of the total assets employed in a manufacturing concern, at least 25 per cent and as high as 60 per cent consists of fixed assets. In contrast, only about 10 per cent to 15 per cent of total assets used in wholesaling is fixed in nature. The reason for this difference is that wholesaling is generally *less mechanized* than manufacturing and as a result requires less investment in expensive machinery and installations. As warehousing becomes more automated, however, fixed assets may be expected to increase in relative importance.

Capital Needs for Merchandise Inventories. Since inventory is the most important single asset, attention is given to it first. The value of inventory needed in a business in a given line of trade depends largely on expected sales volume. The relationship between inventory and sales is usually expressed in the form of a turnover ratio.[1]

Average rates of inventory turnover for selected kinds of wholesale business are contained in Table 16. With these figures it is a simple matter

TABLE 16

TYPICAL RATES OF INVENTORY TURNOVER FOR SPECIFIED
KINDS OF WHOLESALE TRADE, UNITED STATES

Kind of Business	Turnover Rate (Times per Year)
Automotive Supply	4.0
Coal and Coke	48.5
Drugs	6.2
Dry Goods (General Line)	4.9
Electrical Supply	6.5
Electrical Appliances	6.5
Footwear	6.1
Frozen Foods	7.8
Furniture	5.4
Grocery (General Line)	12.0
Hardware	4.1
Industrial Supply	4.8
Lumber, Building Supply	8.3
Plumbing and Heating	4.9

Sources: Based on typical figures reported by members of trade associations in recent years.

[1] See Chapter 20 for a discussion of the significance of turnover rates in the planning and control of merchandising operations.

to approximate the inventory investment needed in a business, assuming that its sales volume has been properly estimated through some form of market analysis. To illustrate, suppose that it has been decided to establish an automotive supply house and that annual sales of about $1.5 million are expected. The average annual rate of turnover in this trade is given in Table 16 as 4.0. This figure represents a ratio of the *cost of goods sold* to average inventory, since inventory is valued on a cost basis rather than at selling prices. It is necessary, therefore, to estimate the *cost* equivalent of $1.5 million in sales. In the automotive supply line, gross margins are in the neighborhood of 25 per cent of sales. The cost equivalent of $1,500,000 is, therefore, $1,125,000 ($1,500,000 times 75 per cent). The average inventory needed to support this level of sales is set $281,000 ($1,125,000 divided by 4).

In estimating inventory needs for a new business, care must be taken to allow for the necessarily slow process of "getting off the ground." Sufficient inventory should be on hand to support the volume of sales to be attained when operations have reached full scale, not the volume of sales for the first month or several months. The logic of this statement rests on the concept that adequate breadth and depth of inventory are basic requirements in building a business. If stocks are skimpy, sales may never reach the level estimated at the outset. This implies, of course, that turnover is bound to be slower in the early stages of the new enterprise, but this is part of the price of admission.

Capital Needs for Accounts and Notes Receivable. The investment required in receivables in a wholesale enterprise depends on four factors: the expected volume of sales, the proportion of sales to be made on a credit basis, the terms on which credit is extended, and the effective terms of repayment or the average collection period. On the average, around 85 per cent of all sales made by wholesalers and manufacturers' sales branches involve the extension of credit. This varies, however, from as little as 30 per cent in such lines as automobiles to virtually 100 per cent in dry goods, jewelry, and certain other trades. Similarly, the amount of receivables on the books at a given time varies with sales fluctuations in accordance with the period for which credit is used and the proportion of customers taking advantage of cash discounts.

The several factors affecting capital needs for receivables are conveniently summarized in a ratio of *sales to receivables,* which serves as a basis for initial financial planning. Illustrative sales-to-receivables ratios for several kinds of wholesale business are given in Table 17. These ratios can be used in much the same way that turnover rates were used to estimate inventory requirements. Thus, for example, the ratio of sales to receivables in the dry goods trade averages around 8.0. If a projected establishment in this kind of business is expected to attain sales of $2 million,

TABLE 17

TYPICAL RATIOS OF SALES TO RECEIVABLES FOR SPECIFIED KINDS OF
WHOLESALE TRADE, UNITED STATES

Kind of Business	Sales to Receivables (Times)
Automotive Supply	9.4
Drugs	9.5
Dry Goods (General Line)	7.8
Electrical Supply	9.0
Floor Coverings	7.1
Footwear	8.1
Grocery (General Line)	27.0
Hardware	9.1
Industrial Supply	6.5
Jewelry	6.1
Plumbing and Heating	8.7
Tobacco Products	16.0

Sources: Based on typical figures reported by members of trade associations and by firms analyzed by credit reporting and similar agencies, such as Dun & Bradstreet, Inc., and Robert Morris Associates.

the required investment in receivables will amount to $250,000 ($2,000,-000 divided by 8). It will be noted that it was not necessary to convert sales to a cost basis as with inventories, since receivables are valued at selling prices and are directly comparable with net sales. Nor was it necessary to use credit sales as the dividend, because practically all sales in this line of trade are made on credit, and hence credit sales and net sales are approximately the same for purposes of this computation.

The procedure just described serves as a basis for estimating the amount of capital needed for receivables *on the average* at a given level of sales. Of course, receivables will not reach this level in a new concern for a period of several weeks or months. In the meantime, capital needs to support this asset will be somewhat less. It is advisable to plan on financing the full amount, nevertheless, since otherwise capital will be drained from other assets as receivables mount.

In addition to providing for capital to finance customers' purchases of merchandise, many wholesale enterprises also undertake to finance retailers' store fixtures, remodelings, and even the construction of new stores. As noted in Chapter 8, this type of financial assistance has grown in importance since World War II and in some lines of trade has become a competitive necessity.

Fluctuations in Working Capital Needs. As indicated in the foregoing paragraphs, inventory and receivables normally comprise from 70 to 80 per cent of total capital needs in a wholesale enterprise. The financing of these assets is complicated by the fact that the requirements are subject to recurring fluctuations, so that the amount of capital needed varies from month to month and even from week to week.

The most important cause of fluctuations in working capital needs is *seasonal variation in sales volume*. Inventory is carried primarily to *support* anticipated sales, while receivables are *created* by sales. Thus, fluctuations in inventory requirements tend to precede changes in sales, while receivables follow such changes. The importance of this seasonal variation obviously depends on the kind of business. In certain lines sales in peak months may be two or more times as great as sales in off-season months. Just prior to and during the peak months, inventories must be built up; in the months following the season, heavy receivables must be carried.

A method of planning for regular seasonal variations in sales and capital needs is discussed in Chapter 20. Since the causal factor is sales, such planning is basically a merchandise planning rather than a financing function. There must, however, be close coordination between merchandise planning and finance personnel if the planning is to be effective.

A second cause of varying working capital needs is found in *cyclical* fluctuations in the general level of economic activity. The effects of these variations are similar to those of seasonal changes, but planning for them is much more difficult because business cycles are largely unpredictable. When a "recession" does occur, as in late 1957 and early 1958, wholesalers have great difficulty in making the necessary adjustments in inventories. Many economists believe, in fact, that the process of working off surplus inventories is a major factor in accentuating business declines and vice versa in the case of expansions.

Fluctuating working capital needs also arise from various kinds of special promotions, which may or may not be related to regular selling seasons. Some manufacturers, for example, conduct promotional events annually or semiannually. If the line is an important one to the wholesaler, he will find it necessary to expand inventories to support the sale.

Periodic variations in working capital needs, such as indicated above, constitute one of the most important and distinctive features of financing in mercantile organizations, both wholesale and retail. Some types of capital sources, notably the commercial bank, were evolved primarily to provide temporary financing to meet such needs. Thus the ebb and flow of inventories and receivables determine, in large part, the financial structure of a wholesale enterprise.

Estimating Fixed Asset Requirements. Fixed asset requirements vary greatly, depending on the kind of business and other factors, such as the method of operation. All wholesale enterprises need some kind of building, office fixtures, and warehouse equipment. In addition, unless the establishment is to be operated on a cash-and-carry basis, some type of delivery equipment will be required.

The size of building needed by a wholesale concern can be estimated on the basis of typical sales per square foot ratios, such as those shown in Table 14, Chapter 17. For example, average space productivity in the hardware trade is around $34 per square foot (in 1954 dollars). If a proposed new enterprise is expected to have sales of $2.5 million (also in 1954 dollars), about 73,500 square feet of warehouse space will be needed. This figure may be adjusted upward or downward if the business is to be operated on some basis other than the conventional; for example, if a large percentage of the goods is to be drop shipped rather than warehoused, less space would be required. In any event, it is usually wise to plan space needs with possible future expansion in mind.

Once space requirements have been determined, capital needs can be estimated on the basis of typical building costs per square foot in a given area and for a given type of construction. These differ in various areas and should be determined through consultation with local contractors or commercial architects. In the mid–1950's, typical building costs for a new one-story warehouse were in the neighborhood of $8 to $9 per square foot.

Capital requirements for fixtures and equipment must be estimated directly on the basis of individual needs. While still small in comparison with inventories and receivables, assets of this type have grown tremendously in importance in recent years. A new wholesale establishment in the grocery trade, for example, must be outfitted with fork-lift trucks, tow trains, pallets, pallet racks, electronic or similar equipment, and other expensive items. These run into many thousands of dollars. By way of contrast an agent or broker can set up shop with virtually no fixed assets beyond a desk and filing cabinet.

Some idea of the kinds of equipment and fixtures needed in various lines of wholesale trade can be gotten from the discussion of warehousing and order-handling methods in Chapters 23, 24, and 25.

Other Capital Needs. When a new enterprise is established, the original capital must include some provision for operating expenses during the initial stages when sales volume is still low. Just how long a period must be so covered will, of course, depend on the nature of the business and the need for its services in the community chosen as a location. As a rule of thumb, it is probably wise to provide for out-of-pocket expenses for one inventory turnover period—that is, if the typical rate of turnover in a particular line is six times a year, two months' operating expenses should be included in the estimate of initial capital requirements. Also, some provision must be made for the expenses of organizing the business, including licenses, taxes, incorporation fees, legal fees, and so on.

SOURCES OF CAPITAL

Once the capital requirements of a wholesale enterprise have been determined, management must proceed to meet these needs from the various sources. These can be classified as *equity sources* (capital contributed by owners) and *debt or creditor sources* (capital borrowed from others). There is in effect a third source to the extent that assets may be *rented* or *leased* rather than purchased. All of the current and fixed assets of a business must be financed in one or more of these ways.

In analyzing potential sources of capital, it is useful to distinguish between those from which capital is obtained for *permanent needs* and those designed for *temporary use*. This distinction is based on the fact that capital needs vary in a given business from time to time over and above a permanent minimum which is required for the life of the enterprise. As will be apparent from the discussion that follows, some sources of capital are adapted primarily to one type of need and some to the other.

Equity Capital. Equity capital consists of the investment made in a business by its owners. At the commencement of a new firm, the proprietor, partners, or stockholders must supply a substantial portion of total capital needs from their own savings. As the business prospers, progresses, and grows, earnings may be retained and plowed back into the business or additional new equity capital may be acquired.

Typically, the founders of a new business have difficulty in raising sufficient equity capital and attempt to substitute trade credit or personal loans for it. This procedure is dangerous since lenders are reluctant to supply funds to a firm unless its financial structure includes an adequate proportion of equity. Just what is an "adequate proportion" will of course depend on circumstances, but there is usually a minimum below which it is unsafe to venture. Some idea of the proper ratio between equity and debt in various kinds of wholesale trade can be gotten from the typical figures in Table 18. Such figures are widely used by suppliers, banks, and other lenders as tests of the financial soundness of potential credit risks. It will be noted that in no case is the ratio of equity to debt less than 1.0, and in most lines of trade it ranges between 1.2 and 2.0. Of course, these averages reflect primarily the financing of *established* wholesaling concerns. In a new enterprise the ratios would usually be somewhat lower. Nevertheless, it is probably a good rule of thumb to say that the owners should contribute at least half of the total capital needs for sound financing.

Owners' equity in a business should increase as the enterprise grows in size. This is accomplished primarily through the retention of profits in the business as opposed to paying them out in dividends or in excessive withdrawals by proprietors or partners. For some years retained earn-

TABLE 18

RATIO OF NET WORTH (EQUITY) TO DEBT FOR SPECIFIED
KINDS OF WHOLESALE TRADE, UNITED STATES

Kind of Business	Net Worth to Total Debt (Times)
Automotive Supply	1.7
Drugs	1.2
Dry Goods (General Line)	1.9
Electrical Supply	1.1
Floor Coverings	1.2
Frozen Foods	1.0
Furniture	1.9
Grocery (General Line)	1.3
Hardware	1.8
Industrial Supply	1.0
Lumber, Building Supply	1.4
Plumbing and Heating	1.5
Tobacco Products	1.1

Sources: Based on typical figures reported by members of trade associations and by firms analyzed by credit reporting and similar agencies, such as Dun & Bradstreet, Inc., and Robert Morris Associates.

ings have been the most important single source of new capital in American corporations, a trend that has been encouraged by the prevailing high rates of taxation on personal incomes. Between 1947 and 1956, "trade" corporations (retail and wholesale) obtained almost 40 per cent of their total capital needs from this source.[2]

When major expansion of a business is planned, it may be necessary to secure additional equity capital through the sale of stock or from contributions by the owners of an unincorporated concern. Because most wholesale corporations are small and closely held, very few of their securities are publicly traded. Perhaps a half-dozen of the stocks listed on the New York Stock Exchange could be classified as those of wholesale corporations, including such organizations as McKesson & Robbins, Inc., and Butler Brothers, Inc. A larger number of wholesale stocks is traded on regional exchanges, but for the most part stock must be sold (if at all) over the counter or directly to local investors in a community.

Equity capital should be regarded as the basic and most important source for *permanent* capital needs. These include fixed assets (except to the extent that these can be financed through long-term borrowing), the minimum requirements for such current assets as merchandise inventories and receivables, and at least the minimum working capital needs of the business to care for current payroll and other expenses.

[2] Based on data reported in "Financing the Expansion of Business," *Survey of Current Business,* U. S. Department of Commerce (September, 1957), 10.

Long-Term Borrowing. Some kinds of fixed assets can be financed in part through long-term borrowing. Probably the most common illustration is the loan secured by a mortgage on real estate. Larger companies may also obtain long-term capital through the issuance of bonds, which may be secured by specific fixed assets or based on the general credit of the company. If the firm's credit standing and general reputation are good, it may also be possible to borrow on the basis of long-term *notes,* with a maturity up to ten years. Like bonds, such notes may or may not be secured by tangible assets.

Except for loans secured by real estate, long-term borrowing is confined largely to large, established companies. One large distributor of industrial chemicals and scientific supplies, for example, has outstanding almost $3.5 million in long-term debt as compared with $21 million in total assets. A new enterprise or a smaller concern would have difficulty in borrowing to a comparable extent.

Intermediate Financing by Equipment Suppliers. When expensive equipment is purchased, such as a tabulating or a computing installation, the manufacturer will usually make intermediate-term credit available to the purchaser. Payments are made at regular intervals, usually monthly, over a period of one to five years, and the credit is secured by chattel mortgages or conditional sales contracts. The cost of such credit is usually low because of the security involved and the supplier's desire for sales. A new concern may, however, have difficulty in obtaining this kind of financing because of the uncertainty of its credit standing.

Leasing and Renting of Assets. Frequently a wholesale enterprise has an alternative to buying certain kinds of fixed assets which can be rented or leased instead. Buildings can be rented if a suitable structure is available on this basis, and in some cases warehouses have been built, sold, and leased back. In some lines of business as many or more companies rent rather than own their buildings. Other types of assets that can be leased include delivery equipment, certain kinds of materials-handling equipment, and tabulating and computing machines.

When assets are rented or leased, the cost is usually higher since the owner must be expected to earn a profit. Capital is, however, freed for other uses (especially for investment in inventory) on which the wholesale concern may be able to get an even higher yield. Another advantage inherent in leasing is that the total cost of occupying a building or of using other assets can be treated as deductible operating expenses for tax purposes.

Trade Credit. Most suppliers extend trade credit to wholesalers on the sale of merchandise. By definition, trade credit is limited almost entirely to temporary capital needs, although some concerns continuously finance a large part of their inventories in this fashion.

The principal advantage of trade credit in comparison with bank loans is its availability to firms not eligible for the latter, or which have exhausted their lines of credit temporarily. To be offset against this, however, is the higher cost of trade credit. If a supplier sells on terms of 2 per cent cash discount in 10 days, net 60 days, the cost is 2 per cent for 50 days or 14.4 per cent per annum. In most lines of business it is customary for wholesalers to take cash discounts even when necessary to borrow from other sources for that purpose. Concerns that fail to take such discounts operate at a substantial disadvantage because of their higher interest costs and loss of preferential standing. Despite this, trade credit represents an important source of capital because inventories can be financed at least for the discount period (say, 10 days) in this way. Thus, at any given point in time, most wholesalers owe more to trade creditors than to banks. Most of these balances are, however, cleaned up in time to take advantage of cash discounts.

Bank Loans. An important source of working capital for most wholesale enterprises is the commercial bank. The common procedure in borrowing from banks is to establish a *line of credit,* which is a standing agreement on the part of the bank to lend up to a certain amount. Loans can then be obtained as needed without delay and without specific collateral and the line of credit itself can be revised if conditions dictate. Banks also make *secured* loans in which some collateral is pledged by the borrowing concern, such as inventory, receivables, or equipment.

A basic advantage of bank loans is their low cost as compared with most other forms of current financing. Typical bank rates of interest per annum on short-term business loans in the 1950's averaged about 4 to 5 per cent. Interest rates vary, of course, depending on the size of the loan, the financial condition of the borrower, and general economic conditions. Furthermore, the *true* cost of a bank loan is considerably higher than the stated interest rate, since, for one thing, must banks require that a borrower maintain a reciprocal balance of approximately 20 per cent of loans outstanding. This means, in effect, that if $10,000 is borrowed, $2,000 must be left in the bank; the borrower really has the use of only $8,000. If the stated interest rate is 5 per cent on such a loan, the true cost is 6¼ per cent, since $500 is paid annually for the use of $8,000. Furthermore, as the loan is discounted (i.e., the interest is deducted in advance) less money is available to the borrower and hence the rate is somewhat higher.

Bank loans should never be considered as a source of capital for permanent needs. Most banks, in fact, require that companies with regular lines of credit periodically "clean up" their outstanding loans. This rule is not universally applied, but it reflects the basic objective of banks to supply *temporary* capital to business and industry. An exception to this general statement is found in *term loans* which are made for periods of one to ten years. Usually such loans are secured by fixed assets and are amortized on a systematic basis over the period of their duration, but such loans are seldom made to wholesalers.

Use of Inventory as Collateral for Loans. When loans cannot be obtained on an unsecured basis, merchandise inventory may be used as collateral. This is feasible during periods when inventories are being built up in anticipation of a heavy selling season, or during temporary lulls in sales when some inventory becomes surplus. The amount that can be thus borrowed depends in part on the kind of goods involved, since banks and other lenders require a considerable "cushion" against possible shrinkage in their value. For standardized, nonperishable commodities, loans may sometimes amount to as much as 90 per cent of market value, but a more typical figure would be 60 to 70 per cent.

When inventory is used as collateral, the lender usually demands a *warehouse receipt* as protection against removal of the goods. Such receipts are issued by public warehousemen on goods stored in their establishments or on the borrower's premises in a *field warehouse*. In the first instance, the borrower leaves the receipt with the bank and cannot withdraw the goods until the loan has been repaid and the receipt recovered. Field warehousing makes for more flexibility, so that goods may be sold as loans are reduced.

Because most wholesale concerns have adequate warehouse space of their own, use of field warehousing is particularly important to them. This arrangement calls for the public warehouseman to segregate a part of the wholesale warehouse from regular stocks by the use of chicken wire fencing or some other temporary constructional device. An employee of the wholesaler is put in charge of the field warehouse, acting as a temporary agent of the public warehouseman. This method avoids the needless expense of transporting the goods to and from the public warehouse establishment and payment for space in such an establishment when the borrowing company has its own space available, in addition to other advantages.

Receivables Financing. Another common form of collateral for loans from banks and other financial institutions is found in accounts receivable. Two distinct types of receivables financing should be differentiated: *ordinary discounting* of accounts and the more complex arrangement known as *factoring*.[3]

In ordinary receivables financing, the lending institution purchases open

---

[3] For a more detailed analysis of the two forms of receivables financing, see Theodore N. Beckman and Robert Bartels, *Credits and Collections in Theory and Practice* (6th ed.; New York: McGraw-Hill Book Co., Inc., 1955), pp. 197–203.

book accounts as they arise or makes advances in anticipation of such accounts. The borrower's customers are *not* notified of the arrangement, and in the case of defaults the lender *does* have recourse against the borrower. This type of financing was developed by commercial finance companies and is still dominated by them, although many banks later adopted the method.

Because receivables financing involves relatively high administrative costs (transactions occur on a daily basis), its costs are much higher than on ordinary bank loans. Usually the rate is quoted on a per diem basis, ranging from 1/52 of 1 per cent to 1/40 of 1 per cent depending on the percentage of face value of the receivables that is advanced. These rates are equivalent to about 10 per cent per annum on the money actually borrowed.[4] It should be recognized, however, that the borrower must pledge substantially more in receivables than he actually gets in cash. The additional receivables serve as a "cushion" to the lender covering bad debts and other forms of shrinkage in value. Thus the lender assumes little or no risk and yet charges interest at a rate considerably higher than that prevailing on unsecured short-term loans. For this reason, receivables financing should be employed only when other sources of current funds have been exhausted or in unusual circumstances such as to take advantage of a very advantageous purchase.

Factoring differs from ordinary receivables financing in at least three important respects. First, the factor assumes the entire credit and collection function, while in ordinary receivables financing the borrower continues to operate his own credit department just as though the accounts were not being discounted. Second, and as a direct result of the first point mentioned, the borrower's customers *are* notified of the factoring arrangement and make their payments directly to the factor. Third, when accounts are factored, there is no recourse to the borrower when defaults occur. The factor purchases the accounts outright and assumes all risk connected with them.

Factoring is one of the oldest methods of business finance, tracing its origins to ancient times. In the United States it has traditionally been associated with the textile industries. Since the 1930's, however, factoring has spread to other industries and is now being used both by manufacturers and by wholesalers in such lines as dry goods, furniture, hardware, housewares, apparel, paint, shoes, and toys. Because it requires notification of customers, factoring is still sometimes regarded as a sign of financial weakness in industries other than those in which it has become customary. This attitude has, however, diminished greatly since the 1930's.

[4] Clyde William Phelps, *Accounts Receivable Financing as a Method of Business Finance,* Studies in Commercial Financing No. 2, Commercial Credit Company (Baltimore, 1957).

The cost of factoring includes two elements: interest on money advanced, and a charge for performance of the credit and collection function, including losses from bad debts. The interest charge is usually around 6 per cent per annum, while the service fee ranges from under 1 per cent to about 2 per cent of the face amount of receivables.

Small Business Administration as Possible Source of Capital. Under certain conditions it may be possible for a wholesale enterprise to secure much needed capital from or through the intervention of the federal Small Business Administration. This agency was first established by an act of Congress in 1953, and in 1958 it was made a permanent independent agency (Public Law 85–536). Among other things, it is authorized to make business loans, directly or through participation with banks and other financing organizations, to a small business concern up to $250,000 and with a maximum maturity of ten years. For such purposes a small wholesale business is a concern with annual sales of $5 million or less and the loans are made to finance "business construction, conversion, or expansion, or the purchase of equipment, facilities, machinery, supplies, or material; to supply working capital;" and the like.

It should not be inferred from the above that it is an easy matter to secure a loan from this agency under normal conditions. In the first place, there are some stringent requirements for qualification. Second, there are a number of conditions under which the law forbids the making of business loans. Finally, there is a greater opportunity for a manufacturer to secure a loan than for a wholesaler, partly because the former may furnish more employment and partly because he may engage in the manufacture of products that are helpful to the national economy or significant from the standpoint of national defense. It would be difficult indeed for a wholesaler to establish such grounds satisfactorily. Nevertheless, it is of some importance to know of this possible additional source of capital that might be tapped under propitious circumstances. Probably more significant may be the financial counseling provided by the Agency's field offices, which may include the arranging of conferences with bankers, creditors, and others, in an endeavor to solve a difficult financial problem that may be faced by the wholesale concern.

19

ORGANIZATION OF A WHOLESALE BUSINESS

Following the basic decisions bearing on the establishment of a wholesale enterprise in a particular line of business at a specific location, and after adequate provision has been made for the necessary capital, the next major problem is that of organizing the business in terms of personnel and by merchandise classifications or groupings. Ordinarily, the term "organization" denotes a group of *people,* implemented and cooperating under proper direction for the effective accomplishment of certain objectives. In this sense it means a division of the work to be done and its assignment to individuals within the firm. It includes, further, a definition of relationships among persons, their duties, and the facilities to be used in performing the various tasks. There would seem to be no valid reason, however, why the term should not also be applied to the *merchandise* handled by the enterprise. Organization of this sort is usually designated by the term "departmentization." In this chapter, both phases of the subject are treated in some detail.

The organization structure in terms of personnel and functions is generally shown in the familiar *organization chart,* several of which are presented in this chapter. Organizational relationships are much too complex, however, to be depicted adequately on any chart, a point to be kept in mind in analyzing the structural parts of an organization shown on a chart.

There are several aspects to the problem of organizing the work and personnel of a wholesale enterprise, which vary in importance depending on the nature and size of the business. Some of the more important ones treated in this chapter are: the *separation of functional components* in the work of the enterprise; differences in organization structure according to *ownership,* and *integration* with other activities; and *departmentization* in terms of merchandise lines.

Benefits of Proper Organization.[1] In many wholesale enterprises, especially very small ones, there is no *formal* organization. Executives in such companies have no organization charts, no manuals, and often regard these devices as useless and wasteful. "We have no organization—everyone just pitches in and does what is needed," expresses the essence of this philosophy. Actually, of course, the absence of a *formal* organization is not the same as the lack of *any* organization. Some organization is inevitable even in the smallest companies, if only by sheer accident. Relationships of authority and responsibility and channels of communication will be developed by the members of any organization, despite the failure of its executives to specify what these relationships should be. It is even possible for some small enterprises to function quite well on this basis, but it is not very likely.

Neglect of organization usually reflects ignorance of its importance. If the benefits of proper organization were known, and if the risks inherent in relying on informal and accidental relationships were appreciated, more attention might be given to the job of designing an appropriate organization structure. Briefly, the benefits of proper organization include: *more effective specialization and division of labor; better fixing of accountability; established channels of communication;* and a *basis for training and promotion.* Each of these may be examined briefly.

Specialization and Division of Labor. Economists since Adam Smith have recognized the fundamental importance of specialization and division of labor as determinants of productivity. It is obvious that a worker can become more skilled at a task if he spends full time at it than would be possible if he did it in conjunction with several other and unrelated activities. Yet it is fairly common to find employees scattering their efforts among sundry tasks in smaller wholesale houses. Systematic analysis of a company's objectives and the kinds of work necessary to accomplish them, leading up to a formal organization plan, would usually avoid this error. Each employee is then assigned definite and related tasks in which he can become something of a specialist.

Accountability for Performance. One of the worst features of an informal organization is the difficulty of establishing accountability for performance. Since no one has definite responsibility for a job, no one is at fault when it is not done or when it is done poorly. This naturally leads to the well-known process of "passing the buck" when trouble arises. Just

---

[1] In this section and the one following, some use is made of concepts and principles developed by Prof. Ralph C. Davis and contained in his *Fundamentals of Top Management* (New York: Harper & Bros., 1951) and in his book on *Industrial Organization and Management* (3d ed.; New York: Harper & Bros., 1957).

as bad is the opportunity which is created for "empire-building," that is, the accumulation of excessive authority by one or more executives as a means of enhancing personal prestige.

Channels of Communication. Proper organization insures definite, recognized channels of communication within an enterprise. In the absence of such channels it it difficult for top management to know what is going on at the operative level, and vice versa. There is an opposite danger of blocking intracompany communications by rigid adherence to chains of command, but this is not a valid argument against organization per se.

Training and Promotion. Setting up a formal organization structure forces management to think about potential replacements for present executives, which is important if the company is to have stability and continuity. Definite provisions can be made for assistants to executives, with duties set up partially as a training ground for eventual promotion. The goal should be for each executive to have a replacement ready at all times.

Stages in the Evolution of an Organization. In the smallest wholesale enterprises all of the functions of the organization are combined in one man, who is owner, manager, and worker at the same time. In the largest enterprises there are many highly specialized departments and divisions and hundreds or even thousands of employees. There may appear to be little or no relationship between these extremes, but in actuality the large organization represents a natural and evolutionary outgrowth of the functions originally embodied in a one-man business. Between the two extremes, there are several distinct stages in the evolution of the organization.

An early phase in the development of an organization is the *separation of managerial and operative levels.* This occurs when the business becomes too big for a single individual to handle, and he hires one or more employees to work under his direction. As the business grows and activity reaches beyond the periphery of direct observation, the work is usually subdivided into unspecialized departments, the division of responsibility being made according to individuals rather than on the basis of functions. Almost all authority still vests in the head of the enterprise, whose organization assumes a *military* aspect. It is this kind of development that is still largely responsible for the illogical allocation of duties in many wholesale places of business rather than on a functional basis.

The separation of duties according to *levels* which starts very early continues with the growth of an enterprise. In Figure 4, no fewer than six different levels of authority and responsibility are shown. At the top are the *owners* of the business (stockholders in a corporation), who exercise ultimate authority over it. Next in line are the owners' representatives, the *board of directors,* who provide top administrative management and set broad policies. Within the policy framework established by the directors,

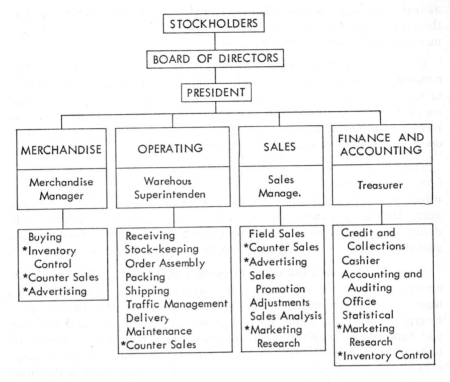

*Functions which may be assigned to different major divisions, as indicated.

FIGURE 4. Major Functional Divisions of a Wholesaling Organization

day-to-day administration is handled by the *president or general manager.* Below the president come *divisional executives,* such as the merchandise manager and the sales manager, who are responsible for managing a particular functional segment of the business. Within each division are smaller organizational units headed by supervisors in the merchandise division, *merchandise departments;* in the finance division, the *credit department.* Finally, within each department or section are employees on the *operative level,* not shown separately in Figure 4. These levels are completely separated only in very large enterprises. In establishments operated by wholesalers and by functional middlemen, most of which are unincorporated or small closed corporations, the top three levels (owners, directors, and general management) are usually combined in the person of the proprietor or a small group of partners or corporate officials.

The separation of managerial and operative levels and the later separation of different levels of management are, in effect, *vertical divisions* of the functions of a wholesale organization. At the same time this vertical division is being made, a *horizontal division* also takes place. To permit specialization in tasks, the basis for separating them is *functional* rather than one of degree of authority. The general principle to be followed in dividing the work is that of *functional similarity;* that is, tasks which are similar in nature or which require similar training, experience, and skills should be grouped together. Functional divisions in a wholesale enterprise are discussed in some detail in the next section.

A third phase in the evolution of an organization, which usually follows the separation of managerial and operative levels and the division of functions, is *departmentization* according to merchandise lines, which is the subject of the concluding part of this chapter.

MAJOR FUNCTIONAL DIVISIONS

At an early stage in the development of a wholesaling organization, proper division of labor requires separation of the major functions of the business. While there are many differences in the functions performed by various types and classes of wholesale establishments, the work of most of them can be divided into four major areas of functional responsibility. These four major divisions are *merchandise, operating, sales,* and *finance and accounting.* Each of these major areas should be assigned to an executive who reports to the *president* or other top executive. A general outline of the four functional divisions is shown in Figure 4, which also indicates some of the more important activities within each division.

The Merchandise Division. Since buying is one of the most essential functions of wholesaling, the merchandise division is of utmost importance, except for those relatively small houses that sell principally on an exclusive agency basis the goods of one or a few manufacturers. The merchandise division is in charge of a *merchandise manager,* or in smaller houses may be handled by the general manager of the firm. Under the division head are buyers[2] who purchase goods for the merchandise lines or departments under their jurisdiction. It is the responsibility of the merchandise manager to supervise the work of the buyers; to assist them in the preparation of buying plans; and to coordinate the over-all merchandising program of the organization.

Because stock control records form the basis for buying procedures, the maintenance of such records is logically a part of the merchandise division's task. Sometimes this division is also in charge of *house* or *counter* sales activities, that is, sales to customers who visit the establishment to

[2] In some lines of trade, where goods are bought by the wholesaler from the same sources year after year, more or less on a contractual basis, the original buying arrangement may be made by the head or other top executive of the wholesaler with the actual purchases from time to time to be effected by a buyer commonly referred to as the purchasing "agent."

make their purchases. As noted below, however, this task is more logically placed under the control of the sales division. Still another function occasionally assigned to the merchandise division is that of stock-keeping, but this is done only when the organization is divided into almost completely autonomous merchandise departments.

The Operating Division. Probably next in importance in the average wholesale house is the warehousing function. In fact, the *warehouse* in wholesaling corresponds to the *store* in retailing, the meaning of the two words being essentially the same. Consequently, a major divisional executive, the *warehouse superintendent,* is placed in charge of this phase of the organization. His responsibilities include all physical handling of goods from receiving through stock-keeping, order assembly, packing, and delivery or shipment via common carriers. The superintendent hires, trains and discharges warehouse personnel and may, in larger organizations, have specialized staff assistants for such tasks. Finally, he assumes full responsibility for the physical condition of the building, its fixtures, and equipment.

As shown in Figure 4, counter sales are sometimes under the control of the operating division and may be made by warehouse personnel. This is usually undesirable for several reasons, but nevertheless is a common arrangement in practice.

The Sales Division. Under the sales manager are grouped all selling activities of the organization, both personal and nonpersonal. In practice there are frequent exceptions to this. One of these is the management of *counter sales,* which, as already noted, may be handled by the merchandise or the operating division. Where feasible, counter sales should be placed in the sales division, since counter personnel must apply the sales policies established by the sales manager and his assistants. Again, when counter sales are not under the jurisdiction of the sales division, the opportunity that exists for real sales efforts when customers visit the house is often neglected.

Another part of the selling function which may not be assigned to the sales division is *advertising*. While advertising is closely related to selling, it is often placed in the merchandise division, because in the preparation and distribution of catalogs, which frequently is the main advertising activity, the buyers claim to possess greater knowledge of the work because of their intimate acquaintance with the merchandise. Sometimes the credit-and-collection function is placed in the sales division on the theory that more effective cooperation of salesmen in securing credit information about customers, and in making collections, is thus made possible.

Specialty salesmen may be placed under the jurisdiction of the merchandise manager and the respective buyers whose goods are sold exclusively by such salesmen, but it is generally felt that a sales manager is better fitted to select, train, compensate, manage, and supervise salesmen and their activities than any other individual in the enterprise. For that reason, he alone should be charged with this responsibility, even though salesmen are specialized according to merchandise departments.

Sales analysis and marketing research sections may be attached to the sales division, since the information developed in these sections is of significance primarily as a basis for sales-planning and policy-making.

The Financial and Accounting Division. This division is generally headed by the treasurer or secretary-treasurer of the company. Under him are placed the functions of credits and collections, office management, and accounting, with a credit manager, an office manager, and a controller in charge of their respective subdivisions. In addition to maintaining general supervision of all these activities, it is the treasurer's special task to handle the financial accounts of profit and loss and the capital accounts of capital stock, bonds, and investments. It is his further duty to receive all money and deposit it in banks designated by the Board of Directors; pay all vouchers that have been audited and approved for payment; keep in custody all notes receivable, securities, and negotiable papers; make arrangement for the proper financing of the company's current needs and for the settlement of its obligations; and pay the salaries of the officers and department heads, which is usually done out of a special bank account maintained for the purpose.

Cashiers must record all cash transactions in the cash book or journal and keep subsidiary records on notes receivable and payable. They handle petty cash disbursements, pay the salaries of the general office staff, and prepare checks for the signature of the treasurer so that remittances can be handled. The credit manager and his staff are charged with the responsibility of maintaining receivables in sound condition and keeping losses from bad debts down to a minimum, but they must also maintain sales volume at a maximum by accepting as many risks as possible and cultivating customer good will.

The office manager supervises the general office staff, including the order and billing departments or sections. He is responsible for the opening and distribution of incoming mail, for typing and stenographic personnel, office supplies, and filing of records. The accounting department, in charge of the controller, makes all the necessary entries of the various transactions of the firm, prepares the payroll, takes off trial balances at intervals, prepares balance sheets and profit and loss statements as required, and maintains a statistical section for the analysis of the records.

When punched-card or electronic data processing equipment is employed, the personnel is assigned to a machine accounting section under the controller. Because of the special skills required for using this equipment, a skilled and trained person must be put in charge of this section, which may have several full-time employees. Inventory control, sales analysis, and statistical reporting may be handled within the machine accounting section, since the information is often developed as a by-product of its order-processing and invoicing activities.

Organization of a Wholesale Hardware House. Typifying the general form of organization of a wholesale business just discussed is the hardware wholesaler with a sales volume of around $10 million whose organization is depicted in Figure 5. Even here certain peculiarities because of special conditions are to be noted. For example, the house in question has for some years been engaged in the general hardware business, and when electrical supplies, radios, and automobile accessories were added to the line of merchandise, the sales manager had little knowledge of the new goods and their selling qualities; hence, a separate sales manager for these items was hired. Similarly, when the company decided to sell mill supplies to industrial users, specialty salesmen were employed to cultivate the factory trade and a sales manager was hired to supervise their activities. Furthermore, because of special circumstances, the work of preparing and maintaining the catalogs up to date is in the financial and accounting division rather than in the merchandise or sales parts of the organization. The chart for this firm generally follows, however, the pattern that has been indicated above, and the organization therein depicted can be adapted with only minor modifications to the requirements of any medium-sized or large wholesaler in any of the jobbing lines.

VARIATIONS IN ORGANIZATION STRUCTURE

Most wholesale enterprises follow the basic pattern of organization set forth in the preceding section of this chapter, at least in its broad outlines. Details naturally differ between firms, but these are not of great importance. There are, however, some basic departures from the pattern that call for further analysis. These differences arise from one or more of several factors: the kind of goods handled, breadth and diversity of the line, functions performed and methods of operation, nature of ownership, integration with manufacturing and/or retailing, number of establishments operated, territory covered, and so on.

Because the impact of these factors varies so much, it is not possible to analyze all of the possibilities in the limited space available. By way of *illustration,* three actual organization plans are presented in the following paragraphs. These include a large multi-unit drug organization; a voluntary chain wholesaler in the food trade; and an industrial distributor handling a limited number of franchised lines.

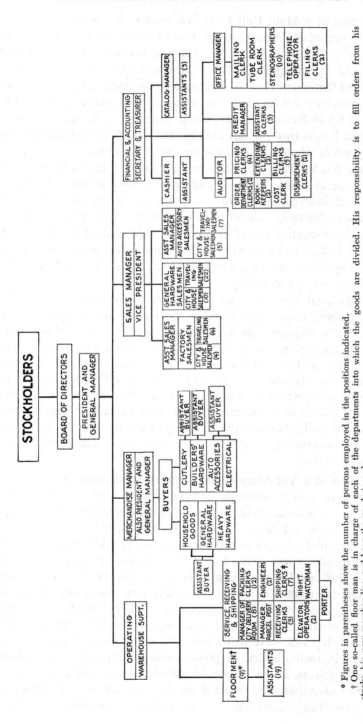

FIGURE 5. Organization Chart of a Wholesale Hardware House

* Figures in parentheses show the number of persons employed in the positions indicated.
† One so-called floor man is in charge of each of the departments into which the goods are divided. His responsibility is to fill orders from his stocks, bin new merchandise, and keep the goods in order.
‡ Including truck drivers.

Organization of a Multi-Unit Drug Wholesaler. As the first example of variations in organizational structures, that of a very large multi-unit drug wholesaler is illustrated in Figure 6. This firm is one of the largest in the wholesale field, operating about 85 regular wholesale drug houses throughout the United States and Hawaii, and engaging in manufacturing operations as well as merchant wholesaling. The company's divisions are responsible to a home office in New York City, where general policies are formulated. Each division has its own organization as well, roughly comparable to that of an independent wholesaler in the same line of business.

Within the headquarters organization (not shown) are major executives in charge of merchandising (selling and buying) for the firm's three major lines: drugs, chemicals, and liquors. A personnel vice-president is responsible for labor relations, over-all personnel policy, and related problems. Another major executive not often found in independent wholesale firms is the financial vice-president, whose duties encompass provision of capital to the divisions (the company's common stock is traded on the New York Stock Exchange) and accounting.

At the divisional level, as shown in Figure 6, the chief executive is a division manager, responsible directly to one of several district vice-presidents. Each division manager, in turn, is given full authority over operations in his locality. An exception to this is found in the accounting department, the head of which reports to the comptroller at headquarters rather than to the division manager. Otherwise the divisional organization follows the basic pattern described earlier in this chapter, with major executives in charge of sales, buying (for each of several departments), operations, and credit. Because the company sells both to drugstores and to industrial and institutional users, separate sales forces are maintained for these customer classes.

Organization of a Voluntary Chain Grocery Wholesaler. The organization structure of a large wholesale grocery house is shown in Figure 7. This particular wholesaler sells almost entirely to retailers who belong to one of the several voluntary chains sponsored by the house. In sharp contrast to the drug wholesaler just discussed is the relatively unimportant position occupied by the selling function. As is true of many other food wholesalers, this firm has no salesmen in the customary sense of the term. Since customers are committed to purchasing from the company through their voluntary chain membership agreements, it is not necessary to solicit business on a regular basis. Instead, *sales supervisors* are employed within the Merchandising and Advertising Division, whose job it is to *assist retail store owners* in their display, in point-of-consumer-purchase advertising, and related problems. Likewise, the advertising department is not engaged in preparing advertisements directed to dealers, but with planning and executing advertising campaigns aimed at ultimate consumers *on behalf*

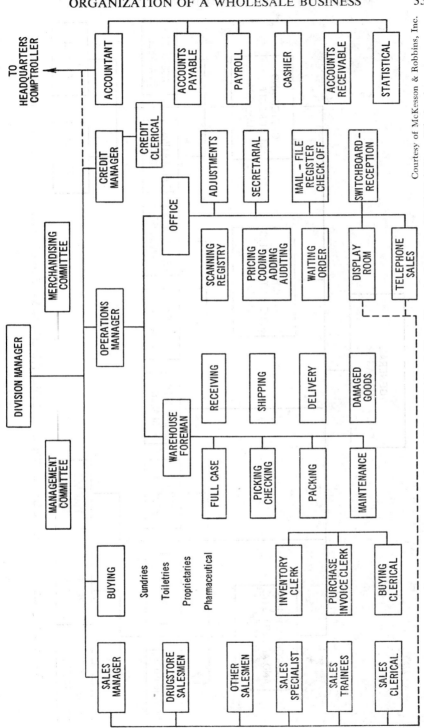

FIGURE 6. Organization Chart of a Typical Division (Wholesale Drug House) of a Large Multi-Unit Drug Wholesaler

Courtesy of McKesson & Robbins, Inc.

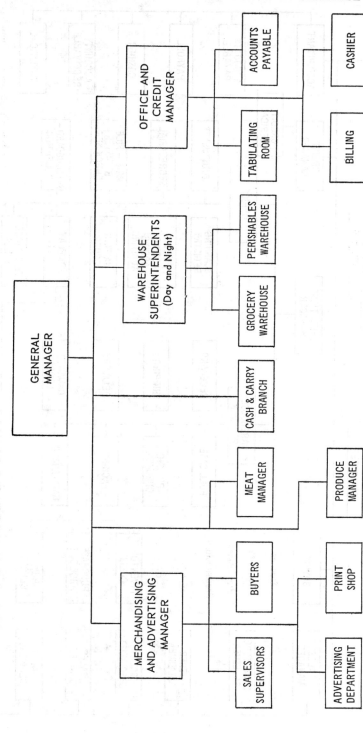

FIGURE 7. Organization of a Large Grocery Wholesaler Selling Primarily to Members of a Voluntary Chain Which It Sponsors

of the member stores. The merchandising and advertising activities of this firm closely resemble the corresponding functions in a corporate food chain, which have served as models for such wholesalers since the 1930's.

Two warehouse superintendents are shown, one for the company's daytime operations and one for a night shift. For reasons explained at a later point in this text, it is fairly common for grocery houses to operate on a two-shift basis, receiving goods during one shift and assembling orders during the other.[3] Another feature largely peculiar to the grocery trade is the use of separate warehouses and warehouse personnel for the grocery and perishables lines, arising from the differences between the two in handling characteristics.

Like most large grocery wholesalers and food chains, the company described in Figure 7 uses an IBM punched-card system of order-processing and stock control.[4] As a result, a tabulating room is shown under the office and credit manager, with a trained machine accountant in charge of the clerical personnel. The credit-and-collection function is of little importance here, since the retailers are required to pay on a "blank check with order" basis.

Organization of an Industrial Distributor Handling Franchised Lines. Figure 8 represents the organization structure of a large industrial supplies distributor employing a total of about 80 persons. This wholesaler is a corporate division of a company in another industry, and an executive committee is used as a sort of Board of Directors to transmit orders from the parent organization. Operating authority rests in a General Manager, assisted by an Assistant General Manager.

The major point of difference noted between Figure 8 and the basic functional organization shown in Figure 4 is the absence of the Merchandise Division. The reason for this lies in the fact that this distributor handles only a few merchandise lines on an exclusive basis, with little change in these lines from year to year. Basic merchandising decisions arise infrequently and are handled by the Executive Committee or by the General Manager. Otherwise the functions of buying are routine in nature and can be delegated to the Purchasing Section within the Operations Division.

All sales activities are concentrated in a Sales Division, which includes field salesmen as well as telephone and counter sales persons, this being an important method of sale in the industrial supply field. Field salesmen here include both engineers who design and service certain products and general-line salesmen.

In the Purchasing Section of the Operations Division separate sections are provided for the functions of *expediting* special orders and back orders

---

[3] See Chapter 23.

[4] For a discussion of such systems, see Chapter 25.

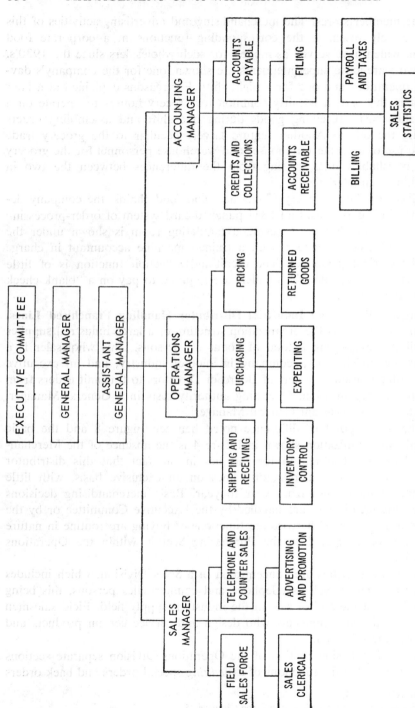

FIGURE 8. Organization of an Industrial Distributor Selling a Limited Number of Franchised Lines

placed with suppliers, and the handling of *returned goods*. These problems are of greater significance in the industrial field than for consumer goods because of the lack of standardization in customer needs and the frequent handling of "rush" orders needed to prevent shutdowns in customers' plants.

DEPARTMENTIZATION

When a wholesale business operates on a fairly large scale, it is extremely difficult, if not impossible, for the general manager or the merchandise manager to maintain effective control over all parts of the business concerned with the buying, warehousing, selling, and handling of the goods. At this point a further division of effort can be made in the organization by departmentizing in terms of merchandise lines. Departmentizing permits closer control and a higher degree of specialization, but beyond a certain point it may give rise to offsetting disadvantages. These factors are discussed briefly in the following sections.

Nature and Extent of Departmentization. *Departmentization* is a segregation of the goods handled by a wholesale enterprise into groups or classes known as departments. In its simplest form departmentization is merely an accounting device adopted for purposes of financial control over buying and inventory levels. Thus, even in a very small firm, it is possible to segregate sales, inventory, and other accounts so that sources of difficulty can be located more easily and remedial action taken promptly.[5]

It is but a slight step from the departmentization of accounting records to the departmentization of the *merchandising division* of an organization. Each department may be assigned to a separate buyer who has responsibility for controlling its inventories, selecting sources of supply, and executing purchasing procedures. If the volume of business does not warrant a full-time buyer for a given department, several related departments can be assigned to a single person. When this type of departmental organization is used, it is also common to segregate the perpetual inventory control records and personnel and place them under control of the appropriate buyers. Again, depending on the volume of business, other clerical tasks, such as pricing invoices, may also be divided along merchandise departmental lines.

Storage and handling of goods in the warehouse are frequently organized on a departmental basis. This is especially common among large wholesalers in such lines as dry goods, who operate in multistory warehouses. The merchandise department becomes the basic *unit* for purposes of stock layout, and warehousemen work only in a specific departmental area. A

---

[5] Analyses of sales and costs by departments are discussed in Chapters 27 and 29, respectively.

similar plan is sometimes found in drug warehouses where each order-picking "station" may serve one or more merchandise departments.

Departmentization may also affect the organization of the *sales division.* Separate salesmen may be used for the departments, and sometimes each department manager (buyer) has complete authority over his own sales-men, along the lines to be found in a large retail department store. A compromise system is to have certain salesmen designated as *specialty men,* supplementing and assisting the *general salesmen* who make the customer contacts and handle the entire line, or cultivating certain classes of customers.

Only in very extreme cases are *all* of the aforementioned activities organized on a departmental basis. The best example of this may be found in certain general line dry goods houses, where

. . . each department is almost a separate business insofar as operations are concerned. As a result the salesmen have to write separate orders for each department instead of one order covering the customer's entire purchase. This type of organization also pyramids overhead . . . by requiring the services of an excessive number of department heads . . . [6]

More commonly the departmental form of organization is applied only to the extent of separate accounting records, separate buyers, and (to a certain extent) in the storage and handling of goods in the warehouse.

Benefits of Departmentization. The benefits of departmentization have already been suggested in the preceding section. One of the primary objectives of departmentization is that it permits the exercise of effective control of merchandise inventories, purchases, and sales. It *correlates* these *merchandising activities* through the facilities which it affords for frequent inventories, so that purchases may be gauged by expected sales on the one hand and existing stock on the other. *It also enables the management to locate slow-moving items and to allocate responsibility* for stock accumulation to certain departments. It thus serves as a rough index of the degree of success with which each department is managed, and affords a basis for planning operations to rehabilitate the backward departments. At the same time, departmentization *points to the profitable departments* in which optimum rates of stock turnover and satisfactory gross margins of profit are achieved. When operating expenses, properly allocated to each department, are deducted from its gross margin, the net profits of each department can be definitely ascertained.

Departmentizing the merchandise often permits greater *specialization in buying* and thereby secures advantages which come from a more intimate knowledge of merchandise, its sources of supply, price movements,

[6] *Dry Goods Wholesalers' Operations,* by John R. Bromell, U. S. Department of Commerce (Washington, D. C.: Government Printing Office, 1949), p. 15.

and conditions of demand. Likewise, when salesmen handle only a limited number of items in a particular department, their product knowledge is often greater and the service given to customers is correspondingly better. This is of prime importance in the sale of complex technical products such as machine tools or materials handling equipment.

Another advantage inherent in departmentization is that it *tends to fix responsibility* for the operations of each merchandise department upon its manager. Finally, it provides a *basis for comparison* of departments among themselves and with similar departments of other wholesalers engaged in the same business. Departmentization may thus help to stop expensive leaks, speed up the rate of stock turnover where it is sluggish, enforce better marketing practices, and prevent the aggressive selling of unprofitable items.

Limitations. There is a point of diminishing returns in departmental specialization, just as there is in functional specialization within an organization. When all functions of an enterprise are decentralized to departments, there is usually a great deal of wasteful *duplication of effort*. Obviously it is more economical to prepare a single sales order and send out a single invoice for each customer than to repeat these clerical operations several times. Often it is also needless duplication to have more than one salesman call on a given customer. Thus, unless different lines are sold to separate customer groups, or customers have several specialized buyers who must be contacted, departmentization of the sales division may cause excessive selling costs.

Another problem that arises with a departmental form of organization is the *difficulty of coordinating efforts*. Each department head must be given a certain degree of independence in budgeting purchases or in selecting sources of supply. On the other hand, each department's policies must conform to those laid down at the top level of the company. For example, the several buyers' estimates of purchase requirements for a given period must be compatible with the over-all financial controls on the business as a whole. This means that compromises must be worked out, which requires considerable time and effort as well as tact and diplomacy on the part of the merchandise manager. Despite these limitations, it is inconceivable that a wholesale business can operate with optimum efficiency without a practical departmentization of the large number of merchandise items in which it deals.

Bases for Departmentization. While no rules can be laid down for rigid and universal application in classifying the stock of a wholesale firm into departments, there are nevertheless certain factors that usually govern the determination as to what items should be placed in a given classification. Probably the most important of them is the *nature of the goods*. The items of merchandise in each department should be of an allied and supplementary character. Thus, the rug department of a wholesale dry goods house may contain rugs, linoleums, lace curtains, lace nets, scrims, marquisettes, cocoa and rubber mats, upholstery goods, shades, brass goods, curtain poles, cretonnes, printed draperies, and carpet sweepers. Here is a logical grouping of goods that are allied in use and in purchase by both retailers and consumers. For the same reason coffees and teas form a logical combination, although they are frequently combined with spices because they may be purchased by the same buyer, and with pea-nuts which can be roasted in the coffee-roasting equipment.

A second basis for determining whether a certain group or class of merchandise is to be placed in a separate department is the *importance of the line from the standpoint of volume.* In the plumbing supply trade, for example, steel pipe usually accounts for an important proportion of the total sales; thus the separation of this line for purposes of control is generally justified. The same may very well be true for such items as sugar or canned milk in the wholesale grocery trade, or for cotton dress goods in a dry goods establishment.

A third factor is the *profitableness of the items* under consideration. If an item or line of goods bears a wide margin and sales are sufficiently substantial, such goods may be singled out and placed in a separate department for special attention and aggressive sales promotion. The relatively long gross margins on tea explain why this merchandise is frequently placed in a separate department in the grocery trade. On the other hand, low-profit margins may also be a reason for separate departments. The customary low markups on sugar practically eliminate opportunities for a fair profit on this highly competitive item, except as it may result from speculative buying; therefore, close control is necessary to insure that losses are not incurred continuously, especially because the volume of sales in such goods is generally substantial.

Storage and handling requirements of a product comprise a fourth factor to be considered in determining a proper departmental classification. Since all the merchandise items in a given department are usually placed together in the warehouse, goods of similar bulk and other physical char-acteristics, other things being equal, are more likely to be placed together than items that are dissimilar in these qualities. When special racks are provided for merchandise in drums or barrels, it is logical to place all such merchandise in the same department unless other considerations dictate a different grouping. Such items as narcotics or ammunition frequently constitute a department, because of the security or safety regulations which necessitate specialized and segregated storage facilities. It may also be advisable to form a separate department for items that require cold storage, since their location is necessarily determined by the existing physical facilities.

A fifth factor is the nature of *sales effort and product knowledge* required for a line. A good illustration is the practice of setting up a special department for an individual manufacturer's line, in return for which an exclusive agency for the line or other inducements may be obtained. Similarly, goods sold under a controlled brand may be placed in a separate department so that better measures of the effectiveness of promotional efforts can be obtained.

Finally, a practical consideration in any departmentization is the *experience of the personnel* of the organization. Gas and oil stoves may be grouped with electrical appliances and fittings in one hardware house merely because one of the buyers happens to be familiar with both lines, while in another firm they are not combined, but each is put under the jurisdiction of a separate buyer.

Number of Departments. In any attempt to departmentize the merchandise of a wholesale firm, the problem of how many departments to create comes to the forefront. To answer such a question categorically is impossible. Among the factors influencing such a decision are the size of the house, diversification of the merchandise, profitableness of certain lines, degree of sales effort required on some items, and the relative importance of the different lines handled. When the house operates on a small scale, the goods are not highly diversified, all items bear about the same margin of profit, and approximately the same sales effort is required in selling the goods. Few departments will therefore be established. Thus a small wholesale grocery firm may have but 7 or 8 departments consisting of canned foods, farinaceous goods, bakery products, confectionery, tobacco, miscellaneous edibles, and miscellaneous nonfood products. A large concern in the same line of business may have 25 or more departments.

The number of departments into which the thousands of items handled by wholesalers are classified may vary from 2 or 3 to as many as 70 or 80 for some of the large concerns with national coverage. Even two houses doing about the same volume of business annually, and operating in the same line of trade, may have a different number of departments, depending upon whether they both handle private branded merchandise, whether each has taken on side lines, whether they engage in manufacturing activities, and upon the special requirements of the territories they serve.

Because these factors vary a great deal among wholesale enterprises, departmentization should be carried out only after a systematic study has been made by a competent investigator. Such a study should be based upon complete information concerning the following factors: (1) the classes or types of merchandise handled; (2) the volume of business in each class in dollars and as a percentage of total sales; (3) the profit margins on each class of merchandise; (4) any special sales effort required, either by contract with sources of supply or for other reasons;

(5) the number of buyers and their qualifications, based upon past experience; (6) the special storage or handling requirements, if any, for any merchandise items; and (7) the nature of control, whether it is intimate and personal or whether it is of a formal character requiring numerous reports and a complex system of records.

As an illustration of the varying number of departments that might be formed in one line of merchandise, a typical percentage division of sales of a plumbing equipment and supplies wholesaler is presented in Table 19.

TABLE 19

TYPICAL DIVISION OF SALES OF PLUMBING EQUIPMENT AND SUPPLIES BY
MERCHANDISE CLASSIFICATIONS AS BASIS FOR DEPARTMENTIZATION

Merchandise Classification	Per Cent of Total Sales
1. Enamel Ware	15.5
2. Pottery	3.5
3. Closet Combinations and Parts	5.7
4. Plumber's Brass	5.7
5. Sort Pipe	4.6
6. Sort Pipe Fittings, etc.	2.6
7. Water Heaters and Range Boilers	2.8
8. Laundry Tubs	0.7
9. Lead Goods	2.7
10. Plumbing Specialties	1.6
11. Pipe, Steel and Wrought Iron	16.5
12. Fittings	7.5
13. Valves, Brass and Iron	2.2
14. Boilers and Radiation	10.2
15. Heating and Steam Specialties	2.3
16. Plumbers' Tools and Equipment	1.2
17. Well Goods	2.5
18. Tanks	0.8
19. All other Plumbing and Heating Material	5.6
20. Miscellaneous other sales	5.8
Total	100.0

All of the lines listed in the table might be grouped in a single department by a hardware wholesaler with sales of $5 to $10 million, for whom they would probably represent about 10 per cent of total volume. For a plumbing equipment and supplies wholesaler of $5 to $10 million annual volume, on the other hand, the number of departments would be almost as inclusive as the list of merchandise classifications shown in the table. For a plumbing supply wholesaler, however, whose sales are only about one-tenth to one-third of this amount, as few as six departments might be a desirable number. After taking into consideration the various factors enumerated above, the following departmental arrangement might be evolved as the most satisfactory: (1) enamel ware; (2) pottery, closet combinations and parts, and laundry tubs; (3) plumber's brass, sort pipe, sort pipe fittings, lead goods, plumbing specialties, fittings, valves, plumbers' tools and equipment; (4) water heaters, range boilers, boilers and radiation, and heating and steam specialties; (5) steel and wrought iron pipe; and (6) well goods, tanks, all other plumbing and heating material, and all miscellaneous goods. Such an arrangement in a firm of this size permits effective control of merchandise inventories, purchases, and sales and enables the wholesaler to enjoy the other benefits of departmentization without excessive cost.

20

STOCK TURNOVER
AND MERCHANDISE
PLANNING

In several succeeding chapters, attention is given to the basic whole-saling functions of buying, warehousing, and selling merchandise. These functions are closely related, and should be conceived as an integrated whole rather than as separate and discrete phases of wholesale management. The relationship among these functions can best be summed up in the concept of *merchandise planning*. All wholesale enterprises are basically organizations seeking to select, obtain, and sell the right merchandise, in the right quantities, at the right prices, and under the right circumstances and conditions. Buying, warehousing, and selling are all aspects of merchandise planning viewed in this sense. Goods are bought and stored only in anticipation of sales; selling efforts are made only on the basis of goods available or procurable for sale.

Because of the interdependence of these activities, coordinated merchandising plans must be made at the top level of a wholesale organization. A basic tool for summarizing such plans is the *merchandise budget,* which specifies desired levels of inventory and purchases on the basis of expected sales. Methodology for preparing such budgets is outlined in the last part of this chapter. Before examining budgeting procedures, however, it is necessary to understand the concept of *stock turnover* which underlies them.

STOCK TURNOVER

The relationship between sales of goods and inventories carried in a wholesale enterprise is expressed in the rate of *stock turn* or *turnover.*

Attainment of a satisfactory rate of stock turnover is one of the most important goals of management in wholesaling. For this reason, the rate of turnover is widely used as a general measure of managerial efficiency as well as in planning purchases.

Computing the Rate of Stock Turn. Stock turn actually refers to the disposal and replacement of a given *amount* of merchandise; however, the term has come to mean the *rate* at which a given stock of goods is sold and replaced during a given period. This rate is usually computed on an annual basis and measures the frequency or the number of times a given inventory is disposed of and replaced during the year.

To obtain the rate of stock turn, it is necessary to divide *total* sales during the year by the *average* inventory carried throughout the year. This may be done on the basis of cost price, selling price, or physical units of sales, providing that both sales and inventory data are figured on the same basis. This computation is illustrated as follows:

$$\frac{\$1,000,000 \ \text{(sales at cost)}}{\$200,000 \ \text{(average inventory at cost)}} = 5 \ \text{(annual rate of stock turn)}$$

While the cost basis is much to be preferred, the same result is usually obtained if selling prices are used. Assuming an average gross margin of 15 per cent of selling prices for the cost figures just given, the computation is as follows:

$$\frac{\$1,176,470 \ \text{(sales at selling price)}}{\$235,290 \ \text{(average inventory at selling price)}} = 5 \ \text{(annual rate of stock turn)}$$

If the situation is such that a significant portion of the merchandise has been sold by marking it down to a lower price than that at which it was carried in inventory, a lower rate of stock turn will be secured by the selling price method than on a cost basis. If markdowns after inventory amounted to 10 per cent of total sales in the situation just illustrated, the result would be as follows:

$$\frac{\$1,058,820 \ \text{(sales at selling price)}}{\$235,290 \ \text{(average inventory at selling price)}} = 4.5 \ \text{(annual rate of stock turn)}$$

Obviously, this amount of markdowns would rarely, if ever, be experienced in a wholesale concern operating on a gross margin of only 15 per cent. For all practical purposes, then, the selling price basis or the cost price basis yields about the same result when computing the rate of stock turn for the business as a whole.

The difference in bases used may be of some importance in ascertaining the rate of stock turnover for specific items of merchandise, particularly those of a perishable nature, or those that are greatly influenced by style considerations. Where this is the situation, the cost basis is favored over the selling price basis, because it reflects more accurately the true physical movement of goods. If proper records are kept, however, the turnover rate for specific items is usually obtained in terms of physical units, as follows:

$$\frac{1{,}440 \text{ (sales in physical units)}}{240 \text{ (average inventory in physical units)}} = 6 \text{ (annual rate of stock turn)}$$

This method is practical only when the physical units are homogeneous; therefore, it cannot be used for computing the stock turn rate for entire merchandise departments, other merchandise classifications, or for the business as a whole. To be sure, it is theoretically and sometimes actually possible to use tonnage figures for this purpose, dividing sales in tons by average inventory in tons.

Determining Average Inventory. In computing the rate of stock turn, special precautions must be taken to insure that an *average* inventory is used: that is, an inventory that is *typical* of the entire year's stock. If an inventory is taken only once a year, this is approximated by a computation as follows:

$$\text{Average Inventory} = \frac{\text{Opening Inventory} + \text{Closing Inventory}}{2}$$

When semiannual physical inventories are taken, the computation is made in the following manner:

$$\text{Average Inventory} = \frac{\text{Opening Inventory} + \text{Midyear Inventory} + \text{Closing Inventory}}{3}$$

Actually, neither of these methods is entirely adequate in practice. The turnover rates computed from annual or semiannual physical inventories are usually not typical because most firms attempt to reduce stocks to a minimum just prior to periodic physical counts, in order to minimize the clerical labor necessary for taking inventory. More important, to be useful in current control of operations, turnover figures are needed more frequently than is possible when they are computed solely on the basis of actual and complete physical inventories. Consequently, more frequent inventory data must be obtained by other means. These include, as will be evident from a discussion in a subsequent chapter, modified physical inventories, statistical inventory systems, and perpetual inventory controls. In the absence of any of these types of inventory systems, some kind of *estimate* based on the experience of an executive should be used in preference to the atypical and infrequent figures derived from actual and complete physical counts.

It is not necessary to compute the rate of stock turn only on the basis of the past calendar or fiscal year. The current stock turn rate may be determined for any combination of periods for which sales and inventory figures are available and then adjusting the figure to an annual rate. For example:

$$\frac{\$100,000 \text{ (sales at cost during past three months)}}{\$50,000 \text{ (average inventory at cost during past three months)}} = 2 \text{ (stock turn rate for } \tfrac{1}{4} \text{ of year)}$$

$$2 \times 4 = 8 \text{ (annual rate of stock turn)}$$

Variations in Turnover Rates. Rates of turnover vary considerably between different lines of trade, between individual enterprises in a given line of trade, and between various lines of merchandise in a single house. In 1955, for example, the average number of turnovers was 3.7 for hardware wholesalers, 4.9 for industrial distributors, 5.8 for drug wholesalers, and as high as 23.5 for tobacco wholesalers.[1] As an illustration of variations within a trade, the average 1957 rate of turnover for industrial distributors was 4.6 in the middle west, against 4.1 in the far west. Similarly, drug wholesalers in Metropolitan New York achieved a typical turnover of 6.6 times in 1955, while those in the Rocky Mountain–Pacific Area averaged 5.5 turns. The lower rates of turnover characteristic of houses in the western United States are due, of course, to their greater distance from suppliers and consequent need to order in larger quantities and to carry heavier stocks. Other variations within a trade arise from differences in the size, merchandise lines, policies, and general managerial efficiency of the different concerns.

Even within a single house, the different lines of merchandise sell at varying rates of speed. In the grocery trade, for example, in a house that turns its stock 10 or 12 times a year, a fast-moving item like sugar is turned about once every 10 days or about 36 times annually. On the other hand, slow-moving items like spices and fancy canned goods may turn but once or even less each year.

Advantages of Rapid Stock Turnover. Within definite limits, management in a wholesale enterprise should seek to maximize the rate of stock turnover. The benefits of a rapid turnover permeate all marketing activities of an organization. Higher turnover can lead to *increased sales, lower markdowns,* and *reductions in certain classes of operating expense.*

The effect of increased turnover on *sales* comes about through the greater flexibility enjoyed by buyers when capital is not constantly tied up in excessive inventories. They can take full advantage of opportunities for

[1] Average or typical figures reported by members of trade associations in the specified lines of business.

special prices and deals, and this should carry over in facilitating sales to customers. Moreover, salesmen are probably motivated to greater efforts when handling clean, fresh, and timely goods rather than having constant pressures exerted by management to dispose of slow-movers.

The relationship between high turnover and low *markdowns* of original selling prices is obvious and requires no further elaboration.

With respect to *operating expenses,* it should be emphasized that only certain *kinds* of expense decline as turnover is increased; other kinds of expense, as explained later, behave in the opposite manner. The expenses that decline are principally those of *possession*—interest on capital invested in inventory, insurance, property taxes, and costs of providing warehouse space. The relationship of such expenses to turnover is shown graphically in Figure 10.

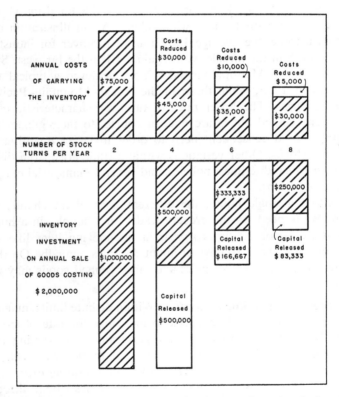

* For purposes of this illustration, it is assumed that the costs of carrying the inventory are as follows: interest on capital invested in inventory, 4 per cent of inventory value; insurance, 1 per cent of inventory value; variable warehouse expense, 1 per cent of inventory value; and fixed warehouse expense, $15,000 per year.

FIGURE 9. Hypothetical Annual Costs of Carrying an Inventory Investment, on an Annual Sale of Goods Costing $2,000,000, at Specified Rates of Stock Turnover

The advantages of a high turnover rate are reflected ultimately in increased net profits and a higher return on invested capital. Higher profits on investment are obtained both through the reduction in operating expenses and through the release of capital invested in inventory. These factors are illustrated in a hypothetical example in Figure 9. Here, costs of carrying the inventory and the amount of capital needed are both shown to decrease as turnover rises. Comparing a turnover rate of 8 with a turnover of 2, the reduction in expenses is 60 per cent ($45,000 reduction from a total of $75,000) and capital investment is reduced by 75 per cent ($750,000 reduction from $1,000,000). These figures, while merely hypothetical, suggest the importance of adequate stock turnover in successful wholesaling.

Limitations to Rapid Stock Turns. While rapid stock turn is an index of good merchandising, there are several reservations. There seem to be definite limits beyond which a quickening in the movement of goods may bring trouble in the way of stock shortages and loss of trade. To avoid such shortages, back orders, and dissatisfied customers, adequate inventories must be carried by the wholesaler. They should be large enough and sufficiently well balanced to enable him to meet the normal requirements of his trade, for it is his function to supply the wants of his customers at all times with least friction. If the wholesaler attempts to pare down his stocks too severely and to keep the goods flowing through his warehouse beyond certain limits, he fails to that extent to perform the function of storage.

A very rapid rate of turnover can also have an adverse effect on the cost of goods and on certain elements of the wholesaler's operating expenses. While the cost of carrying the inventory (as reflected in such items as interest on capital invested in stock, cost of storage, insurance, and so on) decreases as the rate of stock turn increases, the cost of *acquiring* merchandise increases as the stock turn rate is carried beyond reasonable limits. The most important disadvantage of excessive turnover is in the usually higher *merchandise costs* incurred through buying in smaller quantities. Also, if skimpy stocks are carried and small quantities are ordered very frequently, more people have to be employed in purchasing and stock control, an unnecessarily large amount of time is consumed in record-keeping, a large quantity of expensive purchase and control records is used, and the transportation costs per unit of merchandise are increased. This is illustrated in Figure 10, where the relationships between the *cost of possession* and the *cost of acquisition* at various turnover rates are indicated.

Other factors that militate against undue rapidity in the rate of stock movement are to be found in the seasonality of certain goods, location of the wholesaler, quantity-buying opportunities, private-branding policy, and the desire for speculative profits. When goods are either produced or

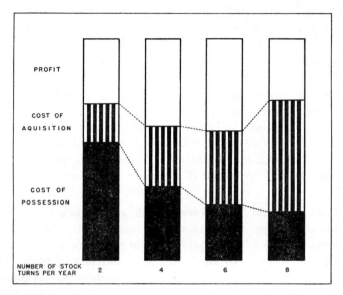

The cost of acquiring the inventory is reflected in such items as purchasing, receiving, telephone bills, accounting, and bill paying. The cost of possessing the inventory is reflected in such items as insurance, taxes, interest on capital, warehouse space, wages, and obsolescence.

FIGURE 10. Illustration of the Nature of the Relationship Between the Cost of Acquiring an Inventory and the Cost of Possessing an Inventory, and the Resulting Profit as the Rate of Stock Turnover Is Increased

consumed seasonally, such merchandise very often must be bought by the wholesaler considerably in advance and in large quantities. This tends to reduce the rate of stock turn. Similarly, advance buying in large quantities may be dictated by the distance of the wholesaler from his sources of supply. For example, a hardware wholesaler in Texas usually carries larger inventories in proportion to sales than one located in Ohio or Pennsylvania. Quantity purchases may also be desirable because of the more advantageous prices at which goods can be bought and possible savings in freight rates. It is then a question of measuring the loss resulting from a more sluggish turnover against the price and other cost advantages obtained.

When a wholesaler embarks upon a policy of selling goods under his own label, he assumes certain responsibilities, one of which is uniformity in the quality of his products. To insure a high degree of uniformity, it is often necessary to buy the entire season's supply in advance. Concerns thus operating usually have a lower rate of stock turn and may incur larger expenses; but because of the wider margin which private branded goods normally bear, they may end the year's operations with a higher net profit percentage. Finally, when a rise in prices is anticipated the desire for speculative profits may prompt the wholesaler to purchase in large quantities, in the hope that anticipated enhanced profits will more than offset whatever additional costs are incurred through a slowing up in the turnover rate.

Increasing the Rate of Stock Turn. Neither understocking nor overstocking is desirable, both being dangerous practices for the economic well-being of the wholesaler. Most firms, however, suffer more from overstocking, and it may not be inappropriate at this juncture to point out some of the ways in which such a condition can be remedied and a more rapid, but at the same time justifiable, rate of stock turn attained.

One of the ways of accomplishing this result is through a *simplification of stocks,* that is, a reduction in the number of varieties carried, particularly those of a parallel nature, and the elimination of items for which calls are few and infrequent. Another possibility is to resist buying new merchandise without first determining its salability and especially its probable effect upon the items or lines already carried. A wholesaler should refrain from adding to his line goods that are intrinsically slow-moving, and which merely split sales with other competing brands in stock.

A third way of increasing the rate of stock turn is through *proper departmentization.* Rates of turnover for the entire stock are a general indication, but they do not point specifically to the offenders. A detailed classification of merchandise makes it possible to ascertain the correct rates of turnover by both items and departments. Just as important, departmental turnover rates can be used as performance measures for the buyers in charge of each department. Each buyer can be held specifically accountable for attaining a satisfactory turnover rate.

Since buying depends so much on the exercise of good judgment and upon certain other factors affecting demand, such as weather, which are difficult to predict, it is inevitable that mistakes will be made, and that some goods are purchased which linger in the warehouse. When permitted to accumulate, such goods slow down the rate of stock turn and eventually result in losses from depreciation. A wise policy to pursue is to *dispose of slow-moving goods as soon as their inactivity is discovered,* either through special sales effort, higher commissions to salesmen, price reductions, or by other means.

The most potent of all devices to increase the rate of stock turn, without at the same time incurring the danger of understocking, is that of *accurate knowledge of the condition of the stock* and every component part thereof. Such information can best be obtained through the maintenance of adequate stock records. These records must be designed to show needed information about stocks, rate of movement, and purchases of *individual items* or narrow *categories* of merchandise to be useful in controlling the level of inventory. Turnover measures *in themselves* will not do this, at least not turnover rates for an entire enterprise or an entire department.

Methods of securing information about stocks for items or narrow categories of items, and the uses of such information in a stock control system, are discussed and evaluated in Chapter 25.

Turnover Rates Distinguished from Inventory-Sales Ratios. Measures of the rate of stock turnover are sometimes confused with ratios of *inventory to sales* commonly used in economic analysis and in current control of inventories by business executives. There are two differences between the rate of turnover and an inventory-sales ratio for a given business. First, in an inventory-sales ratio the method of computation is just the reverse of that used in arriving at a turnover rate; that is, inventory at a given time is divided by sales for a corresponding period rather than vice versa. Second, and more important, in computing an inventory-sales ratio the value of inventory is commonly taken on a *cost* basis while sales are expressed at *selling* prices. Thus, the relationship of the two quantities is distorted by the inclusion of the gross margin in one term of the ratio but not in the other. To illustrate, suppose a wholesale house made sales of $1.2 million in a year, had an inventory amounting to $240,000 at cost values, and attained an average gross margin on sales of 20 per cent. The ratio of inventory to sales would be 20 per cent ($240,000 divided by $1.2 million). It is *not* correct to say, however, that the rate of stock turn was 5 times. Instead, sales must be reduced to a cost basis, resulting in a figure of $960,000. The rate of turnover was, therefore, 4 times ($960,000 divided by $240,000).

Ratios of inventory to sales, while differing from stock turnover rates, are useful in several ways. Such ratios provide the economic analyst with an important indicator of business conditions. An increase in the inventory ratio beyond normal levels is frequently indicative of excessive accumulation, which may contribute to a recession in general business activity. Studies of business cycles over a number of years have indicated the value of current inventory-sales or stock-sales ratios for analyzing both expansions and contractions.[2]

In addition to their use in economic analysis, these ratios are a most valuable tool for management in a wholesale enterprise as well as in other kinds of business organizations. The published statistics of sales and inventories contained in the monthly *Wholesale Trade Reports* of the Bureau of the Census can be used to develop such ratios for wholesalers in various lines of business. Similar data are collected and published in the *Survey of Current Business* and its supplements. With current information about a specific line of trade, executives can judge their own inventory levels as

---

[2] See, for example, Doris M. Eisemann, "Bank Credit and Inventory Cycles," and Thomas Stanback, "Cyclical Behavior of Manufacturers' Inventories Since 1945," both in *American Statistical Association Proceedings* (Business and Economics Section), 1957.

well as gains and losses in relation to sales volume and thus control over-stocking and understocking in their firms.

Merchandise Planning and the Merchandise Budget

One of the most important applications of the concept of stock turnover is in the quantitative planning of merchandising operations. A basic tool of planning and control over merchandising is the *merchandise budget,* which summarizes merchandising plans in dollar terms. The purposes of such a budget, procedures for establishing it, and its use as a control instrument are outlined in this section.

Nature and Purposes. A merchandise budget is a *plan* of sales, inventories, merchandise receipts, purchases, and cash disbursements for a future period. Like other kinds of budgets, it is expressed in *dollar* terms.

There are several reasons for the use of merchandise budgets. First, a budget acts as a *guide to action* in buying. It shows how much must be purchased in a given period of time to support an expected volume of sales and buyers can place their orders accordingly.

Second, and closely related to the first reason, the budget provides a means of *control over investment in inventories.* A major objective in preparing the budget is to *balance* stocks with sales for a given period and to avoid both *over*investment, with the accompanying sluggish movement of goods, and *under*investment, which often leads to losses of sales.

A third reason for setting up a merchandise budget is to provide management with a basis for *evaluating the performance of buyers.* When buying responsibility is divided among two or more executives, each buyer can be judged in terms of his accomplishment of the quantitative goals laid down in the plan for the departments or other areas in his charge.

Steps in Preparing the Budget. In the preparation of a merchandise budget for a specified future period, a rather definite procedure is followed. First, an estimate is made of sales volume for the total period and this is broken down into monthly sales. Expected sales become a logical starting point for the budget since purchases are made primarily in anticipation of sales.

The next step, once sales have been estimated, is to determine the amount of inventory needed to achieve the expected sales. On the basis of needed inventories, receipts of merchandise into the warehouse are scheduled. From this schedule a plan of purchases is drawn up, with due allowance for delays in the delivery of goods. Finally, a schedule of cash disbursements is made on the basis of the orders to be placed.

The preparation of a merchandise budget is illustrated in a hypothetical example in Table 20. Here the procedure for estimating each factor, start-

TABLE 20

ILLUSTRATION OF PROCEDURE FOR ESTABLISHING A MONTHLY MERCHANDISE BUDGET

Month	Expected Sales Per Cent of Annual Total (1)	Expected Sales Amount (2)	Expected Sales at Cost (3)	Required Inventory Beginning of Month (4)	Required Receipts During Month (5)	Required Purchases During Month (6)
January	10.0%	$1,000,000	$800,000	$1,500,000	$740,000	$650,000
February	9.0	900,000	720,000	1,440,000	560,000	600,000
March	8.0	800,000	640,000	1,280,000	640,000	560,000
April	8.0	800,000	640,000	1,280,000	480,000	460,000
May	7.0	700,000	560,000	1,120,000	440,000	520,000
June	6.0	600,000	480,000	1,000,000	600,000	660,000
July	7.0	700,000	560,000	1,120,000	720,000	–
August	8.0	800,000	640,000	1,280,000	–	–

Explanation:

Col. (1), based on past experience and/or trade averages for seasonal distribution of sales.

Col. (2), computed by applying per cent of annual sales (Col. 1) to expected total annual sales, in this case $10,000,000.

Col. (3), computed by multiplying expected sales for each month by the expected ratio of the cost of goods sold to sales—in this case 80 per cent.

Col. (4), determined on the basis of goal annual rate of stock turnover of 6 times. For all months except January and June, beginning inventory equals expected sales at cost multiplied by 2. In these months, because of especially high or low sales, the normal ratio is modified as explained in the text.

Col. (5), required receipts for a given month equal expected sales (at cost) plus required inventory at the end of the month (beginning of following month) minus inventory at beginning of month.

Col. (6), equals one-half of the required receipts for the current month plus one-half of required receipts for the next month, based on assumption that the average time elapsing between ordering and receipt of goods is half a month.

ing with expected sales, is explained. More detailed attention is given to each factor in the paragraphs that follow.

Sales Planning. The data in Columns 1 and 2 of the table are illustrative of *expected monthly sales* for a wholesale enterprise. As shown there, the monthly sales estimates are derived from a sales forecast for the entire year, distributed among the various months on the basis of the firm's past experience or typical experience in the trade. The sales forecast for the year is, of course, the basis for many plans other than the merchandise budget itself. In the sales division the forecast is used to determine territorial potentials, salesmen's quotas, and in some cases their compensation. In most organizations preparation of the forecast is the responsibility of the sales manager, with advice and assistance from other divisions including the buyers. Detailed consideration of sales forecasting methods and problems is, accordingly, deferred to the section of this book which deals with sales management. At this point it is simply assumed that the necessary estimates have been made and are to be used as the basis for planning merchandising operations.

Because inventory figures are commonly on a cost basis, it is necessary to convert the monthly sales estimates to the same basis, as shown in Column 3. Here it is assumed that the average gross margin of the firm is 20 per cent of sales, so that the cost of sales is equivalent to 80 per cent of sales (100 per cent minus 20 per cent). There is some danger in the use of broad averages like this, especially if they relate to the enterprise as a whole. When separate budgets are drawn up for each department, the average departmental cost-to-sales ratio should be more reliable because of the greater homogeneity of goods.

Planning Required Inventories. The next step in the budgeting procedure is to determine the amount of inventory needed in each month to support the expected volume of sales. This is done by applying the desired rate of stock turnover to expected sales. Since turnover is a ratio of cost of sales to inventory, it is a relatively simple matter to compute the amount of inventory needed for an estimated volume of sales. In Table 20, it is assumed that the *goal* turnover rate is 6 times annually, or one-half turn per month (6 divided by 12). Thus, for a given month, the inventory on hand at the beginning of the month should equal twice the expected volume of sales (at cost) for the month. For all of the months shown in the table, *except* January and June, the required inventory (Column 4) was obtained by doubling the expected sales at cost (Column 3). For these months, however, slight modifications were made in the average turnover rate. January is indicated as a month of high sales activity, while June is a period of abnormally low volume. For this reason inventories have been set at *more than* twice sales in June and at *less than* twice sales in January. This reflects the fact that turnover tends to decline as business falls off, because it is not feasible to cut stocks below a certain level without suffering excessive "outs" and "shorts." Conversely, as sales pick up, it is not necessary to expand stocks in proportion, since much of the increase usually comes in a relatively small number of fast-moving items. Establishing proper relationships of beginning inventory to expected sales for each month calls for seasoned judgment based on experience in the effects of such factors in a particular line of trade.

Scheduling Receipts. Determination of the amount of goods that should be received into stock in a given month is a routine matter once required inventory levels have been set. For each month, the required receipts must be sufficient to provide for expected sales *plus or minus* any net change in inventory during the month. To illustrate, expected sales at cost for June are assumed to amount to $480,000. To this must be added the required inventory at the *end* of June, that is, at July 1, which amounts to $1,120,000. Then, from the sum of these two figures ($1,600,000), the inventory on hand at the beginning of June ($1,000,000) is deducted. The result, or $600,000, is the value of goods that must be received into stock during the month. Thus, in a month when a net *increase* in inventory is planned, receipts will exceed sales by the amount of that increase. Receipts for June could be computed by adding the net inventory increase of $120,000 ($1,120,000 minus $1,000,000) to the expected sales at cost of $480,000. On the other hand, in a month when some *decrease* is planned in stocks, such as January used in the example, receipts are less than expected sales. When no change is to be made in inventory (for example, March), receipts should equal sales at cost.

Planning Purchases. Purchases can now be planned, at least in a rough fashion, in accordance with the scheduled receipts of goods into stock. In the illustration, it has been assumed that it takes, *on the average,* half a month to fill a purchase order; that is, half a month elapses between the placing of an order and the corresponding receipt of goods. This means that, in the first two weeks of a month, orders should be placed for goods to be received in the second two weeks; in the second two weeks, goods should be bought for receipt in the first two weeks of the month following; and so on. The figures in Column 6, representing required purchases for each month, have been computed by adding one-half of the receipts for the current month to one-half of the receipts for the following month. For January, total purchases of $650,000 include $370,000 to be received during January plus $280,000 to be received during February. A similar procedure was followed for each of the months shown.

It will be noted that it was necessary to estimate sales for eight months in order to arrive at purchase plans for only six months in the illustration in Table 20. The reasons for this should now be apparent. To plan receipts during a given month, it is necessary to know what inventory is needed at the *end* of that month, which in turn depends on expected sales for the month following. Then, to plan purchases during a given month, it is essential to know the amount of receipts during the next month in order to allow for the time lag in delivery. Thus, to plan purchases for June, it was necessary to estimate receipts for July, which necessitated inclusion of a planned sales figure for August.

Some Reservations. The procedure outlined in the preceding sections for scheduling receipts and purchases must be modified to a certain degree in practice, especially in dealing with style goods and with other merchandise seasonally consumed and/or manufactured. Dry goods wholesalers, for example, may place orders at the beginning of the season for about 60 per cent of their total requirements, with deliveries to be spaced as nearly as possible to actual needs, but subject to some negotiation with suppliers.[3] Thus the amount actually received and the amount purchased in a given month may be quite different from the figures derived from a budget such as that illustrated in Table 20.

Planning Cash Disbursements. An important use of the merchandise budget is in the scheduling of cash disbursements. The treasurer or other chief financial officer must plan to have sufficient cash available to meet the commitments made by the merchandise division. Cash disbursements will follow purchases closely, usually by about 10 days. Since most wholesalers attempt to take all or almost all cash discounts, it is important that a schedule be established for making the necessary payments. If it develops at this point that the needed cash will not be available, and if arrangements cannot be made for additional financing, some modification in purchasing plans may have to be made.

Merchandise Budgeting in Practice. As may be apparent, the budgeting procedure outlined in this chapter is a formal and rather complex process. In many wholesale enterprises no such formal procedure is followed. In fact, no written plans at all may be prepared, particularly in smaller firms. Even in these organizations, however, some attention must be given to planning and coordinating sales, inventories, receipts, purchases, and payments. If it is not, serious problems are bound to arise. The very common overstock condition of financially weak enterprises often results from inadequate planning. Inability to make payments in time to take cash discounts is another difficulty that may issue from the same cause. In a successful wholesale enterprise it is essential that either a formal or informal merchandise budget be used to avoid these and other difficulties.

[3] J. V. R. Porteous, "The Importance of Stock Turnover . . . and How to Attain It," Address to the Midyear Meeting of the Wholesale Dry Goods Institute, July 23, 1953.

21

BUYING POLICIES AND PROCEDURES

The fundamental purchasing objective of having the right goods, at the right time, in the right quantities, at the right prices, and under the right conditions, gives rise to the need for specialized buying skill. General methods for planning and controlling *how much* is bought during a given period of time were outlined in the preceding chapter. In this chapter consideration is given to the more difficult tasks of determining *what* is bought, *where* it is secured, and in what *quantities* purchases are made.

Importance of the Buying Function. The necessity for specialized, technical buying has been accentuated during the course of the twentieth century by an enlarged variety of goods in demand, the increasing number of parallel brands of the same type of article, and the growing number of sources of supply. While the old adage that "goods well bought are half sold" has lost much of its strength and emphasis has shifted to the selling function, it remains true, particularly in wholesaling, that goods bought in accordance with sound marketing principles will be sold most readily and with the least expenditure of money and effort.

Buyers can contribute much to the success of a business, or they can lead it to bankruptcy; as a result, they occupy an important position in the organization of a wholesale enterprise. Not only do they generally hold executive positions but there are several of them in every house of some size. This organizational status reflects the importance of the contribution made by competent buying to a firm's over-all success.

Buying or purchasing for a wholesale house differs radically from mere ordering. Ordering is the carrying out of a purchasing transaction in accordance with a planned procedure for buying predetermined amounts of

378

certain types and qualities of merchandise from sources already decided upon. Buying, on the other hand, is more inclusive and intricate. It implies, first of all, an accurate anticipation of demand from customers. Sources of goods to supply this demand must be carefully selected in the light of certain factors; correct quantities to be purchased must be determined on the basis of estimated sales, existing stocks, and general conditions of supply and demand; methods of buying must be chosen; a correct purchasing procedure must be developed; and when the goods arrive provision must be made for receiving and pricing them. Thus, the buying function really begins long before orders are placed and ends only after the goods have been received, priced, and made available for sale.

BUYING POLICIES

In a wholesale enterprise hundreds or thousands of different items are bought from many different sources of supply. In the course of a year a great many individual purchasing decisions must be made. Obviously it is impractical and wasteful to make each of these decisions without regard to consistency or coordination. Consequently, in any well-managed enterprise, definite buying *policies* are established for the guidance of day-to-day operations.

In many ways, the kinds of merchandise bought and handled give a wholesale enterprise its fundamental character. Decisions about merchandise lines bought affect sales, warehousing, and other aspects of the business as well as buying per se. Buying policies are, therefore, set within a framework of certain *general* policies which were treated in Chapter 16. Among these are policies relating to the number, types, and completeness of merchandise lines; under what conditions new lines will be added; to what extent, if any, private brands will be carried; and relationships with suppliers such as exclusive agency agreements.

Within the framework of an organization's general merchandise line policies, there are a number of policies formulated by the buyers. These normally include such matters as the *quantity to be bought at a given time,* desirability of *concentrating purchases,* and *selection of suppliers.*

Quantity Buying and Small-Lot Purchases. Although the total quantities purchased over a period of time are determined by the estimated sales for the period, the wholesaler has considerable freedom with regard to the size of individual orders placed with suppliers. Thus the decision whether to follow a general policy of buying in large lots or to purchase minimum requirements at frequent intervals is a matter of major importance.

Among the advantages of quantity buying are: (1) lower list prices may be obtained by the purchaser; (2) special price concessions in the form of advertising allowances, extra discounts, or "free deals" are sometimes granted by the seller; (3) important savings in transportation costs can be realized; (4) fewer orders need be placed, so that purchasing costs are reduced; and (5) occasionally the due dates for paying invoices may be postponed by the seller. In a "sellers' market," that is, in a time of general scarcity and when sellers "are in the saddle," wholesalers attempt to buy in large quantities whenever possible in order to be sure of having a supply of merchandise for their customers. Since a "sellers' market" is usually characterized by a rising price level, wholesalers have an added incentive to engage in speculative buying whereby they attempt to make a profit on price movements as well as on the performance of their normal functions. Speculative buying in large quantities is also practiced by some wholesalers under more normal conditions as well, because the frequent fluctuations in the manufacturers' prices for many commodities provide opportunities for extra profits on well-timed purchases.

The fact that losses are likely to be incurred is only one of the disadvantages of speculating on price movements through quantity purchases. Buyers responsible for purchasing a large number of items may not have the time or facilities for judging market trends of specific commodities. There is always the danger that they will concentrate more on the trend of the market than on the normal buying function, with the result that stocks may accumulate far in excess of any reasonable needs and may become seriously unbalanced. If a firm does decide to engage in speculative buying, sound practice dictates that this plan be recognized as a deliberate business policy; that adequate provision be made for careful interpretation of price movements; and that the merchandise purchased on a speculative basis be departmentized or otherwise segregated in order to measure the results of the policy.

In addition to the risk of incurring speculative losses, other disadvantages of quantity buying are: (1) it ties up more capital in merchandise and increases carrying costs, including those of storage, interest, and insurance; (2) it makes for inflexibility in the merchandising program; and (3) it increases the risk of losses resulting from deterioration and obsolescence.

Especially in times of uncertainty, many wholesalers let their fears of inventory losses carry them to the opposite extreme policy of "hand-to-mouth" buying. This policy, which is largely attributable to a similar buying plan first initiated by retailers, has resulted in higher wholesaling costs. To some extent, however, it has been a logical result of improved transportation facilities. The maintenance of reserve stocks by certain manufacturers at accessible places from which the wholesaler's orders can be filled promptly has been at once an outgrowth of and a contributing factor to hand-to-mouth buying.

Nevertheless, small-lot buying is not without its disadvantages. It tends toward understocking which is just as undesirable and uneconomical as overstocking, the former resulting in *outs* and substitutions both of which create ill will, and the latter in higher operating expenses. While small-lot buying by the wholesaler reduces losses incident to unfavorable price changes on a falling market, by the same virtue it minimizes the possibility of making speculative profits on rising markets. Besides, there are certain conditions, such as surround the purchase of seasonal goods, which necessitate large-quantity purchases several months or a year in advance. There may also be opportunities to buy large blocks of merchandise at unusually attractive prices, sometimes even below the cost of manufacture. Finally, it is one of the wholesaler's main functions to maintain large reservoirs of stocks; consequently, when he attempts to pass back to the manufacturer the burden of carrying stocks, he is undermining his own position by shirking his major responsibility and thereby encouraging the manufacturer to do his own wholesaling.

Determining the Optimum Purchase Quantity. As just indicated, there are both advantages and disadvantages in large-quantity buying. At least theoretically, there is an *optimum* purchase quantity under given cost conditions for each item stocked by a wholesale enterprise. This is a purchase quantity that minimizes total costs. If all of the factors mentioned in the preceding discussion could be measured accurately, it would be a relatively simple matter to compute this optimum quantity from a formula. Indeed, there are several versions in common use of the same basic formula for calculating optimum purchase quantities. It is true that these formulas have been more widely used in industrial purchasing than by wholesalers, but there is no valid reason why they cannot be applied to the latter type of buying problem, at least as it relates to staple commodities.

Formulas for determining the optimum purchase quantity vary in form, but all are quite similar in concept. One such formula is as follows:

$$Q = \sqrt{\frac{2YS}{IC}}$$

in which Q is the optimum purchase quantity per order, Y is the expected annual usage in units, S is the cost of placing an order, I is the total carrying charge per annum (including interest, risk, deterioration, obsolescence, and storage) expressed as a percentage of the value of the inventory; and C is the unit cost of the item being bought.[1]

This formula states, in effect, that the optimum purchase quantity (Q) varies *directly* with the square root of expected sales and with the square root of purchasing expenses; and that it varies *inversely* with the square root of dollar carrying charges.

[1] Thomson M. Whitin, *The Theory of Inventory Management* (Princeton, N.J.: Princeton University Press, 1957), pp. 31–42. This reference also has an excellent bibliography of books and periodical articles on this and related subjects, tracing the development of economical purchase quantity formulas back to the mid-1920's.

To illustrate, suppose that a firm uses 12,000 units annually of an item costing $5 per unit; and, further, suppose that studies have revealed the cost of placing an order to be $5 and the annual carrying charges 20 per cent of the value of average inventory.[2] The optimum purchase quantity is then computed by substituting these figures in the formula:

$$Q = \sqrt{\frac{2(12,000)\ (\$5)}{(.20)\ (\$5)}}$$

$$= \sqrt{\frac{120,000}{1}}$$

$$= \sqrt{120,000}$$

$$= \text{about } 346$$

This means that costs would be minimized in this case by ordering between 320 and 350 units at a time and placing 34 or 35 orders per year.

Trial and error will confirm that this is the optimum purchase quantity. If 35 orders are placed for 343 units each, then total costs will include:

12,000 units at $5 each	$60,000.00
35 orders at $5 each	175.00
20 per cent carrying charge on average inventory of $857.50 (equal to half of average order amount)	171.50
	$60,346.50

If 20 orders were placed for 600 units each, total costs computed on the same basis would amount to $60,400; if 50 orders were placed monthly for 240 units apiece, total costs would equal $60,370. Thus, the optimum purchase quantity reflects a *balancing* of opposing cost tendencies. The nature of these factors can perhaps be understood more clearly by referring back to Figure 10 in Chapter 20, which expresses the same idea graphically for the concept of stock turnover. It should be apparent that this is simply another way of looking at the same facts, since the over-all rate of turnover for a group of items is an average of turnover rates for each item in the group. These rates are determined by the number of orders placed and average quantity ordered during the year.

The example used in the foregoing paragraphs may be misleading, since it does not take into account *quantity discounts* on purchases. These discounts, which are offered by most manufacturers, are often the most important of all the cost factors affecting the optimum purchase quantity.

---

[2] Empirical studies in the manufacturing field have shown ordering costs to vary from around $2 up to as much as $10, while carrying charges are commonly estimated at 2 per cent to 3 per cent monthly or 24 per cent to 36 per cent annually.

They can be incorporated into the formula by a relatively simple modification, as follows:

$$Q = \sqrt{\frac{2 Y (S + B)}{IP}}$$

in which the notation is the same as before, except that B is the "fixed charge" included by the supplier in his price and P is the "base price" paid per unit above and beyond this fixed charge.

This formula assumes that when quantity discounts are offered, the price really consists of two parts: a fixed dollar charge (B) which must be paid regardless of quantity ordered; and a unit price (P) paid for each unit *in addition to* the fixed charge.[3]

In addition to the problem of allowing for quantity discounts, there are several other limitations to the formula approach analyzed above. In the first place, it is very difficult to obtain accurate and meaningful measures of the cost factors required for use of the formula, especially the costs of deterioration and obsolescence. Usually some kind of "judgment" figures must be used. A second basic drawback is that the formula approach is designed for routine buying. It has little or no application to buying fashion goods, where "obsolescence" is overwhelmingly the most important factor to consider. Even for staple commodities, the formula approach does not take account of price movements and must therefore be modified by the judgment of the buyer. Third, as stated above, the formula makes no allowance for possible cost savings through lower freight rates on larger shipments, which may be substantial on many items handled by wholesalers.

Despite these and other limitations, computation of optimum purchase quantities offers a promising avenue to enhancing the efficiency of wholesale buying. As long as it is regarded as a *supplement* to experienced judgment and not as a *substitute* for it, there is little danger that factors outside of the scope of the formula will be ignored.

The policy adopted by a firm on quantities bought is closely related to its policy on *frequency of purchases*. When goods are of a staple character and when price movements are not important, it may be feasible to determine the optimum purchase quantity and then simply place the required number of orders at equal intervals during the year. In such cases the policy on quantity bought automatically determines the frequency with which orders are placed. In practice the matter is seldom this simple. For various classes of goods different buying methods are used, and it is often

---

[3] To be sure, quantity discounts are not actually quoted in this manner. Instead, different prices or trade discounts are offered for varying quantities. Nevertheless, the expression used in the formula represents the cost structure that *underlies* a supplier's quoted schedule of discounts.

desirable to place orders at irregular intervals. For seasonal goods market activity centers in certain months of the year, when the bulk of purchases must be made, supplemented by *reorders, fill-ins,* or *emergency* orders. *Jobs* are bought as opportunities appear and as the needs of the business justify. Manufacturing conditions may also have a bearing on the frequency of purchases. Some goods may be produced only to order while others are generally manufactured to stock. The former must be bought long in advance and in large amounts, while goods of the latter type can be secured as needed.

Concentration of Purchases. The number of sources from which wholesalers buy their goods depends upon many factors, among which are the importance of style considerations, the degree of merchandise specialization, the use of selective distribution in a given line of business, the choice of channels of supply, and whether the wholesaler operates on an exclusive agency agreement. When a wholesaler deals in staple goods, handles a limited line of merchandise, represents certain producers exclusively or selectively, and buys largely from agents and others who represent a number of manufacturers, the sources of supply are apt to be less numerous.

Some buyers contend that it is desirable to concentrate the purchase of their requirements and to buy regularly from a limited number of sources than to scatter orders widely. This procedure may enable them to obtain larger discounts, more favorable credit terms, better service, and prompt delivery. The buyers become more familiar with the merchandise items handled and the tendency to overbuy is reduced to a minimum. In addition, the firm enjoys the status of a preferred customer to be favored by suppliers in a "sellers' market." This point was brought into relief acutely during World War II and in the Korean conflict.

On the other hand, some firms prefer to scatter their orders widely among many vendors. Such a policy is said to keep the buyers on the alert for special offers that may come from firms not normally patronized or from newly established concerns. This is particularly true in such trades as dry goods where, though the market is fairly concentrated in a few leading centers, producers operate on such a small scale, manufacture such a limited assortment of merchandise, and styles change so rapidly that buyers must be constantly in search of new sources of supply. As a result the average wholesaler in this trade normally buys from 1,000 to 1,500 sources. For staple items in this trade, purchases are made from about half as many sources as are used for goods subject to rapid style changes.

Similar situations are encountered in other lines of business. For example, since many canneries operate on a small scale, are seasonal in operation, specialize in a limited number of items, and are located in producing areas, it becomes necessary for the wholesale grocer to draw supplies of these goods from widely diversified and distant regions at different times of the year. Other reasons for scattering purchases among a large number of sellers are lack of special inducements by producers to encourage concentration, and unwillingness of many manufacturers of limited capacity to tie up their trade with a few outlets which might affect their independence.

Policy on Sources of Supply. The fundamental question, *from what general class of suppliers a vendor is to be chosen,* is usually determined before the problem of choosing a particular manufacturer to fill a specific order arises. A number of factors enter into the formulation of policy on this matter. Manufacturers' policies with regard to functional discounts, cash discounts, and credit terms influence the decision. In some lines of business, wholesalers prefer to deal with manufacturers who offer price protection through resale price maintenance in states where that is possible.

Many wholesalers resent the practice of manufacturers of selling both through them and direct to retailers, particularly where sales are made to the smaller retailers who generally buy from wholesalers. This feeling was most intense in the depression years of the 1930's when many manufacturers resorted to almost any means in order to secure sales. In the wholesale dry goods trade, for example, it was claimed that business has been "confused, disorganized and, to an extent, demoralized, by the selling policies of the very manufacturers who depend most largely on wholesale distribution" because of sales of a minor portion of their product to retailers at the same price charged to wholesalers. This, it was alleged, "produces an unfair competitive situation, which definitely discriminates against those retailers who are supplied through wholesalers, and gives an unjust advantage to those retailers who are supplied by the manufacturer direct."

In this situation a list was prepared for use by wholesalers, if they chose to do so (since coercion or suggestion that it be followed would be contrary to law), rating the various manufacturers of dry goods according to their selling policies, consisting of those who (a) sell only through wholesalers; (b) sell regular goods through wholesalers only, but manufacture goods under buyers' specifications and labels for national chains and mail order houses; (c) sell regular or identified products only to wholesalers and large metropolitan department stores, allowing a reasonable differential to wholesalers; (d) sell their regular products generally but allow a reasonable differential to wholesalers; (e) sell regular goods to wholesalers, large department stores, national chains, and mail order houses and allow no differential in price to wholesalers; (f) sell the same goods to both wholesalers and retailers at substantially the same price; (g) announce one selling policy and practice another; and (h) those who failed to supply any information concerning their selling policy.

Because the circulation of this list amounted to collective action against manufacturers who sold direct or who failed to grant satisfactory discounts, the Federal Trade Commission ordered The Wholesale Dry Goods Institute, Inc., to cease the practice.[4] This no doubt served as a warning against any other cooperative efforts by wholesalers to influence suppliers' distribution policies. In the "sellers' market" prevailing during World War II and the years immediately following, such actions would have been impractical anyway, since wholesalers were anxious to take goods wherever they could find them. With the return of a buyers' market in the late 1950's, however, there were signs of renewed friction between manufacturers and wholesalers in various industries. While there have been no known actions by *groups* of wholesalers against suppliers with unpopular policies, wholesalers have continued on an *individual* basis to give preference to those who sell exclusively through the distributor channel or who allow reasonable functional discounts. It is certainly in their long-run interest to pursue such a policy, at least in those cases where other considerations are approximately balanced as between alternative sources of supply.

Selection of Specific Vendors. Within the limitations imposed on the buyer by the firm's major policies and particularly by the policy on the *types* of suppliers to be patronized, considerable freedom still exists for the selection of vendors.

At a given time, and within these limits, a buyer's selection of vendors is based upon the net price and margin available, handling of freight charges, sales potential, sales and advertising support, returned goods policies, packaging, and the integrity and financial standing of the manufacturer.

Prices and Margins. Obviously one of the most important considerations in choosing a supplier, assuming goods are of about the same quality, is *price*. Differences between alternative suppliers may take the form of differing *net* prices or differing *discounts* from the same list price. In either case what is of prime concern to the wholesaler is the margin available to him. Because price is so important, most buyers probably start by comparing prices and then modify this comparison by considering some of the additional factors briefly discussed below.

Freight Charges. Closely related to the matter of price is the treatment of freight charges. One supplier may appear to charge a lower price than another; but unless both prices are on an equal basis as to freight costs (either delivered or f.o.b. plant), invoice prices can be misleading. For

---

[4] *United States of America Before the Federal Trade Commission In the Matter of the Wholesale Dry Goods Institute, Inc., Its Officers, Directors, and Members, Order To Cease and Desist,* F.T.C. Docket No. 3751, November 24, 1941. Affirmed by the Circuit Court of Appeals, Second Circuit, in 1943; see 139 F.2d 230.

reasons to be discussed in Chapter 22, the wholesaler is interested in *landed cost* (including freight) rather than just invoice prices.

Sales Potential, Sales Support. The widest margin imaginable would be no inducement to handle a product line if the dollar sales potential is deemed to be too small. Indeed, the very wide margins given on certain specialty lines, such as fancy canned foods, are attributable primarily to their low dollar potential. On the other hand, if extremely rapid turnover and large volume can be expected, as on cigarettes or heavily advertised foods and drugs, narrow percentage margins may be quite satisfactory. The sales potential is partly determined by basic market potential for a type of product, but is also affected by the quantity and quality of advertising effort, sales promotion, training of salesmen, and other forms of sales support given by the manufacturer.

Returned Goods Policies. A supplier's policy on returned goods may be a critical factor. For example, on certain novelty toy and housewares items sold through drug channels, wholesalers will refuse to handle a line unless a liberal guaranty is made. This policy results from unfortunate experiences with inadequately financed or even unscrupulous firms selling untried products.

Packaging. A manufacturer's packaging is important to the wholesaler in several ways. First, packaging in some lines is part of the over-all sales and advertising program and may spell the difference between adequate and inadequate potential. Second, packaging is a major factor in handling methods and costs in the warehouse. Third, weak packages break in handling and may result in excessive losses. Packaging may also be related to the unit of sale for an item. For example, in the industrial supplies field a cooperative effort has been made by members of the two leading trade associations to encourage "decimal packaging" by manufacturers. Under this system 10 units of an item, such as a hacksaw blade or a file, are packaged together, and no fewer are sold at a time. This facilitates the elimination of unprofitable orders from customers for one or two units.

A final consideration regarding packaging has to do with the handling of package *changes*. In the food field especially, many products are frequently sold on "deals"—two for the price of one, one-cent sales, and the like—involving temporary package changes. Furthermore, complete package changeovers are a common occurrence for the same products. If a manufacturer does not cooperate with his distributors during such changes by giving adequate warning and/or by guaranteeing against losses on old stocks, he cannot expect much cooperation from them.

Integrity and Financial Standing. None of the afore-mentioned policies on the part of a manufacturer mean very much unless they are undertaken in good faith and with intent to follow them through. Consequently, a supplier's general reputation and record of past dealings are not to be ignored. It is also desirable to avoid manufacturers who are in financial difficulty or who are otherwise unstable unless, of course, they are patronized only for highly standardized goods in general supply.

Information Concerning Sources of Supply. Information concerning the various factors that are relevant to the selection of sources of supply may be obtained from a number of sources. One of the best is the history or past experience with vendors as contained in the buyer's order file or record system. Manufacturers' salesmen who call at the house add much to the buyer's fund of knowledge, particularly with regard to new developments which may be in their early stages. It is good practice to record information obtained from salesmen and to file it for future reference. Manufacturers' catalogs and price lists provide a large amount of valuable information. In many lines of trade standard sizes have been adopted so that catalogs may be carefully indexed and systematically filed for ready reference.

Most buyers make frequent use of trade directories and registers. Probably the best known of these is *Thomas' Register of American Manufacturers,* an annual listing of manufacturers in all lines of business. In its five volumes, this directory lists both products and companies alphabetically. For each company a symbol is used to indicate the amount of its invested capital. Another popular general directory is *McRae's Blue Book,* which contains over 4,000 pages. In addition to these general directories there are specialized publications in nearly every line of trade. Illustrative are *Topics List Book,* a biennial directory of manufacturers of drugs and pharmaceuticals; *Canners Directory,* for canned foods; and *Source of Supply Directory* in the paper trade. Many trade directories contain information on product developments, prices, and market conditions in addition to the basic information on sources of supply.

Trade journals, which are available for almost every line of business, are valuable in several respects. Articles and editorials contain reports on the development of new products, new styles, selling policies, trends in distribution, and so on. Usually, there is a section that lists important changes in personnel and new companies that have been formed. Furthermore, the advertisements in trade journals are of a technical character and present specifications and other information of value to the buyer. Information concerning the trade publications in most lines of business is available in *Business Publication Rates and Data,* published monthly by Standard Rate and Data, Inc.

Trade Associations exist in most of the important lines of wholesale trade. These associations do a considerable amount of research and contact work and furnish a large amount of useful information to their respective memberships. Purchasing agents, such as Oliver Bros., Inc., and the Biddle Purchasing Co., offer a comprehensive current index of sources, on a subscription basis. The nature of the information supplied by these companies has already been discussed in Chapter 13. Conventions and exhibits provide an opportunity for buyers to come into contact with suppliers and other buyers, particularly at the beginning of buying seasons. Wise buyers obtain catalogs of their competitors by various means and search them for new ideas concerning products, suppliers, and favorable price offerings. In addition, many wholesalers are not reluctant to exchange information directly with their competitors and, in fact, may have an informal agreement to pass on reports concerning new types of merchandise or sources of supply. Exchange of such information is also a major function of the *buying groups* of wholesalers in various lines of trade, discussed in some detail in a later section of this chapter.

The vendors' financial credit reliability is rated by Dun & Bradstreet, Inc. Similar information can be had from special mercantile agencies; from manuals published by Standard & Poor's Corporation, Moody's Investors Service, and the Fitch Publishing Company; from various trade associations; credit interchange bureaus; and from sellers of allied lines of merchandise.

BUYING METHODS AND PROCEDURES

Much has been written on the subject of the buying procedure followed by large manufacturers and large retail stores, but little literature on this business activity is available that relates to the wholesaling field. In a manufacturing plant the buying procedure is usually the responsibility of a single individual designated as the purchasing agent, though in very large concerns a whole department may be organized under his direction. The purchasing agent buys principally materials, equipment, and supplies at the request or upon the requisition of others within the organization. Purchases are made on a basis of quality, price, terms, and service, with little attention being given to salability of the item except in certain limited cases. Finally, the purchasing agent has no connection with, or responsibility for, the sales operations of his firm.

In a retail store of considerable size, buying is diffused among a number of department heads who assume the responsibility for the sale of the goods they purchase. Most of the demands for merchandise originate within the buyer's own sphere of influence. Furthermore, buyers for retail stores deal in finished goods, so that the element of style and the question of brands must be thoroughly considered.

Buying for wholesale houses resembles in some respects that of the retail store, in some points that of the manufacturer, and in some ways it differs from both. Like the retail buyer, the buyer for a wholesale firm deals in finished goods and must consider styles and brands. Most of the demands for goods originate within his own sphere of influence and not from others in the organization. Although the wholesale buyer is to some degree responsible for the resale of the items he purchases, except in the smaller concerns, he has little direct connection with the actual sales efforts of the organization.

Buying Methods. There are several basic methods of buying merchandise for a wholesale enterprise. Goods may be bought from traveling salesmen employed by the various suppliers, by mail, by visiting some central market place, through resident buyers and purchasing agents, through brokers, or through a buying group of independent wholesalers. In some lines of business practically all purchases are made by a wholesaler at his home office when manufacturers' salesmen call. This is especially true of staple goods, although large quantities of seasonal and style goods are also bought in the same way. This method is economical from the standpoint of the wholesaler; stock can be checked at once in order to determine the size of the order; and other members of the firm can be consulted about new items. The chief drawbacks to buying from salesmen are the inability to compare simultaneously the merchandise of rival sources, and the difficulty in securing special concessions, which may be possible on a visit to the market.

Many hardware and grocery wholesalers buy the bulk of their goods by mail or telegram through the aid of manufacturers' catalogs, registers, trade directories, or on the basis of previous experience. For trade of this type, buyers are precluded from going to market, because organized markets for such purposes are nonexistent; furthermore, the same types of merchandise or even the same brands are often bought year in and year out. It should also be noted that practically every wholesale firm uses mail, air mail, or telegraph for fill-ins, reorders, and emergency items, a method which in economy ranks next to buying from salesmen. It also facilitates buying when a large number of sources exists, goods are carefully and exactly described, and quotations are available through up-to-date catalogs and discount sheets on practically any article in a given line, whether stocked or not.

Buying at market centers has some distinct advantages. It enables buyers to study market conditions, to note and sense style movements, to inspect a wide variety of merchandise, to discover new sources of supply, and to observe the activities of other buyers. When actual purchases are made on such visits, special terms and other arrangements are sometimes feasible.

For dry goods, New York stands out as the primary market to which buyers from all over the United States gravitate, visiting it at frequent intervals depending largely upon the distance of the wholesaler and whether continuous connections are maintained through a buying office. Even the most distant wholesalers send their buyers to New York from twice to ten times a year. A large amount of this trade is also attracted to Chicago, because of the important concentration of selling offices in the Merchandise Mart, and to Hollywood. In the furniture industry, visits to the Chicago, Grand Rapids, Los Angeles, and High Point, N. C., markets are made regularly because of the concentration of manufacturing plants in those vicinities and the semiannual exhibitions that have become customary in the trade. The extent to which actual purchases are made on such trips varies considerably. Some buyers make the trips primarily for the purpose of observing general conditions in their field, securing first-hand impressions, and seeking out new sources of supply. On the basis of this knowledge they are then in a position to buy later from visiting salesmen or by mail.

In some lines of trade it is common for wholesalers to join together in *buying groups* for the purpose of securing better prices, for representation in central markets if such markets exist, and for a sharing of experience among members of the group. Ordinarily, buying groups are composed of noncompeting houses, which set up an office under a paid manager, buy in large quantities through the office, and have suppliers bill the central office for goods bought. Some group organizations even maintain warehouses, stock merchandise, and redistribute to members' places of business.

The legality of wholesalers' buying groups is sometimes subject to question. If the organization maintained by such a group acts in a brokerage capacity, receiving fees or commissions from suppliers and directly or indirectly passing them on to its members, it would no doubt be in violation of Section 2(c) of the Robinson-Patman Amendment to the Clayton Act. This section prohibits the receipt or acceptance, as well as the payment or granting, of such fees or commissions except for services rendered to the party which pays or grants them. This has been well established by the many cases adjudicated by the Federal Trade Commission and the federal courts which passed on appeals.[5]

More often the buying group is interested primarily in securing goods for its members at lower or favored prices than those available to non-member wholesalers. These lower or favored prices may be in the nature of larger quantity discounts based on total purchases by the group or they may take the form of rebates on goods resold by the group organization to its members or to other wholesalers. In any such instances action may, of course, be taken by the Federal Trade Commission against the

[5] See Chapter 15 for fuller treatment of the Robinson-Patman Act and its major implications for wholesaling.

seller for an alleged violation of Section 2(a) of the Robinson-Patman Act, for the seller must stand ready to justify such price discrimination by means permitted by the law and discussed in Chapter 15.[6]

Action may also be taken in such cases against the buying groups themselves for alleged violation of Section 2(f) of the Act, which prohibits a buyer from knowingly inducing or receiving an illegal price discrimination. Illustrative are the several complaints issued by the Federal Trade Commission charging buying groups of automotive wholesalers[7] with such a violation of the law. It was charged, among other things, that the offices of these buying groups were "mere bookkeeping devices to induce favored prices" from suppliers. The charges were denied by the defendants. In the answer filed by one group (F.T.C. Docket No. 6889) it was asserted that the buying group "organization is a bona fide business operation," that any lower prices received are legally cost justified by the services rendered by the group to suppliers in "warehousing, advertising, selling, educating purchasers in the use of new products, and saving volume and expense of processing orders and invoices."[8] Actually, of course, a buyer charged with a violation under Section 2(f) need not justify the price differential as would be required of a seller charged with a violation of Section 2(a) of the law. If the buyer had ample reason to believe that, in the light of what he does for a seller, the latter should be able to justify the price discrimination he would probably be acquitted of the charge. Also the buyer might prove that he is functionally different from and not in competition with the discriminated purchasers, hence the discrimination would not be illegal.

Purchasing Procedure. Regardless of the method used to buy goods or the source of supply from which they are obtained, certain steps must be taken in carrying out purchasing procedure. In most kinds of wholesale enterprises this procedure can be standardized to a high degree and carried

---

[6] A case in point is the complaint by the Federal Trade Commission (F.T.C. Docket No. 7032), issued in February, 1958, charging Thermoid Co. (Trenton, N. J.), with price discrimination in favor, among others, of group buying jobbers by allowing such groups a rebate or refund rate, which amounted to 15 per cent of the purchase price in 1956, on all goods bought, while independent or nonmember wholesalers received such a rebate only on goods which they resold to other jobbers or wholesalers. Consent order to Cease and Desist was issued October 3, 1958.

[7] See, for example, Federal Trade Commission action against *Borden-Aicklen Auto Supply Co., Inc.,* and others (Docket Nos. 5766 and 5767), involving 17 jobbers who are members of Mid-South Distributors with headquarters in Memphis, Tenn., and 8 members of Cotton States, Inc., with main office at Andalusia, Ala. Order to Cease and Desist issued March 12, 1959; *Metropolitan Automotive Wholesalers Cooperative, Inc. et al.* (Docket No. 5724), New York City, with 17 jobber members. Order to Cease and Desist issued March 27, 1959; *Warehouse Distributors, Inc. et al.* (Docket No. 6837), concerning 28 Southeastern jobbers, Consent Order to Cease and Desist issued August 28, 1958; *Hunt-Marquardt, Inc. et al.* (Docket No. 6765), Consent Order to Cease and Desist against 14 New York and New England jobbers issued January 12, 1959.

[8] Answer filed January 31, 1958.

out as a routine matter by clerical employees. This does not imply that the judgment factor in buying can be eliminated, since (as previously indicated) the timing of purchases and the amounts ordered depend in part on business conditions and probable price trends. Furthermore, there are many phases of buying that cannot be routinized, as in the purchase of style goods or the selection of new items and the dropping of old ones. Nevertheless, the bulk of purchases can often be handled by subordinates following a prescribed procedure with approval of the buyers.

The basic steps in any purchasing procedure include *anticipation of need, determination of source of supply, execution of purchase order,* and *follow-up of order.* In addition, some provision must be made for the handling of *back orders and adjustments.* Each of these steps is discussed in the paragraphs that follow.

Anticipation of Demand. The first step in the purchasing procedure is anticipating the demand for merchandise. As indicated in Chapter 21, the buyer is limited in his total purchases by the merchandise budget for his department. The problem here is one of using his "open to buy" wisely by determining the specific kinds, qualities, and price lines of merchandise that are in demand at any time and the quantities of these goods that are required to satisfy the needs of the trade. By means of various systems discussed in Chapter 25, it is possible to ascertain just what goods require reordering and in what amounts. In addition, buyers constantly study the requirements of their customers through personal visits to retail stores and through "want lists," that is, lists kept of items not in stock for which customers have asked. They also study markets, watch the lines of merchandise offered by mail order houses (since their catalogs anticipate needs long in advance) and by competitors, and in other ways attempt to anticipate future needs of the trade.

Purchase Records. The next step is to decide from whom to buy the desired merchandise. This is a problem of major importance that has already been discussed in a preceding section of this chapter. It was indicated at that point that the buyer's record of past relationships with suppliers is an important source of information. In cases where a department head buys a large number of items and must choose between numerous competing sources, a record is indispensable to intelligent purchasing.

The simplest plan in use by wholesalers is an *ordinary card index of suppliers.* When this system is used, one card is made out for each vendor, showing what items can be bought from that source, terms of sale, and prices. Comments regarding past dealings are frequently written on these cards, particularly if there has been anything unusual about the relationships with a supplier. This system has the advantage of being simple and inexpensive to maintain. It is usually quite inadequate, however, because it provides no information concerning the quantities purchased, the quality of goods received, the amounts rejected, and similar items. Furthermore, this system necessitates the maintenance of a cross-index in order to determine what manufacturers produce a given article that is to be ordered.

A slightly more complex plan in use by a large number of wholesale distributors provides for a *commodity purchase record,* similar to that shown in Figure 11. Such a record shows when the goods were ordered, when received, the quantity purchased, the list price per unit, the discount

| INVOICE NUMBER | DATE INVOICE | DATE RECEIVED | QUANTITY | UNIT | LIST PRICE | COST | | | PURCHASED FROM |
						DISC'T	FRT.	NET COST	
COMMODITY			BRAND		PACK				NUMBER

FIGURE 11. Commodity Purchase Record

from list price, freight charges, net cost, and from whom the purchase was made. In some firms additional information is placed on the cards by the use of symbols to designate credit terms, method of shipment, the condition of merchandise upon delivery, and so on. This plan overcomes the disadvantages of the simple card index of suppliers, but it is relatively expensive to maintain. For this reason, many firms use this system only for fairly important commodities and rely on other information sources for items that are ordered less often or in smaller quantities.

Some firms maintain, in addition to a commodity record of purchases, a listing of purchases under the name of each supplier. This *vendor record* system provides the same type of information as the commodity purchase record. It is not generally used because of the added expense, but it frequently proves very valuable in that it furnishes at a glance a complete history of relations between buyer and seller.

The various inventory records are also exceedingly useful in making a selection of vendors, as are catalogs and price lists from manufacturers, and the other sources of information previously enumerated.

Purchase Orders and Files. The next step in purchasing procedure is the execution and handling of purchase orders. All orders should be in writing, even when first placed over the telephone or by telegram, in order to avoid mistakes and misunderstandings. They are signed by the buyer, and may also require approval of the merchandise manager. Ordinarily, the purchase order is prepared in triplicate, the ribbon copy going to the vendor, one copy to the accounting department or treasurer, so that payment may be anticipated, and one copy being retained by the buyer. When a fourth copy is prepared it is sent to the receiving department to be used when the shipment arrives, for checking purposes. An additional copy is often sent to the vendor with the request that he indicate the price at which each item ordered is accepted, and return to the purchaser as an acknowlecgment.

Considerable effort has been devoted by wholesalers and by their trade associations to develop the best form for the purchase order, one which minimizes the time and cost of clerical labor in preparing the many orders placed. An example of a standardized form developed by one trade association is presented in Figure 12.

Integrated Data Processing. A further step in simplifying the purchase order routine, along with certain other office procedures, is the concept of "integrated data processing." This is a system of *automatically* carrying out the transcription of information or data used repetitively. In the conventional purchasing procedure the same basic information regarding the item to be bought, supplier, and other details must be transcribed by a typist from a buyer's requisition. In large houses it is common for a backlog of orders to accumulate at certain times, often resulting in delays and out-of-stock conditions. Integrated data processing facilitates the placing of orders by eliminating the typing of items used repetitively on many orders. Instead, such information is stored permanently on a *punched tape* made of paper and filed in the vendor file or in the perpetual inventory file by individual items if such records are maintained. The tapes are then "read" by typewriters especially designed for the purpose, which automatically type the information on a purchase order, leaving blank only those things that must be determined individually for each order.

An illustration of a purchase order prepared by integrated data processing equipment is shown in Figure 13. In this example all the information in the shaded parts of the form was typed automatically from the "common language" tapes.

Use of integrated data processing systems is quite limited in the wholesaling field at present. In one wholesale grocery organization serving hundreds of stores in a voluntary chain, all purchasing procedures are built around such a system. Buyers are supplied with purchase orders typed *in advance* for all items handled by a given salesman. The buyer then fills

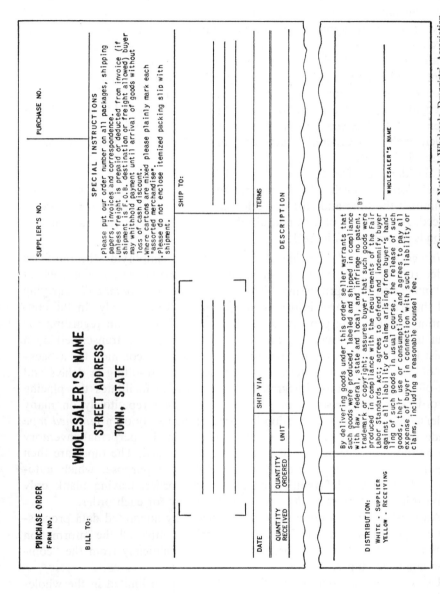

FIGURE 12. Standardized Purchase Order Form Recommended by a Trade Association of Wholesalers

Courtesy of National Wholesale Druggists' Association

in the quantity desired and prices for items ordered after a sales interview has been conducted. As a result of installing this system, the firm was able to reduce the clerical workload by one-half and at the same time eliminate backlogs and delays almost entirely.[9]

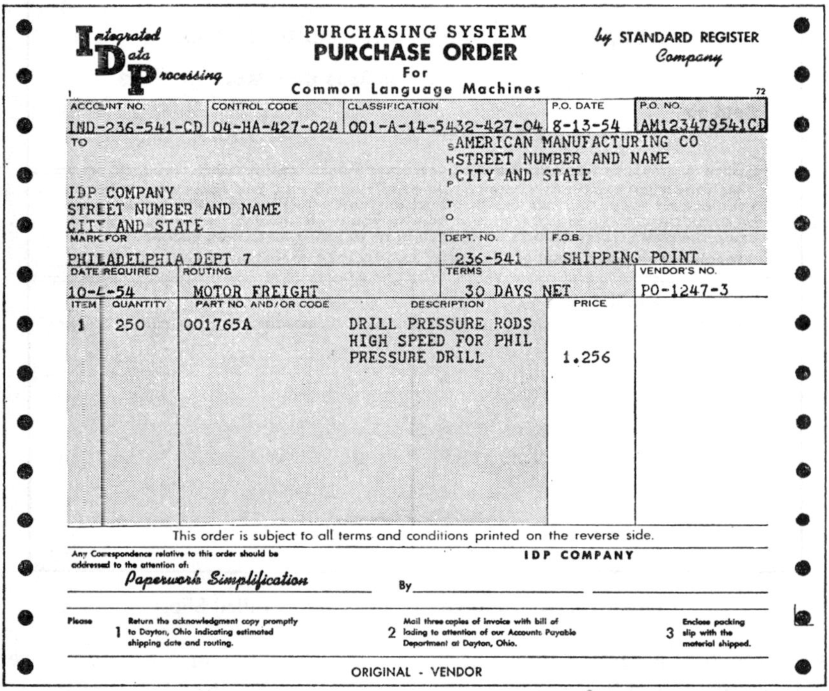

Integrated Data Processing

PURCHASING SYSTEM
PURCHASE ORDER
For
Common Language Machines

by STANDARD REGISTER Company

ACCOUNT NO.	CONTROL CODE	CLASSIFICATION	P.O. DATE	P.O. NO.
IND-236-541-CD	04-HA-427-024	001-A-14-5432-427-04	8-13-54	AM12347954lCD

TO
IDP COMPANY
STREET NUMBER AND NAME
CITY AND STATE

SHIP TO
AMERICAN MANUFACTURING CO
STREET NUMBER AND NAME
CITY AND STATE

MARK FOR	DEPT. NO.	F.O.B.
PHILADELPHIA DEPT 7	236-541	SHIPPING POINT

DATE REQUIRED	ROUTING	TERMS	VENDOR'S NO.
10-4-54	MOTOR FREIGHT	30 DAYS NET	PO-1247-3

ITEM	QUANTITY	PART NO. AND/OR CODE	DESCRIPTION	PRICE
1	250	001765A	DRILL PRESSURE RODS HIGH SPEED FOR PHIL PRESSURE DRILL	1.256

This order is subject to all terms and conditions printed on the reverse side.

Any Correspondence relative to this order should be addressed to the attention of: *Paperwork Simplification*

IDP COMPANY

By ____________

Please 1 Return the acknowledgment copy promptly to Dayton, Ohio indicating estimated shipping date and routing. 2 Mail three copies of invoice with bill of lading to attention of our Accounts Payable Department at Dayton, Ohio. 3 Enclose packing slip with the material shipped.

ORIGINAL - VENDOR

Courtesy of The Standard Register Company

FIGURE 13. Purchase Order Form Prepared Automatically by Integrated Data Processing Equipment

Purchase Order Files. Since at least one copy of each purchase order is retained by the buyer, the necessity for a proper filing method becomes apparent. The purchase order copy is usually filed by name of supplier in order to facilitate reference when the order is modified, delayed, or other changes are brought about as a result of correspondence. All such changes must be noted on it, so that when the goods are finally received it will be possible to determine whether the manufacturer has complied with the terms of the agreement; if not, the matter is made the subject for adjustment. This file is also used in following up orders delayed in transit. Such a file loses much of its value, however, unless a cross-index card file is kept by commodities.

[9] "Superfast Purchasing," *Paperwork Simplification,* published by The Standard Register Company, Dayton, Ohio, Number 40, Fourth Quarter, 1955.

Handling Customer Back Orders. Another file that must be maintained in the buyer's office relates to back orders. When an order from a customer has been assembled, it is checked in the shipping room. If it is

The City Dry Goods Company
"BACK ORDER" AND "OUT" MEMORANDUM

Kansas City, Mo.   19__

Sold to

WE VERY MUCH REGRET OUR INABILITY AT THIS TIME TO FILL THE FOLLOWING ITEMS IN YOUR RECENT PURCHASE. WE EXPECT TO RECEIVE THE ITEMS WHICH HAVE BEEN PLACED ON BACK ORDER AND SHALL FORWARD THEM TO YOU UPON ARRIVAL. WE SHALL NOT RECEIVE THE ITEMS LISTED AS OUT SOON ENOUGH TO WARRANT A FURTHER RECORD.
IF FOR ANY REASON YOU DO NOT WISH THIS BACK ORDER TO FOLLOW PLEASE ADVISE US.

Back Order				Out			
STOCK NO.	QUANTITY	DESCRIPTION	PRICE	STOCK NO	QUANTITY	DESCRIPTION	PRICE

FIGURE 14. Notice to Customer of Items Filled Short

discovered that a certain item has been *filled short* because the goods were not in stock, the shipping clerk prepares an *out slip* showing the name of the customer and the item thus missing. The buyer then orders the merchandise on the basis of this information, notifies the customer of the action (see Figure 14), and files the *out slip* in a *back order* file according to *commodity*. At the same time a separate sales order is prepared for the customer, giving the items that were *filled short,* and placed in a file according to *customers*. When the *short* item is received, the *out slips* are checked, and the *back order* is forwarded to the stock room for filling.

Follow-Up of Orders and Adjustments. One of the duties of a buyer is to follow up his purchase orders and to see to it that they are properly accepted. If acceptance of an order is not indicated or delivery of the merchandise is not forthcoming after ample time has been allowed, inquiry must be made of the vendor. In some cases the Traffic Department of the wholesaler may be called upon to trace large shipments and to expedite their movement to the warehouse. It is also the buyer's function to adjust overages and shortages in shipments and to instruct the Traffic Department what claims are to be filed with the carriers.

22

WHOLESALE PRICES AND PRICING POLICIES AND METHODS

Prices play a dominant role in American economic life. The typical businessman turns to the financial section of his daily paper to see what has happened to the prices of the commodities he handles. Buyers and sellers scan the wholesale price quotations from the major commodity exchanges and market centers in order to make important business decisions. Farmers depend upon the current market price quotations provided for them by the U. S. Department of Agriculture. So vital is the knowledge of wholesale prices to the daily routine of business that many agencies have developed to provide price information. In addition to the agricultural market price reports, the government, through its Department of Labor, collects and compiles current wholesale and retail price data on a wide range of commodities. Leading newspapers, and especially the commercial press, devote entire sections to wholesale price quotations and related information. Many private agencies and economic services issue specialized price data for clients. Telephone, telegraph, cable, radio, and television are used in a highly organized, world-wide network of price reporting. In short, all businessmen are price conscious and keenly alert to the factors influencing the prices of the wares they buy and sell.

What is the reason for this universal interest in wholesale prices? What are wholesale prices and how are they determined? What economic and business functions do they perform? These questions are examined in this chapter because they are of vital importance to all wholesaling organizations.

399

Nature and Importance of Prices. Price may be defined as the money value of a specified quantity of a given commodity or service. It emerges after, and only after, a market transaction has been consummated. Its importance lies in the fact that it is closely related to costs and profits, particularly the latter.[1] Unless a business receives sufficiently high prices for the goods it sells to cover its money outlays, it cannot survive indefinitely. Unless the prices received include also a margin, however small, of net profits, the major business incentive for the owners is absent.

Less obvious, but more fundamental to society, as a whole, is the significance of prices as a regulator of the economic system. Since prices, in the long run, must be high enough to cover costs, inclusive of profits, prices exert a strong tendency to regulate, more or less automatically, the delicate functioning of the economic mechanism. The allocation of economic resources to appropriate uses in production as well as the distribution of the resulting flow of income is largely determined, in a competitive society, by the price-profits relationship. Profits are the chief motivating force, but profits stem from prices. When prices become relatively high in one industry as compared with others because of increased demand for the products of that industry, other factors (such as cost of production) remaining unchanged, profits also tend to become higher than the prevailing level. As a consequence, enterprise, capital, and labor are attracted to that field, production increases, competition is enhanced, and prices and profits tend to fall. Conversely, when demand falls off for the products of an industry, there is a tendency for prices to drop until profits are reduced to such a point that production is discouraged.

These and other price functions interest students of wholesaling, because the prices through which this regulatory action takes place are largely wholesale prices, determined in wholesale markets. A brief review of the theory of price determination is necessary to a clear understanding of wholesale prices.

Theory of Price Determination.[2] Traditional economics explains *market price* determination in terms of the forces of supply and demand, and this explanation has become an accepted part of the common parlance of the market place. Briefly, this explanation assumes freedom of competition between thoroughly informed buyers, on the one hand, and between equally well informed sellers, on the other, no one of which is large enough to influence price by his actions. It assumes further that, in this free market, both demand and supply schedules are highly elastic and that, as a

---

[1] The economist includes normal net profits as a part of cost, whereas the accountant considers profits as a residuum over and above money outlays. From either viewpoint they form a part of price.

[2] For a detailed analysis of this subject, see George J. Stigler, *The Theory of Price* (New York: The Macmillan Co., 1946).

result, the competitive drive of buyers and sellers eventuates in an equilibrium price which clears the market. In other words, a single price emerges which satisfies all marginal producers or sellers, that is, those sellers who are responsible for the last increments of supply because their offerings would not be forthcoming if the price were lowered slightly. Sellers who operate at lower costs than the marginal ones are satisfied because they obtain an additional profit from the price that is high enough to keep the marginal sellers in the market. In addition, the marginal buyers (those unwilling to pay any more than the market price) are satisfied, as are also the buyers who are willing to pay more than the market price but do not need to do so because a sufficient supply is available at a lower price.

Few economists leave their explanation of price with this oversimplified and highly abstract statement of a most complex phenomenon. For a basic and more realistic explanation of prices use of market price analysis is made only as a starting point, and one must push far back into the recesses of the market to grasp and utilize the varied practices which prevail there in order to build a sound and adequate theory of how prices are actually determined in the rough and tumble world of business.

Thus the careful economist explains that the actual market is seldom a competitive market, but one in which the market forces range the full gamut from a large measure of competition to what approximates complete monopoly, but usually lies somewhere between the extremes. Similarly, it is pointed out that demand and supply schedules are seldom completely elastic but may range from the inelastic to the highly elastic. It is recognized that the same commodity in the same market may have, not a single price, but a number of prices prevailing at the same time, depending upon who the buyer is.

A complete discussion of price determination does not stop with the superficial forces of supply and demand but looks behind them to the more permanent forces of the utility of the goods, on the demand side, and to the variation in cost conditions which underlie supply. In the final analysis, price theory leads back to the explanation of the prices of the basic economic factors of production, the wages of labor, the rent of land, interest on capital, and profits of enterprise. Furthermore, a complete discussion of prices investigates the price system as a whole. No price is independent of a great many other prices; in fact, the price structure consists of a complex web of interacting and reacting prices, so integrated that it is difficult, if not impossible, to unravel their pattern and understand their manifold ramifications. Businessmen are constantly making potentially damaging decisions because some change in the price structure, which seems remote to their affairs, is not taken into consideration. Thus, for example, the imposition of a tax on whale oil was allowed to pass unchallenged by the automobile industry since it appeared to have no direct relationship to the normal business and price structure of that industry. It was discovered, too late, that this tax threatened to destroy the Norwegian market for American automobiles since whale oil exports to the United States constituted the chief source of dollar exchange with which automobiles were purchased by that country.

PRICE POLICIES

The foregoing brief discussion of price determination in theory provides only a general background for the task of setting prices in a wholesale enterprise. To the wholesaling executive, in fact, theoretical analyses often appear completely unrelated to pricing practices. There are several reasons for this. First, as most economists would readily admit, price theory has not yet progressed beyond a very generalized and oversimplified stage. This is not intended as a criticism, since price-making is a complex process and very difficult to synthesize into workable principles. Perhaps equally important, businessmen seldom see their own pricing problems in the same light as the theoretician. What the economist explains in terms of generalized supply and demand forces, the individual businessman sees only as isolated actions by competitors or customers. These differences do not, however, detract from the value of sound theory. They merely point up the need to analyze price policies from both theoretical and practical viewpoints.

Pricing decisions, like buying decisions, arise very frequently in the typical wholesale enterprise. Hundreds or thousands of different items must be priced, and each price quotation must be changed as conditions dictate. As a result, individual pricing decisions are usually the province of the buyers for their respective departments or merchandise lines. General guidance for these decisions is provided by certain policies laid down by management. Some of the more important types of such price policies are discussed in this section, while methods of arriving at specific prices are treated in the next section.

Distinctive Pricing Problems of the Wholesaler. A distinction should be made at the outset between *wholesale prices* and *prices charged by wholesalers*. The former term is much broader and more inclusive than the latter, and in common parlance means an entirely different thing. "Wholesale prices" in the broad sense include the prices charged in *all* wholesale transactions, covering the sales of manufacturers, farmers, and other physical-goods producers as well as those of all wholesale establishments. Indeed, the Wholesale Price Index compiled and published by the United States Bureau of Labor Statistics does not even take wholesalers' prices into account. It is based, instead, on prices quoted by manufacturers and by other physical-goods producers in "primary markets," including organized commodity exchanges and f.o.b. factory prices of manufactured products.[3] Since wholesalers' margins tend to be relatively stable, however, this index is still useful for determining trends in prices charged by them. In the discussion that follows, primary emphasis is given to the price policies of wholesalers, although the pricing problems of other wholesale enterprises are quite similar.

In contrast with manufacturers and retailers, wholesalers must contend with certain distinctive problems in arriving at proper price policies and methods. Among these may be mentioned the nature and extent of competition, frequency and magnitude of price fluctuations, influence of manufacturers' policies, and the number of items to be priced.

Nature and Extent of Competition. Active rivalry among competing sellers is characteristic of most segments of the American economy. Thus, manufacturers, wholesalers, and retailers must all be alert to the actions of other firms which serve the same markets. The competitive situation of the wholesaler is, however, distinctive in some aspects. Manufacturers can, by promoting brand names heavily, differentiate their products from others of a similar nature and thus mitigate the directness of competition in some degree. Retailers can appeal to patronage buying motives of particular customer groups, or offer special customer services, and in effect differentiate themselves from other stores. Wholesalers can use both of these techniques to some extent, but ordinarily price is a determining factor in the buying decisions of their customers. For this reason price competition can generally be said to be *more direct* and *more intense* for the wholesaler than it is on other levels of distribution.

Not only is the wholesaler faced with direct and intense competition, but he must compete with several distinct *types* of rivals. These include on the one hand, direct-selling manufacturers, functional middlemen, wholesalers in the same line of business, and wholesalers in other lines; and, on the other hand, integrated retail concerns, buying groups, and direct-buying industrial users. The nature of this competition should be clear from the analysis of the wholesaling structure and of its component parts presented in Part I of this book.

Price Fluctuations. Wholesale prices, including those charged by wholesalers, fluctuate much more frequently than do those of manufacturers or retailers, although the magnitude of the fluctuations is not usually as great. The major wholesale markets are well organized and are highly sensitive to changes in supply and demand factors. Dealers usually operate in large quantities where slight changes involve substantial amounts, and they are

---

[3] The Wholesale Price Index is described in Chapter 6 in connection with its use to adjust wholesale trade volume to a constant price basis. For a more complete statement, see "A Description of the Revised Wholesale Price Index," *Monthly Labor Review* (February, 1952), 180–87.

thus quick to react to relevant market news and information. Producers' prices, those paid at the farm or at the factory, tend to follow closely prices in the wholesale markets because the purchaser usually intends to resell the goods in a wholesale market. On the whole, fluctuations in producers' prices are less frequent but somewhat more violent than in subsequent wholesale transactions. Markets on the producers' level tend to be less well organized and many producers, especially where processing is involved in contradistinction to original production, attempt to stabilize or maintain prices on differentiated products. Wholesale prices fluctuate much more frequently than prices in retail markets. This is true because, in the latter type of market, customary and convenient prices are quite common; it is impractical to re-mark goods frequently; it is not convenient to make changes in fractional amounts; and the wider operating margins are usually adequate to absorb minor variations in the retailer's cost of goods over a short period of time. Fluctuations in retail prices are more violent, because they usually occur only after relatively important changes have taken place in wholesale prices through cumulative small changes.

Manufacturers' Policies. Most wholesalers are somewhat restricted in their price determination by the actions of their manufacturing suppliers. Manufacturers of branded merchandise often suggest or maintain resale prices, and wholesalers must conform to these prices. The importance of this factor obviously varies among different lines of trade and between states, depending on legislative provisions for price maintenance. The use of suggested prices in the determination of specific prices is discussed further in a subsequent section of this chapter. It is mentioned here merely as a general restriction within which many wholesalers must operate.

Number of Items Carried. The typical manufacturer produces a limited number of items. The price of any one item is, consequently, a matter of some importance with substantial effects on sales volume and net profits. For this reason price policies in manufacturing concerns are usually established by top management, often through a committee of executives. In contrast, the typical wholesaler carries thousands of different items. Except for certain "key" lines, the prices of individual items are not of major importance; or, at any rate, sheer numbers prevent top management from concerning themselves with individual items. This factor explains the use of various "formula" approaches to pricing for broad groups of items rather than treating the price of each item separately and distinctively. Large-scale retailers face the same situation, of course, but because of the much greater number of items generally stocked by wholesalers this factor is accentuated for them.

One Price vs. Varying Prices. A major price policy to be established by the management of a wholesale enterprise is the choice between a *one-*

price policy and a *varying-price policy*. Stated briefly, a one-price policy requires that all customers in a given class who buy in equal quantities and under similar conditions of sale be charged the same unit price. A varying-price policy, on the other hand, makes prices the subject of individual negotiation.

Of the two, the varying-price policy is much older. Since ancient times traders have haggled and bargained over prices, and in many parts of the modern world this is still true. In the United States and other industrialized nations, however, the trend has been away from this practice. Beginning in the early nineteenth century, department stores and other retailing institutions adopted one-price policies of varying degrees of strictness. The logic of a one-price policy in a retail store is apparent. Price-marking of many small items practically requires such a policy. Furthermore, the time spent in bargaining with many ultimate consumers and the mechanical difficulties, as well as the reluctance of management to delegate such authority to relatively unskilled clerks, preclude the use of varying prices. These factors are of much less significance, of course, for retailers handling such products as automobiles, electrical appliances, or furniture, and varying prices are far more common in these trades.

Wholesalers as a group have never adopted the strict one-price policy characteristic of most retail trades. One reason is that most wholesalers serve more than one class or type of customer. Distinctions in customer classes may be drawn between industrial users and retailers; between chains and independents; between stores affiliated to the wholesaler in a voluntary group, and those not so affiliated; and so on. The validity of these distinctions is subject to certain legal restrictions, as indicated below. So long as customers in each class are treated alike, a one-price policy prevails. The lines between customer classes may be difficult to define sharply, however, and this contributes to the complexity of administering such a policy.

Another major reason for the use of the varying-price policy at the wholesale level is the much greater importance of individual transactions. When goods are bought and sold in large quantities, even small differences in unit prices may loom large. Closely related to this is the very active competition characteristic of wholesale marketing. While ultimate consumers may not be aware of and concerned about small variations in prices among competing sellers, retailers and industrial users generally are. The varying-price policy permits such competition to be met and provides a greater flexibility than can be attained under a one-price policy. Then, too, wholesale prices are more sensitive to market conditions and fluctuate frequently. Hence the price charged to a given type of customer on one day may be higher or lower than that charged to a similar customer on the preceding day because of altered supply and demand factors. Because of these frequent changes, even a strict one-price policy can apply only for very limited periods of time.

Despite all of these arguments for a varying price policy, there is a definite tendency among wholesalers to adopt the one-price policy. Undoubtedly, the most important reason for this lies in the provisions of the Robinson-Patman Act of 1936. Other factors also contribute to the change, including ethical considerations, desire to keep customer good will, difficulty of controlling salesmen, and mechanical problems incident to varying prices.

The Robinson-Patman Act. This law, discussed in some detail in Chapter 15, has practically forced many wholesalers to adopt at least a nominal one-price policy. Under Section 2 of the Act, a seller is prohibited from discriminating in price between competing customers on goods of like grade and quality, where the effect may be ". . . to substantially lessen competition." Any difference in price may fall under this provision unless it can be justified in one of two ways. If the discrimination can be shown to arise from differences in the seller's costs of serving the customers in question, it may be permissible. The second method of justification is to demonstrate that a lower price was given to meet "in good faith" the competition of a rival. There is in effect a third defense; since the law applies only to price discriminations that may tend to lessen competition, such differences may also be justified if given to noncompeting customers.

The "cost savings" defense of price discriminations applies primarily (but not entirely) to *quantity discounts* granted to large buyers. When large purchases do in fact reduce costs, including those of selling, delivery, and clerical order-processing, the savings can legally be passed on to the buyer. As shown in Chapter 29, certain expenses are usually lower in relation to the selling price of an article when large quantities are sold and handled. The discount given must not *exceed* the actual cost saving, however.

Probably the most important defense of varying prices under the Robinson-Patman Act for wholesalers is that of meeting competition. The intensity of competition has already been mentioned as one of the valid reasons for a varying-price policy from an economic point of view. From this angle as well as for purposes of adherence to the law, it is essential that the competitive offer be bona fide and not merely an excuse. Many retailers will take advantage of a wholesaler's salesman if they know he is permitted to meet lower offers of competitors. In the tobacco trade, for example, it is claimed that "it is common practice among sharp-shooting retailers to play one distributor against another by falsely claiming one has quoted a lower price."[4] Meeting such spurious offers is undesirable from a

---

[4] Harry B. Patrey in collaboration with Joseph Kolodny, *Successful Methods of Wholesale Tobacco Distribution* (New York: Foresight Publications, 1957), p. 16.

managerial viewpoint as well as illegal. For obvious reasons, however, it is very difficult to distinguish between real and imaginary price competition.

Finally, it is believed to be perfectly legitimate to establish price differentials among distinct classes of customers, providing these classes are noncompetitive with one another. This permits charging one price to an industrial or institutional user and another to a retailer, since these groups are clearly not competitive. Likewise, it is apparently permissible to differentiate retailers served as members of a voluntary chain from others not so affiliated. Thus, it is common practice among wholesalers sponsoring voluntaries to serve members on a "cost-plus" basis, that is, by adding a predetermined cost factor to the wholesaler's invoice cost, while nonmembers pay somewhat higher prices determined by other means. This method is based, however, on differences in the cost of servicing the two groups since they presumably *are* competitors. By the same token, apart from cost savings and meeting competitive offers, it would not be legitimate in most cases to differentiate chains from independent retailers as customer classes.

Other Factors Favoring a One-Price Policy. Above and beyond legal restrictions, various economic factors have contributed to the trend toward a one-price policy. One of these is the ethical consideration of *fairness.* Many wholesalers describe the one-price policy as a "clean" way of doing business as opposed to the "chiseling" that arises from varying prices. Certainly, the varying-price policy invites haggling by customers and may result in unfavorable treatment to those who eschew such practices.

Another disadvantage of varying prices is the possibility of losing customer good will. When some customers are allowed to bargain for lower prices, others quickly discover the fact and resent it. Frequently, these customers are the more loyal and desirable ones, and it is preferable to keep their patronage even at the expense of losing some who insist on negotiations.

A varying-price policy usually requires that salesmen be given authority to determine prices charged their customers. Since prices are an important determinant of net profits, this is a major delegation of authority and responsibility and may be questioned on these grounds alone. Some authorities, in fact, regard it as an *abdication* rather than a *delegation.* Weaker salesmen may consistently give in to buyers, thus undermining the whole price structure.

Finally, a varying-price policy leads to mechanical difficulties in order-handling and accounting. The whole problem of maintaining records is greatly complicated by introducing an additional factor that must be carefully controlled. In many lines of trade each order must be "priced" by a clerk before shipment to a customer in order to prevent sales at unauthorized prices. The time required for this task and the chances of error are greatly increased when prices vary. Varying prices are virtually impossible when mechanical tabulating equipment is used to process orders and print invoices. One of the economies of this equipment is its automatic extension of dollar amounts (multiplying quantities by prices), which cannot very well be done if prices are changed on practically every order.

Special Price Policies. Policies must be developed by management to handle pricing of various "special" classes of sales outside of the ordinary course of business. Two important examples are *drop shipments* and *"plus business."*

While some wholesalers specialize in drop-shipping and have no warehousing facilities at all, most of them treat drop shipments as a special method of operation supplementing warehouse sales. In a drop shipment the merchandise is transported from the manufacturer or other supplier directly to the customer without passing through the wholesaler's place of business. This may be done on custom orders or on large quantities, especially carloads or truckloads. It is particularly common when goods are bulky, such as paper, metals, plumbing goods, or machinery, on which the savings achieved by eliminating handling, warehousing, and reshipment are substantial.

Because warehousing expenses are eliminated on drop shipments, wholesalers almost always reduce their prices to pass along these savings to the customer. This is perfectly legitimate so long as the price reductions do not exceed actual savings. Often, however, discounts are granted far in excess of any reasonable estimate of the savings. This happens because costs are not known accurately or because no share or an inadequate share of overhead costs (general administration, office, and the like) is allocated to the drop shipment. Competition may further reduce prices on drop shipments to the point where actual direct costs are not even covered. When this happens, the drop shipment results in an out-of-pocket loss.

The problem of "plus business" is quite similar to that of drop shipments. "Plus business" refers to business obtained from customers other than those ordinarily served and hence is regarded as "pure gravy" by the wholesaler. As with drop shipments, some wholesalers allow their enthusiasm over the increased volume to cloud their better judgment on pricing. The margin on plus business may be set at a low level merely to cover the direct costs, that is, the net additional costs incurred in getting the business. An example is the sale of electrical appliances to a residential contractor by a distributor whose regular trade consists of retailers. The appliance manufacturers have been anxious to get this type of business, partly because of the opportunity to engage in special advertising of their lines. As a result such sales have been made at extremely low prices, sometimes at acknowledged losses.

In establishing policies on drop shipments, "plus business," and other similar special cases, the wholesaler must be extremely cautious and should consider long-run effects as well as immediate gains or other benefits. Apart from the obvious folly of incurring out-of-pocket losses, special low prices tend to weaken the over-all price structure and lead to dissatisfaction on the part of customers. Those who have secured lower prices on special transactions may ask for the same prices on all their purchases. Those who have not secured the special prices will resent it and deal with the wholesaler accordingly. For these reasons, in addition to the risk of violating the Robinson-Patman Act provisions, goods sold to special classes of customers should be priced with due regard to actual costs including a fair share of overhead expenses.

METHODS OF PRICE DETERMINATION

The policies discussed in the preceding section provide general direction to the buyers or others responsible for setting prices on each item stocked by a wholesale enterprise. Within this framework, individual prices are usually determined by more or less definite formulas. While these formulas differ considerably as to details, most of them can be classified in one of two basic categories. The first is to set prices on the basis of *costs,* while the other is to adhere to *competitive* prices. These approaches underlie the pricing methods of manufacturers, retailers, and others, as well as those of wholesale enterprises. Actually, as will be apparent from the discussion that follows, the cost and competitive approaches are not mutually exclusive. No seller can ignore either his costs or competition for long. The distinction is largely a matter of which approach is *emphasized* in a particular situation.

Application of the Cost Approach. Simply stated, the cost approach sets the price of an item at its actual total cost, including a fair amount of net profit. Theoretically, it requires that the *landed cost* be first determined for each item. By this is meant the manufacturer's list price, less all relevant discounts and deductions, plus the amount of freight-in and drayage-in paid by the wholesaler. To this, a margin is added to cover the operating expenses incurred in buying, warehousing, selling, and administration, as well as a net profit. In practice the matter is not this simple. The main problem in its application is the difficulty of determining merchandise costs and operating expenses for each of the thousands of items stocked in a typical wholesale establishment. Apart from the mechanical problems and incident costs of recording and computing the necessary data, it is usually impractical to attempt to allocate operating expenses to individual items on any fair basis. Consequently, the cost approach customarily takes the form of adding a predetermined margin percentage to the average landed cost of the inventory on hand of an item at a particular time. This means that the information necessary to arrive at a price is (1) an accurate measure of landed cost and (2) a margin percentage to be applied to a group of items.

Importance of Proper Cost Determination. As implied in the preceding paragraph, intelligent pricing requires an accurate knowledge of costs incurred in obtaining the merchandise. Knowledge of merchandise costs is also important for several reasons other than price determination. Even where cost is not the main or only basis for price determination and other factors largely govern, it is important to know the cost in order to determine the gross margins that are actually obtained, or the extent of the losses that may have to be incurred on specific items. Because many wholesale prices are extremely sensitive and fluctuate from day to day, proper pricing demands keen judgment and broad knowledge of current market conditions and probable future developments.

Another important reason for determining cost accurately is that the wholesaler may wish to sell to certain customers on a *cost-plus* basis. Certain wholesalers have special classes of customers, such as large institutional users or company-owned stores of mining companies, which may desire to buy at the wholesaler's actual landed cost plus a certain fixed percentage service charge to cover operating expenses and to provide a fair profit. Some voluntary group wholesalers follow a practice of selling to retailer members on this basis. In such cases it is necessary to determine the cost accurately, by some method agreeable to the various parties involved. Parenthetically, it should be noted that the wholesaler may be in violation of the Robinson-Patman Act if the difference between the actual price arrived at on this basis and the price paid by other customers of the same general class for goods of like grade or quality cannot be justified by savings effected in the methods of sale or delivery or by the quantities in which the merchandise is sold or delivered to such purchasers. A wholesaler may also be in violation of the state unfair trade practices acts that prohibit sales below cost as defined therein.

An additional reason for ascertaining cost is that the landed cost must be known for inventory purposes in order to determine the profit or loss which has been experienced by the firm on its operations as a whole during the accounting period. A closely allied use of cost may be made for valuing inventories for income tax or other tax purposes.

Methods of Cost Determination. It is a simple matter to determine the landed cost of merchandise in a specific shipment by use of the supplier's invoice and the carrier's freight charges. It is usually difficult to know the exact cost of a given unit of merchandise in stock, however, because different lots of the same article may have been purchased at different prices. The sensitivity of many wholesale prices and their quick reaction to changes in conditions of supply and demand must be taken into account in the costing technique. Several methods may be used in determining the per-unit cost as a basis of pricing goods bought at various figures. It should be noted here that a method may sometimes be used in determining the cost for pricing purposes different from that used for inventory purposes. When different methods are used, it is primarily because of tax considerations and special provisions of the tax laws. The use of a particular cost determining method may be advantageous and satisfactory to authorities for purposes of evaluating an inventory for payment of property taxes whereas some other method may be desirable for price-setting purposes. Similarly, the use of still a different method may be favored for evaluating the inventory for determining the profit on which the amount of income tax is based.

One of the procedures used for pricing purposes is the *last purchase method.* This procedure merely uses the unit cost of the last purchase and is similar to the *last in, first out* ("lifo") method used for inventory and income tax purposes. Another is the *replacement cost method,* which disregards the actual cost of any shipment but follows instead the current market price, that is, a per-unit cost based upon the prevailing cost of a new lot of the same article that might be purchased in the customary quantities. This method requires the use of a new cost figure every time there is a change in a supplier's price regardless of whether any purchases are made at that price. A third method is that of *first in, first out* (fifo), in which the cost of the articles of each lot of merchandise is exactly the amount paid for them, so that the unit cost is the one which applies to the oldest lot. When that lot is exhausted, the unit cost of the next purchase is used. While this method is relatively simple, it requires keeping track of each purchase, and on a falling market it may not be possible to secure the higher prices warranted by the cost of the older merchandise.

The two most common methods of cost determination in use are the *weighted average* and the *weighted moving average.* In computing the cost per unit by the weighted average method, all the merchandise costs of a given item are added together *periodically* and averaged by the number of units. No distinction in pricing is made between goods of one lot and those of another for identical articles, though different prices may have been paid for them at time of purchase. The procedure is illustrated as follows: A wholesale grocer has in stock 900,000 lbs. of sugar in 100-lb. bags of 10-lb. packages, consisting of various lots, with costs indicated as follows:

Purchase	Quantity	Landed Cost per 100 lbs.	Quantity × Cost
1st	100,000 lbs.	$7.50	$ 7,500
2d	400,000 lbs.	7.69	30,760
3d	400,000 lbs.	7.72	30,880
Total	900,000 lbs.		$69,140

If the sum of the quantities multiplied by the costs ($69,140) is divided by the total quantity on hand (900,000) a *weighted average cost* of $7.68 per 100 lbs. is obtained. Under this system the cost of $7.68 is used for some time, even though subsequent purchases are made at different prices. At regular intervals a new weighted average cost is computed on the basis of the actual cost of the various lots *then* in stock. The main defect in this plan is the lag behind the current market price. When prices are rising, the weighted average, being determined at infrequent intervals, is below the market price; and the reverse is true on a falling market.

For this reason the *weighted moving average* is to be preferred. According to this plan, a new unit cost, and hence price, is determined after each purchase unless the goods are bought at the current moving average cost. The cost is computed by adding the quantities purchased at the different prices and also adding the amounts paid for each lot, and then dividing the sum of the amounts by the total number of units on hand. This procedure is illustrated as follows, again with reference to the same type of an inventory of sugar:

Date	Quantity	Landed Cost per 100 lbs.	Quantity × Cost
April 1	100,000 lbs. (on hand)	$7.50	$ 7,500
April 1	400,000 lbs. (received)	7.69	30,760
	500,000 lbs.		$38,260

$$\frac{\$38,260}{500,000} = \$7.65 \text{ (weighted moving average cost)}$$

April 16 .... Sold since April 1	300,000 lbs.		
April 17	200,000 lbs. (balance on hand)	$7.65	$15,300
April 17	400,000 lbs. (received)	7.72	30,880
	600,000 lbs.		$46,180

$$\frac{\$46,180}{600,000} = \$7.70 \text{ (weighted moving average cost)}$$

Determination of Margin To Be Added to Landed Cost. If a business is to continue in operation and yield a fair net profit to its owners, adequate gross margins must be added to landed cost in arriving at prices for the various items handled. This does not necessarily mean that each and every individual item must return any predetermined amount of net profit; indeed, many items are usually handled on very narrow margins of profit or even at a loss. To some extent this results from ignorance of expenses incurred in handling an item, due to failure to use adequate cost accounting techniques.[5] Even when costs are accurately known, margins may be limited by competition, by manufacturers' policies, or by other factors. Nevertheless, it is still true that over-all net profits are dependent on securing

[5] For a discussion of these techniques and their applications in wholesaling, see Chapter 29.

adequate gross margins on the goods handled; hence the importance of this factor in pricing.

In actuality, the margins (or markups on cost) used for pricing purposes are fairly uniform in a particular line of business and have become well established as customary trade practices. An extensive study of pricing techniques in four major wholesale trades showed that the use of "average markups" was one of the most important single methods used, both in the opinion of the buyers as well as in frequency of occurrence.[6] Such margins are commonly established on a departmental basis rather than for individual items.

Margins may be expressed as a percentage of *cost* or of *selling price*. Thus, if an item is bought for $5 and resold for $6, the gross margin is equivalent to 20 per cent of cost or 16⅔ per cent of selling price. It is generally preferable to relate gross margins to selling prices rather than cost, since this facilitates comparison of margins with operating expenses and other factors customarily determined on the basis of net sales.[7] In practice some wholesalers still use the cost base as 100 per cent because of long-established custom or for other reasons. When cost is used as the base, it should be computed as *warehouse landed cost* and after all applicable discounts and freight-and-drayage-in have been taken into account. Since this may be difficult to compute for each of several thousand items on a current basis, many buyers use invoice cost instead. The wisdom of this practice is questioned, since it means that margins must cover inward freight as well as internal operating expenses and net profit. This may be hard to do in the light of the pattern of rapidly rising freight rates in the post-World War II era.

Deviations from Normal Margins. The basic limitation of prices based on average or customary departmental margins is that they do not allow for differences in the expenses associated with different merchandise items. This may best be explained in terms of an example. Suppose that a plumbing equipment and supplies wholesaler stocks two types of water heaters, one costing $20 and the other $24. These would be included in the same department, and if departmental margins were employed, the same percentage factor would be added to both. If this margin were 33⅓ per cent of selling price, the heater costing $20 would be priced at $30 and the better-quality heater at $36. The *dollar* gross margin would thus be

[6] Aaron J. Alton, "Formation of Prices by Wholesalers in Specified Lines of Business," unpublished Ph.D. dissertation carried out under the supervision of the senior author and deposited in the library of The Ohio State University, 1956, pp. 106–10.

[7] The term "markup" is often used to designate the amount added to cost, expressed as a *percentage of cost*. Markup also differs from gross margin in that *markdowns* may affect selling prices and thus reduce margins actually achieved. In this chapter, emphasis is placed on gross margins (based on selling price) for reasons explained in the text.

20 per cent greater on the higher-priced heater than on the lower-priced one. It is doubtful, however, that the expenses incurred are correspondingly higher. Costs connected with investment in inventory might be; and perhaps somewhat greater selling effort and cost would be needed to move the more expensive item. On the other hand, physical handling expenses are likely to be about the same regardless of dollar value, and clerical and administrative expenses are likewise unrelated to product costs. As a result, the heater costing $24 should technically be marked up less, *percentagewise,* than the $20 product.

Apart from cases such as that just described, use of departmental margins can be criticized on other grounds. It is generally believed that expenses vary inversely with the *rate of stock turnover* for various items. As explained in Chapter 20, several categories of expenses decline as turnover increases, including those of storage, interest, insurance, taxes, deterioration, and obsolescence. This is as true for an individual item as it is for all goods combined. Variations in turnover should, therefore, be reflected in higher or lower margins. Rates of turnover may not be known for each item, however, and only the more obvious and gross differences are ordinarily taken into account in actual practice. There is some evidence that, although buyers are aware of the influence of turnover on costs and believe that it should be reflected in prices, measures of turnover are not often used systematically in varying margins.[8]

Again, it is known that expenses vary among items within a department because of differences in selling effort required, bulk and weight, special handling requirements, servicing needs, repackaging, special licenses needed, and a number of other factors. Due to the extreme complexity of measuring such factors accurately, they do not in practice exert much influence on margins.

Application of the Competitive Approach. Competitive pricing, stated simply, involves the setting of prices at or near those quoted by competitors for identical or very similar goods. In the study of pricing practices previously mentioned, it was found that buyers generally regard competition as the single most important factor to be considered in pricing.[9] Actually, it is difficult to separate "competition" from "typical markup or margin" as a distinct pricing method. The two are interrelated in that competition tends to determine, at least in the long run, the margin that can be achieved in a particular line of business or on a given type of merchandise. Competition also has a more direct influence on prices, since at a given time deviations from traditional margin policies must be made to meet the prices of rival firms. Especially in times of economic stress, margins may be ignored almost entirely as a result of unusually intense pressures. Conversely, when

8 Alton, *op. cit.,* p. 111.
9 *Ibid.,* p. 105.

goods are in short supply the *lack* of competition may enable a wholesale enterprise to secure abnormally wide margins. An extreme case is the practice of charging "what the traffic will bear."

Adherence to the policy of competitive pricing obviously requires some techniques for determining the prices charged by competitors. In most established lines of trade there are periodicals carrying price information, varying in detail from simple indexes of changes to systematic listings of prices quoted by producers or large distributors. An example of the latter is *Platt's Oilgram* in the petroleum industry. In addition to periodicals, *salesmen* are an important source of price information, which they obtain from customers and other trade contacts. Such information must always be interpreted carefully, however, since some customers will deliberately mislead salesmen in order to obtain concessions. Another important source of price data is found in *retail outlets,* where prices are usually marked on the goods on the shelves. A knowledge of retail gross margins permits translation of consumer prices to their wholesale equivalents. This technique is employed by wholesalers and chains in the grocery field. Miscellaneous sources of price information include reports of *purchasing agents, informal contacts of executives,* and *government price indexes.* Collection of all pertinent news, and its application to price determination, calls for considerable skill and judgment and is one of the most important responsibilities of a buyer in a wholesale enterprise.

Influence of Manufacturers' Policies. Despite their independence, wholesalers do not have complete freedom in pricing the goods they buy. An important consideration, which varies in its impact among different lines of business, is the price policy adopted by suppliers. For a number of reasons, manufacturers often seek to control resale prices on their products at both the wholesale and retail levels.

The most complete form of price control by manufacturers is known as *resale price maintenance* or "fair trade." This system, legalized by state laws beginning in the 1930's, permits the owner of a trade mark or brand name to set a minimum or a specific resale price for distributors and/or retailers. The subject is discussed in some detail in Chapter 15.

Apart from contractual resale price maintenance, manufacturers' policies may affect wholesalers' pricing methods in a number of ways. Some suppliers print suggested prices in their catalogs or price lists, but make little or no attempt to insure adherence to them. Others follow a strict policy of selective or exclusive distribution and will withdraw their line from a wholesaler who violates suggested prices. There is evidence to suggest that wholesalers' compliance varies directly with the amount of policing done by their suppliers. As might be expected, buyers are more likely to cooperate when the margins allowed by a supplier are adequate; consequently, manufacturers adopting this policy must usually establish margins at or near those customary for the wholesalers on that merchandise.[10]

Price Records. After the price has been determined, it is necessary that it be recorded in a convenient fashion. In a retail store the price is indicated in actual amounts, or by code, on the label attached to each unit of the goods, on the container in which the goods are displayed for sale, or on the shelf on which the merchandise is placed. In the wholesale field this is generally impractical for several reasons. In the first place, most sales cover fairly large quantities rather than individual units; hence there is no need for attaching the price to each unit. Second, the wholesale prices change frequently, thus marking on a unit basis involves too much expensive repricing. Third, most of the goods are stored in original packages that are not opened until orders have to be filled in amounts less than the package contains.

For these reasons the thousands of items handled by the typical wholesale house have their prices recorded in *price lists*. In making up these lists, the buyer enters in his *price book* enough information to identify the item, with its price, which may be given in symbol form. From this book an *official price list* is prepared, which may consist of a loose-leaf price book, or the data may be placed in the house catalog, which then becomes the guide for all salesmen. Price lists are, in addition, generally furnished to all salesmen. These are prepared in loose-leaf form so as to keep them up to date more readily. As changes in prices take place, they are recorded in the home office in a *price change book,* from which they are transferred to the official price list and thence to the price lists of the salesmen that are brought up to date weekly or biweekly. *Price change orders* may be issued from time to time, and, when the changes are important, salesmen may be notified by mail or wire. Only when the salesmen are constantly informed as to what goods are available and at what price is it possible to reduce *back orders,* substitutions, and quotations of unprofitable prices.

---

[10] Alton, *op. cit.,* chap. vii.

23

THE WAREHOUSING FUNCTION IN A WHOLESALE ENTERPRISE

One of the most important functions of the wholesaling system is the warehousing of goods as they pass through the channels of distribution. To the layman, indeed, the terms "wholesaling" and "warehousing" are practically synonymous. From the viewpoint of suppliers and customers, moreover, warehousing of stocks near the point of demand is regarded as a vital service of wholesale organizations. In this chapter and in the one following, warehousing activities and their management in a wholesale enterprise are discussed and analyzed.

Nature of the Warehousing Function. As indicated in subsequent sections of this chapter, warehousing methods have undergone many changes since 1940, and this process of change is continuing at an accelerating rate. In large part these changes in *methods* reflect a more basic change in the *conception* of warehousing and its purposes. The traditional concept of warehousing, until about the time of World War II, was primarily one of providing *storage* for goods carried in stock. Through the 1930's, the principal efforts of most wholesalers had been directed toward developing better selling techniques and searching for ways in which to increase sales volume. Physical operations connected with the merchandise were in a large measure neglected, with the result that, in the early 1940's, warehousing methods and practices in most firms were little different from those of 25 years previously. So long as operating expenses did not increase and so long as the established warehouse personnel assembled and delivered orders on time, wholesalers could and did continue the traditional practices.

Just prior to and during the war years, sales became less of a problem, and wholesalers were faced with the burden of handling an expanded volume of business, at the same time losing experienced warehouse employees to the armed forces or to the more remunerative "war industries." Rising labor costs, the results of inexperienced help and an increasing wage scale, ate away at profit margins at a time when it was difficult or, because of government regulation, impossible to obtain compensating price increases. These factors accelerated a trend which had its inception among more progressive wholesalers some years before—a trend emphasizing the *movement* of goods as the principal warehouse function rather than *storage* —a trend which closely connected warehousing operations with the buying and selling activities of the firm. As a direct outgrowth of the increased emphasis on movement of goods through the warehouse rather than a static holding of goods, it was recognized that *all* of the physical handling activities involved in buying, storing, and selling goods are integral parts of warehousing. This implies that all such activities—including receiving, internal movement, storage, protection, order assembly, packing, shipping, and related operations—should be planned and managed as an integrated whole. Some materials-handling authorities refer to this concept as "automated" warehousing.

Technological progress in materials-handling machines and equipment has played a large part in the development of the modern concept of warehousing. Some of the more important changes in methods and equipment, discussed in more detail later in this chapter and in the next, include: (1) the use of one-story warehouses in which the movement of goods is horizontal rather than vertical; (2) emphasis on "turnover operation," which calls for buying with reference to minimum inventory levels rather than speculative opportunities, and determining markups with reference to expense ratios rather than taking what the market will bear; (3) the use of skids and pallets in handling unit loads of merchandise by mechanical methods wherever practicable; and (4) the use of an assembly line technique of order-filling that is correlated with sales procedure.

While these are the common ingredients of what is called "streamlined warehouse operation," it should not be inferred that all of these factors must be present in order to obtain the advantages of improved handling. In many cases one-story buildings are not feasible because of conflicting locational needs; or the use of certain types of handling machinery may not be applicable because of the nature of the goods being warehoused. Even in these cases, the basic concept of a *flow* of merchandise through the warehouse should be employed, with whatever modifications in its application that may be necessary.

ELEMENTS OF THE WAREHOUSING PROCESS

Many factors affect the warehousing methods that are and should be used in a wholesale enterprise. Among these are certain *characteristics of the goods* being handled, including size, weight, value, and perishability; *characteristics of the market* being served, especially in terms of the number of suppliers and customers and the frequency with which goods are bought and sold; and the *size of the enterprise* itself. Each warehousing situation must, therefore, be analyzed with reference to these and other pertinent factors. Even before this can be done, intelligent planning requires that management: (1) recognize the importance of warehousing; (2) appreciate the benefits to be obtained by proper methods; (3) understand the basic sequence of warehousing activities; and (4) be aware of the major problems to be resolved. These prerequisites are common to all warehousing, whether it is performed by a wholesaler, a manufacturer, or a retailer, and regardless of the kind of business or its size.

Importance of Warehousing. The importance of warehousing in a wholesale enterprise can be measured in at least two ways: (1) the costs incurred in performing the function, and (2) the magnitude of the investment in inventory which is directly affected by warehousing.

According to Census and trade association data, expenses connected with warehousing represent 35 to 40 per cent of total operating expenses for most kinds of wholesalers. This includes the costs of occupancy and of delivery as well as direct expenses of warehouse operation. Warehousing costs are just as important, if not more so, in wholesale establishments operated by manufacturers and retailers.

Not only are warehousing expenses of substantial absolute and relative magnitude, but they are in many respects *more subject to control and possible reduction* through careful management than are other classes of expense. Warehousing activities are carried on within the wholesale establishment; are subject to continuous supervision; and are more susceptible to quantitative measurement than are, for example, selling or buying operations. Furthermore, there is constant pressure for lower warehousing costs from a variety of sources, including integrated wholesaling organizations as well as other wholesalers. Especially in older wholesale companies, it is common to find that the greatest opportunities for reducing total expenses are in the warehouse.

Warehousing has a direct bearing on the effectiveness with which capital is utilized in merchandise inventories. When warehousing techniques are inefficient, inventory turnover is likely to be sluggish; obsolete goods accumulate; and excessive damage and deterioration occur. When warehousing is planned, organized, and controlled systematically, on the other hand, turnover is increased, stocks are fresh, and the whole tempo of operations is speeded up. Because merchandise inventory is usually the most important single asset of the wholesale enterprise, warehousing has a significant indirect effect on net profits in addition to its direct effect on operating expenses.

Advantages of Proper Warehousing. In view of the importance of warehousing in wholesale establishments, the benefits or advantages derived from adhering to proper warehousing principles and procedures must be recognized. Good warehouse arrangement provides the basis for a location file covering all merchandise carried in stock, so that the location of any of the thousands of merchandise items can be determined at once. Not only can the assigned location be determined but, in a properly operated concern, the right merchandise actually is in the correct location at all times, thus keeping "outs" and "shorts" on the order assembly line to a minimum.

A second benefit of good warehousing is that it facilitates a logical classification of merchandise into departments for control purposes. Third, proper warehouse operation provides for a layout of merchandise that enhances speed and efficiency in filling orders. Fourth, the physical condition and the arrangement of stock have a direct bearing on the facility with which stock records controlling merchandise movements are kept. A fifth advantage to be gained from proper warehousing is a favorable effect on total operating costs. This may be brought about in a number of ways. Use of modern handling methods reduces the labor expense in warehouse operation. A clean and orderly arrangement reduces insurance and maintenance costs, and a proper rotation of stocks keeps losses from obsolescence and deterioration to a minimum. An additional benefit is that a well-ordered warehouse contributes to a higher level of morale among the employees, reduces injuries, and enhances the productivity of labor and equipment. Finally, proper warehousing contributes to the maintenance of good relationships with customers, since orders are filled promptly and with a minimum of "outs."

Warehousing Activities. The work of the warehouse is the responsibility of the warehouse superintendent who, as was pointed out in Chapter 19, is usually in charge of the operations division of the organization. Working under the superintendent are such employees as receiving clerks, car unloaders, porters, handling equipment operators, elevator operators, stockmen, order assemblers, shipping clerks, dray loaders, janitors, and watchmen.

Warehousing activities include all operations that are common to service wholesalers, retailer-owned warehouses, chain store warehouses, and manufacturers' sales branches with stocks. These activities can be thought of as an integrated sequence of operations, briefly discussed below:

1. Warehouse operations begin when the goods arrive at the warehouse. Certain aspects of receiving having to do with checking for identity with purchase orders, checking for quality and quantity, and so on, are part of the buying function. These activities may or may not be carried on under the jurisdiction of the warehouse superintendent as indicated in a later part of this chapter. Regardless of the type of receiving system utilized, there are certain physical aspects that necessarily constitute a warehousing operation. These have to do with the *unloading of cars or drays* at the sidings or receiving platforms and the unpacking or uncrating of certain types of shipments.

2. By some means or other, after shipments have been unloaded or accepted from carriers, they must be moved from the unloading areas and *placed in storage in assigned locations.* This may be done by manual handling or by various mechanical or semimechanical methods discussed in a later section of this chapter.

3. A substantial portion of the goods that are bulky and that are purchased in large quantities is usually kept in reserve stocks not readily accessible to order assemblers. The third step then involves *bringing merchandise from the reserves to the forward stocks,* as the goods on the order assembly lines become depleted. Again, this operation may be performed by manual or by mechanical methods.

4. *Assembly of order* is the fourth step in the movement of goods through the warehouse. Since most retailers or other customers buy in small quantities, involving at the minimum a broken case lot and at the maximum only a few cases of a single item, there is usually no alternative to manual handling of goods in fairly small quantities. Various semimechanical devices can be utilized, however, in speeding up this process while at the same time minimizing the amount of labor cost. A part of this phase of the operation involves checking of the order after final assembly.

5. In lines of business where goods are ordered in small quantities, as in the drug trade or in lines where much of the merchandise is packed by the manufacturer in small containers as in the hardware field, all or part of the assembled order goes to the *packing* room. Here packers select shipping cartons to accommodate the loose items, giving attention to weight distribution throughout the container, the fragile character of some items, and the strength of the container.

6. After being checked and packed, the merchandise goes to the *shipping* department and is delivered to customers. Cartons must be stenciled, tagged, or crayon-marked if delivery is to be effected by a common carrier.

If the wholesaler has his own delivery system, it may be necessary to mark only the cartons packed in the packing room.

In addition to these activities relating to the movement of goods, the warehouse superintendent is also responsible for the cleanliness and the general condition of the stock. He is charged with the maintenance of the building and of the equipment used in the warehouse. He must see to it that all goods are stored in accordance with sound warehousing principles, and he must re-examine the merchandise layout and operating methods from time to time with a view to effecting economies and speeding up operations.

Major Problems To Be Resolved. In planning the warehouse operations of a new enterprise, or in evaluating those of an established concern, four major problems must be resolved. First, the proper *type of warehouse building* must be selected or constructed, giving attention to location factors as well as to the handling methods to be used in it. Second, the *layout* of the warehouse must be designed so as to facilitate efficient operation. Third, *methods and equipment* must be selected for each of the major warehousing activities outlined briefly in the preceding section. Fourth, *controls and records* must be devised so as to maintain proper levels of inventory, minimize pilferage and deterioration, and provide a basis for evaluating the performance of warehouse employees.

In the remainder of this chapter attention is given to the first two items, dealing with building and layout, and to the third and fourth points insofar as they apply to receiving, internal distribution, and storage of goods. In the next chapter, methods, equipment, and control systems as applied to order assembly, packing, and shipping are analyzed. The closely related subject of inventory control is treated in Chapter 25.

THE WAREHOUSE BUILDING

One of the first problems to arise in the establishment of a new wholesale enterprise is the design and construction of the warehouse building. As indicated in previous chapters, this decision hinges in part on factors of location and financing. The warehouse is, however, more than just a place in which to store goods. Its design has an important bearing on the merchandise handling methods used, and should be conceived with a view toward the most efficient possible operation.

General Type of Building. Basically there are two types of warehouses in use by the wholesalers in lines of business requiring a large amount of storage space. These consist of (1) the older and more familiar multistory warehouses designed for vertical storage, and (2) the newer one-story buildings that involve horizontal storage of merchandise. As a result of the tendency to cluster wholesaling businesses in a concentrated area, the

FIGURE 15. The Old Multistory Building of Hibbard, Spencer, Bartlett & Co., Located in the Center of Chicago

FIGURE 16. The New One-Story Building of Hibbard, Spencer, Bartlett & Co., Outside the City of Chicago

vertical warehouse has predominated in the regular jobbing lines. Since the middle 1930's, however, there has been a marked trend toward the single-story type, a trend that has been greatly accentuated by the experience of government warehousing operations during World War II when speed in the mass handling of equipment and supplies was a prime essential and when great experimental developments in horizontal handling methods by mechanical means could be undertaken without regard to cost. The advantages of horizontal handling of some types of products have become more apparent to many progressive wholesalers, with the result that numerous new buildings are being located in outlying areas where the ground cost permits the construction of a type of warehouse in which these advantageous features may be incorporated (see Figures 15 and 16).

The extent of the shift to one-story warehouses is indicated by Census data on the subject, which show that over half (55.3 per cent) of all warehouse space occupied by wholesalers in 1954 was in single-story buildings.[1] Since no such information was collected for earlier years, it is not possible to make any accurate comparisons. It is known, however, that prior to 1940 most wholesalers of any substantial size occupied multistory structures. Use of one-story buildings is of greatest relative importance in lines of trade handling bulky commodities, since opportunities for savings in handling costs are greater. Thus, the highest proportion of one-story warehouse space in 1954 was found among beer and ale distributors (83.6 per cent), followed by automotive wholesalers (66.6 per cent) and industrial machinery and equipment wholesalers (65.1 per cent). At the opposite end of the scale, for the above-mentioned reason or because of special circumstances peculiar to a given line of trade, one-story buildings were of *least* importance among general line dry goods wholesalers (14.8 per cent), general line wholesale druggists (21.0 per cent), and clothing, furnishings, and footwear distributors (26.7 per cent).

Advantages of One-Story Buildings. Several factors account for the shift to one-story warehouse buildings, which has taken place among established firms as well as newer enterprises. The most important advantages are a *reduction in operating expenses* and *lower construction costs,* the former being by far the most significant.

Operating economies in a one-story building cut across the entire warehousing process. In receiving, it is possible to have railroad spurs and truck docks inside the building, with unloading surfaces on exactly the same level as the floor of the warehouse. This makes possible the use of various types of handling equipment for unloading and moving goods into stock which would be very difficult, if not impossible, in a multistory warehouse. Loss of time due to waiting for elevators is eliminated. Super-

[1] *1954 Census of Business, Wholesale Trade, Warehouse and Cold Storage Space,* Bulletin W–2–5 (Washington, D. C.: Government Printing Office, 1957), Table 5A.

vision is generally easier and greater flexibility can be attained by shifting warehousemen from one task to another as needed. For these reasons labor costs are almost invariably lower in the one-story warehouse, in some cases as much as 50 per cent less for the same volume of business.

Basic construction costs per square foot of floor space do not differ greatly as between one-story and multistory buildings. The total cost of the building for a given volume of business is likely to be lower when it is single-story, however, for several reasons. Most important, the percentage of total space usable for storage is higher because of the elimination of elevators, stairwells, chutes, and other means for vertical movement of goods and people. In multistory buildings such nonoperating area occupies from 10 per cent to as much as 20 per cent of total space.

Construction costs may also be lowered in a one-story building by virtue of the fact that such buildings are usually fire *resistant* rather than fully *fireproof*. Furthermore, it is not necessary to excavate for a basement beneath a one-story building and walls are of lighter-weight construction since they support only the roof. Thus, the total investment needed for a given volume of business is almost certain to be less in a single-story structure.

Not only are construction costs lower, but space can be made *more flexible* in a one-story warehouse. To meet an emergency need for a large amount of space to care for an incoming shipment, it is not necessary to transfer merchandise to different floors to make the space, nor to resort to the alternative of storing the new shipment in surplus space on a number of different floors. Space flexibility made possible by the single-story building simplifies departmental layout and facilitates order-handling. The arrangement of stock on one floor makes it possible to use a "once-around, assembly line" method of filling orders. Training periods to familiarize order clerks with the stock and its location on several floors are shortened and clerical work is reduced by obviating the necessity for the preparation of extra order copies for each floor.

Limitations of One-Story Building. The one-story building is not to be considered as a panacea for all the warehousing problems of the wholesaler. The operating advantages of horizontal handling methods must be carefully weighed against location factors, and the original cost, maintenance cost, and depreciation cost of power equipment for materials handling must be compared with that of the operating equipment required in a vertical warehouse. It must not be forgotten that newer handling methods can be incorporated to some degree in the older type of multistory building and that, if other factors such as have been previously enumerated make a central location essential, high ground costs and the difficulty of securing adequate land in an established wholesaling district probably prohibit the construction of a large one-story building. Even if an outlying location is feasible, the advantages of horizontal handling can be realized to a substantial degree only where operations are on a fairly large scale, where very large quantities of the same kind of merchandise are handled, and where the merchandise is heavy or bulky relative to its value with the result that storage and handling costs become an important part of total operating expenses. There is every indication that large service wholesalers in such lines as hardware or groceries will make increasing use of one-story buildings in outlying locations, whereas small firms, or those engaged in lines of business where buyers visit the market to compare style and quality, or limited-service organizations that do not have a sales force or delivery facilities, may derive many more advantages from a location in an established central wholesale district than they could ever hope to gain from a streamlined one-story building.

WAREHOUSE LAYOUT

Once the general type of building has been chosen, its interior space must be laid out and apportioned among the various phases of warehousing activity. There are two aspects of this problem: (1) the over-all layout pattern and (2) the location of specific merchandise items within the order assembly area which comprises the major part of most warehouses. General layout patterns are discussed in this section, while *merchandise* layout is reserved for treatment in connection with order handling methods discussed in the following chapter.

Approach to Layout Planning. The objective of layout planning in a wholesale warehouse is to facilitate speed and economy in handling operations. Just how this is achieved will depend on a great many circumstances, but there are a few general rules that are of value.

The layout should be so designed that goods, in passing through the warehouse, move from one step in the sequence to the next with a minimum of back-tracking. The reason for this is that handling expenses vary directly with the *distance* that a given physical volume of merchandise must be moved. Hence, to minimize costs, it is necessary to minimize movement distance. A straight-line layout in which goods pass from receiving to reserve stocks to active stocks to packing and shipping is probably ideal from this point of view. Depending on the shape of the building, however, it may be necessary to bend the line or even to follow a "loop" pattern.

Another general rule is that there should be a distinct *separation* of the various steps in the handling sequence. A common violation of this rule is the combined receiving-shipping area found in many warehouses. When these activities are conducted in the same part of the building, the result is almost inevitably confusion and delays. Trucks must wait for access to the docks and warehouse employees "bump into each other." Preferably, receiving and shipping—which are the beginning and end of the handling sequence—should be located at opposite ends or sides of the warehouse.

Layout planning can be accomplished in large part with scale drawings or 3-dimensional models prior to actual construction. A useful technique in analyzing alternative layout plans is the *flow process chart* widely used in manufacturing plant layout. A simple form which can be used in flow process analysis is illustrated in Figure 17. This form summarizes the

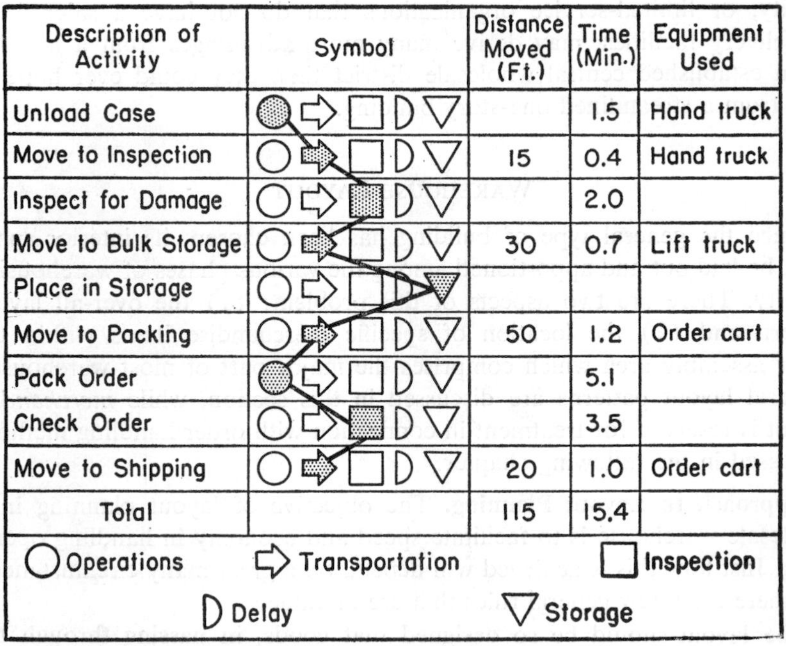

Description of Activity	Symbol	Distance Moved (Ft.)	Time (Min.)	Equipment Used
Unload Case	◉⇨☐D▽		1.5	Hand truck
Move to Inspection	○⇨☐D▽	15	0.4	Hand truck
Inspect for Damage	○⇨▨D▽		2.0	
Move to Bulk Storage	○⇨☐D▽	30	0.7	Lift truck
Place in Storage	○⇨☐D▼			
Move to Packing	○⇨☐D▽	50	1.2	Order cart
Pack Order	◉⇨☐D▽		5.1	
Check Order	○⇨▨D▽		3.5	
Move to Shipping	○⇨☐D▽	20	1.0	Order cart
Total		115	15.4	

○ Operations   ⇨ Transportation   ☐ Inspection
D Delay   ▽ Storage

FIGURE 17. Illustration of Flow Process Chart in Analyzing Warehouse Layouts or Methods

operations, distance, and time required for a handling procedure, as determined from direct observation or from a drawing or model of a proposed new method. By comparing the time, distance, and equipment involved in alternative layouts, it is possible to determine the most efficient to be adopted.

General Layout Patterns. The details of warehouse arrangement vary considerably even among progressive wholesalers in the same lines of business, but certain general similarities among concerns in all lines may be noted, which depend largely upon the nature of the building. In high multi-story buildings, which occupy a very small amount of ground space, the dimensions of any of the floors are usually not large enough to accommodate a complete selection of reasonable quantities of all items carried in stock. In such houses order assembly lines are not generally used. The merchandise is arranged on the various floors according to similarity of items, weight, bulk, frequency of sale, and other such factors to be discussed in the next chapter. Merchandise items for customer orders may be assembled simultaneously on all floors and conveyed to a main order assembly or packing area on the ground floor.

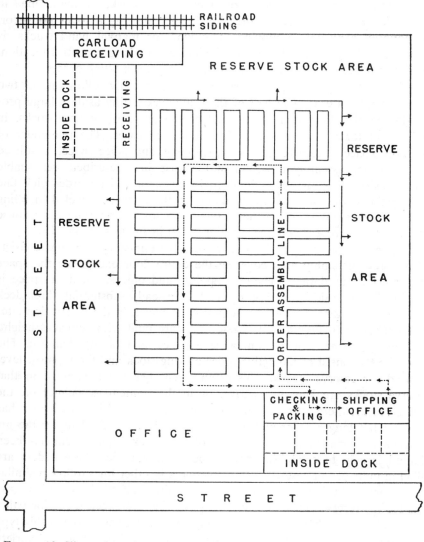

FIGURE 18. Illustration of a Complete Assembly Line Type of Plan for a One-Story Drug Warehouse

In multistory buildings of large floor dimensions and in one-story buildings, progressive wholesalers set aside part of the usable space for an order assembly area and another part of the building space for reserve stocks. In the multistory buildings the ground floor is usually devoted to office space, receiving, checking, packing, and shipping activities. One or more of the lower floors above the ground level constitute the order assembly line, and the upper floors are utilized for reserve stocks of full case goods, frequently stored on skids or pallets. Suitable quantities of all merchandise items, in full cases or in open-shelf stock, are maintained in the order assembly area. An order pick line, utilizing a roller conveyor, a monorail conveyor, a moving "tow-line," or manual hand trucks, is brought to the goods, rather than bringing the goods to a central location. This minimizes the distance traveled by employees in filling orders.

Wholesalers operating one-story warehouses usually follow one of two basic layout patterns. The first of these involves setting aside a large proportion of the floor area for the detached storage of reserve stocks, in pallet unit loads or in stacks of individual full cases. The remainder of the floor space, except for receiving, shipping, and office space, is utilized for an order assembly area. As in the case just described, reasonable quantities of all items are maintained in this area and an order pick line is brought to the merchandise to minimize the distance traveled in filling orders. Two plans of this general type, one for a wholesale drug house and one for a grocery concern, are illustrated in Figures 18 and 19.

The second basic type of layout pattern for one-story buildings consists of an order assembly area covering the entire floor except for the space that must be used for receiving, shipping, and offices. No floor space is specifically set aside for reserve stocks. Instead, substantial three-deck racks are used throughout the warehouse, as shown in the illustration later in this chapter in Figure 21b. These racks are built with sufficient height, so that each level can accommodate a pallet load of merchandise. The lower levels consist of the active order picking stock and the topmost level is used for reserve stocks. This arrangement has the advantage in that reserve stocks are kept just above, or in the immediate vicinity of, the active stocks, thereby facilitating inventory and replenishment; it also has a somewhat longer order pick line than would be required under the arrangement discussed above. The use of this stock arrangement has been limited largely to establishments in the grocery trade where orders are filled in units of full cases. A few wholesalers in other lines follow a similar plan, however, using the open space above the shelf stock of broken case lots for the reserve stocks of such items and the three-deck racks for pallet unit loads of merchandise that is usually sold in full cases. When this type of layout pattern is established, an order pick line of the "towline" variety normally circulates through the entire floor area.

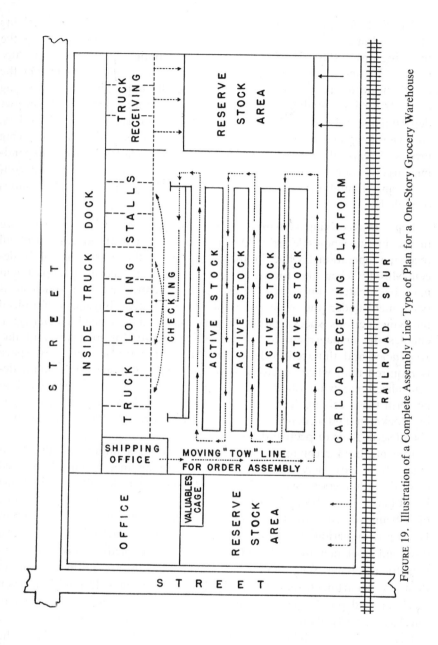

FIGURE 19. Illustration of a Complete Assembly Line Type of Plan for a One-Story Grocery Warehouse

RECEIVING

The first step in the sequence of warehousing activities is the receiving of goods bought from suppliers. The specific activities that make up the receiving process consist of (1) accepting incoming shipments from suppliers, (2) accepting goods returned by customers, (3) transporting the merchandise to the receiving room or area, (4) unpacking, (5) checking contents for both quality and amount, (6) distributing goods to the proper departments and floors, (7) handling invoices and returned goods orders, and (8) keeping receiving records. The manner in which the receiving process is carried on varies considerably among wholesale firms, depending largely upon the characteristics of the merchandise, size of the concern, and limitations which may be imposed by the physical facilities occupied.

Types of Receiving Systems. Two general types of receiving systems are in use in the wholesale field. One provides for centralized control of all receiving operations, while in the operation of the other control is decentralized. When the former is used, a separate receiving department may be created; but when receiving is decentralized, the function is performed under the supervision of the respective buyers. Centralized receiving permits specialization in personnel and enhanced efficiency; it enables the management to allocate responsibility for mistakes and discrepancies and thus reduce leaks to a minimum; furthermore, less space is required than when receiving is decentralized. On the other hand, decentralized receiving obviates the necessity for a separate personnel to perform the receiving function; the work can be done in their spare time by stockmen and order-fillers who may be more familiar with the merchandise in their respective departments.

Decentralized receiving is subject, however, to a number of disadvantages. It is extremely difficult to keep incoming merchandise separated from the other goods on the floor and to prevent order-fillers from using it until after it has been checked. More space is devoted to receiving, some of it being set aside for the purpose in each department or on each floor. During rush periods incoming goods may remain unchecked for several days and stockmen and order-fillers may be so occupied as to require extra help for receiving. When goods in a single shipment are destined for more than one department, difficulties arise in checking them. In addition, when receiving and purchasing are combined and checkers have easy access to purchase records, there is a tendency to be lax in checking the goods.

Decentralized receiving, nevertheless, is essential or advisable when the goods are so technical that the average clerk in the receiving department cannot properly identify them; when the goods are bulky and extra handling must be eliminated; when incoming merchandise is received largely during dull seasons so that idle stockmen can be used to advantage; or when the volume of business is too small to justify a separate receiving personnel.

Regardless of whether a centralized or decentralized system is used, there is a certain amount of receiving that must be done in a central place near the unloading platforms. This includes the acceptance of incoming shipments, the counting of shipping packages or containers, and inspection for visible damage as evidenced by "bad order" shipments. These activities must be completed prerequisite to the signing of a receipt for the carrier or for the truck driver of the supplier.

Checking Incoming Merchandise. After merchandise is received and placed into storage in the warehouse, the identity of each individual shipment may be lost. It is, therefore, essential that the checking of each shipment be done as soon as possible after it is accepted. It is usually impossible to check each shipment immediately, because receipts of l.c.l. shipments tend to be bunched in the early hours of the day. To avoid confusion and mixing of shipments, it is advisable to allot a definite amount of space for each shipment, through the use of bins when practicable, or by laying out the floor space in systematically numbered squares, each square providing space for a single shipment.

In checking shipments, attention must always be given to three considerations and, frequently, to a fourth. First, to prevent substitution on the part of suppliers, the goods must be checked for identity, as evidenced by a careful description, with what has been ordered. Second, the quantity of merchandise in the shipment must be definitely determined to insure that the proper amount is paid to the supplier. Third, the condition of the goods must be examined to determine if there is any concealed damage that was not apparent when the shipment was accepted. These factors are checked by the regular checking personnel, by one of three general methods in common use by wholesalers: the invoice check, the complete blind check, and the partial blind check.

In addition, some kinds of goods must be checked carefully for quality. This is a merchandising function and should be handled by the buyer or his assistant rather than by the checker. When a separate check of this kind is required, it should be made coincident with the quantity check, if practicable, and at least before the goods are placed with the regular stock. It is obviously impractical to examine every piece of merchandise in the shipment unless the goods are of a very high unit value. The usual procedure, therefore, is to examine various items selected at random from the shipment.

Checking Against the Invoice. In checking incoming goods against the invoice, the following procedure is common. When the invoice is received by the buyer who placed the order, he checks the items thereon against his copy of the purchase order to note discrepancies, if any. He then places the invoice number on his order copy and the order number on the invoice, so as to connect and identify the two forms.

The invoice is then kept either by the buyer or else in the receiving room until the goods arrive, when they are checked against it in order to determine whether the items stated on it have actually been received and are in good condition. It then constitutes the receiving report and is sent, together with the freight bill, to the buyer, who approves it, if satisfactory, and forwards the two documents to the accounting department.

The use of this method makes it easy for the checker to identify an item and the quantity. It is quick and economical and, if an apparent discrepancy is found, the goods are rechecked immediately, thus insuring against unwarranted claims. At the same time checking by this method is liable to be done carelessly and haphazardly. Having an invoice before him, the checker may mark the amounts as correct without carefully counting each item; he is thus apt to check from the invoice rather than from the merchandise. In addition, invoices may be mislaid or late in arriving; in such cases blind checking must be resorted to or else the receiving room will be clogged. Finally, invoices are frequently mutilated beyond recognition in the checking room.

The Complete Blind Check. In using the complete blind check system, the checker lists the item and quantity as called off by another person, known as the caller, on a form designated as the receiving slip or ticket (see Figure 20). When checking is completed, this form is sent to the buyer where it is compared with a copy of the purchase order or the invoice. Where there is disagreement, a recount is indicated.

In some large firms the receiving report is prepared in quadruplicate.[2] One copy is sent directly from the receiving department to the stock record department. The original and two copies accompany the goods to the appropriate goods storage department. The goods storage department indorses the original and one copy, returns the original to the receiving department for filing, sends a copy to the stock record department, and files the unindorsed copy. The stock record department enters the goods in inventory after receipt of two copies which are in agreement and sends one copy to the buyer. The buyer then makes up a purchase file consisting of the invoice, the purchase order, and a copy of the receiving report. This file is then sent to the accounting department for auditing and payment. An important feature of this plan is that the operations of each work station are checked and reported on by one or more of the other stations.

2 See John R. Bromell, *Effective Use of Wholesale Drug Warehouses,* U. S. Department of Commerce, Industrial Series No. 68 (Washington, D. C.: Government Printing Office, 1947), pp. 32–35.

Receiving Ticket

THE ELECTRICAL WHOLESALE CO.
INDIANAPOLIS, INDIANA

Date_____

Order No._____

*The Following Material Has Been Received Via*_____ *Charges $*_____

*From*_____

COUNT	CAT. NO.	NAME OF MATERIAL	REMARKS

Material described above received in good order_____ Signed_____
                                                    Date   *Receiving Clerk*
*Via*_____ *Charges, $*_____ Cases_____Cartons_____Crates_____
                                    Bags_____Pkgs._____Bbls._____

FIGURE 20. Receiving Slip, Ticket, or Report

The blind check system is the most accurate method of checking, neither checker nor caller knowing what goods are expected or in what amounts. It also withholds from the checker any knowledge of the costs of the goods, as invoices are kept in the buyer's office until sent to the accounts payable division. The system is very expensive, however, since it consumes much time in preparing a complete record of the contents. The items may not be easily identifiable, and the checker may be unable to determine the exact description of the goods. Moreover, when a packing slip is enclosed with the shipment, the purpose of this method is defeated, unless a complicated system of multiple checks, similar to that just described, is employed.

The Partial Blind Check. A third method of checking incoming goods consists in a combination of the invoice check and the blind check system. Under this plan itemized invoices with quantities omitted are furnished to the checkers. When the goods are checked, the quantity of each item is inserted in the appropriate space provided for the purpose. The receiving invoice goes through the same routine as the receiving slips.

An invoice with the quantity of each item left blank may usually be secured from suppliers by special request on the purchase order form; otherwise, the items are listed in the office on a separate sheet of paper. This plan of checking combines the advantages of both the preceding systems. A partial blind check is much more accurate but not quite as speedy as the invoice check. On the other hand, it is slightly less accurate than the complete blind check, but it is much faster and more economical in operation.

Receiving Records. It is necessary that a number of records be prepared and kept by the receiving personnel in the course of normal operations. The number and type of these records vary according to size of the concern, physical facilities utilized, and type of receiving and checking systems in use. The most important receiving records in use by wholesalers are the receiving register, the receiving report, the daily receiving register, and the floor record.

Receiving Register. Regardless of whether a centralized or decentralized receiving system is used, receiving registers are generally kept by the personnel accepting shipments. This register usually provides the following information: receiving serial number, date or time of arrival, name of shipper, name of carrier, number of packages, weight, freight charges, apparent condition of shipment, and initials of the person accepting the shipment. When a shipment is accepted and entered in the register, the receiving number is stamped or written on the carrier's or vendor's receipt and on the invoice or receiving report. Thereafter the shipment is identified by that number only. This procedure facilitates tracing of disputed shipments, for without it the identity of any shipment is difficult to determine.

Receiving Report. Use of the receiving report has already been discussed in connection with the description of the blind check system (see Figure 20). The usual form of the receiving report or receiving ticket provides for the recording of the following information: number of the report, time of arrival of shipment, number or name of the checker and caller, name of the supplier, the transportation agency, the quantity and description of each item of merchandise, and the condition of the goods.

Daily Receiving Ledger. If receiving is decentralized and shipments are checked against invoices, itemized receiving reports are unnecessary. In such cases a daily receiving ledger may be maintained by all departments to show the date of the invoice, name of the shipper, transportation agency, date of the receipt of goods, and the name of the person checking the shipment.

Floor Record. If merchandise is received on more than one floor, a floor record becomes a necessity. All goods must be recorded as soon as they are removed from the elevator or other conveyor in order to determine whether the merchandise received at the unloading platform reached the proper receiving area. If part or all of a shipment is misplaced, it is possible to locate it immediately by examining the records kept for each floor.

Disposition of Incoming Merchandise. Most wholesalers lack the facilities to store all goods in regularly assigned departmental space in the order-picking area. Reserve stocks of some goods are frequently maintained on upper floors, in nearby rented buildings, or in public warehouse space. Bulky merchandise, large quantity purchases motivated by favorable price offerings, and seasonal merchandise purchased ahead of the selling season are typical of incoming shipments in this category. Some goods may, in fact, be moved directly from receiving to the shipping area. In the industrial supply line, for example, merchandise ordered especially for a particular customer is handled in this way and is known as a "dock sale." Extremely fast-moving goods may be treated in similar fashion in the grocery and other consumer goods trades. It is customary for the buyers or other officials to issue instructions to the receiving department relative to the disposition of the merchandise.

Sometimes instructions may be given in advance of receipt of the merchandise so that goods destined for the reserve storage areas can be forwarded to these areas directly from the freight terminals. The shipment is then checked and a memorandum is issued by the receiving department to the buyer interested in or concerned with the shipment.

In many other establishments instructions as to whether goods are to be delivered to the respective departments or sent to the reserve storage areas are issued only after the goods have been checked by the receiving department and a report has been sent to the buyer. The buyer then notes the intended disposition on this report and returns it to the receiving manager who takes action accordingly.

Receiving Returned Goods. An important phase of the receiving function is that which deals with goods returned by customers for exchange or credit. Goods are returned by customers for a number of reasons. Errors in filling orders, defective merchandise, undesirable substitutions, and undue delay in delivery on seasonal or special orders all contribute to merchandise returns. Some unscrupulous customers who have overbought or who have erred in the choice of merchandise may attempt to rectify their mistakes by returning excess merchandise or undesirable items to the wholesaler. In addition, returns may be caused by overselling on the part of the wholesaler's salesmen who were too eager to swell their commissions by volume sales.

Some system must be devised for the handling of returned merchandise in order to protect the house against abuse on the part of unscrupulous customers; to safeguard the firm's good will by demonstrating an eagerness to correct all mistakes; to provide a means of handling returned merchandise that has been used for display purposes and has therefore become soiled or deteriorated; to discover reasons for returns so that causes

for the situation may be eliminated wherever possible or at least minimized; and to maintain the accuracy of stock records.

Complaints regarding unsatisfactory merchandise are usually first made
to the wholesaler's salesman, who is in many instances authorized to effect
all such necessary adjustments. The salesman should be thoroughly familiar
with the company's policy concerning returns and should handle each case
in a tactful and diplomatic manner, particularly when it becomes necessary
to refuse a request for an adjustment.

If it is considered advisable to accept merchandise for return, the salesman fills out a "Returned Goods" form in duplicate, noting the description
and quantity of the merchandise and the reason for the action. Both copies
of the form are sent to the buyer, who retains the original and sends the
duplicate to the receiving manager. Upon arrival of the goods, the receiving manager checks them against the returned goods form and enters the
pertinent information in a returned goods receiving ledger. A notation is
made simultaneously on the duplicate returned goods form, and this is
sent to the buyer, who may inspect the goods and issue instructions relative
to the disposition to be made of them. At the same time the buyer informs
the customer of the disposition of the returned merchandise and the
amount of the allowance or credit given. This amount is noted on the
original of the returned goods form, which is then forwarded to the accounting department for proper recording and other handling.

In a number of cases goods are returned by customers without the consent of the salesman and without notifying the wholesaler of the intention
or reasons for such action. When this occurs, a receiving clerk makes out
the returned goods form in duplicate, registers the necessary information
in a returned goods ledger, and sends both copies to the buyer. From
this point on, the routine is not essentially different from that just described, except that delays may occur before instructions are issued for
the final disposition of the goods, since they may have been returned unjustly and some correspondence may be necessary before an agreement is
reached as to the adjustment.

Returning Goods to Suppliers. Wholesalers frequently have to make returns of goods to suppliers for reasons similar to those noted for returns
by retailers and other customers to wholesalers. It is advisable to have all
such returns of goods to suppliers, as well as all adjustments concerning
prices, rebates, shortages, and so on handled in the merchandise or purchasing department. This department is best fitted for such work, since it
has occasion to deal with the manufacturers and therefore is familiar with
their policies and attitudes.

Regardless of the origin of a complaint, the whole matter of dealing with
the manufacturer is turned over to the buyer concerned as soon as it is
decided what merchandise is to be returned or what adjustment is to be

sought. All records and correspondence must be properly filed, so that they are readily available when needed. Once a month or at other intervals, when checks to manufacturers are prepared, the buyer or his assistant examines the file in order to note the status of individual complaints and to determine whether or not full payment or any payment at all is to be made. The accounting department can then be advised of delays or part payments on account of returns or adjustments pending at that time.

INTERNAL DISTRIBUTION AND MOVEMENT OF GOODS

After receiving and checking, the next step in the sequence of warehousing activities is the distribution of goods to storage areas. As indicated in the section dealing with layout, separate areas are often devoted to reserve and active stocks. In such cases at least some merchandise must be handled twice, first from receiving to reserve stock and then from reserve to active stock. Regardless of whether or not reserve stocks are segregated from active stocks, goods can be moved either by manual means or by any one of a variety of mechanical methods. This section deals with alternative techniques for internal movement of goods and with the conditions under which each is used to best advantage.

Traditional Handling Methods. The traditional method of handling merchandise in wholesale warehouses has been on a case-by-case basis. If only short distances are involved in handling and if the goods are not too heavy, the operation is often completely manual, with the worker carrying one or two cases from an unloading to a storage area. More often, the movement of merchandise is facilitated by the use of two-wheel or four-wheel hand trucks. The use of these trucks, however, still necessitates the manual case-by-case handling at both ends of the haul. In wholesale establishments that have not undertaken modernization programs, this method of handling case goods still largely prevails. Furthermore, under some conditions there may be little or no alternative to manual methods of distributing goods within the warehouse. When an establishment operates on a very small scale or when the goods are of low bulk and/or high unit value, the savings to be realized through mechanical equipment may not offset the relatively high fixed costs. It is still usually possible, however, to improve handling methods through better layout, better training of warehouse personnel, or in other ways.

Modern Handling Methods. Many wholesalers, however, have realized that a large part of their warehouse expense is attributable to the high labor cost involved in repetitive case-by-case handlings; as a result, they have emulated developments in industrial plants and government warehouses in order to reduce costs and speed up operations. By far the most important of these developments has been the recognition of the *unit load*

FIGURE 21a. Illustration Showing a Low-Lift Platform Truck Handling a Skid Load of 225 Cases of Soap

FIGURE 21b. Illustration of Handling by a High-Lift Power Fork Truck of a Number of Boxes of Goods for Storing on Upper Tier of Warehouse

FIGURE 21c. Illustration of Use by Battery-Powered Fork Truck of Two Pallets
Loaded with Bags of Flour for Storing 16 High in Four Tiers

Courtesy of the Baker-Raulang Company and the Electric Industrial Truck Association

FIGURE 21d. Illustration of Loading Right into the Box Car of Palletized Load

441

principle. This principle may be stated as follows: the more pieces or pounds of merchandise it is possible to combine in a unit that can be moved in a single handling operation, the lower the cost of moving each piece or pound and the shorter the time required to move a given physical volume of goods.

Two methods of handling unit loads are in general use by progressive wholesale establishments. One involves the utilization of platform *skids,* which are usually handled by power lift trucks or hand-operated jacks; the other consists of the use of *pallets,* which are handled by high-lift power fork trucks. Mechanized handling of unit loads on skids and pallets is illustrated by the reproductions shown in Figure 21 (a, b, c, and d).

Skids are platforms resembling sledges in appearance. They are usually of wood construction, although many are reinforced with metal, and a few all-metal skids are in use. The older skids usually have two wooden runners, of the same length as the skid, that elevate the platform some 10 to 12 inches off the floor. The open space under the skid platform allows the insertion of a hand jack or the platform of a power lift truck. The skid can be raised off the floor slightly and the load moved from one place to another as a unit. The improved skids are usually mounted on four metal legs, leaving space open on all four sides under the skid. This adds to flexibility, as it permits the elevation to be effected from the sides as well as from the ends of the skids. A number of sizes of skids are in use in wholesale establishments, a rather common size being 48 by 72 inches. Since the weight of the load is concentrated on the runners or on the legs, it is generally impossible to stack one skid on another without causing damage, unless the merchandise below is protected.

Pallets differ from skids in several important respects. The pallet is a flat wooden platform, usually about 6 inches thick, consisting of planks fastened to both sides of cross timbers. The forks of a high-lift fork truck are thrust into the space between the planking of the pallet and the load is lifted by the elevator action of the truck, carried to the allotted space in the warehouse, and lowered into the proper position. The forks are removed from the pallet as the truck backs away from the stack. Pallets are of varying sizes, but are usually much smaller than skids. The largest size in general use is 48 by 48 inches, and 3-foot pallets are very common. The weight of the pallet load is evenly distributed over the entire lower surface of the pallet. This equal weight distribution, together with the elevator mechanism of the truck, permits high tiering of several pallet loads, provided each load is stacked level so as to support additional pallets.

The lower height of pallets and the greater flexibility through high tiering make the pallet superior to the skid wherever high ceilings are available and advantageously usable. For this reason pallets are generally favored by wholesalers with one-story buildings. Wholesalers who make use of the unit load principle in multistory warehouses, however, tend to favor the use of skids. In such buildings ceiling heights normally do not permit double or triple decking, and the larger amount of waste space caused by the higher elevation of the skid is considered more than offset by the larger unit loads which can be handled by that means.

Regardless of which method is used, the unit load is formed as the car or the dray is being unloaded, the load is carried to the reserve stock as a unit, and later brought to forward stocks as a unit. Case-by-case handling is eliminated on all movements of merchandise between the time of unloading and order assembly. Possibly in the future, case-by-case handlings during unloading operations will be eliminated by receipt of merchandise which has been formed into pallet load units by manufacturers. Although a considerable amount of progress in this direction has been made in the manufacturing field, developments in the wholesale trade are hampered by several factors. Lack of standardized handling procedures on the part of wholesalers keeps manufacturers from shipping merchandise in standard unit loads that cannot be handled by many of their customers. Then there is the problem of what to do with the empty pallets. The wholesaler would accumulate great stocks of pallets in a short period of time. Pallets have generally been too expensive to be discarded after a single use. On the other hand, freight rates applicable to the return of empty pallets have been so high that this practice has not been encouraged. A partial solution to this problem in some cases has been found in the use of disposable pallets made of corrugated paper. The strength of such pallets is limited, however, and the cost is rather high when the pallets are used but once.

Advantages of Palletized Unit Loads. Wholesalers making full or partial use of palletized unit loads enjoy a number of operating advantages relative to other wholesalers who continue to rely upon manual handling methods. These advantages, shown below, also accrue in large measure to wholesalers using skids for unit loads.

1. *Lower Handling Costs.* Substantially lower handling costs are effected by the reduction in the number of individual package handlings required. The benefits derived from handling loads in pallet units may be illustrated by the results of a time and motion analysis of actual observed conditions as applied by one materials handling expert to a hypothetical handling problem. It is assumed that 1,000 cases of merchandise of a given size and weight must be moved a distance of 200 feet and restacked in an orderly manner. The actual costs of handling such a movement obviously will vary according to individual circumstances, but the relative costs of performing this task by various alternative methods, assuming a labor cost of $1.50 per hour and an electric truck operating cost of $0.75 per hour, are indicated as follows:

   a) Simple Manual Operation: Worker removes one case from old stack;

carries it 200 feet; places it on new stack; and returns to repeat operation. Total labor time, 38.3 hours. Cost, $57.45.

b) Two-wheel Hand Truck: Worker removes cases from stack individually; loads five cases on two-wheel hand truck; pushes truck 200 feet to new stack; stacks cases individually; and returns to repeat operation. Total labor time, 16.6 hours. Cost, $24.90.

c) Four-wheel Hand Truck: Same as (*b*) above, but with each load consisting of 20 cases. Total labor time, 11.6 hours. Cost, $17.40.

d) Conveyor System: Worker at old stack removes cases individually; places cases on a conveyor system; cases are removed by another worker 200 feet away and stacked. Total labor time, 10 hours. Total cost disregarding expense of conveyor operation, $15.00. It should be noted that labor time will not vary with the length of the movement because the conveyor is in continuous operation, transportation man-hours being zero.

e) Electric Fork Truck System: Worker removes cases from old stack individually; stacks 60 cases on pallet (five rows high, each row four cases long and three cases wide); truck operator picks up unit load; drives 200 feet; places unit load into position on new stack; returns and repeats operation. Total labor time, 5.5 hours (5 hours stacking and 0.5 hours truck operation). Labor cost, $8.25. Truck operation cost, $0.375. Total cost, $8.63.

f) Electric Fork Truck System Handling Previously Palletized Shipment: Old stack is stacked in unit loads on pallets. Truck operator inserts fork into pallet; lifts pallet and drives 200 feet to new stack; returns and repeats operation. Total labor time for truck operation 0.5 hours (no stacking required). Labor cost, $0.75. Truck operation cost, $0.375. Total cost. $1.13.

In wholesale warehouses where the unit load principle is used, the initial unloading and placing in storage is accomplished by method (*e*). All subsequent handlings prior to order filling can be accomplished by method (*f*). While the difference in cost indicated above may be exaggerated for most cases, it is very substantial. Even the most antiquated wholesale houses seldom employ to any degree methods (*a*) and (*b*). Moreover, in a comparison of costs consideration must be given to the cost incurred in palletizing and otherwise preparing the goods for mechanical handling.

2. *Rapid Movement of Goods.* The speeding up of the flow of merchandise is a natural result of the unit load principle that is obvious from the preceding discussion. Speedy operations smooth out labor requirements and make it possible to handle heavy seasonal shipments without halting regular operations. Demurrage charges can be eliminated or substantially reduced and drays are not kept stationary for long periods. When the occasion demands, additional space can be secured in the warehouse by a quick rearrangement of unit loads.

3. *Maximum Utilization of Storage Space.* The use of unit loads makes it possible to stack merchandise to ceiling heights in most cases. The electric fork truck makes high tiering possible that could not otherwise be effected because of the difficulty of handling heavy items by manual methods. Some wholesalers have found it possible to increase the capacity of their warehouses by 20 to 50 per cent by the use of pallets.

4. *Good Housekeeping.* Since unit loads are immovable without the lift truck, units that have been properly placed are not moved unless there is reason for so doing. High stacking necessitates an orderliness that is frequently not observed in handling merchandise on an individual case basis.

5. *Physical Inventories Facilitated.* Unit loads of standard sizes reduce the time and cost required for taking inventory. It is easier and more accurate to determine the number of pallet loads in a stack and multiply this number by the number of cases per load than to ascertain the number of individual cases in a large stack.

6. *Less Merchandise Damage.* Most losses due to damaged merchandise occur while goods are being handled or moved. If unit loads are used, individual pieces are handled less frequently, thereby reducing the chance of damaging materials. This assumes, of course, that the unit load is handled by a well-trained and conscientious operator.

Evolution of Mechanized Handling Methods. Mechanized handling of unit loads is sometimes mistakenly regarded as a recent technological development. Actually, fork lift trucks were first developed as early as 1919.[3] Over the years handling equipment has been improved in many ways. A major problem with the earlier fork lift trucks, for example, was the large amount of aisle space required for maneuvering between stacks of merchandise. This has been substantially reduced as a result of technical improvements in the design of the trucks. Another significant change has been the higher stacking made possible by stronger lifting mechanisms. Grocery warehouses, in which palletized handling has been carried further than in most other lines of business, are now commonly built with 20-foot ceiling clearances. This permits stacking of goods to a height of three pallets on the top deck of a triple-decked pallet rack, for a total of five pallets in each segment of floor space. The effect on costs is quite important, since maximum utilization can be made of *cubic* space. In the 1950's, a warehouse with a ceiling height of 15 feet cost around 40 cents a cubic foot to build, while a structure with a 20-foot clearance cost only a little over 30 cents a cubic foot.[4] In other words, increasing the cubage by a

[3] *Unit Loads—Their Handling-Shipment-Storage,* The Electric Industrial Truck Association (Chicago, 1947), p. 4.

[4] William H. Meserole, "Warehousing Costs Can Be Cut in Half," *Flow* (April, 1954).

third through higher ceilings adds very little, if anything, to total construction cost.

A development in the 1950's that promised even further economies in warehousing was the *clamp* method of handling, whereby a clamp attachment is used on a truck in place of a fork attachment used in palletized handling. A unit load of goods can then be lifted and moved by the clamp truck without stacking on a pallet or skid. This method is illustrated in

Courtesy of *Modern Materials Handling* magazine and The Procter & Gamble Company

FIGURE 22. Clamp Truck Handling Unit Load

Figure 22. Its advantage, of course, is the elimination of pallets and their cost, which is quite substantial in large-scale operations. Operating time compares quite favorably with palletized handling.[5] The basic limitation of clamp handling is that the size of the containers being handled must be highly standardized and relatively strong. If size is not standardized, the load is likely to slip and serious damage result. If the containers are too fragile, on the other hand, the pressure of the clamp may crush them. For this reason clamp handling has found its greatest use so far among manufacturers, who are able to control the standardization of containers for their own products.

Limitations to Mechanized Handling of Unit Loads. The full benefits of handling unit loads with skids, pallets, or clamps can only be realized on internal handlings of merchandise after cars and drays have been unloaded and until orders are assembled. For reasons already given, the wholesaler can continue to expect to receive most incoming goods in individual case units. Furthermore, he cannot assemble orders by means of unit loads without eliminating one of the principal reasons for his existence—that of breaking bulk and supplying goods to retailers and other customers in small quantities, as needed.

The degree to which mechanized handling methods can be utilized in warehousing operations varies with the size of the house and the line of business. Unless goods are received in quantities of 20 to 30 cases or more, economical unit loads cannot be formed. In the grocery trade almost all the merchandise is purchased in sufficient quantities to take advantage of mechanized handling, even in the smaller concerns. Unit loads, therefore, have almost revolutionized handling methods in that field. On the other hand, a large proportion of the wholesale hardware or the wholesale drug merchant's purchases is in amounts of less than 10 cases. In such lines only partial use can be made of unit loads, with considerable variation according to the size of the establishment. All wholesalers, however, should be completely alert to the savings that can be effected by such methods and incorporate modern techniques wherever possible.

Finally, extensive damage to shipping containers and their contents may result if the power and strength of modern handling equipment is allowed to become misdirected. A faulty pallet, an unsteady tier, a careless or inexperienced truck operator, are all potential sources of great losses, in spite of the fact that *proper* unit load handling can reduce merchandise damage. Skill in operating fork and lift trucks is not easily or quickly acquired. Equipment has its own idiosyncrasies, and there are differences in control responses among different makes of equipment.

[5] "Now Clamps Handle Small Cartons Too!" *Modern Materials Handling* (June, 1957).

Therefore, a proper training and supervision program is a prerequisite to economical operation by mechanical methods.

Other Types of Equipment. In addition to the familiar two-wheel and four-wheel hand trucks and the power-driven lift trucks and fork trucks just described, wholesalers use various other devices to handle merchandise in the warehouse. Fork trucks themselves are highly flexible equipment. Most models are so equipped that the forks designed for pallet handling can be removed and replaced with other attachments especially designed for hauling loads such as rolls of paper, drums, barrels, etc.

Tractor-trailer systems are sometimes used. This type of system is a *hauling* rather than a *handling* device and involves the use of an electric or gasoline-propelled tractor drawing a number of four-wheel trailers in train. Its principal use is in connection with fairly long hauls of large shipments. In the wholesale field the use of this system is largely restricted to long one-story buildings that do not have unloading facilities at various locations along the length of the warehouse.

In some hardware and mill supply houses and in some specialty concerns and manufacturers' sales branches, power cranes are used to handle individual items of heavy equipment. Cranes are available in a number of standard types and capacities, but are sometimes designed for the performance of a particular job in an individual warehouse.

Various types of conveyor equipment are commonly used in wholesale warehouses. Small portable gravity conveyors are frequently used in unloading operations, particularly in houses that do not use skids or pallets. These gravity conveyors are also used in shifting merchandise stocks within the warehouse. Naturally, only short movements on the same floor level can be effected by the force of gravity. To overcome this difficulty, it is not uncommon to find a series of portable gravity conveyors connected by means of elevating power-driven conveyors. This is illustrated in Figure 23, which shows the common "skate-wheel" type of conveyor with a power-operated "booster" section in use in a grocery warehouse.

The most frequent use of conveyor equipment is on order assembly lines. Power-driven roller conveyor systems, permanently installed, run the length of the floor in the order-picking areas of some houses and are used to carry baskets in which loose order items are placed at various stock locations as required. Some houses use a monorail conveyor. This involves a single rail mounted near the ceiling throughout the order assembly area. Carriers for order baskets are suspended from the rail by means of casters, and are pushed from one order assembly station to another. A few houses make use of an overhead power-driven moving chain to which order assembly trucks may be attached. The trucks, each holding a separate order, are pulled through the order assembly area at a slow rate of speed and are loaded with the merchandise selected from the de-

Courtesy of The Rapids-Standard Company, Inc.
FIGURE 23. Gravity Conveyor with Power-Driven "Booster" Section

partmerts through which they are passing. If the rate of movement is too rapid for the order-pickers, the trucks may be detached for a while and later hooked back to the "tow-line."

In addition to the mechanical or semimechanical equipment, various installations, such as chutes and dumb-waiters, are constructed in multistory buildings to facilitate the movement of goods. Chutes are of two main varieties. Circular chutes, built like coiled springs, are commonly used where more than two floors are connected. The other type of chute, built like a straightaway ramp, is just used between two floors. Chutes are used in receiving, replenishing forward stocks, and in sending assembled orders to packers; obviously, their use is confined to downward movements. Dumb-waiters are employed to economize on the use of elevators for small interfloor movements of merchandise. The use of scales, counters, and shelving is obvious, and the use of "drum-racks" and "half-decks" has been explained in another connection. Finally, it may be observed that thoughtful employees, seeking more efficient methods of doing their various jobs, account for a wide variety of special purpose "homemade" equipment that is used in a large number of concerns.

Forward Stock Replenishment. Where the active order-picking stock is separated from the reserve stock, provision must be made for replenishing the forward stock. This involves determining (1) the quantity of merchandise to be maintained in the forward stock and (2) the method by which the forward stock is to be replenished. Each of these problems can be solved only by the individual wholesaler with reference to factors peculiar to his own establishment. Certain general observations may be of value, however. The quantity of merchandise kept in forward stock must not be so large that space becomes a problem and the order-picking walk unduly extended. On the other hand, the supply must be large enough that "outs" on the order assembly line are avoided. Thus the quantity depends upon the bulkiness and the sales volume of individual items and upon the method used for stock replenishment.

Stocks of merchandise may be replenished in a number of ways. In almost all houses of any substantial size, the individual order-picker or stock clerk works in a limited area, which contains the forward stock of only one department or a few departments. In line with one replenishment system, the order-picker or stock clerk in charge of a particular section fills out a stock requisition form that is taken to the reserve stock department. The stock clerk draws the needed merchandise, takes it back to his own area, and stores it properly. This method is generally used where the forward stock consists largely of relatively small quantities of individual items stored on open shelves.

A second method is favored when both the forward and reserve stocks are maintained in fairly large quantities of full cases. The stock clerk writes out a requisition, which is turned over to the reserve stock department. In this case, however, the goods are brought to the forward stock by other employees, frequently in skid or pallet loads handled by mechanical methods.

In one-story warehouses where the "three-deck level" layout pattern is followed, no requisitions are used. Active stocks on the lower levels are replenished by means of electric fork trucks, which merely lower another pallet load into the assigned position.

Replenishment of forward stocks is not effected from reserve stocks in the case of all items that are carried. Not all items are purchased in sufficient quantities to require a reserve stock. The forward stock in some instances, then, consists of the entire supply of the item, which can be replenished only upon receipt of an additional shipment from the supplier.

ESSENTIALS OF WAREHOUSE OPERATION AND SUPERVISION

Good Warehousekeeping. Certain fundamental principles must be observed, irrespective of line of merchandise or size of business, type of building, or layout design employed. Proper warehousing calls for the assignment of a definite place for each item in stock and for proper supervision to insure that each item is in the allotted location. Stock is located with reference to sound layout principles. A control book or a location file is maintained, showing the location of each item according to the division, section, shelf, cabinet, drawer, bin, or bay in which it may be found.

Fixtures must be adapted to each type of merchandise. When no special fixtures are required, space for storing is laid off on the floor in blocks, each one properly identified by a number or letter. Stock is properly stacked and arranged within the space allotted. Each lot of goods is kept separated by a small but distinct break between adjoining lots of merchandise. Bags and paper board or fiber board containers are best stacked in interlocking fashion, on large low platforms or on pallets or skids, while wooden cases are piled one on top of the other. Stock consisting of a large

Courtesy of The Rapids-Standard Company, Inc.
FIGURE 24. "Flow Rack" for Storage of Active Stocks

number of small items must necessarily be stored in bins, cabinets, drawers, or on shelves, which must be of a size and dimension to accommodate the merchandise without waste. Each fixture must be conspicuously identified by a letter or number, or both; location designations should also be stenciled or tacked on the fixtures.

Economies can often be effected in connection with the handling of fast-moving items, which sell in broken case lots, by segregating such items from the remaining shelf stock and filling orders directly from open cases instead of having the items shelved. Many tobacco wholesalers, for example, keep cases of the fastest-selling brands of cigarettes in the order-packing room itself, either above, below, or adjacent to the packing tables.

When goods are subject to physical deterioration, provision must be made for proper rotation of stocks. A strict "first-in-first-out" principle of order-filling must be employed, since shipment of spoiled or stale merchandise leads to costly returns and loss of good will. An ingenious device for insuring rotation of tobacco stocks is illustrated in Figure 24. Each brand of merchandise is assigned to one or more tracks in the "flow rack." The track is a short segment of roller conveyor set up on a slight incline so that stocks put in at the rear will slide to the front, where order pickers remove them as needed. Under this system it is practically impossible to violate the "first-in-first-out" rule. Similar devices are used by manufacturers and wholesalers of baked goods, candy, coffee, frozen foods, ice cream, and other perishable or semiperishable goods.

Cleanliness, both in substance and appearance, is another prerequisite to good stock keeping in the warehouse. Commodities that are odoriferous, such as matches and insecticides, must be placed at a distance from items like sugar and coffee. Likewise, common salt, which tends to absorb moisture and odors, must not be placed near tobacco or certain breakfast cereals. All floors in the warehouse must be kept clean and in good repair at all times; no rubbish or obsolete goods are allowed to accumulate; fallen boxes are replaced immediately; broken lots are kept at a minimum. Aisle-ways and all equipment used in the warehouse, including chutes, conveyors, elevators, stairs, and so on, always remain free from obstructions.

Labor Supervision in the Warehouse. In spite of a trend toward the use of labor-saving devices in warehouse operation, labor cost continues to be a very important proportion of the typical wholesaler's operating expenses. In smaller concerns the warehouse superintendent personally supervises the activities of all the warehouse employees. In larger firms the superintendent is assisted by a number of foremen, each of whom may be responsible for certain types of activities. The problem of handling labor efficiently must be solved by the talent of the warehouse foreman. The difficulty of this task has increased as a result of a tendency toward greater specialization in activities and in equipment. Formerly, most warehouse employees did a little bit of everything, and it was a simple matter to shift workers from one job to another as the occasion demanded. This is no longer the situation, at least in the larger and more progressive houses. Certain employees operate handling equipment, some unload cars and drays, others assemble orders, and still others work in the packing room. Carpenters, mechanics, painters, and janitors may be employed for maintenance and housekeeping activities. In some houses union regulations prevent shifting a man from one job to another. In others, where this is not the case, many workers have little knowledge of the duties of many of the other employees in the same establishment. This situation results in costly interruptions and idleness if work does not flow smoothly through the warehouse.

The work to be accomplished must be carefully studied and planned in advance insofar as practicable, in order that the proper amount of work and the right number of employees are available at each station. Workers are not to be assigned extremely specialized duties if this can be avoided. For example, it is desirable to have order-fillers replenish and arrange stocks when there is a lull in order-filling activity; case goods are brought to forward stocks by electric trucks when cars and drays are not waiting to be unloaded; and order-checkers double as packers or dray loaders. Foremen are alert constantly for congestions and bottlenecks and for idleness and assign workers to different but related tasks within the limits of freedom available to this end.

The trend toward specialization has several implications for selection and training procedures. Many activities in a streamlined operation require a high degree of skill, necessitating a scientific selection of employees. Aptitude and intelligence tests may be administered to ascertain the probability of a new worker's success in some jobs. Careful analysis of each job in the warehouse helps to determine the qualifications for the job and which other jobs are closely enough related so that a combination of activities will not result in a loss of the advantages accruing from specialization. Definite and carefully prepared training programs permit the rapid instruction of new workers in the correct performance of their duties. In addition, complete and accurate performance records serve as a basis for recommendations for promotion, transfer, or dismissal.

Light and Color in the Warehouse. Adequate light and the proper use of color in the warehouse create a working atmosphere that has a favorable effect on operations. Satisfactory illumination reduces labor costs and other operating expenses in a number of ways. A large volume of merchandise can be handled in a minimum amount of time because of the ease with which checking, sorting, and stacking are performed. Losses owing to discrepancies in checking, breakage, water damage, and so on are easily detected and more readily controlled than under conditions where merchandise is stored in improperly lighted rooms. Adequate lighting decreases the number of accidents, enhances efficiency, and raises the level of morale among the workers, with a resultant lowering in labor turnover.

In one-story buildings it is possible to rely on natural light to a high degree. Many streamlined warehouses have a skylight system of one type or another extending across the entire roof area, making the general use of artificial light unnecessary during daylight hours. On the other hand, inadequate lighting has been characteristic of most multistory warehouses because of a managerial emphasis on immediate out-of-pocket expenses as reflected in utility bills, rather than on the somewhat less tangible but more important long-run advantages of proper illumination.

A rule to follow in this regard is that the warehouse should be so illuminated that the fine print of a newspaper can be read without strain at any place where an employee is working. Ceiling lighting fixtures, as a rule, give ample light where merchandise is stacked in open areas, whereas lower fixtures must be used in most aisles where merchandise is stored in racks, shelves, or bins. Adequate candle power must be used, and all fixtures and globes must be cleaned regularly in order to obtain the full benefit that can be derived from the lighting system. An illuminating engineer may be consulted to determine where and how needed light should be provided. Some progressive wholesalers who have done this have replaced all old fixtures with modern fluorescent installations capable of providing what appears to be light equal to daylight over the entire floor area. Switches are so arranged that it is not necessary to illuminate an entire floor or division when light is needed in only one small section.

The advantages to be derived from the proper use of color are similar to those that may be gained from adequate lighting. Only relatively few wholesalers, however, have acted upon the recognition that some colors reflect light while others absorb it, and that some color combinations create a pleasant and restful atmosphere while others produce a gloomy or depressing one. In a number of new or renovated buildings a plan similar to the following has been used: ceilings, upper walls, and upper pillars are painted white to get the maximum reflection of light; lower parts of the side walls are painted blue for pleasant atmosphere and a cleaner appearance; bins, shelves, and other fixtures are painted gray to prevent direct glare, and because gray does not soil easily; and fire equipment, obstructions, and other danger spots are painted red for easy recognition. As in the case of lighting systems the wholesaler may profit from the recommendations of a specialist in determining the proper use and combination of color to facilitate operations in the warehouse.

24

ORDER-HANDLING
AND TRAFFIC
MANAGEMENT

The sequence of warehousing activities outlined in the preceding chapter is completed with the assembly of orders for customers, packing, and shipping. Between the receipt of goods from sources of supply and their eventual shipment to customers, sales efforts must of course be made to secure orders. Thus, from a strict chronological viewpoint, this discussion of order-handling procedures should follow Chapters 26 and 27, which deal with the selling function. Order assembly, packing, and shipping are, however, integral parts of warehousing and are carried out by warehouse personnel under the supervision of the operations manager. The type of order form used by salesmen, also treated in this chapter, is closely related to order-handling procedures.

Sources and Types of Sales Orders

The basic document around which office and warehouse activities for order assembly are built is the *sales order.* Progressive wholesalers, chain store organizations, and manufacturers have recognized that proper design of sales orders can contribute to efficiency of operations and are devoting considerable attention to the subject.

Sources of Sales Orders. Orders from customers flow into a wholesale house from at least four distinct sources. Outside salesmen may be one channel, either bringing in their orders personally or transmitting them by mail, wire, or telephone. Some customers send in their own orders regularly by *mail* or follow this practice in the intervals between salesmen's calls. Many customers, especially those residing in the same city or metropolitan area, frequently order goods by *telephone,* while out-of-town customers resort to this method for emergency purchases. Finally, the customer may visit the wholesale house and place the order in person with a house salesman. These sources are of unequal significance to houses operating in different lines of trade. In a hardware house many more orders are secured from customers who place orders by mail through the catalog at their disposal than is true in a drug firm where a large proportion of the orders is obtained through salesmen or via the telephone direct from customers. A dry goods wholesaler, on the other hand, secures a large proportion of his orders from customers who select merchandise while visiting the house. The relationship existing between the wholesaler and his customers also has a bearing on the method of ordering. In the grocery trade retailers belonging to voluntary chains almost invariably mail in their orders while unaffiliated independents usually prefer to give their orders to a salesman.

The source of an order has an important bearing on the number of order copies to be made out. If the orders are taken by salesmen, it is good practice to prepare the sales order in duplicate, a copy for the customer and the original to be sent to the house. A third copy is sometimes made and retained by the salesman. Some houses require their salesmen to use indelible pencils and to make three or four carbon copies of the order, which are used to assemble simultaneously the order items from different parts or floors of the warehouse. As another method of facilitating order filling procedure, some wholesalers have differently colored order forms for goods stored in various parts of the building or even for individual departments. Thus the salesmen may be required to write up sales for all items stored on the second floor on a green order form, for goods on the third floor on a pink order form, and so on.

A different procedure may be followed when orders are taken by telephone. When telephone orders consist primarily of *fill-ins* for customers who ordinarily place orders with the salesman, a clerk will make out an original and perhaps one carbon copy manually. When, on the other hand, regular orders calling for many different items are placed over the telephone, either directly by the customer or by a salesman who has taken the order, the *audio transcription* method may be used. Under this system, the order is dictated into a mechanical device and a phonograph record or tape created. This record may then be transcribed by typists into as many copies as needed. A variation on the system involves the direct use of the record by a clerk who removes punched cards from a tub file while listening to the playback.[1] This eliminates transcription of the order altogether and may effect a substantial reduction in clerical expense.

---

[1] Theodore H. Allegri, "Recording Salesmen's Orders," *Marketing Activities,* U. S. Department of Agriculture, February, 1956, pp. 16–17. For a discussion of the tub file system of inventory control, see Chapter 25.

Blank Sales Order Forms. Every wholesale concern provides forms on which are recorded the various items of merchandise sold to a customer. These sales order forms are of two basic types, the classification depending upon whether the form is a *blank* upon which the salesman or the customer must enter the description of the items, the quantity ordered, the price, and other essential information, or whether the item descriptions, prices, and so on are *preprinted* on the form with the result that only the quantity of the desired items need be indicated.

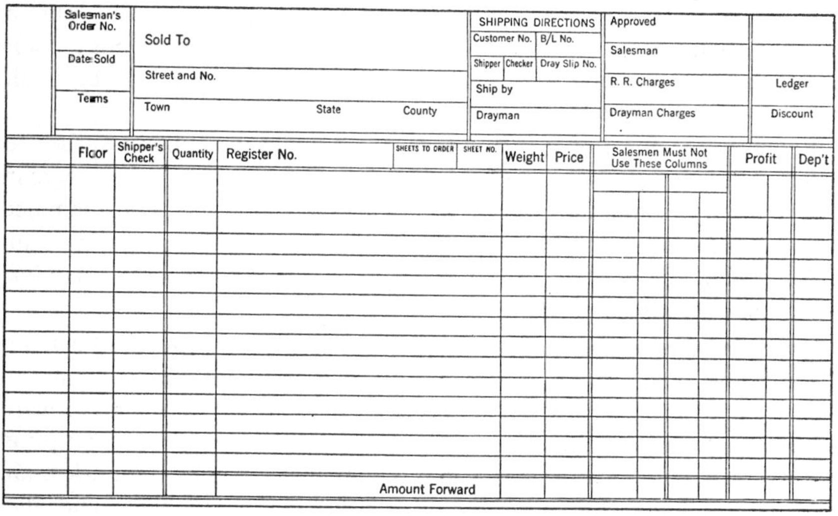
Salesman's Order No.
Date Sold
Terms
Sold To
Street and No.
Town
State
County
SHIPPING DIRECTIONS
Customer No.
B/L No.
Shipper
Checker
Dray Slip No.
Ship by
Drayman
Approved
Salesman
R. R. Charges
Drayman Charges
Ledger
Discount
Floor
Shipper's Check
Quantity
Register No.
SHEETS TO ORDER
SHEET NO.
Weight
Price
Salesmen Must Not Use These Columns
Profit
Dep't
Amount Forward

FIGURE 25. Sales Order Form Used by a Grocery Wholesaler

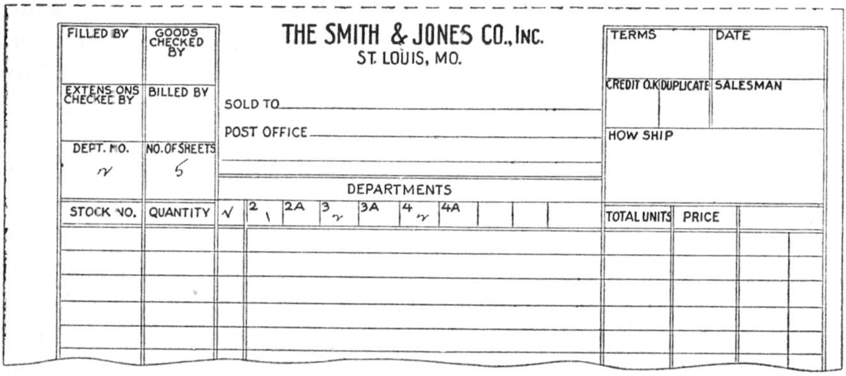
FILLED BY
GOODS CHECKED BY
EXTENSIONS CHECKED BY
BILLED BY
DEPT. NO.
NO. OF SHEETS
THE SMITH & JONES CO., INC.
ST. LOUIS, MO.
SOLD TO
POST OFFICE
DEPARTMENTS
STOCK NO.
QUANTITY
√
2
2A
3
3A
4
4A
TERMS
DATE
CREDIT O.K.
DUPLICATE
SALESMAN
HOW SHIP
TOTAL UNITS
PRICE

FIGURE 26. Simplified Sales Order Form Used by a Dry Goods Wholesaler

The preponderant majority of wholesalers in most lines of business use blank forms similar to those shown in Figures 25 and 26. The size and contents of such a sales order form differ with the line of business, variety of merchandise handled, location of the customer, and other factors. For example, it is not uncommon for a wholesaler to have one sales order form for city trade and another for *foreign* or out-of-town customers, usually consisting of those located outside the seller's free delivery radius. The differences between the two are that the form for city trade is smaller, because such customers buy more frequently and order fewer items at any one time; also, it contains space for the driver's name in place of information about routing the shipment. In out-of-town orders, routing—whether by parcel post, express, or freight, and over what specific road—must be indicated. Sales order forms may also be differentiated by separate colors for regular orders, for rush shipments, and for customers waiting in the warehouse for the goods.

Whatever the form of a sales order, it must always contain spaces for proper customer and salesman identification, description of the merchandise, quantity sold, the price at which the sale was consummated, terms of sale, the date sold, and remarks. It also provides a varying number of spaces for checking the responsibility for the numerous handling and filling operations.

Preprinted Order Forms. Preprinted order forms are condensed catalogs of the wholesaler's stock of goods. The various merchandise items are listed by departments in the same order as they are arranged in the warehouse. For each item there is usually shown a code number, description, package size, number of packages in the minimum shipping unit, price, and other data, although the space for price is frequently left blank and filled in by the salesman from a current price list. Samples of preprinted order forms are shown in Figures 27 and 28.

Several advantages may be derived from the use of preprinted order forms. Confusion in the office and on the assembly line resulting from incomplete and inaccurate descriptions is eliminated. The time required for preparing orders is reduced, and the entire line of merchandise is brought to the attention of the salesman or the customer every time an order is placed. In addition, the listing of items in warehouse sequence eliminates much waste motion and loss of time in filling orders.

The use of preprinted order forms has been largely limited to wholesale establishments in the grocery trade, more particularly to chain store warehouses and voluntary group wholesalers who maintain a punch card system of inventory control as discussed in Chapter 25. This is by no means exclusively the case, however, as such order forms offer important advantages whether or not this method of inventory control is adopted. It is a common misconception that preprinted forms can be used economically only when the number of items carried is relatively small. It is true that, even in the grocery trade, the listing of some 1,500 to 2,500 items

COLUMN 4

	Pack		Price
	Cod Fish Cakes		
A428	24-10oz. Beardsley	20c—18%	3.90
A430	24-10oz. Gorton Ready-to-Fry	21c—15%	4.25
	Fish Flakes		
A440	24-7oz. Gorton	23c—14%	4.75
	Kippered Snacks		
A446	50-¼'s Happy Landing	12c—27%	4.35
A448	100-¼'s Happy Land'g	12c—29%	8.50
	Herring		
A458	24-8oz. Bismark	20c—22%	3.70
A456	24-8oz. Sliced Marinated	17c—25%	3.07
A457	12-16oz. Sliced Marinated	27c—21%	2.54
	Mackerel		
A469	20lb. Pails Canadian Fillets	21c each—24%	7.20
A475	24-15oz. Davis	23c—22%	4.30
A472	12-12oz. Gorton Fillets	30c—21%	2.85
A473	24-14oz. Gorton Fresh	23c—21%	4.35
A470	24-5¾oz. La Playa Fillets	15c—19%	2.90
	Salmon		
2 A490*	24-1's Some Brand Pink		
A499*	24-½'s Some Brand Some Variety		
	Sardines		
A507*	50-¼'s Golden Eagle Oil	15c—22%	5.80
A503*	48-1's Tall Sea Ace Calif. Natural	23c—20%	8.85
	Tuna Fish		
A528*	48-½'s Pyramid Yellow Tail	35c—20%	13.50
	FRUIT JUICES		
	Apple Juice		
A542	12-qt. Shurfine	19c—27%	1.67
	Apricot Nectar		
A543	48-12oz. Hearts Delight	2/25c—27%	4.40
A544	12-46oz. Heart's Delight	39c—19%	3.80
	Blended Juice		
A554	24-2's Old South Swt.	2/23c—20%	2.20
	Grape Juice		
A562	24-pt. Penn Treaty	27c—20%	5.15
2 A564	12-qt. Penn Treaty	49c—17%	4.90
	Grapefruit Juice		
A578	24-2's Life Guard Nat.	3/25c—16%	1.68
A599	12-46oz. Deep South Nat.	21c—15%	2.15
	Lemon Juice		
A615	48-5½oz. Exchange	3/19c—32%	2.05
A616	24-12oz. Realemon	29c—38%	4.30
	Lime Juice		
A624	24-2's Apte	21c—20%	4.00
	Orange Juice		
A637*	24-2's Deep South Nat.	2/23c—23%	2.10
A639	24-2's Exch. Calif.	15c—21%	2.85
A641	12-46oz. Exchange, Nat.	33c—17%	3.30
	Orange-Apricot Juice		
	Peach Nectar		
A652	48-12oz. Heart's Delight	2/25c—29%	4.25
	Pineapple Juice		
A662*	24-2's Some Brand		
	Prune Juice		
A678	12-qt. Del Monte	25c—20%	2.40

COLUMN 5

	Pack		Price
A674	24-12oz. Sunsweet	12c—30%	2.00
A676	12-qt. Sunsweet	25c—13%	2.60
	Tangerine Juice		
A682	24-2's Pasco	10c—23%	1.85
	B FRUITS		
	Apple Sauce		
B2*	24-2's Penn Treaty	19c—25%	3.40
1 B4	12-303's Gl. Mott's	19c—31%	1.55
B3	24-2's Shurfine Apple Sauce	17c—24%	3.10
	Apples		
B12	12-30oz. Musselman's Apple Pie Apples	34c—16%	3.40
	Apricots		
B23	12-2½gl. Del Monte Whole Unp.	35c—18%	3.45
B25	48-1's Del Monte Halves	23c—18%	9.00
B26*	48-1's Demand Halves	21c—22%	7.80
B37	24-2½'s Penn Treaty Whole Peeled	39c—24%	7.10
	Blueberries		
B50	24-300's Little Darling	29c—23%	5.30
	Cherries		
B47	24-2½ Felice Fcy. R. A.	45c—18%	8.80
1 B51*	48-1's Hunts R. A.	32c—23%	10.75
B54	24-2's Hunts R. A.	39c—24%	7.10
B55*	48-1's Libby's R. A.	33c—21%	12.50
	Cranberry Sauce		
B58	24-16oz. Conway's Whole Berry	24c—25%	4.30
B61	24-16oz. Minot	23c—24%	4.20
B64	24-16oz. Ocean Spray	20c—12%	4.20
B62	24-16oz. Penn Treaty	24c—25%	4.30
	Fruit Cocktail		
1 B78	48-1's Tall Hunts, Fcy	27c—22%	10.00
B80	24-2½ Hunts, Fcy	42c—18%	8.20
1 B82	24-2½ Del Monte	41c—17%	8.15
B86	48-1's Del Monte	26c—18%	10.05
B75	48-1's Libby	26c—17%	10.05
B76	24-2½'s Libby's	39c—13%	8.10
B88	48-1's Penn Treaty	29c—23%	10.60
2 B90	24-2½'s Penn Treaty	45c—23%	8.30
	Fruit Salad		
	Grape Fruit		
B113	24-2's Zeneda	19c—23%	3.50
	Peaches (Halves)		
B124	24-2½ Budget	27c—21%	5.10
B126	24-2½ Del Monte	30c—15%	6.05
B132	24-2½ Hunt's	31c—26%	5.50
B128	24-2½ Libby's	33c—25%	5.90
B133	48-1's Hunt's	19c—21%	7.15
1 B130	24-2½ Penn Treaty	33c—21%	6.20
B135	24-2½ Val Vita	27c—25%	4.85
	Peaches (Sliced)		
B144	24-2½ Budget Home Style Y. F.	29c—23%	5.30
B145	24-2½ Budget Y. C.	27c—20%	5.20
B137	48-8oz. Demand	12c—27%	4.20
B162	24-2½ Hunts	31c—24%	5.62
B143	24-2½ Libby's	33c—24%	6.00
4 B146	24-2½ Penn Treaty	33c—20%	6.30
1 B147	48-1's Penn Treaty	21c—24%	7.60
	Pears		
B172	24-2½ Budget	39c—21%	7.35
B178	24-2½ Libby's	45c—20%	8.60
B180	24-2½ Mission Peak	43c—21%	8.15
B183	48-1's Penn Treaty	27c—21%	10.25
B184	24-2½ Penn Treaty	47c—22%	8.75
	Pineapple Sliced		

COLUMN 6

	Pack		Price
	Pineapple Crushed		
1 B216	24-2½ Del Monte	30c—13%	6.25
2 B209	24-2's Libby's	26c—20%	4.95
6 B218	24-2's Penn Treaty	27c—24%	4.93
	Plums		
	Fresh Prunes		
B234	24-2½'s Flavora Choice	25c—19%	4.85
B238	24-2½ Snider's Fcy	27c—21%	5.08
	Prepared Prunes		
B248	12-2½ Del Monte Ready To Serve	30c—19%	2.90
B330	24-2's tin Heart's Delight Nectarized	22c—29%	3.75
	Maraschino Cherries		
B259	24-4oz. Shurfine	16c—24%	2.90
B261	24-8oz. Shurfine	27c—22%	5.05
	FRUITS (Dried)		
	Apricots		
	Currants		
B278	24-11oz. Dover	15c—23%	2.75
	Dates		
B282	12-7¼oz. Dromedary Pitted	25c—22%	2.33
	Figs		
B290	24-8oz. Black Mission	17c—27%	2.95
B292	24-8oz. Calif. Layered	20c—24%	3.65
	Peaches		
B302	24-11oz. Del Monte	21c—20%	4.00
	Mixed Fruits		
	Dromedary Peels		
B353	12-3oz. Citron	12c—30%	1.00
B354	12-3oz. Lemon	12c—30%	1.00
B356	12-3oz. Orange	12c—30%	1.00
B357	12-3oz. Pineapple	21c—22%	1.90
	Prunes		
B320	24-1lb. Penn Treaty Ex. Lge. Prunes	23c—24%	4.20
B319	24-1lb. Del Monte Lge.	23c—23%	4.20
B322	24-1lb. Sunsweet Lge.	23c—24%	4.15
B323	24-2lb. Sunsweet Lge.	41c—20%	7.85
	Raisins (Seedless)		
B333	48-1lb. Del Monte	17c—23%	6.25
B335	24-15oz. P.T. Seedless Raisins	16c—22%	3.00
	MINCE MEATS		
B365	12-20oz. Ex. Family	55c—21%	5.20
B366	12-2lb. Ex. Family	85c—25%	7.65
B367	12-18oz. Keystone	37c—20%	3.55
B368	12-2lb. Keystone	65c—23%	6.00
B369	12-18oz. Marvel	29c—21%	2.75
B370	12-2lb. Marvel	45c—24%	4.10
B364	12-1¾lb. Social Club	47c—19%	4.55
	PAPER PRODUCTS		
	Cleansing Tissues		
1 B386	48-200's Ponds Facial (Fair Trade 15c)	31%	4.92
B388	72-200's Scotties	13c—30%	6.50
	Toilet Tissue		
3 B418*	100 Some Brand		
	Napkins		
B393	50-80's Graco	2/29c—23%	5.52
B400	50-80's Seda	2/29c—20%	5.78
	Sanitary Napkins		
B420	48-12's San-Nap-Pak (Fair Trade 2/59c)	29%	10.12
	Towels		
	Waxed Paper		

ITEMS MARKED * ARE AVAILABLE ONLY IN LIMITED QUANTITIES

Courtesy of the Quaker City Grocery Company, Philadelphia, Pa.

FIGURE 27. Inside Page of One Type of Preprinted Order Form

Items circled are items ordered by the customer, and the number prefixed to an item indicates the number of packages of the circled item desired by the customer.

1	2	3	4	PAGE NO. 4F				USE THIS FORM FOR ORDER	
								FROM	TO
				SUGGESTED RETAIL		COST		DESCRIPTION	

1	2	3	4	SUGGESTED RETAIL	COST		DESCRIPTION
						1	
				4 2	7 9 7	2	P E A C H S L I H S R & W 2 ½
				1 5	2 8 0	3	P E A C H Y C S L I R & W 8
				3 1	5 9 7	4	P E A C H H V S A U N T M A R Y S 3 0 3
				3 1	6 0 7	5	P E A C 8 S L 1 U N T M A R Y S 3 0 3
				4 9	9 5 8	6	P E A C H H V S A U N T M A R Y S 2 ½
				4 9	9 4 8	7	P E A C H S L A U N T M A R Y S 2 ½
				2 5 |A| 4 7 0	8	P E A C H H V S Y C D E L M 3 0 3
		2		3 1	3 0 5	9	P E A C H S L Y C D E L M B F
				2 5 |A| 4 7 0	10	P E A C H S L Y C D E L M 3 0 3
				3 5 |A| 6 8 5	11	P E A C H S L Y C D E L M 2 ½
				4 3 |A| 8 2 1	12	P E A C H E L B S L D E L M .2 ½
				3 5	6 8 5	13	P E A C H H V S Y C D E L M 2 ½
				4 3 |A| 8 2 1	14	P E A C H E L B H V S D E L M 2 ½
				3 1 |A| 6 0 3	15	P E A C H S L I R R O V 2 ½
				3 1	5 6 8	16	P E A C H H V S O V 2 ½
				3 3 |A| 3 1 6	17	P E A C H S P I C E L I B 3 0 3
				3 3	6 3 7	18	P E A C H S L H U N T S 2 ½
				3 3	6 3 7	19	P E A C H H V S H U N T S 2 ½
				2 9	5 4 0	20	P E A C H H V S H I L L T O P 2 ½
						21	
						22	P E A R S
						23	
				2 9	5 4 5	24	P E A R S R & W 3 0 3
				4 5	8 2 8	25	P E A R S R & W 2 ½
		2		3 3	3 9 6	26	P E A R S H V S R & W 8
				2 9 |A| 5 6 7	27	P E A R S H V S S T O K 3 0 3
				3 1 |A| 5 6 9	28	P E A R S H V S D E L M 3 0 3
				4.5 |A| 8 6 5	29	P E A R S M E L B A D E L M 2 ½
				1 7 |A| 3 1 0	30	P E A R S S L D E L M B U F
				2 5	4 6 0	31	P E A R S B A R T I R R E G O V 3 0 3
						32	
						33	P I N E A P P L E
						34	
				3 5	6 6 6	35	P I N E A P C H D E L M 2
				3 5 |A| 6 9 7	36	P I N E A P S L D E L M 2

FIGURE 28. Preprinted Or[...]

requires a number of large pages with several columns to each page. One large grocery chain uses a preprinted order form listing almost 10,000 items. Most, however, are much smaller than this. Some wholesalers carrying extensive lines, both in the grocery trade and in other kinds of business, circumvent this difficulty by using a separate preprinted form for each merchandise department. In this way the number of pages comprising any one order is reduced to the number of departments from which merchandise is ordered. A limited number of progressive wholesalers in lines such as drugs and hardware have made partial use of preprinted forms, with con-

PACK	%	F	ORDER DAY **4**	ORDER DAY **3**	ORDER DAY **2**	ORDER DAY **1**
		1				
4	21	2	14012	14012	14012	14012
4	22	3	14014	14014	14014	14014
4	20	4	14022	14022	14022	14022
4	18	5	14024	14024	14024	14024
4	19	6	14026	14026	14026	14026
4	19	7	14028	14028	14028	14028
4	20	8	14038	14038	14038	14038
4	18	9	14039	14039	14039	14039
4	20	10	14040	14040	14040	14040
4	19	11	14042	14042	14042	14042
4	20	12	14043	14043	14043	14043
4	20	13	14044	14044	14044	14044
4	20	14	14045	14045	14045	14045
4	19	15	14054	14054	14054	14054
4	23	16	14060	14060	14060	14060
2	21	17	14154	14154	14154	14154
4	19	18	14172	14172	14172	14172
4	19	19	14176	14176	14176	14176
4	22	20	14190	14190	14190	14190
		21				
		22				
		23				
4	22	24	14304	14304	14304	14304
4	23	25	14308	14308	14308	14308
4	25	26	14310	14310	14310	14310
4	19	27	14322	14322	14322	14322
4	23	28	14342	14342	14342	14342
4	20	29	14344	14344	14344	14344
4	24	30	14346	14346	14346	14346
4	23	31	14350	14350	14350	14350
		32				
		33				
		34				
4	20	35	14550	14550	14550	14550
4	18	36	14554	14554	14554	14554

m with "Tear-Off" Strips

siderable success. This procedure involves segregating the fast-moving or most active items in the warehouse and listing them, in identical arrangement, on the order forms. The more numerous slow-moving items are not so listed, but are written up separately on regular blank order forms.

Although a small number of items in the line is not a prerequisite to the use of a preprinted form, reasonably large individual orders are essential. Even in grocery houses that generally use preprinted forms, such forms are not used for very short orders. For such short orders regular forms are used instead, because the preprinted forms are expensive to produce and, because of their bulkiness and first-class postage rate applying thereto, are costly to mail into the house. Furthermore, little confusion is likely to result in the warehouse in filling an order consisting of only a few lines.

Finally, it should be noted that the preprinted form is feasible only where most of the merchandise items are of a staple nature and are regularly carried in stock. It could not be used economically in businesses, such as are found in the produce trade, where the kind and quality of items fluctuate from week to week and from season to season; neither is it to be recommended for houses handling a large amount of style merchandise that is ordinarily purchased by sample or by inspection.

When preprinted order forms are used, they are typically revised on a weekly basis. This has certain disadvantages, especially in terms of printing costs. Depending on the number of items, wholesale grocers' order forms cost from about 25 cents to as much as $1.50 per copy to produce.[2] One solution to this problem is found in the type of form shown in Figure 28. This form is prepared every four weeks, with four "tear-off" strips to be used for weekly orders by the retailers. The customer enters the desired quantity on the order strip opposite the commodity description. A space is also provided for the retailer to enter his own stock records as he examines his inventory weekly.

Examination of Figures 27 and 28 reveals some of the additional kinds of information provided for the convenience of customers. Grocery wholesalers usually give a *suggested retail price* (S.R.P.) based on shopping of prices advertised by chains and other competitors. The *cost* to the retailer is quoted in terms of a case or other standard ordering quantity rather than per unit. Also commonly shown is the retailer's *gross margin* as a per cent of sales ("%") if he uses the suggested retail price. Approximate *rates of turnover* at the retail level, based on the experience of the wholesaler's customers, may be given. Thus the preprinted order serves at once as a catalog and price list of the wholesaler's or chain warehouse stock and as a guide to the pricing and merchandising of the retail store operators.

Card Order Catalogs. A new type of order form developed in the 1950's consists of *cards* designed to be processed by automatic tabulating equipment. The catalog used by the customer, illustrated in Figure 29, is similar in concept to the strip order form shown in Figure 28. Instead of writing in the desired quantity of each item on the strip opposite the commodity description, the customer marks the quantity on a card using a special "mark-sensing" pencil. These marks are converted into punched holes by a

2 "The Lessons Taught by a Hundred Good Examples—A Study of The Grocery Order Form," The National-American Wholesale Grocers Association (Mimeographed, Not Dated).

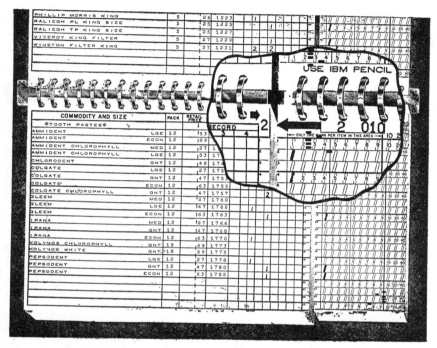

FIGURE 29. Card Order Catalog. Reprinted by permission from "IBM Card Order Plan." Copyright 1955 by International Business Machines Corporation.

special machine in the warehouse office. The cards then form the basis for creating a printed order for warehouse use and for invoicing.

The card order catalog method is obviously limited to wholesale establishments equipped with electronic data processing equipment. Thus far it has been adopted by only a few of the larger and perhaps more progressive chains and wholesalers in the grocery trade. When used in conjunction with certain types of stock control systems, it offers significant economies in office procedure.[3] Use of cards for ordering seems certain to increase in the future, although some feel that cards will in turn be obsoleted by other ordering media, particularly by punched tapes.

PROCESSING OF ORDERS BEFORE ASSEMBLY

In every wholesale enterprise a definite procedure must be established for the handling of orders. While the details of these procedures vary somewhat, they all contain the same basic steps. These are: (1) processing of orders prior to assembly; (2) actual assembly of orders; (3) processing of orders after shipment, and (4) packing and shipping. Each of these steps is further analyzed in the remainder of this chapter.

[3] See Chapter 25.

As orders come into the office, they must be processed to prepare them for warehouse operations. This involves *registration* of the order, *credit-checking, price-checking,* and *transcription* or *copying.*

Registration. When an order is first received in the office, it is sent to a clerk, who enters it on a register, usually consisting of an ordinary day book. Spaces are provided for the time the order was received, name of the customer, and a serial number for the order; in addition, provision is made for checking out the order after it has been filled.

In some houses where the sales order is used for order-filling purposes, the location of each item on the order as to floor or department is marked, at the time of registration, in a special column provided for this purpose.

There are several reasons for registering orders as soon as they are received. In the first place, registration assures greater regularity in order-filling, each order being handled, as far as possible, in accordance with the sequence in which it was received. To accomplish this, the serial number usually is stamped or written in a prominent place on the order form used for filling purposes. Second, registration serves as a check on the movement of orders through the house. Thus, it will always be known how much time has elapsed from the receipt of an order to its checking out. Another reason for registration is that it prevents losses and misplacements of orders. Any order that is not filled in a reasonable amount of time can be traced through the various operations in order-handling. As a last result, if an order is actually lost, the customer can be recontacted, whereas in the absence of registration the loss of an order might easily go unrecognized until a complaint is received.

Credit-Checking. After registration, the order is usually sent to the credit department for approval, unless it is strictly a cash transaction. Some firms prefer to secure credit approval even before an order is registered, for if it is rejected by the credit department, registration is unnecessary. It is also an optional matter whether to secure credit approval before prices are checked or vice versa. There are several reasons for passing on the credit worthiness of the risk before checking as to the prices appearing on the order. The main reason is that there is usually a greater likelihood of turning an order down because of a poor credit standing than of turning it down on account of price misunderstandings. In a sellers' market, characterized by a rising price level and a shortage of goods, and even in more normal times when the price level is only slightly rising or is fairly stable, the probability of losing an order because of a price misunderstanding is slight. Many wholesalers feel that it is advisable to initiate work in the credit department, because this operation may require considerable time, particularly if a complete investigation must be undertaken, as with a new customer or when an old customer becomes financially weak or embarrassed.

Because of the very important nature of the work of the credit department, the procedures in handling the credit phase of the transaction are discussed separately in Chapter 28.

Checking Prices. If credit-checking is the second step in order-routing, orders are checked next to determine if the prices at which goods have been ordered by the customer or quoted by the salesman are acceptable to the house. This price-checking work may be done by the general or territorial sales manager, by buyers, assistant buyers, or by a price record clerk, depending upon whether prices are sensitive and fluctuating, and whether a one-price or varying-price policy is pursued. In firms handling staple lines of merchandise with few price changes the order clerk may be given access to the official price list in order to do this checking. If the quoted price is too high the figures are changed; but if too low, the order may be delayed pending adjustments by correspondence with the customer. When such a delay becomes necessary, the order must be returned to the register clerk for filing, pending final action. When the new price is finally accepted by the customer, the order is registered again under the new date and sent on its way. A similar procedure is followed when the order cannot be approved for credit and an attempt is made to resell it on a cash basis.

Unless price fluctuations are frequent and substantial, complete price-checking of every order may be unnecessary. Many firms find that a *sample* checking of orders turned in by the various salesmen is adequate.[4] The salesmen who persistently make errors or who deliberately make unauthorized concessions on prices will soon be located in this fashion and appropriate corrective action taken. Apart from this, inadvertent price errors are likely to be few in number and can be held within predetermined limits by judicious sampling.

Some firms believe that an order should first be checked as to prices before it is sent to the credit department, for, if it is not accepted because of errors in quoting prices, no credit investigation is necessary and much time and expense are thus saved. As has been indicated, in many firms price-checking is a relatively simple operation that can be performed speedily and at little cost, with the result that the firm does not lose much if the order is later turned down on account of credit. On the other hand, if salesmen are given considerable leeway in quoting prices, the approval of prices so quoted becomes an important matter. This is, of course, modified by the Robinson-Patman Act, which, in effect, prohibits charging customers in the same class, on goods of like grade or quality, different prices that cannot be justified by differences in the costs of selling and delivering

---

[4] *Methods of Handling and Delivering Orders Used by Some Leading Wholesale Grocers,* Marketing Research Report No. 13, U. S. Department of Agriculture (Washington, D. C.: Government Printing Office, 1952), p. 15.

to these customers, unless the seller can prove that lower prices are granted to meet competition from another seller. Another reason for checking prices before credit is that in a buyers' market there may be frequent occasions to turn down orders because of unsatisfactory prices. This is true because customers are reluctant to accept any upward revision in the prices that may have been quoted; therefore it may take considerable time to reach an understanding when prices are in dispute. Obviously, no rule as to whether prices or credit should be checked first can be laid down categorically for uniform treatment by all houses in all phases of the business cycle. This is a matter to be determined by the individual wholesaler according to the circumstances of his own operation.

Transcription or Copying of Orders. The third step in preliminary order processing is the transcription or copying of orders for use in warehouse assembly and subsequent office handlings. If the original orders or copies of the sales order which have been prepared by the salesmen are used for order-filling purposes, no order recopying or modification is necessary. Some wholesalers, however, prefer to make in the office sufficient additional copies of the entire order so that items can be assembled from all parts of the warehouse simultaneously. In many firms this is still done by typists who rewrite orders completely. This is a costly procedure, however, except by the audio transcription method previously referred to, and some companies have eliminated it by using duplicating machines of various types (Copyflex, Ozalid, Ditto, Apeco Uni-Matic Auto-Stat, etc.) to make copies from the original submitted by the salesman, even for invoicing purposes.

Among wholesalers who use automatic data-processing equipment, orders are typically transcribed for warehouse use by machine methods. When the "tub file" system is used, punched cards are pulled by clerks for each item called for on the order; these cards are fed into a printer which prepares a warehouse copy, automatically eliminating any items that are not in stock. A slightly different procedure is used when "batch billing" or computer systems of inventory control are employed, but with essentially the same end result.[5] The tabulating machinery automatically sorts the items into warehouse sequence if this differs from the sequence on the preprinted order form. It may also be used to divide the original order into several parts, one for each floor of a multistory warehouse or for each section of a one-story building. Obviously this processing greatly facilitates assembly of orders by warehouse personnel, since it avoids the necessity of rearranging the order at that point.

A procedure followed by some wholesalers for preliminary processing of orders is that of *scanning* and *editing*. This is necessary only when the

[5] See Chapter 25 for a discussion of the tub-file, batch-billing, and computer systems of inventory control.

original order or photocopies of it are to be used for assembly in the warehouse. Scanning involves a coding of the items listed on an order to indicate the departments or work stations from which they are to be picked in the warehouse. When warehouse employees are experienced and know their stock well, they can scan orders themselves. When warehousemen do not have an intimate knowledge of the goods and their locations, it may be preferable to have one or more specialized persons in the office perform the function for them. *Editing* is likewise designed to make actual assembly of the order faster and easier. The editing clerk deciphers items written by the salesman and elaborates the commodity description if necessary. This avoids loss of time in the warehouse assembly line as order-pickers attempt to "decipher" the order.[6]

ORDER ASSEMBLY

From a cost standpoint, the most important step in the entire warehousing process is the assembly of orders. The typical wholesale enterprise handles hundreds of orders daily, calling, on the average, for several different items per order. Each item or "invoice line" ordered must pass through several distinct physical handling and control operations. Because of this continuous flow of work, the majority of warehouse employees are usually engaged in order assembly and this phase of warehousing requires more time than any other.

Efficient assembly of orders requires that a definite procedure be followed, based on careful study of the firm's particular requirements. It further requires a logical system of stock arrangement and identification in locating goods within the warehouse.

General Methods of Order Assembly. While order-filling procedures vary with regard to details, one of three general methods of procedure is usually followed. These are: (1) filling the order from an assembly line by means of the original preprinted order form or a copy thereof prepared by mechanical means; (2) using the original sales order form or a single copy thereof as a work sheet for all floors and merchandise departments; and (3) filling the order simultaneously on the basis of a separate copy of the order for each floor or department concerned. Regardless of the method used, provision is almost always made for giving rush orders precedence by identifying them with a special stamp or color of order form.

Assembly Line Order-Filling. Filling the order directly from the preprinted order form is the simplest and the most economical of the three

---

[6] For an analysis of scanning and editing functions in the wholesale drug trade, see Albert B. Fisher, Jr., *Warehouse Operations of Service Wholesale Druggists* (Columbus, Ohio: Bureau of Business Research, The Ohio State University, 1948), pp. 105–7.

methods. It is most practical when the physical facilities permit the arrangement of all merchandise items on an assembly line, but, as has been indicated, partial use can be made of this method for segregated fast-moving items. Use of this method of order assembly is obviously limited to circumstances previously stated, under which a preprinted order form is practical.

The assembly line is usually divided into a number of work stations because an order-picker can become familiar with the stock of one department or of a few departments much more completely than he can learn to know the stock of all departments. After checking, the order form is sent to the order-picker at the beginning of the assembly line. He selects the goods from his work area and places them on a roller conveyor, a continually moving "tow-line," or on a hand truck that is drawn from one station to the next. The order form moves with the assembled goods, each order-picker adding merchandise from his respective department or departments as the order line moves through his area. Items of an individual order are kept together throughout the process, with the result that the order is complete and ready for checking when the end of the assembly line is reached. The assembled order is then moved to the packing room, if it contains broken case lots; otherwise, the order is ready for the shipping department. If only partial use is made of the preprinted form, one of the other methods must be used for filling the balance of the order.

Filling an Order from a Single Copy. In many multistory buildings, orders are filled from a single copy of the blank order form as written up by the salesman. When this method is used, it is necessary, first, to indicate opposite each item the number or symbol of the floor or department in which it is located, and second, to send the order by messenger or pneumatic tube to the topmost floor from which some of the items are to be filled. An order-filler of this department assembles the items of the order, checks them, records the time the work was completed, initials the form, and sends it together with the merchandise to the next lower floor represented on the order. The order continues on this journey through the warehouse until all goods called for have been assembled, whence it may be sent to the broken package room for less than original package lots and finally to the packing room (see Figure 30).

Filling from a single copy of the sales order is feasible when the merchandise is not bulky (else the movement of goods from department to department becomes too cumbersome); when most orders call for merchandise in one or two departments; or when the firm operates on a small scale and goods are stored in a limited space so that order chasers can quickly follow an order through to completion. In any event, there is delay in filling orders by this method, since but one department can work on an order at any one time, and if an order is held up in a single department

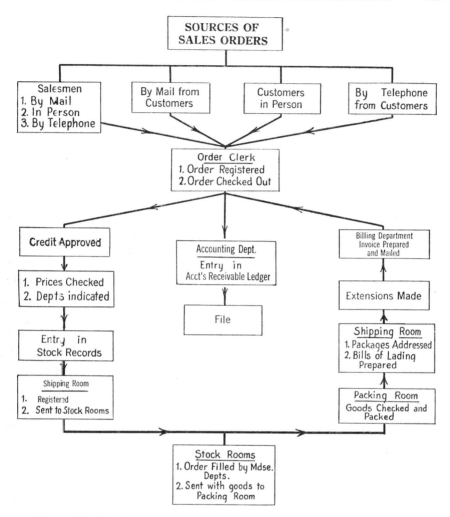

FIGURE 30. Course of Sales Orders when a single copy is used as a work sheet for filling by all merchandise departments concerned

others are prevented from filling it. Moreover, this method of filling orders is costly in comparison with the alternatives. There is usually more waste motion when order chasers are used than when an assembly line is brought to the goods; on the other hand, when goods are required to go through all merchandise departments, handling costs are higher than when the order is filled simultaneously from all departments or floors.

Filling an Order Simultaneously. When orders are filled simultaneously on all floors or in all departments, separate order copies or order forms are prepared by the salesmen or are transcribed in the office by methods discussed above. The procedure used in filling an order by this method is illustrated in Figure 31. Each copy or page of the order is identified by the same order number, but the sheets are numbered serially. All copies, together with the original order, are sent to the shipping room where the order is registered on a shipping ledger, and a location is assigned for assembling it in the packing, shipping, or city delivery room, such information being stamped on all copies of the order. The copies are next distributed to the respective departments, where the merchandise is filled and sent directly to the assigned location via chutes, spiral gravity conveyors, elevators, declining tracks, and the like. This plan obviates the necessity of transporting merchandise from department to department, permits simultaneous filling, and prevents undue delays.

Various modifications of this method have been adopted. Some houses work it on a floor basis rather than by departments. In houses where individual floor dimensions are relatively large, each floor may be laid out in the nature of an assembly line, and the various pages of the order are filled in a manner that makes possible most of the advantages of assembly line order-filling in a one-story warehouse. This is particularly true of wholesalers in the grocery trade who transcribe individual floor orders from preprinted order forms. Other wholesalers, principally those who use complete copies of the order for each floor, follow the same procedure on each floor as when the entire order is assembled from a single copy. The only difference in the two methods, then, is that in the one case the work on different floors is carried on simultaneously. Another variation that is more or less common is to prepare floor sheets (copies of the order) only for goods ordered in full packages, using the original for filling items ordered in broken packages, especially when no central broken package room is maintained. In such cases, the full package items may be filled on the assembly line principle, whereas the original order is handled in the filling of broken package merchandise in the same manner as when a single copy is used for filling the entire order.

Stock Arrangement for Order Assembly. Regardless of which method of order assembly is followed, some attention must be given to the efficient arrangement of stocks within the active or forward stock areas. This arrangement should be so designed as to (1) facilitate speedy location of items called for on orders, and (2) minimize the ton-mileage needed for order assembly.

The principal factors to be considered in locating individual items within the order assembly area are the *departmental organization* of the firm, *velocity of merchandise movement* or *turnover, weight, bulk, shipping unit, value, physical deterioration,* and *legal requirements.*

Traditionally, wholesalers have laid out their warehouse stocks on the basis of departments, with all goods in a given department kept in the

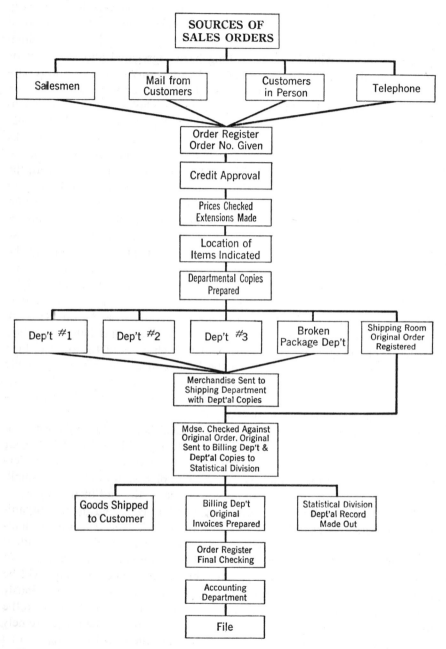

FIGURE 31. A Simplified Procedure Diagram showing the course of an order when all departments concerned fill it simultaneously on the basis of departmental copies of floor slips

same general area. Exceptions have long been made for very heavy or very bulky goods, which are stored on the first floor or in the basement of a multistory building or near the shipping docks in a single-story building. Also, very fast-moving items have long been segregated and stored at or near the packing and shipping rooms. Apart from these exceptions, departmental layout was seldom violated until recent years.

Since the end of World War II, progressive wholesalers have come to recognize certain limitations in this traditional pattern of stock arrangement. The main difficulty is that the departmental classification of stocks is designed primarily for merchandise-planning and control purposes, which may or may not coincide with proper warehousing procedures. In the warehouse, where *physical* handling is the prime consideration, it is more logical to arrange goods in accordance with their handling characteristics. This may best be explained in terms of an example. Suppose that orders are assembled in a grocery warehouse on an assembly line such as those shown in Figures 18 and 19. An order-picker starts at the beginning of the line and traverses all or most of it, selecting the items listed on his copy of the order. These items all differ as to velocity of movement, weight, bulk, and otherwise. If no attention is given to these factors, the order-picker is likely to find that heavy or bulky items must be put on the truck at the early stages of the assembly line, while small and light goods are located near the end. Worse yet, items with high rates of turnover (which are called for on most orders) will be located near the beginning, while slow-moving items are at the end. All of this means that the worker must push a greater weight farther—the number of *ton-miles* will be greater—than if the layout had been designed with these factors in mind.

Ideally, if ton-mileage is to be minimized, items with high rates of turnover and those that are bulky and/or heavy will be located as near the end of the assembly line as possible. When this is done, the order-picker can traverse the greater part of the line picking up only a few small, light items, adding the greater number as he nears the end of the route.

When the ton-mileage principle is applied fully, departmental organization of active stocks virtually disappears. This is true because the handling characteristics of turnover, bulk, and weight apply to individual *items,* not to departments as a whole. For example, in the category of canned soups in a grocery house, a few brands and types of soups will be very active, while most others will be relatively slow-moving. Obviously not all soups can be put in the same place if attention is to be paid to the ton-mileage concept. It is not enough merely to segregate the few extremely fast-moving, very heavy, and very bulky items; these factors vary among individual items by fine degrees.

The fullest application of the ton-mileage principle is found in the so-called *slot system* used in the most progressive grocery warehouses. Under this system, items are assigned to warehouse locations ("slots") in accordance with their handling characteristics, no regard whatever being given to merchandise departments. This implies that the warehouse sequence differs from that of the order form, since goods must be listed by types for convenience of ordering by retailers. Since the order form sequence and the warehouse sequence differ, a *warehouse order assembly* form must be prepared in the office with the goods listed as they appear in the assembly line. Two methods are in use for this sorting operation. If a punch card

SELECT FOR: Johnson's Supermkt. 1885 River Road City		DATE: July 22/— ORDER-PICKER: PB CHECKER: J.N.B.							
Quan.	Slot Nos. 0–999	Quan.	Slot Nos. 1,000–1,999	Quan.	Slot Nos. 2,000–2,999	Quan.	Slot Nos. 3,000–3,999	Quan.	Slot Nos. 4,000–4,999
		1	1,012						
2	183								
				3	2,487				
1	242								
		1	1,721					2	4,761
5	641								
						2	3,875		

FIGURE 32. Transcription of Order Form for Use in Order Assembly

system of inventory control is used, the tabulating equipment can automatically rearrange the sequence of goods by slot number. If this is not possible, a clerk rearranges the order manually, using a form such as that illustrated in Figure 32. When an order is received, the goods appear in departmental sequence as shown in Figures 27 and 28. The slot number of each item also appears on the order form or is inserted by the salesman from a code book. A clerk then goes through the order, transcribing only the quantities and slot numbers onto the warehouse copy shown in Figure 32. From this copy, on which the items are arranged in slot number sequence, warehouse personnel assembles the order.

When the slot system is used, goods may readily be shifted from one slot to another as the occasion demands. These slots, identified only by numbers, correspond to a person's mailing address and are used only in the warehouse, not by the customer in ordering. If the rate of turnover for an item increases, because of seasonal factors or special promotions, its slot can be changed to allow for the situation. Another advantage of the system is that it practically eliminates the reliance traditionally placed on the memory of warehouse personnel for locating items. In older concerns it is common to find that the warehouse foreman and a few of the senior employees serve as "walking encyclopedias" for searching out items. When the order calls for an item by slot number, it is necessary only to find the corresponding tag or marker on the shelf or pallet rack.[7]

To date, the slot system has not been widely adopted. It is more common to find modified departmental systems of stock layout, with a greater or lesser number of items being singled out for special treatment on account of their velocity of movement, bulk, or weight. Without question, however, the trend is toward greater use of numerical stock arrangement.

Whether or not the regular stocks are arranged departmentally, in most warehouses certain goods must be stored in special facilities because of their perishability, high value, small-order quantities, or legal requirements. Such goods as candy, dairy products, frozen foods, and the like must be refrigerated for obvious reasons. Valuable goods, such as cigarettes, jewelry, or small electrical appliances, must be stored in a "valuables cage" to minimize pilferage. This is often combined with the "broken-package room" from which orders for less than a standard shipping unit (usually a case) are filled. Finally, products like narcotics and ammunition must be stored separately on account of strict legal requirements. Orders calling for such goods may be filled simultaneously from the special stock rooms and from the regular stocks, then combined at the shipping dock for forwarding as a unit.

Mechanization of Order Assembly. The high cost of order assembly results from the fact that it is largely a manual operation. In view of the great economies effected by mechanizing receiving and internal distribution of goods, wholesaling executives have long sought means of applying similar techniques to order assembly. Thus far, actual applications of mechanized order-filling systems have been rather limited, primarily because of the expense involved in their experimental design. By the early 1950's, however, it was at least theoretically possible to construct a completely automatic warehousing system including all phases from receiving to order assembly.[8]

---

[7] For further analysis of the slot system, see W. H. Meserole, *The Spatial Organization of Goods in a Wholesale Warehouse*, Address Before a Management Seminar for Executives in Paper Distribution, The Ohio State University (Mimeographed, 1954); Fisher, *op. cit.*, pp. 90–98. For a description of a complete "slot" system in a grocery warehouse, see "Behind It Are New Ideas to Speed the Goods," *Business Week* (February 26, 1955), 42–46.

[8] "The Push Button Warehouse," *Fortune* (December, 1956), 140 ff.

In several warehouses mechanized order-filling devices were being tried on a limited scale by early 1958. A large drug wholesaler on the West Coast, for example, installed a series of inclined chutes containing stocks of fast-moving items which feed goods onto conveyors. The system includes five conveyors, each of which handles a single order at a time. When an item is listed on an order, an employee releases the desired quantity by activating a gate at the end of the chute. The conveyor then moves the order to the packing room where it is combined with other goods assembled by traditional methods, and then shipped. At first, only 1,800 out of the 34,000 items stocked by the wholesaler were picked automatically.[9] A somewhat similar device is said to have been developed by the Hickok Manufacturing Company for assembling orders of men's furnishings.

Another development in the mechanization of order assembly is the electronic tow truck used in a few grocery warehouses. This truck automatically moves through the order assembly line, stopping only at items called for on a particular order. It is controlled by punched cards prepared in the office at the same time the original store order is processed and the invoice prepared.[10] Thus "automation" eliminates the need for searching by the order-picker almost altogether.

In view of these and related developments, it seems likely that completely mechanized order assembly will some day materialize. Moreover, it will probably be possible to integrate such a system with inventory control, using one or more of the methods described in the next chapter. When this "breakthrough" occurs, warehousing procedures will be revolutionized.

PROCESSING OF ORDERS AFTER ASSEMBLY

During and after the actual assembly of orders in the warehouse, certain additional office processing operations must be carried out. These include *extensions, billing, entry in stock records, checking out, posting,* and *filing.* Depending on the order-handling system used, these operations may precede or follow the shipment of orders to customers.

Extensions. After the goods have been prepared for shipment, the original sales order is returned to the office, where prices are re-examined for substitutions, and extensions are computed and entered in the proper column. In some houses, extensions are made when prices are first checked. If, however, a concern experiences many substitutions, or a large

[9] "Automation Gets It Wholesale," *Business Week* (March 15, 1958), 156–60.
[10] R. M. Winslow, "Automation in Food Wholesale Distribution Centers," in Robert D. Buzzell (ed.), *Adaptive Behavior in Marketing,* Contributed Papers at the December Conference of the American Marketing Association (Columbus, Ohio, 1956), p. 45.

number of orders have to be *filled short*, it is wiser to postpone making extensions until after the order has been filled.

Billing. A separate organization may bill goods to city trade, while another handles invoices to out-of-town customers. This is often done because invoices are usually required for orders delivered by the wholesaler before the goods leave the warehouse; out-of-town orders are usually delivered by common carriers so that shipments may be made before invoices are mailed.

As a general rule, invoices (see Figure 33) should not be prepared until the order has been filled although some houses prepare them in advance, making extensions later. The number of copies of an invoice varies in practice to a considerable degree, anywhere from two to nine or ten. Even when the same number of invoice copies is prepared by two houses, their

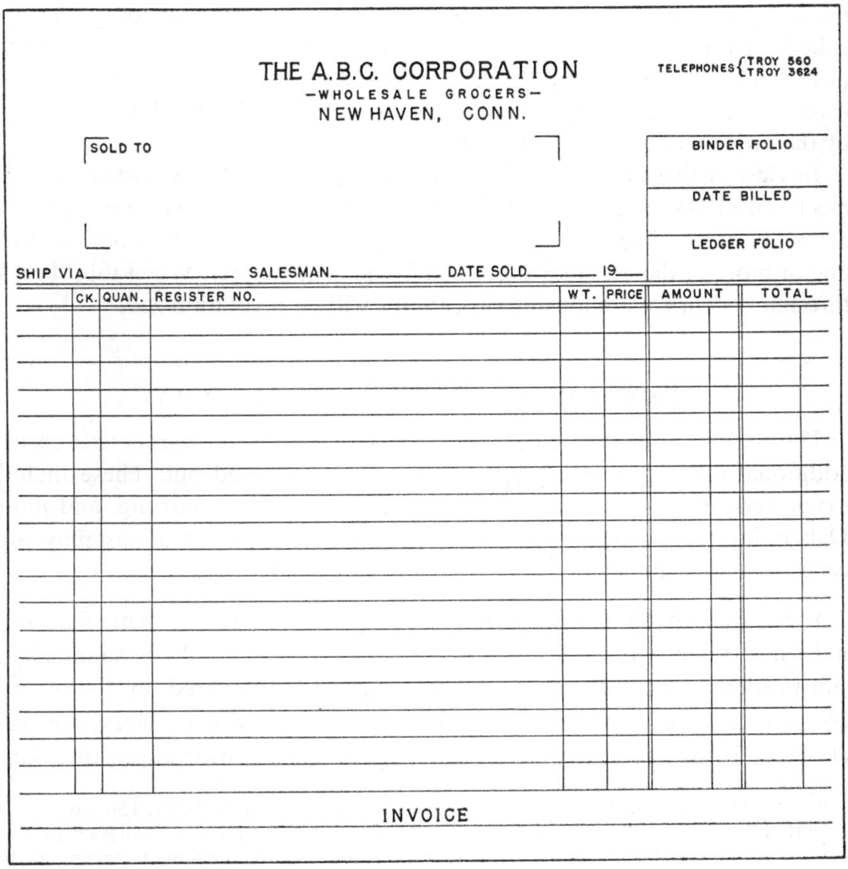

THE A.B.C. CORPORATION
—WHOLESALE GROCERS—
NEW HAVEN, CONN.

TELEPHONES { TROY 560
TROY 3624

SOLD TO

BINDER FOLIO

DATE BILLED

LEDGER FOLIO

SHIP VIA_____ SALESMAN_____ DATE SOLD_____ 19___

CK.	QUAN.	REGISTER NO.	W T.	PRICE	AMOUNT	TOTAL

INVOICE

FIGURE 33. Form of Invoice

destinations may differ greatly. The ribbon copy must always be sent to the customer, and a second copy used for posting to the ledger. Beyond this there is little uniformity. In preparing several copies of an invoice, continuous interfolded or manifold forms may be used so as to eliminate the necessity for numerous operations. Ease of preparation makes it possible to supply extra copies of the invoice to serve one or more of the following purposes:

1. Shipping label or packing slip
2. Shipping order for filling purposes
3. Copy for shipping record and file
4. Copy for entries on stock records
5. Separate copy for pricing
6. Office copy
7. Duplicate for receipt from customer
8. Delivery sheet in case of local deliveries
9. Back-order
10. Salesman's copy
11. Sales department copy
12. Commission copy for clerk who figures salesmen's compensation
13. Branch office copy
14. Credit department or collection copy

How many copies of an invoice to prepare and what their destinations should be depends largely upon the past experience of the house and upon special conditions under which it operates. Some houses make out a bill of lading in triplicate in the same operation as the invoice by means of continuous forms, and others have one or more statements prepared at the same time. The latter are used as reminders if payment is not forthcoming when due.

If the punch card system of perpetual inventory and accounting is used, the invoice is usually prepared when the order is received or while it is being filled in the warehouse. This can be done because there is little danger of "outs" or substitutions on orders. Where the perpetual inventory is accurately maintained, there are shipping units in the warehouse for all unit control cards in the file; conversely, if the house is out of an item, there are no cards in the file and the item will not be billed. Invoices are prepared by an automatic accounting machine in the same manner as individual floor order forms are transcribed, and may be prepared in the same operation if desired. If orders are filled directly from the preprinted order form, then billing must become a separate operation.

A form of automatically transcribed invoice is shown in Figure 34. The identification data at the top of the invoice are printed from a prepunched "customer" card. Each line of the invoice is automatically printed from the item unit control cards, pulled from the "tub" file as units of merchandise are ordered. All information that is punched on these cards can be printed on the invoice. The office copies contain all information shown on the customer's invoice and, in addition, have an extra column in which are recorded the wholesaler's costs for the various items. Totals are cumulated and are automatically printed after the last item card has passed through the machine. Detachable delivery receipts are often provided on such forms when delivery is made by the wholesaler's trucks (see Figure 34).

Occasional errors in invoicing come about when the stock of a particular item is very low and there is a discrepancy between the perpetual in-

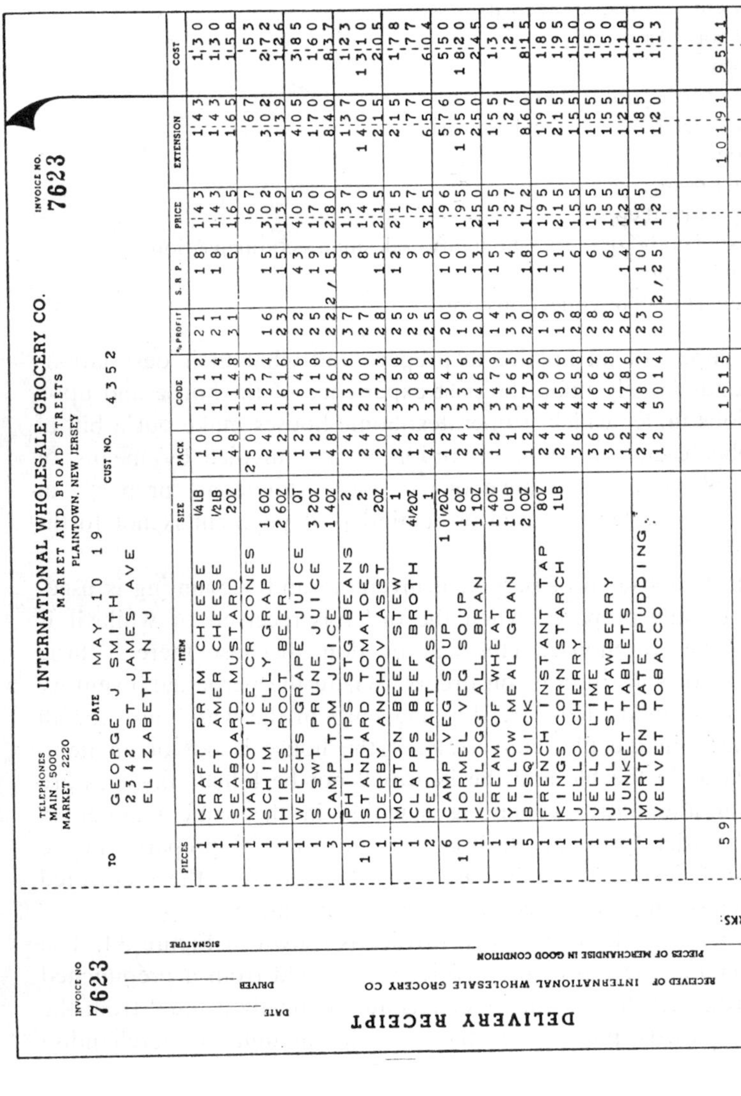

DELIVERY RECEIPT

INVOICE NO 7623

DATE ______ DRIVER ______ SIGNATURE ______

RECEIVED OF INTERNATIONAL WHOLESALE GROCERY CO

PIECES OF MERCHANDISE IN GOOD CONDITION

REMARKS:

TELEPHONES MAIN · 5000 MARKET · 2220

INTERNATIONAL WHOLESALE GROCERY CO.
MARKET AND BROAD STREETS
PLAINTOWN, NEW JERSEY

INVOICE NO. 7623

DATE MAY 10 19

TO GEORGE J SMITH
2342 ST JAMES AVE
ELIZABETH N J

CUST NO. 4352

PIECES	ITEM	SIZE	PACK	CODE	% PROFIT	S. R. P.	PRICE	EXTENSION	COST
1	KRAFT PRIM CHEESE	1/4 LB	10	1012	21	18	1 43	1 43	1 30
1	KRAFT AMER CHEESE	1/2 LB	10	1014	21	18	1 43	1 43	1 30
1	SEABOARD MUSTARD	2OZ	48	1148	31	5	1 65	1 65	1 58
1	MABCO ICE CR CONES		250	1232			67	67	53
1	SCHIM JELLY GRAPE	16OZ	24	1274	16	15	3 02	3 02	2 72
1	HIRES ROOT BEER	26OZ	12	1616	23	15	1 39	1 39	1 26
1	WELCHS GRAPE JUICE	QT	12	1646	22	43	4 05	4 05	3 85
1	S SWT PRUNE JUICE	32OZ	12	1718	25	19	1 70	1 70	1 60
3	CAMP TOM JUICE	14OZ	48	1760	22	2/15	2 80	8 40	8 37
1	PHILLIPS STG BEANS	2	24	2326	37	9	1 37	1 37	1 23
10	STANDARD TOMATOES	2	24	2700	27	8	1 40	14 00	13 10
1	DERBY ANCHOV ASST	2OZ	20	2733	28	15	2 15	2 15	2 05
1	MORTON BEEF STEW	1	24	3058	25	12	2 15	2 15	1 78
1	CLAPPS BEEF BROTH	4 1/2OZ	12	3080	29	9	77	77	77
2	RED HEART ASST	1	48	3182	25	9	3 25	6 50	6 04
6	CAMP VEG SOUP	10 1/2OZ	12	3343	20	10	96	5 76	5 50
10	HORMEL VEG SOUP	16OZ	24	3356	19	10	1 95	19 50	18 20
1	KELLOGG ALL BRAN	11OZ	24	3462	20	13	2 50	2 50	2 45
1	CREAM OF WHEAT	14OZ	12	3479	14	15	1 55	1 55	1 30
1	YELLOW MEAL GRAN	10LB	1	3565	33	4	27	27	21
5	BISQUICK	20OZ	12	3736	20	18	1 72	8 60	8 15
1	FRENCH INSTANT TAP	8OZ	24	4090	19	10	1 95	1 95	1 86
1	KINGS CORN STARCH	1LB	24	4506	19	11	2 15	2 15	1 95
1	JELLO CHERRY		36	4658	28	6	1 55	1 55	1 50
1	JELLO LIME		36	4662	28	6	1 55	1 55	1 50
1	JELLO STRAWBERRY		36	4668	28	6	1 55	1 55	1 50
1	JUNKET TABLETS		12	4786	26	14	1 25	1 25	1 18
1	MORTON DATE PUDDING		24	4802	23	10	1 85	1 85	1 50
1	VELVET TOBACCO		12	5014	20	2/25	1 20	1 20	1 13
59				1515				101 91	95 41
TOTAL PIECES				TOTAL WEIGHT				TOTAL EXTENSION	TOTAL COST

Courtesy of International Business Machines Corporation

FIGURE 34. Invoice Form Transcribed by Automatic Machine Billing

ventory and the physical stock. For example, there may be one unit control card left in the file but no corresponding unit of merchandise in the warehouse. The item extension is printed on the invoice when the order is received, the discrepancy is noted as the order is filled or checked, and a separate credit memorandum is prepared for the customer. In the opposite situation, when the order is filled directly from the preprinted form and the file shows an "out" for an item that is actually in stock, a separate invoice is prepared for the one item after the discrepancy is noted in checking the invoice against the assembled order. These situations occur very infrequently in a well-managed concern, for they can arise only as the result of a combination of two factors, a low stock and an erroneous perpetual inventory record.

Entry in Stock Records. If a perpetual inventory system is maintained, each sales order or sales invoice must pass through the hands of the clerks making entries in the stock records. At what point in the procedure this should be done is a matter of controversy. Some authorities insist that entries in the stock records should be made as soon as the goods are priced and the order is approved for credit. This assumes, however, that orders are filled exactly in rotation, that no substitutes will be effected, and no deviations will be made in the number of units filled. For fast-moving stocks of a nontechnical nature this is hardly possible; hence it is far better to wait until the order is actually filled. In firms that use the punch card system for stock control, the adjustment of stock records is taken care of as unit control cards are withdrawn from the "tub" file in connection with order transcription or billing.

Checking Out. When the order has gone through the above operations, its work is about finished and it should be sent to the register clerk who checks it out, thus keeping track of every order until completed.

Posting. The order is then sent by the order register clerk to the accounting department. Here the customer is charged with the proper amount in the sales, cash, or accounts receivable ledger, as the case may be, and such other records are prepared as are deemed necessary for good management. Posting is also done from a copy of the invoice in many houses. Departmental copies of the order are commonly used for statistical purposes and then discarded.

Filing. The final step in the routing procedure is to file the original order and also one copy of the invoice. The latter may be used for analysis of sales, as a basis for adjustment of claims, and for other purposes. Such files are usually kept for a period of five or six years, depending in part upon the statute of limitations in the territory in which the house functions.

PACKING AND SHIPPING

Packing and shipping operations may be performed by the same department or the two functions may be separated. In either event there must be close cooperation between them and in rush hours the personnel may be transferred from one activity to the other. The shipping department, in turn, may be divided into city and country divisions, the former taking care of city packing and delivery, and the latter preparing orders for parcel post, freight, express, or long-distance truck shipment.

Packing and Checking. As has been shown in the earlier discussion in this chapter, merchandise may reach the packing room via two methods. If the order is filled from a single copy of a preprinted or ordinary order form, the filled order reaches its destination as a unit, having been built up as it passed through the various departments. If the order is filled simultaneously by means of duplicate copies, the merchandise is sent directly to the packing or shipping rooms from the individual order-fillers.

Regardless of the procedure followed in filling orders in the stock rooms, when the merchandise is assembled in the packing room it must be checked by packers against the original order, and all outs, substitutions, and shortages carefully noted. *Out slips* are prepared if the order cannot be filled entirely, and errors are corrected as discovered.

In some wholesale houses checking is decentralized, and is performed at each order-picking station.[11] The main advantage of this method is a saving in the time required to correct errors. It suffers from the disadvantage, however, that collusion between order-pickers and checkers is facilitated and pilferage may increase. Still another variation in procedure is *sample-checking,* in which only valuable items are checked on each order. At intervals, orders are checked completely to ascertain which order-pickers, if any, are exceeding a reasonable rate of error.[12] If picking errors are relatively few, and if warehouse personnel is experienced and honest, sample checking is probably adequate to control the assembly process.

After the order has been checked, the packer proceeds to pack the goods and prepare them for shipment. Packing is still largely a manual operation, although some mechanical equipment has been devised for its performance. Many tobacco wholesalers, for example, use *tying machines* which automatically tie bundles with twine in a matter of a few seconds.[13]

When orders are shipped largely or entirely in full cases, as is true in the grocery business, no packing is necessary. Goods are then sent directly

---

[11] Fisher, *op. cit.,* pp. 117–19.

[12] *Ibid.,* pp. 119–20; *Methods of Handling and Delivering Orders Used by Some Leading Wholesale Grocers, op. cit.,* pp. 22–24.

[13] Harry B. Patrey in collaboration with Joseph Kolodny, *Successful Methods of Wholesale Tobacco Distribution* (New York: Foresight Publications, 1957), pp. 522–23.

from the warehouse to the shipping room and checked as they are loaded onto trucks.

Methods of Shipment. Depending on the line of business and market area served, orders may be shipped by any of several methods. Some wholesalers, as in the hardware trade, ship many orders by common carrier or parcel post. On the other hand, establishments serving local market areas deliver most orders with their own trucks. On orders picked up by customers, obviously, no shipping at all is necessary. Shipping activities are among the responsibilities of the *traffic manager,* as indicated in the next section.

TRAFFIC MANAGEMENT

There are two kinds of merchandise movement or traffic in a wholesale concern. The *internal movement* of goods, which is part of the work of the warehouse personnel and the respective merchandise departments, includes such operations as checking, pricing, distributing to departments and floors, assembling for storage and handling, packing and order-routing. The *external movement* of goods centers around the functions of receiving, shipping, and local delivery, and represents the core of activity of the traffic department. The term traffic management is restricted in this discussion to the external transportation problems and activities of the wholesaler.

Traffic management is not always recognized as an important wholesaling activity; however, not only is the performance of such functions in a wholesale house a vital necessity, but, when properly discharged, it may accomplish numerous savings and result in the elimination of waste. If the wholesale house is a large one, traffic management is the function of a separate department in charge of a traffic manager, but in smaller concerns this duty is customarily assigned to some one in the shipping room, usually the shipping clerk. The person responsible for the work should possess, in addition to a formal training in transportation and traffic management, a certain amount of practical experience that will enable him to speak the *traffic language* and readily develop and maintain favorable contacts with carriers, freight agents, switch clerks, rate clerks, and even the yard crew. He should be familiar with all available transportation facilities for the movement of both inbound and outbound shipments, and thoroughly conversant with the various express and freight classifications.

Traffic Management and Receiving. Most activities in which the receiving department is engaged do not relate directly to the external movement of goods, but there are some functions connected therewith which demand attention of a traffic expert. These activities are outlined below:

1. Routing incoming shipments in order to effect economies in transportation and to expedite receipt of the goods. Having complete knowledge

of the best routings from a given source of supply to his warehouse, the traffic manager should pass such information on to vendors. Since the wholesaler normally pays the freight on incoming goods, he usually designates the route over which they shall be shipped. Suggestions as to routing are normally accepted by the manufacturer even when the latter pays the freight.

2. Tracing undue delays in transportation or lost shipments. In doing this, the traffic manager must be able to estimate the location of a shipment by the time-distance between source of supply and destination. This can be done through a familiarity with the average rate of speed per hour for freight by the different types of carriers.

3. Carting *from* terminals is another receiving problem which is closely allied to carting *to* terminals on outgoing shipments; hence the problem of carting is treated here in its entirety. One of the chief questions to be decided is whether to use the equipment of the firm or to hire such independent agencies as transfer and trucking companies. Common carriers have tended to assume responsibility for this function through the adoption of so-called *store-door delivery* service, whereby the carrier not only *delivers* less-than-carload freight to the consignee but also *collects* the goods from the consignor. This service offers several advantages, some of which inure to the benefit of the wholesaler and others to the benefit of the carrier. It reduces the number of vehicles crowding about terminals, relieves traffic congestion, facilitates full loads with incidental savings, and enables the railroads to handle a greater volume of goods through their freight terminals. The unloading of merchandise directly from the freight car to the truck for immediate delivery contributes to greater economy. Otherwise, goods must be unloaded and placed in the freight house, the consignee must be notified of their arrival, and finally, the goods must be stored until called for. Other benefits which accrue from such a unified plan result from the fact that collection and delivery of shipments decrease idle time of expensive carting equipment. There tend to be fewer idle and motionless cars on railroad tracks and thus a larger supply of them is available. The wholesaler is relieved from the necessity of engaging in transportation which can be best performed by specialized agencies. The greatest impetus, however, to the widespread adoption of this plan has been the competition which railroads have faced from long-distance trucking companies that both collect the shipments from consignors and deliver them to the doors of consignees.

4. The traffic manager also supervises the unloading and weighing of merchandise in order to minimize demurrage charges and to make the goods quickly available so that sales may be expedited and cancellations and back-orders reduced to a minimum. Weighing is of especial importance when freight is paid by the receiver, or when shipment is in less-than-

carlots. Claims against carriers or vendors may arise from shortages thus discovered.

5. Auditing of freight bills, embracing an examination of the classifications assigned to each item on the bill and a verification of extensions should be handled by a traffic expert. When audited and found correct, freight bills are approved and filed with the corresponding bills of lading. If discrepancies are disclosed, a basis is furnished for claims, since payments to carriers are usually made immediately upon receipt of the goods although a limited amount of credit may be extended by railroads to shippers on their approved list.

6. It is the function of the traffic department to handle the claims resulting from discrepancies in incoming shipments. Such claims are filed against the carriers if they have arisen out of *bad-order* shipments, *concealed loss or damage,* and errors in freight bills. In filing a claim against a carrier, all data in substantiation thereof are presented, including the original bill of lading, the original invoice or a certified copy thereof, the original freight bill showing notation of loss or damage as made and signed by the carrier's agent, and, if the loss is concealed, the copy of the inspection report which was made out by the agent when the damage was discovered must also be presented. The chief reasons for claims against vendors, except where merchandise is returned, are shortage, damage for which they are responsible, overcharges, and misrouting. Even when these claims are prepared by merchandise department managers, the traffic department keeps records of them and follows them through to a satisfactory adjustment.

7. Another duty of the traffic department is to arrange for insurance adequate to protect the wholesaler's interests in, and liabilities for, goods in transit. When the wholesaler purchases goods f.o.b. point of shipment, he takes title to the merchandise at the origin and assumes the responsibility for all damage or loss that is not directly attributable to the negligence of the shipper or carrier. Similarly, when selling on an f.o.b. destination or delivered basis, he is responsible for goods being transported to customers, except for the liability of the carrier. Thus insurance arrangements are important with respect to both receiving and shipping activities. Insurance is often required when there are gaps in the continuous liability of carriers in the handling of a shipment; when the liability of the carrier is limited, as may occur if several carriers or different types of carriers handle a shipment; when the liability of the carrier is limited, as is the case when goods are shipped at declared or reduced valuations; when a shipment contains dangerous articles that are likely to damage goods of other shippers or the equipment of the carrier; and under other special circumstances.

8. Records and statistics on inbound shipments are a useful tool in traffic management. A record of inbound tonnage, especially over con-

trolled roads, that is, roads chosen by the receiver, is desirable, as is a file of freight bills, a record of claims filed, a claim pending file, and a transfer file for settled claims.

Traffic Management and Shipping. The principal functions of the traffic department in connection with shipping operations, in addition to carting to terminals and arranging for the necessary insurance, are as follows:

1. Outgoing shipments are routed in order to reduce costs of transportation to customers, to increase speed of delivery as a service to the trade, and to prevent damage to perishable merchandise. In routing such shipments there is usually a greater variety of transportation facilities from which to choose, but very often the means of shipment—whether by freight, express, truck, water route, or air, as well as the particular carrier—are designated by the customer when placing the order.

2. One of the shipping tasks of the traffic department is that of packing. This work is done with due reference to the safety of the goods, cost of packing material, labor costs, and the effect of a given type of packing and material upon the classification rate. The nature of the goods often determines the type of packing, the general trend being away from heavy wooden boxes to the lighter and less expensive containers made of composition board, light woods, and fiber or pulpwood.

3. Another function is the marking of freight for shipment. Markings should be durable and legible showing only the essential points, such as identity of the shipper, consignee, and of the goods. Checking weights and classifications is also necessary. Freight rates vary, not only with the nature of the goods and method of packing but also according to the commodities combined in a package. Consequently, no goods of two different classifications are included in the same package, where the freight is a significant item, since the entire package would take the highest rate classification applicable to any of the contents. The contents are carefully described so as to obtain the lowest rate classification possible. *Cost book catalogs* and *freight classification books* are helpful in ascertaining exact weights and in securing a billing terminology for honestly describing them so as to obtain rates materially lower than charged if the designations were less exact.

4. Weighing shipments, both carload and smaller quantities, is another shipping room activity. Freight charges are arrived at by multiplying the weight of the shipment by the authorized rate, hence weights must be recorded on the bill of lading. A distribution list is made out showing weights of the different packages, when shipping in small amounts, to facilitate proper allocation of cost to the different customers. Platform scales are used for weighing goods on trucks, track scales are provided for weighing carload shipments, and different types of portable scales are used for other purposes.

5. In connection with all shipments that are not called for by carriers, the ordering of empty railroad cars, trucks, or trailers to be spotted for loading falls in the province of the traffic manager. He must also know how to stow the cars to attain maximum efficiency and a minimum shifting of goods. Whether heated, refrigerated, or other special cars or trucks are needed must likewise be determined. To supervise the loading of goods to prevent damage, and to see that all packages are called and checked against a record previously prepared by the shipping room are additional activities of the traffic department.

6. Rate information to the sales department is furnished by the traffic department to enable salesmen to quote prices which will meet competition. This is especially true when it is necessary to equalize rates by prepaying all or part of the freight bill. Claims for customers against carriers are commonly handled by the wholesaler who maintains a traffic department, even though the customer pays the freight, since few retailers know the exact procedure. The traffic department maintains records of outgoing traffic operations as well as those of receiving activities mentioned previously. If many large rail shipments are made, this work includes a record of sales tonnage, by carriers; a record of all cars ordered, showing date the car was ordered, date of delivery on the switch, when it was set, loaded, taken out, the initials and number of the car, and name of consignee; the amount of prepaid freight, by customers and salesmen; and a file of shipping tickets showing a complete record of each shipment.

Management of Local Delivery Operations. Another responsibility of the traffic manager is that of managing local delivery activities. In most lines of business it has become customary for wholesalers to deliver orders with their own equipment or with equipment leased from cartage firms in the immediate vicinity of the warehouse. In fact, the relative economies of truck shipment have led to an extension of what was once considered the "local" market area, with truck deliveries now commonly being made over distances up to 100 miles and even more.

Whether to own a fleet of trucks or to contract local deliveries to a firm specializing in this type of service is a question calling for an important decision. In making the choice, a comparison of the contract cost and the estimated cost of performing the service by owned equipment is the main factor, although consideration is also given to the comparative flexibility of the two systems, the lack of control over employees of the contract hauler, the capital investment required for delivery equipment, physical facilities required for garaging and servicing of owned equipment, managerial problems, and other similar factors. If a fleet of his own trucks is operated by the wholesaler, there is the continuing problem of determining the type of equipment to use. A large number of small trucks usually provides a more flexible system, but is also more costly to operate than a smaller number of large trucks capable of carrying the same loads. When the physical volume of shipments is large as in the grocery trade, economical operations are frequently achieved by the use of a tractor-trailer system. Since there are several trailers for each tractor, the tractors do not have to stand idle while trailers are being loaded or unloaded.

Whether to make a specific charge to the customer for the cost of delivery is another problem requiring attention. In densely populated markets, where small areas are involved, the cost of delivery is generally absorbed into the total operating expenses. In sparsely populated areas, however, the concept of "local" may involve long distances, resulting in markedly different costs of delivering to different customers. When this is the situation, there is frequently a separate charge for the wholesaler's delivery service in terms of specified monetary amounts or as a percentage of sales. In some houses such charges are based on a combination of weight and distance factors, with the charge increasing in direct proportion to the distance traveled in making the delivery. In other firms a territorial arrangement is used of the postal zone rate type, with the same charge applying to all customers within a given area.

Routing and controlling the movement of local delivery equipment is another problem. The territory must be zoned to prevent overlapping and to insure delivery according to schedule. Every delivery department maintains route sheets showing the movement of all vehicles, also a file of copies of all orders receipted by customers. It is often necessary to coordinate delivery routes with salesmen's routes and to schedule delivery runs so that customers get their merchandise as soon as possible after the salesman's call. The best route to be followed within each delivery zone is a matter that must be determined largely by trial and error. Preferably, the traffic manager should make trips with each driver in order to familiarize himself with streets and traffic conditions. If the routes are carefully planned, overtime of drivers can be minimized and expenses thus controlled. Experiments have shown that when routes are not planned by the traffic manager, excessive delivery cost inevitably results.

Finally, accurate expense records showing the cost of maintaining and operating the individual items of equipment are indispensable to efficiency and service. Cost per truck, per mile, and per ton-mile are measures that are computed from properly kept records as aids in deciding such questions as whether to own equipment or contract the delivery service, the types of equipment to operate, and the amount of delivery charges to be made.

25

INVENTORY CONTROL

Closely connected with warehousing and order assembly procedures is the system of *inventory control* or *stock control* used in a wholesale enterprise. Inventory control also affects, and is affected by, most of the other major management functions. It serves as a guide to *buying* and is often a part of this division in the organizational structure. It contributes to effective *selling* by maintaining the adequate stock assortments so essential to continued business relationships with customers. Finally, it underlies the whole method of *merchandise-planning* and the concept of *stock turnover* through which buying, stock availability, and selling are coordinated. Since inventory control touches on so many phases of operations, it is clearly one of the most important managerial tools in a wholesale house. Thus it is not surprising that the presence or absence of a well-conceived inventory control system is often one of the big differences between a well-managed business and a struggling concern leading to ultimate failure.

Nature and Purposes of Inventory Control

As will be seen in subsequent parts of this chapter, there are several types of inventory control systems and many variations of each of them. Regardless of system and procedural details, the basic nature and purposes of inventory control are the same in any wholesale business.

Inventory Control Defined. In a broad sense "inventory control" designates any and all procedures and records intended to prevent running out of goods and at the same time to avoid costly overstocking. In this sense inventory control obviously includes the whole technique of merchandise-planning discussed in Chapter 20. Merchandise-planning in dollar terms is not, however, true inventory control. It is an administrative control over investments in inventory, exercised at the departmental level and for the business as a whole. Such a system may show, for example, that Department A has exceeded its planned inventory levels and that some reduction is in order. It does not tell *why* such overstocking occurred and *where.* Neither does it provide any adequate control over "outs." More basically, it fails to provide any day-to-day guidance to buyers or others responsible for purchasing, who must determine *how much* to buy of *each item* and *when.*

Inventory control in a more definitive or in its fullest sense includes all procedures and records designed to show, on an *item-by-item basis,* (1) how much is in stock and/or on order at any given time and (2) when the item should be reordered. This requires a vastly more complex system than that used in merchandise-planning. Information must be collected, recorded, and analyzed for each of the thousands of items typically carried by a wholesale concern. It goes without saying that such systems are expensive to operate. Yet, as one authority in the field has commented, ". . . no expense incurred by the distributor can be as easily justified as the cost of maintaining an effective inventory control system."[1]

Purposes of Inventory Control. The basic purpose of inventory control is implied in the definition given in the preceding paragraph. Since the system indicates when an item should be ordered, it serves as a *guide to buying.* In large part, it replaces the guesswork and "judgment" of the old-time buyer with concrete, exact information. This does not imply that buying becomes automatic under an inventory control system. The need for skill in buying remains, but the buyer's time and energies are freed from routine clerical tasks and may be directed to more important matters.

In addition to guiding buying activities, inventory control serves a number of other purposes. First, in conjunction with the financial controls discussed in Chapter 20, it makes possible the efficient use of investment in inventory by optimizing the rate of stock turnover. Second, and equally important, it helps to reduce "outs," substitutions, and back orders, and thus indirectly contributes to enhanced customer satisfaction. Third, it provides a basis for the control of pilferage and other causes of stock shortages. Fourth, it makes possible the early detection of slow-moving items and the taking of prompt corrective action. Finally, it facilitates a smooth physical flow of goods through the warehouse and, by reducing the inventory needed to support a given sales volume, alleviates space problems.

The Reorder Point. One of the two main objectives of an inventory control system is to avoid running "out" or "short" of any item, or at least to hold "outs" and "shorts" within predetermined limits. This is accomplished primarily through the setting of *reorder points* for each item. When

---

[1] Joseph Kolodny in *Successful Methods of Wholesale Tobacco Distribution* (New York: Foresight Publications, 1957), p. 182.

an item reaches its reorder point, the buyer more or less automatically places an order with the supplier.

The theory underlying the use of reorder points is shown schematically in the top part of Figure 35. Here it is assumed that an item sells at a uniform rate of 40 units per day and that the standard ordering quantity is 1,200 units as determined by the methods discussed in Chapter 21. It is also assumed that it takes *exactly* 5 days to receive goods from the supplier after an order is placed. Given this information it is easy to set

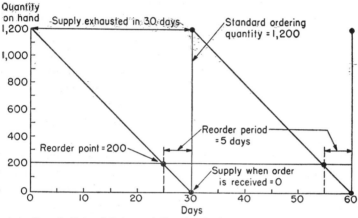

Case A: Rate of Sales and Reorder Period Certainly Known

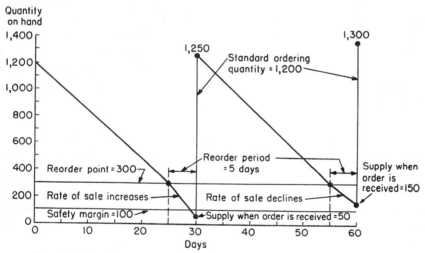

Case B: Safety Margin to Allow for Uncertainty Regarding Rate of Sale (or Reorder Period)

FIGURE 35. Schematic Diagram of the Use of Reorder Points in Inventory Control

up the control system. Since it takes 5 days to receive goods, the *reorder point* should be set at 200 (5 days times 40). Whenever the stock reaches this point an order is placed; when the order is received the stock on hand will have reached zero. All that is needed is a method of ascertaining when the stock reaches 200 and the rest is automatic.

The matter is not, however, this simple. In the first place, the rate of sale and the reorder period (time required to receive an order) are not known exactly; these factors change according to season, general economic conditions, and chance variations. Thus it is necessary to provide a *safety margin* in establishing reorder points, as shown in Case B of Figure 35. Here the safety margin has been set at 100 units; the reorder point then becomes 300 (200 plus 100). If the rate of sale increases, as shown in the first 30-day period of the example, the supply may fall below the reserve. On the other hand, if demand falls off, as in the second 30-day period of the example, the stock on hand at the time the new order comes in will be more than the minimum of 100. It is also possible that the reorder period will deviate from 5 days, which would have effects similar to those just indicated.

Safety margins used in establishing reorder points are usually determined on the basis of prior experience. Often there is a tendency to allow for maximum variations, with resulting excess stocks. For example, if it takes a week to replenish the stock of an item, the reorder point may be set at the *maximum* weekly demand, and stocks would never be depleted. But it may be preferable to allow stocks to run out once in a while if the average inventory can be reduced substantially thereby. The degree of safety that is desirable varies, of course, for the different types of commodities.

A more systematic approach to setting reorder points was being developed experimentally in the mid-1950's. This approach is based on an application of probability theory and makes it possible to hold the chances of running out of an item within predetermined limits such as one in a hundred or one in twenty.[2]

INVENTORY CONTROL THROUGH VARIOUS SYSTEMS

In a wholesale house inventory control is attained through inventory systems. Essentially, an inventory is a periodic counting and recording of merchandise and its estimated worth. It may be taken at definite intervals or maintained continuously. Many modifications and variations of inventory methods may be found in actual practice, but generally all inventory systems in use by wholesale firms may be classified into six types.

---

[2] For an explanation of this method that is applicable to wholesaling as well as to retailing, see William S. Peters, "Control of Stocks in Grocery Retailing," *Journal of Marketing,* XXII (October, 1957), 148–53.

1. Actual Physical Inventory
2. Physical Inspection
3. Continuous "Stock-Taking"
4. Tickler Method of Inventory
5. Purchase Record System of Inventory Control
6. Real Perpetual Inventory

The first four types of control require physical contact with the goods, while the remaining two are achieved mainly through records. These methods of control are adapted to different lines of business and each is suited to special conditions. Inasmuch as large varieties of merchandise may be handled by a single wholesale house and the circumstances underlying the operations of any one concern may differ from those of another, it is to be expected that houses in the same line of business will use different methods of stock control. Even in a single establishment two or more methods of control may be utilized for different classes of merchandise. Furthermore, adaptations of any one type of control must be made to the personnel and any special characteristics of the firm adopting it.

Actual Physical Inventory. Irrespective of the method used in determining monthly, weekly, daily, or perpetual inventories, the actual physical inventory cannot be eliminated. When properly taken, it is the most accurate of all inventory systems yet devised, is the only means of checking upon the accuracy of other methods of stock control in use, and is superior to the alternative methods in unearthing leaks and losses. Such an inventory, therefore, must be taken at least once or twice a year. If the supplementary records maintained are inadequate, actual physical inventories should be taken at more frequent intervals, probably once a month, although the validity of such practice, at least in most businesses, is questionable, as is shown below.

Before taking an actual physical inventory, certain preparations must be made. All merchandise must be arranged in an orderly manner and in accordance with the classifications in use. Broken packages are filled or taken to the broken package room, containers are repaired and replaced, and the warehouse is cleared for speed in the inventory process. A responsible official of the company supervises the work, in which he is assisted by the various department managers and buyers. In taking this kind of inventory, each item in stock is actually counted, whether in the warehouse of the company, in outside warehouses, on the shipping floor, in the receiving department, or in the broken package room. Furthermore, the goods must be inspected for quality, age, and general condition. Spoiled, deteriorated, shopworn, and obsolete goods are set aside and excluded from the regular inventory.

To accomplish the counting and inspection, two principal methods are used by wholesalers, the tag method and the inventory sheet method. When tags are used one person acts as both counter and marker. Under this plan it is not necessary to close up the plant and cease business operations while the goods are inspected, counted, measured, or weighed, but only for a short time while the tags are being gathered. A tag similar to that shown in Figure 36 is prepared for each article. To prevent loss, the tags

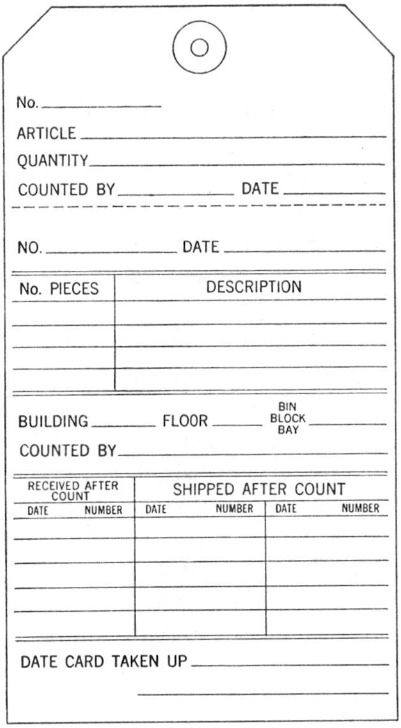

No. ______

ARTICLE ______

QUANTITY ______

COUNTED BY ______ DATE ______

NO. ______ DATE ______

No. PIECES	DESCRIPTION

BUILDING ______ FLOOR ______ BIN BLOCK BAY ______

COUNTED BY ______

RECEIVED AFTER COUNT		SHIPPED AFTER COUNT			
DATE	NUMBER	DATE	NUMBER	DATE	NUMBER

DATE CARD TAKEN UP ______

FIGURE 36. Physical Inventory Tag

are numbered consecutively and a given series of numbers is assigned to each person participating in taking the inventory. The tag is perforated into two parts, and when the quantity of an article is determined it is posted both on the stub and the detachable part; it is then wired to the merchandise or container. On the lower part, spaces are provided for the recording of additions to and withdrawals from stock since the count, and for the date the tag is taken up. When all items have thus been tagged, the detachable parts are collected and taken to the office where the items and quantities are copied on inventory forms similar to that shown in Figure 37.

A variation of the tag method of physical inventory is to record the inventory count on punch cards. These cards may become the permanent inventory record or the inventory may be posted to inventory sheets

Stock No.	Description	Quan-tity	Cost Price	Present Market Value	Per	Inven-tory Exten-sion	Totals	Proof Extension
	Amount Forward							
.....	....	....	...	....	...	....	...	....
.....	....	....	...	....	...	....	...	....
.....	....	....	...	....	...	....	...	....
.....	....	....	...	....	...	....	...	....
.....	....	....	...	....	...	....	...	....
.....	....	....	...	....	...	....	...	....

Department_____Sheet No____

Date_____19__ Details of_____Stock_____

Called by____Entered by____Priced by____Calculated by____Verified by__

Sheet No.

Stock

FIGURE 37. Physical Inventory Sheet

by manual or mechanical means. A type of physical inventory punch card, designed for automatic machine sorting, computation, and listing of the inventory, is shown in Figure 38.[3] Almost any type of information such as department number, description of the item, quantity on hand, cost price, selling price, gross margin, warehouse location, initials of the counter, and so on, may be recorded on cards of this kind, according to the needs of the individual firm. The cards are numbered and prepunched in order to account for all cards issued. The item numbers and descriptions are pre-printed and prepunched on the cards by mechanical equipment before the cards are issued, or are filled in manually by the inventory clerk at the time of the counting. If the latter procedure is used, the counter writes the item number and the quantity on the left-hand part of the card and on the stub, as shown in Figure 38. The same information is marked on the right-hand part of the card in the numbered spaces by means of a pencil which is sensitive to electric impulses, and for that reason this form is generally referred to as a "mark-sensed" card.

The recorded information can then be punched automatically as the card goes through a machine specially designed for that purpose. Cost in-

[3] Supplies and equipment for punch card systems of physical inventory and other accounting and control purposes are furnished by International Business Machines Corporation and Remington Rand Division, Sperry Rand Corporation. A somewhat similar type of card, which is punched and sorted and has the extensions computed by manual operations, is supplied by the Royal-McBee Company, makers of "Keysort" cards. The manner in which "Keysort" cards are handled is indicated in a following section of this chapter dealing with punch card systems of statistical and perpetual inventory.

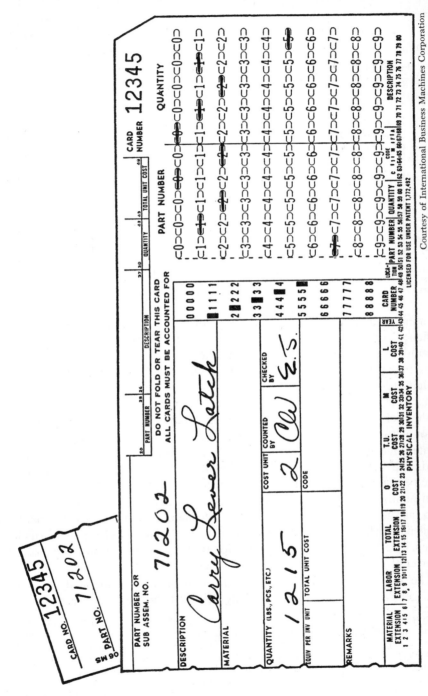

Courtesy of International Business Machines Corporation

FIGURE 38. "Mark-Sensed" Punch Card for Automatic Computation and Sorting of Physical Inventory Item Records

formation and selling prices, if desired, are also entered on the card and punched. The inventory is figured by running all cards through an accounting machine that automatically multiplies the price by the quantity and carries a cumulating total. The letters of the alphabet can be punched on these cards as well as numbers; thus the item description can be punched. As the individual cards pass through the machine, all information that has been punched on the card can be automatically printed, in one action, as a line on an inventory listing sheet. This system requires the use of expensive equipment and specially trained personnel.

This type of physical inventory is not generally used unless such equipment is already employed by a firm for other accounting and control purposes. Both the manual and the automatic punch card physical inventory systems are particularly well adapted to branch house or chain operations where it is desired to bring all inventory records together for combined analysis. If the proper information is recorded and punched, the entire group of cards for the whole organization can be sorted according to departments and items, extensions can be made, and the cards can be resorted in any desired manner, all in a very short period of time.

If the inventory sheet method is used, the work is usually done by a pair of employees, one calling and inspecting the merchandise as it comes, and the other entering the description and quantities on the sheet. After the first count, checker and caller change places and go over for a second time the entire stock to which they were assigned. Sometimes the sheets are exchanged with another pair working in a neighboring section, for rechecking. All sheets are numbered in the office to prevent losses.

The inventory sheets containing the items and quantities are submitted to buyers for pricing, either at cost or market value or according to whatever policy the concern has chosen to follow. Then the items are extended; that is, the number of units of each article is multiplied by the price and totals are entered for each sheet. To enhance accuracy in this work, responsibility is allocated for every operation by requiring each clerk to initial in the appropriate place the nature of the work done. An additional column may be provided for extensions, so that after the first column of extensions is made it can be torn off at a perforated place and the extensions made a second time, after which the two are compared to insure accuracy.

From the foregoing description it is apparent that the actual physical inventory cannot be used as a sole method of stock control. To do so would necessitate taking such inventories at frequent intervals. This would be a dreaded ordeal, since it usually requires closing down the plant and calls for much preparation of the stock in the warehouse. Likewise, pricing is a difficult task, and the calculating of extensions and verifying them are tedious operations representing much clerical work and time diverted from regular business. Moreover, the job of inspecting and counting the merchandise is unpleasant. As a result the work is rushed through, and salesmen and others not interested are often pressed into service. The outcome is that there are errors in the count, in the description or identification of the items, in the recording of quantities and prices, and in making extensions and verifications, as well as in adding up totals. Thus, while the actual physical inventory is the most accurate of all when properly taken, serves as a check on others, and helps to discover shortages and merchandise of poor quality, the conditions under which it is usually taken militate against its frequent use. Every attempt is made to take such an inventory when the stock is the lowest, such as the end of the fiscal year or in the middle of the summer before goods for the autumn season are received.

It is sometimes reported that wholesale concerns in the grocery trade take physical inventories each week, because warehouse operating conditions are more favorable to inventory-taking in that line; this, however, is generally in the nature of *continuous stock-taking,* which is discussed in a following section, rather than a complete physical inventory which may be used properly for accounting purposes.

Physical Inspection. This method of stock control is by far the simplest yet devised, is the easiest means of keeping track of stock movements, and is the most economical. It simply requires placing responsibility on some persons for reporting items which are running low, although on occasion the system may also call for reports on slow-moving items. This responsibility may be assumed by the buyers themselves or may be placed upon stock clerks, order-fillers, or even porters. The buyer may make a regular trip daily through the warehouse or through the portion for which he is responsible, familiarizing himself with the stock and at the same time compiling lists of wants and slow-movers. When others are charged with that responsibility they are furnished with a want list, in which items that are being rapidly depleted are entered and called to the attention of the buyers. These are sometimes supplemented by special reports, such as those obtained when vendors' salesmen call or when important orders are placed by mail. If the task is assigned to a single person, the work is usually so divided that one floor is inspected each day. This method of control is the least scientific and most haphazard. Its application is limited to those lines of business, like groceries, where numerous units of a given article are constantly kept in stock and the merchandise can be so arranged as to make possible an estimate of conditions, based upon a quick inspection.

Continuous "Stock-Taking." This method of inventory, sometimes called *count of stock* control, resembles in some ways the actual physical inventory, but differs from it in the following respects: (1) only *whole* goods are counted, that is, merchandise in original containers and no broken packages; (2) goods are not inspected for their physical condition;

(3) in stock-taking rechecking the count is eliminated; (4) since no values are used there is no need for pricing, extension, verification, or totaling. The elimination of much of the work attendant upon an actual physical inventory makes possible the continuous use of the stock-taking method of physical count. Special forms may be provided on which to report the condition of stock. *Low* reports indicate an impending shortage on fast-moving items; *out* reports are prepared when immediate reordering is essential. *Short lists* serve the same purpose as *out* reports.

This inventory method is used solely for the control of purchases with the view of reducing outs and shortages, preventing stagnant stocks, and securing a maximum turnover. Under this plan the merchandise is counted weekly, biweekly, or monthly; the work is done regularly by stock clerks or on Saturdays with the assistance of outside salesmen. The information is recorded on stock sheets such as that shown in Figure 39. On this sheet,

ITEM - DESCRIPTION, PACK, ETC.	ORDERING GUIDE		1-4	1-11	1-18	1-25	2-1	2-8	2-15
Uncle John's Remedy Large Size - 24's	MIN. 10	INV.	10	31	21	10	32	21	
	ORD. 30	ORD.	30			30			
		REC.		30			30		
John Doe's Tonic Large Size - 24's	MIN. 40	INV.	60	40	20	105	82	60	
	ORD. 100	ORD.		100					
		REC.				100			
Etc.,	MIN.	INV.							
	ORD.	ORD.							
		REC.							

FIGURE 39. Page from Stock Book Used in Periodical-Count Method of Stock Control

the vertical columns represent dates on which stock is counted. For each item listed on the sheet, spaces are provided for recording stock on hand, on order, and for receipts. The column headed "Ordering Guide" shows the minimum stock (reorder point) and the maximum. When the minimum is reached, an order is placed for the maximum amount.

A careful study of the information on these sheets over a period of time will disclose the intervals normally elapsing between date of placing an order and date of receipt of the merchandise, and indicate the amount of stock on hand in relation to sales and to orders placed for which no goods have as yet been received.

The periodical count involved in stock-taking is best adapted to concerns in which the merchandise is stored in original packages as received from manufacturers, containing a comparatively large number of individual units, and to concerns whose sales are large in number but are made in small quantities. If sales are relatively few and individually substantial, it would be more economical to install a real perpetual inventory system. Similarly, too much time would be required in counting the items if the goods consist of many articles, of which but few units each are kept in stock. This method of control has some of the characteristics of an actual physical inventory and some of the features of a real perpetual inventory, since it is a unit control method rather than one of values. It is not as accurate as these, however, and cannot be used for accounting purposes, nor is it adapted to all kinds of business.

Tickler Method of Inventory. The tickler method of inventory embodies some of the characteristics of the real perpetual inventory in that it deals with physical units rather than values and includes all goods whether in original containers or in broken packages. At the same time, the figure is obtained through a physical count which is not true of the real perpetual inventory, nor is the count taken frequently enough to deserve the designation "perpetual." This method of inventory is based on the assumption that various items in a wholesaler's stock, particularly in certain departments, move at different rates of speed. Therefore, to inventory all items with the same frequency would be wasteful and uneconomical. To eliminate such waste effort, the items are ticklered to come up for inventory at intervals which are determined largely by their respective rates of turnover.

Under this plan some items are given attention weekly, some biweekly, and others at longer intervals. In establishing the tickler, flexibility is essential so as to allow for shifts in the intervals at which articles are to be counted. Sheets are then made out, each containing items of the same inventory interval. These sheets are so filed that they come up automatically at the designated time. The figures recorded on these forms are transferred to stock control cards, on which may also be information on orders placed, goods received, sales made, and other data thought necessary. The tickler principle is frequently applied to the stock-taking method of inventory just described, according to which the merchandise is classified for counting purposes on the basis of stock activity. When a merchandise department contains a large number of items of comparatively low unit value and unit control is desired, the tickler method affords the only practical solution. It has a further advantage in that inventory work can be distributed evenly and made a routine matter.

Purchase Record System of Control. The purpose of a purchase record plan, which can hardly be called a system of stock control, is to afford a clue for estimating roughly the quantities of merchandise on hand, the frequency of placing orders, and the amount that should be ordered at given intervals. The system is flexible; it can be kept for short periods only, during which it is desired to check on the activity of certain goods such as those that have been suspected of inactivity, or it can be kept continuously for some important items. The purchase record may consist of a card similar to that shown in Figure 40, one for each commodity, or on the basis of manufacturers from whom supplies are obtained. The stock may be counted at frequent or infrequent intervals. The record is usually maintained for a period of six months, a physical inventory being taken

Article		Brand		Size		Number		
Location		Inventory:		Date		Quantity		
				Date		Quantity		
Date Ordered	Quantity Ordered	Date Received	Quantity Received	List Price	Discount	Delivered Cost		Unit Cost
. . . .	. . . .	. . . .	. . . .	. . . .	. . . .	. . . . . .	. . . . . .	. . . . . .
. . . .	. . . .	. . . .	. . . .	. . . .	. . . .	. . . . . .	. . . . . .	. . . . . .
. . . .	. . . . . .	. . . .	. . . .	. . . .	. . . .	. . . . . .	. . . . . .	. . . . . .
. . . .	. . . . . .	. . . .	. . . .	. . . .	. . . .	. . . . . .	. . . . . .	. . . . . .
. . . .	. . . . . .	. . . .	. . . .	. . . .	. . . .	. . . . . .	. . . . . .	. . . . . .
. . . .	. . . .	. . . .	. . . .	. . . .	. . . .	. . . . . .	. . . . . .	. . . . . .
. . . .	. . . .	. . . .	. . . .	. . . .	. . . .	. . . . . .	. . . . . .	. . . . . .
. . . .	. . . .	. . . .	. . . .	. . . .	. . . .	. . . . . .	. . . . . .	. . . . . .

Total Quantity Purchased_____

Frequency of Purchases_____

FIGURE 40. Commodity Purchase Record for Inventory Control

at the beginning and at the end of that period. In examining the relationship existing between the date orders are placed and the date the goods are received and between these in relation to stocks on hand at the beginning and at the end of the period, it is possible to determine how often orders for the item should be placed and for what amount.

This method may sometimes be used as the sole guide to a buyer in purchasing. It is particularly adapted to firms or departments dealing in nontechnical staple articles and to merchandise that is handled in comparatively large amounts but sold in small lots of little value. Under these circumstances a real perpetual inventory is either not essential or too expensive to operate. The purchase record is used as an alternative to some of the continuous physical inventory methods of control.

Real Perpetual Inventory. A real perpetual inventory is a continuous record of every item in stock, showing receipts, withdrawals, and balance on hand. It is a running balance showing the amount on hand at all times of each item in stock. The principle underlying it is relatively simple: goods on hand at the beginning of the period, reckoned in physical units, plus goods purchased, less goods sold, brought up to date currently, equals stock on hand. The application of this principle, however, is far from simple, for in the average wholesale house there are great varieties of merchandise for which the individual posting by item demands much more than receipts, withdrawals, and balance on hand. If a modern system is installed which provides for all the essential information on one record, it is also necessary to post orders placed, cancellations, purchases returned to manufacturers, returned goods from customers, exchanges, and so on, in order to arrive at correct figures of additions to or withdrawals from stock. This requires not only clerical work for maintenance of records, but also calls for a routing through the stock record room of many forms from which the postings are made. The preparation of an extra copy of some of these forms may be needed in order to expedite their movement through the house.

The data for the real perpetual inventory records are obtained from various sources. Information on orders placed is taken from copies of purchase orders. If any of the goods ordered are cancelled, a copy of the letter or order requesting the cancellation is sent to the stock record room. If no extra column is provided for this information, cancellations are recorded in red ink below the purchases to which they apply and are deducted. Actual receipts are recorded from copies of receiving reports or from copies of invoices. If goods are returned to a vendor a copy of the returned goods order or debit memorandum, as it is sometimes called, is furnished the stock clerk for entry in red ink below receipts, unless a special column is set aside for such postings. Sales are posted from sales orders either before or after the orders have been approved for credit and either before or after they have been filled, depending upon whether a strict or lenient credit policy is followed by the house and whether the firm experiences many outs and makes substitutions. If there is a possibility of orders being held up for credit investigation, they should first be handled by the credit department and afterwards by the stock record clerk. Similarly, if goods are always in stock and substitutions are not practiced to any extent, the sales orders may first be routed through the stock record room and then to the shipping department for filling. If goods are returned by a customer, a receiving report or credit memorandum is sent to the stock record clerk for entry in red ink in the sales column.

The routine of posting sales presents a considerable task, especially when there are a large number of small sales which multiply the number of entries for a given item and entail heavy expense. In many firms, the stock control records occupy a large amount of space, frequently being filed horizontally in multidrawer cabinets that run the length of a large office room. It is advisable, therefore, that all postings for a particular grouping of merchandise be made at one time in order to keep waste motion in moving back and forth among the drawers to a minimum.

Several methods are used in actual posting from sales orders. In some houses, a given product is chosen and all orders or invoices containing that item are sorted together and the item is posted. This procedure of posting one item at a time is followed until all items are entered. Another method is to record the first item on each invoice or order, then the second, and so on. All one-item orders are thereby eliminated in the first run and the two-item orders on the second. A third way is to prepare a tally sheet on which the total quantity of each item sold during the day is listed; from this the postings are made to the stock records in totals only. Still another method is the use of unit posting slips for each item sold. These are sorted together at the end of the day, added up, and one total is posted in the record.

Because of the complexity of application, the perpetual inventory method of stock control is not adapted to all kinds of wholesaling or to all kinds of merchandise in a given wholesale concern. Such an inventory is most practical:

1. When seasonal goods or style merchandise is involved, the purchases of which require exact knowledge of quantities sold during similar seasons in preceding years in order to gauge requirements for the current season.
2. When the goods are of a technical or strategic nature and it is absolutely necessary to have on hand, for immediate delivery, whatever may be demanded by the trade. If continuous records are not maintained, the possibility of running short of some items and overstocking in others is too great. This is particularly true of industrial distributors; electrical supply concerns; hardware firms; wholesale houses handling automotive accessories, replacement and repair parts to machinery; and drug wholesalers for certain serums, antibiotics, and other emergency items.
3. When the line of merchandise is not adapted to frequent stock-taking and yet unit control is desired. This would be true when the number of items handled is large but the quantities of each are relatively small and require careful weighing or measuring or other close scrutiny to ascertain the amount on hand.
4. When the merchandise has a relatively high unit value, as is the case of ready-to-wear apparel, furniture, high-grade jewelry, mechanical refrigerators, radios, washing machines, rubber tires, and batteries. The expense of posting such items on stock records would be relatively small when compared to the value of the merchandise.
5. When the number of products handled is relatively small, so that the task

would not be too burdensome and costly, although wholesalers handling as many as 60,000 or more items are known to maintain a real perpetual inventory system because the technical nature of the goods demands it.

6. When sales are made in substantial quantities, even though the goods are of a low unit value, making the number of postings reasonable. Concerns whose stocks are active but average sales small would probably find the cost of posting and maintaining the necessary equipment and records more or less prohibitive.

7. When complete control is required by law, as in the sale of narcotics, spirituous liquors, and similar items.

One essential feature of a real perpetual inventory is that a separate record should be maintained for each item in stock. Some wholesalers find this too expensive and yet see the value of unit control on a continuous basis. Consequently, they combine several items on a single card or sheet, thereby reducing both installation cost and the expense of posting. A dry goods wholesaler, for example, may post on a single record all hosiery of a certain size regardless of brand, price, color, or shade; or a record may be kept for hosiery of a certain quality or brand irrespective of size, color, or shade. This is a modified and not a true real perpetual inventory, which loses much of its effectiveness. Another point which is desirable is that *quantity order* and *balance on order* should be shown. Probably the most significant feature, however, is that showing quantity received, sold, and balance on hand. To prevent overstocks, the record should provide for the establishment of an ordering point for replenishment. When to place an order for a given item and the number of weeks' supply to order are determined largely by a planned turnover program. Space also should be allowed for the cost price of each item and for a monthly recapitulation of sales for the preceding and current years, respectively, which presents a valuable barometer of fluctuations in sales, seasonal, cyclical, or those resulting from changes in the design or style of the commodity.

These various points are illustrated in Figure 41, where a small section of a visible index "Kardex" file cabinet is shown.[4] The data concerning a particular item are kept on three separate cards (see Figure 42), which are centralized in the upper and lower flaps of a single pocket. The form in the upper left-hand corner provides a record of orders placed, shipments received, and cost of the item. In the upper right-hand corner, another form provides for recording a summary of monthly and annual sales for a period of fourteen years (both sides of the cards are used). The third form in the lower flap of the pocket is an in-out and balance record of receipts and sales that shows the quantity that should be on hand at any one time.

[4] Kardex is the trade-mark for visible index filing equipment supplied by the Remington Rand Division, Sperry Rand Corporation.

Courtesy of Remington Rand Division, Sperry Rand Corporation
FIGURE 41. Section of a Visible Index "Kardex" File Drawer

Permanent or semipermanent data, such as the description of the item, monthly usage, ordering point, and so on, are inserted in the visible celluloid strip and do not have to be retyped as the cards are changed. A manually adjusted signal, which is moved as postings are made, indicates at a glance the condition of the stock relative to the order point for each item in the file system without having to open the pockets to examine the perpetual inventory figures.

Numerous signaling systems have been devised to show how many weeks' or months' supply of stock there is on hand, when the predetermined minimum has been reached, when seasonal items should be bought, how much of an overstock condition exists at any given time, when an order was placed, what items are out of stock, when the last sale of a slow-moving item was made, and other points of information. While some simple and easily operated method of signaling is useful in guiding buyers, it is easy to overdo it and attempt to supply so much detailed information that the personnel becomes enslaved to the records.

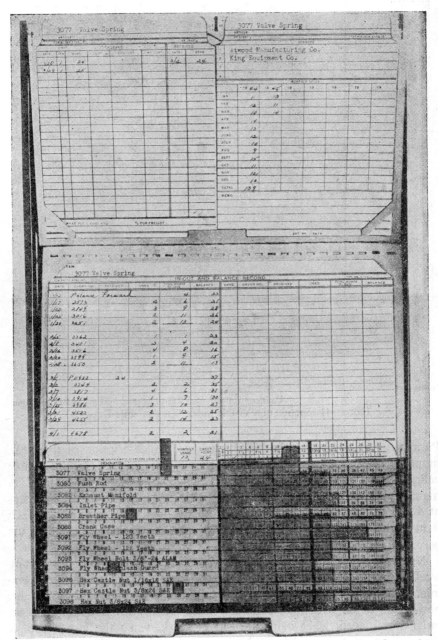

FIGURE 42. Perpetual Inventory Record Containing Complete Information
on an Item

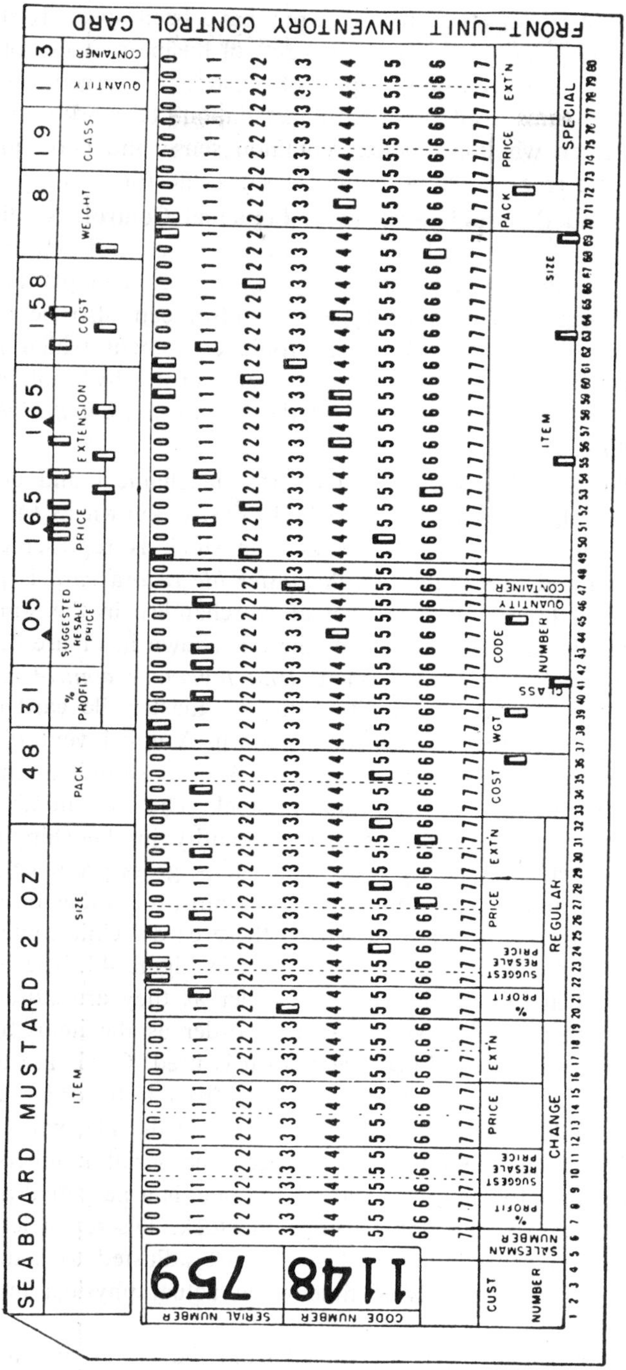

FIGURE 43. Sample of Unit Inventory Control Card as Used with Punch Card Systems of Statistical and Real Perpetual Inventory

Courtesy of International Business Machines Corporation

Virtually hundreds of stock record forms have been specially designed for different wholesalers to suit varying kinds of business, scales of operation, degrees of specialization, types of customers served, personnel peculiarities, and sums available for the installation. To work out the best system for a given wholesale house, common sense and good judgment are essential, and records are no complete substitute for either.

Mechanical and Electronic Systems of Perpetual Control. As discussed in the preceding section, real perpetual inventory control requires considerable clerical effort for the manual posting of sales, receipts, and other movements of goods. The same type of control can also be achieved through the use of mechanical or electronic equipment which replaces manual posting in large part. The three systems in use by wholesale concerns in the 1950's for this purpose include the *tub file, batch-billing,* and *computer* methods.

Tub File System. The oldest of the three mechanical and electronic systems of control, dating from the early 1930's, is known as the *tub file* system. Under it, each *unit* of each item in stock is represented by a punched card stored in a "tub" file. A *master file record card* is punched with information describing each item of merchandise in the warehouse. This card is almost exactly the same as the one shown in Figure 43 except that no serial number is printed on it. *Unit inventory control cards* are automatically reproduced in quantity from the master file card or from another "set-up" card that is used for a pattern. A unit inventory control card, as shown in Figure 43, is made up for each shipping unit (case, dozen, gross, barrel, etc.) of every item in stock. The code number of the item, the serial number of the card, the quantity in the shipping unit, warehouse location, cost, selling price, extensions, gross profit percentage, department or commodity class number, and almost any other information desired by a particular firm are shown on these cards. Unit control cards are kept in a tub file similar to the one shown in Figure 44. The items are usually arranged in this file in the same order as they are stored in the warehouse, which may also be in the same order as the items are listed on the order form if a preprinted order form is used. Cards are added to the file as items are received and are pulled from it by order clerks as merchandise is sold. Thus the number of cards in the file, which can be ascertained by taking the difference between the serial numbers of the front and rear cards for any item and adding one, is a perpetual inventory record of the number of shipping units in stock. Discrepancies due to pilfering, errors in order-filling, and so on, are adjusted to actual stock conditions at regular intervals of time when actual physical inventories are taken.

The unit control cards that are pulled from the file as merchandise is sold are used for printing warehouse order copies and customer invoices.

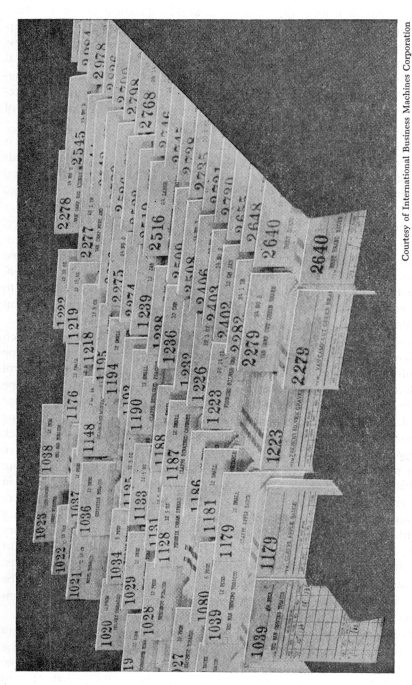

FIGURE 44. Illustration of a Section of a Real Perpetual Inventory Control "Tub" File

These cards then form the basis for a weekly statistical inventory. They are run through machines, which sort the cards by departments or merchandise classifications and cumulate the cost, selling price, and gross margin. The ending inventory for each department in terms of *value* is ascertained by subtracting sales at cost from the sum of the opening inventory and the receipts during the week. In this manner a departmental statement of profit and loss and a statement of inventory condition in terms of monetary units are provided.

In some wholesale houses where the number of merchandise items is very large, it is not considered practical to have all the unit control cards in a central location. In place of a tub file, these firms usually have a metal container for the cards at each bin or other place in the warehouse where the individual items are stored. The cards are not pulled until the order is filled by the stock clerk. They are then placed in another container, which moves with the order and goes to the office after the order is completely assembled. From this point on, the cards are analyzed in the same manner as when a tub file is used. When broken-case sales are common, as in the drug trade, several types of cards for each item may be used to designate different quantities. Thus a card with a blue stripe may represent one unit; a green stripe, three units; and a yellow stripe, one dozen.

A variation of the punch card system involves the use of cards which are hand-punched, sorted, and extended by manual means. The same type of information can be recorded as is usually found on the unit control cards designed for automatic machine tabulation. A sample of this type of card is shown in Figure 45. The cards are perforated around the edge and desired information is punched through the proper perforation, leaving an open slot. A needle is run through a given perforation in a whole block of cards, the cards are manipulated by hand, and all cards which have been punched in this perforation then drop free of the remaining group. In this way, it is possible to sort out all cards representing merchandise in a given department, sold by a salesman in a given district, purchased from a given supplier, and so on. The cards are serial numbered and kept in a tub file, the serial numbers furnishing the basis for the perpetual inventory figures. The spaces at the bottom of the card, shown in Figure 45, are for use after the order is filled, in connection with sales or customer analysis. Although all sorting, computing, and listing from these cards must be done by hand, the operation can be carried out by nonspecialized employees and without the use of any expensive machinery.

Batch-Billing System. Since the late 1940's, a series of developments in data processing equipment and systems has led to rapid changes in the perpetual inventory control methods used in wholesale enterprises. The first of these changes was the adoption, after about 1950, of the *batch-billing* technique, also known as "line-billing" or "electronic-billing." This

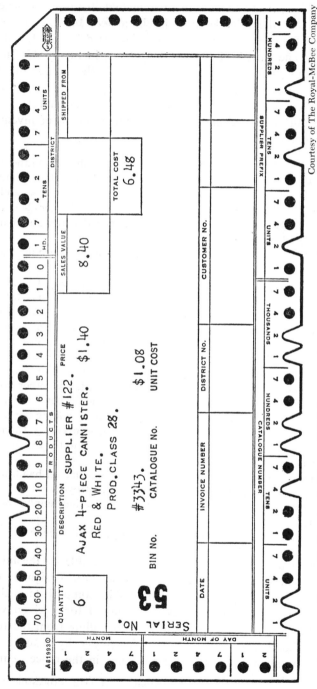

FIGURE 45. Sample of a "Keysort" Unit Inventory Control Card for Hand Sorting and Manual Extensions

Courtesy of The Royal-McBee Company

system is similar to the tub file method in that it utilizes punched cards. It differs in that the tub file itself is eliminated. Instead of having one punched card for each *unit* in stock, only one card is used for all units of a given item. The card is similar to that shown in Figure 43. In addition to the descriptive information on unit cost and other items, the card also shows the *quantity on hand* at a given time. As goods are received or shipped, it is constantly updated to show the new stock level.

The procedure followed under a batch-billing system of inventory control may be summarized as follows:

1. As orders are received, a card is punched for each item on the order, that is, for each *invoice line* (thus the term "line-billing"). These cards contain customer identification number, commodity code number, and quantity ordered. If the card order system is used (see Chapter 24), the mark-sensed cards can be transformed into punched cards automatically instead of by key-punching.
2. Similar cards are punched for merchandise received since the last processing of the inventory cards.
3. Either once or twice daily, all receipt cards and order cards are sorted by commodity. The receipt cards are placed behind the master inventory card, followed by the order cards, and a blank card is filed behind each group. This blank card will become the new master inventory card.
4. All master cards, receipt cards, and order cards are processed by an electronic calculator in a "batch" covering accumulations during an entire day or half a day, depending on the volume of operation. The calculator first punches the commodity description, weight, and other constant information into the blank card which will become the new master inventory card. It then computes a new inventory balance by adding the receipts and deducting the orders. At the same time, a new inventory *value* and *unit cost* are calculated by adding the value of receipts to the existing inventory value and dividing by the total quantity.
5. New master inventory cards showing a new balance on hand, total value, and unit cost are filed. Old master cards are destroyed.
6. Order cards are re-sorted by customer identification number and used to prepare invoices.
7. Invoices are sent to the warehouse for filling and shipment.[5]

The development of this system was made possible by the introduction of the first sufficiently rapid electronic calculator designed to handle punched cards. It offers several advantages in comparison with the tub file method. First, fewer employees are required for a given volume of orders, because the manual operation of card pulling from the tub files is eliminated. Second, card-punching is easier physically than card-pulling, which leads to enhanced morale and efficiency in the office. Third, much

[5] *Inventory Control and Material Accounting,* IBM Data Processing Series (The International Business Machines Corporation, 1955), pp. 39–41.

less floor space is required when the bulky tub files are removed. Fourth, there is less waste of cards, since price changes must be made on only one master card rather than on several dozen or hundreds in a tub file. Fifth, seasonal peaks are handled more easily, since the physical quantities ordered do not affect the work load in the order-processing section. Sixth, the system is more accurate; errors in card-pulling under the tub file system are rather frequent.

Finally, and perhaps most important of all, batch-billing makes possible more frequent control reports to buyers and other management personnel, leading to closer control over inventories. This is true because a complete "stock status" report can be prepared by tabulating the master cards (one card per item) rather than tabulating the thousands of unit cards in a tub file. Some of the reports commonly used in conjunction with batch-billing are illustrated in Figure 46. The "Inventory and Stock Movement" report is usually issued weekly. The others shown, the "Out Report" and the "Below Minimum List," are daily reports, since out-of-stock and below-minimum conditions call for prompt action by the buyers.

The principal disadvantage of batch-billing is that order-processing is slower than under the tub file system. Since cards must be punched in the office after receipt of orders rather than just pulled from tub files, shipment to stores may be delayed by as much as one day. This difficulty can be partly overcome when the card order system is used, since this eliminates the need for punching through the automatic conversion of mark-sensed order cards. Batch-billing is generally preferable to the tub file system when a relatively small number of items is stocked, most items are active, and customers order infrequently and in large quantities. These conditions often apply to a warehouse servicing a chain or voluntary chain of large supermarkets. If, on the other hand, a large number of customers place frequent orders for small amounts or if "rush" orders are common, the system is less adaptable to these conditions than is the tub file method.

Computer Systems. Following rapidly after the introduction of batch-billing techniques, still another new system of perpetual unit control utilizing the *file computer* was developed in the mid-1950's. Under this system all inventory information is stored in the computer itself, with no punched cards or written records except those used in putting in or taking out data from the machine.

One type of file computer consists of a series of disks like phonograph records, each one containing up to 1 million magnetic spots (see Figure 47). The data for each item in stock are recorded by sending an electric current through these spots. Through a complex system of coding, a series of magnetic spots may be used to record the name of an item, current inventory balance, unit cost, and other information such as that shown on the punched card in Figure 43. Information on receipts, orders, other additions and deductions from stock, and price changes is fed into the computer by punched cards or by punching keys on a keyboard (shown on the right of Figure 47).

The computer is controlled by "programs," consisting of wired panels which control the operations of the data-processing section. For example, the program calls for all order cards to be deducted from the balance on hand. The processing section automatically performs this deduction and computes a new balance, storing it on the magnetic disks. Information is taken out of the computer in the form of punched cards or typewritten reports, prepared automatically (shown on the left of Figure 47).[6]

The computer system combines the advantages of the tub file and batch-billing techniques. Since no tub file of cards is required, all of the benefits of batch-billing listed in the preceding section are also derived from use of the computer. As no card-punching is needed, the time-lag in order-processing by the batch-billing technique is also substantially reduced. Against these advantages must be set the much higher cost of a computer installation; one user reported a net addition to operating expense of $200 a month over and above that of batch-billing, even after allowing for uses of the installation for other than inventory control purposes.

To date, computer systems of inventory control have been used to a limited extent. As early as 1955, two or three specially built computers had been installed for this purpose. In 1956 the first computer designed for this type of work was offered for sale on a regular basis and several were put into operation in 1957 and early 1958. It was said that over a hundred computers were on order by chains and wholesalers in the grocery trade in mid-1958.

Evaluation of Mechanical and Electronic Systems. All three of the perpetual unit control systems discussed in the preceding sections are expensive to install and operate. All require complicated equipment and technically trained personnel. In some cases special physical arrangements must be made for the equipment, such as air conditioning to prevent damage to the delicate mechanisms. In view of these costs, consideration should be given to the conditions under which such systems are feasible.

Certainly one important consideration is the *size* of the enterprise. In a very large wholesale or chain store warehouse, installation of data-processing equipment may replace several full-time clerical employees. Thus the monthly rental or amortized purchase price can be offset, at least in part, by reductions in payroll. Possibly, smaller wholesale concerns can get the benefits of mechanized control without buying an entire installation.

---

[6] Space does not permit a full description of the workings of a computer, nor does the present discussion require it. For additional information, see "Business Week Reports to Readers on Computers," *Business Week* (June 21, 1958); *Data Processing by Electronics,* Haskins & Sells (New York, 1955).

INVENTORY AND STOCK MOVEMENT REPORT

WEEK ENDING 2-15-5-

BUYER	VENDOR	CODE	ON ORDER	PACK	DESCRIPTION—SIZE	RECEIPTS	MINIMUM	QTY ON HAND	NO WEEKS ON HAND	AVERAGE WEEKLY MOVE	1ST WEEK	2ND WEEK	3RD WEEK	4TH WEEK
1	1	1248		12	GOOD LUCK LEMON FILL	10	10	48	6	8	7	6	11	9
1	1	1249		12	GOOD LUCK LIME FILL		7	29	29	1	1		2	1
1	1	1251		12	GOOD LUCK COCONUT FILL		10	37	5	7	10	4	6	8
1	1	1252		12	GOOD LUCK CHOC FILL		10	31	5	6	5	7	10	2
1	1	1986		12	FRH WORSTERSHIRE 5 OZ		50	103	9	11	17	10	9	10
1	1	2025		48	FRENCH CRM SL MUST 6 OZ	50	50	53	3	15	17	11	18	17
1	1	2026										3	16	14
1	1	2027										6	7	8
1	1	2468										5		
1	1	2469										5		
1	1	2470										5		

DAILY OUT REPORT

DATE 2-14-5-

BUYER NO.	CODE NUMBER	PACK	DESCRIPTION AND SIZE	CASES SHORTED	ORDERS SHORTED	DOLLAR VALUE
3	2812	24	CHASE & SANBORN REG COFFEE 1 LB	11	10	266.64
3	3089	24	TENDERLEAF GREEN TEABAGS 16 PK	5	5	30.00
3	3318	12	INSTANT SANKA COFFEE 4 OZ	6	6	99.36
3	3846	30	SWAN SOAP THRIFT PK REG 5 PK	1	1	16.56
3	3925	24	ARMOUR SUDS 19 OZ	5	5	43.20
3	3951	10	OXYDOL NEW DETERGENT GNT	33	22	247.50
3	3969	10	RINSO BLUE GNT	31	13	232.50
				92 ✲	62 ✲	935.76 ✲

BELOW MINIMUM LIST

DATE: 2-15-5-

BUYER NO.	CODE	PACK	DESCRIPTION	SIZE	ON HAND	MIN. QTY.	ORDER
3	2812	24	CHASE & SANDBORN REG COFFEE	1 LB	42	50	
3	3089	24	TENDERLEAF GREEN TEABAGS	16 OZ	18	30	
3	3951	10	OXYDOL NEW DETERGENT		76	100	
3	4682	24	SKIPPY CREAM PEANUT BUTTER	1 LB	16	20	

FIGURE 46. Inventory Control Reports Prepared by Punched-Card Processing Equipment. Reprinted by permission from "IBM Accounting and Chain or Wholesale Grocery Distributors." Copyright 1955 by International Business Machines Corporation.

Printed Output

This versatile, new serial printer—with tape-controlled carriage—prepares reports at speeds up to 80 lines per minute, depending on the number of printing positions per line.

Card Output

This unit punches output data from 305 RAMAC into IBM cards, in any desired format, at speeds up to 100 cards per minute. Punching and printing can occur at the same time.

Processing

Within this section are magnetic cores, electronic circuitry and a magnetic drum to store programs, rearrange information and perform arithmetical and logical processing of data. A wired control panel contributes to logical decision making, as well as ease of programming.

FIGURE 47. "RAMAC" File Computer for

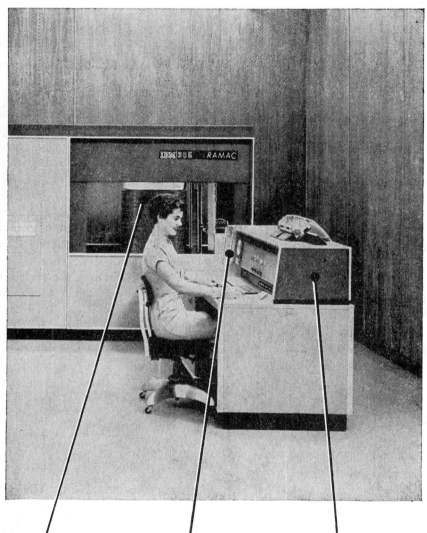

Disk Storage

Any record stored here can be located directly, at random, without searching through unwanted information. Capacity is 5,000,000 alphamerical characters, stored as magnetic spots on the 50 rotating metal disks, visible through the protective glass cover.

Card Input

This unit transfers data from punched cards into 305 RAMAC at speeds up to 125 cards per minute. Card reading can occur simultaneously with other programmed operations. Several transactions can be recorded in one card to accelerate data input.

Interrogation and Supervision

From this console, by means of the transmittal keyboard, memory can be interrogated for specific facts—at any time. Answers are automatically typed by the receiving typewriter, mounted on the console. The various console indicator lights and switches aid in monitoring operations.

Courtesy of International Business Machines Corporation

Use in Real Perpetual Inventory Control

The manufacturers of such equipment maintain "service bureaus" in a number of cities which process punched cards for a number of clients on a fee basis.

Even in fairly large firms, it is doubtful if the complete cost of an electronic control system can be justified solely in terms of reduced clerical expense. Consideration must also be given, then, to the *improvements in control* and *general management* made possible by faster availability of better information. The use of a computer in a medium-sized grocery chain, for example, made possible a 15 per cent reduction in inventory at the same time that the number of stores of the supermarket type was increased from 21 to 27.[7] But the benefits of improved control are not limited to inventory. Punched card and computer systems are also used to process other kinds of information, including the data resulting from analyses of sales and costs, payrolls, and special studies of various types. All of these advantages should be considered in evaluating the cost of a proposed system, although at times it may be most difficult to put an exact dollar value on them.

[7] Wayne E. Brown, President of Big Bear Stores, Inc., Columbus, Ohio, quoted in an advertisement appearing in *Business Horizons,* Vol. I (Summer, 1958), 6.

$$26$$

MANAGEMENT OF THE SELLING FUNCTION

This chapter and the one following deal with the management of the selling function in a wholesale enterprise. There is an old maxim to the effect that "Nothing happens until you make a sale." While this can easily be misinterpreted to mean that the other functions are unimportant or auxiliary, it does point up the fact that all the activities of buying, warehousing, inventory control, and some others are intended substantially to contribute to the ultimate objective of selling goods and are essential functions of a wholesale business. Attention may now be turned to the management of the activities *directly* involved in selling. These include advertising, sales promotion, certain types of customer services, management of the personal sales force, and analysis and control of selling activities.

Scope of Sales Management. The term "sales management" has traditionally been used to designate the management of the sales force, including selection, training, compensation, and supervision. This is actually just one part of sales management although, of course, a very important one. In a true sense sales management embraces the planning, organization, and control of *all* selling activities, not just those of the salesmen. Specifically, the task of sales management in a wholesale enterprise includes:

1. *Determination of Sales Objectives.* This aspect of sales management is frequently misunderstood. Many sales executives would define their objective as being simply "to sell as much as possible." While this may be a valid over-all objective, other things being equal, it is of little help in formulating proper sales policies. In the first place, greater sales volume per se may not be consistent with *more profitable volume*. Profits may

actually be decreased by an increase in volume if, for example, the larger volume is obtained by cutting prices, or in the form of unprofitable small orders, or by extending the market area beyond certain limits. The sales objectives of a wholesale concern should, therefore, specify what *kinds* of sales are desired in terms of commodities, customers, territories, and other criteria. The objectives should also indicate *how* sales are to be obtained. There is frequently an alternative, for example, between attempting to secure the dominant share of business from a smaller number of customers *versus* a small share of the purchases of a large number of customers.

As an illustration of the way in which sales objectives should be formulated, the following goals have been set by one leading wholesaler:

 a) To get the largest possible share of the purchases of each customer and to make the company the dominant supplier in its market area
 b) To increase the total volume of sales
 c) To increase the volume of *profitable* sales
 d) To assist dealers in merchandising activities so as to increase their sales to ultimate consumers
 e) To become the dealer's friend and trusted counselor

There is, of course, no standardized formula for devising sales objectives. They should be based on accurate knowledge of the situation confronting a particular firm in its competitive setting.

2. *Establishment of Sales Policies.* Sales policies should be designed to achieve the wholesaler's objectives. For example, the objective of providing merchandising assistance to dealers may be implemented by a compensation policy that motivates salesmen to perform such tasks; by a training policy that emphasizes retail display or store planning; and by various other policies. An important aid in establishing sales policies is the quantitative analysis of sales, discussed in Chapter 27.

3. *Sales Force Management.* In a wholesale concern the principal method of securing sales is through the field or "outside" sales force. Hence the selection, training, compensation, supervision, and control of salesmen still make up a major responsibility of management and usually require most of the time of the principal sales executive. These phases of sales management are treated in the latter part of this chapter.

4. *Advertising, Sales Promotion, and Customer Services.* In addition to the management of the sales force, the selling function embraces a number of more or less supplementary activities such as advertising and sales promotion. Closely related to these are certain types of customer services such as product information, store planning, and cooperative retail advertising, which are of increasing importance in most lines of business.

5. *Coordination of Sales with Other Functions.* Finally, because the selling function touches on so many other phases of operation in a whole-

sale enterprise, provision must be made for coordination with other divisions in the organization. This is ordinarily carried out by teamwork among the executives in charge of sales, buying, warehousing, and control, with the general supervision of top management. The important thing is that the need for coordination be recognized and provided for by regular meetings, clear-cut lines of authority and responsibility, and definite procedures to be followed in the event of disagreements. If this is not done, conflicts are likely to arise. For example, the sales manager may favor handling any product requested by a customer regardless of the potential demand. Some concerns actually have "museums" containing such items in their warehouses. This policy is likely to be resisted, for obvious reasons, by the buyers, the warehouse manager, and the controller. Similar conflicts may arise on the matter of credit policies; merchandise budgeting; or delivery scheduling. In such cases the conflicting interests must be balanced for the maximum good of the enterprise as a whole.

ADVERTISING AND SALES PROMOTION

In comparison with personal selling, the amount spent by wholesalers for advertising is small. For most lines of business, such expenditures are but from one-twentieth to one-tenth of the amounts that are expended for personal selling. For example, the average ratio of advertising expense to net sales among tobacco distributors is 0.07 per cent; for hardware wholesalers, 0.3 per cent to 0.4 per cent; and for industrial distributors, 0.3 per cent. Only in a few lines such as alcoholic beverages, coffee and tea, and automotive tires and tubes are advertising expenses typically as much as one-fifth to one-fourth of personal selling expenditures. While this provides an index of the relative importance of the two forms of sales and promotional activity, it perhaps also indicates the neglect of many wholesalers to take full advantage of the modern force of advertising.

Status of the Wholesaler with Respect to Advertising. The wholesaler appears to be in a peculiar position with reference to advertising and his use of it. He is not like the manufacturer who advertises chiefly to gain recognition, preference, or insistence for his own products, nor like the large advertisers in the retail field, such as department stores and specialty shops, who deal principally in style goods or in merchandise for which frequent price appeals are desirable. His stock in trade is primarily a large variety of parallel lines for which it is not wise to advertise aggressively since such sales effort would tend largely to shift buying habits from one brand to another, and not necessarily increase his total sales. Consequently, wholesalers have assumed the role of *distributors,* leaving to the manufacturer the task of creating demand for his products. The small amount of consumer advertising done by wholesalers is designed to support private brands for which some have assumed commercial responsibility. The bulk of the wholesaler's advertising is directed to retailers and industrial users rather than to the ultimate consumer, and is confined to catalogs, circulars and other direct mail literature, and to a little advertising in trade papers.

The Sales Catalog. Typically, the most important advertising medium used by wholesalers is the catalog, which lists and describes the items carried. With the limited amount of mail order wholesaling now done, the catalog has become largely a supplementary device to assist the salesman in his work. Even so, the preparation and distribution of a catalog is the major item of advertising expense in many wholesaling firms, and the catalog is an important source for mail and telephone orders in businesses where it is not feasible for the salesmen to call at very frequent intervals.

Catalogs may be compiled from materials supplied by manufacturers in the form of loose-leaf pages, or a wholesale concern may print its own catalog, using electrotypes provided by suppliers. The former practice is, for obvious reasons, much the cheaper of the two and is employed by many small wholesalers and by virtually all manufacturers' agents. Larger wholesalers usually print their own catalogs, because manufacturers' pages often contain generalized selling appeals that make the book unduly bulky and tend to "clutter it up." Moreover, information contained on suppliers' pages is not standardized in format or content, and this may confuse buyers and salesmen who desire quick reference to pertinent information.

A compromise between the use of manufacturers' catalog pages and the printing of an entirely new catalog has been developed through the co-operative efforts of several wholesale trade associations. Under this plan, manufacturers supply printed catalog material to distributors, following a standardized layout and using a standardized typography. The distributor then "pastes up" the material, and it is reproduced by the photo-offset process. This method reduces preparation costs substantially since no electrotypes are needed for reproduction and no proofreading of distributors' catalog copy on the part of the manufacturer is required.[1]

If a separate catalog is to be prepared, the task may be carried out by the wholesalers' own advertising departments or by specialized catalog-building companies. These companies, which are used principally by small wholesalers, study a firm's line of merchandise, survey the market area and the firm's sales records to determine the distribution list, prepare and print the catalog, and distribute it. Large wholesale houses that operate on a sectional or regional basis usually prepare and distribute catalogs in their own organization, with only the actual printing contracted to an outside

---

[1] "A New Look at the Distributor's Catalog Plan," Report of the Joint Committee on Catalogs, National Industrial Distributors' Association and Southern Industrial Distributors' Association, 1958. The recommendations of this committee have also been adopted by the National Wholesale Hardware Association and the National Association of Sheet Metal Distributors.

firm. In some cases complete printing facilities are owned and operated by the wholesaler.

The preparation of the catalog is the responsibility of the advertising manager, though in a large house there is usually a catalog manager working under the direction of the advertising manager. The entire book is carefully planned in outline form. This requires listing all items by departments, with the individual items grouped in natural classifications to facilitate location by buyers. Page dimensions, quality and weight of paper, and the number of copies are other items that must be planned, as they have an important bearing on the cost of the operation. The number of copies is determined largely by the customer and prospect list, which should be carefully analyzed to ascertain whether all those listed thereon justify the cost.

A specimen page is usually prepared to determine the general layout, decoration of the page, and the approximate number of pages required. Using this page as a model, a complete "dummy" catalog is built, resembling the desired final product in every possible way. After this is approved, plates are made and proof pages are printed and checked. It is then necessary to make a complete index, with various cross references. A colorful cover that attracts attention is designed, the printing and binding operation is completed, and distribution is effected.

Such an operation is an expensive undertaking, particularly if the number of items is in the tens of thousands and most of the items have to be illustrated and described in detail. For this reason many wholesalers publish catalogs only every three or four years, and issue supplemental price sheets and new item and discontinuance notices on strips of mimeographed paper to be inserted. During such a period of time, a catalog can become so obsolete that it consists largely of corrections, most of which are kept up to date by salesmen, but not by customers. To get around this difficulty, many firms publish a loose-leaf catalog. All corrections or additions are in the form of standard complete pages, which may call for the elimination of obsolete pages. Catalog-building then becomes a continuous process. The salesmen always have a neat and orderly selling aid, but even under this system it is difficult to get customers to insert new or to delete obsolete material. This has led some wholesalers to the practice of preparing small special catalogs to be distributed at frequent intervals, for example, twice a year, to those customers handling the kind of merchandise listed. This practice saves the expense of distributing a complete catalog to all customers, most of whom may handle only a portion of the kinds of items carried.

Other Advertising Media. In addition to the sales catalog, other advertising media commonly used by wholesalers include *direct mail* circulars or brochures, *trade periodicals,* and *advertising specialties*. Direct mail advertising is used principally in connection with special promotions, seasonal sales, and the like. Advertising in trade periodicals may be of the institutional type and is generally designed to pave the way for salesmen's calls. Advertising specialties include such items as calendars, pens, and memo pads. Sometimes it is possible to use a specialty item that ties in with the customer's ordering procedure and thus reminds him of the wholesaler at the best possible time. For example, retailers may be given "want books" to be used in recording products needed, and which at the same time remind them of the wholesaler as a source of supply for these items.

Cooperative Institutional Advertising. Wholesalers have long been subjected to criticism as "unnecessary middlemen" and pressure has been exerted by both suppliers and customers for more direct distribution. To aid in combating such criticism, some concerns have used advertising to promote the use of wholesalers in the channels of distribution. This type of advertising is usually conducted by trade associations rather than by individual firms. An example is shown in Figure 48. This advertisement, minus the picture part at top half of page, is built around just one of the many selling points that could have been used and was scheduled to appear in eight periodicals.

Participation by Wholesalers in Manufacturers' Promotional Campaigns. While wholesalers are often not in a position to advertise extensively on their own behalf, they play an important role in the campaigns carried on by their suppliers. Wholesalers' salesmen are in constant contact with retailers, and are in an excellent position to "merchandise the advertising" to them. Cooperation with suppliers is especially close when the wholesaler works on an exclusive franchise basis, as in the case of household electric appliance distributors. In this industry the major manufacturers introduce their annual new lines to distributors and key retailers at exhibits held at the factories.

When a wholesaler handles a wide variety of products, there is an obvious need to be selective in cooperating with suppliers. A number of criteria may be used in choosing the lines to which emphasis is to be given. One factor is *sales volume,* which is determined through a quantitative analysis of sales such as that described in the following chapter. A second criterion is the *profitability* of the line to the wholesaler. The supplier's *distribution policies* may be taken into account, preference being given to those who sell only to wholesalers. On the basis of these and other considerations, the wholesaler may select a limited number of "key lines" and give them full support. Promotional efforts by other suppliers may be given a complete "cold shoulder" or treated with relative indifference.

USE OUR CAPITAL to cut your storage space costs

Using our large steel stocks saves you the costs of a big chunk of expensive storage space. And you can free-up and convert this tied-up space to more productive, profitable use. That's good business.

Since our labor, our equipment cuts your steel, does preliminary processing for you . . . you save the investment—the costs—of using your own labor and equipment. You save handling expense and other inventory costs. Whatever your steel need, there's a nearby Steel Service Center set up to serve you quickly from stock.

If you're putting steel in your inventory because you think it's a bargain, compare *all* of your costs of possession with the cost and *freedom-from-risk* of buying steel from your Steel Service Center. Use this chart. Or, to be more precise, get the booklet, "What's your real cost of possession for Steel" from your convenient Steel Service Center. American Steel Warehouse Association, 540 Terminal Tower, Cleveland 13, O.

The American Steel Warehouse

...YOUR STEEL SERVICE CENTER

COST OF POSSESSION FOR STEEL IN YOUR INVENTORY

Per ton delivered
Cost of capital:
Inventory
Space
Equipment
Cost of operation:
Space
Materials handling
Cutting & burning
Scrap & wastage
Obsolescence
Insurance
Taxes
TOTAL

COST OF FREEDOM-FROM-RISK STEEL FROM YOUR STEEL SERVICE CENTER

Per ton, cut-to-size, and delivered
TOTAL

Courtesy The American Steel Warehouse Association

FIGURE 48. Cooperative Institutional Advertising by a Wholesale Trade Association

Some of the more aggressive wholesalers actually take the initiative in coordinating their sales and advertising efforts with those of their suppliers. An outstanding example is McKesson & Robbins, Inc., a nationwide chain of drug wholesale houses. This firm organizes its efforts around a "weekly sales calendar" consisting of promotional plans, week by week, for a six-month period. The company may approach certain suppliers with a proposed campaign, offering its own cooperation in exchange for consumer advertising support by the manufacturer.[2] During one Christmas season McKesson & Robbins was said to have enlisted over 5,000 retail drugstores in a nationwide gift promotion featuring the products of 26 different manufacturers.[3] While this is not representative of the typical wholesaler's participation in his suppliers' promotional efforts, it does indicate the scope of the possibilities in this area.

Cooperative Advertising Programs for Customers. A phase of advertising that has assumed increased importance for many wholesalers is that of conducting cooperative advertising programs for their customers. Such programs are most extensive among wholesalers sponsoring voluntary chains, as in the food trade. The sponsoring wholesaler performs several functions: (1) he collects advertising allowances from manufacturers on behalf of the members of the group; (2) newspaper advertisements are prepared for insertion over the group name, or mats are provided for use by individual stores; (3) direct mail circulars are printed for use by members; (4) radio and television commercials may be produced for the group as a whole; (5) point-of-sale materials, such as window displays and banners are provided; and (6) a public relations program may be conducted for the benefit of the entire group. These functions can be performed by the wholesaler with much greater effectiveness than by the individual stores since full-time specialized personnel is employed to carry them out.

While not as extensive as the programs of voluntary chain groups, many wholesalers not affiliated with such organizations also provide their customers with various types of advertising assistance. The concept underlying all programs of this character is that the wholesaler's sales are best promoted by helping dealers of consumer goods sell more to ultimate consumers.

Determining the Advertising Appropriation. Many factors enter into the determination of the size of advertising appropriations made by wholesalers. Among them are the nature and variety of goods handled, volume

---

[2] "McKesson and Robbins: Salesmen," *Fortune* (July, 1952), reprinted in George H. Brown (ed.), *Readings in Marketing from Fortune* (New York: Henry Holt & Co., 1955), pp. 26–31.

[3] *Retail Memo,* Retail Department, Bureau of Advertising of the ANPA, Inc., December 13, 1957.

of sales, extent of private-brand merchandise, territory covered, exclusive agency representation, degree of selective distribution, and the general value attributed to advertising. Sometimes no special amount is set aside for advertising, each attempt at promotion being handled separately and on its own merits. When an appropriation is made in advance for the ensuing fiscal period, which is the usual procedure, one of several methods is followed. A certain part of the past year's sales or profits, gross or net, may be devoted to advertising. A similar method is to set aside a percentage of anticipated sales, gross or net, for the coming year. A third plan is to follow the example of competitors. If it is customary in the trade to issue catalogs or to use billboards, deviations may be undesirable and advertising may be used more for protection than as a constructive selling force.

Occasionally, an arbitrary amount is set aside for advertising, without much regard for past and future sales, or the activities of competitors. Usually it is about the same amount as has been spent for the preceding year. When this procedure is followed, there is a tendency to curtail the appropriation for advertising when it is most needed, as in times of depression. The feeling is that the firm cannot afford to advertise, but this attitude is as unscientific as is the determination of an arbitrary sum for sales promotion. When a firm believes in the value of advertising, it may follow an opposite plan, and put all the money it can obtain into advertising, and steadily reinvest a part of its profits in that fashion, on the assumption that the percentage of selling costs decreases as the amount spent for advertising increases.

Probably the best way of ascertaining how much to spend for advertising is by a combination of the above methods. The task to be accomplished should be first defined, the competitive and other conditions surveyed, and the possible advertising media determined. Past experience should be relied upon, but changes in policy, anticipated increases or decreases in sales volume, expected changes in business conditions, and anticipated sales resistance must also be taken into account.

Sales Promotion. It is difficult to draw exact lines of demarcation between sales promotion and personal selling on the one hand and between sales promotion and advertising on the other. The term is used here to designate those selling activities that "supplement both advertising and personal selling, coordinate them, and render them more effective."[4] Among the sales devices of this type used by wholesale concerns are *display rooms, trade shows,* and *exhibits.* In a sense all of the customer services discussed in the next part of this chapter might also be classed as sales

[4] Cf. Theodore N. Beckman, Harold H. Maynard, and William R. Davidson, *Principles of Marketing* (6th ed.; New York: The Ronald Press Company, 1957), p. 408.

promotion, but these services are of sufficient importance to justify separate treatment.

Display rooms are commonly used in connection with cash-and-carry trade, but are sometimes set up even in establishments with little of this kind of business. The display room may resemble a retail store, and in a few cases "supermarket" rooms have been set up with self-service counters, carts, and check-out counters.[5] In addition to regular merchandise lines, the showroom may be used to promote sluggish items at "bargain" prices and to display and demonstrate new merchandise lines to potential buyers.

One problem encountered in the operation of a display room is that ultimate consumers may seek to buy in it at "wholesale prices." This difficulty is accentuated by the trend to make showrooms more attractive, even to the point of installing glass fronts. Another drawback is that a display room requires considerable floor space on the valuable ground floor. Despite these limitations, many concerns find that the display room is worthwhile in terms of increased sales. One concern is said to have secured an average of two new customers per day in the first year of operating such a room.[6]

Trade shows and exhibits are of special importance for concerns handling complex technical products. Distributors in the hardware, plumbing and heating, and industrial supply trades often conduct periodic shows under their own sponsorship, with suppliers invited to participate by setting up displays and manning them with specialty salesmen.

CUSTOMER SERVICES

In the struggle to maintain their competitive position, wholesalers have found it necessary to make many changes in the nature and extent of the services they render for their customers. The objective of all such services is, of course, to develop and maintain a lasting business relationship with the customer. Properly conceived services can be a potent device in achieving this objective. Except in the case of exclusive distributorships, wholesalers can seldom offer anything unique in the way of merchandise; the customer can almost always buy the same or a very similar product elsewhere. The *services* given by the wholesaler *can* be made unique, however, and thus help to differentiate and distinguish one concern from another.

The kinds of services that are given by wholesalers depend on several factors, including the line of business, types of customers served, and the competitive situation. In the discussion that follows, therefore, it is not

[5] Harry B. Patrey in collaboration with Joseph Kolodny, *Successful Methods of Wholesale Tobacco Distribution* (New York: Foresight Publications, 1957), p. 452.

[6] Jack Lewin, "Permanent Product Display Room Pays Off for Wholesaler," *American Paper Merchant* (October, 1957), 25–26.

meant to imply that *all* or even *most* wholesalers perform each and every service mentioned. The list is merely *illustrative* of the kinds of customer services that have proved successful under various circumstances.

Promotional Assistance. Among the wholesalers serving retail stores, undoubtedly the most important form of assistance is in the area of sales promotion. More specifically, wholesalers aid and assist dealers in matters of *advertising, display,* and *special promotional items.* In connection with advertising, wholesalers may advise dealers of cooperative advertising arrangements and advertising allowances available from manufacturers; prepare layouts and even produce completed advertisements; and supply circulars, catalogs, and other materials for use by retailers. As indicated in a previous section of this chapter, in a voluntary chain the wholesaler assumes practically the entire responsibility for these matters. Even in the absence of formal arrangements, progressive wholesalers have assumed the initiative in giving their customers professional help. For example, in the hardware trade (where voluntaries are not at all common), a survey disclosed that almost 80 per cent of the wholesalers provide circulars and catalogs and nearly 75 per cent supply newspaper mats.[7]

Display assistance includes the advising of dealers as to what products to display and when; helping them obtain special displays from manufacturers; and, in some cases, actually setting up window or counter displays. These tasks are typically assigned to the salesman, who may be offered special compensation in return for taking the time away from regular selling duties. This type of service is among the most popular from the retailer's standpoint. It is interesting to note, for instance, that of the ten most popular kinds of assistance mentioned by retail druggists in a survey, three had to do with display.[8]

In furnishing special promotional goods to retailers, wholesalers emulate the promotional strategy of the corporate retail chains and thus enable the independents to compete on a more nearly equal basis. In the grocery trade, weekly meat, produce, and other food items are featured in advertisements prepared by the wholesaler. Hardware wholesalers, on the other hand, more commonly provide *monthly* specials. In either case, the purpose is to capitalize on price appeals at the consumer level.

Store-Planning. Another phase of customer service is that of store-planning, including the location and design of new stores, assistance in layout and fixturing, and renovation of older stores. Some wholesalers, especially those operating voluntary chains, take the initiative and seek out proprietors for stores financed and constructed by the wholesaler. Some operate

[7] "The New Look in Wholesaling," special section of *Hardware Retailer* (May, 1958), 32.

[8] *The Retailer Looks at His Service Wholesale Druggist,* Bulletin No. 47, The National Wholesale Druggists' Association (New York, not dated), pp. 11–12.

store-planning departments with full-time specialists who draw up recommended layouts including allocations of space among the various lines handled by the retailer.[9] Several plans are used in furnishing dealers with fixtures. One is for the wholesaler to buy and resell the fixtures, which may be procured under a special contract from a manufacturer. Another is to refer leads obtained from dealers to a fixtures producer or distributor, with the wholesaler sometimes guaranteeing the retailer's credit and earning a commission on all sales. *Remodelings* of older stores include both layout-planning and fixture modernization, and in this the wholesaler may assist the dealer in securing long-term credit from a bank or other source of capital. McKesson & Robbins, Inc., is said to have assisted one out of every eight drugstores in the United States with remodelings or construction of new stores within a four-year period.[10]

Sales-Training. Wholesalers' salesmen render an important service to retailers in connection with the training of retail salespersons. Most small retailers, for obvious reasons, cannot afford specialized staff personnel to conduct training activities; nor do most store proprietors have the time or inclination to perform the task themselves. The wholesaler's salesman provides training both on the job and in special meetings, which may be held in classrooms at the wholesale establishment and may involve a variety of visual aids. The training is designed primarily to supply clerks with selling points for the goods handled, but may also extend to the fundamentals of salesmanship, stock control, and other appropriate subjects.

Product Information. As a part of the basic function of selling, wholesalers must obviously transmit information about their products to customers and prospects. Above and beyond this, a more formal type of informational service may be set up for the benefit of retailers or industrial users. Perhaps the most extensive development along this line has been in the drug trade, where wholesalers employ pharmaceutical specialists to advise druggists about new items, their composition, their uses, and so on. The need for such a service arises from the flood of new drug items appearing in rapid succession, and the inability of manufacturers' "detail men" to contact all retailers with sufficient frequency to keep them informed.[11]

[9] E. M. Johnston, "Servicing the Retail Merchant's Needs," *Proceedings of the 29th Annual Convention,* National Wholesale Dry Goods Association (New York, February, 1956), p. 10.

[10] George W. Kauffman, "Changing Patterns in Drug Wholesaling," in Robert D. Buzzell (ed.), *Adaptive Behavior in Marketing,* Contributed Papers, December Conference of the American Marketing Association (Columbus, Ohio, 1957), p. 56.

[11] "Why a Pharmaceutical Department?" The National Wholesale Druggists' Association.

Other Customer Services. The list of services provided by wholesale concerns for their customers could be greatly extended. Among the others that may be noted are the following:

1. Accounting and stock control systems and records
2. Price tags, labels, and the like
3. Preparation of tax returns
4. Legal advice
5. Assistance with general management problems

A problem that arises in connection with all of the foregoing customer services is that of charging for them. Traditionally, wholesalers have absorbed the costs of special services in their over-all operating expense, with no special charges being made. Competition may not permit this, however, in which case customers utilizing a particular service such as advertising or store-planning may be asked to pay all or most of the cost. When the aid is of a continuing nature, such as newspaper mat service, a regular weekly charge may be levied.[12] Many of the services are still rendered, however, by most wholesalers without any specific or direct charge for them. Naturally, the costs thus incurred are an integral part of the wholesaler's cost of doing business. To the extent that they result in larger sales volume and improved business relationships that make for more concentrated buying by customers, such costs are more than offset by the benefits secured.

Selection and Training of Salesmen

Management of personal-selling activities is composed of several distinct phases. These include the *selection, training, compensation,* and *supervision* of salesmen and the *planning* and *control* of sales efforts. Each of these phases is considered in the discussion in this chapter and in the one that follows.

Types of Salesmen. The sales force of a wholesale concern may comprise several different kinds or types of salesmen. Most of them are usually engaged in *field* or *"outside" sales,* calling on retailers and/or industrial and commercial users. This sales force, in turn, may be broken down into *general line* and *specialty* salesmen if specialized knowledge is essential to the handling of one or more lines; and into *city* and *country* salesmen, the former operating in the metropolitan area in which the house is located. In some lines of trade there are *counter salesmen* and *telephone salesmen*

---

[12] Rudolph L. Treuenfels, "Some Additional Observations," in W. David Robbins (ed.), *Successful Marketing at Home and Abroad,* Contributed Papers, 40th National Conference of The American Marketing Association (Boston, Massachusetts, 1958), pp. 416–22.

in addition to the regular sales staff. Finally, some salesmen may be assigned to merchandising and other duties related to selling and designated as *store supervisors* or by a similar title. This practice is followed by wholesalers who sponsor voluntary chains among their retailer customers.

These classes and types of salesmen are important since the type of selling assignment affects the methods used in management. In the selection and training of a telephone salesman, for example, far more emphasis would be placed on the ability to speak clearly and make rapid reference to catalogs than for a regular field salesman.

Analysis of the Selling Task. The first step in the selection of salesmen for a wholesale house is to make an accurate and detailed analysis of the duties which they are called upon to perform. Consciously or unconsciously every sales manager has a prescription for the kind of men he wants. He should, therefore, prepare a job description indicating the kind of position available, duties required, how they are to be performed, and the qualifications of the candidate which are essential to effective performance. Such an analysis leads to better methods of selection, training, supervision, compensation, and promotion. In addition to direct-selling duties, a wholesaler's salesman performs a number of nonselling duties including the securing of credit information, collection of due and overdue accounts, handling of claims, making adjustments, winning over disaffected customers, checking mailing lists in his territory, helping dealers in ways previously indicated, and preparing reports for officials of his company. In some consumer goods lines, the function of the wholesaler's salesman has become one of selling merchandise *for* his customers rather than *to* them. He has in a sense ceased to be only a salesman and has become a sales manager for his trade.

To perform these duties and to sell goods effectively on a continuous basis, the wholesaler's salesman must possess a composite of characteristics known as "personality" which enables him to create and maintain a good impression upon buyers and prospects. He must enjoy good health and follow correct habits of life. This is particularly true of traveling salesmen whose duties are exacting and strenuous. The salesman must be a person of good character, including such qualities as veracity, reliability, self-control, fairness, loyalty, sincerity, decency, and sobriety. In the absence of these characteristics, a salesman's sporadic brilliant achievements may be offset by losses during periods of aberration. To these characteristics must be added a good measure of business sagacity. This implies an ability to grasp the significance of circumstances, to understand facts quickly and to discuss them with thoroughness, foresight, and mental alertness. Adequate education is essential in a good salesman. This is rapidly coming to mean a college education, since so many customers have had that opportunity, although equivalents in experience and self-education may be equally good, and occasionally even better.

Other qualifications that are more or less taken for granted relate to tact, punctuality, initiative, resourcefulness, concentration, executive ability, self-confidence, and knowledge of the goods, his firm, its policies, and human nature. Most of these qualities can be developed through training, others are perhaps more fundamental and inherent. Practical experience in selling is occasionally required of a candidate for a sales position, and some attention is given to his marital status, age, voice, size, and the like. The entire process of determining the attributes essential to success in selling for a wholesale house is changing and in need of exhaustive scientific study.

Sources of Salesmen. Salesmen may be secured by a wholesaler from several sources. One of the principal sources is the firm's *own organization.* Men thus chosen can be watched during their period of employment in other capacities and only those who seem to possess desired qualifications are promoted. These men are presumably familiar with the house, its policies, the managing personnel, and most important, with the merchandise. Stockmen and order-fillers or young office employees are frequently promoted to sales positions. These men usually have "sticking" qualities, thereby reducing sales force turnover and the cost incident thereto; they are also as a rule loyal to the house and regular in their work. Often, however, a man who has spent a number of years in the office or warehouse finds it difficult to make the adjustment to a job in selling. His loyalty to the house is no assurance that he is able to withstand the forces of competition in the field. Houses that are most successful in recruiting salesmen from within the organization are those which establish a definite policy of doing this and keep this policy in mind when hiring men for certain inside positions.

Probably the next most important source for wholesalers' salesmen is *competing concerns.* Salesmen hired away from competitors are already trained in most aspects of the business and, if assigned to the territory which they previously cultivated, they may divert trade from their former employers. Some wholesalers refrain from hiring competitors' salesmen because they have much to unlearn and many acquired habits to alter, because they sometimes may take advantage of their new position and seek further advances in remuneration, because they can usually be hired only at advanced figures, or because the practice is regarded as unethical unless the salesman had first severed his connections with the old employer.

Retailers who have failed in business for reasons other than inefficiency, or retail store clerks, are often promising candidates. They are familiar with the line of goods, consumers' attitudes toward the various products, and the problems confronting retailers. Usually they have been disciplined to working long hours without large compensation, and, in the case of clerks, a job as a wholesaler's salesman represents an advancement in which they strive hard to make good.

Among the other methods of recruiting salesmen are *newspaper classified advertising,* advertising in *trade publications,* local *employment agencies, placement offices* of colleges of commerce, and other organizations. Colleges of commerce have increased in importance as a source of salesmen, because many graduates have demonstrated an ability to apply the general principles learned to individual sales situations. Some wholesalers, however, are reluctant to take on new graduates because many expect too much in the way of compensation and advancement, and lack a willingness to learn the details of a wholesale house's procedures by doing more or less menial work in the early stages of their employment. Finally, the aid of the company's own sales force may be enlisted. Knowing approximately what qualifications are required, the company's salesmen may choose likely candidates from among their friends and acquaintances.

Selection Methods. The problem of selecting salesmen from among applicants is basically one of identifying and measuring the qualities that are known to make for success in the job. Unfortunately, all too little is known about these qualities beyond generalities which are of little help in selection procedures. It is largely for this reason that most wholesalers rely on personal impressions and judgments of potential sales personnel. In better-managed firms these *subjective* methods of selection have largely been replaced by more scientific techniques, which are of definite value despite the gaps in knowledge regarding the prerequisites for effective selling.

Among the methods that have been found useful in selecting salesmen are *personal interviews, application forms, rating scales,* and *psychological tests.* The personal interview gives the sales manager an opportunity to size up the applicant's personality, knowledge, and other pertinent qualifications. This interview can be effectively supplemented by a rating scale on which the characteristics are arranged either alphabetically or in order of their importance. A value is assigned to each characteristic on the basis of the company's experience, thereby reducing guesswork. Application blanks which may be filled out before or after the interview are an aid in reaching a decision. They disclose certain characteristics and give an idea of the applicant's experience, education, and accomplishments. In one type of application blank quantitative weights are assigned to those factors, such as experience, education, or age, which can be measured. Psychological tests have long passed beyond the experimental stage and are now in wide use for a variety of purposes, but relatively few wholesalers, except for large sectional and national concerns, have resorted to them in selecting salesmen. Finally, it is important to check references given by the applicant. Sometimes a salesman can be chosen almost entirely on the basis of recommendations of references known to be impartial and shrewd judges of a person's qualities.

Training Salesmen. The old belief that salesmen are born and not made is now recognized as generally unsound and fallacious. It has given way to a realization that a competent sales force can be built through correct training. While it is essential for would-be salesmen to possess certain innate qualities, such as those discussed above, the ability to sell can demonstrably be developed by appropriate training. Under all circumstances, newly hired salesmen should be trained in order that they may acquire the necessary knowledge in the shortest possible time, and substitute the experience of others for their own "trial and error" means of learning. A good training course necessarily deals with the company's organization and policies, products handled, trade to be cultivated, selling methods that have been found successful, and the selling and nonselling duties which salesmen will be called upon to perform.

The most common method of training in use by wholesalers is to require the new salesman to spend a certain period of time in the house where he can browse around, observe conditions, and ask questions. After he has accumulated a rudimentary knowledge of some of the points enumerated above, he is assigned to an experienced salesman, whom he accompanies on a regular route. If the older salesman uses correct methods, and has the analytical ability to discover and correct faults properly, the training of the novice may prove entirely satisfactory.

Of the more formal and systematic methods of training salesmen, there is a great variety. Some require only practice, others combine practice with study and lectures. Training may be given in concentrated courses of study and lectures or in the form of continuous service or training "on the job." One large wholesaler operating a chain of establishments on a nationwide basis has the following combination of training methods for new salesmen: a one-year training course covering all aspects of the company's operations; weekly examinations and interviews with an individual in the firm designated as "sponsor" to the new man; assigned readings in literature published by manufacturers, trade associations, and others; and attendance at regular sales meetings.

Sales-training does not cease after a new man has been assigned to a regular territory. Formal training becomes less important, naturally, and may consist only of infrequent meetings and refresher courses. Training dealing with new products, product service, and the like is often provided by the manufacturers whose lines are carried by the wholesaler. Finally, there is a certain amount of training inherent in the program of sales *supervision* discussed in the next chapter.

COMPENSATION OF SALESMEN

The task of devising a satisfactory method of compensation is a perplexing sales management problem. This is particularly true as far as wholesalers are concerned because the wholesaler's salesman is almost always expected to perform many more activities than merely selling a given volume of goods. As nonselling activities increase in importance, the development of proper compensation methods becomes even more difficult. Furthermore, only in the largest firms are selection procedures, formalized training programs, and supervision methods developed to the high degree that has become rather commonplace in the sales organizations of large manufacturing firms. In the typical wholesale house a relatively small sales force is guided by a single executive with no staff assistants. The result is that selection, training, and supervision activities are largely on a personal basis, while the compensation plan is the principal formal instrument for accomplishing the sales objectives of the firm.

Objectives of a Sales Compensation Plan. A well-balanced compensation plan that is designed to meet certain objectives assists the wholesaler in attaining a high level of marketing productivity that is compatible with current sales opportunities. Among the more important of the objectives that may be achieved by a good plan are the following:

1. It directs the salesman's efforts to those activities that are profitable to his employer. These activities include rendering the kind of service to customers that induces them to concentrate purchases with the firm; securing new and profitable accounts; educating the customer to the necessity of ordering in sufficient quantities to make his orders profitable for the wholesaler to handle; selling merchandise with good profit margins; and the performance of other services that enable the salesman's employer to operate more effectively and efficiently.

2. It causes the salesman to give proper consideration to the interests of his customers. Only by acting for their interests, as well as the interests of the employer, can the salesman render the kind of service that makes for long-run success. The good salesman does not *over*sell or *under*sell his customer, and he does what he can to help each of his customers become a successful merchant and an efficient businessman.

3. It causes the salesman to give due regard to the interest of the manufacturer of the merchandise that he is selling. If the compensation plan emphasizes service to the manufacturer, it aids considerably in developing closer and more amicable relations between the latter and the wholesaler.

4. It stimulates the salesman to put forth his best efforts in the accomplishment of his tasks. The plan incorporates features that encourage each salesman to do his best at all times.

5. It attracts to the sales organization men of the proper type for the

work to be accomplished and it helps to keep them satisfied employees of the firm.

Problems in Devising a Compensation Plan. There is no one best method of compensating wholesalers' salesmen, just as there is no one best method of selling or advertising merchandise. Practically every plan in use has its elements of strength, and each may be satisfactory under certain conditions. But a plan that may be adaptable to most wholesalers in the hardware or drug trades cannot be used by all wholesalers in those trades, nor may one plan always be applied to all the individuals on any one sales force. Within the same trade, no one system of compensation is used to the exclusion of other plans—for just as trades differ, so wholesale organizations within the same trade have fundamental differences requiring individual treatment.

Regardless of the line of business, size of the firm, diversity of the line of goods actually handled, territory covered, and other factors, the wholesaler is confronted with three major problems in devising a satisfactory compensation plan. First, the total amount of compensation, or at least the minimum amount, that is to be paid over a period of a year must be determined. Second, a method of attaining that amount of total compensation must be evolved. This may include a salary, commission, profit-sharing, or bonus type of plan, or a combination of several of these. Third, provision must be made for distributing that total amount by weeks, months, quarters, or other periods of time, because the way in which the salesmen receive their income may be fully as important as the total amount earned during the year.

Characteristics of a Good Sales Compensation Plan. In order to solve the problems that have been indicated and in order that the objectives of the plan may be attained, certain general requirements or tests that experience has demonstrated are necessary for a sound compensation plan must be fulfilled. These requirements are:

1. *Adequacy.* The compensation provided by a good plan is adequate from the standpoint of services rendered by the salesman and provides an income sufficiently high to enable the salesman to maintain a standard of living that is commensurate with the importance of his position and is compatible with that of the customers whom he serves.

2. *Simplicity.* A plan that is easily understood by both the salesman and the company and has few complicating factors is preferred over other plans. However, simplicity is not to be worshiped over other essential characteristics; actually, it is a characteristic of secondary importance.

3. *Proportionate Reward.* The pay is proportionate to the volume of sales, to the profitableness of the salesman to the house, and to the results

accomplished. The salesman doing a better piece of work than his fellows is given a greater reward.

4. *Incentive.* The plan stimulates the salesman to do and want to do those things that will produce profitable sales over a long period of time.

5. *Protection for Customers.* The plan is designed to discourage any actions that are detrimental to the best interests of customers.

6. *Flexibility.* It is flexible enough to operate effectively during all seasons of the year and is adaptable enough to meet the normal variations that occur in the course of business.

7. *Low Operating Cost.* A minimum amount of clerical help is needed to compute the salesman's earnings. In some cases, the cost of additional clerical help may be considerably overbalanced by the returns from that effort. Wherever possible, however, the plan should be devised to utilize existing basic clerical operations rather than to create new ones.

8. *Promotion.* The plan incorporates some provision for promotion in pay and reward for continuous service. In many instances the primary opportunity for promotion is that of advancement in position, but, in addition, some periodic increase in pay for those salesmen who render long and loyal servce is desirable.

9. *Uniform Earnings.* The plan enables the salesman to earn a reasonably uniform income each month, as his expenses are relatively regular from month to month. It is difficult for most salesmen to adjust their living standards wisely to an income that varies from time to time. This requirement by no means precludes the payment of bonuses at intervals less frequent than the length of regular pay periods.

10. *Promptness.* Prompt reward is given the salesman for the service he renders. A salesman is more apt to be stimulated by an incentive plan if his reward follows closely upon the heels of accomplishment. The fact that most profit sharing plans fail to meet this requirement is one of their principal drawbacks.

11. *Fairness.* A final characteristic of a good compensation plan, but not the least important, is that of fairness. A good plan is fair to the employer and to the salesman. An employer is not expected to make unreasonable contributions to the salesman; likewise, the salesman is protected against conditions that are beyond his control.

Not every salesman's compensation plan can measure up 100 per cent to all of these requirements, but comparison of any plan against these "ideal" standards will help to locate weaknesses which may be susceptible of improvement.

Salary Plans of Compensation. The more important plans of compensating salesmen in use by wholesalers are of the following types: straight salary, commission on sales, commission on gross profit, sliding commission, salary and commission, salary and group commission, salary and departmental commission, bonus plans, and profit sharing systems. From this list it is apparent that the salary or commission plans predominate, although there are many variations and modifications of both.

The *straight salary plan* is the simplest method, salesmen are assured of a certain income, they are relieved of anxiety, the house has more control over its sales force, and much more promotional work can be done through salesmen. Furthermore, it is more difficult for a competitor to hire away a salesman who is on a straight salary, and the plan does not present to the employer any serious problems of adjustment during times of depression or in periods of inflation.

Among the disadvantages of the straight salary plan are: it limits a salesman's earning power over short periods of time, it fails to furnish the incentive to push sales or to concentrate on new and hard-to-sell items, and it is open to charges of favoritism. Unless the salary is frequently revised there is a tendency to overpay poor salesmen and underpay good producers. Then there is the perennial question of whether *efforts* or *results* should be the basis for fixing a salesman's salary, since the salary is fixed at the beginning of the year, in ignorance of the sales volume that would be obtained during the year. In times of stress there is also a tendency to discharge salesmen rather than reduce their salaries, for fear of resentment and disruption of the force, when its loyalty and aggressiveness are most needed.

The straight salary plan is used principally under special circumstances, such as for compensating new salesmen until they establish themselves, for paying men opening new territories or operating in marginal sales areas, or for paying men whose work is somewhat different from that of other salesmen. This plan is also used in trades where salesmen do considerable promotional work or perform an unusually large number of nonselling tasks. Moreover, the plan is widely used when companies find it difficult to measure sales performance or when close control over salesmen's activities is desired.

Because of the weaknesses of the straight salary plan of paying regular salesmen, the salary is often combined with the commission on sales method in order to minimize the bad points of each and, at the same time, retain the good features of both. When this plan is used, a fixed salary is agreed upon, with the understanding that sales shall constitute a certain multiple thereof and a specified commission is paid on all sales in excess of this figure.

Commission Plans of Compensation. Commission plans of compensation are used primarily when wholesalers desire to emphasize sales volume. They are especially popular with companies selling specialties, and have also proved successful for many companies that introduce new products frequently.

The *straight commission on sales* is used when most of the items handled yield substantially the same margin of profit. Under this plan there is a constant incentive for the salesman to be alert, extra exertions are immediately rewarded, there is no limit on a salesman's earnings, the ratio between sales force expense and sales remains constant, unprofitable salesmen eliminate themselves, and the plan is very simple to operate. Furthermore, arguments regarding salary adjustments are avoided, and the salesman assumes more of the executive attitude because he feels that he is practically in business for himself. On the other hand, the sales manager has less control over his salesmen who are paid according to results, the plan places a premium on sales *volume* rather than *quality* sales, immediate results are stressed, prospects are not cultivated intensively, there is a tendency to *high-spot* the territory, and when permitted to vary prices the salesman is prone to quote the lowest price in order to secure the business and his commission.

The *sliding commission* plan of paying salesmen varies the rate of commission with the volume of business. Ordinarily, a quota is established on which the standard rate of commission is based. All excess sales are divided into steps of equal size or interval, with a higher or lower rate of commission for each step or graded increase in sales. This plan of compensation seems to be well adapted to one-sale specialty goods, but is not particularly suited to the wholesaling field generally. The advantages inherent in this plan are that the salesman is strongly motivated to push sales since he is practically in business for himself, the unprofitable salesman eliminates himself, and sales cost is low for small volume. All the disadvantages of the straight commission plan apply, but usually to a stronger degree. A variation of the sliding commission plan is the *stepped-up commission* method, in which higher rates are paid on successive increments in business. In such cases a certain quota is set on which the salesman receives a given percentage. For the next step of, say, $10,000 in sales, he receives a somewhat higher rate of commission, and on the following step of, say, $5,000, he secures a still higher rate of compensation.

Commissions are often figured on gross profits instead of net sales, that is, each salesman's commission is figured on the gross profit obtained from his own sales. This tends to direct his effort to the goods producing the highest margin. It also prevents a salesman from quoting the lowest prices to customers or from pushing loss leaders and items bearing narrow margins. The profit-sharing rate of commission can be adjusted to compensate salesmen for different costs of traveling and for varying degrees of competition in sales territories. This plan overcomes many of the objections to a straight commission or a sliding commission method. It requires, however, a substantial amount of clerical work; it is difficult for the salesman to understand the plan and to compute his earnings; and the plan is open to charges of manipulation.

Probably the most flexible type of commission system is the *group commission* method, in which varying commission rates are paid on different groups of commodities. Such commissions are usually combined with a base salary which guarantees the salesman a minimum income and which is counted as part of the commission. In its simplest version, the commodity groups are set up on the basis of the *gross margin* accruing to the concern. Other factors may be taken into account as well, such as the *distribution policies of the supplier* or *handling expenses required*. Some wholesalers pay a commission based on the "net margin" or difference between gross margin and direct expenses associated with a commodity group as determined by a cost analysis. Thus, for example, one item may have a gross margin of 20 per cent and direct handling expenses of 10 per cent, while another has a gross margin of 25 per cent and direct expenses of 18 per cent. A higher rate of commission would then be paid on the first item despite the fact that its gross margin is smaller. This system takes into account the fact that net profit does not necessarily vary directly with gross margin, and is therefore a refinement of the group commission based on gross margin alone. It is especially well adapted to concerns handling a wide variety of products bearing different margins and with different cost characteristics such as bulk, weight, or spoilage.

Still another factor that may be used in varying the rate of commission is the average *line extension* or the value of the average customer order for an individual item. For example, if an item is sold at $2.50 per dozen and the average customer order is 3 dozen, the average line extension is $7.50. This factor is important because many operating expenses are relatively constant regardless of the amount ordered, varying primarily with the number of invoice lines to be processed. Illustrative are such costs as order-processing in the office, order-picking, checking, and clerical expenses of posting orders to stock control records.[13] As a result, the net profit of the wholesale concern tends to vary directly with the value of the average line extension. This being the case, the salesman can be stimulated to make more profitable sales by varying the commission in accordance with the line extension as well as gross margins and other factors.

Group commission plans generally provide the greatest flexibility of all types of compensation systems. Special commission rates can be set for new products, for sluggish items, or for other special circumstances. A basic disadvantage is that it requires considerable clerical work, since

---

[13] This point is developed further in Chapters 29 and 30.

every invoice must be coded and sales records must be maintained for each salesman by product groups.

It is common for wholesalers to combine a *drawing account* with the various commission plans of compensation, which is in one way a loan against commissions yet unearned while in another way it resembles a minimum salary, particularly when the drawing account is guaranteed. The purposes of the drawing account are to help the salesman to finance himself between pay days, and to provide a minimum income. In most cases the salesman's drawing account is determined by past performance and by business conditions in the trade. There is no agreement among companies regarding the size of drawing accounts, but they are seldom more than 75 per cent of anticipated commissions. At certain periods, either monthly, semiannually, or yearly, the amount of the salesman's advance is deducted from his earned commissions. If the balance is in favor of the salesman, he receives the difference in a lump sum. Should there be a deficiency, the company may carry the debt over into the next period, unless it is in the nature of a guaranteed minimum salary, and the salesman is required to pay it back from his future commission earnings. More often, the deficiency is disregarded and the loss is absorbed without holding the salesman responsible for the commissions received but unearned.

Bonus Plans and Profit-Sharing Systems of Compensation. The plans of compensation discussed in preceding paragraphs are sometimes supplemented by a *bonus,* which is a payment made annually or semiannually in a lump sum as a means of augmenting the salesman's income, the purpose being, of course, to stimulate salesmen to greater effort. The bonus may be based on sales, net profits, or some other criterion, or may rest on the discretion and judgment of the management. Usually, bonuses are based on certain achievements and upon completion of certain prescribed tasks, such as setting up store displays, getting new accounts, or conducting training sessions for retail clerks. If a point system is used to determine the bonus, a given value may be assigned to each of the tasks, with penalties imposed for failure to accomplish certain requirements.

Profit-sharing plans have as their major objective that of unifying the interests of salesmen and the organization, and the development of loyalty and initiative. Usually, they have not worked out satisfactorily, except as supplementary means of compensation, because net profits are affected by many factors beyond the salesman's control. If the plan also requires a sharing of losses, salesmen are unable and unwilling to bear their share. These methods of compensation gained some headway during the 1920's, but the years of depression that followed gave them such a setback that they have not regained their former status.

Salesmen's Expenses. Traveling and other expenses incurred by salesmen in line of duty are an integral part of a compensation plan for a wholesaler's sales force. When large territories are covered, salesmen's expenses may actually exceed compensation. Some firms include salesmen's expense in the salary or commission; others pay a fixed allowance at definite intervals; while another plan is to reimburse salesmen for expenses actually incurred. The first procedure eliminates the necessity for expense reports, and the amount used for the purpose is likely to be smaller than when the firm pays expenses as incurred. Skimping on expenses, however, may prove disadvantageous, and salesmen may fail to cover their territory adequately. It is also difficult to determine what part of the compensation should be allowed for expenses, since salesmen's expenses do not necessarily vary with the volume of business secured. The third method necessitates extra reports and vouchers, but it gives the sales manager more control over his force. The salesmen can be directed to visit communities or customers that are relatively inaccessible, to live and travel in a manner determined by the company, and to carry out plans which require large expenditures. Salesmen's expense problems are multiplied by the use of automobiles. If salesmen use their own cars for traveling, the company may pay all expenses as reported, it may compensate them on a mileage basis, or may make a flat weekly or per diem allowance. If the company furnishes the cars, the problems of depreciation, use of the car for personal purposes, cost of operation, repairs, and upkeep must be faced.

SALES-PLANNING

A certain amount of planning of anticipated sales is indispensable, whether the firm operates strictly on a budget basis or controls its operations informally. Comprehensive and accurate information on expected sales volume is of utmost importance in the control and internal management of every modern wholesale establishment, for such knowledge is used as a basis for the proper determination of desired inventories, purchases, sales and promotional activity, and financial management of the business. The need for sales-planning in connection with merchandise-budgeting was pointed out in Chapter 20. As indicated in the subsequent discussion, such plans also serve as a basis for controlling the activities of salesmen, and the plans may be employed in connection with the compensation system as well.

Planning Total Sales. The first problem in planning sales is a determination of the total volume of business that is expected for the firm during the period covered by the budget. This is usually six months or a year, depending on the kind of business. In arriving at the total figure, consideration must be given to *current volume; recent trend in volume; changes in market potential; general business conditions; changes in company policies, product lines, or personnel; and changes in the competitive situation.*

Current Sales Volume. The starting point for a sales forecast is the current level of sales. Wholesaling is a fairly stable kind of business in most lines of trade and, unless there are good reasons for believing otherwise, the presumption is that the status quo will be maintained at least for the short period covered by the plan. Moreover, the existing level of sales reflects all of the many forces at work within and without the organization and should be maintained unless changes occur in one or more of these factors. This means that if a firm had a sales volume of $5,500,000 in a given year, the same amount will be anticipated in the year following in the absence of radical changes.

Recent Trend in Sales. Most companies experience a certain amount of growth or decline over a period of time, which can be measured in terms of a *trend* in sales. If consistent increases have been achieved in each of several preceding years, averaging about 5 per cent per annum, then a similar increase would normally be expected in planning sales for the next year. To continue the hypothetical illustration from the preceding paragraph, the figure of $5,500,000 would be increased to $5,775,000. Great care should be exercised in applying an increase or decrease of this kind. It should be borne in mind that past trends do not *necessarily* extend into the future; and especially that sales trends are not regular and consistent. Sales in a particular year may, therefore, differ markedly from the amount that would be expected on the basis of a trend projection.

Changes in Market Potential. The sales of an individual wholesale enterprise represent but a part of the total market potential for the lines it sells in its territory. Because sales are obtained out of the total market potential, independent estimates of this potential are of great importance in sales planning. Such estimates can often be obtained from trade associations or periodicals or through special studies. As an illustration of the methods used by wholesalers to determine market potential, some firms in the dry goods trade base their estimates on average sales per 100,000 population, per $1,000,000 of disposable personal income, and per $1,000,000 of retail general merchandise sales in a given territory.[14] Use of several factors in this fashion permits checking of one against the other to achieve maximum accuracy. Assuming that about a 1 per cent increase is expected in the market potential, the illustrative sales forecast might be raised from $5,775,000 to $5,830,000.

General Business Conditions. Changes in general business conditions, as revealed by fluctuations in total consumer income, the level of employment and unemployment, degree of utilization of industrial capacity, and similar indicators, obviously will have an effect on the sales of a wholesale

[14] Fred W. Chapman, Jr., "The Need for Territorial Analysis," *Proceedings of the 29th Annual Convention,* National Wholesale Dry Goods Association (New York, February, 1956).

enterprise. General business conditions are closely related to changes in market potential discussed in the preceding paragraph, but are not the same thing. Different industries and lines of business are affected in different ways by general conditions; some kinds of wholesale firms may actually suffer very little in times of economic stress, while others are practically forced out of business altogether. If general business conditions are expected to decline about 4 per cent, the forecast of $5,830,000 might be lowered to $5,600,000.

Company Policies, Products, and Personnel. Future sales may be affected materially by changes in an enterprise's policies, product lines, and personnel. An example of a policy change that would affect sales is that of credit terms. If a stricter attitude is adopted toward debtors, or if the credit period is shortened, sales will no doubt decline; and the converse is also true. Other important policies are those touching delivery, product service, salesmen's calls, and pricing.

Changes in product lines have an obvious effect on total sales. If new items are added, and assuming that they are not merely duplications of existing items, sales gains should result. If, on the other hand, an important line is lost, a measurable decline must be anticipated.

Company personnel, especially salesmen, contributes to the level of sales obtained. When a top salesman leaves a wholesale house, he may actually take customers with him to a competitor or to his own business. Less direct, but often just as important, are the contributions of nonselling personnel such as the credit manager or even the truck drivers.

Major changes in these internal factors are not frequent in most organizations. Assuming they are to remain about the same, no change would be made in the forecast of $5,600,000 indicated in the previous section.

Changes in Competition. Outside of the organization itself, a major determinant of its sales is the competitive structure for the lines carried. As suggested in Chapter 18, the competition faced by an enterprise includes all similar firms and, in addition, various kinds of related middlemen and direct-selling manufacturers. If an electrical goods wholesaler were attempting to evaluate the factor of competition in his sales forecast, he would consider not only other electrical wholesalers but also direct-selling manufacturers, retail chain organizations, agents and brokers, and wholesalers in related lines, such as industrial equipment and hardware, to the extent of the lines in question.

In the hypothetical example used throughout this section, supposing that competition is expected to decline somewhat so that 5 per cent more sales might be expected as a result, the forecast of $5,600,000 could be increased to approximately $5,900,000. This, then, would be the estimate of total sales for the coming year, arrived at by successive modifications of the current year's level of sales in the light of known or expected changes in relevant factors that determine marketing opportunities.

Distribution of Total Sales by Types. After a forecast of total sales for the enterprise has been formulated, it should be broken down into classes and types. One such division is between city and country sales, the latter referring to business secured from customers outside of the metropolitan area in which the concern is located. This separation can be made on the basis of the ratio obtained in the past between sales in the two types of markets, modified, of course, by their respective market potentialities. If the wholesaler operates over an extensive area, it may be advisable to divide the territory into a number of districts and allocate the anticipated volume by these districts.

Total city and country sales, respectively, are next divided into merchandise departments. Ratios established by past performance are very helpful. They are modified, of course, by additions to or deletions from the line of merchandise, changed buying habits and consumption patterns, the level of income payments which affects the proportion of consumer incomes expended for durable or luxury items that may be included in the line of goods handled, changes in sales policies or advertising plans, and other similar factors.

Salesmen's Quotas. The final step in sales planning is the determination of what part of the total volume of sales, by merchandise departments, is to be expected of each individual salesman in a given territory. Quotas thus set for each salesman enable him to know in advance how much business he is expected to produce and the approximate proportion of that business that should be produced in the more important lines of merchandise. In addition, they provide the management with a basis for compensating the salesman and a means of evaluating his performance.

In setting up a distribution of sales estimates by salesmen the goal is to arrive at a sales figure for each man that can actually be realized. Quotas impossible of attainment are to be avoided, because they defeat their own purpose.

The two most important factors to be considered in effecting this distribution on a quota basis are past performance and potential sales. Past performance cannot be used alone, for this assumes that each man has done a satisfactory job in the past. This past-performance factor is more important for the wholesalers' salesmen, however, than it is for the manufacturers' salesmen. The manufacturers' salesman is usually the sole representative in his territory for the line of products handled, and he can reasonably be expected to obtain a given proportion of the total potential sales as indicated by a market index. The wholesaler's salesman, however, is in competition with other wholesalers' salesmen and with other forms of competition. Because retailers and other customers are usually solicited by several salesmen carrying the same merchandise items, the amount of sales obtained by a wholesaler's salesman is largely conditioned by his individual ability, personal relationships with customers, price policies of the concern, accessibility of the house, transportation and delivery costs, credit terms, and other such factors. Past performance of the salesman reflects all these factors and indicates what may be expected in the future if the same salesman continues to operate under similar conditions. If, for example, a 5 per cent increase in total sales volume is anticipated, it appears sound therefore to apply this percentage increase to past sales of each individual salesman unless there is a very specific reason for doing otherwise. The same holds true for the amount of sales expected for each salesman by merchandise departments.

It is desirable to check quotas arrived at on this basis, however, against some measure or indicator of the potential sales in each territory. *Specific* market indexes calculated by involved statistical techniques are often used by manufacturers to estimate territorial potential sales of one product or a number of closely related items in a product family. Indexes of this kind are not well adapted for use in the typical wholesale enterprise. Because of the large number and variety of items carried, a *general* market index that shows the market opportunity for a wide variety of products is more suitable.

Among the general market indexes available for use are population, family buying income, industrial production, automobile registrations, and retail store sales. Common sense and experimentation tell the wholesaler which of these is most suitable in any individual case. Data on population and retail store sales are available from the censuses of Population and Business. There is always the danger, however, that census data do not accurately reflect current conditions. More recent data may be available from local agencies of government, chambers of commerce, and so forth. Very valuable in this connection are the current estimates provided in the annual "Survey of Buying Power" issue of the magazine *Sales Management*. This source provides generally reliable *estimates* by cities and by counties on such items as population; number of households; total retail sales for all types of stores and for food, general merchandise, and drugstores; effective buying income (disposable personal incomes) as a total and on a per household basis; and the amount of farm income.

For certain lines of wholesaling a more specific index may well be used. For example, a grocery wholesaler may base his quotas on sales of food stores, total or by certain lines of merchandise. An electrical wholesaler may use the number of homes wired for electricity as a basis. Each of these may be modified by other factors, such as per capita income.

If it has been decided, for example, to use total retail sales as a measure of potential volume for the wholesaler, the procedure involves determining the total for the market areas covered by the wholesaler, and the percentage accounted for by each political division for which data are available. Since the *county* is the smallest unit for which data are consistently available, it is convenient to draw territory boundaries on a county basis. In this way the percentage for each salesman's territory can be calculated. If two or more salesmen operate in the same county, the potential for that county may be distributed among them according to population (which is available for small divisions), the number of retail outlets, the number of accounts called on, or on some other basis that appears reasonable under the particular circumstances.

The resulting figures cannot be used indiscriminately in quota-setting. In some parts of a wholesaler's market area, competition from other wholesalers may be more intense than in other areas. Salesmen working at a distance from the house obtain only a small proportion of the business on bulky or heavy items, unless the firm prepays freight or makes deliveries without charge. Chain and department stores take a larger proportion of the business in the urban than in the rural areas. Therefore the reliability of all types of general indexes is limited, so far as the wholesaler is concerned, by circumstances of this nature. Such indexes must be modified after taking into consideration competition, distance, and other pertinent factors.

When an index of potential sales, so modified, reveals that some salesmen have not performed properly in the past, there is justification for an increase in their quotas as determined on the basis of past performance. Such increases must not be so large as to be discouraging to the salesman, because important changes in accomplishment can never be expected immediately. When increases are so made, it is advisable to pick out certain lines of merchandise or certain classes of customers, in which the salesman has been weak, for additional concentration. Thus the salesman sees in a specific manner how the increase is to be achieved.

Yearly quotas are broken down into shorter time periods, usually months, according to the seasonal nature of the business. A system is usually provided whereby salesmen are informed at intervals of their progress so that they may gauge the amount of exertion necessary to achieve the desired results.

27

SALES ANALYSIS
AND CONTROL

Scientific management of selling activities in a wholesale enterprise is predicated on an accurate knowledge of sales *opportunities* and *results*. Such knowledge is obtained in part through regular supervision of salesmen and from records of their operations. For the most part, however, comprehensive knowledge of this character is gained through periodic analyses of sales results in order to reveal strong and weak points, indicate trends in the business, and evaluate the performance of personnel. Through such an analysis sound sales policies can be formulated for the supervision of salesmen and others concerned with the selling function. On the basis of sales policies and the programs formulated to carry them out, effective sales control is accomplished.

SALES SUPERVISION

The need for sales supervision and direction is so apparent as to require little elaboration. Even experienced salesmen need such help; up-to-date facts should be supplied, as well as continuous training, since new and improved methods of selling are being constantly evolved. Because many wholesalers' salesmen usually operate at a distance from the house and always more or less independently, supervision is necessary to correlate their efforts with those of the firm. Furthermore, a salesman is kept in close touch with headquarters since conditions change rapidly, prices are revised, new lines are added, and old lines dropped. Finally, no salesman is likely to work to capacity if he is not supervised and stimulated by a superior, for self-imposed pressure is seldom as consistently productive as that emanating from the home office.

Elements of the Supervision System. A system of supervision and control of salesmen includes personal contact with a sales executive who can inspire his subordinates. This is achieved by requiring the salesmen to report to the home office at frequent intervals or by the sales manager's spending some of his time with his men in the field. The latter has often proved most effective in stimulating sales. Sales conferences for the discussion of sales points of individual lines, ways of assisting customers, and similar matters constitute another component part of a supervisory plan. A third feature consists of supervision through reports and records. Among the reports that have been found most useful are route sheets which are filled out by the home office when routing is controlled (see Figure 49), daily reports of calls and sales (see Figure 50), expense reports, automobile expense reports, and reports on complaints and adjustments. Usually salesmen are also required to submit credit reports and separate reports on collections. Where salesmen recurrently and regularly call upon the same trade and are charged with the duty of making collections, the collection report is usually combined with the daily report on calls and sales.

THE AMERICAN SUPPLY CO.
LANSING, MICH.

SALESMAN'S ROUTE SHEET

Week beginning.................................*I shall make the following towns on the day, date and in the order named below.* *(Signed)*.................................

DAY	DATE	TOWN	DAY	DATE	TOWN

My address each day will be as follows:

DAY	DATE	TOWN	CARE OF
MON.			
TUES.			
WED.			
THURS.			
FRI.			
SAT.			
SUN.			

COPY OF THIS REPORT MUST REACH US FRIDAY MORNING PRIOR TO THE WEEK FOR WHICH IT IS MADE.
☞ KEEP A RECORD OF THIS REPORT AND INQUIRE FOR MAIL, TELEGRAMS OR TELEPHONE CALLS AT ALL ADDRESSES GIVEN.

FIGURE 49. Salesman's Route Sheet Form

The following content is rotated and represents a form.

THE WESTERN WHOLESALE CO.
CINCINNATI, OHIO

Salesman's Daily Report

Date _____ 19___

Day _____

DAILY WORK SUMMARY

Calls Made _____
Orders Secured _____
Future Orders Secured _____
New Accounts Secured _____
Accounts Collected _____
Total Amount Collected $_____

Give Us Any Information Which Will Make it Possible for Us to Write Each Individual a Personal, Friendly Letter.

"OUT OF TOWN." When the buyer is out of town, give his name, tell where he was and what he was doing, if possible.

INFORMATION. If the dealer asks any questions or wants information or says anything which suggests our writing a letter, tell us about it.

CHANGES IN THE STORE. If the dealer enlarges or remodels his store — if he puts in a new front — if he puts in new show cases, shelving or equipment — tell us so we can write him and compliment him on his progressiveness.

FAMILY AFFAIRS. We want to be able to write to the dealer concerning such personal affairs as illnesses and deaths. Tell us also of such events as children returning home from college or similar intimate conditions in which we are interested.

CONCERNING THE SALESMAN. Wherever the house can write the dealer and say anything to help to make the salesman increasingly "solid" with the dealer, give us the information.

NOTE: THIS REPORT IS TO BE SENT TO US WITHOUT EXCEPTION EACH WORKING DAY.

Customer's Name	Located at	Sold Yes No	Collection Amount	Future Yes No

Hotel _____ Town _____ Salesman _____

FIGURE 50. Salesman's Daily Report Form

It is normally not sufficient for the sales manager to check whether or not a salesman included a certain town in his itinerary. It is possible to visit the town in question and call on only two instead of five or six desirable prospects or customers located therein. The report on calls and sales throws light on this point and serves as a check on the frequency of calls on the same trade and on the reasons why orders were not secured. It helps to establish a given salesman's effectiveness through the relationship between calls and sales. It also enables the salesman to survey his acomplishments for the day, thereby often spurring him on to renewed effort. The psychological effect of reporting regularly is wholesome, and the daily report obviates the necessity for much correspondence. From the various reports required of salesmen, their movements can be checked and recorded on maps by means of pins with colored heads. The salesman's attention can thus be called to his derelictions, if any, and more complete, regular, and intensive coverage assured.

Time-and-Duty Study. An important aid in the supervision and control of salesmen's efforts is the device known as "time-and-duty study." By this is meant a detailed analysis of the manner in which the salesmen spend their time and the methods by which they perform their duties. To make such a study, it is necessary to break down the salesman's job into the individual components that can be recognized and recorded. There may be as many as 20 or more common discernible components. These may be grouped according to activities taking place inside the customer's place of business and those taking place outside; each of these two groupings in turn may be divided into "productive" and "nonproductive" activities. A sample that contains an adequate representation of the better and the poorer salesmen is then selected for the study. The criteria for this selection include not only dollar volume of sales but volume in relation to potential, gross margins obtained, and other measures of performance that are discussed in a following section. Salesmen operating under significantly different conditions, as city salesmen and country salesmen, are always analyzed separately.

A competent and trained observer, not ordinarily associated with the firm, accompanies each of the salesmen for one or more regular working days; he records and classifies the exact amount of time spent on each of the various elements of the job, and he makes notes of other observations not subject to precise quantitative measurement. The timing must be conducted in such a way that the salesmen are not aware that they are a part of an investigation of this nature; otherwise, their work would likely be conditioned by such knowledge. Obviously, this requires considerable ingenuity on the part of those planning and carrying out the study.

The results of two time-and-duty studies, dealing with city and country wholesale drug salesmen, respectively, are summarized in Table 21 and

TABLE 21

COMPOSITION OF THE AVERAGE WORKING DAY FOR CITY AND
COUNTRY WHOLESALE DRUG SALESMEN, BY TYPE OF ACTIVITY

Type of Activity	City Salesmen (Average Working Day—7.2 hours)	Country Salesmen (Average Working Day—10.1 hours)
Time Spent Inside Stores	54.3%	62.9%
Time Spent Outside Stores:		
Travel Time	23.9	22.6
Meals	7.0	8.4
Other Time Outside Stores	14.8	6.1
TOTAL	100.0%	100.0%
Average Calls per Day	6.2	7.3
Average Minutes per Call	36.8	49.9

Sources: Robert N. Skinner, *A Time and Duty Study of City Wholesale Drug Sales-men*, unpublished M.B.A. thesis on deposit in the library of The Ohio State University, 1958, pp. 11, 12, 17; James J. Mischler, *A Time and Duty Study of Country Wholesale Drug Salesmen*, unpublished M.B.A. thesis on deposit in the library of The Ohio State University, 1958, pp. 9, 13.

Figure 50. While intended merely to be illustrative, these data are no doubt representative of conditions that exist in many wholesale concerns. As shown in the table, there is a substantial difference in the length of the working day for city and country salesmen as well as in its distribution among various types of activities. This indicates the necessity of treating the two groups separately in any further analysis.

Perhaps the most valuable finding to be obtained from time-and-duty studies is the determination of differences between efficient and inefficient salesmen, as illustrated in Figure 51. For this comparison, salesmen were classified on the basis of the efficiency with which they utilize their time. It is interesting to note that there was a close relationship between this classification and the ratings previously given the same salesmen by their superiors on the basis of other criteria.

The information provided by a study of this kind furnishes a basis for specific and positive recommendations for the training of the less efficient and the new members of the sales force. Salesmen may be trained to increase the amount of their productive time in various ways, among which are the possibilities for (1) utilizing waiting periods for checking the dealer's stock; (2) minimizing the amount of general conversation not related in any way to the selling task; (3) approaching the interview in a direct business-like manner to cut down on the time spent in waiting for interviews; (4) interviewing the dealer in the rear of the store where interruptions are not so likely to occur; and (5) better planning of sales calls to reduce trips back to the car in order to bring in samples, literature, and the like. A similar analysis of the time spent outside of customers'

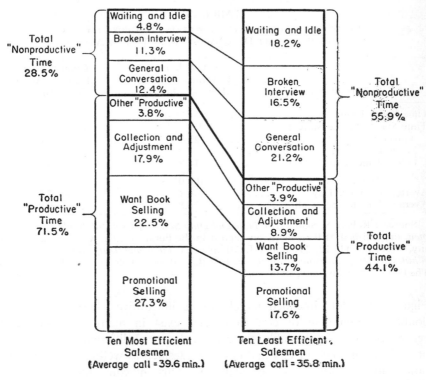

FIGURE 51. Distribution of Time Spent on Average Sales Call by Ten Most Efficient and Ten Least Efficient City Wholesale Drug Salesmen

Source: Based on data from Robert N. Skinner, *A Time and Duty Study of City Wholesale Drug Salesmen*, unpublished M.B.A. thesis on deposit in the library of The Ohio State University, 1958.

places of business also reveals methods of increasing productive time. Illustrative of these are fewer trips to the wholesale house, particularly by city salesmen, and the use of parking lots rather than long searches for free parking places.

In connection with the time study, the exact manner in which the best and the poorest salesmen use their productive hours may be observed. This is accomplished by noting the effectiveness of different types of selling arguments, the number of different merchandise items mentioned to the customer, and the proper use of display materials and samples. The analysis of carefully recorded information of this kind furnishes a basis for constructive recommendations, which, when carried out, result in substantial returns by way of increased selling effectiveness.

Studies of this kind are substantial undertakings that require expert planning and involve considerable expense. For this reason, they cannot be carried on easily by small- or medium-sized wholesalers. This type of study, however, is well adapted to cooperative undertakings by groups of wholesalers in the same line of business whose salesmen operate under similar conditions. In the individual firm, the sales manager can approach this type of information by such means as more frequent observations of the individual salesman's activities, conferences with customers of the firm whenever the opportunity is present, and interviews with capable manufacturers' salesmen who occasionally travel with the wholesaler's representatives.

SALES ANALYSIS AS A PHASE OF SCIENTIFIC MANAGEMENT

The essence of successful management in wholesaling as in all business is management based on pertinent facts properly interpreted, or *scientific* management. In contrast, unscientific management reflects operation without adequate information on which to build sound business policies. It is true that many fine old wholesale houses whose founders never heard of scientific management have succeeded, but they no doubt practiced sound management which they had learned in the hard school of experience. Today successful business is built more surely and speedily by taking full advantage of the vast and growing body of organized knowledge concerning sound business policy and practice. Scientific management, first applied in manufacturing, has gradually pervaded all fields of business.

The Profit Motive in Management. Management is not an end in itself but a means to an end. That end normally is the making of profit. Profit constitutes the dominant motivating force of the competitive régime which generally characterizes the American economy. The wholesaling segment of our economy is subject to the same competitive influences. In the final analysis, the success of any wholesaling activity is measured principally in terms of profits.

Inadequate net profits, or net losses, are generally caused by insufficient gross margins, a limited volume of business, high operating expenses, or a combination of these factors. It follows, therefore, that the principal means by which net profits can replace losses or can be increased above those now enjoyed by a wholesale enterprise are through (1) a widening of gross margins, (2) an increase in sales volume, (3) a reapportioning and redirection of the sales effort into more profitable channels, and (4) control of operating expenses, often resulting in a curtailment without sacrificing essential functions and services.

Wider Gross Margins. The ability of a wholesaler to secure a wider gross margin is limited by two circumstances. In the first place, the wholesaler is in competition with other wholesalers and with other types of wholesaling institutions. An attempt to enhance margins by increasing prices to customers, therefore, results in an offsetting competitive disadvantage in the form of losses in sales volume. The second circumstance limiting the ability to increase gross margins is that the matter is not entirely under the control of the wholesaler, but is usually the prerogative of the manufacturer or other supplier. Many manufacturers make it a policy to maintain resale prices through resale price maintenance legislation, advertising the retail price to consumers, exclusive agency agreements, and other means. Thus the wholesaler, being limited by competition on the one hand and by manufacturers' policies on the other, usually does not have much freedom with regard to prices charged to customers, and can often secure a wider gross margin only by inducing manufacturers to grant larger trade or functional discounts.

Manufacturers, however, tend to resist wholesalers' requests or pressures for wider gross margins, usually because such attempts are unsupported by factual evidence. If studies are made which show the amount of selling effort required for a given product, the storage and handling expense incurred in wholesaling the item, the quantities in which the item is customarily purchased and delivered by the wholesaler to his customers, the maximum practical turnover rate that can be attained, and other pertinent information, then the case can be laid before the manufacturer on a factual basis. When this is done and the conclusions are warranted, most manufacturers, particularly those who rely heavily on wholesalers for the distribution of their products, are willing to grant larger discounts to wholesalers in order to provide an adequate compensation for the essential services rendered and a reasonable net profit on wholesaling of the product.

Increased Volume of Business. When conditions are propitious, as during the upward movement of the business cycle, it is not exceedingly difficult to enhance net profits through an increase in sales volume. Normally, however, it is much harder to attain larger profits in this manner than through alternative methods. If additional selling effort is applied, by cultivating a more extensive territory or by cultivating the present market more intensively, a point of diminishing returns is often quickly reached when the larger volume is matched against the higher selling costs. This is frequently true because the wholesaler is not well situated for creating additional primary demand for the products in which he deals. Increases in sales volume are often obtained at the expense of competitors who retaliate by increasing sales pressure or by cutting prices.

The most effective way for a wholesaler to increase sales volume probably resides in enhanced efficiency in the performance of all his operations so that he can operate profitably on a lower margin or provide better services to the trade than are afforded by his competitors. A redirection of the sales effort and a closer control of operating expenses, both of which are in themselves methods of increasing net profits, contribute to the wholesaler's ability to accomplish this end.

Reapportioning and Redirecting the Sales Effort. While it is difficult to secure wider profit margins from manufacturers and to increase sales volume through additional sales efforts, a redirection of sales effort along more fruitful lines is a very effective method of increasing net profits. This may result in an increased volume of sales or it may result in approximately the same or a lower sales volume secured at a higher profit ratio. It involves a planned program of marketing research to discover and explore new opportunities and requires the careful analysis of internal records, particularly sales records, to determine the manner in which past efforts have been directed or allowed to meander. This permits attention to be concentrated on customers who buy in larger quantities, on products that have a high unit value and carry a wide gross margin, and so on. Such a program concentrates on efforts aimed at increasing the over-all effectiveness of the organization through greater sales efficiency achieved by the proper utilization of facts. Total operating costs, in the absolute, may increase, decrease, or remain the same; but relative costs are thus reduced or are held constant while improved services are rendered through a better utilization of the time and efforts of employees and of the capital invested in the business.

Control of Operating Costs. Under all ordinary circumstances, especially when business travels a descending spiral into a recession, a very effective way of increasing net profits (or curtailing losses) is through a positive program directed specifically toward a reduction of operating expenses and the close control of all business operations affecting costs. There are indeed few wholesale houses—whether independently operated, or owned and operated by manufacturers, chains, or cooperatives—in which there is no opportunity to eliminate wastes and inefficiencies or to enhance efficiencies through the application of scientific cost analysis. When accounting records are properly set up, expense items are systematically classified with a view to subsequent analyses, and general expenses are allocated intelligently, the costs of performing various activities can be ascertained. By means of such standards, inefficiencies are noted and corrected. This method of increasing net profits is particularly attractive to the progressive wholesaler, for the matter of reducing operating expenses is largely under his own control, being but indirectly influenced by sources of supply or by external conditions. Furthermore, a saving in a dollar of expense is equivalent, other things being equal, to a dollar added to net profit. Of course, sometimes an *increase* in expenses may result in better service, larger sales, and hence increased profits. In any event, control of operating costs is not an approach to be used exclusively, but rather one to supplement others for the proper guidance of a scientific-minded management. Some approaches to the problem of expense control are discussed in Chapters 29 and 30.

PURPOSES AND TYPES OF SALES ANALYSIS

From the foregoing it is apparent that one of the two principal methods of achieving the goal of maximum net profit is through the proper direction of sales effort. This, in turn, requires a factual foundation which can be obtained only through analysis of actual sales results over a period of time.

General Nature of Sales Analysis. The term "analysis" means, of course, a *breakdown* or *distribution* of some total into its component parts. In the case of sales, the breakdown can be made in terms of amounts and percentages of total on the basis of departments, by size of order, by customers, by sales territories, and for various other bases of classification. The analysis may be supplemented by a study of the gross margins obtained for each basis of classification investigated. When this is done, it is necessary to enter the cost on each line of the house copy of the invoice so that gross margins may be computed by order lines or for invoice totals and tabulated according to customers, departments, salesmen, and so on. Sales analyses are also frequently coupled with corresponding analyses of operating expenses, so that effort can be channeled in the most *profitable* directions, as far as net results are concerned, as well as in those producing the greatest *volume* or approximately profitable results as judged, for example, by gross margins.

All types or phases of a sales analysis are not made with the same frequency. For example, analysis of sales and gross margins by salesmen may be made continually as an adjunct of the sales compensation plan. Analyses by size of order, on the other hand, may be made infrequently and even on a sample basis, the sole motive being guidance in policy determination.

For the facts discovered by sales analysis there is no practical substitute. In every instance in which such analyses have been made for the first time or after a long period of time, so far as is known, the facts brought to light have amazed the management and their disclosure has been invariably followed by some corrective action of a constructive nature.

Analysis by Merchandise Departments. One important type of sales analysis, perhaps the most commonly used in practice, is on the basis of merchandise *departments* or other merchandise classifications. This shows which lines of merchandise produce the greatest volume and which the smallest. Table 22 illustrates the results of such an analysis for a wholesale automotive firm. The figures, based on sales during a 13-week period, covered more than 25,000 invoices with more than 76,000 line

TABLE 22

ANALYSIS OF SALES AND LINE EXTENSIONS BY MERCHANDISE
DEPARTMENTS IN A WHOLESALE AUTOMOTIVE FIRM

Department	Per Cent of Total Sales	Number of Line Extensions	Average Line Extension
Replacement Parts	34.2%	38,322	$ 5.62
Automotive Accessories	15.6	12,816	7.67
Shop Equipment	14.7	1,083	85.51
Shop Supplies	7.8	16,653	2.95
Radios	7.5	405	116.67
Radio Parts and Supplies	7.3	4,437	10.37
Tires	5.2	1,452	22.56
Television Sets	4.8	187	161.71
Batteries	2.9	847	21.57
TOTAL*	100.0%	76,202	$ 8.27

* Total sales for 13-week period: $630,000.

extensions. In addition to the ranking of departments in terms of total volume, the table shows the number of invoice lines covered by sales in each category and the average line extension.[1]

A slightly different form of sales analysis is illustrated by the data in Table 23. These figures, reflecting a year's business for a full-line tobacco wholesaler, include a breakdown of dollar gross margins as well as of volume. Such an analysis clearly indicates which lines contribute most to total gross profits. In the example given, cigarettes, although accounting for almost two-thirds of sales volume, contribute less than one-third

TABLE 23

ANALYSIS OF SALES AND GROSS MARGINS BY MERCHANDISE DEPARTMENTS
FOR A PERIOD OF ONE YEAR FOR A TOBACCO WHOLESALER

Merchandise Department	Sales		Gross Margin		
	Amount	Per Cent of Total	Per Cent of Sales	Amount	Per Cent of Total
Cigarettes	$1,483,733	62.7%	2.84%	$ 42,138	30.88%
Candy and Fountain ..	354,960	15.0	11.69	41,495	30.41
Cigars	262,670	11.1	8.93	23,456	17.19
General Sundries	137,251	5.8	14.86	20,395	14.95
Tobacco	82,824	3.5	3.79	3,139	2.30
Drug Sundries	44,962	1.9	12.99	5,841	4.28
TOTAL	$2,366,400	100.0%	5.80%	$136,464	100.00%

Source: Based on composite figures for 16 full-line tobacco distributors as reported in Harry B. Patrey in collaboration with Joseph Kolodny, *Successful Methods of Wholesale Tobacco Distribution* (New York: Foresight Publications, 1957), p. 11.

[1] The significance of the average line extension was mentioned briefly in Chapter 26 and is developed further in Chapter 30.

of gross profit. On the other hand, candy and fountain goods, because of the much wider margin they carry, contribute nearly one-third of dollar gross profit but only 15 per cent of sales. Because of the value of such figures as guides in the establishment of sales policies and in their modifications, many firms prepare sales analyses of this kind monthly or even weekly.

Sales analysis may be carried beyond departments into even narrower classifications of goods. For example, within a single department, sales figures may be obtained for each major supplier's line. If it is found that one or two lines account for practically all of the sales and gross profits within some homogeneous category, parallel lines may be dropped or handled on a "special order" basis only. This permits a reduction in the inventory carried to support the sales of a particular classification of goods.

Analyses of sales by merchandise departments are of various forms, depending upon the interests of individual firms. From the facts obtained through such an analysis, the firm may be led to a greater concentration of sales effort on goods with a high average line extension and reasonable volume, and less upon those that already produce large volume but whose line extension is very low. When gross margins are analyzed along with sales, management is aided in its work of setting prices on individual items in order to obtain a more satisfactory gross margin rate for the business as a whole. The most profitable commodities, from the standpoint of total dollar gross margins, may thus be determined. In some cases the management may realize that it has devoted a very large amount of sales effort to a particular group of items because of a high gross margin percentage, but that the effort has not been worthwhile from the standpoint of sales or dollar gross margins realized on these items. In other cases, opportunities for aggressive promotion of high margin items, which have been neglected in the past, may be discovered.

Analysis by Salesmen. An analysis of sales by salesmen may proceed in several different directions. Total sales are classified by salesmen in order to determine what proportion of the total has been obtained by each man on the sales force. The results of such an analysis, conducted for the wholesale automotive firm previously mentioned, are shown in Figure 52. The proportion of total gross profit accounted for by each salesman may be analyzed in a similar manner. Such analyses are frequently made on a routine basis in houses where a commission plan of compensation is in force. Only salesmen operating under like conditions and selling the same products to the same kinds of customers should be compared on this basis. Even so, there is a weakness in judging the accomplishments of salesmen on the basis of such a comparison, because it assumes that each salesman should have produced about the same volume as each of the other salesmen.

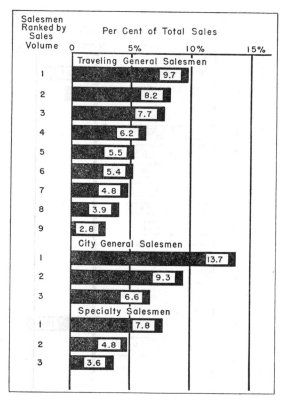

FIGURE 52. Analysis of Sales by Salesmen According to the Proportion of Total Sales Volume Obtained by Each Salesman in a Wholesale Automotive Firm

That this is usually not the situation is recognized by most sales managers. It is therefore necessary to express the sales accomplishments of each salesman as a percentage of the amount of sales that he is expected to achieve. When salesmen's quotas are used as the basis of comparison, the management is frequently surprised to learn that the salesman with the largest volume may not be the best producer; that some salesmen who have produced about the same volume of business as others may actually have done a much better job; and that various salesmen differing widely in actual volume of sales achieved may be on about the same level as far as accomplishment in terms of potential is concerned. Situations similar to these are clearly indicated if the data presented in Figure 52 are compared with the results shown in Figure 53. For example, the traveling general salesman who ranked first in the proportion of total sales volume on Figure 52 ranked fourth on Figure 53 when his sales are related to the quota assigned to him on the basis of his territory potential.

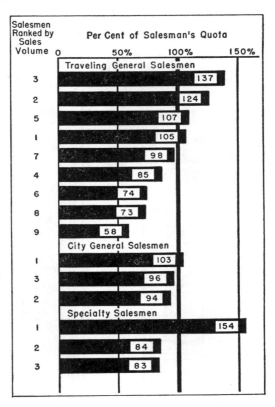

FIGURE 53. Analysis of Sales by Salesmen According to the Percentage of a Hypothetical Quota for Each Salesman in a Wholesale Automotive Firm

As a supplement to the above types of analyses, each salesman's total sales volume may be analyzed by merchandise departments as shown in Figure 54. This is accomplished in the same manner as a departmental analysis for the firm as a whole.

Since each outside salesman normally operates exclusively in a given territory, this analysis furnishes a territorial picture of business. When a salesman's territory is large, however, additional territorial analysis, with counties or combinations of counties used as control units, may be worthwhile as a means of analyzing the firm's business throughout its trade area.

Sales analysis by salesmen or territories reveals when territories are too large to be adequately covered by a salesman and when a territory is too small or does not have sufficient potential business to provide adequate compensation for a salesman's efforts. It shows which salesmen are comparatively successful, and it reveals those who have been able to get

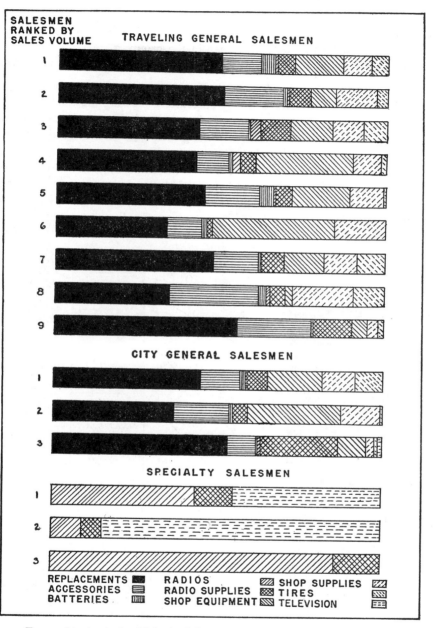

FIGURE 54. Analysis of Sales by Salesmen and by Merchandise Departments in a Wholesale Automotive Firm

by with only a small amount of effort expended. The analysis by merchandise departments uncovers the lines in which the weak salesmen have done the poorest job. Armed with this information and guided by the results achieved by the better salesmen in the group, a sales manager can proceed to train his sales force intelligently and on an individual basis.

Analysis by Customers. A third important phase of a complete sales analysis is that of analyzing sales by customers, showing the amount each customer purchased from the house during the period under investigation. If there are important differences among the customers served by the house, each type or class of customer should be analyzed separately. Thus, in a large wholesale hardware firm the trade may be divided into city customers and country customers, and each of these groups in turn may be divided into retailers and industrial consumers. Retailers may be broken down into regular hardware stores and other types of stores,

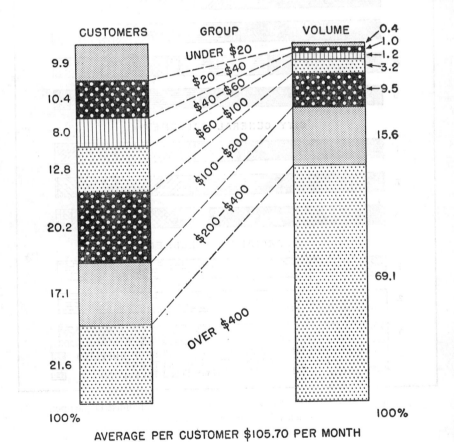

AVERAGE PER CUSTOMER $105.70 PER MONTH

FIGURE 55. Customer Analysis, by Monthly Purchases

whereas it may be desirable to classify industrial users according to manufacturing plants and repair shops, or on some other basis.

Figure 55, which is the result of such an analysis and is believed to be typical of many wholesale houses, shows how little business is contributed by a large percentage of the customers and what a small proportion of the customers yields the bulk of the volume. To make the business of the former group more profitable to the house, it becomes necessary to study the possibilities of each customer. Every effort should be made to secure a larger volume of business from a promising account through a concentration of purchases, or to sell him more merchandise that bears a high margin. When business potential is lacking, it may be best to eliminate those customers who contribute too small an amount of trade, first by calling on them at less frequent intervals and then by gradually dropping them from the list. Time thus saved by salesmen can be utilized to greater advantage either in cultivating new trade or in more intensively serving more profitable accounts from which even greater volume may be forthcoming.

By analyzing each type or class of customer separately, the management learns which groups contribute the greatest volume and offer possibilities for more intensive cultivation. If such studies are made periodically, trends are established and sales effort is directed accordingly.

Analysis by Size of Orders. Closely allied to an analysis of sales by customers is the analysis by the size of individual orders. Figure 56 shows a distribution of sales orders by size groups. It reveals a very bad situation, believed to be typical of conditions in many firms that have not taken positive corrective action. It may be noted that, of all the orders in the wholesale house for which the analysis was made, 13.1 per cent averaging over $100 each accounted for 52.8 per cent of the total business. At the other extreme, 4.5 per cent of the orders were under $4 each and supplied an aggregate business of only 0.2 per cent of the total volume obtained by the house from all customers. Not only are small accounts unproductive from the standpoint of volume, but the cost of serving such accounts frequently equals or exceeds the gross profit obtained. (See Chapter 29 for a discussion of expense analysis as related to order size.)

The "small order problem" is a common one in many lines of business, especially among wholesalers handling such lines as tobacco products, beer and wine, and other convenience goods distributed through many small outlets. Several approaches to the problem have been formulated by progressive concerns.[2] Certainly the first step should be to acquaint the company's salesmen with the nature and significance of the problem.

[2] William R. Davidson, "Handling the Small Order Problem," Presentation at the 1957 *Wholesale Management Course* conducted by The Ohio State University in cooperation with the National Association of Wholesalers.

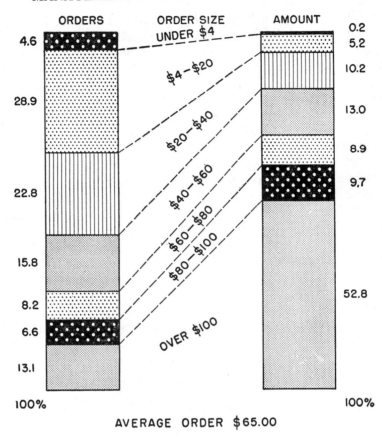

ORDERS   ORDER SIZE   AMOUNT

UNDER $4

$4 – $20

$20 – $40

$40 – $60

$60 – $80

$80 – $100

OVER $100

ORDERS		AMOUNT
4.6		0.2
		5.2
28.9		10.2
		13.0
22.8		8.9
		9.7
15.8		
8.2		52.8
6.6		
13.1		
100%		100%

AVERAGE ORDER $65.00

FIGURE 56. Sales Volume, by Size of Order

This may be further implemented by reducing the frequency of calls on customers who persist in giving small orders and by reducing salesmen's compensation on orders below a specified minimum.

Company policies regarding services given and pricing may also be employed to discourage small orders. For example, customers placing such orders may be (1) refused credit, (2) forced to pick up their goods at the warehouse, (3) required to pay freight and additional service charges, or (4) charged higher prices through the adoption of a quantity discount schedule.

Educational efforts can be directed at customers themselves, since placement of frequent small orders is as unprofitable for the buyer as the seller. The advantages of concentrating purchases can be pointed out and various inducements offered to do so. As a last resort, some concerns adopt a minimum order size and simply refuse to accept orders below this amount. The ability to follow this course of action is limited, it should be noted, by the suppliers' desire to get "100 per cent distribution" and by the fact that many small orders are placed by regular and profitable customers because of unusual circumstances or by new customers who are worth cultivating.

Analysis by Method of Sale. Sales may also be analyzed in other than the principal ways indicated above. Sometimes they are classified by the method of sale, showing number of orders and dollar volume of sales obtained by outside salesmen, mailed into the house direct by customers, received over the telephone, or secured directly from customers calling in person. When this is done periodically, shifts in the buying habits of customers become apparent as they begin to develop rather than after such shifts have become marked, and the management is guided accordingly. Such an analysis may well be tied in with an analysis by salesmen's territories, a relatively large number of mail or phone orders from any given salesman's area indicating that he is perhaps not covering his territory adequately.

Analysis by Terms of Sale. Another type of analysis is by terms of sale, showing total cash and credit business, the latter being further classified according to length of the credit period if such variations are significant to the concern. Sometimes a variety of terms is offered to customers without the management's being aware of which terms are most popular with the trade. An analysis of terms granted on sales orders reveals those terms that are favored by customers and may lead to the elimination of terms that are only rarely elected.

There is usually considerable difference in the terms granted by a wholesale house and those actually taken by customers, and sales may be analyzed on this basis also. When cash discounts are offered for payment within 10 days, for example, it will usually be found that many customers do not mail remittances until the tenth day with the result that the accounts are outstanding longer than has been planned. Furthermore, some customers make a practice of taking cash discounts even when submitting payment long after the discount period has expired. As the terms actually taken by customers have an important bearing on the interest cost of carrying accounts receivable and may influence bad debt losses if not carefully observed, it is important that the management keep itself informed in this regard.

Analysis of Returned Sales. The control of returned goods is a perplexing problem in a wholesale operation, because of the extra costs that it entails. When the amount of goods returned for exchange or credit becomes excessive, it endangers the wholesaler's profit. The first task is to discover reasons for the returns. As stated before, these may include defective merchandise; unaccepted substitutions; a change of heart on the part of the customer, particularly when he has overbought or the price has declined; errors in filling orders; overselling by zealous salesmen; late delivery; errors in pricing; on-approval sales; and c.o.d. shipments made without first securing permission of the consignee. Some of these causes may be readily removed, others can be reduced only with great difficulty.

An analysis of returned sales, based on the credit memos issued by the company, throws light on the subject. Such analyses are made by merchandise departments, by salesmen, by customers, and by reasons for the returns. Furthermore, the returns made from each salesman's territory are analyzed by reasons for making the returns as a means of discovering which salesmen are responsible for a large percentage of the returns, and to what extent they are caused by zeal to load up customers or by inability to close sales properly. Through such an analysis errors for which the house is responsible can be corrected and the spotlight focused upon those salesmen and customers who may be the chief contributors to the problem.

METHODS OF OBTAINING DATA FOR SALES ANALYSIS

Information needed for purposes of sales analysis can be secured in a number of ways. In firms using punch card equipment or computers for order-processing and inventory control, information by customer type, salesman, size of order, or on any other pertinent basis for analysis is usually included on the cards or other media employed in invoice preparation. Sales analysis in such cases becomes a *by-product* of routine daily accounting procedures and summary tabulations can be prepared as often as needed with little added cost. In most firms, however, sales analysis represents a *special* rather than a regular type of procedure and is done only at rather infrequent intervals. The discussion that follows is oriented primarily to this typical situation.

Preparing Data for Analysis. Among unenlightened wholesalers, a frequent objection to sales analysis is that the *expense* of gathering together, tabulating, and summarizing the almost countless details that enter into such a study is out of proportion to the benefits to be derived. Actually this is a misconception. The data required for a complete sales analysis are readily available from the firm's own records, or can be so available if the records are designed with a view to subsequent use and analysis. As pointed out above, it is neither necessary nor desirable to carry out all phases of a complete analysis continuously or even at very frequent intervals. Moreover, the work required for an analysis is relatively simple and can be done by routine office employees after the procedure is once set up and put into operation by a competent official or by an outside consultant.

A statistical copy of the invoice is usually the basic source for most of the information required. The form of this copy is essentially the same as the original that is mailed to the customer, but extra columns or spaces are often provided for information, such as costs or gross margins, which the firm desires to keep from the customer. An invoice copy designed for purposes of continuous or periodic sales analysis contains most or all the following information:

1. Name of the customer
2. Address of the customer (street, city, county, and state)
3. Name of the salesman handling the account
4. How the order was actually received (salesman, phone, house call, mail)
5. Company order number, or invoice number
6. Date of shipment
7. Credit terms granted
8. Whether customer is an old or a new account
9. Kind of customer (hardware dealer, general store, wholesaler, industrial user, etc.)
10. Description of each item
11. Department number of each item
12. Quantity purchased for each item
13. Price of each item
14. Price extension for each item
15. Cost of each item
16. Cost extension for each item
17. Gross margin for each item
18. Total amount of the sale
19. Total gross margin on the sale

At first glance, this may appear to be a sizable list, but a careful inspection reveals that most of this information is already available on invoices used by firms that have never made any sales analysis. Even if provision is made for the complete list of these informational items, it usually represents only a partial departure from previous practice. It may not be necessary to include all the information listed above on the invoice copy of a particular firm; but if there is a reasonable possibility that some particular information may be needed for subsequent analysis and if the information can be recorded without appreciable expense, then it is economical to make provision for it in the first place.

The activity of recording and extending costs may seem to be a burdensome undertaking; but if this information is kept current, it is easily placed on the order copy from which the invoice is prepared at the time when prices are checked. Many firms that make sales analyses do not compute the gross margin for each invoice line, but only for the invoice total. While this precludes direct analysis of gross margins by merchandise departments, it provides for such an analysis by salesmen, customers, methods of sale, and any basis for which the invoice *total* can be used.

Some of the information can be coded for quick tabulation in special boxes at the bottom or top of the invoice, as shown below:

Sales-man	Customer Class	Custo-mer	City	County	State	Account (Old) New
12	6	1416	3	16	2	

Tabulating and Summarizing Sales Data. There are two basic methods of tabulating and summarizing sales analysis data. These are (1) by posting information to columnar "work" sheets and (2) by the use of punch cards. If, for example, an analysis of sales by salesmen and by merchandise departments is to be made under the first method, the following procedure is used: the invoices are sorted according to salesmen and then a separate columnar work sheet is set up for each salesman; columns are provided for each merchandise department, and price and cost extensions are posted to the appropriate columns, as shown in Figure 57. If there are a large number of merchandise departments or if many merchandise classifications are analyzed, it may be necessary to use more than

Analysis of Sales by Salesmen and by Merchandise Departments

Salesman: Brown

Invoice Number	Invoice Total		Order Line Extensions by Departments				De
	Amount of Sale	Cost of Sale	Department A		Department B		Pr
			Price	Cost	Price	Cost	
8432	26 43	19 56	4 50	3 75	15 60	10 13	
			2 13	1 86			
8697	58 96	42 00	10 05	9 12	11 76	9 02	
8698	10 76				2 35	1 76	
8730	4 50	3 75			4 50	3 75	
8742	16 71	14 20	7 50	6 02			
8743	9 13	7 75	1 10	84	2 36	2 01	
8758	113 45	98 76	20 45	18 21	8 42	7 26	
			5 76	4 98	3 76	2 98	
			10 43	9 01			
8759	14 76	12 58			3 13	2 76	
8764	29 56	25 42	2 15	1 85			
8769	46 58	36 00	15 08	12 75			
8775	121 75	98 25			26 00	24 10	
					29 50	20 75	
8787	9 76	5 13	9 76	5 13			
8789	44 58	36 40	10 20	8 04	8 75	6 98	
Totals	506 93	399 80	99 11	81 56	116 13	91 50	
Gross Margin	107 13		17 55		24 63		
Gross Mar. %	21.13%		17.71%		21.21%		

FIGURE 57. Form of Work Sheet Suitable for Hand Tabulation of Sales Analysis Data

one such sheet for the analysis of each salesman's sales. Totals are then added and checked and the results are posted to summary records.

A variation of this plan involves the use of automatic bookkeeping machines. The carriages of these machines are shifted automatically from column to column by the operator; the proper amount is entered in each column; and columnar totals and a grand total are automatically added, carried in the machine, and printed on the analysis sheet at the completion of the posting.

If the punch card system is used, a separate card is made out for each line of the invoice. Usually the identification information is punched from coded data as illustrated above while merchandise, price, and cost information is punched on the cards from the order lines in the body of the invoice. Cards designed for machine tabulation similar to that shown in Figure 43 or cards designed for hand-sorting like the one shown in Figure 45 may be used. While a considerable amount of time may be required for the preparation of a large number of cards, this may be more than offset by the rapidity with which these cards may be sorted and re-sorted if a number of cross-classifications are to be used.

28

CREDIT AND OFFICE
MANAGEMENT

Two closely related phases of management in a wholesale enterprise are those of credit management and office management. Much of the routine work of the credit department is clerical in nature and is performed by office personnel. Thus, in some organizations, responsibility for both credit and office management is assigned to the same executive. Even when this is not the case, there is need for a close coordination between clerical duties related to credit-granting and collections and those associated with other major functions of the business.

CREDIT MANAGEMENT[1]

In most lines of trade the extension of credit to customers in connection with their purchases is an important function of the wholesale concern. Often 90 per cent or more of total sales is made on a credit basis. Credit is usually both a competitive necessity and an important means of promoting business. Moreover, as shown in Chapter 18, a substantial portion of the total assets of a wholesale concern is typically invested in accounts and notes receivable. Proper use of credit in building sales as well as effective employment of the capital invested therein requires careful attention to the management of the credit function. This may be broken down

[1] The subject of credit and collection management is so complex and specialized that only a presentation of a few high spots in outline form can be made here. For a comprehensive treatment, see Theodore N. Beckman and Robert Bartels, *Credits and Collections in Theory and Practice* (6th ed.; New York: McGraw-Hill Book Co., Inc., 1955), and *Credit Management Handbook,* prepared and edited by the Credit Research Foundation, Inc., of the National Association of Credit Management (Homewood, Illinois: Richard D. Irwin, Inc., 1958).

into three main phases: the evaluation and selection of credit risks, collection of accounts, and over-all control of credit.

Organizational Responsibility for Credit Management. In larger wholesale concerns with a fairly high degree of personnel specialization, responsibility for the extension of credit is assigned to a credit manager. He, in turn, may report to the controller or treasurer or directly to top management; or, in some cases, he is a part of the sales division. In any event the credit manager should have considerable independence in making and enforcing decisions within the policy framework laid down by top management.

The qualified credit manager combines the attributes of a banker, a detective, and a salesman. He has the banker's respect for money, the detective's ability to sense dishonesty, and the salesman's appreciation of a good customer. He familiarizes himself thoroughly with the strengths and weaknesses of the firm's regular customers and is able to appraise accurately the credit risk of new accounts. Not only is he responsible for approving a credit line for a customer, but he or one of his assistants passes on the credit aspect of every order received from the customer. His is the responsibility, also, for following through on collections from delinquent accounts. In brief, his principal duties are to keep losses at a minimum and sales at a maximum. To exercise the nicety of judgment that is essential in securing a proper balance between these two objectives requires a technique that is highly intricate. Many volumes have been written on this subject; hence, it is possible in the following paragraphs merely to indicate a few of the essential elements of granting credit and the collection of accounts. Finally, it is his major responsibility to make the most effective use of the capital invested in the receivables.

EVALUATING CREDIT RISKS

A certain amount of risk is inherent in the extension of credit. Indeed, to attempt the avoidance of risk altogether would eliminate, for practical purposes, the need for credit management. The essence of effective credit management is *profitable* risk-taking through the careful evaluation of risks attaching to individual customers and transactions. Within the basic policies of the enterprise, the credit manager must evaluate each risk in the light of certain fundamental criteria, utilizing information obtained from a number of sources.

Basic Criteria for Evaluating Risks. The problem of evaluating credit risks arises in a wholesale concern whenever an application for credit is received from a new customer. Decisions must be made, first, whether or not to grant credit at all; second, in what amounts; and third, under what terms or conditions. The second and third questions may also arise from time to time in connection with established customers when changes in credit limits or revisions in customary terms seem advisable or when difficulties are encountered in collections. The basic factors to be taken into account in answering these questions are commonly referred to as the four "C's" of credit—Character, Capacity, Capital, and Conditions.

Authorities in the field of credit generally regard *character* as the most important single consideration in passing on a potential account. Character may be defined as the aggregate of mental and moral qualities of a customer or prospect that determine his dependability in meeting business obligations. By its very nature, it is a difficult attribute to measure. It must be judged on the basis of the risk's past record for business and personal dealings and other things which reflect "willingness to pay."

While character tends to determine willingness to meet obligations, ability to meet them is largely governed by financial *capacity*. In wholesale credit-granting, capacity is measured primarily in terms of earning power or management efficiency of a business. This must be modified, however, in light of the concern's financial structure, especially the relationship between equity and debt.

The *capital* of a debtor, measured in terms of tangible net worth, serves as protection to the wholesale concern granting credit. While it is generally assumed that credit will be repaid out of current receipts, capital acts as a kind of reserve from which payment could be made in case of financial difficulty.

Finally, the risk involved in granting credit is affected by general prevailing and anticipated business *conditions*. These are not, of course, within the control of individual debtors, but the degree of risk that a wholesale concern is willing to assume naturally varies with such conditions. During periods of expansion and prosperity, greater risks will be taken on the theory that even marginal businesses will succeed. Conversely, when conditions are poor, risks will be rejected that otherwise might be quite acceptable. There are also some business, economic, or legal environmental factors, not necessarily general in character, that may affect all members of a given industry or trade. All these must be taken into account in dealing with members of the affected industry or trade.

Sources of Information Regarding Credit Risks. In applying the "C's" of credit to individual credit risks, the "C" relating to conditions need not be given separate treatment, as it has a bearing on *all* customers and prospects, at least in a given industry or trade. Assuming a general appraisal of this environmental factor that is of equal applicability to all affected risks, the search for information on a specific risk is confined to the remaining three "C's" of credit. Facts on these are obtained from a number of different sources, including *mercantile agencies, credit inter-*

change bureaus, trade references, salesmen, attorneys, banks, and *directly from the subject or risk.*

Largest and best known of the mercantile agencies is Dun & Bradstreet, Inc., the only *general* agency of its kind now operating. Subscribers to the Dun & Bradstreet service obtain information regarding credit risks from its reference book and from individual reports supplied for a fee on request. The reference book lists over 2,600,000 names of business firms in the United States and Canada, classified geographically. For each name symbols are used to designate "financial strength" (tangible net worth) and "composite credit appraisal," based on previous payment record and other relevant factors. In many cases these ratings may be sufficient to pass on a credit application, especially if the amount involved is small. If more information is desired, a report is obtained giving the history of the concern, its general methods of operation, financial information, and payment record in some detail.

While Dun & Bradstreet, Inc., is the only *general* mercantile agency, there are a number of *special* mercantile agencies that provide similar services to creditors. Illustrative are the Manufacturers' Clearing House in the plumbing supply trade and the Lyon Furniture Mercantile Agency covering furniture and appliance dealers.

Credit interchange bureaus facilitate the exchange of experience among mercantile creditors in a given city or area. Most of these bureaus are operated under the auspices of the National Association of Credit Men, although some exist as offshoots of trade associations. Each bureau is owned and operated independently by a local association of credit men, and information is exchanged between bureaus under the coordination of the Central Credit Interchange Bureau in St. Louis. Members of a bureau submit their experience with a customer to the bureau whenever a report is in preparation at the request of a member. This report shows the combined record of the risk in dealings with other trade creditors, including, for each creditor, length of time the account has been sold, date of the last sale, highest recent credit extended, amounts owing and past due, terms of sale, payment habits, and pertinent comments. This information is all designed to help answer the basic question "Can and does he pay?"

Trade references are usually secured from a prospective customer at the time he applies for credit. These references may then be used to request information from other creditors directly rather than through an interchange bureau. The value of such references is limited by two considerations: first, the customer is likely to give only favorable references, omitting any creditors with whom his record has been poor; second, and more basic, direct inquiries consume much valuable time and effort.

Nevertheless, there are some circumstances under which direct inquiries may be desirable or necessary.

Attorneys and banks are often in a position, by the nature of their business, to provide valuable information on credit risks. Attorneys may be compensated directly for making credit reports, or indirectly through placement of any collection work that arises in a given community. Banks, on the other hand, usually furnish credit reports free of charge on a reciprocal basis, since they are also interested in obtaining similar information on prospective borrowers.

Almost invariably wholesale concerns utilize their own salesmen as a source of credit information. This is logical, since the original application for credit usually comes as a result of an order being obtained. The salesman may be asked to fill out a report covering such items as the physical appearance and location of the business, approximate value of inventory and fixtures, and local reputation of the customer. Salesmen often object to doing this type of work, since it takes time away from selling duties. To overcome such objections, careful coordination of sales and credit activities is needed.

Finally, credit information may be secured directly from the prospect or customer in the form of financial statements and through interviews by the credit manager. Financial statements secured in this way are likely to be more current and complete than those obtained through mercantile agencies or other indirect sources. They are also more likely to be signed and the items arranged in a preferred or desired order. Such statements are carefully analyzed, partly through the use of certain standard ratios, to determine the character, capacity, and capital strength of the business.

Setting Credit Limits. On the basis of information obtained from the sources outlined in the preceding section, the credit manager decides whether or not an application for credit should be accepted. Equally important are the decisions regarding the *amount* of credit to be extended and the *terms* on which it is to be handled. Effective control is best achieved if a quantitative limit is set on the amount of credit to be allowed. Such limits are not to be rigidly applied, but are very useful as *guides* to management action. Some credit men criticize the use of quantitative limits on the ground that they are necessarily arbitrary and hence useless. Probably as a result of this attitude, credit limits are sometimes set and then largely ignored. When this is done, it is certain that credit limits have little value. On the other hand, it is probably just as bad to set limits and observe them without exceptions. A more balanced view is that the limits should be used as danger signals. Within the predetermined limits, credit authorization on customer orders can be routinized and delegated to office personnel. When an order is received in excess of the limit, it can be sent to the credit manager for further consideration. This saves the valuable time of the credit manager and obviates the wasteful practice followed by some concerns of requiring his approval on *all* orders.

There is no ready-made formula for computing quantitative credit limits. Two basic approaches are used, one based on the customer's *ability to pay* and the other on his *merchandise requirements*. Ability to pay in this connection is measured by the customer's purchases during a given period, minus his estimated obligations to established creditors. The remainder represents the amount available to pay a new supplier. The other approach, based on the customer's requirements, is applied by estimating the *share* of purchases of lines handled by the wholesale concern which it can reasonably expect to receive during a given period of time, divided by the concern's average rate of receivables turnover.[2] The result represents the maximum amount of credit allowed to the customer at any one time.

COLLECTION POLICIES AND PROCEDURES

The second major phase of credit management is the collection of overdue accounts. Most debtors, of course, meet their obligations promptly and require little in the way of special collection effort. It cannot be assumed, however, that all customers will pay when due. In extreme cases, some may attempt to avoid payment or delay it beyond reason. Short of this, many debtors fail to pay when due on account of adverse general economic conditions or personal circumstances. In both cases collection efforts must be employed to achieve control of capital invested in receivables and minimize losses from bad debts.

Variations in Collection Policies. The collection policies pursued by wholesale concerns vary considerably among different lines of business and among individual firms in the same trade. All such policies are, of course, intended to accomplish the same basic objectives; but specific policies differ in accordance with trade custom, competitive conditions, and other factors.

Collection policies should provide for differentiated treatment of overdue accounts on the basis of the degree of risk involved. Some customers must be recognized as poor risks, requiring stricter treatment than others. Conversely, good risks are treated with deference since their continued patronage is desired and care must be taken not to antagonize them. This distinction is simple to state but very difficult to apply. The problem is to identify the poor risks. Most of these will presumably be weeded out in the initial evaluation and refused credit in the first place; but no matter how efficient the system, some of these risks are bound to obtain credit and thus give rise to the majority of collection problems. Classification

[2] For a more detailed exposition of both methods, see Beckman and Bartels, *op. cit.*, pp. 565–70.

of a customer as a poor risk, if not achieved by the evaluation procedure prior to granting credit, must be based on the results of subsequent experience as revealed in the various steps of the collection process. Besides, it is the responsibility of the credit manager to accept calculated risks if he is to help in maximizing sales.

Collection policies may be characterized as "strict" or "lenient." This distinction is, of course, one of degree. When a strict policy is pursued, collection efforts will be commenced earlier, will be repeated at more frequent intervals, and may also differ in kind from those used under a lenient policy. Not only do some wholesale concerns have generally stricter policies than others, but within a given firm stricter policies are applied in dealing with less desirable credit risks.

OUTSTANDING ACCOUNTS

Month Ending_____19___

NAME	120 days	90 days	60 days	30 days	Current	Total

FIGURE 58. Summary of Outstanding Accounts Receivable, Classified by Age

Locating Overdue Accounts. In a wholesale enterprise that sells to hundreds or even thousands of accounts, some definite system must be used to identify past-due accounts. One method is to maintain duplicate copies of all sales invoices, filed according to maturity dates. Each day the invoices currently due are checked against the ledger and if they have been paid are destroyed. Unpaid invoices are used as a basis for notifying the credit manager of overdue accounts on which the collection process is to be commenced.

After overdue accounts have been identified, a report is drawn up, summarizing those that are 30 days past due, 60 days past due, and so on. An example of such an "age analysis" of accounts is shown in Figure 58. This type of report facilitates control over the credit operation, since the credit manager (and top management) can see at a glance how many accounts are overdue, as well as the amount thus involved, and which customers are responsible.

A "tickler file" of delinquent accounts may also be used, consisting of cards filed by dates. As the various steps in the collection process are taken, the card for an account is moved forward to the date on which the next step is to be used. Clerical personnel can then determine, by referring to the day's cards, what actions are to be carried out during the day.

Steps in the Collection Process. The collection process used by a wholesale business consists in a series of predetermined steps to be taken at specified intervals and in a planned sequence. Among the more important collection efforts used in mercantile credit are *repeat statements, letters and telephone calls, personal visits, collection bureaus and agencies,* and as a last resort, *legal action.*

Repeat statements (duplicates of original invoices marked "reminder" or "second notice") serve as a gentle reminder that payment is overdue and may be sufficient to get results from customers who have neglected payment through simple carelessness. Likewise, collection letters and telephone calls in the early stages of delinquency are phrased in terms of reminders and are worded tactfully. At this stage it should be assumed that the customer is willing to pay and every effort should be made to avoid antagonizing him with threats or "dunning."

Collection may also be attempted through the wholesale concern's salesmen at an early stage of delinquency. Often a major portion of the salesman's time is devoted to collections and related activities (see Figure 51, Chapter 27).

When it becomes apparent that an overdue account is caused by more than simple neglect, stronger and more personalized collection steps are taken. While simple form letters are often sufficient in the early stages, later collection letters are carefully planned. Appeals may be made to the debtor's sense of fair play, self-respect, or sympathy. Implied threats may also be incorporated in such letters. If these fail, still stronger measures are taken. One is to notify the debtor that, unless payment is received, a draft will be drawn upon him and sent to his bank.

At various stages of the collection process, the efforts of an individual firm's collection department may be supplemented by outside assistance. Some of the credit bureaus operated by wholesale trade associations offer such assistance to their members. One national association, for example, invites member firms to submit names of delinquent accounts. The association then sends a series of four letters with increasingly strong appeals. A fee of 2.5 per cent of the amount collected through the bureau is charged. This procedure may be more effective than similar letters emanating from the creditor himself, since the debtor may fear jeopardizing his standing with all members of the trade association rather than with just one supplier.

When the preceding collection methods are unavailing, the final step in the *normal* collection process is to turn the account over to an attorney or collection agency. If their efforts also fail, suit is brought against the debtor by an attorney on behalf of the creditor. There are, of course, other measures which creditors can take under varying circumstances, including repossession of the merchandise, attachments, composition settlements, and the use of bankruptcy proceedings.

CONTROL OF CREDIT OPERATIONS

As in all other phases of wholesale management, effective performance of the credit function requires control over credit operations. Because credit-granting is a very complex function with several distinct objectives, a variety of measures and indexes must be employed. Several benefits are attained by the use of such measures. First, they serve as a basis for evaluating the performance of the credit department, especially when standards of accomplishment are available for comparative purposes. Second, by comparing results over a period of time, trends in credit performance can be gauged. Third, realistic standards can be used in planning future operations.

The more widely used control measures for wholesale credit activities are the *credit sales index, rejection index, average collection period and receivables turnover rate, bad debt loss percentage,* and *collection percentage.* Inasmuch as the bulk of the business in a wholesale house selling on credit is done on credit, the credit sales ratio to total sales is not very significant and hence not discussed here.

Rejection Index. As previously stated, one of the objectives of credit management is to maximize credit sales insofar as is consistent with minimum losses from bad debts. A useful measure of accomplishment for this objective is the rejection index, or percentage of credit applications rejected. When this percentage exceeds past experience or typical trade experience, credit policies should be reviewed since they may be too strict.

Average Collection Period. The average collection period is the average number of days taken by customers to pay their accounts. It is computed by dividing the receivables outstanding at the end of a period (a month or a year) into the total credit sales for the period and then dividing the result into the number of days in the credit period. For example, suppose that a wholesaler had outstanding receivables amounting to $100,000 at the end of a month and sold a total of $40,000 on credit during the month. The average collection period is 75 days ($40,000 divided by $100,000 = 40 per cent, divided into 30 days = 75). To put it another way, the receivables outstanding at the end of a month represented 75 days' worth of credit sales.

A derivative of the average collection period is the receivables turnover rate, analogous to the inventory turnover rate discussed in Chapter 20. This is computed by dividing the average collection period into the number of days in a year. Thus, if the average collection period is 75 days, the rate of receivables turnover is 4.8 times annually (360 days divided by 75 = 4.8 times).

The average collection period varies considerably between different kinds of wholesale business, depending in part on the customary terms of sale. Typical figures for several lines of trade are given in Table 24. As an

TABLE 24

AVERAGE COLLECTION PERIOD AND TYPICAL BAD DEBT LOSSES AS A
PER CENT OF SALES FOR WHOLESALERS IN SPECIFIED KINDS
OF BUSINESS

Kind of Business	Average Collection Period (Days)	Bad Debt Losses (Per Cent of Sales)
Automotive Parts and Accessories	36	0.25%
Drugs	35	0.09
Dry Goods (general line)	45	0.10
Electrical Supply	38	0.19
Floor Coverings	48	0.26
Footwear	46	0.24
Furniture	40	0.19
Grocery (general line)	14	0.06
Hardware	36	0.16
Industrial Supply	50	0.14
Plumbing and Heating	43	0.33
Tobacco Products	18	0.07

Sources: Average collection period based on experience reported to various trade associations and credit reporting agencies including Dun & Bradstreet, Inc.; bad debt losses as reported in the *1954 Census of Business, Wholesale Trade—Credit, Receivables, Bad-Debt Losses—Merchant Wholesalers,* Bulletin W–2–3 (Washington, D. C.: Government Printing Office, 1957), Table 3A.

example of extreme variation, the average collection period for grocery wholesalers was only 14 days as compared with between 45 and 50 days in dry goods, footwear, and floor coverings. The principal reason is found in the terms of sale commonly used: in groceries, net 7 days or even C.W.O. (cash with order); in dry goods, 2/10 n/60.

OFFICE MANAGEMENT

The office of a wholesale house is the focal point for observing and controlling the major activities of the business. In line with modern practice, scientific management is increasingly applied to wholesale office operations. The essence of office practice is adequate and efficient record-keeping for the various departments of the business, coupled with a smooth, swift flow of work. Successful leaders in wholesaling, as in other types of business activity, have learned that best results are achieved by placing office operations in charge of a professionally competent office manager wherever possible.

Office Functions. While the term "office" is usually used to designate a physical *place* where certain activities are carried on, it is more useful to conceive of the office as a series of *functions* in a wholesale business that may be carried on in one or several places.[3] The functions of the office include the preparation, processing, and storage of business records of all kinds; computations such as extension of invoices; and communications, both within the organization and outside it. Thus the office is the nerve center of the business through which information is transmitted.

Office functions cut across all the major divisions of a wholesale enterprise. Some of these functions have already been discussed at various points in earlier chapters. Preparation of purchase orders, for instance, was treated in connection with buying procedures in Chapter 21; methods of handling customer orders were analyzed in Chapter 24. There is no need to repeat these discussions here. At this point it is intended merely to show the relationships among various types of paperwork and to discuss the organizational arrangements for handling them.

Centralized vs. Decentralized Office Management. Office tasks in a wholesale concern may be centralized, decentralized, or a combination of both methods. The degree of centralization that is desirable depends on several factors, especially the size of the concern and the complexity of its paperwork. "Centralization" does not necessarily refer to physical facilities, but also to organizational responsibility and authority.

When the business is large enough to justify subdivision of operations into major merchandise departments and/or branch houses, it is common for the heads of these units to want their own office forces. This is sometimes permitted, but only under the general supervision of the office manager for the entire business. Just as the sales manager supervises all sales activities of branch houses, so is the office manager best qualified functionally to control the departmental or branch office staffs. The office manager can quickly determine whether or not the work load of a particular department is heavy enough to justify one or more full-time workers. Undoubtedly, gains in efficiency accrue from specialization in departmental office work where technical terms and customs differ from those in other departments. On the other hand, the office manager knows when better service can be rendered by centralized procedure. His opinion, rather

---

[3] Charles B. Hicks and Irene Place, *Office Management* (New York: Allyn & Bacon, Inc., 1956), pp. 4–6.

than that of the merchandise department manager, is worthy of the more serious consideration, since he is the expert in office procedure and organization.

While the purchasing, sales, credit, warehouse, traffic, and other separate departments of the larger wholesale houses can frequently justify separate offices for certain of their record-keeping operations, many office activities of a business are more efficiently performed by a central office. This office, in turn, may be subdivided to handle the different office functions.

A well-organized office maintains a *mail room* with which is frequently combined a messenger service. Incoming mail is quickly sorted and distributed to the appropriate divisions of the company. Orders, whether coming through the mail, over the telephone, or directly from the salesmen, are usually routed to an *order department,* where they are recorded, duplicated, and copies routed to the credit department for checking, the warehouse for filling, and to such other divisions as the needs of the particular business may dictate. A *stenographic pool* may be maintained to expedite secretarial service. Centralized offices also maintain *computing departments, billing departments, accounting departments, central files,* and such facilitating sections as *office supplies and equipment.* Special needs of particular lines of business often dictate additional sections.

Analysis of Office Procedures and Records. One of the major contributions that can be made by a specialized office manager is that of analyzing office routines and records with a view toward simplifying them. There is a general tendency among buying, sales, and other management personnel to multiply paperwork without due regard to its utility or cost. The office manager should have the authority to review all requests for additional records or office service. In doing so, he asks such questions as: What is the objective to be served? What is the nature of the operation? What other executives or departments may be involved or interested? How can the job be done most economically? Before complying with the request, he works out an accurate estimate of the cost to be checked against the goal or objective sought. If the cost of doing the task is greater than the value to be derived from it, that particular operation is reappraised.

The office manager takes the over-all view of the company in establishing and carrying out the office work of the business. Typing and stenographic work are good examples. Much money is wasted by thoughtless and inefficient handling of these essential functions of every business. Each executive and department head usually wants his own private secretary, yet very few have a sufficient volume of dictation and allied work to keep a competent secretary fully occupied. The result is either halfhearted attempts to provide "busy" work or a sheer waste of time and money. A central stenographic pool, properly operated, can perhaps meet this situation. If such a pool is formed, key executives may be allocated their own secretaries, but these persons are also kept available for other work when the respective executives do not require them. The use of mechanical dictating equipment is recommended for stenographic pools.

By scientific study of the work load, the office manager is able to maintain a higher level of service at a lower cost. What is true of stenographic service is also true of filing, bookkeeping, billing, machine operations, inventory control systems, and the whole range of office operations.

The Smaller Wholesale House. The great majority of wholesale houses operate on a scale that hardly justifies the elaborate subdivision of the office positions outlined above. Nevertheless, efficient operation of office functions is fully as important to the small as to the large wholesaler. Indeed, the smaller business is sometimes even more careful to avoid waste and lost motion in office work since it has smaller capital reserves.

For efficient operation, the progressive smaller wholesaler familiarizes himself thoroughly with the minimum record-keeping essential to achieve such an end, and avoiding costly and intricate systems of accounting, he installs the simplest methods available which provide adequate guidance. Counsel from experts in the field of accounting and office management and advice from the U. S. Department of Commerce can be sought with profit.

The smaller wholesaler cannot ordinarily afford an office manager. He or his partner must serve in that capacity as well as in many others. Instead of divisions of the office with specialists in charge, the small operator has a single small office with but one or two office workers. Particular care is exercised in the selection and training of office helpers, since the need is for versatile workers who can turn their hands to typing, filing, bookkeeping, checking credit records, maintaining inventory controls, and performing the many other tasks of a busy wholesale office.

Where the large wholesaler keeps office costs down by hiring less experienced persons to work under the supervision of specialists, the small wholesaler finds that it pays to offer a premium salary to his general utility workers. By selecting superior talent, he keeps the quality of his office output high and his costs not excessive, though perhaps not comparable with those of a larger office on a percentage of sales basis.

29

ANALYSIS AND CONTROL
OF OPERATING EXPENSES

As indicated in Chapter 27, one of the two most fruitful methods of increasing net profits in a wholesale enterprise is through the control of operating expenses. It should be pointed out at the outset that the term "control" is not synonymous with expense "reduction." It is true that one objective of expense control is the reduction of costs through elimination of waste and by way of enhanced efficiency. It is also true, however, that control may be achieved by *increasing* expenditures, if they are more than offset by profits derived from greater sales volume or wider gross margins resulting therefrom. The basic purpose underlying expense control is proper direction and channeling of expenditures into the most profitable courses.

Control of operating expenses in a progressive wholesale concern is achieved principally through (1) adequate classification of expenses, (2) comparative analysis of expenses and expense ratios, (3) analysis of expenses for various segments of a firm's operations, and (4) expense-budgeting.

EXPENSE CONTROL THROUGH THE ACCOUNTING SYSTEM

The basic source of information on operating expenses is the accounting system, which provides a continuous record of receipts and expenditures. If the system is properly designed with control applications in mind, it is a powerful tool for management in and of itself. Moreover, it furnishes the basis for special cost analyses that may be made from time to time.

Prerequisites of Expense Control. An adequate accounting system is obviously a basic prerequisite of effective expense control. To be adequate the system must provide account records that are complete, accurate, current, and capable of being classified meaningfully. The necessity for complete and accurate expense records is quite clear; legal requirements and reasonable control make them essential. In addition, expense information must be current. Instead of waiting until the end of the year for the information concerning profits earned, losses suffered, and expenses incurred, as is customary in some concerns, the progressive wholesaler obtains such information at more frequent intervals, usually monthly. In this way leaks and losses can be checked before it is too late and other activities can be examined and controlled.

A monthly statement of expenses and of profit and loss can be prepared without the necessity of actually closing the books. Adjustments are made for certain items of the trial balance taken off the ledger in the usual way, such as goods received but not paid for, unpaid expense, accrued payroll, depreciation, bad debts, prepaid expenses, interest accrued, taxes accrued, and such other adjustments as will make possible a correct picture of the company's accomplishments during the month. If it is not feasible to take a physical inventory, the cost of goods sold can be estimated by the average gross margins obtained on the sales for each merchandise department. If accurate and detailed statistical inventories are maintained, this information is available as a matter of course.

Bases for Classifying Expense Accounts. In setting up the accounting system, several possible bases for expense classification should be kept in mind. The simplest type and the one around which the original accounts are usually built, although even here there are exceptions as in advertising expense and bad debts, is the so-called *natural* classification. Under this system, expenses are identified and recorded on the basis of their nature or object. For example, accounts are usually set up for wages, rent, insurance premiums, utilities, office supplies, and other such categories. Each of these may, in turn, be shown in greater and more useful detail. Wages, for instance, may be broken down into office wages, warehouse wages, and so on.

If the basic expense accounts are kept in sufficient detail, it is also possible to utilize a *functional* classification. Under this system expenses are segregated according to the type of activity for which they are incurred. Some of the major functional expense categories common to all wholesale enterprises include selling, warehousing, delivery, and general administration. As in the case of natural expense classes, these major categories may be subdivided. Selling expense, for instance, may be broken down into advertising, field sales, house sales, telephone sales, and traveling.

Very often the accounting system is built upon a *hybrid* classification of expenses reflecting both natural and functional factors. In the Census of Business, for example, wholesalers' operating expenses are classified as administrative, selling, shipping, delivery, warehouse, occupancy, and others. As indicated in a later section of this chapter, similar breakdowns are used by many wholesale trade associations in their collection and publication of typical figures for various trade groups. This is designated as a hybrid classification of expenses because, in the first place, one of the major categories (occupancy) is not functional but natural. Second, some of the major functions of a wholesale concern, such as buying, are not segregated. Third, as will be apparent from subsequent parts of the chapter, the functional groupings are not sufficiently detailed to permit allocation of expenses to products, customers, orders, or in making other special types of cost studies. These comments are not intended as criticisms of the hybrid expense classification. For purposes of day-to-day accounting and control, the system is quite adequate and, in fact, greatly superior to a purely natural classification of expenses.

Whatever basis is used for classifying expenses, if the system is to be employed for meaningful analysis intended to achieve control, certain rules should be followed in defining and segregating the various categories:

1. A separate account must be set up for every item of expense and no *miscellaneous* group of appreciable size can remain. A miscellaneous account properly includes only such items as are incapable or, because of size, unworthy of analysis. Although it is impossible to set definite rules for rigid universal application, it is generally desirable that miscellaneous expenses do not amount to more than 2 or 3 per cent of total operating expenses and that any one item in the miscellaneous group does not amount to more than 0.5 per cent.

2. The number of different items in the classification must not be excessively large. Even though an item may be distinct and separable, it should not be set up separately if the amount is so small as to be insignificant. To do otherwise is only to confuse the issue. Attention is properly centered on those items that may respond to corrective action with some worthwhile saving; it must not be diverted by items offering no possibility of compensating for the heed given them.

3. Insofar as possible, the accounts must be set up in such a way that all specific expenditures charged to an account are homogeneous, at least to the degree that they are uniformly affected by changes in the volume of business. For example, salesmen's compensation is usually properly separated from salesmen's traveling expenses, because the former is often expected to vary nearly in proportion to sales volume while the latter lags a good deal on account of the more or less fixed elements included therein.

Uniform Systems of Account Classification. A knowledge of operating expenses for a wholesale concern, however detailed, does not in itself provide a basis for expense control. The amounts spent for various purposes and the relationships existing among expense categories must be judged in relation to some kind of *standard* or *norm*. Comparisons with results for previous years may be helpful, especially in determining the causes of trends in expenses and profits, but there is also a need for stand-ards not based on the firm's own experience. Otherwise, there is a tendency merely to perpetuate the past, including both its weak as well as strong points.

The need for objectively determined standards of operating expense has led to the development of *uniform* accounting systems by groups of whole-sale concerns, especially through their trade associations. Typical figures collected from firms using the same expense accounts may then be used by individual firms in evaluating their own results.

As illustrations of uniform expense classifications, those used by four leading wholesale trade associations are shown in Figure 59. In all cases a combination of functional and natural categories is used, as in the Bureau of the Census system.

Comparison of the systems of expense classification shown in Figure 59 serves to bring out some interesting similarities and differences. Basically, all employ the same major functional categories except for the function of *purchasing* which is segregated by the National and Southern Industrial Distributors' Associations. Within the major categories certain differences may be noted which reflect variations in typical methods of operation. In the hardware and industrial supply fields, for example, separate accounts are maintained for inside salesmen, indicating the importance of this method of selling as compared with drugs, where inside sales are of rela-tively little consequence. In the case of drug wholesalers a separate account is shown for *tabulating equipment expense,* reflecting the widespread use of punch-card equipment among firms in this line of business. Even greater differences could be observed by comparison with such lines of trade as steel and aluminum distributors, who perform numerous fabri-cating functions, such as slitting, cutting, edge-rolling, and annealing.[1] Such differences are to be expected, since functions performed by wholesale concerns vary somewhat in degree and sometimes in kind, according to the line of trade in which they operate, and must necessarily be reflected in the expense classification system.

Comparison of Operating Results. On the basis of a standard account classification, the operating expenses for a period just ended can be com-pared with a corresponding previous period, with average results for a number of previous periods, or with the results experienced by other firms similarly operating. This is usually done by expressing each expense item as a percentage of net sales and as a percentage of total operating expenses. Both these bases are desirable. In the first place, some expense items involve a small dollar amount so that variations appear insignificant when

[1] See *Distribution Cost Analysis for Metals Distributors—Manual of Instruction* (American Steel Warehouse Association, Inc., and National Association of Aluminum Distributors, 1956).

National Wholesale Druggists Association	National Wholesale Hardware Association	National and Southern Industrial Distributors' Associations*
ADMINISTRATIVE: Management Salaries Other Executive Salaries Office Payroll Payroll Taxes, Group Insurance, Retirement Tabulating Equipment Telephone and Telegraph Stationery, Printing, Office Supplies, Postage Taxes (excluding real estate, payroll, and income) Bad Debt Expenses Other Administrative OCCUPANCY SELLING: Salesmen's Salaries and Commissions Salesmen's Travel Other Selling Payroll Other Selling WAREHOUSE: Warehouse Payroll Other Warehouse DELIVERY AND TRUCKING: City Delivery and Trucking Country Shipping	ADMINISTRATIVE: Management Salaries Office Salaries General Office: Postage, Stationery and Supplies Telephone and Telegraph Maintenance, Depreciation, and Repairs on Equipment Miscellaneous Office Legal, Collection, and Auditing Donations and Charity SELLING: Advertising House Salesmen's Compensation Traveling Salesmen's Compensation Traveling Salesmen's Expenses WAREHOUSE AND HANDLING: Heat, Light, Water, Power Repairs and Depreciation on Equipment Boxing and Packing Delivery Store and Warehouse Salaries FIXED CHARGES AND MISCELLANEOUS: Charges Against Owned Real Estate Rent Insurance (excluding building and trucks) Taxes, Licenses (excluding real estate and income)	ADMINISTRATIVE AND GENERAL: Executive Salaries Executive Travel Legal and Professional Taxes and Licenses Donations Dues and Subscriptions Other Insurance (excluding fixtures and equipment) Credit and Collection Miscellaneous Administrative OCCUPANCY: Maintenance Employees' Salaries Depreciation—Buildings Repairs and Maintenance—Buildings Insurance—Buildings Real Estate Taxes Interest on Mortgage Rent Heat, Light, Water, Power SELLING: Outside Sales: Traveling Salesmen's Compensation Traveling Salesmen's Expenses Traveling Salesmen's Automobile Expenses Depreciation on Automobiles Inside Sales and Sales Administration: Salaries and Wages Traveling Expenses Repair and Maintenance—Store

* For each of the 7 functional classifications there are also separate accounts for "Group Insurance, Profit-Sharing, Bonuses, and Pensions" and for "Payroll Taxes."

FIGURE 59. Uniform Systems of Expense Classification Used by Four Leading Wholesale Trade Associations

Sources: Adapted, with slight modifications, from recent publications of the respective trade associations.

National Wholesale Druggists Association	National Wholesale Hardware Association	National and Southern Industrial Distributors' Associations*
	FIXED CHARGES AND MISCELLANEOUS (*Cont.*): Social Security and Other Employee Benefits Interest Bad Debt Losses Other Miscellaneous	SELLING (*Cont.*): Equipment Insurance—Store Equipment Advertising Catalog Expense Miscellaneous Selling WAREHOUSE OPERATING: Salaries and Wages Packing Materials Repairs and Maintenance—Warehouse Equipment Depreciation—Warehouse Equipment Insurance—Warehouse Equipment Miscellaneous Warehouse DELIVERY: Drivers' Wages Truck Operation and Maintenance Depreciation—Trucks Outgoing Cartage, Freight, Express Miscellaneous Delivery PURCHASING: Salaries and Wages Traveling Miscellaneous Purchasing OFFICE: Salaries and Wages Outside Office Services Stationery and Supplies Postage Telephone and Telegraph Depreciation—Office Furniture and Equipment Repair and Maintenance—Office Furniture and Equipment Insurance—Office Furniture and Equipment Miscellaneous Office Expense

FIGURE 59—*Continued*

expressed as a percentage of sales (for example, rent and bad debt losses), but such variations may be very significant when expressed as percentages of total operating expenses. Second, variations in very important expense items may be exaggerated when the operating expense base alone is used. Use of the two bases thus provides a double perspective with which to gauge the importance of deviations from expected, average, or previously realized results.

TABLE 25

COMPARISON OF OPERATING EXPENSE RATIOS FOR A HYPOTHETICAL WHOLESALE CONCERN WITH TYPICAL FIGURES FOR CONCERNS OF COMPARABLE SIZE IN THE SAME LINE OF BUSINESS

Expense Category (All Items Expressed as Percentages of Net Sales)	Typical Trade Figures	Hypothetical Wholesaler, Inc.
Net Sales	100.00%	100.00%
Cost of Goods Sold	82.50	83.53
Gross Margin	17.50	16.47
Operating Expenses:		
ADMINISTRATIVE:		
Management and Executive Salaries	1.32	1.40
Office Salaries (including payroll tax)	2.04	2.46
Telephone and Telegraph	0.20	0.32
Stationery, Office Supplies	0.23	0.28
Bad Debts	0.08	0.17
Other Administrative	1.07	1.36
Total, Administrative	4.94	5.99
OCCUPANCY	0.50	0.77
SELLING:		
Salesmen's Compensation	2.00	2.07
Salesmen's Travel Expenses	0.49	0.62
Inside Sales Payroll	0.52	0.77
Other Selling Expenses	0.25	0.29
Total, Selling	3.26	3.75
WAREHOUSE:		
Wages and Salaries	2.21	3.00
Other Warehouse	0.18	0.29
Total, Warehouse	2.39	3.29
DELIVERY AND TRUCKING:		
City Delivery	0.42	1.03
Freight, Express, Parcel Post	0.74	0.67
Total, Delivery and Trucking	1.16	1.70
TOTAL OPERATING EXPENSES	12.25	15.50
NET PROFIT BEFORE TAXES	5.25	0.97

The basis for each computation must be dollar net sales or operating expenses for the time period, establishment, or groups of establishments to which the expense data are applicable. The danger of computing operating expense percentages for one period on the basis of another period's dollar sales must be avoided; otherwise, the comparison is meaningless and may prove misleading.

The data in Table 25 furnish an example of comparative analysis of operating expenses. Ratios for the individual firm are listed side by side with typical figures for houses of comparable size in the same line of business. By confining the comparison in this way, variations arising principally from differences in the scale of operation are avoided. Many trade associations, in publishing the results of periodic cost surveys, classify the reporting firms on the basis of several factors including size, geographic region, and other pertinent differentiating factors.

The figures in this table may be used to illustrate the way in which comparative analysis contributes to expense control. Obviously, the hypothetical wholesaler has experienced unsatisfactory results, earning a net profit of less than 1 per cent of sales while similar firms earned more than five times as much. Why were his earnings so low? Comparison of the various expense categories sheds considerable light on the question. In the first place, the concern's gross margin was more than one full sales percentage point lower than the typical gross margin. This may have resulted from failure to secure adequate price concessions from suppliers, to price the goods properly, or, more likely, to push high-margin items in the merchandise line.

Not only was the gross margin narrower, but the firm's operating expenses were substantially higher than typical. No one class of expense serves to account for the discrepancy; in fact, all five major classes of expense were higher. Comparative analysis makes it possible, however, to pinpoint the areas offering opportunities for the *greatest* potential improvement. For example, city delivery expense is more than twice as high for the firm in question as for typical firms. If this class of expense alone could be brought in line with average trade experience, net profits could be increased by about two-thirds. Some of the other types of expense that vary greatly from the typical figures are occupancy (50 per cent higher), inside selling (50 per cent higher), and bad debts (more than twice as high).

Comparative analysis serves to focus the attention of management on these areas. It does *not* show *why* these classes of expense are too high or otherwise vary from the typical; it does *not* tell management what corrective actions are needed if such are necessary. These questions can be answered only by more intensive study of each cost item in which the unfavorable deviation is substantial. City delivery routes, for example, may be studied with a view to minimizing backtracking and overlapping. Delivery policies may be at fault, with too frequent deliveries of small orders. Whatever the cause, management is guided to the areas needing greatest improvement through comparative expense analysis.

SPECIAL FORMS OF EXPENSE ANALYSIS

Need for Further Analysis. The comparative analysis of costs by kind of expense, made possible by an adequate account classification, is simple and economical. Such an analysis can be used by any wholesaler, no matter how small his operations, to provide some general information for cost control purposes. Whenever weaknesses are of considerable importance, they are revealed and a search for the specific cause of the unfavorable showing can be undertaken.

The analysis by kinds of expense, however, is definitely limited in its value. While it may show that wages paid to warehouse employees were more than expected, it is not ascertained whether the total costs of filling orders or handling merchandise by such employees were excessive. Similarly, while salesmen's traveling expenses may appear too high, this kind of analysis does not reveal, for example, whether calls are being made on certain customers whose business cannot possibly justify the expense involved or whether, in another case, the poor showing is due entirely to bad situations in only three of the twelve salesmen's territories. Analysis by nature of the cost items is insufficient, because it does not fix responsibility or provide specific answers to questions relating to the efficiency with which functions are being performed, the commodities on which to concentrate sales effort or drop from the line, the customers to cultivate or cease calling on, the territories to cultivate or withdraw from, the sales methods to employ and the prices to charge, and so on.

Answers to these questions must be sought through special types of expense analysis, carried out at relatively infrequent intervals. The premise from which such analyses proceed is that different segments of the total operation of a wholesale concern vary in profitability, some even being conducted at a loss. If these segments, such as customers or product lines, can be isolated and identified, control can be achieved by adapting policies to the situation. In other words, profitable segments of the business can be cultivated and emphasized and unprofitable segments de-emphasized or even perhaps eliminated.

Analysis by Functions and Subfunctions. The most useful type of expense analysis, a prerequisite to most other types, is on the basis of *functions* and *subfunctions*. As indicated previously, regular accounts may be kept on a semifunctional basis as illustrated in Figure 59. True functional analysis goes far beyond this and segregates costs for *each distinct kind of activity* performed in an enterprise. The nature and purpose of functional analysis have been well expressed as follows:

. . . [functional cost analysis] starts from a different premise [than does natural expense analysis]; namely, that expenditures are not made merely to secure goods and services, but rather to achieve certain objectives through the performance of specific functions. Salaries are paid, supplies are purchased, taxes and insurance are paid to store . . . [products], to fill customers' orders for these products, to ship the orders, to check credit, to keep customers' accounts, etc. . . . When we know the costs of these functions, we can allocate them to the various products which we sell, and we can then prepare a statement showing the relative profitability of different products.[2]

It is not possible to set up a list of functions and services that will fit all wholesalers. The number of functions and services performed by different wholesalers, even by those in the same line of business, varies widely and there is also considerable variance in the organizational setup of similar establishments. Inasmuch as the primary purpose of functional analysis is cost control, the classification of functions and services must coincide with *organizational responsibility* for the performance of such activities. Little can be done to control the cost of an activity, the responsibility for which cannot be fixed. Thus each wholesaler must establish his own classification of functions and services for cost analysis according to the circumstances of his own business.

The functional classification used by the U. S. Department of Commerce in many of its wholesaling cost studies, however, is illustrative of an arrangement that can be used by many small- and medium-sized establishments. Four major functional cost groups, three of which are subdivided, are recognized. These are as follows:

1. Maintenance
   a) Storage
   b) Investment in merchandise
2. Movement
   a) Handling
   b) Order routine
   c) Delivery
3. Promotion
4. Reimbursement
   a) Payments
   b) Collections

Where the above arrangement does not appear suitable, different functions and subdivisions thereof may be established. In large firms, where the division of labor is carried to a high degree, the functional classification may well be much more detailed than that shown above.

As an example of a more detailed functional classification of expenses, a system developed by a manufacturer for the use of his distributors included the following:

2 *Ibid.,* Section I, p. 1. Parenthetical phrases supplied.

1. Stock investment
2. Stock storage
3. Order-handling and accounting
4. Outgoing material-handling (including delivery)
5. Incoming material-handling
6. Customer-financing
7. Buying costs
8. Building costs (occupancy)
9. Administrative costs
10. Selling costs[3]

This list of functions is essentially a subdivision of that previously given. *Storage* and *investment* correspond to the subdivisions of *maintenance*. *Order-handling and accounting* is the same as *order routine,* while *outgoing* and *incoming material-handling* are slight modifications of *handling* and *delivery,* and so on. The degree to which functions are subdivided depends on the degree of specialization in a given concern. The function of material-handling, for example, may be broken down into receiving and checking incoming shipments, full case order-picking, broken case order-picking, checking, packing, and shipping. It is desirable to classify functions in as great detail as possible, so that sources of difficulty can be pinpointed and so that functional costs may be allocated, for example, to customers or product lines with a high degree of accuracy.

Allocation of Natural Expenses to Functional Groups. Once the functions and subfunctions have been identified, the next step in the analysis is to redistribute operating expenses into the functional categories. This redistribution is merely a reshuffling of the same expense items shown on the regular accounts. Allocating costs to functional groups in no way affects total expense, which is identical regardless of the basis of classification.

Some natural classes of expense can be assigned *directly* to functional groups. For example, if the functional categories developed by the U. S. Department of Commerce previously indicated are employed, natural expense categories directly attributable to the functional groupings would include:

	Direct Natural Expense Categories
Functional Groups	
1. Maintenance	
a) Storage	Cost of Outside Storage (in public warehouses)
b) Investment in Merchandise	Insurance on Inventory Taxes on Inventory

[3] "Distribution Cost Accounting for Net Profits," *Industrial Distribution* (July, 1957), 106–36.

Functional Groups	*Direct Natural Expense Categories*
2. Movement	
a) Handling	Wages of Employees Engaged Full Time in Handling
	Rent or Amortization, Repairs, Maintenance, and the like, of Handling Equipment
b) Order Routine	Wages of Office Employees Engaged Full Time in Order Routine (registering, editing, and otherwise processing orders)
c) Delivery	Wages of Truck Drivers
	Cost of Outside Trucking Service
	Repairs, Maintenance, and Depreciation of Trucks
	Freight, Express, Parcel Post
3. Promotion	Advertising
	Catalog and Price List Expense
4. Reimbursement	
a) Payments	Wages of Office Employees Engaged Full Time in Reimbursement
b) Collections	Wages of Office Employees Engaged Full Time in Collections
	Bad Debt Losses

In addition to the above-mentioned classes of expense, many categories of costs cannot be directly attributed to functional groupings and must therefore be *allocated* among them. Rent, for example, is in large part a cost of storage, but also constitutes a part of the costs of "payments" and "collections," because part of the space is used to house these functions. If a salesroom or counter is maintained, some part of rent may also be attributable to "promotion."

The next step in a functional analysis of costs is, then, the allocation among functional groupings of those natural classes that are common to two or more of whatever functions are recognized. This may be done by time studies, space measurements, counts, managerial estimates, and other methods. The manner in which certain expense items may be allocated to the functional cost groupings shown above is indicated in Table 26. The bases or factors used are merely intended to be illustrative; variations may be worked out according to particular circumstances whenever a different functional classification of expenses is employed. The number of indirect functions to which certain expense items have to be allocated varies in different circumstances. In some cases, where there is very little overlapping of activities, warehouse wages can be charged directly by providing separate wage accounts for each activity. Again, since general administration is itself considered a function, the need for allocation of such items as executive salaries is eliminated. If selling and promotion are recognized as

TABLE 26

ALLOCATION OF TYPICAL NATURAL EXPENSE ITEMS TO FUNCTIONAL COST GROUPS

Expense Items	Basis for the Allocation of Expense Items to Functional Cost Groups	Functional Cost Groups to Which Expense Items Are Assigned
Sales Salaries and Expense	Time Study	Order Routine and Promotion
Warehouse Wages	Time Study	Handling, Storage, and Investment
Office Wages	Time Study	Order Routine, Reimbursement, or Other Functions
Rent	Space Measurement	All Functional Groups
Executive Salaries	Managerial Estimate	All Functional Groups
Social Security Taxes	Amount Added to Wages	All Functional Groups

one function, sales salaries and expense can be charged direct, eliminating the need for allocation of this item.

By adding together the direct expenses and the appropriate portions of the indirect expense items, the cost of performing each function or activity is ascertained. For purposes of cost control, the results of the analysis are more suitable when the number of indirect expense items is small. It becomes difficult to hold any individual responsible for the costs of collections, for example, if any sizable proportion of the cost is the result of an arbitrary managerial estimate of the division of some item such as managerial salaries. For reasons such as this, it is advisable to carry the classification of natural expense accounts as far as possible and thus reduce the number of indirect expenses to a reasonable minimum. If a functional classification of accounts recognizing such activities as the following is used, the amount of allocation of indirect expenses is very small or can be practically eliminated:

Selling and promotion
Buying
Receiving and shipping
Trucking (subdivided into):
　Trucking incoming goods
　Trucking country shipments
　City delivery
Occupancy and warehousing
Investment in merchandise
Credit and collection
Office and accounting
General administration

While the degree of functionalization is somewhat less complete because of greater overlapping in this instance, the arrangement is often more suitable because all the important natural expense items usually can be classified under such headings.

Application of Functional Analysis of Costs. When the costs of performing various recognized functions are ascertained, the analysis can be extended in various ways. Functional costs can be related to merchandise departments, individual commodities, salesmen's territories, customers, methods of sale, or order-size groups and can be applied in other ways to assist in policy determination. The principle of such application of functional cost analysis is that the characteristics of different departments, territories, and so on require more or fewer functional services. When the costs of functional services are known and the amounts of functional services required in a given case are ascertained, then the costs of serving different territories, operating different departments, and so on can be determined. Where unsatisfactory conditions are noted, the analysis also shows what may be expected from remedial action. This is possible, because every unprofitable operation can be analyzed in various ways and, with a knowledge of functional costs, the effects of changes in policy usually can be foreseen.

The manner in which extended applications of functional cost analyses are made is as follows:

1. All costs of functions that are specifically and directly applicable to the analysis in question (departments, customers, territories) are segregated for direct application. Examples are buyers' salaries for departmental analysis, outgoing freight for customer analysis, or salesmen's salaries for territorial analysis.

2. All cost items that are specifically inapplicable to the object of the analysis are segregated and completely excluded from the analysis. Examples are the cost of private brand advertising on manufacturers' brands of goods, or salesmen's salaries for orders received by mail from customers not solicited by salesmen.

3. For each remaining functional activity, a unit of measure is selected to determine the amount of service rendered or required by the particular object of the analysis. The unit of measure is used to allocate indirect functional costs to individual departments, territories, or other segments of the business being analyzed. One of the prerequisites of a system of cost allocation is *simplicity of operation,* lest the clerical expense outweigh any gain that might result from accurate knowledge. The use of the simplest or most convenient means of allocating costs, however, often violates a second prerequisite, that of *equity in the distribution of the cost burden* among the various segments of the business. The task of the analyst is to strike a satisfactory balance between these prerequisites so that meaningful results are provided at a reasonable cost.

In allocating functional costs to various segments of a business, two criteria should be employed, namely, *responsibility* and *benefit*. Whenever possible, each segment of the business is charged with the share or portion of the variable marketing effort for which it is responsible. For example, sales territories are "responsible" for merchandise handling expense in proportion to the number of merchandise units handled in filling orders for each territory and are charged accordingly. Similarly, merchandise departments are "responsible" for inventory investment expense in proportion to the dollar value of goods carried in inventory for each department. It is impossible to allocate all indirect costs on the basis of this criterion, however, because in some cases responsibility cannot be determined or measured. In such cases, it is necessary to allocate indirect costs according to the benefit derived from the performance of a given function. The use of this criterion depends on the assumption that different segments of the business benefit in some measurable way as a result of certain costs being incurred even though these segments are not directly responsible for the expenditures. Storage costs, for example, do not vary with customer characteristics, as customers are in no way responsible for the amount of cost incurred for this activity. It is reasonable to assume in most cases, however, that customers "benefit" from the performance of the storage function in proportion to the volume of their purchases, and storage costs may be allocated according to this basis or factor. In the same way, merchandise departments are not directly responsible for the amount of credit and collection expense incurred, but it may well be assumed that individual departments benefit from credit and collections in proportion to their sales.

Expenses by Merchandise Departments. One of the important extensions of functional cost analysis is by merchandise departments. If it is intended to carry such an analysis to the point of determining net profit for each department, all functional costs are either charged directly or are allocated to departments.

Direct Costs. It is often possible to identify the following items of cost as expenses directly chargeable to individual departments:

a) Salaries of departmental buyers
b) Salaries and wages of departmental buyers' clerical assistants
c) Compensation and expenses of departmental specialty salesmen
d) Costs of owning and operating special equipment or facilities for storage or delivery, such as a special building for one department or refrigerated trucks for special commodities
e) Departmental advertising and sales promotion
f) Taxes and licenses applicable to individual departments or commodities, as those applying to liquor, cigarettes, margarine, etc.
g) Special wrapping and packing materials when these are an important item of expense

Items such as the above are deducted from whatever functional costs are otherwise recognized. The number of indirect functional costs recognized for purposes of departmental analysis is usually fairly small. This is true because the cost of an analysis mounts rapidly as the number of functions and allocation bases is increased. Any of the lists of functional costs given previously in the section on analysis by functions performed is illustrative of indirect functional costs which may be used in this type of analysis, although in larger firms the major functions may be further subdivided to relate each activity more directly to some measure of variability.

Allocation of Indirect Costs. While it is not possible to cover here all the methods and bases used for allocating the indirect functional costs, the following are suggestive of those most commonly used by wholesalers that have undertaken analyses of this kind.

1. SELLING AND PROMOTION. Such primary expense items as general salesmen's compensation and traveling expense, other sales traveling expense, sales manager's salary, general advertising, catalogs, and miscellaneous selling expense constitute the cost of the selling and promotion function. The salesman-hour is probably the best unit for measuring this functional service. The amount of time spent on the merchandise of each department may be ascertained by means of a time-and-duty study as discussed in Chapter 26, or from salesmen's reports on their own activities if the number of departments is not so large as to make this too complicated in practice. Although a time study may be expensive, this may be carried out on a limited sample basis and the cost justified by the continuing use of the information over a fairly long period of time. Only actual solicitation time need be considered, because traveling and waiting time can be distributed on the same basis as solicitation time.

When the time basis is not practical, the distribution of budgeted sales by departments is sometimes used to allocate selling costs. The theory that has been used to justify this basis is that the organization is set up to achieve planned sales and that departments are responsible for selling costs incurred in proportion to the amount of sales budgeted for each. This basis is properly used only when the amount of sales effort applied is about in the same proportion, by departments, as budgeted sales. The distribution of dollar gross margins is a third allocation factor often used with considerable justification, on the ground that more effort is required to sell high-margin than low-margin merchandise.

A fourth plan calls for distribution of selling and promotion expense on the basis of the *actual* volume of sales secured for each department. While this plan is easily applied and commonly used, it usually has little merit since it does not take into account the difficulty of selling different lines of merchandise. The use of sales results as an allocation basis follows the "benefit" criterion rather than that of "responsibility" and therefore may not be in proportion to the amount of effort applied.

In some cases it is advisable to consider selling and promotion as separate functions and to allocate the costs of each on different bases. If this is done, the cost of salesmen's activities may be allocated on the basis of a time study or some other suitable factor and sales supervision and general promotion items on the basis of the budgeted sales dollar.

Assuming that $750 of promotion expense spent in a given month is to be allocated to departments on the basis of the budgeted sales dollar, the calculation would then be:

Department	Budgeted Sales	Per Cent of Total	Distribution of Promotion Expense
A	$ 15,000	10	$ 75
B	75,000	50	375
C	30,000	20	150
D	30,000	20	150
	$150,000	100	$750

2. BUYING. As previously stated, salaries of buyers and their clerical assistants, together with certain other miscellaneous expenses connected with the activity of buying, are often directly chargeable to departments. In many cases, however, a buyer purchases goods for more than one department and the work of whatever assistants he may have is distributed in a similar manner. Total buying expenses are not allocated to all departments; rather the expenses associated with each buyer are allocated to the departments for which he is responsible. The dollar volume of purchases made for the respective departments is sometimes used as a basis. If the departments differ greatly as to turnover, unit value of products, and number of items, this basis may not be equitable. The use of the number of items ordered, number of orders placed, or number of items stocked usually results in a more appropriate distribution of such expense.

3. RECEIVING AND SHIPPING. The cost of the receiving and shipping function, which consists largely of the wages of employees engaged in these activities, varies with the amount of merchandise handled. The kind and variety of merchandise determines the best allocation basis. If the merchandise is fairly homogeneous among the various departments, a weight factor or some other physical measurement basis such as the number of cases or other packages can be properly applied. In some situations the number of line extensions per department on customer invoices is a suitable basis. Frequently some standard handling unit is developed on the basis of tests and analyses. A case of goods, for example, may be considered as a standard unit and odd items such as barrels, sacks, or broken case lots treated as multiples or fractions of a standard unit, according to their time-of-handling relationship to the standard handling unit.

In large firms where shipping and receiving activities are not closely related, it is desirable to recognize them as separate functions or activities for cost analysis purposes. Receiving is sometimes a relatively simple activity and shipping complicated and vice versa or, for short periods of time, the quantities received for a department may be quite different from the quantities shipped. Thus receiving may be allocated according to standard handling units, weight handled, or invoice line extensions on vendors' invoices. Shipping may be treated separately on the same or similar bases but applied specifically to outgoing shipments.

4. TRUCKING. The cost of trucking consists of such natural expense items as wages of drivers and helpers, gasoline, oil, grease, tires and repairs, depreciation, insurance, taxes and licenses on trucks, garage expenses, and so on. Various difficulties are encountered in allocating trucking costs. If the same trucks are used for various activities, it is necessary to allocate costs to the subfunctions of trucking incoming goods, trucking country shipments, and city delivery. The best single measure for distributing trucking expense to these subfunctions is the number of truck hours spent on the various activities. It is often necessary to modify this, however, because running time and stopping time have a different significance for cost purposes and the relative importance may vary considerably between the subfunctions. Of course, if different trucks are used for different purposes, most of the trucking costs can be charged directly, and if some of the subfunctions are not performed the problem is further simplified.

The cost of trucking incoming goods and the cost of country shipments are often allocated to departments on the basis of weight handled per department, but this sometimes has to be modified by bulk if there are important differences in this respect among the merchandise in the various departments. A physical measurement basis is not usually suitable for city deliveries because frequent stopping, unloading, and making the actual delivery are such a large part of the total cost. The number of delivered orders containing merchandise from each department or the number of line extensions on city-delivered orders is a better basis. If such basis is used, departments in which typical orders are small are charged with an adequate share of the total delivery cost and departments in which orders tend to be large are not overcharged.

5. OCCUPANCY. If occupancy is recognized as a single function, it may include such cost items as rent, light and heat, depreciation on buildings, taxes and insurance on buildings, depreciation and operating costs of warehouse equipment, warehouse wages and salaries, and warehouse maintenance and repairs. The cost of this function may be allocated to departments on the basis of the proportion of the total usable space occupied by the merchandise inventory. For most purposes the number of square

feet is an entirely satisfactory measure; but if there are important differences in the ceiling heights in various parts of the building or if "half-decks" or other space-saving devices are used, the number of *cubic* feet is preferred as a factor for allocation.

Occasionally, a space measurement does not reflect the variable elements in all of the expense items indicated above. If this is the situation, it is better to divide this cost function into storage and handling activities. The cost of items associated with storage can then be prorated to departments on the basis of the amount of space occupied and the cost of handling activities on the basis of standard handling units, weight, number of packages handled, or line extensions on customer invoices, whichever is most suitable.

6. INVESTMENT IN MERCHANDISE. When investment is recognized as a cost function, it pertains only to the necessity of carrying an inventory of merchandise. It always includes such items as taxes and insurance on merchandise, and may also include interest. Whether interest on own investment as well as that on borrowed capital is to be regarded as a cost is subject to some differences of opinion. Often interest is not considered as a cost of operation and in such cases cannot be logically included in a functional cost analysis. It must be included, however, if it is desired to determine the net profit for the various segments of the business. Interest on inventory investment can be charged as a departmental cost only if interest on the various asset investments pertaining to all functions is also charged. When this is done, interest cost must be an imputed interest calculated at the prevailing current rate of interest on the actual asset value, rather than a sum which is limited to the amount of interest actually paid on borrowed funds. The reason for this is that the use of borrowed funds is frequently an arbitrary matter and the allocation of only interest actually paid would result in unduly high charges to some functional activities and very little to others; it would also vary from time to time, depending upon how the management chooses to finance the inventories.

Inventory investment expenses are distributed to departments on the basis of the ratio of the dollar value of the inventory of each department to the total inventory. The inventory figures used must be typical of the time period for which the analysis is being made. If the period is a month, the average of the beginning and ending inventories is a satisfactory basis; but if a longer period is involved, the average is derived from a number of actual or estimated monthly inventories.

7. CREDIT AND COLLECTION. This cost function includes such items as interest on receivables, credit department expenses, collection fees and expenses, and bad debt losses. Usually this function is not directly related to departmental characteristics and must be allocated according to the criterion of "benefit" rather than "responsibility." Allocation may be on

the basis of the distribution of net sales by departments. In situations where cash sales are an important amount or where cash sales have characteristics different from credit sales, this cost is distributed on the basis of departmental *credit sales* rather than total sales.

8. OFFICE AND ACCOUNTING. Included in this cost function are such varied items as all general office wages and salaries other than executive salaries, telephone and telegraph, postage, stationery, office supplies, depreciation, insurance and taxes on office equipment, and miscellaneous office expenses. In small firms where the office work is carried on by only a few employees, all performing a variety of activities, these diverse items are considered as a single function and prorated to departments by a single allocation base. Dollar volume of sales has often been used for this purpose, but this is not satisfactory because it frequently does not reflect the amount of office work required by different departments. The distribution of customer invoice line extensions by departments is a better basis as it corresponds rather closely to the amount of functional service required by each department.

In medium-sized and larger firms, where there is a separation of activities, the so-called office and accounting function is divided into a number of separate functions that are treated individually. The activities of billing, pricing of invoices, and keeping of stock or sales records are allocated to departments according to the number of sales transactions or invoice line extensions per department. Customer and cash receipts accounting are closely related to credit and collection expenses. Such expenses may be allocated on the basis of dollar sales or number of transactions, whichever appears more suitable. It may be advisable to treat other items of office expense as part of general administration discussed below.

9. GENERAL ADMINISTRATION. This item includes such costs as executive salaries, legal expenses, donations, and other miscellanous expenses. Such costs may be allocated to other cost functions before the extension of the analysis to merchandise departments as was indicated for executive salaries in Table 26. General administration, however, is often treated as a separate cost function in order to avoid the necessity of allocating such indirect costs to functional activities on an arbitrary basis. The cost of this function, if it is so recognized, must nevertheless be allocated to merchandise departments if net profits by departments are to be determined.

Obviously, the responsibility for expenses of this kind cannot be accurately fixed, or rather, a basis for so doing cannot be determined at a reasonable cost. The result is that the bases commonly used for the allocation of such expenses are of necessity somewhat arbitrary and open to question. Bases that have been commonly used are the departmental distribution of gross profit, net sales, or budgeted sales. The reasons for the use of these bases are the same as those indicated for the allocation of selling and promotion expenses according to the same bases. Another basis which has some merit is the proportionate amount of total functional expense allocated to the various departments by means of factors recognized in good accounting practice. The argument for the use of this basis is that the various departments require the attention of the general administrative staff roughly in proportion to the costs of the other functional activities for which the departments are responsible or from which they derive a benefit. Probably a better way to allocate administrative costs is to examine the way in which executives spend their time and to charge the various operative functions accordingly. These costs are then allocated to departments as part of the various functional costs by a measure related to each individual functional activity of which administrative activity is an element. It is doubtful, however, if this costly refinement can in most situations be justified by the increased accuracy from the analysis.

If it is too costly to determine a logical basis for allocating indirect cost items, such as administrative expenses; or if it is impossible to do so, it is better not to allocate them at all. The results of the analysis may be more meaningful for managerial purposes if only the direct costs and those functional costs for which a dependable basis of measurement is available are charged to departments (or other segments of the business). Administrative expenses and other indirect cost items may be considered a residual group to which each department is expected to make a reasonable contribution. In many cases this is clearly preferable to arriving at a "net profit" of dubious validity—one that might have been quite different if other allocation bases had been selected arbitrarily. If a complete analysis of *all* costs is required or desired, the management must be aware of the extent to which arbitrary (as contrasted with logically defensible) allocation has been used. Allowance must then be made for a generous margin of safety in the interpretation of the results before action is taken or policies are changed because of the uncertain factors in the costing process.

Importance of Departmental Analysis. The analysis of expenses by merchandise departments is useful for controlling the costs of doing business and for various aspects of policy determination. The analysis shows which departments are making a profit and which, if any, are not. If a department is not earning a net profit after the allocation of all expenses, it does not necessarily mean that the department should be eliminated. In this connection, the distinction between *escapable* and *nonescapable* costs is important. Some expenses charged to a department are escapable in the sense that if the department were eliminated, the expenses would be eliminated. If a buyer devotes full time to a single department, his salary is an escapable departmental expense. So is the investment in inventory of goods for a particular department. On the other hand, if a department were discontinued, there would probably be little if any reduction in such costs as general administration, office payroll, and accounting expense.

Using the distinction between escapable and nonescapable expenses, a departmental profit-and-loss statement might be set up somewhat as follows:

	Dept. A	Dept. B	Dept. C	Dept. D	TOTAL
Net Sales	$100,000	$150,000	$80,000	$170,000	$500,000
Cost of Goods Sold	70,000	130,000	60,000	140,000	400,000
Gross Margin	$ 30,000	$ 20,000	$20,000	$ 30,000	$100,000
Escapable Expenses	10,000	21,000	6,000	13,000	50,000
Contribution to Nonescapable Expense and Net Profit	20,000	(1,000)	14,000	17,000	50,000
Nonescapable Expenses	7,000	4,000	15,000	4,000	30,000
Net Profit	$ 13,000	($ 5,000)	($ 1,000)	$ 13,000	$ 20,000

NOTE: Parentheses indicate a loss.

This example, while deliberately exaggerated, illustrates the kinds of results that can be achieved through departmental expense analysis. Of the four departments, only two (A and D) showed net profits. One of the losing departments (C) did, however, make a contribution above and beyond its escapable expenses. If this department were eliminated, the nonescapable expenses allocated to it would remain, and total net profits would actually be reduced. On the other hand, Department B did not even cover its direct expenses. If this situation cannot be corrected through revisions in prices or expense reduction, the department should probably be dropped. This course of action may be limited, however, by the fact that the line is one that customers expect the concern to handle and that, if eliminated, would cause them to take their business elsewhere.

While the results for any given period are meaningful, the departmental analysis of expenses is most valuable when conducted at frequent intervals. When comparable results for successive periods such as months, quarters, or seasons are available, trends in costs and profits are established and unsatisfactory conditions are noted as they begin to develop rather than after they have become serious. Furthermore, the results of remedial action that may have been instituted in the past can be observed and changes made if warranted.

Expenses by Individual Commodities. The analysis of expenses by departments discussed above does not always provide the necessary information on the relative profitableness of different types of merchandise. Particularly is this true when a single department contains items or groups of items that are substantially dissimilar in important characteristics. Consequently, attempts are sometimes made to allocate expenses to individual items or commodities, as an aid in determining what specific items are to be discontinued, merely carried, or pushed aggressively. Through a study of this kind, coupled with one of turnover by items, it may be possible to reduce the number of items carried and the expenses associated therewith without appreciably affecting the volume of business.

The analysis by individual commodities is merely an extension of the analysis by departments. The same procedure is used throughout, except that few, if any, cost items can be charged directly to individual commodities. Because of the large number of items carried in most wholesale houses, this kind of analysis is too expensive to be carried on regularly or completely. It is usually undertaken only when an unsatisfactory or questionable profit condition has been observed for one or more specific merchandise departments.

Analysis of expenses for individual commodities or narrow groups of products often reveals rather startling differences in their profitability. For example, the results of one such analysis are shown in Table 27. On one product line this company experienced a *net loss greater than the gross margin*. Also of interest are the following comments of an executive in the firm in question.

Product Code 01 . . . was favorable product. On this product, we put out more effort, increasing our inventory from $19,226 to $54,195 and increased our sales from $269,959 to $385,057 . . . In the case of Product Code 03, we had substantial sales and gross profit and were reluctant to drop it. Price structure changes which the manufacturer had already initiated has [*sic*] changed the loss of 0.28% to a 4.12% profit. Product Code 07 looked almost hopeless . . . On this item we substantially increased our selling price in an effort to reduce our losses. If this does not [succeed] . . . within the coming year, we plan to eliminate the product. In the meantime, we are reducing our inventory so that we can be in a position to drop the product group completely with a minimum inventory loss.[4]

Expenses by Salesmen's Territories. The analysis of expenses by merchandise departments was discussed in considerable detail, because once the principles and difficulties are understood, the same techniques may be applied to the analysis of expenses by other segments of the business such as territories, customers, customer-classes, order-size groups, or methods of sale. In most wholesaling firms, it is advisable to analyze operating expenses by salesmen's territories. While the gross profit is not affected by the geographical distribution of sales, net profit is influenced greatly by delivery costs, customer density, competitive conditions, and other factors that vary among the territories served.

Territorial cost analysis differs from departmental analysis only in that different items constitute the direct expenses and different allocation bases

---

[4] "Distribution Cost Accounting for Net Profits," *op. cit.*, p. 119.

TABLE 27

ANALYSIS OF SALES, GROSS MARGIN, AND OPERATING EXPENSES BY INDIVIDUAL PRODUCT LINES IN A WHOLESALE CONCERN

Product Code	Product Sales	Cost of Goods Sold	Gross Profit	Gross Profit as Per Cent of Sales	Allocated Expense	Expense as Per Cent of Sales	Net Profit	Net Profit as Per Cent of Sales
01	$296,959	$239,528	$57,431	19%	$38,156	13%	$19,275	6%
02	44,888	36,742	8,146	18	6,946	15	1,200	3
03	144,868	120,684	24,184	17	24,588	17	(404)	—
04	23,831	18,574	5,257	22	5,026	21	231	1
07	13,064	9,659	3,405	26	7,224	55	(3,819)	(29)
08	7,665	6,453	1,212	16	1,886	25	(674)	(9)
10	2,161	1,621	540	25	548	25	(8)	—
11	24,962	16,424	8,538	34	4,562	18	3,976	16
14	42,437	34,044	8,393	20	7,123	17	1,270	3
18	18,729	16,940	1,789	10	3,521	19	(1,732)	(9)
19	50,032	41,734	8,298	17	8,954	18	(656)	(1)
20	29,421	20,606	8,815	30	6,376	22	2,439	8
24	52,062	42,300	9,762	19	7,826	15	1,936	4
28	72,077	42,527	29,550	41	16,078	22	13,472	19
TOTAL	$823,156	$647,836	$175,320	21%	$138,814	17%	$36,506	4%

NOTE: Parentheses indicate a loss.

Source: "Distribution Cost Accounting for Net Profits," *Industrial Distribution* (July, 1957), 112.

or factors must be used for some of the indirect expense items. Among the expense items that are often directly chargeable to territories are the following:

   a) Salesmen's salaries and commissions
   b) Salesmen's traveling expense including depreciation and maintenance of automobiles if owned by the firm
   c) Outward freight, express, and parcel post
   d) Salesmen's telephone, telegraph, and postage expense
   e) Samples used by salesmen
   f) Salesmen's supplies

For the most part, the indirect functional costs can be allocated to territories on the same basis as to departments. In some cases, however, the allocation bases previously used do not reflect the differences in the amount of functional service required by territories. When trucks are used for delivery, the allocation of delivery expenses on a physical measurement basis such as weight, bulk, or a standard handling unit that is suitable for departmental analysis penalizes the territories near the house. Thus the physical measurement basis must be modified by the average distance covered in making deliveries to each territory. This involves distributing a proportion of the total trucking cost to territories on the basis of physical measurement and a portion on the basis of distance. Such proportions can be determined only by a study of the relative importance of each through analyses of the specific circumstances. Since territorial sales are a composite of all departments, it is obviously impractical to attempt the distribution of expenses associated with occupancy or storage on a space measurement basis. Such expenses are usually distributed in accordance with sales, the assumption being that a given dollar volume of sales in one territory requires as much investment in inventory and storage space as a similar amount of sales in another territory. This seems warranted unless special circumstances dictate another approach to the problem.

The other indirect functional costs can be allocated as a general rule on the bases previously indicated. Factors such as standard handling units, invoice lines, budgeted sales, and gross margins are determinable for territories as well as for departments and reflect the variability of certain items of cost by territories. As in the case of departmental analysis, territorial analysis need not be carried to the point of determining net profit. Territories that do not yield more than their direct costs and the semidirect costs allocated on a clearly defensible basis are unquestionably unprofitable. In the case of other territories, it may be just as meaningful to know the amount of the contribution to nonanalyzed expenses as an arbitrarily determined "net profit." This does not mean that suitable allocation bases for administrative or general expenses cannot be determined, but rather that often the cost of determining reliable bases of measurement may be out of proportion to the added benefits obtainable.

This kind of analysis helps to locate unsatisfactory areas and, since each territory is usually served by a single salesman, responsibility for performance is fixed. When the information is combined with the results of sales analysis and other measures of salesmen's performance, as discussed in the preceding chapter, the proper type of corrective action is indicated. This may require increasing the number of calls made, adjusting delivery charges, making less frequent calls and deliveries, or intensifying promotional effort. The situation may sometimes appear so hopeless that complete withdrawal from the territory or territories in question is the best solution. The results of the analysis can then be used to forecast what may be experienced in the future as a consequence of the elimination of some costs and the shifting of portions of inescapable or fixed costs to different territories. They can be used in a similar manner to foresee cost relationships that would come about from adding new territories to the operating area.

Expenses by Customers. In Chapter 27 the need for an analysis of sales by customers was emphasized. Such an analysis, while providing usable information, is usually not adequate unless supplemented by a study of costs. The need for an analysis of costs by customers is based on the fact that some customers require more units of functional service, relative to sales and profits, than others.

The following are suggestive of different ways in which costs may be analyzed by customers:

a) By individual customers
b) By customers classified according to volume of purchases
c) By customers classified according to average order size
d) By customers classified according to type: as industrial consumers and retailers, each group being further divided as circumstances warrant

Such analyses are not generally carried on continuously or at very frequent intervals. They are usually made only when a need is recognized for determining in greater detail the reasons for an unsatisfactory showing of one sort or another or for the determination of discount schedules applicable to each type of customer.

Analysis by individual customers is too costly in application to be of benefit to most wholesaling establishments. If the number of customers is small, however, and most of them account for a sizable volume of business, the expense of this analysis is not excessive. Such an analysis is merely a logical extension of the procedure used for territorial analysis, with the exception that usually there are no expense items that can be charged directly to customers. For example, expenses associated with salesmen's activities must be prorated according to the number of calls made or, if this is unsatisfactory, according to the amount of time spent with each customer.

Most of the information obtainable from an analysis by individual customers can be supplied by an analysis according to volume-of-sale classifications. Data on customer classes are almost always stated in dollars. The number of customers per class and the proportion of total sales volume per class are often available from sales analysis information. If a large number of classes are set up for *sales* analysis purposes, it may be advisable to combine these into a smaller number for *cost* analysis purposes. A large number of classes tend to increase the cost of making an analysis and the results are usually confusing. About six or eight classes are sufficient in most cases, with the classes chosen so that there are a fairly large number of customers in each class and significant differences between classes.

If a territorial analysis reveals important cost differences between territories, the analysis by volume classes is best conducted on a territorial basis. Since the cost of a salesman's call or the cost of delivery may vary considerably between territories, it is often misleading to allocate such costs to all customers of the house in a given volume class on the same basis. It frequently happens that customers in a given volume class may be profitable in one territory and unprofitable in another. It may at times be proper and economical to group several territories that are similar as to the costs that vary between territories for the purpose of making customer analyses. When the differences between territories are not important or when a wholesale house operates on a local scale, the analysis is carried on for the firm as a whole. The procedure is the same in either case except that territorial cost and sales data are used when the analysis is made by subdivisions of the market area.

Usually there are no expense items that can be charged directly to groups of customers. The procedure is one of grouping various expense items in terms of functional activities and distributing functional costs to the various volume-size classes. In any wholesale establishment, functional costs may for this purpose be divided into three groups: (1) expenses that can be closely related to customers, (2) expenses not closely related to customers but for which a reasonable allocation basis is available, and (3) expenses that bear little or no relationship to individual or classes of customers. The expense items in each of these classes vary somewhat from establishment to establishment, as do the allocation bases that measure their variability. The following discussion is suggestive, however, of allocation bases that are suitable under most circumstances. A wholesaler should not, however, adopt suggested allocation bases without studying special circumstances pertaining to his own operations.

Various bases are used for allocating costs that are closely associated with customers. All direct costs of salesmen including salaries, commissions, and traveling expense can be distributed according to the number of calls made on customers in each class. It is usually advisable to modify the average cost per call by the average size of order for each class. In some cases it is modified by the average time required for orders of varying sizes if this information is available from time studies or can be obtained without incurring expense out of proportion to the benefits derived. Delivery costs can be allocated according to average delivery costs. Expenses associated with order-handling are allocated by the number of orders for each class, the number of order line extensions, or some factor that takes into consideration both number of orders and order line extensions. Credit and collection costs including the clerical cost of handling receivables are allocated on a cost per customer basis, sometimes modified by credit ratings if significant differences exist between such ratings and volume classes.

Certain expenses are not so closely related to customers but are capable of being distributed on a reasonable basis. Sales administration and supervision expenses can be allocated in proportion to the amount of direct salesmen's cost previously allocated to volume classes. Costs associated with buying activities can be distributed according to the cost of goods sold to each class of customers.

Most of the other expense items have little relation to customers. Among these are general advertising, investment expense, occupancy expense, warehousing expenses not associated with order-handling, and general administration. The proportion of total sales volume accounted for by each class is probably as good an allocation basis for these items as any other that may be selected.

The extent to which an analysis by classes of customers is carried depends on the purpose for which the analysis is made. If the analysis is made to determine (or to justify) price differentials under regulatory statutes, particularly the Robinson-Patman Act, it is necessary to allocate all expense items to all classes of customers in the fairest manner possible. The only exception would be costs that are specifically inapplicable as, for example, credit and collection costs for cash customers.

Another purpose of expense analysis by customers may be to determine which classes are profitable and unprofitable and to arrive at a "break-even" point with regard to a customer's volume of purchases. In this connection it may be advisable to distribute only those expense items that are closely associated with customers and leave the remainder in an undistributed "overhead and profit" category. Just as many types of expenses are fixed with respect to the number of departments operated (non-escapable), many are fixed with respect to the number and types of customers served. It may be determined, for example, that customers of a given type are served at a loss if *all* expenses are allocated including such categories as general administrative expense. If the analysis is confined to direct or escapable costs, however, it may be found that the same classes of customers contribute something to overhead and hence should be retained. From a policy standpoint it would be unwise to drop such customers, although services may be restricted or other means employed to reduce the costs of selling to them or to encourage them to become more desirable customers.

Analysis by Order Size. Closely related to the analysis by customer groups is analysis by size of order. When a detailed functional analysis is made, it is usually found that certain types of costs vary with the number of *line extensions* on an order and size of line extensions, certain others are relatively constant *per order,* while still others vary primarily with the *total dollar value* of the order. Illustrative of the first category are some parts of selling cost, most of the costs of order-routine, order-picking, and broken-package order-packing. In the second group are such activities as accounts receivable posting, sales statistical processing, and shipping. Finally, costs that vary primarily with dollar volume include general administration, storage, and inventory carrying charges.

An important use of expense analyses by order size is to determine a firm's "break-even" point in terms of order size. The reasoning to be applied here is similar to that given in connection with the discussion of analysis by customer groups. Some orders are handled at a loss if all expenses are allocated, but may contribute in some measure above and beyond the direct expenses associated with them. In any event, analysis of expenses by order size is essential if the small-order problem is to be held within reasonable bounds. The common practice, in some lines of business, of handling orders amounting to $5 or $10 is almost certainly unprofitable even when only direct expenses are considered. Just where the minimum order should be set cannot be determined, however, without a quantitative analysis.

Interpretation of the Results of Cost Analysis. An objection frequently directed against the extended applications of functional cost analysis is that the methods of allocating indirect costs result in approximations that are not reliable for purposes of policy determination. This is decidedly true if allocation bases are not selected for their suitability in each individual case. If the detailed cost items are grouped in terms of functions, the number of which depends on the size of firm and the degree of specialization, careful study usually determines some basis of measurement that accurately reflects the variability in the amounts of functional service required by the different segments being analyzed. As has been emphasized at various points of this discussion, for most purposes there is no necessity for allocating costs when defensible allocation bases cannot be determined.

There will always be some borderline cases, no matter how refined the analysis, because of uncertainties in the costing process. But it is not these borderline situations that usually give concern to the management. In many firms where cost analysis is not a routine practice, clearly unprofitable operations often exist that cannot be uncovered by sales analysis or through an analysis of costs by kind of expense. Extended applications of functional cost analysis, while necessarily including approximations to some degree, provide factual information that unquestionably serves as a better guide for policy determination than any guesses or hunches that can be evolved. Even where all segments of the business are profitable and there is no question of substitution or elimination, the *relative profitableness* of the various segments is determined and the sales effort is directed accordingly.

EXPENSE BUDGETING

All the methods of expense control discussed thus far are designed primarily for locating sources of difficulty *after* expenses have been incurred. Adequate control requires more than this. If problems are discovered only ex post facto, corrective action becomes largely a matter of "fire-fighting." In order that such control may be forward-looking as well, it is necessary to plan expenses in advance. Systematic planning in this area takes the form of an *expense budget*. This should not be confused with the *merchandise budget* discussed in Chapter 20, although the two are closely related.

Purposes of Budgeting. The basic purpose of expense-budgeting is to establish maximum limits for the various categories of operating expense. These limits facilitate the control of actual expenses on a current basis. If the budget has been prepared realistically, deviations from it direct the attention of management to potential problems before they materialize or become serious. If a proper classification of expenses is used, the budget also serves to fix responsibility for deviations from expected results on the individuals or groups responsible.

Budgeting Procedure. The main steps in establishing an expense budget are: (1) forecasting sales volume and gross profits, (2) planning fixed expenses, (3) planning variable and semivariable expenses, and (4) adjusting planned expenses as necessary. A reasonably accurate forecast of sales volume is essential because certain classes of expense vary with sales and can be estimated only in relation to a specific sales goal. Methods of forecasting sales were treated in Chapter 26, and for purposes of this discussion it will simply be assumed that a sales forecast has been made.

The second step is to plan *fixed expenses* or those types of expense that do not vary, or vary only slightly, with changes in sales volume. In a typical wholesale concern, fixed expenses might include:

Management compensation (unless some incentive or bonus system related
  to sales volume is used)
Dues, donations, subscriptions, and the like
Repairs and maintenance of equipment
Postage, stationery, office supplies
Rent
Depreciation on equipment and fixtures
Property taxes
License fees and taxes
Fire insurance premiums

The term "fixed expenses" should not be interpreted too literally. In the first place, many such expenses are affected slightly by changes in sales volume. An example would be postage, stationery, and office supplies. The variation in such expense categories is likely, however, to be quite small. It should also be kept in mind that there are virtually no expenses that will not be affected if the change in sales volume is great enough. It may be possible, for example, to accommodate a substantial increase in volume without increasing office and warehouse floor space. Beyond a certain point, however, facilities become overcrowded and acquisition of additional space becomes necessary.

Estimates of fixed expenses are readily made on the basis of previous experience. Unless there are to be changes in circumstances that are known to affect such expenses, expected costs for a future period can be carried forward from the preceding period.

Most of the expenses in a typical wholesale business vary to some degree with sales volume. It is useful to subdivide these into *variable expenses,* that is, those which vary directly and proportionally with sales, and *semivariable expenses,* which fluctuate directly, but not proportionally, with sales. Illustrative of the first class are salesmen's commissions when paid on the basis of sales. When this compensation method is used, commissions can easily be computed once an estimate of expected sales is made.

Probably the majority of operating expenses in the typical wholesale enterprise are of the semivariable class, which present a more complex problem than either fixed or exactly variable costs. Two general approaches may be used in budgeting semivariable expenses. One is to analyze operating results over a period of time to determine the level of each expense category at different levels of sales volume. This procedure suffers from the weakness that the circumstances under which the concern operates may have changed and past results may have little bearing on the future, but in stable, mature concerns, this method is probably as accurate as any. A second approach to estimating semivariable expenses is through the use of functional performance measures. This method is discussed in the following chapter.

The final step in the budget process is to adjust the various expense items to conform to the over-all net profit goal. It may be that the total operating expense, built up from the individual expense classes, is too high to permit the attainment of a satisfactory net profit return. If this is the case, each item should be reviewed and possible expense reductions sought out.

Expense budgets are commonly prepared on an annual basis, estimates being made near the end of one year for operations in the subsequent year. After the annual figures have been drawn up, they should be broken down into shorter time periods, preferably months. This is done for the purpose of obtaining closer control over operations. To be effective for controlling expenses, the budget must also be broken down by detailed classifications. All types of expenses are budgeted for the business as a whole and various items are budgeted for merchandise departments and for territories. In some firms, special circumstances may dictate other major classifications of budgeted expenses.

Requisites of Effective Budgeting. To be useful for purposes of expense control, the budget must meet certain tests. It should be *realistic* and *flexible* and should have the *support of those responsible for incurring expenses.*

Realism in budgeting means that expected results, rather than ideal standards impossible of attainment, are used. For example, if the cost of a salesman's call in a new territory has been excessive and cannot be corrected in the new budget period, there is nothing realistic about budgeting a standard cost that would be considered satisfactory. This may require budgeting a loss for some segments of the business. If, however, a loss is expected from a particular operation, it should be brought to the attention of those concerned, at the beginning of the period, so that the operation can be watched more closely. Thus the budget is not merely the sum total of individual performance standards, but a coordinated and realistic plan for the future.

Flexibility should be present in any expense budget. After all, the budget consists of a series of *estimates,* many of which are in turn based on an *estimate* of sales volume or on other *estimates* of functional performance levels, workloads, and so forth. The fact that these estimates have been reduced to writing does not endow them with any greater accuracy. Hence management must be willing to recognize the possibility that some of the estimates are in error and revise the cost standards or budgets accordingly. This may be done in part by drawing up several budgets in advance, each based on a different level of sales volume within a range of expectations. Flexibility may also be introduced by periodic reviews of budgeted expenses during the year, with revisions being made as warranted by changed conditions or by factors unforeseen or overlooked when the budget was first prepared. Care should be taken not to become *over*flexible, since otherwise the value of the budget as a means of controlling expenses may be destroyed.

Finally, if the budget is to be of maximum value, it must be accepted and understood by the persons in the organization who actually have responsibility for incurring and controlling expenses. The budget should not be handed down from on high, or it may be resented and ignored by those whose performance it is supposed to measure and upon whom responsibility for staying within it rests. To get the support of executives and supervisors, their participation should be sought in drawing up the estimates. Not only are they more likely to accept the budget as realistic, but this procedure encourages each person to think through the various factors affecting expenses under his control and may lead to valuable cost-reducing ideas.

30

PERFORMANCE MEASURES AND STANDARDS

A delicate but highly essential role for management in a wholesaling business is the isolation and precise measurement of the marketing job, its component elements, and the effectiveness of the personnel assigned to the various tasks. Long recognized as a marketing management function, this responsibility has until recently been "played largely by ear." That is to say qualitative, if not emotional, evaluations have all too often sufficed to base judgments. One should not be too hasty in deprecating such a subjective approach. If administered by a wise and experienced manager, who has over many years developed a sensitive "feel" for the business, reasonably good decisions may very well be reached. On the whole, however, modern marketing must utilize the most advanced management technology. This chapter opens the door on modern concepts and methods in this field of managerial responsibility.

PERFORMANCE MEASURES

Isolating the Job. Before performance can be measured, the question, what performance? must be answered. The job or function to be appraised must first be precisely defined. Some functions are simple, others are complex. For example, the job of unloading a railroad box car is easily defined. It may be explained in terms of cases or other physical units of goods handled per hour. Much more complex is the performance of an executive who has to turn his attention from one important decision to another throughout his day. Here the definition of the job in terms suitable for measuring performance is much more difficult, but not impossible.

Fortunately, the majority of workers in a wholesaling business are engaged in activities which fall in the simpler context of repetitive jobs. Among them may be noted the following:

Clerical processing of invoices
Preparation of checks for suppliers
Unloading incoming merchandise
Filling orders
Delivering orders

Responsible management should classify all of its activities into clearly definable job or functional groupings as a first step in performance measurement.

Nature and Purpose. The major objective of functional performance measures is to secure a better tool for cost control. Such measures are not substitutes for, but supplements to, orthodox expense control systems. They measure *work output* for specific job categories and for individual employees. For example, the output of an order-filler in the warehouse who handles full cases only may be measured in terms of the *number of cases* handled per hour, day, or week. This might be 50 cases per hour for one man, 40 for another, and 60 for a third.

These figures are the functional performance measures or *productivity ratios* (ratio of output, cases handled, to input, hours of labor) for this particular job. In anticipation of the subsequent analysis of performance *standards* it may be helpful to note here that a performance standard may be taken for a particular job in a wholesaling business by averaging the performance ratios of all workers on that job. Thus if we take the above illustration, the average number of cases handled per hour by the three workers is 50. If work conditions are identical or essentially similar for all full-case order-fillers, it is possible by this method to measure the relative efficiency of each one against the standard or norm. In addition, functional measures are used to plan personnel needs, to evaluate the progress of individual employees, and to budget expenses. Each of these uses is treated in more detail in subsequent sections of this chapter.

Procedure for Establishing Performance Measures. Establishment of functional performance measures for a wholesale concern includes three basic steps: (1) determination of a logical unit of output measurement for each major function performed, (2) relating the output unit to a measure or measures of resource input, and (3) development of standards or norms of accomplishment.

The first step, and by far the most difficult, is to set up units of output measurement. This must be done for each type of activity separately, and as many different measures are required as there are distinct and separable types of activity. Moreover, the types of output measures used may differ between individual concerns to the extent that different functions are performed and because of variation in the degree of personnel specialization. Obviously, it is not possible to specify any universally applicable set of functional output measures; these must be developed by each concern individually on the basis of a detailed analysis of the functions performed by individuals and groups within the organization. Nevertheless, there is likely to be a high degree of similarity among comparable firms in a given line of business and to some extent uniform performance measures may be employed.

Illustrative of the functional output measures that might be used are a few of the measures developed in an extensive study of service drug wholesalers shown below:

Functional Activities	*Output Measure*
Management (General, Sales, Credit, and Operations)	None
Buying:	
a) Buyers	Number of Items Carried in Stock
b) Stock Counting	Number of Items Counted, Modified by Average Value of Inventory per Item
c) Purchase Invoice Routine	Items Ordered (Invoice Lines on Purchase Orders)
Order Assembly (Picking, Checking, Packing, and Shelving)	Invoice Lines
Shipping	Packages Handled[1]

The basis for determining the appropriate unit of output measurement for each of the above and for many other activities was an analysis of the work performed in each section of the organization. Where an employee performed several distinct duties, the measuring unit was based on the activity to which he devoted most of his time. For example, the clerks responsible for purchase order routine performed some duties not related to the number of items ordered, but these were of a miscellaneous nature and not readily measured.

Examination of the output measures used in this case reveals that they are designed primarily for *repetitive* types of activities. The more complex and the less repetitive a function is, the less susceptible it is to easy measurement. For management, no unit of output at all was established. For some other activities, such as general accounting and general clerical, the measuring unit used (number of active accounts served by the company) is recognized as an indirect and approximate estimate.

Obviously, the functional breakdown and output units employed in the above example could not be adopted by a basically different type of wholesale concern. For example, if mechanical or electronic systems of

---

[1] For a more complete listing, see Albert B. Fisher, "Development of Operating Standards for Wholesalers," *Journal of Marketing*, XIV, No. 2 (September, 1949), 198–210.

inventory control are used in a business, there would be no function corresponding to "stock counting." Functional performance measures must be tailor-made to the set of functions performed in an individual concern or typical of a group of concerns.

The second step in applying functional performance measures is to relate the work output to a resource input used in obtaining the output. Resource input may be measured in "natural" terms such as man-hours of labor or square feet of space, or in terms of dollar cost. For example, one association of wholesalers collects and publishes typical performance figures for various major functions, as follows:

Function and Performance Measure	Typical Figures (1955)
Administration:	
Invoice Lines per Office Man-Hour	21.70
Administrative Costs per Invoice Line	19.5¢
Sales:	
Selling Cost per Invoice Line	12.8¢
Warehouse:	
Invoice Lines per Warehouse Man-Hour	20.65
Warehouse Expenses per Invoice Line	9.9¢[2]

These performance standards may be used by the individual drug wholesaler in much the same way that typical expense ratios are used, that is, as norms against which actual individual company results may be evaluated.

PERFORMANCE STANDARDS

The third step in using functional performance measures is to establish standards of performance. These may be based on average performance within a business or they may be in the form of typical trade figures, such as those given in the preceding paragraph. Another way of expressing the standards is to compute the number of man-hours and/or the dollar costs that should have been required for a given volume of output, and then compare this with actual results. This may be illustrated for the receiving section of the business and made part of a control report for a given period of time, as follows:

	Man-Hours	Wages
Actual	800	$1,720
Standard	760	1,650
Operating Index	95	
Wage Gain or Loss		—$70

The "standard" man-hour allowance and "standard" wage allowance are computed on the basis of a standard or normal level of performance, preferably for the industry. In other words, if 39,750 cases were received

[2] *Facts on Sales, Costs, and Profits of Service Wholesale Druggists—1955*, Bulletin No. 50, National Wholesale Druggists' Association (New York, 1956).

during the period in question and the performance standard is 52.3 cases per man-hour, about 760 man-hours (39,750 divided by 52.3) *should* have been required. This man-hour allowance is then multiplied by the regular wage rate per hour to get the standard wage allowance. The "operating index" is computed by dividing the actual man-hours by the standard (760 divided by 800 = 0.95) to determine the percentage of standard performance actually achieved. In this case, the receiving section operated at 95 per cent of standard during the period in question. The report can also be set up to show, as in the illustration, the gain or loss in expenses as compared with standard. In the receiving section, $1,720 was actually paid in wages, or $70 more than should have been paid if normal efficiency had been attained. Hence there was a "loss" of $70 in this section. This type of report serves to pinpoint the sections or persons responsible for excessive costs and shows exactly how much dollar loss (or saving) each incurred.

Relationship of Performance Measures to Traditional Methods of Expense Control. As previously stated, functional performance measures were developed by wholesale concerns and other types of business principally because of certain weaknesses in the traditional methods of expense control.[3] At the same time, the level of performance attained by a concern is obviously related to its dollar expenses and net profits. This relationship may best be explained by indicating the nature of the weaknesses in orthodox control methods and showing how and to what extent functional measures overcome these weaknesses.

As explained in the preceding chapter, the orthodox approach to expense control places principal reliance on the *comparison* of expense figures with standards or norms derived from a firm's own past experience and from typical trade results. For example, in Table 25 in Chapter 29, a series of expense ratios (percentages of net sales) for an individual firm is compared with typical ratios for other wholesalers of comparable size in the same line of business. The ratio of *warehouse labor* expense for the hypothetical concern is 3 per cent, while the typical figure is 2.21 per cent. Based on this comparison, under the traditional approach, it would be concluded that the wholesaler's warehouse personnel is *less efficient* than normal and that attention should therefore be directed to effecting improvements in procedures, equipment, supervision, or other factors influencing warehousing efficiency.

Wage Variations. The conclusion suggested by comparative expense analysis may not, however, be entirely justified. It is quite possible that

[3] A related development in the field of retailing is the system of "production unit accounting" adopted by the National Retail Merchants' Association (then the National Retail Dry Goods Association) in 1954. This system is explained in the association's *Standard Expense Center Accounting Manual* for 1954.

the warehousing methods used by this wholesaler are *more efficient* than those of comparable concerns, despite the variance in labor costs. The difference may arise, instead, out of variations commonly found in *wage rates* for warehouse workers, which are often more than great enough to explain a difference of the magnitude shown in Table 25.

The effect of variations in wage rates (and other factor costs, such as rent) on expense ratios is substantial. When it is considered that about two-thirds of a typical wholesaler's total expense is in the form of wages and salaries, this factor takes on special meaning. Moreover, when a deviation from a "standard" or "normal" expense ratio is caused by wage or salary differentials, the implications for management action are quite different than if the deviation resulted from inefficiency. A firm paying a premium wage rate is not usually in a position to do much about it. Wage rates may be determined largely by factors outside of the control of any one company. On the other hand, if an excessive expense ratio is caused by factors *other* than wage rates, corrective action is called for. A major reason for the development of functional performance measures has been the desire to neutralize the influence of differences in wage rates when comparing the performance of one firm with another or of a given enterprise in one time period with another.

Other Causes of Variations in Expenses. Even when wage differentials are discounted, expense ratios are still affected by a complex set of factors. Comparison of ratios does not, without further analysis, identify the factors responsible for an excessive cost in one segment of a business or another. This can be explained by another example taken from Table 25. As shown there, the hypothetical wholesaler incurred office payroll expenses amounting to 2.46 per cent of net sales, compared with an average of 2.04 per cent for wholesalers of the same type. Suppose, further, that this concern pays exactly the same rate of wages to office workers as that paid by the typical firm. Why were office payroll expenses higher than normal? A number of explanations are possible, but two major factors are likely to account for the situation: (1) the *functional performance* of office workers in terms of work done, and (2) the office *workload* in relation to the firm's sales volume. This may be explained by examining the office functions of processing sales orders. The work done here consists of registering the orders, editing them for clarity, checking prices, making extensions, and posting the sales to stock control records.[4] The best measure of output for such activities seems to be the number of *invoice lines* on the orders processed. In other words, it takes a certain amount of time to read and edit each line, a certain amount of time to check and extend prices on each line, and a certain amount of time to enter each

---

[4] There are, of course, variations in the procedures followed by different firms in order routine. For further analysis of such procedures, see Chapter 24.

invoice line in stock control records. The invoice line serves, therefore, as a measure of work accomplished in order-processing in the office. Office payroll expense will consequently vary according to the performance of employees as measured by the number of invoice lines processed per man-hour. If two wholesale concerns pay the same wage rate and all other things are equal, the one with the highest output of invoice lines per hour will have a lower office payroll expense ratio.

All other things are not, however, necessarily equal. There may also be differences between firms in the *workload* of order processing activity relative to sales volume. This is conveniently measured by the *average line extension,* that is, the average dollar value per invoice line. Suppose that two firms with the same sales volume pay the same wage rate, and suppose further that the performance of office personnel in the two concerns is exactly equal. But one firm has an average line extension of $4, while the average for the other is $5. If each concern sells $5 million annually, one must process 1,250,000 invoice lines ($5,000,000 divided by $4) while the other handles only 1,000,000 lines ($5,000,000 divided by $5). One company, in other words, has a heavier *workload* relative to sales than the other. If all other things remain equal, the firm handling the heaviest workload will incur a higher ratio of office payroll expense to sales volume.

The significance of the distinction between functional performance and *workload* is in the different types of corrective action that are called for. If it is found that expenses are too high because of poor functional performance (in the office or elsewhere), then the solution may be found in better training, more intensive supervision, or revised procedures. On the other hand, if performance is satisfactory but the workload is heavy in relation to sales, the answer may lie in a revision of *sales* policies, especially those dealing with small orders. Since these are separate and distinct types of corrective action, it is obviously desirable to separate performance and workload factors as causes of excessive cost. This can be done through the use of functional performance measures. This, in fact, is precisely what was done in the example dealing with office payroll in the preceding paragraph.

Other Uses of Functional Performance Measures. The principal purpose of functional performance measures, as just outlined, is to serve as a means of evaluating employee performance and controlling operating expenses. In addition, such measures may be used for several related purposes including the planning of personnel requirements, evaluating the progress of new employees, and expense budgeting.

In planning personnel requirements, functional performance figures are useful in relating estimated workloads to the number of man-hours or employees needed for a particular job. This approach is illustrated in

TABLE 28

DETERMINATION OF THE NUMBER OF OFFICE EMPLOYEES REQUIRED IN A WHOLESALE
DRUG HOUSE ON THE BASIS OF THE NUMBER OF INVOICE LINES HANDLED MONTHLY
AND AVERAGE NUMBER OF LINES PER ORDER

And Number of Invoice Lines Handled Monthly Is:	If Average Number of Lines Per Order Is:						
	9.9 and Under	10.0 to 10.9	11.0 to 11.9	12.0 to 12.9	13.0 to 13.9	14.0 to 14.9	15.0 and Over
	Then—Number of Office Employees Required Is:						
20,000	7.0	6.9	6.7	6.5	6.1	5.7	5.5
40,000	13.7	13.4	13.1	12.7	12.0	11.2	10.7
60,000	20.4	19.7	19.3	18.6	17.6	16.5	15.4
80,000	26.5	26.0	25.6	24.6	23.2	21.8	20.8
100,000	32.7	32.2	31.4	30.4	28.8	27.0	25.2
120,000	39.0	38.3	37.6	36.4	33.8	32.3	30.2
140,000	45.3	44.7	43.5	42.2	40.0	37.4	35.0
160,000	51.5	50.5	49.5	48.0	45.5	42.6	39.9
180,000	57.9	56.9	55.7	54.0	51.2	47.8	44.8
200,000	64.3	63.5	62.0	60.1	56.9	53.1	49.8
220,000	70.6	69.5	68.2	66.1	62.7	58.4	54.8
240,000	77.0	76.0	74.5	72.2	68.4	63.7	59.8
260,000	83.3	82.3	80.7	78.2	74.2	69.0	64.8
280,000	89.7	88.7	87.0	84.3	79.9	74.3	69.8
300,000	96.0	95.0	93.2	90.3	85.6	79.5	74.7
320,000	102.3	101.3	99.4	96.3	91.3	84.8	79.7
340,000	108.7	107.7	105.7	102.4	97.0	90.1	84.7
360,000	115.0	114.0	111.9	108.4	102.7	95.4	89.7
380,000	121.4	120.4	118.2	114.4	108.5	100.7	94.7
400,000	127.7	126.7	124.5	120.5	114.3	106.0	99.7

Source: "How Many People Do You Need to Operate a Wholesale Drug Company?" National Wholesale Druggists' Association, not dated.

Table 28, which shows the number of office employees required in a wholesale drug concern for various workloads measured in terms of invoice lines handled monthly and average number of lines per order. The average number of lines per order must be considered as well as the number of invoice lines, since some office tasks (for example, order registry) are related primarily to the number of orders rather than to the number of lines. The office staff requirements shown in this table could be used by a new enterprise to determine how many persons should be hired, or by an existing business as a rough measure of its office efficiency.

In some wholesale concerns where the workload varies significantly from day to day or from week to week, functional performance measures may be used for short-term personnel planning. In the grocery trade, for instance, the order assembly workload often varies a great deal from one day to the next. Some houses in this trade receive goods during the day and assemble orders at night. During the day, as orders from customers come in, the warehouse superintendent estimates the number of *pieces* to be handled during the coming night. (Virtually all orders are for full-case amounts; hence, no consideration need be given to broken-package business.) On the basis of these estimates and performance standards for the number of pieces normally handled per man-hour, an estimate of the number of man-hours required is made. By late afternoon this estimate is practically complete. The superintendent then determines how much over-time, if any, is to be worked and if it exceeds a predetermined figure, an extra worker will be called in. This technique avoids excessive and costly overtime work and minimizes delays in filling customer orders which might result if the workload were too great for the number of employees on hand.

Performance measures make possible an objective evaluation of the progress of new employees. For obvious reasons, trainees cannot be ex-pected to attain the levels of performance characteristic of experienced workers. But their improvement can be measured in terms of output per hour and standards established for learners with various amounts of ex-perience. For example, a study might reveal that order-pickers attain 30 per cent of standard performance by the end of the tenth week; 60 per cent by the end of the twentieth week; 80 per cent by the end of the twenty-fifth week; and 100 per cent in the thirtieth week.

For expense budgeting, functional performance measures provide a basis for planning workloads and the costs associated with them. They are of value principally for the budgeting of *semivariable* expenses, which neither stay constant in dollar amount (as do fixed expenses) or vary exactly with sales volume (as do variable expenses). The procedure may be summarized briefly as follows:

1. Assuming that a forecast of sales has been made, estimate the amount of functional service or *workload* for each functional work center as re-lated to the expected volume of sales.
2. Multiply the number of units of functional service for each work center by the estimated cost per unit of service or output. This, in turn, is deter-mined by reference to the expected level of performance (such as output per man-hour) and the estimated costs of the resources to be used (such as wage rate per hour).

To illustrate this procedure, suppose that a paper wholesaler expects to attain sales of $3 million in the coming year. The average line exten-sion has been running about $14.50, but is expected to increase to $15. This means that the workload for the coming year will be 200,000 invoice lines ($3,000,000 divided by $15). The number of invoice lines per office man-hour has been averaging around 18, but changes in office procedure are expected to raise this to 20. The number of man-hours of office labor is, therefore, set at 10,000 (200,000 invoice lines divided by 20). The average wage rate is expected to be $1.80 per hour for office workers. Office payroll is budgeted, therefore, at $18,000 (10,000 man-hours times $1.80). If all pertinent variables—the average line extension, lines per man-hour, and wage rate—remain constant, then the ratio of office payroll expense to net sales would also remain constant, and it could be budgeted as a variable expense.

Limitations of Performance Measures. Functional performance measures for wholesale concerns are very similar to various types of efficiency measures used in manufacturing management. Experience in factory management has revealed certain limitations of such measures which, it is believed, also apply to performance measures in wholesaling.[5]

One danger in the use of performance measures is that management may tend to rely too heavily on figures and quotas for their own sake, to the detriment of other factors. If output falls below a predetermined standard, pressure may be exerted on workers to increase it. If, in their zeal to attain standards, supervisors ignore valid excuses for time losses, morale will suffer.

A second limitation of performance standards, and closely related to the first, is that the standards are *averages* and do not take into account the various factors affecting employee efficiency. For example, the output unit adopted for the truck delivery function may be the *number of orders delivered.* But different drivers may encounter varying traffic conditions; or some may handle larger orders, requiring more time to unload, than others. In one study it was found that the time required to cover a non-city delivery route depended on three factors: number of stops (orders), distance covered, and value of orders (which approximates their average size).[6] These three factors were then used in a multiple correlation equation for estimating the time needed to cover a route. This technique is undoubtedly too complex for use in day-to-day control of operations by most wholesale concerns. The important point is, however, that factors influencing performance be recognized and allowed for in evaluating actual results.

A third limitation inherent in functional performance measures is that such measures do not reflect *quality,* but merely *quantity* of output. An order-picker may attain a very high level of efficiency in terms of invoice lines per hour, but only at the expense of accuracy by committing frequent errors. If possible, some measure of quality (such as an error percentage) should be used in conjunction with quantitative performance measures.

[5] Cf. Frank J. Jasinski, "Use and Misuse of Efficiency Controls," *Harvard Business Review,* XXXIV (July–August, 1956), 105–12.

[6] Martin Kriesberg, "Procedure for Measuring Employee Productivity," *Advanced Management* (August, 1952), 6–8.

MEASURES OF SALES PERFORMANCE

An especially difficult problem is encountered in measuring the performance of salesmen in a wholesale concern. Sales duties, by their very nature, are nonrepetitive and hence not susceptible of measurement by the methods discussed in the preceding sections of this chapter. Yet measures of sales performance are needed, since most salesmen work away from the office and cannot be closely supervised.

Sales Volume Alone Inadequate Index. Since the salesman's objective is to make sales, it might be thought that dollar volume would serve as an adequate measure of performance. There are at least two basic limitations to the use of volume standards, even when they are related to territorial quotas. First, the goal of the wholesale enterprise is not just *sales* but *profitable sales*. It is often possible for a salesman to achieve a high dollar volume by concentrating on low-margin items that yield but little profit to the company. Second, and even more important, maximum immediate sales results are often incompatible with long-run success. "High pressure" methods may result in high volume for a short period, but customer good will may be lost and the long-run interests of the wholesale concern will suffer.

Most Relevant Measures. For these and other reasons, sales performance cannot readily be measured by any one statistic or index. Preferably, a *combination* of measures should be used to evaluate the effectiveness of salesmen and supplement the control achieved through reports, field visits, and the like. Among the more important measures of sales performance are the *average daily number of calls,* the *order-call ratio, average order size,* and *sales expense ratio*.

One measure of the amount of work done by each salesman is the *average number of calls* made daily. Of course, if salesmen operate under different conditions, as city and country salesmen do, or call on different types and classes of customers, as retail and industrial, it is necessary to set up separate classifications. When accurate summary records are maintained, showing the number of calls made by all salesmen of a given class, wide variations may be discovered between the performances of high, median, and low salesmen, when ranked on this basis.

Since salesmen cannot be expected to obtain orders at every call made, the *order-call ratio* is a measure of considerable importance in determining sales effectiveness. This is computed simply by dividing the number of orders by the number of calls made. If different types of customers are called upon, it is desirable to show variations in this ratio for each salesman by class of customer. It is usually found that the top salesmen are producing many more orders from the same number of calls than are the poorer salesmen. If this is true, the sales manager can find out what the better salesmen are doing to obtain favorable ratios and pass this information along to the rest of the sales force.

These two measures do not take into consideration variations in the *average size of the orders* sold by each salesman. If this information is not already available from a sales analysis (see Chapter 27), it may be provided for on the daily report form of the salesman, thus giving another indication of sales effectiveness.

Practically all wholesaling firms, whether or not they have a well-developed program of cost analysis, have a record of individual salesmen's salaries, commissions, and expenses. Expressing each *salesman's compensation and expenses as a percentage of the sales volume obtained* by him is another important measure. This shows the percentage of sales volume in each salesman's territory that was required for direct selling expenses, and it focuses attention on those areas where the greatest possible savings in direct expenses can be translated into additional profit.

These measures of performance all have one thing in common. They can be computed and kept up to date with very little effort or expense by the mere utilization of information that is made readily available in the normal course of operations in a wholesaling firm.

Application of Sales Performance Measures. Whether sales performance is evaluated by the results of sales analysis, time-and-duty study, or on any other basis that has been suggested, there is danger in carrying any one measure too far. Measures or standards are not ends in themselves, the objective or end being an increase in efficiency. Any one measure is important only as an indicator in that direction. Every sales executive must recognize that there are important variations between salesmen's territories, such as potential volume, travel time required, competitive strength, and psychological factors in selling not reducible to quantitative measurement. Factors of this kind account for part of the variation that may be observed by the use of standards for comparison. A large part of the total variation, however, is almost always caused by variations in the effectiveness with which sales effort is applied. Particularly when a variety of indicators is used, *the important weaknesses are spot-lighted for correction.* A ratio or a performance standard is never properly used as a club over salesmen or supervisors; objective yardsticks are effective for the control of sales activities only when used as tools to furnish meaningful information to individual employees in order to help them do a better job in their respective areas of operation.

MEASURES OF MANAGERIAL PERFORMANCE

The most complex and difficult of all functions in a business enterprise are those of management itself. Since management plans, organizes, and directs *all* the activities under its control, it is responsible for the over-all net results of these activities. These results can seldom, if ever, be expressed in any one unit of accomplishment. As a result, several different measures of managerial performance must be used and evaluated jointly. Among the more important measures for this purpose are *total operating expense, net profit,* and *market position.* Other measures that should be of some value, but are not yet widely used, are the *value added* by, and *total productivity* of, an enterprise.

Total Operating Expense. The importance of expense control as a means of enhancing net profits was explained in Chapters 27 and 29. Expense ratios for the various departments and divisions of a wholesale concern are used by management in evaluating the performance of the persons in charge of each organizational unit. Similarly, the performance of management can be measured in part by the *total* operating expense of the concern. Total expense ratios may be compared with past experience or with typical trade experience in a particular line of business. The most comprehensive source of information for this purpose is the periodic Census of Wholesale Trade conducted by the U. S. Bureau of the Census. Operating expense ratios for selected types of wholesalers are summarized in Table 29. Similar information is also published for manufacturers' sales branches, petroleum bulk plants, agents and brokers, and assemblers of farm products. These data are available by states and cities as well as on a national basis.

TABLE 29

OPERATING EXPENSES AS A PER CENT OF NET SALES, SPECIFIED
KINDS OF WHOLESALERS, 1954

Kind of Business	Operating Expense Ratio
Automotive Supply	24.7%
Drugs (General Line)	13.6
Dry Goods (General Line)	14.4
Electrical Supply	13.6
Furniture	21.1
Grocery (General Line)	8.2
Hardware (General Line)	17.6
Industrial Supply	20.0
Lumber, Millwork (With yards)	12.5
Plumbing and Heating	16.3
Tobacco Products	5.9

Source: *1954 Census of Business,* Vol. III, *Wholesale Trade—Summary Statistics,* (Washington, D. C.: Government Printing Office, 1957), Table 1A.

While total expense ratios are useful in evaluating the accomplishments of management, great care must be observed in interpreting such figures. The fact that total expenses for a particular firm exceed typical trade

TABLE 30

OPERATING EXPENSES AS A PER CENT OF NET SALES FOR SPECIFIED KINDS OF WHOLESALERS, BY SIZE OF ESTABLISHMENT, 1954

Kind of Business	Annual Sales Volume (In Thousands of Dollars)									
	$10,000 and over	$5,000– 9,999	$2,000– 4,999	$1,000– 1,999	$500– 999	$300– 499	$200– 299	$100– 199	$50– 99	Less than $50
Automotive Supply	—[b]	—[b]	17.1%	20.8%	24.9%	27.1%	27.7%	28.0%	28.4%	31.5%
Drugs (General Line)	15.0%	13.4%	13.4	13.6	13.5	19.1	22.6	–	–	–
Dry Goods (General Line)	14.3	15.6	14.3	14.4	12.7	–	–	–	–	–
Electrical Supply		10.2	17.2	16.1	19.3	22.4	25.8	28.6	32.6	37.7
Grocery (General Line)[a]	9.8	8.2	8.8	8.5	9.0	9.8	11.0	–	–	–
Hardware (General Line)	17.3	16.4	17.3	20.0	19.4	16.3	19.9	–	–	–
Paper (Coarse)	—[b]		14.8	15.8	17.7	17.7	19.8	20.2	21.5	28.1
Plumbing and Heating		14.6	15.4	15.8	16.8	17.3	19.7	20.7	23.1	32.0
Stationery, Office Supplies		18.9	21.7	25.1	28.5	27.9	28.1	27.3	28.1	29.5
Tobacco Products	5.5	4.8	5.2	5.6	7.2	7.3	8.1	7.9	13.0	22.7

[a] Exclusive of voluntary group wholesalers, retailer-owned cooperatives, and cash-and-carry wholesalers.

[b] Believed not to be comparable with other size classifications.

Source: *1954 Census of Business, Wholesale Trade,* Bulletin W–2–2, *Size of Establishment or Firm* (Washington, D. C.: Government Printing Office, 1957), Table 2A.

results is not necessarily an indication of inefficiency. Many factors may affect expenses, including the size of the community in which a concern is located, its scale of operation, functions performed, merchandise lines handled, and so on. The effects of one of these factors—scale of operation —is illustrated in Table 30. As shown there, operating expenses tend to vary inversely with sales volume up to a point, beyond which they increase with greater size. An individual firm's expense ratio should be compared, wherever possible, with others in the same size class, not with an over-all average such as those shown in Table 29. Even then, allowances must be made for other sources of variation mentioned previously.

The fact that total expense ratios are affected by so many variables, many of them beyond the control of management, seriously limits the value of such ratios as measures of performance. If no allowance is made for these variables, an unfair judgment may result. On the other hand, the existence of such influences and the difficulty of obtaining strictly comparable data make it possible to rationalize almost any deviation from expected or normal results. Consequently, total expense ratios serve as just *one* indication of managerial performance to be considered in the light of other measures discussed in the remainder of this chapter.

Net Profits. Since the objective of those who risk capital in a wholesale enterprise is profit, it is natural that managerial performance be evaluated largely by the net profits earned. Indeed, the emphasis on expense reduction noted at various points in this book derives largely from the rigidity of wholesale margins on the one hand and the desire to maximize profit on the other.

In one sense, only *dollar* profits are significant to the owners of an enterprise, since their interests focus on the dollar returns paid out in terms of dividends or withdrawals. The dollar amount of net profit is of little assistance, however, in evaluating managerial performance. Profits must be judged *relative to* some base if their adequacy or inadequacy is to be determined. The most commonly used bases to which profits are related are *sales, total assets,* and *net worth.*

Traditionally, profits are expressed as a percentage of sales just as are gross margins and operating expenses. Typical profit margins (after income taxes) as related to sales are given for selected types of wholesalers in the first column of Table 31. These percentages are quite low as compared with net profits in retailing, manufacturing, and other types of business activity. It must be remembered, however, that capital is usually turned over more quickly in wholesaling than in most other segments of the economy. Thus, a very low profit on sales may still represent a satisfactory return on investment.

The second and third columns of the table contain typical ratios of net profits to *total assets* and rates of *capital turnover,* respectively. The rela-

TABLE 31

Net Profits (After Taxes) as Percentages of Sales, Total Assets, and Net Worth for Specified Kinds of Wholesalers
(Typical Figures During the 1950's)

Kind of Business	Net Profit as Per Cent of Net Sales (1)	Ratio of Sales to Total Assets (2)	Net Profit as Per Cent of Total Assets (3)	Ratio of Sales to Net Worth (4)	Net Profit as Per Cent of Net Worth (5)
Automotive Supply	1.7%	2.5	4.3%	3.9	6.6%
Drugs	2.0	3.4	6.8	10.5	21.0
Dry Goods	1.1	2.3	2.5	3.6	4.0
Electrical Supply	1.3	3.4	4.4	6.5	8.5
Grocery (General Line)	0.4	5.6	2.2	10.1	4.0
Hardware	1.5	2.4	3.6	4.2	6.3
Industrial Supply	2.0	2.1	4.2	4.4	8.8
Plumbing and Heating	1.6	2.5	4.0	4.3	6.9
Tobacco Products	0.5	5.1	2.6	10.0	5.0
Wine, Liquor, and Beer	0.8	3.5	2.8	7.9	6.3

Sources: Based on typical figures reported by members of trade associations and by firms analyzed by credit reporting and similar agencies, such as Dun & Bradstreet, Inc., and Robert Morris Associates.

tionship of profit as a percentage of total assets to profit as a percentage of sales may be summarized in this manner:

$$\frac{\text{Net Profit}}{\text{Total Assets}} = \frac{\text{Net Profit}}{\text{Net Sales}} \times \text{Rate of Capital Turnover}$$

For instance, the ratio of net profit to net sales for automotive supply wholesalers is indicated in Table 31 to be 1.7 per cent. The rate of capital turnover (sales divided by total assets) is 2.5. The ratio of net profit to total assets is, therefore, 4.3 per cent (1.7 per cent times 2.5).

When profits are related to total assets rather than to sales, comparisons between different kinds of business are more meaningful. Profits are earned, after all, as a reward for investing capital in the form of assets. Thus, while profits are quite low in the grocery trade when compared with sales—only 0.4 per cent—they loom much larger in relation to total assets, although still relatively modest.

Finally, net profits may be related to net worth, which represents the investment of the *owners* in a wholesale enterprise. This may yield a picture quite different from profits related to total assets, since the opportunity to use borrowed capital and "trade on the equity" differs from one business to another. Typical ratios of net profits to net worth for selected types of wholesalers are shown in Columns 4 and 5 of Table 31. It will be noted that some lines of trade enjoy very high rates of return viewed in this sense, although their profits may be quite low in relation to sales or total assets. Thus, for example, drug wholesalers earned over 20 per cent on net worth, more than three times as high a rate as automotive supply wholesalers, even though their profits on sales were only slightly higher (2.0 per cent against 1.7).

Market Position. Another important measure of managerial performance is the *market position* enjoyed by the enterprise, especially in upward or downward trends in this position. "Market position" refers to the *share* of the total wholesale market obtained by a wholesale concern in its market area and in the lines of merchandise handled by it. If a concern sells tires and nothing else, its market position is the percentage of total wholesale tire sales made by it in its trading area.

Market position is a better measure of performance than sales volume per se because sales are affected by many factors, such as general business conditions, outside of management's direct control. A general expansion of the market may produce favorable results in terms of low expenses and high profits, but at the same time conceal major weaknesses in management. Conversely, even the best executives may show up poorly in times of general recession. The market position of the firm takes into account these external factors and focuses attention on the *relative* performance of the individual concern.

Accurate measures of market position are difficult to make because of problems in estimating total sales, overlapping of market territories, and the like. Nevertheless, such estimates are indispensable for sales-planning and other purposes as well as for appraising management. Methods of estimating total market potential, to which the sales of the individual firm may be related, have been discussed in Chapter 26.

Value Added and Over-all Productivity. The concepts of value added and productivity were treated in some detail in Chapter 14 in connection with a discussion of the economic contributions of the wholesaling system. These concepts also appear to be useful for measuring the performance of an individual firm and its management. Since they are relatively new and not widely understood, their use in practice is as yet very limited. It is believed, however, that value added is a valid measure of *over-all* output for a wholesale concern and that it can be related to various measures of resource input to ascertain the productivity with which resources are used. This approach would make possible more accurate performance measures for management, somewhat comparable with the narrower functional performance measures discussed earlier in this chapter as applied to workers engaged in repetitive jobs.

Conclusion. In analyzing American wholesaling, this book has attempted to place it in proper perspective both as an integral part of the marketing process and as affected by its economic, social, and legal context. Two major considerations have determined this approach: first, a desire to provide the basis for a better understanding of the true nature and substance of wholesaling in all its ramifications, and second, the need for a managerial viewpoint that would be helpful to the executives responsible for guiding the course of a wholesale enterprise.

At various points attention has been called to the many important changes taking place in the technology and management of wholesaling activities and in the operation of a wholesale business. Indeed, with the accelerating pace, even greater changes in wholesaling may be expected. To assure future progress, it is proper to point out and to urge the need for more scientific research in wholesale distribution. Only thus will the creation of economic values by the wholesaling process come to be more fully appreciated, and only in this way will the wholesaling institutions make their maximum contribution to the economic development and security of our nation.

Appendix

Selected Case Problems

L. & C. MAYERS CO., INC. *v*. FEDERAL TRADE COMMISSION*†

Nature of Catalogs. The evidence shows that the petitioner sent out catalogs in which many of the articles offered for sale were pictorially and descriptively represented. These were sent chiefly to industrial concerns, cooperative buying bureaus, state and local governments, and purchasing clubs. On the covers of such catalogs and at various places therein, the petitioner referred to itself as "Wholesale Jewelers." The articles were set forth in the catalogs at so-called list prices from which the purchasers were allowed a discount of 53 per cent in order to find out the cost to them of each item. The catalogs specifically stated that list prices are not to be confused with retail prices and that the former term is used in order to permit prices to be quoted on which only one discount has to be computed. The catalogs also stated that if one purchased goods at lower prices at any other wholesale jewelers, the difference would be refunded within 30 days.

The Purchasers. The stipulation of facts divides the purchasers from the petitioner into seven classes. The cease and desist order includes but three of these groups, which are as follows:

1. Sales to industrial concerns, public utilities, banks, and other similar organizations of articles not for resale but for use by such organizations where the sales are not in quantity lots.

2. Sales to industrial concerns, public utilities, banks, and other similar organizations buying merchandise not for resale but for the benefit of their employees, the merchandise being shipped by respondent directly to the employee for whom the merchandise is ultimately intended or to the organization purchasing the same, the organization paying the respondent therefor with its check and obtaining reimbursement from the employees, or the employees' money orders or personal checks being forwarded to the respondent by the organization making the purchase.

3. Sales to mutual buying clubs maintained by fraternities, colleges, or universities and to the employees of industrial public utility or similar organizations of articles purchased for the purpose of obtaining benefits in price and otherwise of such buying, where the merchandise purchased by such purchasers is not resold, but is applied to their own use or to the use of members of such organizations.

The order also sets forth a fourth group which prohibits sales not in quantity lots to individuals where the goods are not to be resold. Apparently this was intended to apply to a strictly retail type of business.

* United States Circuit Court of Appeals, Second Circuit. Decided June 6, 1938. (Complaint by the Commission was issued on May 18, 1932. Much of the wording of this case is from the official language used by the Commission and the Court.)
† See Chapter 2.

Findings of Federal Trade Commission. The gravamen of the complaint in this proceeding is unfair competition in selling at retail. The respondent has found that the petitioner represents itself to the purchasing public as selling at wholesale prices, that these prices are higher than the usual and customary prices charged by wholesalers of jewelry to purchasers thereof, and that this deceived the retail buying public and so unfairly diverted trade to the petitioners from competitors who truthfully described their status. If the petitioner was doing a purely wholesale business, as it contends, there could be no unfair competition with retailers since the purchasers would have the wholesale field from which to buy and would not need to pay petitioner's higher prices or buy at retail at all.

Nature of Wholesale Business. As a description of what constitutes a wholesaler, the Commission says:

"A wholesaler of jewelry is one who sells to the trade for resale and seldom, if ever, to the purchasing public, with the exception that sales to industrial concerns, public utilities, banks and other similar organizations, which purchase in quantity lots, i.e., simultaneous sales of more than one of a given item, not for resale, but for use by such organizations, are considered as wholesale transactions. It is the character of sales to the trade that makes and distinguishes a wholesaler."

There is testimony of experts which justifies this definition of a wholesaler. This court in *Great A. & P. Tea Co. v. Cream O'Wheat* (227 Fed. 46) and *Mennen Co. v. Federal Trade Commission* (288 Fed. 774) has ruled in like effect.

Theory of Case. The theory of the Commission's complaint is that the company sells to ultimate consumers; that in aid of such sales it uses catalogs designating itself as a wholesaler and that the purchasing public regards it as such— one selling to retailers at a price lower than the price at which the retailer sells; that consumers infer from this representation that they are buying at the prices at which retailers purchase, thereby saving an amount equal to the retailer's profit, and that the prices as fixed in the catalogs are wholesale prices; but that such is not the fact, and the consumer purchaser is thereby deceived.

Representations Constitute Unfair Competition. The groups to whom the petitioner is directed not to sell representing itself as a "wholesaler" are consumers. There is evidence to justify the finding that the prices at which the petitioner sold were higher than normal wholesale prices. We will not disapprove a finding based upon conflicting evidence. *Federal Trade Commission v. Winsted Hosiery Co.*, 258 U.S. 483; *Federal Trade Commission v. Standard Education Society*, 302 U.S. 112. Since the jewelry was sold to customers "not for resale," they are the ultimate purchasers. The evidence of experts as well as of other manufacturers and jewelers justifies the conclusion of the respondent that the petitioner was not a wholesaler. Such false and misleading representations which have a tendency and capacity to induce the purchase of petitioner's products in preference to the products of others (competitors) constitutes unfair competition within the meaning of Section 5 of the Federal Trade Commission Act (38 Stat. 719; 15 U.S.C.A. 45). *Federal Trade Commission v. Royal Mill-*

ing Co., 288 U.S. 212; *Brown Fence & Wire Co. v. Federal Trade Commission,* 64 F.2d 934, 936 (CCA–6).

Public Interest Involved. Petitioner contends that there is no public interest involved and therefore the order should not be approved. It is in the interest of the public to prevent the sale of commodities by the use of false and misleading statements and representations. *United States v. Winsted Hosiery Co.,* 258 U.S. 483, 494; *Federal Trade Commission v. Balme Co.,* 23 F.2d 615, 620 (CCA–2). Indeed, a representation may be unlawful under Section 5, although the trader makes it innocently. *Federal Trade Commission v. Algoma Lumber Co.,* 291 U.S. 67, 81. It is not necessary that the product so misrepresented be inferior or harmful to the public; it is sufficient that the sale of the product be other than as represented. *Federal Trade Commission v. Royal Milling Co.,* supra.

Enforcement of Federal Trade Commission Order. The order is affirmed and the order of enforcement is granted.

Problem. In the light of current authoritative knowledge concerning the concept of a wholesale transaction, was the discussion in this decision sound in every respect? If not, in what respects was it weak or unsound? Under what law was the action taken and decided? Most important, in the face of this decision, how can one explain the many practices of sellers in interstate commerce who through the mails advertise to ultimate consumers that they sell *at wholesale* and urge consumers to send for *the wholesale catalog?*

CUSTOMER CLASSIFICATION FOR PURPOSES
OF DIFFERENTIATED TREATMENT*

Following are some statements on the subject, as well as references to court decisions, with some of the reasoning used in arriving at them:

1. Cases concerning price discriminations involve primarily three types of discounts: quantity discounts (noncumulative discounts based upon the dollar amount bought at a single time, and usually delivered at a single place), cumulative or volume discounts (based upon the total dollar purchases over a period of time, often for delivery at a number of different places), and functional or trade discounts (discounts which depend upon the distributional status or classification of the customer, with the former applying to those operating on the wholesale level). None of these discounts can be considered valid or invalid, in itself. Validity may be dependent upon other factors, which vary from case to case.

2. Complaints charging that respondent companies in the sale of tile allowed discounts varying from 5 to 15 per cent to certain customers designated as wholesalers, which discounts were denied to other customers designated as contractors, were dismissed in the following cases:

> *United States Quarry Tile Co.,* F.T.C. Docket No. 2951.
> *Superior Ceramic Corp.,* F.T.C. Docket No. 3546.
> *Mosaic Tile Co.,* F.T.C. Docket No. 3548.
> *Pardee Matawan Tile Co.,* F.T.C. Docket No. 3549.
> *Wenczel Tile Co.,* F.T.C. Docket No. 3550.
> *Wheeling Tile Co.,* F.T.C. Docket No. 3551.
> *National Tile Co., Inc.,* F.T.C. Docket No. 3553.

3. The offering of sugar to distributors at lower prices and with price-renegotiation privileges is not a discrimination against a manufacturer who is denied the same privileges, nor is the distributor discriminated against because he cannot obtain delivery commitments for as long a period as can the manufacturer. Although the statute requires that there shall be no discrimination in favor of one purchaser against another, it is still obvious that the seller's discrimination cannot lessen competition unless the customers are indeed competing in the distribution of the product. Where two purchasers are in different levels of the distribution process, differences in price or sales terms offered them do not violate the law. *Chicago Sugar Co. v. American Sugar Refining Co.,* 176 F.2d 1 (CA–7, 1949); certiorari denied (U.S. Sup. Ct., February 6, 1950).

4. The practice of classifying customers according to function (wholesaling, retailing, and the like) and of granting a different discount to each class of customer was protected by a Senate amendment to the Price Discrimination Act which was eliminated in conference.

* See Chapter 4.

640

Comment by the Statement of Managers on the part of the House, Report No. 2951, June 8, 1936. fails to disclose whether trade discounts were intended to be abolished by the elimination of this amendment, as the statement merely reads: "The Senate amendment also contained a provision for classification of buyers, on which they receded."

Inasmuch as customer classification was held lawful prior to the amendment of Section 2 of the Clayton Act by the Price Discrimination Act, however, it seems that the practice may still be lawful under the amended section, as long as the discount is not unreasonably large.

Prior to amendment of Section 2 of the Clayton Act by the Price Discrimination Act, it was held that it was no violation of the section for a manufacturer to sell to wholesalers at one price and to retailers at a different price, even though they purchased in the same quantity. *Mennen Co. v. Federal Trade Commission,* 288 Fed. 774 (CCA–2, 1923); certiorari denied, 262 U.S. 759.

Classification of customers with varying discounts to jobbers, wholesalers, retailers, and consumers was ordered discontinued in *South Bend Bait Co.,* F.T.C. Docket No. 729, in 1922, as a violation of Section 2 of the Clayton Act. The Commission subsequently revoked its order and dismissed the complaint on the basis of the *Mennen* case, *supra.*

5. Four manufacturers of a commercial inoculant used for promoting the growth of leguminous plants were ordered to desist from selling the inoculant to dealer-jobbers at jobbing prices except as to that portion which was resold to dealers. The order required the manufacturers to charge the same price as dealers for that portion of the inoculant sold at retail.

Agricultural Laboratories, Inc., F.T.C. Docket No. 3263.
Hansen Inoculator Co., Inc., F.T.C. Docket No. 3264.
Albert L. and Lucile D. Whiting, trading as the Urbana Laboratories, F.T.C. Docket No. 3265.
The Nitragin Co., Inc., F.T.C. Docket No. 3266.

Problem. 1. Basically, what would be necessary to prove or establish the validity of each of the three types of discounts referred to in item 1 of the above statements and references?
2. What is the significance of the dismissals of cases in item 2 and how does that fit into the decision of item 3?
3. Why were the decisions in cases in item 5 different from those in items 2 and 3?

DURALIGHT AIR DUCTS

DEVELOPMENT OF A WHOLESALE MARKETING PLAN
FOR A NEW PRODUCT*

Avery B. Culver was employed as a cost estimator for a large contracting company. He was an imaginative and thoughtful worker and was always looking for improved methods of doing old jobs.

One problem in particular intrigued him. He had observed the rapid growth in air-conditioning installations. The traditional method made use of metal duct work to carry the cooled or conditioned air from the central plant to the various parts of the structure. This was an outgrowth of the use of metal pipes and ducts for heating systems. Two technical difficulties emerged with the growth of air-conditioning: changing temperatures frequently precipitated moisture within the ducts, which led to rust, and the metal ducts were noisy. To correct these defects, ducts had to be insulated both inside and outside. Various materials were used for this purpose, among them a new synthetic called fiberoid.

Fiberoid is a strong, tough insulating material with many excellent characteristics. Mr. Culver studied its use as an insulating material for metal ducts, for he was greatly conscious of the high cost of insulation. In his spare time he experimented, having in mind the possibility of making ducts out of fiberoid and eliminating the metalwork and the costly insulating job. The problem was how to construct strong and stable ducts from the wide sheets of varying thickness of which fiberoid is made. The sheets could be bent or folded into rectangular ducts rather easily, but how to lock the joining edges and render them air- and waterproof was difficult. One process had been tried with limited market success. It consisted of taping the edges and seams and had been used in residential building, but it was found not suitable for commercial and industrial installations because it lacked rigidity and the assurance that the taped seams would not open.

Mr. Culver hit upon a solution. He perfected a metal locking device which held the fiberoid edges firmly together and provided rigidity and structural strength for the ducts. The air- and water-sealing was accomplished by brushing on an inexpensive mastic compound. He proceeded to have searches made in the patent office and to make application for a patent. At the same time he had a supply of the locking devices made up to test the process further. The results of these tests were very satisfactory.

Mr. Culver next made some comparative cost estimates. The basic cost of metal duct work in his city was 68 cents per unit. Insulating with fiberoid added 99 cents to the cost, bringing the total to $1.67. In contrast, he found that the cost of making and installing his new fiberoid ducts was but 41 cents per unit.

Mr. Culver knew little or nothing about modern marketing methods and

* See Chapter 7.

642

was not sure how to proceed in distributing his new product. Consequently, he consulted a professional marketing economist, Dr. Thomas Black. Making a preliminary evaluation of the potential market, Dr. Black found that non-residential building in the United States was running at an annual rate of $10 billion. Metal duct work in this field, based on actual cost ratios obtained from architects and building cost estimators for nine structures then under contract, averaged 2.7 per cent of total costs. To be on the conservative side, he cut this figure down to 1.5 per cent and estimated the annual rate of air duct work in the United States to be around $150 million.

Dr. Black also obtained a copy of a 1957 report, based on a nationwide survey of commercial and industrial establishments, of the market outlook for commercial and industrial air-conditioning. This report was issued to customers as a marketing service by Du Pont. These and other data he collected and examined assured him that there was a very substantial and growing market for air ducts. He then began work on a marketing plan.

First of all he was concerned about competition. He knew that such a process at such costs would be speedily copied, as patent protection had its limitations. A patent provides protection, it is true, but only after legal action. As one attorney put it, "A patent is a license to sue." Lawsuits cost money.

Dr. Black explained to the inventor, Mr. Culver, that the best protection was to keep the patent pending, to pursue a continuous research program, and to introduce new ideas or improvements on the patent, thus keeping it alive but never getting an actual patent. A *patent pending* status would keep the details secret. But as soon as a patent is issued, it is published or is open to public inspection; it is thus easy for competition to copy it or infringe on it. In a situation like this, aggressive and effective sales promotion to gain and keep the lead in the market would be the best guaranty of success.

It was agreed to establish a corporation to market Mr. Culver's product. The name chosen for the product was Duralight air ducts, and the company was called Duralight Air Ducts, Inc. Two marketing plans were considered. The first was to operate the company as a contractor. The company would bid on contracts and actually install the air ducts itself. The advantage of this plan was that the company would be in complete control of its process and might better be able to meet competition and head off infringements or copying of its product.

Disadvantages of this plan were that it was very costly to organize a company large enough to handle contracts in all parts of the nation and that labor problems might be encountered—such as jurisdictional disputes over which union (metalworkers or carpenters) would have the rights to work on the new ducts. Building codes, which usually specified metal duct work, might also be an obstacle to sales. Since the inventor had but limited capital, he thought the plan impractical.

About this time two of Mr. Culver's friends who were contractors and who had seen the new process offered him $5,000 for the right to use it. When Dr. Black heard of this, he hit upon an alternative proposal for marketing the device. The second plan contemplated the granting of exclusive franchises to carefully selected contractors in different cities and states. After investigating the field of franchise-marketing, he worked out details for a program for air ducts. The plan involved the granting of exclusive franchises on the following basis:

Large city or city-county franchise $10,000
State or provinces, except California (to be treated as two states) $25,000
Foreign state $50,000

The franchises were to be for five years, subject to renewal by negotiation.

In addition to the franchise payment Duralight Air Ducts was to receive 50 per cent of the profits on each contract after recovery by the contractor of the franchise cost during the first year. A minimum annual return to Duralight of $25,000 was required on city franchises and $50,000 on state or foreign franchises. Contractors who wanted the franchise had to furnish information on their financial status and on their volume of business in air duct work over the previous five years. Only strong companies would be franchised. In order to have an independent check on the volume of business done, the contract required the contractor to purchase the patented locking device and the mastic sealing compound from Duralight.

Upon investigation Dr. Black had learned that the metal locking device could be procured in one of three ways: the company could set up its own factory and manufacture the product itself, it could have it manufactured by an American firm, or it could have the item made in Japan. Under the second or third alternatives Duralight would act as wholesaler of the product, even though the product was made to its own specifications. To manufacture the product itself would entail a modest investment in plant and equipment and would require the organization and training of staff. The advantage would be in the control of its product. The cost would probably be somewhat higher than under the second alternative. An American manufacturer said he could fit it into his operation and make the needed runs at times when his equipment might otherwise be idle. He quoted a price that would be hard to match in a new single-item operation. Preliminary investigation indicated that the locking device could be had from Japan at the lowest price even when freight and import duties were added.

In order to test the potentialities of the franchise plan, Dr. Black had the records of several contractors analyzed. He summarized his findings as follows: On a large commercial structure, such as a hotel or office building, the contract for duct work for air-conditioning might amount to $100,000. Under existing technology, costs would average $90,000, leaving $10,000 or 10 per cent net profit. Under the new Duralight Air Ducts process a contractor could underbid his competitors and get the contract, say, for $90,000. His cost would be $22,500 on this process, which would leave him a net profit of $67,500. A royalty payment of 50 per cent of net would cost the contractor $33,750, leaving $33,750 or 37.5 per cent of sales, nearly four times his net by the old method. And he would be providing a much better product. As competition encroached he would still have a considerable margin for underbidding before he got down to his original 10 per cent profit.

It was felt this would be a strong selling point for attracting franchised customers. The franchise plan had a further advantage in that it avoided the necessity of setting up an extensive organization with concurrent requirements for capital. Indeed, this plan could be financed without the sale of stock since several local contractors were eager to get the process.

Emphasis would be placed on the *process* rather than on the patented fittings. A suitable trade-mark, properly registered, would give additional protection.

Dr. Black did not overlook the fact that the Culver process, if successful, would create an extensive market for fiberoid. He held several conferences with regional and headquarters officials of the Fiberoid Corporation and found them quite willing to cooperate with Duralight Air Ducts.

As marketing problems were further studied, the advisability of getting a flow of income started by granting two city franchises at once was weighed. This would yield immediate income of $20,000, thus providing some working capital. Thereafter emphasis would be placed on state franchises. One problem with city franchises was the fact that contractors frequently bid on jobs over a rather wide area. Granting city franchises required a definition or delimitation of territory which might cause difficulty later. Some large contractors might even cover several states in their operations. Thus the state rather than the city seemed to be the best minimum territory, once the business got under way.

A detailed sales budget was worked out which indicated the objectives of the company for specific cities and states. It was contemplated that it might take three years to blanket the United States. It was recognized, however, that once a good staff was organized and a sound promotional campaign launched, the goal might be reached earlier. The first full year was scheduled to produce $1 million gross income made up of franchise payments of $425,000 and royalties from the sale of metal fittings and mastic of $575,000. It was estimated that this volume of income for Duralight would represent something less than $2.5 million annual volume for the franchised contractors. This seemed to be a modest figure to aim at since the total market for duct work had been estimated at $150 million per year.

In view of the superiority of the product and the great cost advantage over the older method, it seemed conservative to expect that the new process might gain 10 per cent of the market in three years. This would yield a gross annual income of between $5 and $6 million to Duralight.

Problem. What problems (in addition to those mentioned) might be expected? How would the Duralight company be classified in the field of wholesaling? Could you outline a different marketing plan?

ASSOCIATED DISTRIBUTORS, INC.*

PROMOTING THE USE OF WHOLESALERS IN DISTRIBUTION

Associated Distributors, Inc., is a buying organization which is owned cooperatively by a group of 16 independent wholesaling companies in the hardware trade. These companies are all located in different cities east of the Mississippi River. Collectively, they operate a total of 27 separate establishments, employ 460 salesmen, and make regular calls on about 12,000 hardware stores and other outlets handling hardware items. The various companies that own Associated differ considerably in sales volume size and radius of operation, but they are all operated in a similar manner and are known in the trade as "regular" or "full-service" wholesalers.

Associated maintains a buying and merchandising office in New York City and a smaller office in Chicago. Policies are established by a board of directors, each member of which is a major operating executive in one of the wholesaling companies. Operations of Associated are administered by an executive director who is a full-time salaried official located at the New York office.

The major functions of Associated are the following: to serve as headquarters for the buyers of the wholesale firms when they visit the market; to collect and disseminate marketing information relating to sources of supply, new products, demand trends, and so forth; to handle actual buying for wholesalers from small and scattered suppliers who have no regular sales contacts; to make group-buying arrangements when the requirements of the various wholesalers can be pooled to obtain better prices, more favorable terms, or other special concessions from suppliers; and to develop merchandising and special sales promotion programs which can be used by the member companies.

At a meeting of the board considerable discussion was given to the increasing proportion of families owning their own homes and living in suburban areas and to the effect of this trend on the wholesale and retail hardware business. Among other things, it was observed that this had resulted in a rapidly expanding retail market for lawn and garden supply items. Materials such as seed, fertilizer, and weed-killer preparations were greatly increasing in sales volume at retail stores. Wholesalers had not benefited much from this trend because of a common tendency for the major producers or packagers of such products to distribute direct to retailers.

The directors were of the opinion that wholesalers could distribute such products more effectively than the processors and could realize substantial sales volume and profit gains if a strong line could be obtained. One of the best-known lines was that of the Liberty Seed Company, and all of the directors were of the opinion that it would be the best line for wholesalers to handle.

The executive director was able to furnish the following information about Liberty: The company did a volume of business in the preceding year of about $10 million in lawn seeds, fertilizer, and related items. This was almost double

* See Chapter 8.

646

the sales volume of about five years previous. Liberty has a policy of selective, direct-to-retailer distribution. Its line is sold in about 5,000 retail stores throughout the United States, and this is believed to be about 15 per cent of the total number of outlets where a reasonably complete line of lawn seeds and related items is sold. The company employs about 20 salesmen who make infrequent calls on the dealers. Much field sales time is spent in selecting and opening new accounts and giving merchandising assistance to very large purchasers. Customers are contacted frequently by mail and usually order altogether by mail. The demand for the company's products is quite seasonal. Most retail sales are made in the periods March–May and September–October. There are several package sizes of a wide variety of specific items. It is difficult for retailers to anticipate demand for individual items, and reorders must be sent to the company for processing. During the peak season it is difficult for the company to keep up with reorders, and it often takes two weeks or more for a dealer to replace stock. This often results in out-of-stock conditions on best-selling items during the height of the selling season. The Company is the heaviest advertiser in the field, has a product line with high consumer acceptance, and offers its products at a modest premium over the prices charged for most nonadvertised brands. Retail prices are established by Liberty, and these are rigidly enforced by discontinuing selling to any known price-cutting dealers.

It was known that the president of Liberty did not have a very high regard for wholesalers. His educational background was in the field of agriculture, and he had been concerned with production problems until the time that he assumed the position of president four years ago. On various occasions, he had been quoted as favoring direct distribution, believing that more aggressive selling was possible by a firm's own representatives than by wholesalers' salesmen who have thousands of items to sell. Furthermore, it was known that Liberty was very pleased with its growth in recent years and that it would be difficult to influence a change in the company's distribution policy.

The directors were, nevertheless, quite impressed by the apparent opportunity for a large volume of profitable sales and decided that every effort should be made to obtain Liberty products for distribution by Associated wholesalers. Consequently, a special committee of board members was appointed to develop a presentation to be used in a conference to be arranged with the president of Liberty. At the first committee meeting it was decided that, in view of a likely unsympathetic initial reception, the presentation must be brief, dramatic, and convincing. It was agreed that it should be presented orally in not more than twenty minutes, so that there would be ample opportunity for questions and discussion. It was concluded, further, that the presentation should have educational emphasis upon the services that regular wholesalers render, but that this treatment should be specifically directed to the Company in question and not handled in a vague and general manner.

Problem. Using the facts given, develop a written presentation designed to accomplish the objective of convincing the president of Liberty Seed Company that its products should be marketed through members of Associated Distributors, Incorporated. Include any exhibits that you consider helpful in visualizing the points contained in the written material.

FEDERAL TRADE COMMISSION v. SYLVANIA ELECTRIC PRODUCTS, INC., and PHILCO CORP.*†

Excerpts from Complaint Issued December 21, 1949. The Federal Trade Commission having reason to believe that the party respondents named in the caption hereof, and hereinafter more particularly designated and described, since June 19, 1936, have violated and are now violating the provisions of Section 2 of the Clayton Act as amended by the Robinson-Patman Act approved June 19, 1936 (U.S.C. Title 15, Sec. 13), hereby issues its complaint against the said respondents stating its charges as follows:

Paragraph Three. Respondent Sylvania sells tubes to approximately 380 authorized distributors of said respondent's products, hereinafter referred to as "Sylvania distributors," located throughout the United States. Said respondent sells its tubes to Sylvania distributors for resale by said distributors to radio servicemen and retail dealers of radio parts and accessories for replacement purposes.

Respondent Sylvania also sells tubes to radio set manufacturers for use as original equipment in radio receiving sets or for resale for replacement purposes throughout the United States.

Respondent Philco is the largest manufacturer of radio receiving sets in the United States. Respondent Philco purchases its tubes from respondent Sylvania and other tube manufacturers and is the largest single purchaser of tubes from respondent Sylvania. Said tubes when purchased by respondent Philco are shipped and caused to be transported by said tube manufacturers, including respondent Sylvania, from the State or States in which the respective plants of said manufacturers are located, to respondent's place of business at Philadelphia, Pennsylvania or to the places of business of respondent Philco's customers located throughout the United States.

Respondent Philco purchases said tubes either for use as original equipment in radio receiving sets or for resale throughout the United States to its authorized distributors of Philco products, hereinafter referred to as "Philco distributors," for further resale by said Philco distributors to radio servicemen and retail dealers of radio parts and accessories, including franchised Philco dealers, for replacement purposes; or for resale through its wholly-owned subsidiary, Philco Distributors, Inc., to radio servicemen and retail dealers of radio parts and accessories for replacement purposes.

Paragraph Five. Respondent Sylvania, in the course and conduct of its business as hereinbefore set forth, has been since June 19, 1936, and now is, discriminating in price between different purchasers of tubes of like grade and quality by selling said products to some of its customers, including Sylvania distributors, at substantially higher prices than it sells such products of like grade

* F.T.C. Docket No. 5728.
† See Chapter 15.

and quality to respondent Philco. Many of said customers paying substantially higher prices are competitively engaged with respondent Philco, or customers of respondent Philco, in the sale or resale of tubes within the United States.

The aforesaid discriminations in price are effected by granting discounts, rebates and allowances to respondent Philco which have the net effect, either directly or indirectly, of reducing said respondent Philco's price to a substantially lower amount than respondent Sylvania charges others of its customers on tubes of like grade and quality. Said discriminations in price generally vary in amount as between the more than 400 types of tubes manufactured by respondent Sylvania. . . .

Respondent Philco is enabled by the aforesaid price discriminations to resell said tubes to its customers, Philco distributors, at substantially lower prices than respondent Sylvania sells its Sylvania distributor customers, on products of like grade and quality. Respondent Philco, through its wholly-owned subsidiary, is thereby enabled, and Philco distributors are enabled and encouraged by respondent Philco, to resell said tubes to radio servicemen and retail dealers at substantially lower prices than products of like grade and quality can be resold by Sylvania distributors or other distributors.

Paragraph Six. Respondent Philco Corporation, in the course and conduct of its business as hereinbefore set forth, since June 19, 1936, has knowingly induced and received and now is knowingly inducing and receiving the discriminations in price as herein described; and has knowingly induced and received and now is knowingly inducing and receiving discriminations from other tube manufacturers on such tubes as said manufacturers respectively have introduced for sale in commerce.

Paragraph Seven. The effect of such discriminations in price as set forth in *Paragraph Five* and *Paragraph Six* herein may be substantially to lessen competition or tend to create a monopoly in the respective lines of commerce in which respondent Sylvania, respondent Philco and customers of both said respondents are engaged, or to injure, destroy or prevent competition with respondent Sylvania, respondent Philco or with customers of respondent Philco.

Paragraph Eight. The foregoing alleged acts and practices of respondent Sylvania in granting the discriminations in price as set forth herein constitute violations of the provisions of subsection (a); and the foregoing alleged acts and practices of respondent Philco in knowingly inducing and receiving the price discriminations as set forth herein constitute violations of the provisions of subsection (f), respectively, of Section 2 of the Clayton Act as amended by the Robinson-Patman Act, approved June 19, 1936 (U.S.C. Title 15, Sec. 13).

Defense of the Case in General Outline. Sylvania's chief defense and the only one considered by the Commission was one of cost justification. For this purpose a thorough cost study was undertaken, under the direction of the controller, by the internal auditors of the company with the assistance of Lybrand, Ross Bros. and Montgomery—the company's independent public accountants.

This study, begun in late February, 1951, was completed by the middle of September, and it involved a total of approximately 3,000 man-hours of work. It was followed by a supplementary study of factory warehousing costs which involved another 400 man-hours of work. It revealed a weighted average price differential in favor of Philco of 15.86 cents per tube and a cost justification of 15.67 cents per tube. The difference that could not be justified by cost savings of 0.19 cents per tube or one-third of 1 per cent of Sylvania's selling price was claimed to be within the *de minimis* concept recognized by the Commission in the United States Rubber Company case, Docket No. 4972.

Philco's defense was mainly to the effect that as a "prudent" business concern it felt that the differential could be justified by the many functions and services that Sylvania eliminated in selling to it as compared to its sales to its own distributors. Furthermore, it was argued that Philco was not on the same plane as Sylvania's distributors but was operating on a different functional level and hence not in competition with Sylvania's distributors; that being the case, it would not be necessary to justify the price differential by cost savings.

Decision of Hearing Examiner Webster Ballinger (Released December 25, 1953). Charges against Philco Corporation of Philadelphia of "knowingly inducing and receiving" discriminatory prices from Sylvania were ordered dismissed by the examiner.

In granting Philco's motion to dismiss the complaint against it, the examiner said the evidence establishes that Philco "knowingly received discriminatory prices." But citing the Supreme Court's June 8, 1953, decision in the *Automatic Canteen Company* case,* he said:

"To constitute a violation of subsection (f) of the Clayton Act, as amended it must be affirmatively alleged and proven, not only that respondent Philco Corporation 'knowingly received' price differentials, but also knew when the purchases were made that the lower prices were not within one of the defenses available under the statute to respondent Sylvania Electric Products, Inc., particularly cost justification."

The examiner accordingly ruled that the allegations in the complaint and the proof were "insufficient" to constitute a violation under Section 2(f).

In issuing an initial order against Sylvania, the examiner held that it had violated Section 2(a) of the Clayton Act by selling replacement tubes to its own distributors at higher prices than it sold products of like grade and quality to Philco. The examiner found that the discrimination in favor of Philco ranged percentagewise from 9 per cent to 93.6 per cent, and dollarwise from 7 cents to 49½ cents per tube type.

The trial examiner, in his initial decision, found that Sylvania's practice of selling tubes to Philco at discriminatory prices "has resulted in injury to competition . . . and if permitted to continue may result in substantial injury." He accordingly ruled that the practice violates Section 2(a) of the Clayton Act unless the discriminations can be "cost justified." He disallowed, however, the cost justification defense offered by Sylvania, primarily on the ground that it involved the use of a "weighted average accounting method" based on actual sales to Sylvania distributors in 1948 and "hypothetical"† sales made to

* *Automatic Canteen of America v. Federal Trade Commission,* 73 S. Ct. 1017, rev'g 194 F.2d 433 (1952).

† In order to use the same product-mix in both cases for comparison purposes.

Philco during the same year. The Sylvania defense was that the weighted average price differential was justified by cost differences.

The examiner ruled, however, that the use of the weighted and hypothetical weighted average in sales prices "has not been established as a sound accounting method for the determination of sale price differences." He said: "The true sale price difference for each type of tube is that shown on the price lists."

The examiner also found that the difference in the cost of marketing tubes to Philco and to Sylvania distributors had been overstated. The Sylvania cost study showed that it cost 17.92 cents to market a tube to Sylvania distributors and 2.18 cents to market a tube to Philco, or a difference in favor of Philco of 15.74 cents. The examiner concluded, however, after disallowing the inclusion of certain items or the method of allocation used, that it cost 15.23 cents to market a tube to Sylvania distributors and 1.31 cents to market a tube to Philco, or a difference in favor of Philco of 13.92 cents.

The items in the marketing cost study which were disallowed by the examiner dealt with cash discounts, research expenses, royalties, sales service section, and sales management.

Order Dismissing the Complaint. Sylvania appealed the case to the Commission, which, on October 1, 1954, issued an order dismissing the complaint against Sylvania. The following statements were contained in this order written by Commissioner Caretta:

Respondent Sylvania in its appeal contends that the price differences shown by the record are not unlawful because of the presence of cost justification and because the evidence fails to establish the requisite competitive injury. Specific exceptions are taken to substantially all of the hearing examiner's findings and conclusions which are adverse to respondent Sylvania's contentions as well as to his order and to certain rulings excluding evidence offered by respondent Sylvania and admitting evidence offered by counsel supporting the complaint. Counsel supporting the complaint, although contending before the hearing examiner that the allegations of the complaint with respect to both respondents are sustained and that respondent Sylvania had failed to establish its defense of cost justification, now state that they will not argue the issues presented by respondent Sylvania's appeal because they have determined that they cannot ask the Commission to sustain the hearing examiner who concurred in their previous view that an order should issue covering those tube types which are not fully cost justified. They further state that the record is clear that the discriminations which are not fully cost justified are largely with respect to a limited number of tube types which are not sold in substantial volume.

We thus have the novel situation of counsel supporting the complaint asking the hearing examiner to find a violation of the law by both the respondents, getting half of what they asked for—a finding of a violation by one of the respondents—and now advising us that no violation which would warrant an order has been proven.

The facts of record show that respondent Sylvania sells replacement tubes to Sylvania distributors at prices higher than those charged respondent

Philco and that many Sylvania distributors paying the higher prices are competitively engaged with Philco Distributors, Inc., a wholly owned subsidiary of Philco, and other Philco distributors in the sale and resale of such tubes. There are approximately 600 types of tubes sold by Sylvania for replacement purposes. Each type is sold in different quantities. Many types are obsolete and are in limited demand. The price differentials between Sylvania distributors and respondent Philco vary as between the different types of tubes.

Respondent Sylvania has offered the defense of cost justification. In support of this defense a cost accounting study was presented. The record contains considerable testimony by experts concerning various aspects of this study. That the study was made in good faith and generally in accordance with sound accounting principles is clearly established. While there are certain items of distribution costs which counsel supporting the complaint originally contended were not proper to consider in computing costs, the basic question presented by the cost study is whether, under the circumstances of this case, it is proper to compare the aggregate price difference on the entire complement of tubes with the aggregate cost difference. In other words, is it proper to use a "weighted average" price in determining the amount of the differential to be cost justified, or should the price differential on each individual tube type be cost justified? Counsel supporting the complaint originally contended, and the hearing examiner held, that it was the price difference for each type of tube which must be cost justified. If a "weighted average" price is used, the price differential between Sylvania distributors and respondent Philco appear to be substantially cost justified. If the individual prices on the different types of tubes are used to determine the amounts of the price differentials, some of the price differences appear to be more than cost justified while others are not entirely cost justified.

There is no showing in this case that the lack of uniformity in the price spread has any competitive significance. There is no showing that the tubes which are in the greatest demand are the ones on which the price spread is greater. To the contrary, it appears that the types of tubes on which the price differentials are larger are in the least demand. Under all the circumstances of this case, we believe that it is proper to compare the aggregate price difference with the aggregate cost difference on the entire complement of tubes sold by respondent Sylvania. Such a comparison shows that respondent Sylvania's cost justification defense has been established. The complaint must, therefore, be dismissed as to both respondents in this proceeding. This determination makes it unnecessary for us to rule more specifically on each of the exceptions to the hearing examiner's initial decision made by respondent Sylvania in its appeal.

Concurring Opinion by Commission Chairman Edward F. Howrey (Released October 27, 1954). In his concurring opinion, the chairman stated, among other things, that insofar as the disputed items are concerned, "All of these items taken together do not add to much in dollars and cents. In fact the elimination of all of them" [as contended by counsel supporting the complaint] "would result in a lack of cost justification, on a weighted average basis, of only $0.0087 per tube. Without passing on the accounting issues involved in the challenged items, and accepting for the moment the correctness of the weighted average method, it seems to me that the amount of $0.0087 per tube is *de minimis*. No cost justification study presented in good faith should be rejected because of such a minor cost deficiency. . . ."

With regard to the use of the weighted average price, the chairman said: "While the use of the weighted average price for the whole line seems reasonable in this case, it might, of course, be quite different where demand was primarily for individual items and the volume of sales depended on price differences and other similar competitive factors. . . ."

He then concluded that "If the cost justification proviso is ever to be administered successfully, the Commission must, in my opinion, approach the problem with a desire to give full credence to the intent of Congress. This intent, as I interpret it, was to make a fair adjustment between the protection of small buyers and the welfare of the consumer—to preserve for the consumer the benefits of mass production and low cost distribution while prohibiting price favors to large buyers that were unrelated and not reasonably attributable to savings created by more economical methods of manufacture, sale or delivery."

"In the light of the foregoing, it seems entirely proper, under the facts and circumstances of this case, to compare the aggregate price difference on the entire complement of radio tubes with the aggregate cost difference. Any other holding would, it seems to me, nullify the proviso insofar as this respondent is concerned."

Problem. Analyze this case for the purpose of (1) determining the application of the Robinson-Patman Act in a specific instance and what is involved in such a procedure, (2) ascertaining the differences in approach under Section 2(a) applicable to the seller and Section 2(f) applicable to the buyer, and (3) indicating to what extent the determinations in this case may or may not be used as precedents for other cases.

STATE WHOLESALE GROCERS *ET AL. v.*
THE GREAT ATLANTIC AND PACIFIC
TEA COMPANY *ET AL.**†

State Wholesale Grocers and Zeigmund Wholesale Grocery Co., Inc., Illinois corporations, called plaintiff wholesalers, and a group of individual store retailers of grocery products and other related goods, called plaintiff retailers, all engaged in business in metropolitan Chicago, brought suit in the district court of the United States for treble damages and for injunctive relief under certain provisions of the Robinson-Patman Act. The action was taken against The Great Atlantic and Pacific Tea Company (called defendant), and certain manufacturers including General Foods Corporation, Morton Salt Company, and other suppliers of grocery products to the A & P stores (called defendant suppliers). In the district court judgment was entered in favor of the defendants, and the case was dismissed. Plaintiffs have appealed to the circuit court, which in major part reversed the decision of the lower court.

Much of the evidence as submitted to the circuit court was stipulated and there was no significant dispute as to the basic facts pertinent to the decision. In the appeal plaintiffs concentrated on their claims that the defendants violated Sections 2(d) and 2(e) of the Act and practically disregarded charged violations of Sections 2(a) and 2(f) which were also included in the district court action.

Some of the salient facts established by the record are briefly stated. *Woman's Day* is a magazine published since 1949 by Woman's Day, Inc., all capital stock of which is held by The Great Atlantic and Pacific Tea Company. It ranks in circulation and advertising among the leading national magazines (such as *Life, Saturday Evening Post,* and *Better Homes and Gardens*) and is of content and quality comparable with *Good Housekeeping, Woman's Home Companion,* and the like. The cost per single copy for printing, publishing, and distributing *Woman's Day* varied from approximately 17 to 21 cents in recent years; it has been selling for 7 cents since 1951 and, until this suit was filed, compared with 35 cents for the other comparable magazines mentioned in the findings of fact.

Woman's Day is and always was obtainable only at A & P stores (except in Colorado where it has no stores and where an independent distributor sells each month about 14,000 copies at a retail price of 15¢ per copy). It cannot be purchased by subscription or any place else. Since its inception it has been identified as the A & P magazine and has carried such identification on the cover since 1953.

Woman's Day is an effective medium for the advertisement of the A & P stores in general. It creates good will among the customers of A & P. It at-

* CCA–7, No. 12178, dated July 25, 1958; certiorari denied, January 26, 1959.
† See Chapter 15.

tracts new customers for A & P and keeps its old ones. It sells approximately 42 million copies a year. It is a promotional operation of A & P and exists solely for competitive benefit to A & P's retail stores.

The annual cost of producing *Woman's Day* exceeds $9 million. Less than 25 per cent of this cost is recovered through the sale of copies. The remainder is received from the sale of advertising space to suppliers and nonsuppliers. Supplier advertisers, which are manufacturers whose products are sold in A & P stores, accounted for about two-thirds of the advertising revenue of the magazine.

While plaintiffs argued that by advertising in *Woman's Day,* suppliers were discriminating in favor of A & P in violation of Secton 2(e) of the Robinson-Patman Act, emphasis was placed on the allegation that there was very definite violation of Section 2(d) of the Act, the relevant language of which is:

"It shall be unlawful for any person . . . to pay or contract for the payment of anything of value to or for the benefit of a customer of such person . . . for any services or facilities furnished by or through such customer in connection with the . . . sale . . . of any products . . . sold, . . . by such person, unless such payment or consideration is available on proportionally equal terms to all other customers competing in the distribution of such products. . . ."

In the district court's decision in favor of the defendants, there was reliance on the fact that "none of the plaintiffs offers for sale a store magazine as apparently no such magazine is available for their distribution"; hence, they "are unable and unequipped to furnish the services for which payment would be made and for which the defendant suppliers in this case pay *Woman's Day.*" Consequently, there could be no violation, under the circumstances, of Section 2(d) of the Act. In this reasoning, the majority of the circuit court disagreed, as indicated by the following statement in its opinion which reversed that of the lower court:

"In determining the proportionally equal terms upon which a seller shall make available any payment or consideration referred to in Section 2(d), the Act requires a frank recognition of the business limitations of each buyer. An offer to make a service available to one, the economic status of whose business renders him unable to accept the offer, is tantamount to no offer to him."

No rulings were made by the circuit court on certain other questions, including the issue of damages. As such issue was not separated in the district court and no objection was raised to such procedure by any of the parties, the matter was remanded to the district court for a ruling and determination.

It should be stated at this point that the circuit court decision does not involve the A & P directly, since it is believed that under Section 2(d) of the Robinson-Patman Act the violation of law can be charged only against the seller (in this case the defendant suppliers) for failure to make available the payment in question under proportionally equal terms. Indirectly, however, A & P would be affected, as suppliers would not be able to buy advertising space in *Woman's Day* under the injunctive relief which the decision gives the plaintiffs.

Problem. In the light of this decision, what action should be taken by A & P? Obviously, it has some alternatives. For one thing, it might make the magazine available by subscription and through other normal outlets like newsstands and drugstores, in addition to selling it through its own stores. That would raise many questions including, among others, one of price at which the magazine shall be sold, since its present price is too low for such distribution. Another possibility is to sell the magazine to an independent organization that will publish and distribute it like any other magazine. It might appeal strongly to such a possible buyer inasmuch as the A & P stores would dispose of large quantities of it through the established channel. This would supply the buyer with a minimum distribution. A third possibility is to appeal the case to the U. S. Supreme Court and argue, among other things, that the advertisers—suppliers as well as nonsuppliers—are getting their money's worth by advertising in the magazine, that the rates are comparable with those paid for advertising in similar publications, and that the fact that nonsuppliers advertise in it and pay the same rate is a good indication that they consider it worth the expenditure. (This was done; but, as indicated, certiorari was denied, and hence there was no opportunity to develop and present these arguments.) There may be some other possibilities. Which way shall be chosen?

LONE STAR AUTOMOTIVE SUPPLY COMPANY, INC.*

FINANCIAL PLANNING FOR EXPANSION

Lone Star Automotive Supply Company, Inc., is located in a rapidly growing metropolitan area in the southwestern United States. The company sells automobile parts and accessories, garage and service station equipment, and related lines to service stations, auto dealers, and garages. Last year was the fourth full year of operation and during this time Lone Star has become one of the three leading suppliers in its trading area.

Two young men, Frank Thompson and George McBlaine, own and operate Lone Star. Both had experience in the service station business prior to forming the enterprise. An original third owner was bought out during the third year of operation. As a result of this experience, the remaining owners are opposed to selling stock in their company and feel that if this were done, they would lose control of its management. With the exception of the cost of buying out the third owner, all earnings after taxes have been reinvested in the business.

Sales of Lone Star Automotive Supply Company have grown as a result of the increasing population of the trading area and of aggressive efforts by the owners. Figures for the first four years were as follows:

Year	Net Sales
19x1	$120,000
19x2	260,000
19x3	375,000
19x4	455,000

For the present year (19x5) sales of $560,000 are expected. It is anticipated that future growth will be at a greatly reduced rate unless the company substantially expands its territory or brings in new merchandise lines such as tires and tubes.

At the end of the first year the owners' net worth represented 46 per cent of total assets. This declined to 30 per cent at the end of 19x2 and declined further (after the withdrawal of the third owner) to 19 per cent at the end of 19x3. In 19x4 it increased slightly to 20 per cent, and reductions in bank loans and accounts payable are expected to increase the figure to around 22 per cent by the spring of 19x5.

Thus far, expansion has been financed primarily by funds supplied by trade creditors. Manufacturers of parts and accessories sell on terms of 2/10th prox., net 30 thereafter, and some of them have given extended terms up to 120 days to Lone Star. At the end of 19x4 trade creditors were supplying approximately 59 per cent of total capital and commercial banks 11 per cent. Bank loans have been employed to finance seasonal needs. The current ratio of the company has never been above 1.79 at the end of the year. Since inven-

* See Chapter 18.

tory makes up the bulk of current assets, the quick ratio has also been quite low. However, the owners feel that the true financial picture is somewhat better than indicated by the balance sheets because of their conservative asset valuation policies. For example, all inventory more than one year old is carried on the books at zero. In terms of original cost there is approximately $15,000 of such inventory.

Balance sheets for Lone Star Automotive Company for the past four years are included in Exhibit A. The "deferred accounts payable" are due between 60 and 120 days. The bank note is for 90 days. The bank overdraft consists of $2,000 in checks written to owners but not cashed and $1,740 in checks written to suppliers but not yet mailed.

Terms of sale to customers are 2/10th prox., net 20th prox. Between 70 and 80 per cent of the customers discount their bills, but some of the remainder present difficult collection problems. Any account more than 30 days overdue is put on a C.O.D. basis. About 10 per cent of the receivables at the end of 19x4 were more than 90 days overdue, and 40 per cent of these are regarded as uncollectible. The company deals with many small service stations and repair garages that are relatively unreliable.

The company opened one small branch in 19x3 and another in 19x4. Both of these establishments have been profitable, and it is hoped that two more small branches can be opened in 19x5. The sales forecast previously mentioned is based on the expectation that two new branches will contribute $60,000 in volume, the remainder of the increase to be obtained by the main establishment and the two existing branches. The proposed branches would require an additional investment of $4,000 in fixtures and equipment. Apart from this no increase in fixed assets is anticipated in 19x5.

Since Lone Star is incorporated, the owners have sought to obtain their compensation entirely through salaries and bonuses, net profits being reinvested in the business. In 19x3 the officers took in bonus $5,000, and in 19x4 this was increased to $7,000.

Exhibit B is an operating statement for the year 19x4. For comparison purposes selected industry ratios are given in Exhibit C.

Problem. Appraise the financial condition of Lone Star Automotive Supply Company, Inc., as of December 31, 19x4. How much capital will be needed for the proposed expansion in 19x5? How should this capital be obtained?

EXHIBIT A

LONE STAR AUTOMOTIVE SUPPLY COMPANY, INC.
Comparative Balance Sheets for Years Ending December 31, 19x1–19x4

	12/31/x1	12/31/x2	12/31/x3	12/31/x4
ASSETS:				
Cash on Hand and in Banks	$ 960	$ 485	$ 1,246	$ 1,128
Accounts Receivable (net)	20,205	29,173	34,172	41,070
Merchandise Inventory	44,100	85,330	125,975	162,322
Total Current Assets	$65,265	$114,988	$161,393	$204,520
Furniture and Fixtures	285	1,035	1,472	1,980
Equipment	1,240	1,670	2,880	3,760
Automobiles and Trucks	2,615	2,615	9,450	9,450
Total Fixed Assets	$ 4,140	$ 5,320	$ 13,802	$ 15,190
Less Reserve for Depreciation	625	1,060	2,340	2,875
Total Net Fixed Assets	$ 3,515	$ 4,260	$ 11,462	$ 12,315
Prepaid Items	310	792	811	1,264
TOTAL ASSETS	$69,090	$120,040	$173,666	$218,099
LIABILITIES AND NET WORTH:				
Bank Overdraft	–	–	$ 1,175	$ 3,740
Accounts Payable within 30 days	$26,662	$ 47,784	69,125	87,536
Deferred Accounts Payable	2,410	21,553	26,670	41,018
Note Payable—Bank	4,500	6,450	29,725	23,600
Accrued Payroll Taxes	870	2,576	3,495	4,623
Reserve for Income Taxes	–	2,417	2,766	4,550
Due to Officers	3,100	3,600	7,150	9,832
Total Current Liabilities	$37,542	$ 84,380	$140,106	$174,899
Capital and Stock	30,000	30,000	30,000	30,000
Surplus	1,548	5,660	3,560	13,200
Total Net Worth	$31,548	$ 35,660	$ 33,560	$ 43,200
TOTAL LIABILITIES AND NET WORTH	$69,090	$120,040	$173,666	$218,099

EXHIBIT B

LONE STAR AUTOMOTIVE SUPPLY COMPANY, INC.

Condensed Operating Statement for the Year Ended December 31, 19x4

		Amount	Per Cent of Net Sales
Net Sales		$455,000	100.0%
Cost of Sales (net of discounts)		336,440	73.9
Gross Margin		$118,560	26.1
Operating Expenses:			
Administrative	$35,775		
Selling	33,400		
Delivery, Shipping	9,730		
Warehouse	6,280		
Occupancy	10,830		
Other	5,915		
Total Operating Expenses		101,930	22.4
Net Operating Income		$ 16,630	3.7
Federal Income Taxes		4,990	1.1
Net Income After Taxes		$ 11,640	2.6

EXHIBIT C

LONE STAR AUTOMOTIVE SUPPLY COMPANY, INC.

Selected Industry Financial Ratios for Wholesalers of Automotive
Parts and Supplies

(Median Ratios)

Ratio	Industry Median
Current Assets to Current Debt	3.37×
Net Profit (after taxes) on Net Sales	2.0%
Net Profit (after taxes) on Tangible Net Worth	6.7%
Net Sales to Tangible Net Worth	3.56×
Net Sales to Net Working Capitala	4.73×
Net Sales to Receivables	9.4×
Net Sales to Inventory	5.1×
Current Debt to Tangible Net Worth	38.2%
Total Debt to Tangible Net Worth	58.2%
Inventory to Net Working Capital	87.9%
Current Debt to Inventory	61.7%
Gross Profit on Net Sales	27.1%

a Net Working Capital equals the excess of Current Assets over Current Liabilities.

Sources: Based on typical figures reported by credit agencies and by trade associations in the late 1950's.

MOSER WHOLESALE GROCERY COMPANY

BASES FOR DEPARTMENTIZATION*

The Moser Wholesale Grocery Company is a general line independent wholesale concern located in a city of about one million population. The company sells a full line of groceries to independent retail food stores, restaurants, bakeries, and institutional buyers, but does not handle fresh meats or produce. Total sales volume is in the neighborhood of $45 million.

Buying and merchandising activities are organized into 28 departments, as shown in the accompanying exhibit. The buyers are responsible for maintaining contact with sources of supply, ordering routine, pricing, maintaining proper inventory levels, and (in the case of private brand goods) negotiating prices and product specifications.

EXHIBIT A

MOSER WHOLESALE GROCERY COMPANY
Merchandise Departments, Commodity Lines, and Gross Margins

Dept. No.	Commodity Lines	Average Gross Margin (Per Cent of Sales)	Buyer
1	SUGAR	2.95	Glassman
2	COFFEE and Coffee Substitutes	9.52	Wells
3	TEA	11.56	Wells
4	EXTRACTS, Spices, Herbs, Seeds, Pet Supplies, Private Label Proprietaries	20.75	Mathews
5	CANNED FRUITS AND VEGETABLES, Canned Fish (except sardines), LaChoy and other Oriental Products	7.41	Davis
6	CANNED MEATS and Sardines	11.40	Graham
7	PRIVATE BRAND CANNED FOODS, Soups, Sauerkraut, Beans, Spaghetti	12.25	Mathews
8	CANNED MILK	9.66	Graham
9	CANDIES, Confections, Gum	11.78	Boggs
10	DRIED FRUITS, Fruit Peels, Nuts	15.28	Davis
11	FARINACEOUS GOODS (Manufacturers' Brands), Flour, Corn, Laundry Starch	5.12	Poster
12	FARINACEOUS GOODS (Private Brands)	8.71	Mathews
13	CONDIMENTS (Manufacturers' Brands), Pickles, Sauces, Relishes, Salad Dressings, Vinegar	10.15	Mathews
14	CONDIMENTS (Private Brands), Bulk Kraut, Salad Oil, Olive Oil, Olives	14.36	Mathews
15	SYRUPS, Molasses, Blended Syrups, Glucose	10.85	Poster

* See Chapter 19.

EXHIBIT A—*Continued*

Dept. No.	Commodity Lines	Average Gross Margin (Per Cent of Sales)	Buyer
16	PRESERVES, Jellies, Jams, Spreads, Maple Syrup, Honey, Mincemeat, Peanut Butter, Apple Butter	9.22	Mathews
17	BULK FISH, Salt, Cheese, Smoked Meats, Lard and Lard Substitutes, Cooking Oils	8.06	Botci
18	BAKING POWDER, Soda, Cocoa, Certo, Chocolate, Crackers, Gelatin, Cream Whip, Mushrooms, Potato Chips, Yeast, Coconut, Pie Fillings	8.23	Wells
19	BEVERAGES, Fountain Supplies (Manufacturers' Brands), Fountain Fruits, Maraschino Cherries, Malt, Malted Milk, Ovaltine, Sauces, Mineral Waters, etc.	12.53	Graham
20	BEVERAGES, same as Dept. 19 but Private Brands	15.75	Mathews
21	CIGARS, Smokers' Sundries, Pipes, Lighters, Cigarette Holders	7.15	Graham
22	CIGARETTES, Tobacco, Snuff	3.51	Graham
23	PAPER AND PAPER PRODUCTS, Bags, Wrapping Paper, Paper Cups and Dishes, Waxed Paper, Towels, Toilet Tissue, Aluminum Foil	19.21	Wells
24	SOAPS AND CLEANSERS, Ammonia, Laundry Soaps and Detergents, Toilet Soap, Bluing, Borax, Lye, Sal Soda, Bleaches	5.99	Wells
25	BAKERS' SUPPLIES, Soda Fountains, Ice Cream Machinery and Supplies, Bulk Powdered Milk, Condensed Milk, Glacé Fruits, Candy, Wrapping Paper for Bakers	14.42	Botci
26	STORE FIXTURES, Electrical and Auto Supplies, Restaurant Equipment	16.50	Botci
27	NOTIONS, Stationery, Toys	12.73	Joyce
28	MISCELLANEOUS NONEDIBLES, Drugs, Fruit Jars, Lanterns, Tubs, Pails, Brushes, Brooms, Baskets, Matches, Tacks, Cordage, Corks, Scoops, Wooden Dishes, Lubricating Oils, Candles, Polishes, Mops, Cleansing Pads, etc.	20.15	Joyce

Problem. Identify and illustrate each of the bases that must have been used in departmentizing this concern. Why do some buyers handle several departments that involve nonrelated merchandise lines?

PLANNING PURCHASES

USE OF A MERCHANDISE BUDGET*

Buyers in the Mitchell Wholesale Company are required to plan their purchases in advance on a monthly basis for each of two six-month merchandising periods. Merchandise budgets are prepared 30 to 60 days in advance of the beginning of each period and submitted to the firm's general manager. On November 1, the buyer in Department A has the following information available:

1. Planned sales for the period January–June, $200,000
2. Typical distribution of sales by months:

January	. . . . . 20%	April	. . . . . . 16%
February	 20	May	 14
March	 16	June	 14

3. Desired inventory on December 31, $85,000; on June 30, $60,000
4. Goal gross margin, 20 per cent of sales; operating expenses, 16 per cent; net profit, 4 per cent
5. Desired rate of inventory turnover, 4 times per year

The buyer also knows, on the basis of prior experience, that there is an average time lag of about one month between placement of an order and receipt of goods.

Problem. Prepare a merchandise budget for the six-month period January–June, showing planned beginning inventory, deliveries during the month, and purchases during the month. What assumption was it necessary to make? Was it a realistic assumption? Of what use is such a merchandise budget to management?

* See Chapter 20.

WAREHOUSE DISTRIBUTORS, INC. *ET AL.**†

On July 10, 1957, the Federal Trade Commission issued a complaint against Warehouse Distributors, Inc., its 28 jobber members dealing in automotive parts and supplies, and some of the officers of these companies, as well as the manager of the organization that was formed and was operating as a buying group for its members. The respondents were charged with knowingly inducing and receiving favored prices in violation of Section 2(f) of the Robinson-Patman Amendment to the Clayton Act.

More specifically, the complaint charged that the members used their combined buying power, through Warehouse Distributors, Inc., to demand and obtain certain price advantages. One of them was to get suppliers, who were selling on a quantity discount schedule, to base their discounts on the combined purchases of all members of the group at the same time that competing wholesalers were allowed discounts only on the basis of their individual purchases. Another was to secure trade discounts from suppliers who did not give them to competing wholesalers. Suppliers who did not grant such discriminatory terms were replaced by others that did make the concessions.

It was the contention of the Commission that the buying group was not a bona fide purchaser of the goods from suppliers but only a device through which the members were billed and paid for the purchases. It was a "mere bookkeeping device for facilitating" price discriminations, the effect of which may be substantially to destroy or prevent competition between suppliers on the one hand and between respondent wholesalers and nonfavored competing jobbers on the other.

Accordingly, an initial decision was handed down by the Hearing Examiner, which was later agreed to by all of the respondents. This resulted in what is known as a "Consent Order to Cease and Desist," released on August 28, 1958. It ordered all respondents to stop inducing and accepting illegal price discriminations from suppliers of automotive products. It forbade them to induce or accept a net price (arrived at after deducting all discounts, rebates, and allowances and taking into account all other selling conditions affecting net price) known by them to be lower than that which the supplier charges other customers, where (1) the seller competes with other suppliers for the respondents' business and (2) the respondents compete with other customers of the supplier or seller.

The Consent Order included the following statement: "The agreement is for settlement purposes only and does not constitute an admission by the respondents that they have violated the law."

Problem. In the first place, was the Federal Trade Commission justified in issuing the complaint on the grounds stated, from both an economic and

* Consent Order to Cease and Desist, F.T.C. Docket No. 6837.
† See Chapter 21.

a legal point of view? In a word, could the buying group possibly justify its position? Second, since a Consent Order has the same effect and force as a regular order to cease and desist and at the same time contains a waiver by the respondents of any right to challenge or contest the validity of the order entered in accordance with the agreement, what is gained by consenting insofar as the respondents are concerned? Third, in view of the above, what is the significance of the statement quoted about not being an admission of a violation of law?

BARISH BROTHERS TOBACCO COMPANY, INC.*

COST-PLUS PRICING

Barish Brothers Tobacco Company sells a line of cigarettes, cigars, candy, and sundries to grocery stores, confectioneries, delicatessens, and proprietary stores. Total sales in the preceding year amounted to $3.5 million. Net earnings after taxes were 0.8 per cent of sales; the gross margin was 7.53 per cent.

In past years, a substantial portion of the company's sales has been made to grocery stores. Since 1946, however, the relative importance of this class of customer has declined steadily. Executives of Barish Brothers attribute this to the growth of corporate chains, voluntary chains, and retailer-cooperative groups at the expense of traditional independent grocers. Most of the grocery wholesalers sponsoring voluntaries and the retailer-cooperatives handle tobacco products and nonfood sundries for their member stores. Barish Brothers have found it difficult to compete with these organizations on a price basis and consequently many established customers have been lost.

The traditional method of pricing in the company has been to add a predetermined markup to the average landed cost of the goods. The markup varied by product line, in the case of cigarettes being about 3 per cent of cost, while for such items as cigarette lighters it was more nearly 20 per cent of cost. The voluntary and cooperative groups, on the other hand, use the cost-plus method of pricing. Under this system a customer is billed at the wholesale cost plus a uniform percentage, which is usually between 3 and 5 per cent. This charge does not include the costs of cooperative advertising programs and other merchandising assistance, which is covered by specific service charges.

Joseph Barish, one of the owners of the company, believes that they should adopt some version of the cost-plus pricing system in order to compete more effectively with the voluntary and cooperative groups and with the regular independent grocery wholesalers who have in many cases copied the system. He proposes that cost-plus pricing be tried for selected customers, generally the largest ones, and that the "plus percentage" be set between 2 and 5 per cent, depending on the size of the order. On sales to smaller outlets the traditional method would be retained, and on sundry items sold under resale price maintenance contracts no such method would be possible. In order to offset the reduction in gross margin caused by adopting this method, he proposes to use a preprinted order form like those employed in grocery chains and cooperative groups. Use of such an order form would also require a rearrangement of the warehouse stocks and a general streamlining of operations. Unless this is done, he argues, more and more business will be lost to competing sellers.

Problem. Is cost-plus pricing feasible for the company? Would adoption of the proposed changes make the company more competitive?

* See Chapter 22.

BROWN WHOLESALE DRUG COMPANY

WAREHOUSING METHODS*

The Brown Wholesale Drug Company was founded in 1912 by two brothers, Albert and George Brown. Control of the firm now is held by the two sons of Albert, Thomas and Albert, Jr., and by the husband of George Brown's daughter, James Davidson. The company has experienced a steady growth and last year had sales of over $6 million. A total of 124 persons are employed by the firm, not counting the 3 members of top management.

Although the Brown Company is profitable, the executives believe it should obtain higher returns than it does. In an attempt to locate possible sources of increased efficiency, a comparison of the firm's operating expenses with those of other drug wholesalers in a similar size group was made. The figures for last year were as follows:

Sales and Expense Items	Brown Company	Typical Figures
Sales	100.00%	100.00%
Gross Margin	17.28	17.21
Operating Expenses:		
Administrative	5.11	5.14
Occupancy	0.54	0.51
Selling	3.51	3.45
Delivery and Trucking	1.44	1.35
Warehouse	3.38	2.72
Total	13.98%	13.17%
NET OPERATING PROFIT	3.30%	4.04%

On the basis of this comparison, it was decided that primary attention should be given to improvements in warehouse operations. No systematic study of warehousing had ever been made in the firm's history. As more space was required, buildings adjoining the company's original warehouse were bought or leased and remodeled to fit its needs.

James Davidson was assigned the task of studying the company's warehousing methods and reporting his findings to the other executives. His first step was to prepare rough drawings of the layout of the warehouse, two of which are reproduced in Exhibit A. The first drawing shows the ground floor, on which receiving and shipping operations are carried on and the offices are located. The other drawing is of the second-floor storage and order assembly areas. The third and fourth floors are similar to the second floor.

The second major step taken by Davidson was to trace the sequence of operations through which a typical item passes from the time it is received until it is shipped. These operations were summarized as follows:

1. Goods are received by truck in receiving area and unloaded to platform.
2. Goods are moved to inspection area and inspected for damage.

* See Chapters 23 and 24.

667

EXHIBIT A

BROWN WHOLESALE DRUG COMPANY

Layout of First and Second Floors of Warehouse

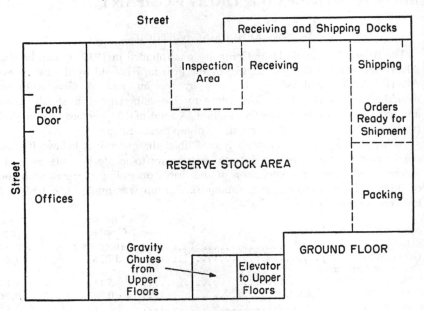

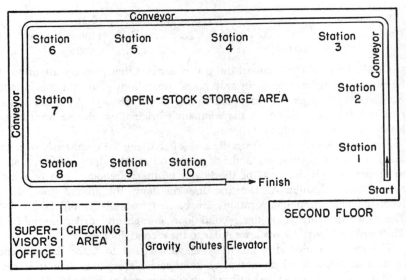

3. Goods are moved to reserve stock area on first floor.
4. Goods are requisitioned by warehousemen from reserve stocks and moved to open shelf areas as needed.
5. Orders are assembled. Storage areas are laid out as shown in Exhibit A with a moving belt conveyor passing around each floor. Warehousemen are assigned to "stations" as shown on exhibit, each man specializing in goods of a single department or, at most, two or three departments. Each order is assembled in a tray or basket, which passes from station to station. At each station the basket is removed from the conveyor, goods are selected from shelves and put into the basket, and it is replaced on the conveyor to pass on to next station.
6. Orders are checked at checking station on each floor and any mistakes corrected.
7. Completed orders are moved to packing area, packed, and sent on to shipping area for loading on outbound trucks.

In observing the activities of warehouse employees for several days, Davidson reached several conclusions with regard to the main problems that were being encountered. First, there seemed to be a great deal of congestion in the receiving and shipping areas. At times incoming shipments almost completely filled the docks and outbound orders could be put on trucks only with great difficulty and loss of time. Second, there seemed to be too many delays on the assembly lines. Pickers at some stations would be idle while others had backlogs of order baskets waiting for their attention. As a result, morale was low in the warehouse and employee turnover high. Newer employees held up more experienced workers, since it takes about three months for a trainee to learn the merchandise designations and locations within his station. A third problem seemed to be poor supervision of the order-pickers. The floor supervisors, all experienced order-pickers themselves, are well regarded by the warehouse superintendent. All of them complain, however, of not being able to cover their areas. Much of their time is devoted to answering questions regarding the location of items or the meaning of abbreviations used by salesmen in writing up orders.

James Davidson reported his findings to the Brown brothers, and a meeting was held to discuss possible improvements in warehousing methods.

Problem. What changes would you suggest in the warehousing practices of Brown Wholesale Drug Company? Give attention to possible improvements in layout, equipment, procedures, and supervision.

SECURITY DRUG COMPANY

SALESMEN'S COMPENSATION SYSTEM*

The Security Drug Company sells a full line of pharmaceuticals, proprietaries, and sundry items to retail drugstores and to such institutions as hospitals and clinics. Total sales volume last year was over $8 million. The firm employs 25 outside salesmen and several telephone and counter salespersons.

The sales manager of the company is dissatisfied with the present system of compensating salesmen. The outside salesmen are paid on the basis of a group commission plan, with the commission on each line depending on the firm's gross margin on that line. A drawing account supplements the commissions. Inside salesmen receive a salary, plus a small commission on sales. The sales manager feels that the system is inadequate because:

1. With commissions based upon gross margins, there is at best but an indirect relationship between the commission paid and the profitability of a line to the company. The handling expenses on various lines differ considerably on account of differences in bulk and turnover; the average line extension for some lines is substantially higher than for other lines; and discounts are given to retailers in various amounts. (These discounts, improperly called "cash discounts," are in reality promotional discounts given to induce the handling of a particular line, and in some cases amount to 5 or 6 per cent of Security's selling price.)

2. The salesmen have the feeling that they are in business for themselves and resist attempts by management to control their activities. As a result most salesmen neglect nonselling duties such as setting up displays, which are regarded as very important by management. Moreover, new lines are often neglected because it is easier for the salesman to push an accepted product than an unknown one.

The sales manager wishes to devise a compensation system that will overcome these difficulties and facilitate the accomplishment of the company's sales objectives. In addition to maximizing dollar volume, these objectives include building the lasting good will of the retailers, assisting retailers in their selling activities, and concentrating on lines that are most profitable to Security.

Problem. In the light of the specific facts of this case and of the general purposes of a sales compensation system outlined in Chapter 26, what kind of system should be adopted by Security Drug Company? (Outline the suggested system in detail, indicating each component as to nature, purpose, and application.)

* See Chapter 26.

FRANKLIN PAPER COMPANY

ANALYSIS OF EXPENSES BY SIZE OF ORDER*

The Franklin Paper Company is a so-called "dual house," handling both fine and coarse paper items. Fine paper lines consist of printing papers, bond stationery, and the like; coarse paper lines include bags, wrapping paper, cups, plates, cellophane, and sundries such as twine, candles, and soap. Fine papers are sold primarily to printers and publishers, while the other lines are sold to industrial users, retail grocery stores, stationery and office supply stores, restaurants, laundries, dry cleaners, and department stores.

Executives of the company have for some time recognized the existence of a small-order problem. While printers and publishers generally buy in substantial quantities, retailers, industrial users, and service establishments often order in small quantities. Salesmen contact these latter customers weekly and fill-in orders are placed by telephone between salesmen's visits. With a few exceptions all orders are delivered by the company's own trucks within the large metropolitan area and surrounding territory served by it.

To arrive at a solution to the problem of small orders, it was decided to make an analysis of operating expenses as related to order size. The first step in this study was to classify all expenses on a functional basis, as shown in Exhibit A. Each expense item is expressed as a per cent of net sales for the preceding year. Salesmen are compensated on a straight commission basis of 6 per cent, but total sales compensation is less than 6 per cent of total net sales because some customers (such as governmental agencies) are handled as "house accounts."

The company's net operating profit (not shown on Exhibit A) was 3.41 per cent of net sales last year.

The next step in the analysis of expenses was to determine how the various classes of expense are related to size of order, if at all. After a careful study of the problem, it was decided to classify all expenses into three groups:

1. *Those affected primarily by the number of orders handled*, including accounts receivable (B–7), sales statistics (B–9), and shipping (D–3). Some categories of expense were found to depend both on the number of orders and on the dollar value of sales; thus city delivery (E–1), country delivery (E–2), and credits and collections (B–8) were divided in half; half of each item was treated as being affected by the number of orders, half as being affected by sales volume.

2. *Those affected primarily by the number of invoice lines processed*, including sales travel expense (A–2), general sales salaries and administration (A–3), telephone order desk (B–3), order-processing (B–4), stock control (B–5), billing (B–6), warehouse supervision (D–4), full-case and broken-case order-picking and checking (D–5 and D–7), unpacking and shelving broken-case goods (D–6), and broken package order-packing (D–8).

3. *Those not directly affected by the number of orders or by the number of*

* See Chapters 27 and 29.

671

EXHIBIT A

FRANKLIN PAPER COMPANY

Functional Categories of Operating Expense as Percentages of
Net Sales, Last Year

Expense Category	Per Cent of Net Sales
A. SELLING EXPENSES	6.83%
A–1 Compensation of Outside Salesmen 5.16%	
A–2 Sales Travel Expense 0.08	
A–3 General Selling and Selling Administration 0.65	
A–4 Advertising and Sales Promotion 0.87	
A–5 Catalogs 0.07	
B. OFFICE FUNCTIONS	5.06
B–1 Purchasing 1.45	
B–2 Accounts Payable 0.18	
B–3 Telephone Order Desk 0.81	
B–4 Order-Transcribing, Pricing, Extending 0.92	
B–5 Stock Control 0.45	
B–6 Billing 0.13	
B–7 Accounts Receivable 0.17	
B–8 Credits and Collections 0.21	
B–9 Sales Statistics 0.05	
B–10 General Office and Accounting 0.69	
C. GENERAL ADMINISTRATIVE EXPENSE	2.41
D. WAREHOUSING EXPENSES	3.00
D–1 Receiving and Checking Incoming Shipments 0.14	
D–2 Storage 1.10	
D–3 Shipping 0.20	
D–4 Warehouse General and Supervisory 0.49	
D–5 Full Case Order-Picking and Checking 0.48	
D–6 Unpacking and Shelving Broken-Case Merchandise .. 0.14	
D–7 Broken-Case Order-Picking and Checking 0.24	
D–8 Broken Package Order-Packing 0.21	
E. DELIVERY EXPENSES	1.51
E–1 City Delivery 1.09	
E–2 Country Delivery 0.42	
F. INVENTORY CARRYING EXPENSE	1.21
TOTAL OPERATING EXPENSE	20.02%

EXHIBIT B

FRANKLIN PAPER COMPANY

Operating Expenses for Orders of Various Sizes with Different
Numbers of Invoice Lines

(Expenses as Per Cent of Dollar Value of Order)

Number of Lines on Order	Total Dollar Value of Order						
	$5.00	$10.00	$25.00	$50.00	$100.00	$200.00	$500.00
1	52.6%	33.8%	22.5%	18.7%	16.8%	15.9%	15.3%
2	73.2	43.1	26.2	20.6	17.8	16.4	15.5
3	89.8	52.4	29.9	22.4	18.7	16.8	15.7
4	–	61.7	33.6	24.3	19.6	17.3	15.9
5	–	71.0	37.4	26.2	20.6	17.8	16.1
10	–	–	56.0	35.5	25.2	20.1	17.0
20	–	–	93.2	54.1	34.5	24.8	18.9

EXPLANATION: Total expense for an order of a given size and with a given number of invoice lines equals $0.95 (constant cost per order) + $0.93 × number of lines + 14.98 per cent of dollar value. For instance, for a $10.00 order containing 2 invoice lines, total cost = $0.95 + $0.93 × 2 + 14.98 per cent of $10.00, or $0.95 + $1.86 + $1.498, a total of $4.308 or 43.1 per cent of the total value of the order.

invoice lines. All other expenses were grouped under this heading, including half of each of the three categories (E–1, E–2, and B–8) mentioned in Group 1, above. These expenses were arbitrarily applied to individual orders on the basis of the dollar value of the order.

The procedure for determining the costs of handling an order was set thus:

1. Expenses affected by the number of orders handled would be computed on a dollars-and-cents per order basis and each order charged with the same cost. By dividing the total of such costs by the number of orders handled, an average of $0.95 per order was computed.

2. Expenses affected by the number of invoice lines would be computed on a cents per invoice line basis and each order charged according to its number of lines. By dividing the total of such costs by the total number of invoice lines processed, an average of $0.93 per line was computed.

3. All other expenses would be allocated to each order in accordance with its dollar value. These costs amount to 14.98 per cent on orders taken by salesmen and 9.18 per cent on orders from house accounts on which no sales commission is paid.

4. The total cost of handling an order is then equal to $0.95 *plus* $0.93 times the number of lines *plus* 14.98 per cent of the value of the order (or 9.18 per cent if from a house account).

On the basis of these figures, a table was constructed showing the expenses connected with orders of different size taken by salesmen. This table is presented in Exhibit B.

Problem. On the basis of the information given in the case, what policy alternatives are presented to the management of Franklin Paper Company? Which ones should be adopted and how should they be implemented?

CENTRAL CITY HARDWARE, INC.

DEPARTMENTAL ANALYSIS OF OPERATING EXPENSES*

Central City Hardware, Inc., is a large, full-service hardware wholesaling concern serving independent retailers and industrial users in and around a city of 800,000 population. The company is organized into 10 merchandise departments, as follows:

Department A–Steel and Heavy Hardware
     B–Contractors' Supplies and Agricultural Implements
     C–Builders' Hardware and Small Tools
     D–Housewares
     E–Electrical Wiring Supplies
     F–Machinery Items
     G–Cutlery; Guns, Ammunition, and Accessories; Athletic Equipment; Bicycles and Supplies
     H–Automotive Accessories and Supplies
     I–Plumbing Items
     J–Paints, Oil and Glass

Each department is assigned to a buyer who has full responsibility for merchandising activities for his lines. Salesmen are responsible to the sales manager, who works with the buyers in developing dealer aids, monthly specials, and other promotional activities. The arrangement of goods in the warehouse is largely departmental except for certain heavy or bulky items that are kept on the first floor of the company's four-story building. Warehouse employees report to a supervisor, but a given employee devotes primary attention to goods in a group of several adjacent departments. Monthly reports of sales, cost of goods, and gross margins are prepared on a departmental basis and monthly statistical inventories are maintained.

The controller of Central City Hardware has felt for some time that periodic analyses of operating expenses on a departmental basis would be of great value to management. The president of the company is doubtful that such analyses would be worth the costs and efforts needed to obtain them. The company employs two full-time accounting persons in the controller's department and their time is occupied with routine posting of accounts, trial balances, and the like.

After considerable study of cost-accounting systems, the controller has devised a simplified method of allocating operating expenses to merchandise departments. The expense classifications and bases for allocating to individual departments are:

* See Chapter 29.

674

Expense Category	*Basis for Allocation to Departments*

WAREHOUSING:

Salaries and Wages ....Approximate percentage of warehouse employees' time spent in various departments, determined by discussion with supervisor and warehousemen

Packing Materials ....Sales, modified by amount of packing required for different types of goods

Rent—Warehouse ....Floor space occupied

DELIVERY:

Truck Expense and Depreciation .....Percentage of total number of deliveries made during a sample period

Freight from Warehouse ....Direct to departments as shown by number of packages on sales invoices

SELLING:

Salesmen's Salaries and Expenses .....Sales

Advertising ....Sales

Catalog ....Number of pages in annual catalog

Sales Administrative ....Sales

ADMINISTRATIVE AND OFFICE:

Executive and General Office Salaries ..Sales

Buyers' Salaries ....Direct to respective departments where possible; otherwise, by volume of purchases

Stationery, Office Supplies, Postage ....Sales

Rent—Office ....Sales

Insurance ....Value of average inventory

Bad Debts ....Sales

Telephone and Telegraph ....Sales

Miscellaneous Expense ....Sales

The chief merit of this system, according to the controller, is its simplicity. The monthly analysis of expenses and net profits or losses by departments requires only about 10 hours of work and can, therefore, be handled without any additional accounting personnel. Several of the department managers feel, however, that the system is unfair and that the profit figures for their departments do not accurately reflect their contributions to the firm's over-all net profit.

Problem. Evaluate the bases used for allocating operating expenses to departments and suggest possible improvements. Would a more complex system of allocation be worthwhile in view of its probable higher cost?

SELECTED BIBLIOGRAPHY

A. General

American Marketing Association. *Journal of Marketing*, Special Issue, "Wholesaling in Our American Economy," XIV, No. 2 (September, 1949).

Beckman, Theodore N., Maynard, Harold H., and Davidson, William R. *Principles of Marketing*, 6th ed. New York: The Ronald Press Co., 1957.

Clewett, Richard M. (ed.). *Marketing Channels for Manufactured Products*. Homewood, Ill.: Richard D. Irwin, Inc., 1954.

Converse, Paul D. "Twenty Five Years of Wholesaling," *Journal of Marketing*, XXII, No. 1 (July, 1957), 40–53.

Converse, Paul D., Huegy, Harvey W., and Mitchell, Robert V. *Elements of Marketing*, 6th ed. Englewood Cliffs, N. J., Prentice-Hall, Inc., 1958.

Engle, Nathanael H. (ed.). *Marketing in the West*. New York: The Ronald Press Co., 1946.

Small Business Administration. *Basic Information Sources on Wholesaling* (Business Service Bulletin No. 83.) Washington, D. C.: Government Printing Office, December, 1954.

Small Business Administration. *Basic Information Sources on Operating Costs and Ratios—Wholesale Trades.* (Business Service Bulletin No. 130.) Washington, D. C.: Government Printing Office, 1955.

The Ohio State University, Bureau of Business Research. *Summaries of Lectures—Wholesale Management Course.* Annual summary of course conducted in cooperation with the National Association of Wholesalers and obtainable from it.

United States Department of Commerce. *Wholesale Trade Report.* Monthly series on sales and inventories of wholesalers by kind of business and by regions.

B. Wholesale Institutions and Industries

Cassady, Ralph, Jr., and Jones, W. L. *The Changing Competitive Structure in the Wholesale Grocery Trade.* Berkeley: University of California Press, 1949.

677

DAVIDSON, WILLIAM R. *The Wholesale Wine Trade in Ohio.* Columbus, Ohio: Bureau of Business Research, The Ohio State University, 1955.

Food Topics [Magazine]. *Sales Service—The Food Broker Story,* in cooperation with National Food Brokers Association. Chicago: Food Publications, Inc., 1957.

GOODSTADT, LEONARD L., "The Distribution of Frozen Foods with Emphasis on the Wholesaler." Unpublished Master's thesis, New York University, 1954.

Hardware Retailer [Magazine]. Special Issues on Hardware Wholesaling (May, 1956, and May, 1958).

HENDERSON, CHARLES M. "Analysis of Wagon Distribution as Used by Wholesalers and Manufacturers in the Marketing of Food Products to Retail Food Stores." Unpublished Master's thesis, University of Pennsylvania, 1951.

HERGET, WALTER C., JR. "Changes in Wholesale Grocery Merchandising." Unpublished Master's thesis, New York University, 1956.

JOHNSON, WILLIAM L. "Where Is the Automotive Wholesaler Going?" Unpublished Master's thesis, University of Pennsylvania, Philadelphia, 1957.

KARAS, MILAN R. "The Contributions Made by Service Wholesalers to the Economy of Hamilton County, Ohio." Unpublished doctoral dissertation, The Ohio State University, Columbus, Ohio, 1951.

KAUFFMAN, GEORGE. "Changing Patterns in Drug Wholesaling," in ROBERT D. BUZZELL (ed.), *Adaptive Behavior in Marketing.* Proceedings of the Winter Conference, American Marketing Association (Chicago, 1957).

KOHN, MERVIN. "The St. Louis Dry Goods Wholesaler in Transition." Unpublished doctoral dissertation, St. Louis University, St. Louis, Missouri, 1957.

LAWRENCE, VICTOR C. "The Industrial Distributor." Unpublished Master's thesis, New York University, 1953.

LEFFLER, MARVIN. *How To Become a Successful Manufacturer's Representative.* Englewood Cliffs, N. J.: Prentice-Hall, Inc., 1952.

LEWIS, EDWIN H. "The Comeback of the Wholesaler," *Harvard Business Review* (November–December, 1955), 115–25.

MILLER, FREDERICK BYERS. "Richmond, Virginia, as a Wholesale Trade Center: An Analysis of its Development and Present Position." Unpublished doctoral dissertation, The Ohio State University, Columbus, Ohio, 1952.

MORRISSEY, WILLIAM H., JR. "The Main Managerial Problems of the Fine Paper Wholesale Merchant." Unpublished Master's thesis, New York University, 1955.

MOSKOWITZ, NORMAN. "The Changing Importance of the Wholesaler in the Plumbing and Heating Industry." Unpublished Master's thesis, New York University, 1956.

NATIONAL FOOD BROKERS ASSOCIATION. *History Defines the Food Broker,* Washington, D. C., not dated; also, *The Food Broker* (Washington, D. C., 1941).

NOLEN, HERMAN C. "The Modern Wholesaler and His Adjustment to a Changing Economy," in W. DAVID ROBBINS (ed.), *Successful Marketing at Home and Abroad,* Proceedings of Convention of the Marketing Association (Boston, 1958), pp. 409–15; also, "Some Additional Observations," by Rudolph L. Treuenfels, pp. 416–22.

O'LEARY, E. B. *Cooperative Wholesaling in Grocery Distribution.* (Monograph No. R–31.) Columbus, Ohio: Bureau of Business Research, The Ohio State University, 1942.

PATREY, HARRY B. In collaboration with Joseph Kolodny, *Successful Wholesale Tobacco Distribution.* New York: Foresight Publications, Inc., 1957.

SATLER, LEONARD. "Wholesale Merchandising in the Carpet Industry." Unpublished Master's thesis, City College of New York, 1950.

SHIRK, A. U. *Marketing Through Food Brokers.* New York: McGraw-Hill Book Co., Inc., 1939.

SMALL BUSINESS ADMINISTRATION. *How Food Brokers Help Small Manufacturers.* (Management Aids for Small Manufacturers No. 63.) Washington, D. C.: Government Printing Office, 1955.

STAUDT, THOMAS A. *The Manufacturers' Agent as a Marketing Institution.* United States Bureau of the Census. Washington, D. C.: Government Printing Office, 1952.

STAUDT, THOMAS A., and LAZER, WILLIAM. *A Basic Bibliography on Industrial Marketing.* (Bibliography Series No. 4.) Chicago: American Marketing Association, 1958, for further references on this subject.

STILL, RICHARD S. "Historical and Competitive Aspects of Grocery Wholesaling in Seattle, Washington." Unpublished doctoral dissertation, University of Washington, Seattle, Washington, 1953.

TAYLOR, JAMES DOWELL. "The Development, Operation, and Role of the Rack Jobber in the American Economy." Unpublished Master's thesis, State University of Iowa, 1954.

TAYLOR, NORMAN E. "The Midland Cooperative Wholesale, Inc., Its History and Analysis." Unpublished doctoral dissertation, University of Minnesota, Minneapolis, Minnesota, 1955.

The Saturday Evening Post [Magazine]. *Joint Marketing Study,* in cooperation with National Food Brokers Association (Philadelphia: Curtis Publishing Co., 1948).

UNITED STATES DEPARTMENT OF COMMERCE, OFFICE OF DISTRIBUTION. *Voluntary and Cooperative Chains.* (Business Service Bulletin No. 206.) Washington, D. C.: Government Printing Office, 1957.

UNITED STATES DEPARTMENT OF COMMERCE, OFFICE OF DOMESTIC COMMERCE. *A Study of Tobacco Wholesalers' Operations.* (Industrial Series No. 62.) Washington, D. C.: Government Printing Office, 1946.

VEREEN, ROBERT. "Modern Developments in Hardware Wholesaling," in ROBERT D. BUZZELL (ed.), *Adaptive Behavior in Marketing.* Proceedings of the Winter Conference, American Marketing Association (Chicago, 1957).

VOLPP, LOUIS D. "The Changing Functions of the Grocery Wholesaler: A Case Study in Des Moines, Iowa, 1929–1954," *Iowa Business Digest,* XXVII (December, 1956), 21–29.

WINSLOW, R. M. "Automation in Food Wholesale Distribution Centers," in ROBERT D. BUZZELL (ed.), *Adaptive Behavior in Marketing*. Proceedings of Winter Conference, American Marketing Association (Chicago, 1957).

C. PRODUCTIVITY, EFFICIENCY, AND GOVERNMENTAL IMPACT

BARANOFF, SEYMOUR. "The Current Opportunities of the Independent, Full-Service Merchant Wholesaler of Manufactured Consumer Goods." Unpublished doctoral dissertation, New York University, 1955.

BAYLESS, JAMES LESLIE. "The Changing Role of the Wholesale Grocer in the Iowa Market." Unpublished doctoral dissertation, State University of Iowa, 1952.

BORRELLO, FRANK. "The Role of the Wholesaler in the American Marketing Structure." Unpublished Master's thesis, New York University, 1954.

BURGHARDT, FRED H. "Industrial Distributor: His Position and Importance in the Industrial Market." Unpublished Master's thesis, New York University, 1951.

BUZZELL, ROBERT D. "Productivity in Marketing: With Special Reference to Drug and Hardware Wholesalers." Unpublished doctoral dissertation, The Ohio State University, Columbus, Ohio, 1957.

CAHN, DAVID. "The Woolen Piece Goods Wholesaler in the United States." Unpublished Master's thesis, City College of New York, 1951.

EUROPEAN PRODUCTIVITY AGENCY, ORGANIZATION FOR EUROPEAN ECONOMIC COOPERATION. *Productivity in the Wholesale Trade*. Paris, 1956.

FEDERAL TRADE COMMISSION. *News Summary*. Periodic news releases dealing with complaints, decisions, and decrees under the laws administered by the Commission.

OSTBERG, HENRY D. "Functional Discounts: Their Economic and Legal Implications." Unpublished doctoral dissertation, The Ohio State University, Columbus, 1957.

Trade Practice Conference Rules: Wholesale Optical Industry (1950); Wholesale Plumbing and Heating Industry (1955). Promulgated by the Federal Trade Commission. Obtainable from the Commission or from such a Trade Regulation Service as that published by the Commerce Clearing House, Inc.

VAN CISE, J. G., and DUNN, C. W. (eds.). "How To Comply with the Antitrust Laws." Commerce Clearing House, Inc.

D. ESTABLISHING, LOCATING, FINANCING, AND ORGANIZING A WHOLESALE BUSINESS

CRITES, DENNIS M. "A Study of Merchant Wholesale Trade in Oklahoma and Other West South Central States." Unpublished doctoral dissertation, Indiana University, Bloomington, 1956.

DONALDSON, ELVIN F. *Corporate Finance*. New York: The Ronald Press Co., 1957.

GUTHMANN, H. G., and DOUGALL, H. E. *Corporate Financial Policy.* 3d ed. Englewood Cliffs, N. J.: Prentice-Hall, Inc., 1955.

HUSBAND, WILLIAM H., and DOCKERAY, J. C. *Modern Corporation Finance,* 4th ed. Homewood, Ill., Richard D. Irwin, Inc., 1957.

Industrial Distribution Magazine, "Organizing for More Sales" (September, 1953), 90–120.

LEWIS, EDWIN H. *Wholesaling in the Twin Cities.* (University of Minnesota Studies in Economics and Business No. 15.) Minneapolis, 1952.

MEADOR, ROWE MORGAN. "An Analysis of the Little Rock Metropolitan Wholesale Market with Special Attention Given to Some Practices of Wholesalers Within the Market." Unpublished doctoral dissertation, University of Arkansas, Fayetteville, 1957.

MITCHELL, H. A. *Wholesale Buying Centers for Retailers in the Deep Central South.* New Orleans: Tulane University, 1949.

NATIONAL ASSOCIATION OF WHOLESALERS. *How To Think About and Plan Insurance for Wholesalers.* Washington, D. C., 1954.

NATIONAL ELECTRICAL MANUFACTURERS ASSOCIATION. *NEMA Industrial Trading Areas.* New York, 1957.

NATIONAL WHOLESALE DRUGGISTS' ASSOCIATION. *NWDA Drug Trade Market Data.* New York, 1956.

RIDLEY, FRANCIS R., JR. "Delineation and Analysis of Wholesale Trading Areas." Unpublished Master's thesis, New York University, 1951.

TOUSLEY, RAYBURN D., and LANZILLOTTI, ROBERT F. *The Spokane Wholesale Market.* (Economic and Business Studies Bulletin No. 18.) Pullman, Washington: State College of Washington Bureau of Economic and Business Research, 1951.

UNITED STATES DEPARTMENT OF AGRICULTURE, AGRICULTURAL MARKETING SERVICE. *Planning a Wholesale Frozen Food Distribution Plant.* (Marketing Research Report No. 18.) Washington, D. C.: Government Printing Office, 1952.

UNITED STATES DEPARTMENT OF AGRICULTURE, AGRICULTURAL MARKETING SERVICE. *Wholesale Market Report Series.* Periodic studies of wholesale food marketing requirements and facilities in specific areas. Washington, D. C.: Government Printing Office.

E. BUYING AND PRICING

ALTON, AARON J. "Formation of Prices by Wholesalers in Specified Lines of Business." Unpublished doctoral dissertation, The Ohio State University, Columbus, Ohio, 1956.

UNITED STATES DEPARTMENT OF LABOR, BUREAU OF LABOR STATISTICS. *Wholesale (Primary Market) Price Index,* monthly; *Prices and Price Relatives for Individual Commodities,* monthly; and *Weekly Wholesale Price Index.* Washington, D. C.: Government Printing Office.

F. Warehousing, Delivery, Order-Handling, Inventory Control

Chadwick, Winslow J. "The Application of Scientific Management Principles in Warehousing with Special Emphasis on Packaged Food Products." Unpublished Master's thesis, Tulane University, New Orleans, 1953.

Electric Industrial Truck Association. "Unit Loads: Their Handling—Shipment—Storage." Chicago, 1947.

Fisher, Albert B., Jr. *Warehouse Operations of Service Wholesale Druggists.* Columbus, Ohio: Bureau of Business Research, The Ohio State University, 1948.

Flow [Magazine]. Special Issue on "Handling Economics for Greater Wholesale Profits," in cooperation with the National Association of Wholesalers (January, 1955).

Harris, Murray P. "Modern Materials Handling Techniques as Applied to the Warehouse Operations of Wholesalers." Unpublished Master's thesis, The Ohio State University, Columbus, 1955.

National Wholesale Hardware Association. *Report on the Warehouse Building.* Philadelphia, not dated.

United States Department of Agriculture, Agricultural Marketing Service. *An Analysis of Some Methods of Loading Out Delivery Trucks of Produce Wholesalers.* (Marketing Research Report No. 15.) Washington, D. C.: Government Printing Office, 1952.

United States Department of Agriculture, Agricultural Marketing Service. *Improving the Truck Delivery Operations of a Wholesale Grocer.* (Marketing Research Report No. 127.) Washington, D. C.: Government Printing Office, 1956.

United States Department of Agriculture, Agricultural Marketing Service. *Methods of Handling and Delivering Orders Used by Some Leading Wholesale Grocers.* (Marketing Research Report No. 13.) Washington, D. C.: Government Printing Office, 1952.

United States Department of Agriculture, Agricultural Marketing Service. *Methods of Increasing Labor Productivity in Multistory and Small One-Floor Grocery Warehouses.* (Marketing Research Report No. 142.) Washington, D. C.: Government Printing Office, 1956.

United States Department of Agriculture, Agricultural Marketing Service. *Use of Recording and Transcribing Equipment in Loading Delivery Trucks of Produce Wholesalers.* (Agricultural Information Bulletin No. 43.) Washington, D. C.: Government Printing Office, 1951.

United States Department of Commerce, Bureau of Foreign and Domestic Commerce. *Streamlined Wholesale Grocery Warehouses.* (Industrial Series No. 18.) Washington, D. C.: Government Printing Office, 1945.

United States Department of Commerce, Bureau of the Census. *Transportation of Fresh Fruits and Vegetables by Agricultural Assemblers.* Washington, D. C.: Government Printing Office, 1958.

UNITED STATES DEPARTMENT OF COMMERCE, OFFICE OF DOMESTIC COM-
MERCE. *Effective Use of Wholesale Drug Warehouses.* (Industrial Series No.
68.) Washington, D. C.: Government Printing Office, 1947.

UNITED STATES DEPARTMENT OF COMMERCE, OFFICE OF INDUSTRY AND COM-
MERCE. *Modernizing and Operating Grocery Warehouses.* (Domestic Commerce Series No. 26—new series.) Washington, D. C.: Government Printing Office, 1951.

VITOLO, EDWARD F. "The Economics of Palletized Materials Handling." Unpublished Master's thesis, New York University, 1950.

G. SALES, ADVERTISING, AND CUSTOMER SERVICES

DAVIS, JAMES H. *Increasing Wholesale Drug Salesmen's Effectiveness.* Columbus, Ohio: Bureau of Business Research, The Ohio State University, 1948.

FREY, ALBERT W. *Advertising,* 2d ed. New York: The Ronald Press Co., 1953.

MAYNARD, HAROLD H., and DAVIS, JAMES H. *Sales Management,* 3d ed. New
York: The Ronald Press Co., 1957.

NATIONAL INDUSTRIAL DISTRIBUTORS' ASSOCIATION. *Survey on Salesmens'
Compensation Plans.* Philadelphia, 1957.

NATIONAL WHOLESALE DRUGGISTS' ASSOCIATION. *The Retailer Looks at His
Service Wholesale Druggist.* New York, 1953.

NATIONAL WHOLESALE HARDWARE ASSOCIATION. *Report on Methods of Compensating Salesmen.* Philadelphia, 1953.

SANDAGE, C. H., and FRYBURGER, VERNON. *Advertising Theory and Practice,*
5th ed. Homewood, Ill.: Richard D. Irwin, Inc., 1958.

SEELYE, ALFRED L., and BASS, FRANK M. *Sales Compensation Methods and
Policies of Texas Wholesalers: Grocery, Drug, Hardware.* (Studies in Mar-
keting No. 2.) Austin, Texas: Bureau of Business Research, University of
Texas, 1957.

SMALL BUSINESS ADMINISTRATION. *Sales Training for Small Wholesalers.* (Small
Marketers Aid No. 11.) Washington, D. C.: Government Printing Office,
1956.

SMALL BUSINESS ADMINISTRATION. *Wholesaler's Customer Analysis.* (Business
Service Bulletin No. 39.) Washington, D. C.: Government Printing Office,
1954.

STEWART, JACK N. "A Study of the Sales Training Program of the Kansas City
Division of McKesson and Robbins, Inc., Wholesale Druggist." Unpublished Master's thesis, The University of Kansas, Lawrence, 1952.

UNITED STATES DEPARTMENT OF AGRICULTURE, AGRICULTURAL MARKETING
SERVICE. *How Some Wholesale Grocers Build Better Retailers.* (Marketing
Research Report No. 12.) Washington, D. C.: Government Printing Office,
1952.

UNITED STATES DEPARTMENT OF AGRICULTURE, AGRICULTURAL MARKETING
SERVICE. *Use of Fieldmen by Wholesale Food Distributors and Affiliated*

Retailers. (Marketing Research Report No. 266.) Washington, D. C.: Government Printing Office, 1958.

UNITED STATES DEPARTMENT OF AGRICULTURE, AGRICULTURAL MARKETING SERVICE. *Views of Independent Grocers on Wholesaler-Retailer Relations.* (Marketing Research Report No. 42.) Washington, D. C.: Government Printing Office, 1953.

UNITED STATES DEPARTMENT OF COMMERCE, SMALL BUSINESS ADMINISTRATION. *How Wholesalers Assist Manufacturers.* (Small Business Aid No. 485.) Washington, D. C.: Government Printing Office, 1949.

UNITED STATES DEPARTMENT OF COMMERCE, SMALL BUSINESS ADMINISTRATION. *How Wholesalers Assist Retailers.* (Small Business Aid No. 486.) Washington, D. C.: Government Printing Office, 1949.

H. CREDIT AND OFFICE MANAGEMENT

BECKMAN, THEODORE N., and BARTELS, ROBERT. *Credits and Collections in Theory and Practice,* 6th ed. New York: McGraw-Hill Book Co., Inc. 1955.

NATIONAL ASSOCIATION OF CREDIT MEN. *Credit Management Handbook,* prepared and edited by the Credit Research Foundation. Homewood, Ill.. Richard D. Irwin, Inc., 1958.

Office Executive [Magazine]. Special Issue, "The Wholesaler and His Office Problems" (February, 1955).

I. EXPENSE ANALYSIS AND CONTROL, PERFORMANCE STANDARDS

AMERICAN STEEL WAREHOUSE ASSOCIATION, INC., and NATIONAL ASSOCIATION OF ALUMINUM DISTRIBUTORS. *Distribution Cost Analysis for Metals Distributors.* Cleveland and Philadelphia: 1956.

Business Week [Magazine]. Special Report on "Computers" (June 21, 1958).

GARROTT, P. B. "Integrated Data Processing Brings Automation in Paperwork," *Automation* (December, 1954; January, 1955; and February, 1955). Reprinted as a Special Report by Standard Register Company, Dayton, Ohio.

HASKINS and SELLS. *Data Processing by Electronics.* New York, 1955.

HECKERT, J. B., and MINER, ROBERT B. *Distribution Costs,* 2d ed. New York: The Ronald Press Co., 1953.

Industrial Distribution [Magazine], "Distribution Cost Accounting for Net Profits" (July, 1957).

LONGMAN, DONALD R., and SCHIFF, MICHAEL. *Practical Distribution Cost Analysis.* Homewood, Ill.: Richard D. Irwin, Inc., 1955.

MONIESON, DAVID D., "Value Added as a Measure of Economic Contribution by Marketing Institutions." Unpublished doctoral dissertation, The Ohio State University, Columbus, 1957.

NATIONAL PAPER TRADE ASSOCIATION, INC. *Manual of Accounting and Costing for the Paper Distributing Trade.* New York, 1949.

NATIONAL WHOLESALE DRUGGISTS' ASSOCIATION. *Facts on Sales, Costs and Profits of Service Wholesale Druggists*. Annual survey of members' operations.

NATIONAL WHOLESALE HARDWARE ASSOCIATION. *Overhead Expense in Wholesale Hardware Distribution*. Annual survey of members' operations.

ROLLWAGE, E. A., and BENNETT, B. V. *Punched Card Accounting Procedures*. New York: National Wholesale Druggists' Association, not dated.

UNITED STATES DEPARTMENT OF COMMERCE, BUREAU OF FOREIGN AND DOMESTIC COMMERCE. *Distribution Cost Analysis*. (Economic Series No. 50.) Washington, D. C.: Government Printing Office, 1946.

UNITED STATES DEPARTMENT OF COMMERCE, BUREAU OF FOREIGN AND DOMESTIC COMMERCE. *Simplified Accounting for Wholesale Grocers*. (Industrial Series No. 76.) Washington, D. C.: Government Printing Office, 1947.

NAME INDEX

SUBJECT INDEX

Budgets
  expense, 612–15
  merchandise, 373–77
Buildings (See "Warehouses")
Bulk tank stations, 100
Bureau of the Census, 41, 51
Bureau of Labor Statistics, 55–57
Buyers, wholesale house, 347–48
Buying
  expense, allocation of, 586, 593, 595, 597, 599
  importance of, 378–79
  information concerning sources of supply, 388–89
  methods and procedures
    anticipation of demand, 393
    back orders, 398
    basic methods, 390–92
    follow-up and adjustments, 398
    purchase orders, 395–97
    purchase records, 393–94
  performance measures, 618
  policies
    concentration of purchases, 384–85
    optimum purchase quantity, 381–84
    quantity vs. small-lot, 379–84
    selection of specific vendors, 386–88
    sources of supply, types, 385–86
Buying group, 206, 391–92
  case problem, 664–65
Buying pool, 206

"Canvassing clerks," 78
Capital productivity, 245–46
Capital turnover, 630–32
Card order catalogs, 462–63
Cash-and-carry wholesalers, 176–78
  operating expenses of, 177
Catalogs, buying from, 390
Census Bureau, definition of wholesale establishment, 41, 51
Census of Wholesale Trade, 87–88, 101
Centers, distribution, 390–91
Centralized receiving, 432–33
Chain store licensing tax, 258
Chain store warehouses, 100, 200–201
Chain wholesalers, 125–26
Chains
  effect of
    on independents, 205–6
    wholesaling, 165–66
  voluntary affiliates of, 207
Chandlers, 78
Channels of distribution
  of industrial goods, 154–55
  of manufactured goods, 89–90

Checking merchandise, three methods of, 433–36
Chutes, 449
Circumventing the wholesaler
  conditions favoring
    availability and competence of wholesalers, 194
    availability of partial substitutes, 194–97
    character of market, 191–94
    circumstances of manufacturer, 189–91
    nature of product, 188–89
  methods used in, 180–82
  reasons for
    competition, 184–85
    desire to buy direct, 187–88
    dissatisfaction with wholesaler, 186–87
    economy, 183–84
    nature of goods, 182–83
Claims, freight, 483
Clamp method of handling unit loads, 446–47
Classification of customers, 280–81
  case problem, 640–41
Classification of operating expenses, 584–90
Clayton Antitrust Act, 258, 261–62
Collection period, average, 578–79
Collections, 575–78
Colonial period, wholesaling in, 75–76
Color in warehouse, 454
Commission compensation plans for salesmen, 537–40
Commission houses, 230–31
Commission merchants, 224–25
Commissions of agents and brokers, 222–23, 229, 231, 232
Commodities, expense analysis by, 604–6
Commodity Exchange Act, 258
Commodity output, related to wholesale trade volume, 92–95
Commodity purchase record, 394
Common law and monopoly, 260
Community, selection of, for location, 313–22
Compensation of salesmen
  bonus and profit-sharing plans, 540
  case problem, 670
  characteristics of good plan of, 535–36
  commission plans of, 537–40
  objectives of, 534–35
  problems in, 535
  salary plans of, 536–37
  salesmen's expenses, 540–41